IT'S OBVIOUS YOU WON'T SURVIVE BY YOUR WITS ALONE

Other Dilbert Books from Boxtree

Shave The Whales
ISBN: 0 7522 0849 7

Bring Me The Head of Willy The Mailboy!
ISBN: 0 7522 0136 0

Always Postpone Meetings With Time-Wasting Morons
ISBN: 0 7522 0854 3

Still Pumped From Using The Mouse
ISBN: 0 7522 2265 1

Access Denied – Dilbert's Quest For Love in the Nineties
ISBN: 0 7522 2421 2

Telling It Like It Isn't
ISBN: 0 7522 2426 3

The Dilbert Principle
ISBN: 0 7522 2287 2 (hardback edition)
ISBN: 0 7522 2470 0 (paperback edition)

The Dilbert Future
ISBN: 0 7522 1118 8

Dogbert's Top Secret Management Handbook
ISBN: 0 7522 2410 7

IT'S OBVIOUS YOU WON'T SURVIVE BY YOUR WITS ALONE

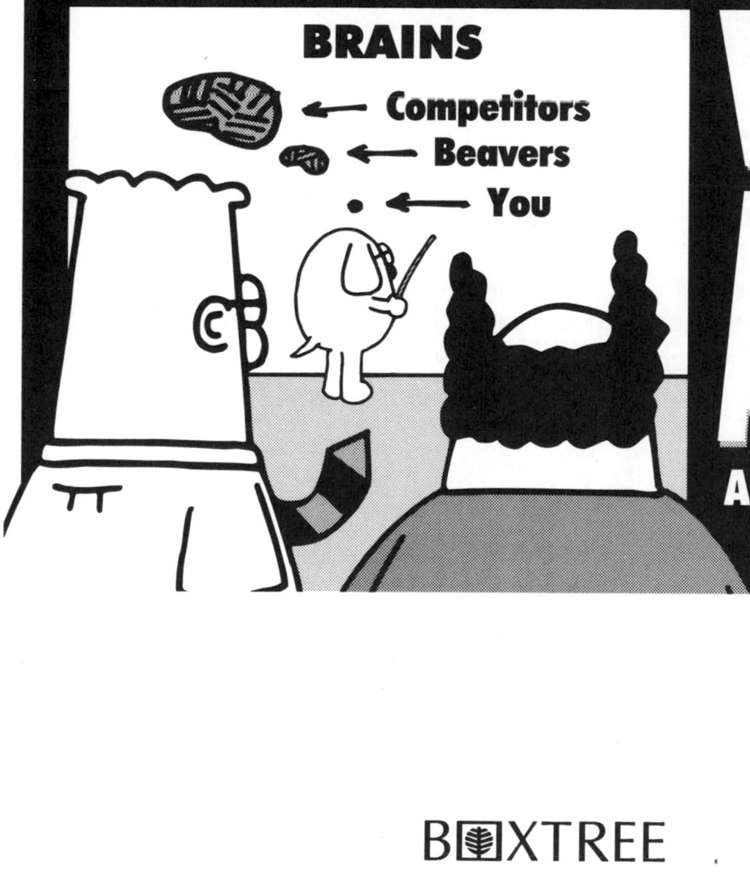
BRAINS
Competitors
Beavers
You

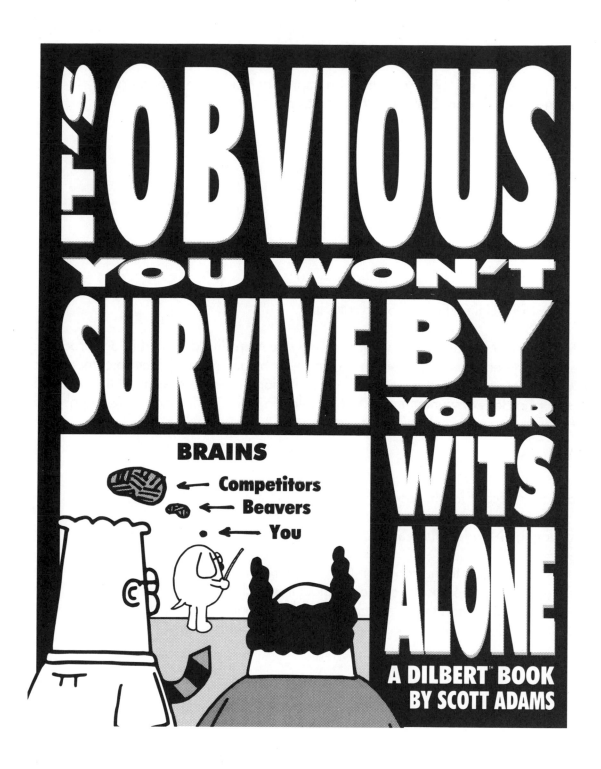

A DILBERT™ BOOK
BY SCOTT ADAMS

BOXTREE

First published in 1995 by Andrews and McMeel, a Universal Press Syndicate Company, 4900 Main Street, Kansas, Missouri 64112, USA

This edition published in 1997 by Boxtree, an imprint of Macmillan Publishers Ltd, 25 Eccleston Place, London, SW1W 9NF and Basingstoke

Associated companies throughout the world

ISBN 0 7522 0201 4

DILBERT®, is a registered trademark of United Feature Syndicate, Inc.

DOGBERT and DILBERT appear in the comic strip DILBERT®, distributed by United Feature Syndicate, Inc.

Copyright © 1995 United Feature Syndicate, Inc.

9 8 7 6 5 4 3 2 1

A CIP catalogue record for this book is available from the British Library

Printed in Italy by New Interlitho S.P.A. – Milan.

Introduction

I created the first five Dilbert books strictly to earn money. This sixth book is being done for love. Specifically, my love of money.

I don't mean I "love" money in some greedy, shallow sense of the word. I mean I actually have feelings for money. I once had a fling with an attractive little five dollar bill. It was wonderful, if you don't count the paper cuts . . . and of course there was the big fight after my tasteless joke about Ford's Theater. But mostly it was good.

It ended like most of my relationships — I traded her for a bag of Ruffles and a Diet Coke. The moral of the story is, "Don't fall in love on an empty stomach," especially if your loved one is accepted as legal tender at convenience stores.

Speaking of hunger, at parties I'm often asked if I see myself more as a writer or an artist. To which I reply, "Excuse me while I freshen my Snapple*." Then I scurry away. I escape because the conversation inevitably degenerates into unpleasant comparisons of my artwork and things found in nature, such as carpet stains and motorcycle accidents.

I'm sure my artwork would be better if I spent more time on it, but I'm a busy guy. Take today for instance; I have to write an exciting introduction for this book. Later I'll be sorting all of my currency into "cute" and "ugly" piles. This stuff doesn't happen by itself.

Here's my point: Wouldn't it be nice if all the annoying people on earth became our personal servants? Well, it's possible. As you may already know, when Dogbert conquers the planet and becomes supreme ruler, anybody who is not on the free Dilbert newsletter mailing list will become domestic servants for the enlightened people who are. Save yourself from that fate by joining now.

The Dilbert newsletter is free and it's published approximately "whenever I feel like it," which is about four times a year.

E-mail subscription (preferred): write to scottadams@aol.com

Snail mail: Dilbert Mailing List c/o United Media
                200 Madison Ave.
                New York, NY 10016

Scott Adams

http://www.unitedmedia.com/comics/dilbert/

* It's not what you think. You're disgusting.

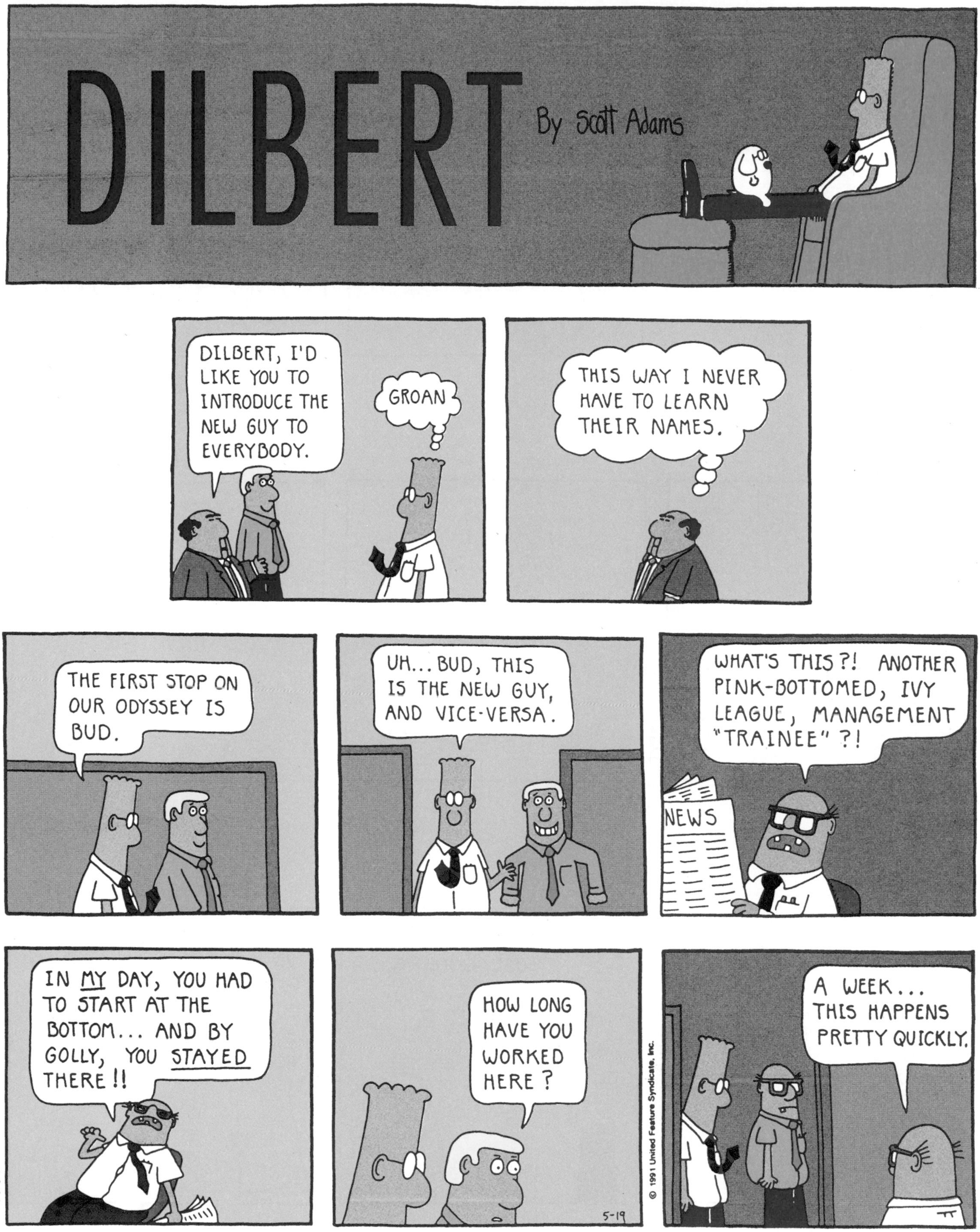
DILBERT
By Scott Adams
DILBERT, I'D LIKE YOU TO INTRODUCE THE NEW GUY TO EVERYBODY.
GROAN
THIS WAY I NEVER HAVE TO LEARN THEIR NAMES.
THE FIRST STOP ON OUR ODYSSEY IS BUD.
UH... BUD, THIS IS THE NEW GUY, AND VICE-VERSA.
WHAT'S THIS?! ANOTHER PINK-BOTTOMED, IVY LEAGUE, MANAGEMENT "TRAINEE"?!
NEWS
IN MY DAY, YOU HAD TO START AT THE BOTTOM... AND BY GOLLY, YOU STAYED THERE!!
HOW LONG HAVE YOU WORKED HERE?
A WEEK... THIS HAPPENS PRETTY QUICKLY.
S.Adams
© 1991 United Feature Syndicate, Inc.
5-19

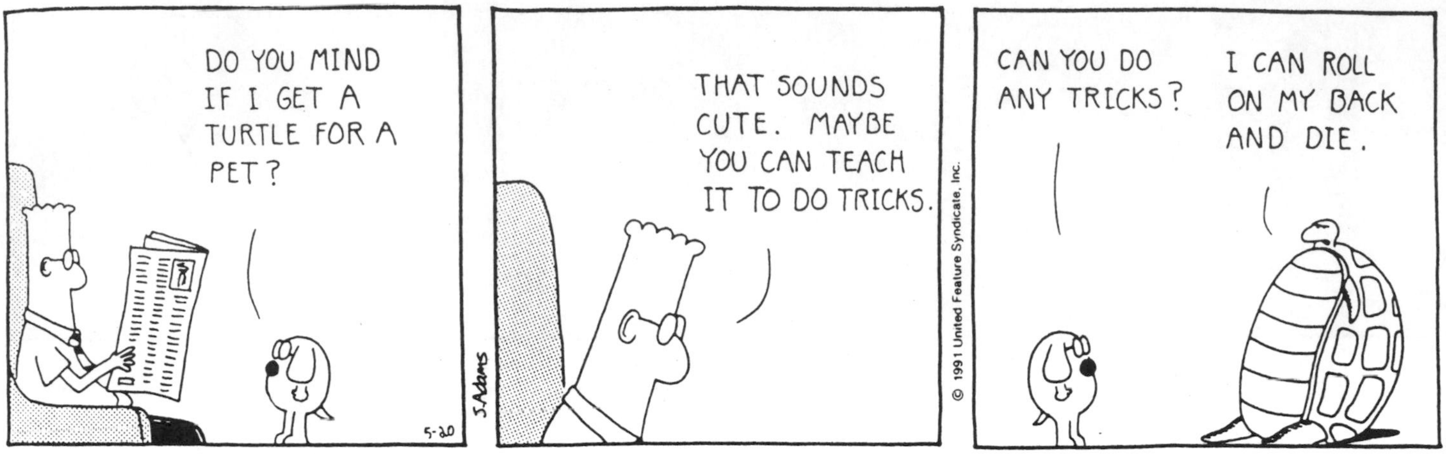
DO YOU MIND IF I GET A TURTLE FOR A PET?
5-20
THAT SOUNDS CUTE. MAYBE YOU CAN TEACH IT TO DO TRICKS.
S. Adams
© 1991 United Feature Syndicate, Inc.
CAN YOU DO ANY TRICKS?
I CAN ROLL ON MY BACK AND DIE.

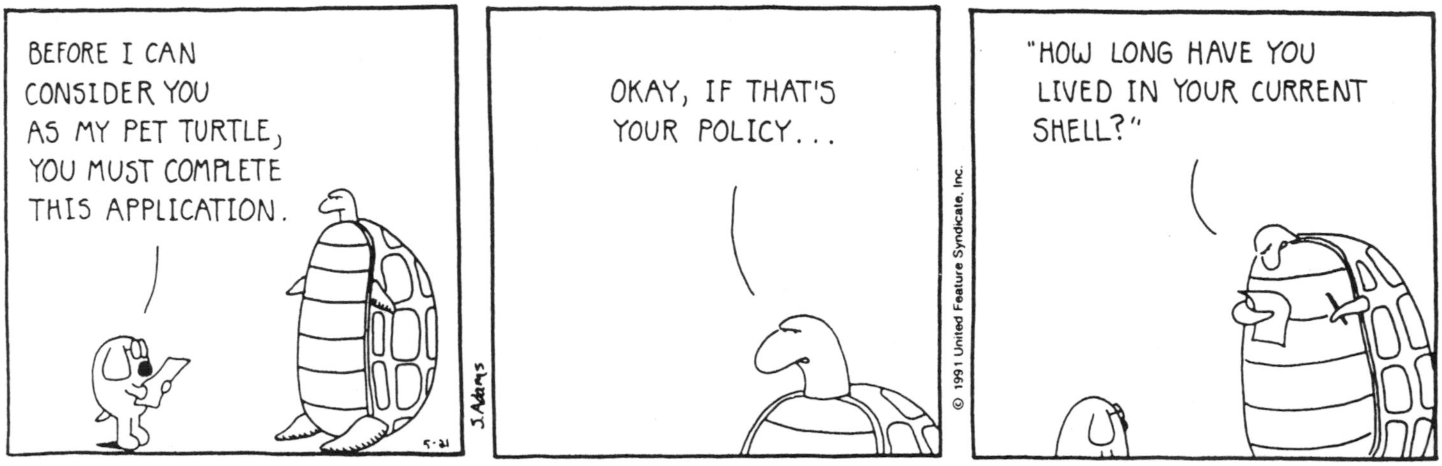
BEFORE I CAN CONSIDER YOU AS MY PET TURTLE, YOU MUST COMPLETE THIS APPLICATION.
5-21
S. Adams
OKAY, IF THAT'S YOUR POLICY...
© 1991 United Feature Syndicate, Inc.
"HOW LONG HAVE YOU LIVED IN YOUR CURRENT SHELL?"

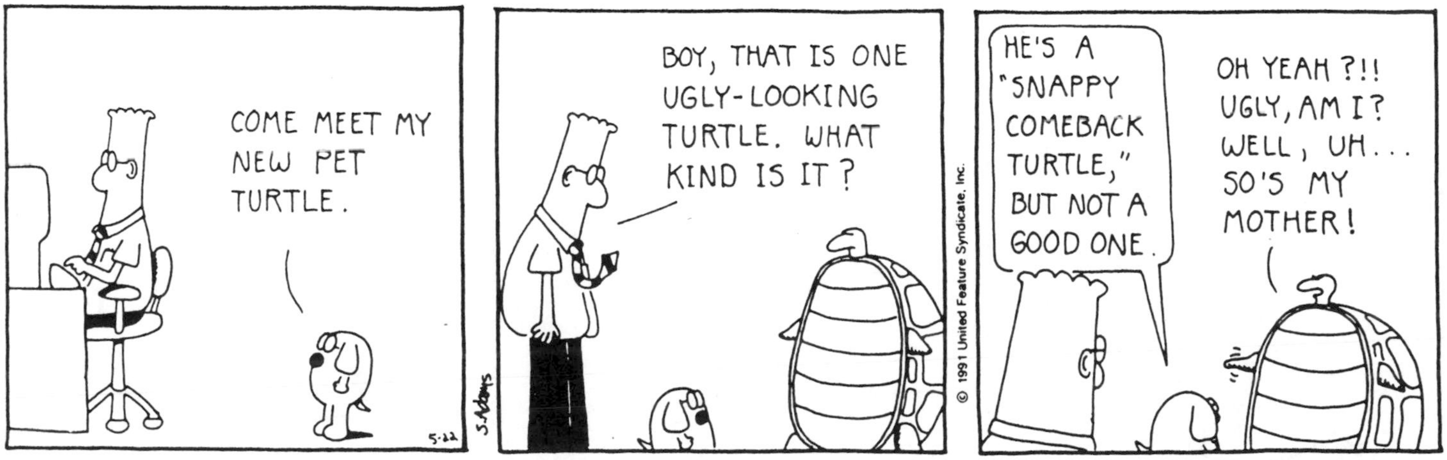
COME MEET MY NEW PET TURTLE.
5-22
S. Adams
BOY, THAT IS ONE UGLY-LOOKING TURTLE. WHAT KIND IS IT?
© 1991 United Feature Syndicate, Inc.
HE'S A "SNAPPY COMEBACK TURTLE," BUT NOT A GOOD ONE.
OH YEAH?!! UGLY, AM I? WELL, UH... SO'S MY MOTHER!

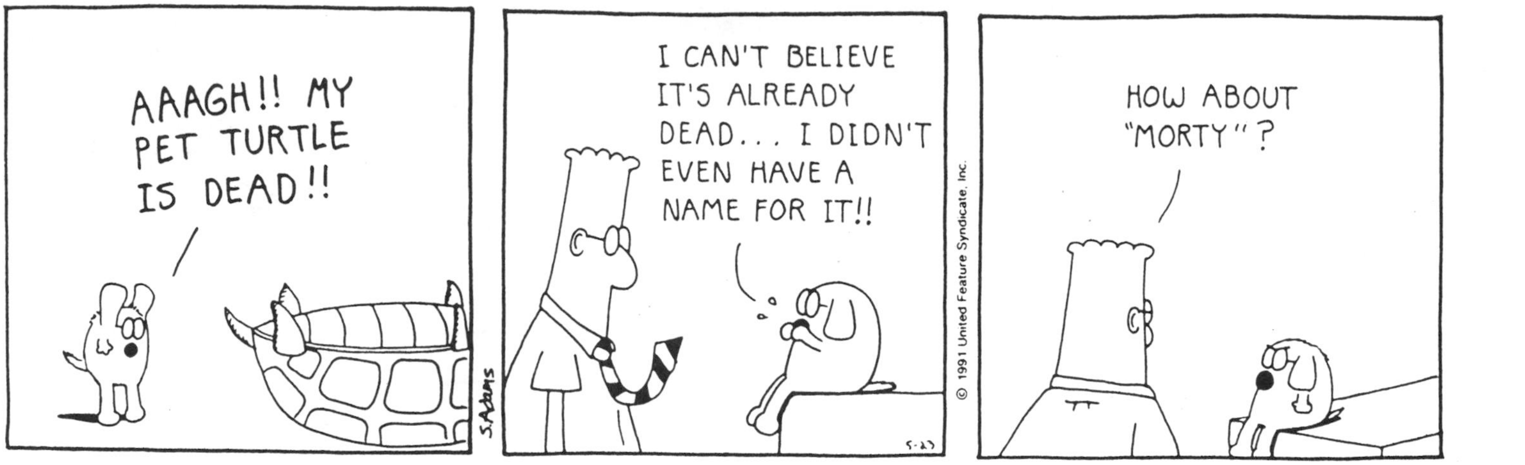
AAAGH!! MY PET TURTLE IS DEAD!!
I CAN'T BELIEVE IT'S ALREADY DEAD... I DIDN'T EVEN HAVE A NAME FOR IT!!
HOW ABOUT "MORTY"?
© 1991 United Feature Syndicate, Inc.

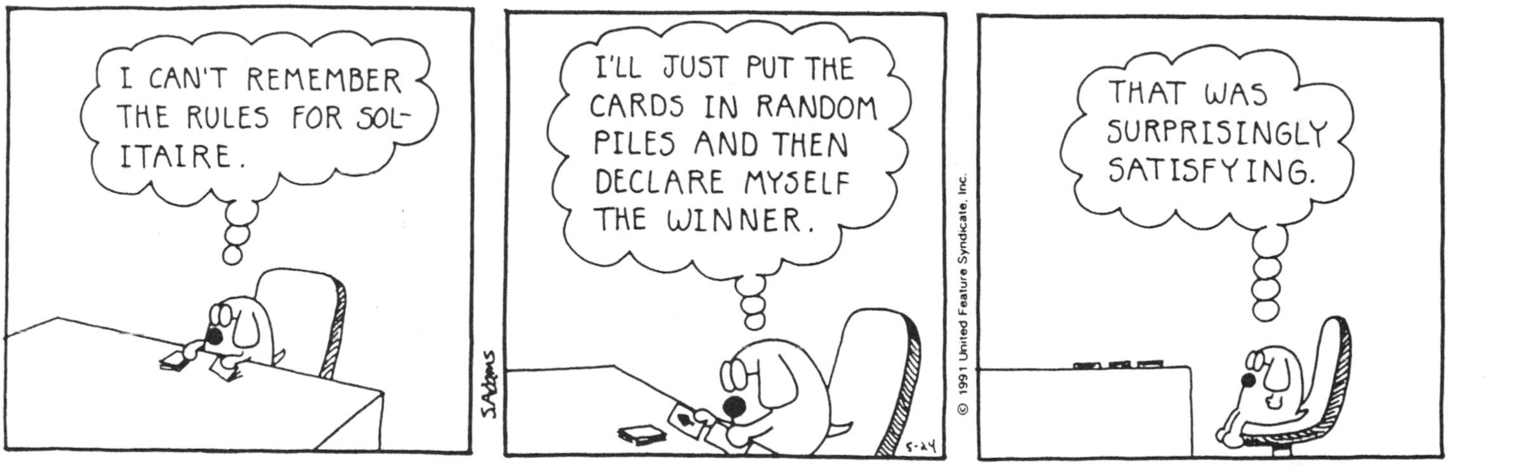
I CAN'T REMEMBER THE RULES FOR SOL-ITAIRE.
I'LL JUST PUT THE CARDS IN RANDOM PILES AND THEN DECLARE MYSELF THE WINNER.
THAT WAS SURPRISINGLY SATISFYING.
© 1991 United Feature Syndicate, Inc.

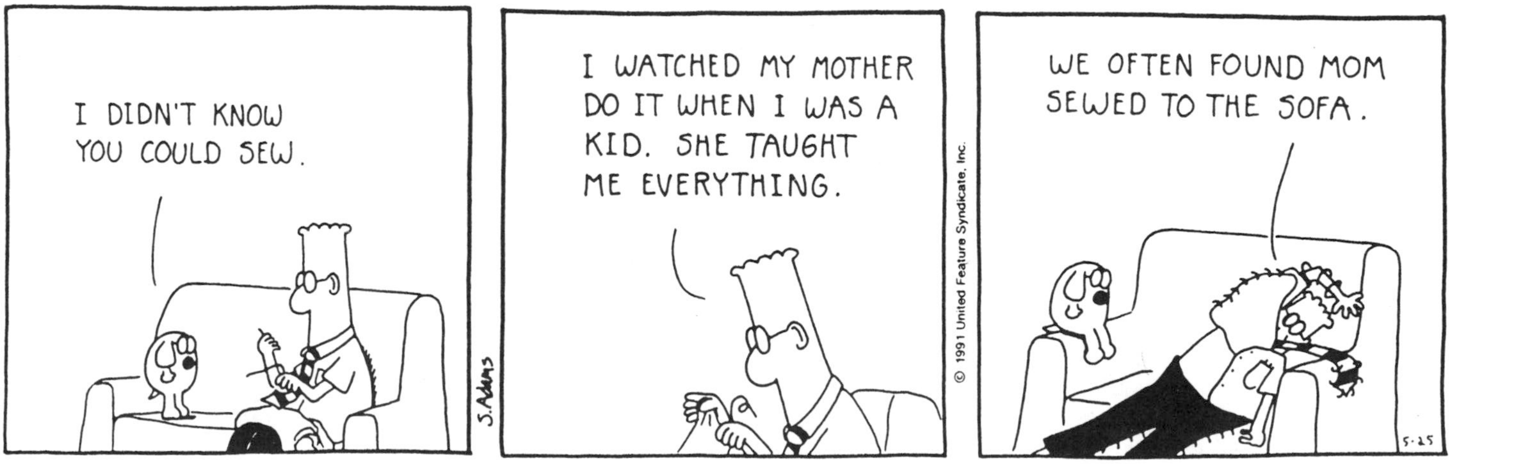
I DIDN'T KNOW YOU COULD SEW.
I WATCHED MY MOTHER DO IT WHEN I WAS A KID. SHE TAUGHT ME EVERYTHING.
WE OFTEN FOUND MOM SEWED TO THE SOFA.
© 1991 United Feature Syndicate, Inc.

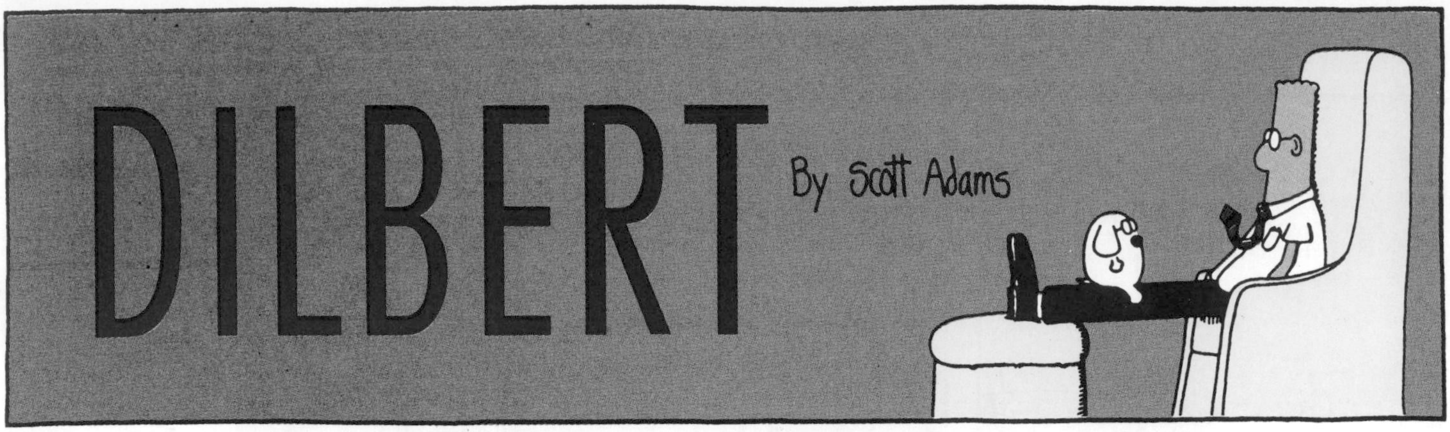
DILBERT
By Scott Adams

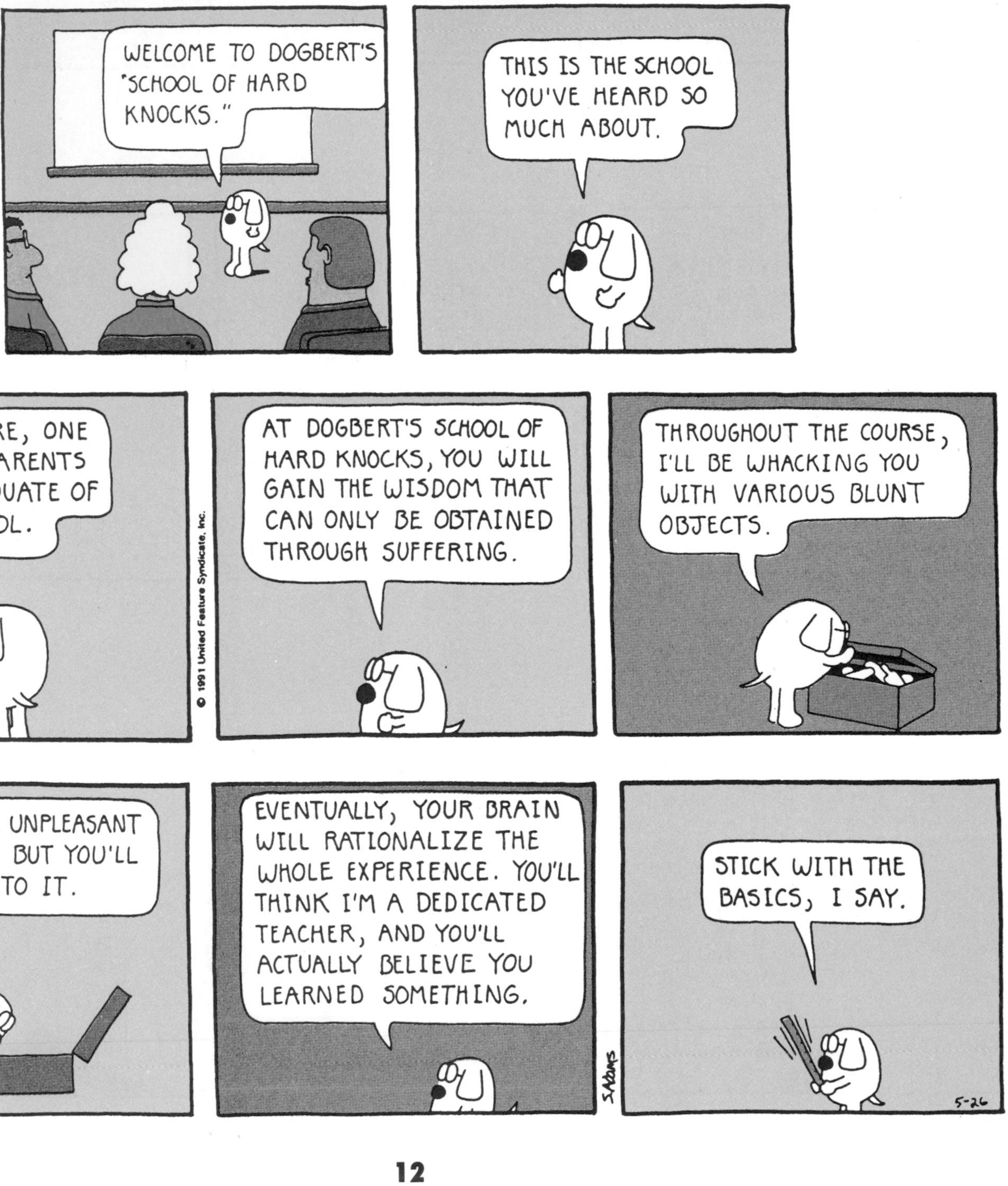
WELCOME TO DOGBERT'S "SCHOOL OF HARD KNOCKS."
THIS IS THE SCHOOL YOU'VE HEARD SO MUCH ABOUT.
CHANCES ARE, ONE OF YOUR PARENTS IS A GRADUATE OF THIS SCHOOL.
© 1991 United Feature Syndicate, Inc.
AT DOGBERT'S SCHOOL OF HARD KNOCKS, YOU WILL GAIN THE WISDOM THAT CAN ONLY BE OBTAINED THROUGH SUFFERING.
THROUGHOUT THE COURSE, I'LL BE WHACKING YOU WITH VARIOUS BLUNT OBJECTS.
IT MAY BE UNPLEASANT AT FIRST, BUT YOU'LL GET USED TO IT.
EVENTUALLY, YOUR BRAIN WILL RATIONALIZE THE WHOLE EXPERIENCE. YOU'LL THINK I'M A DEDICATED TEACHER, AND YOU'LL ACTUALLY BELIEVE YOU LEARNED SOMETHING.
STICK WITH THE BASICS, I SAY.
5-26

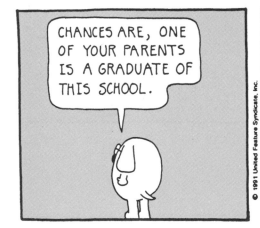

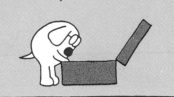

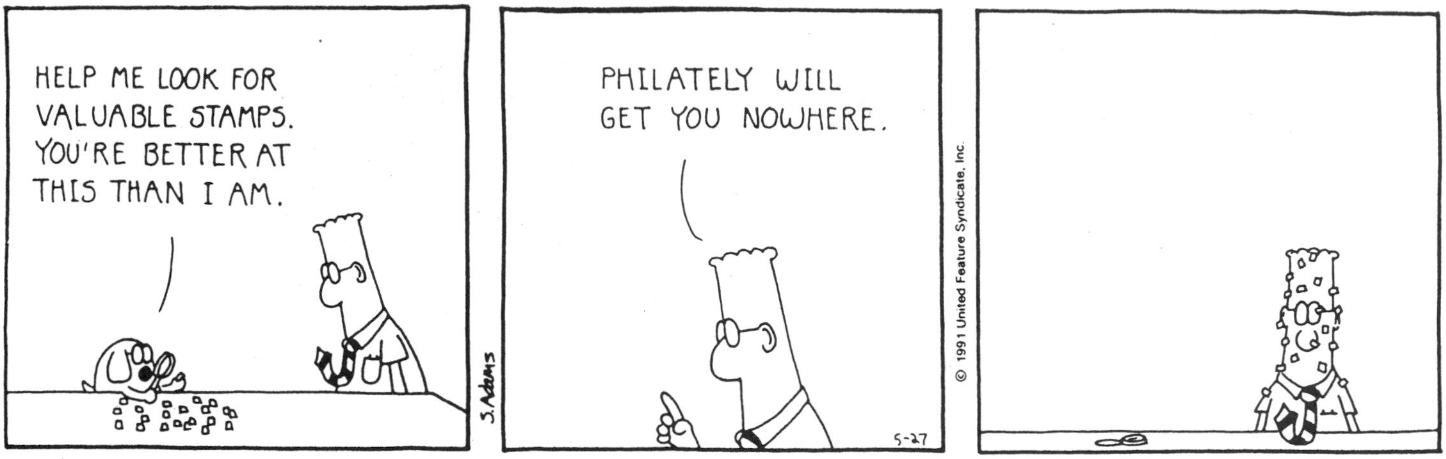
HELP ME LOOK FOR VALUABLE STAMPS. YOU'RE BETTER AT THIS THAN I AM.
PHILATELY WILL GET YOU NOWHERE.
© 1991 United Feature Syndicate, Inc.

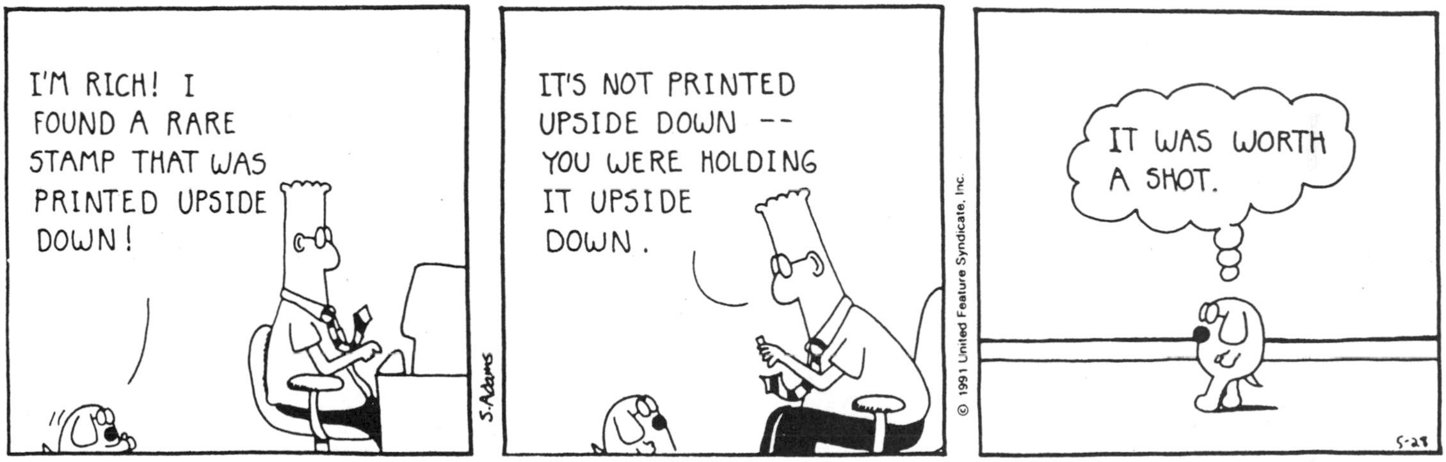
I'M RICH! I FOUND A RARE STAMP THAT WAS PRINTED UPSIDE DOWN!
IT'S NOT PRINTED UPSIDE DOWN -- YOU WERE HOLDING IT UPSIDE DOWN.
IT WAS WORTH A SHOT.
© 1991 United Feature Syndicate, Inc.

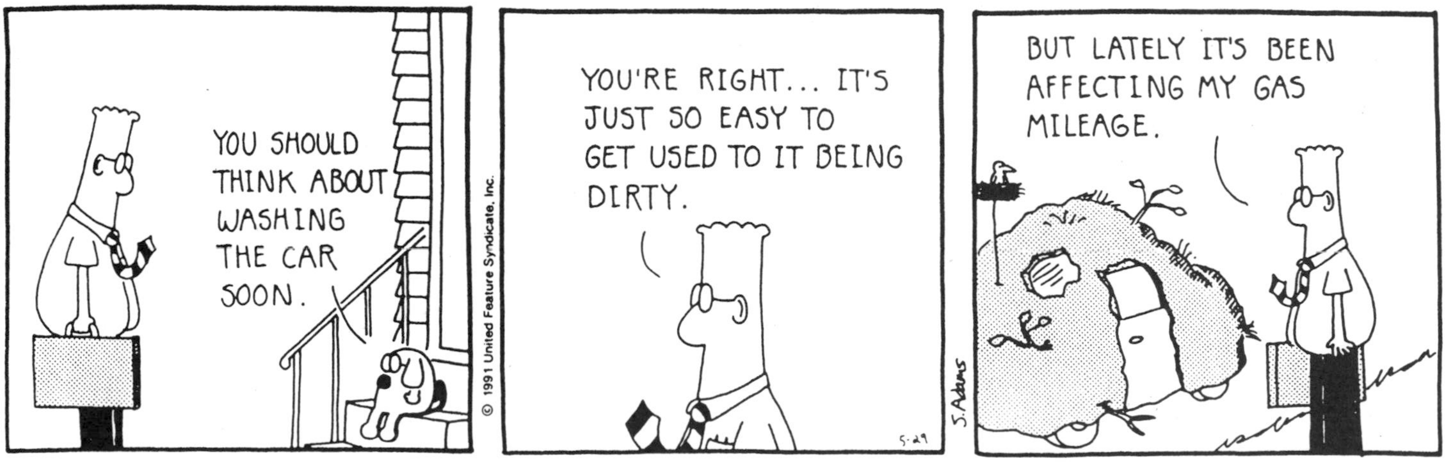
YOU SHOULD THINK ABOUT WASHING THE CAR SOON.
© 1991 United Feature Syndicate, Inc.
YOU'RE RIGHT... IT'S JUST SO EASY TO GET USED TO IT BEING DIRTY.
BUT LATELY IT'S BEEN AFFECTING MY GAS MILEAGE.

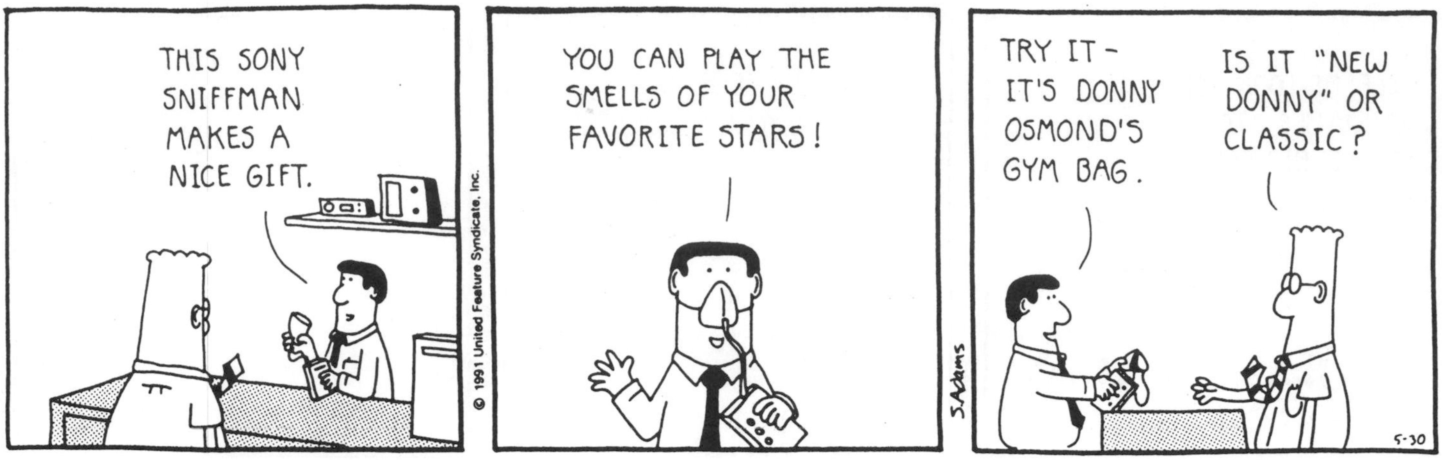
THIS SONY SNIFFMAN MAKES A NICE GIFT.
© 1991 United Feature Syndicate, Inc.
YOU CAN PLAY THE SMELLS OF YOUR FAVORITE STARS!
TRY IT - IT'S DONNY OSMOND'S GYM BAG.
IS IT "NEW DONNY" OR CLASSIC?
S.Adams
5-30

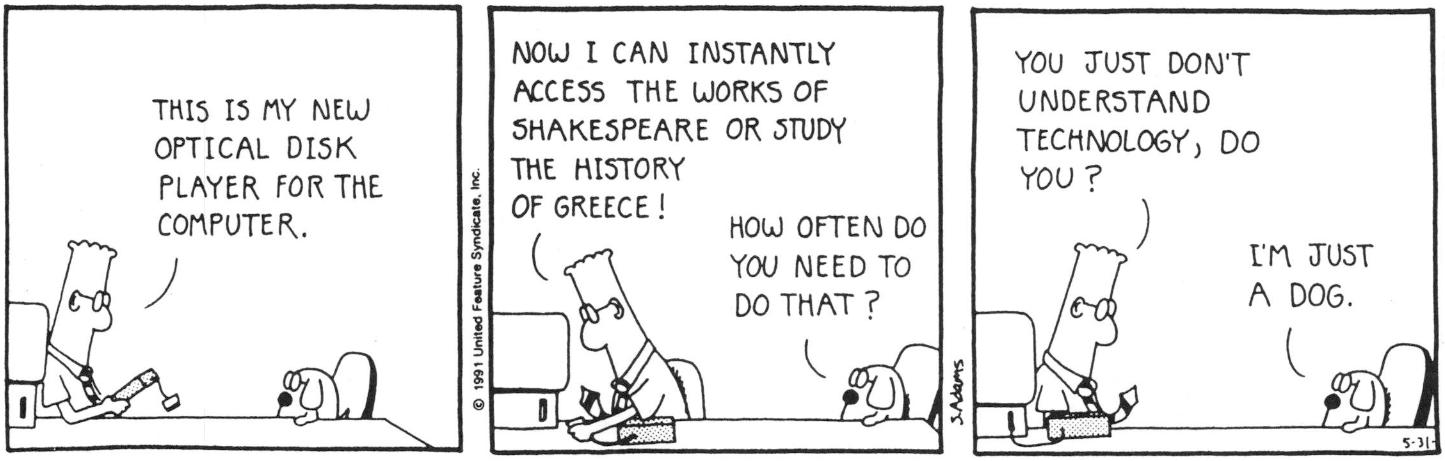
THIS IS MY NEW OPTICAL DISK PLAYER FOR THE COMPUTER.
© 1991 United Feature Syndicate, Inc.
NOW I CAN INSTANTLY ACCESS THE WORKS OF SHAKESPEARE OR STUDY THE HISTORY OF GREECE!
HOW OFTEN DO YOU NEED TO DO THAT?
YOU JUST DON'T UNDERSTAND TECHNOLOGY, DO YOU?
I'M JUST A DOG.
S.Adams
5-31

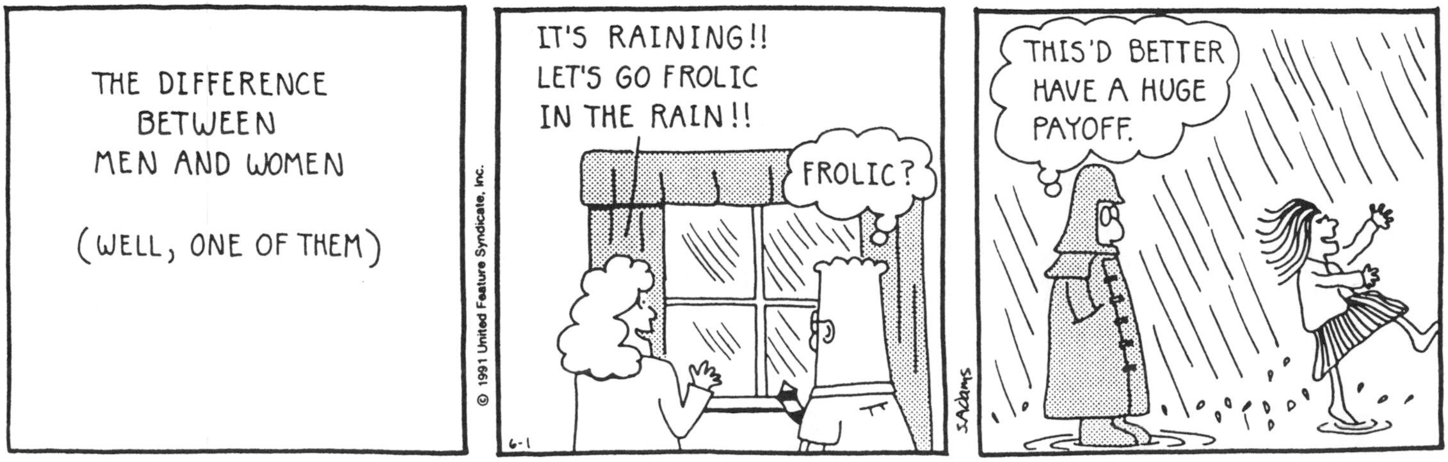
THE DIFFERENCE BETWEEN MEN AND WOMEN
(WELL, ONE OF THEM)
© 1991 United Feature Syndicate, Inc.
IT'S RAINING!! LET'S GO FROLIC IN THE RAIN!!
FROLIC?
6-1
THIS'D BETTER HAVE A HUGE PAYOFF.
S.Adams

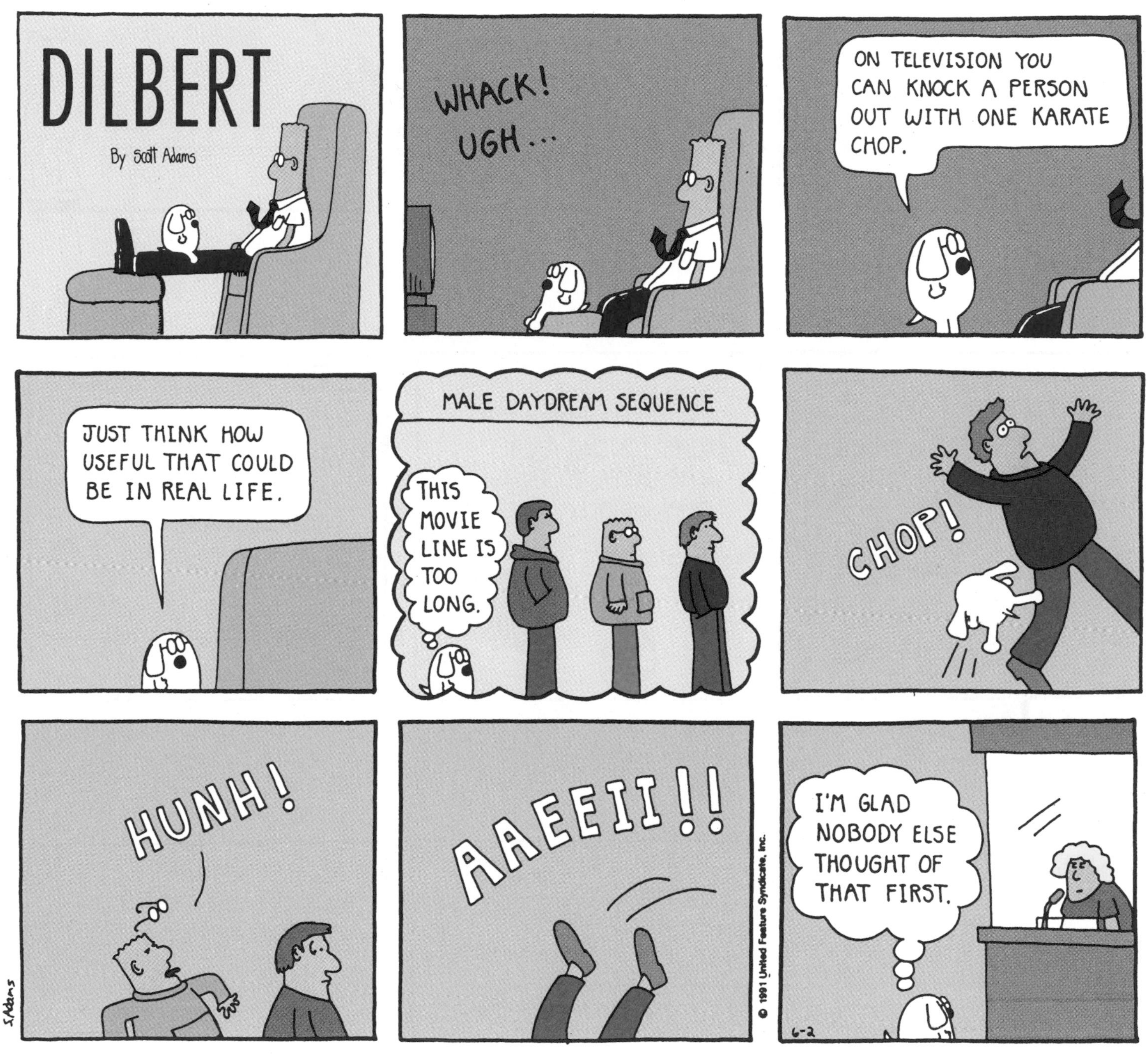
DILBERT
By Scott Adams
WHACK! UGH...
ON TELEVISION YOU CAN KNOCK A PERSON OUT WITH ONE KARATE CHOP.
JUST THINK HOW USEFUL THAT COULD BE IN REAL LIFE.
MALE DAYDREAM SEQUENCE
THIS MOVIE LINE IS TOO LONG.
CHOP!
HUNH!
AAEEII!!
I'M GLAD NOBODY ELSE THOUGHT OF THAT FIRST.
S. Adams
© 1991 United Feature Syndicate, Inc.
6-2

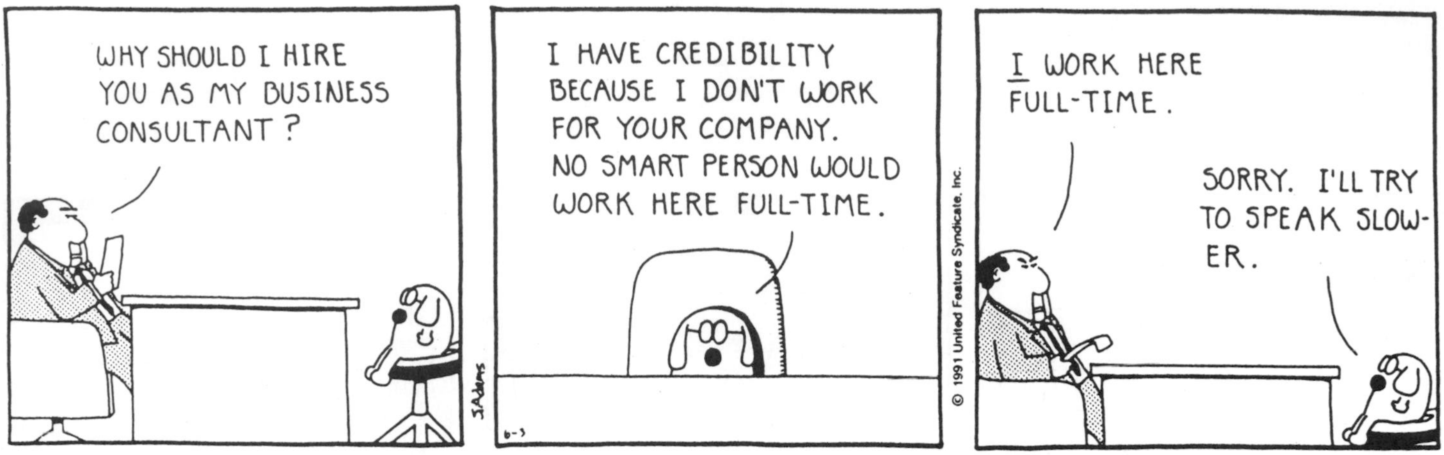
WHY SHOULD I HIRE YOU AS MY BUSINESS CONSULTANT ?
I HAVE CREDIBILITY BECAUSE I DON'T WORK FOR YOUR COMPANY. NO SMART PERSON WOULD WORK HERE FULL-TIME.
I WORK HERE FULL-TIME.
SORRY. I'LL TRY TO SPEAK SLOW-ER.
© 1991 United Feature Syndicate, Inc.

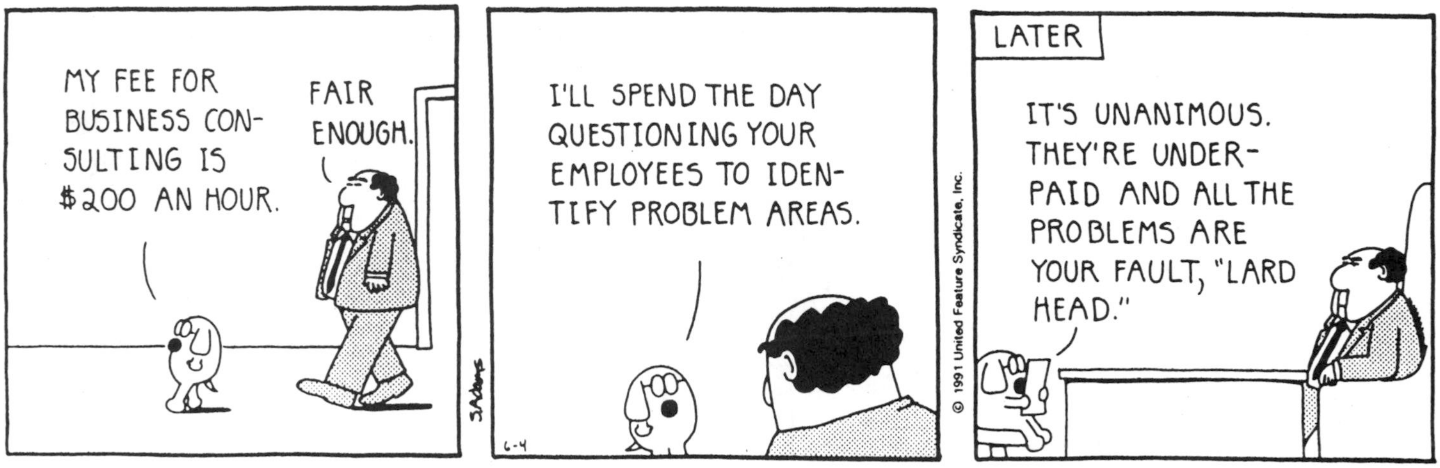
MY FEE FOR BUSINESS CON-SULTING IS $200 AN HOUR.
FAIR ENOUGH.
I'LL SPEND THE DAY QUESTIONING YOUR EMPLOYEES TO IDEN-TIFY PROBLEM AREAS.
LATER
IT'S UNANIMOUS. THEY'RE UNDER-PAID AND ALL THE PROBLEMS ARE YOUR FAULT, "LARD HEAD."
© 1991 United Feature Syndicate, Inc.

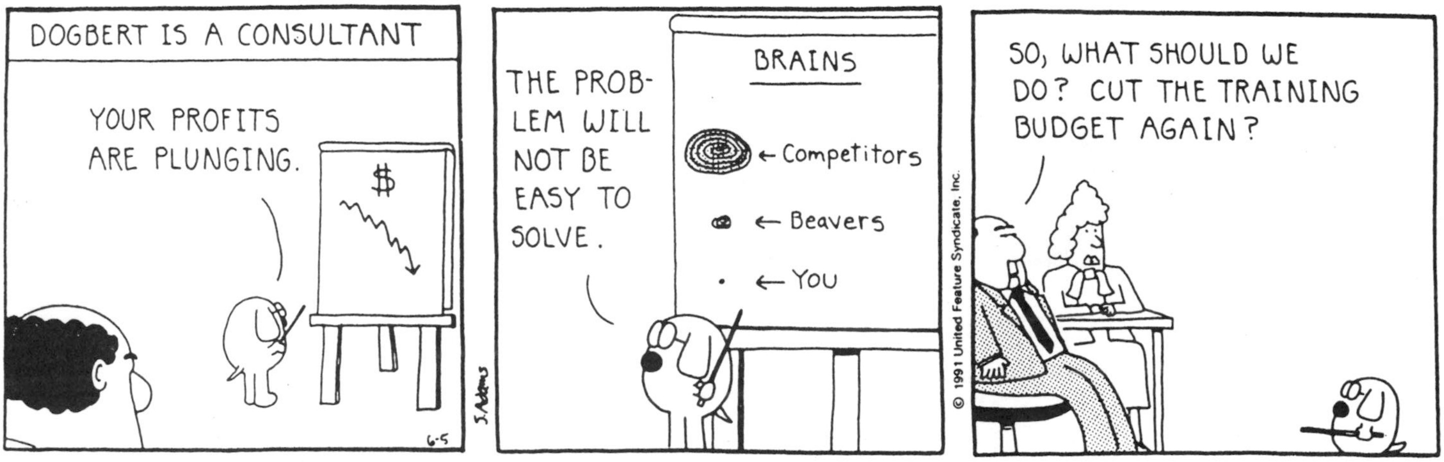
DOGBERT IS A CONSULTANT
YOUR PROFITS ARE PLUNGING.
$
THE PROB-LEM WILL NOT BE EASY TO SOLVE.
BRAINS
← Competitors
← Beavers
← You
SO, WHAT SHOULD WE DO? CUT THE TRAINING BUDGET AGAIN?
© 1991 United Feature Syndicate, Inc.

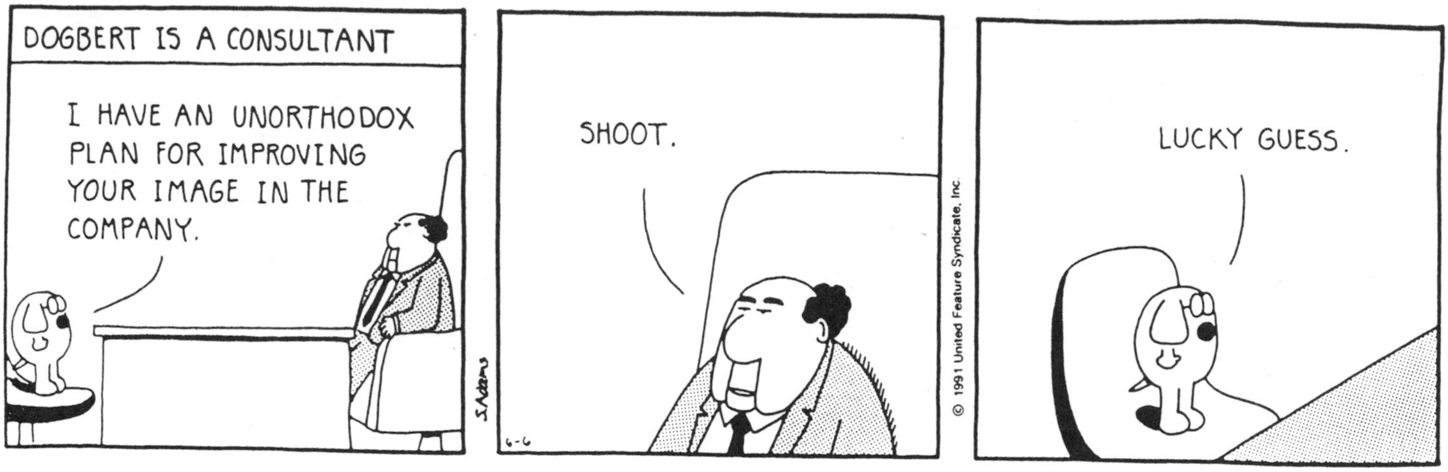
DOGBERT IS A CONSULTANT
I HAVE AN UNORTHODOX PLAN FOR IMPROVING YOUR IMAGE IN THE COMPANY.
S.Adams
6-6
SHOOT.
© 1991 United Feature Syndicate, Inc.
LUCKY GUESS.

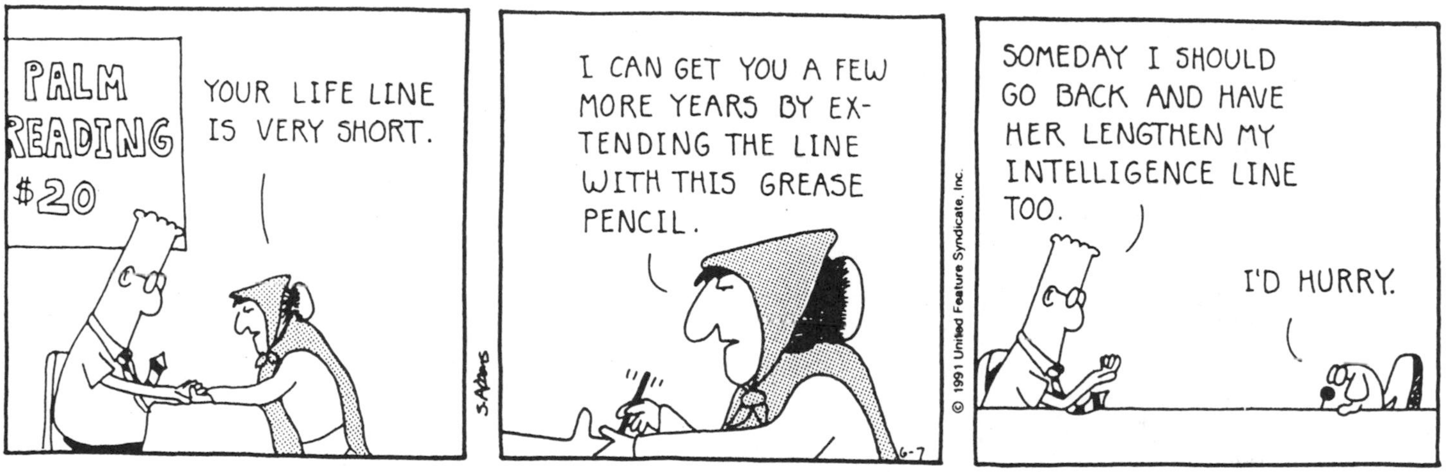
PALM READING $20
YOUR LIFE LINE IS VERY SHORT.
S.Adams
I CAN GET YOU A FEW MORE YEARS BY EX-TENDING THE LINE WITH THIS GREASE PENCIL.
6-7
© 1991 United Feature Syndicate, Inc.
SOMEDAY I SHOULD GO BACK AND HAVE HER LENGTHEN MY INTELLIGENCE LINE TOO.
I'D HURRY.

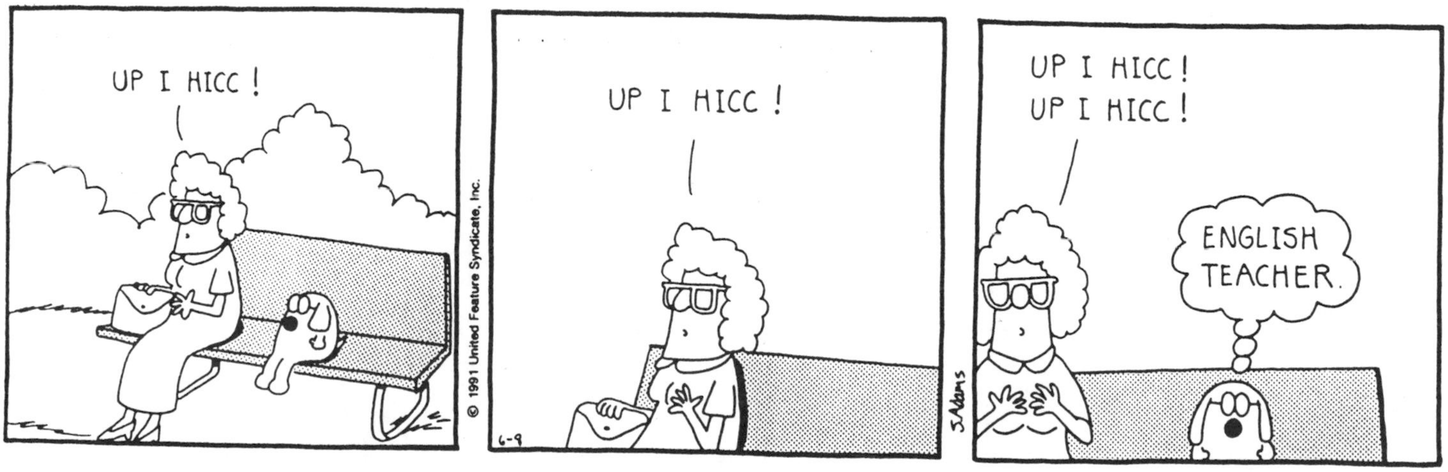
UP I HICC !
© 1991 United Feature Syndicate, Inc.
UP I HICC !
6-9
S.Adams
UP I HICC !
UP I HICC !
ENGLISH TEACHER.

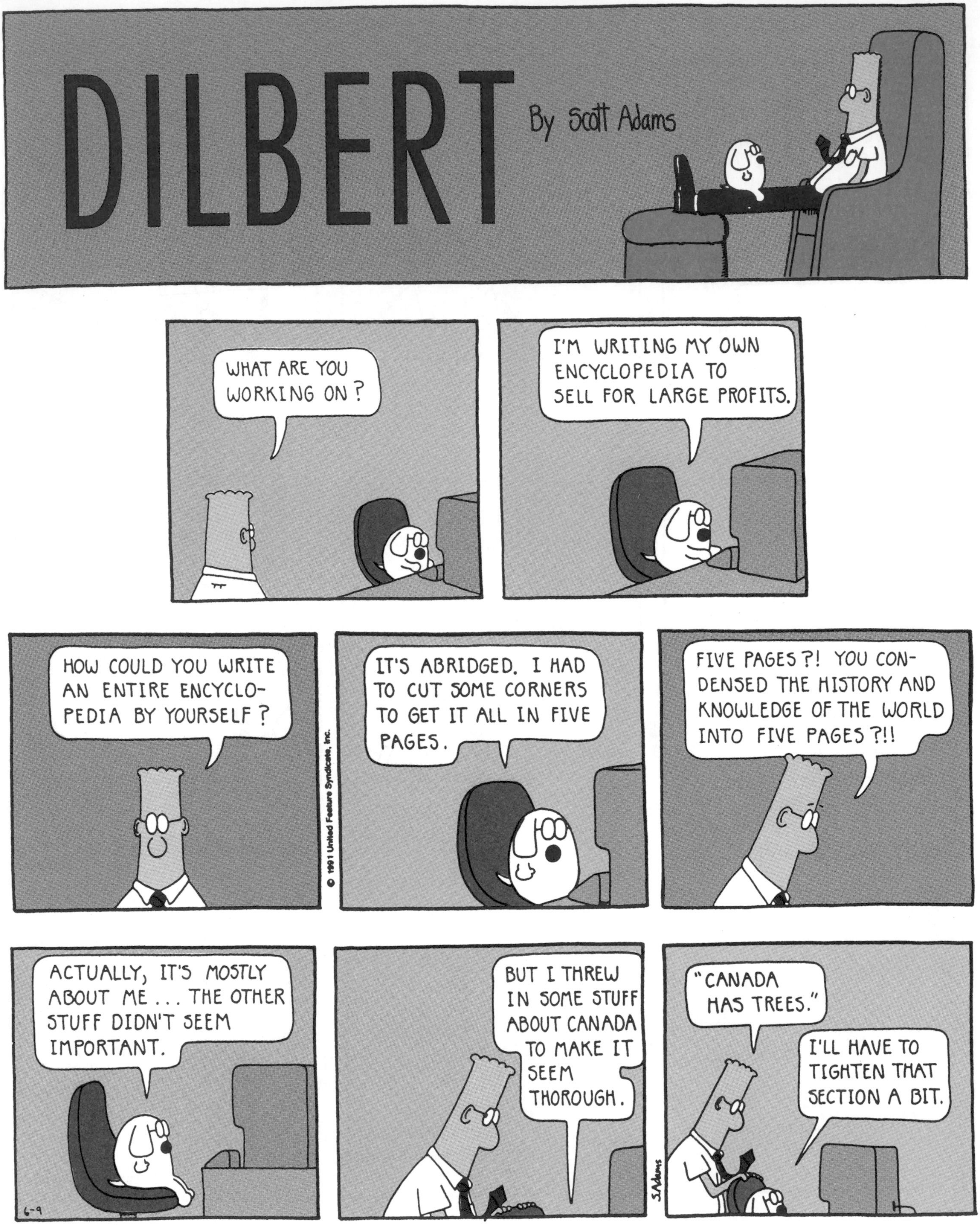
DILBERT
By Scott Adams
WHAT ARE YOU WORKING ON?
I'M WRITING MY OWN ENCYCLOPEDIA TO SELL FOR LARGE PROFITS.
HOW COULD YOU WRITE AN ENTIRE ENCYCLOPEDIA BY YOURSELF?
© 1991 United Feature Syndicate, Inc.
IT'S ABRIDGED. I HAD TO CUT SOME CORNERS TO GET IT ALL IN FIVE PAGES.
FIVE PAGES?! YOU CONDENSED THE HISTORY AND KNOWLEDGE OF THE WORLD INTO FIVE PAGES?!!
ACTUALLY, IT'S MOSTLY ABOUT ME . . . THE OTHER STUFF DIDN'T SEEM IMPORTANT.
6-9
BUT I THREW IN SOME STUFF ABOUT CANADA TO MAKE IT SEEM THOROUGH.
S.Adams
"CANADA HAS TREES."
I'LL HAVE TO TIGHTEN THAT SECTION A BIT.

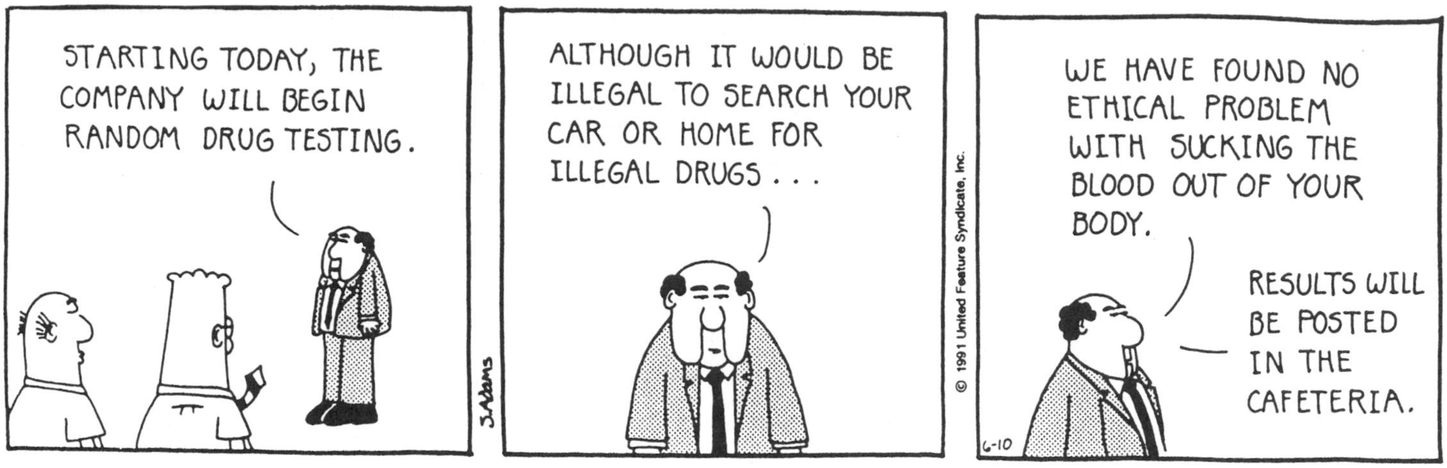
STARTING TODAY, THE COMPANY WILL BEGIN RANDOM DRUG TESTING.
ALTHOUGH IT WOULD BE ILLEGAL TO SEARCH YOUR CAR OR HOME FOR ILLEGAL DRUGS . . .
WE HAVE FOUND NO ETHICAL PROBLEM WITH SUCKING THE BLOOD OUT OF YOUR BODY.
RESULTS WILL BE POSTED IN THE CAFETERIA.
© 1991 United Feature Syndicate, Inc.
6-10

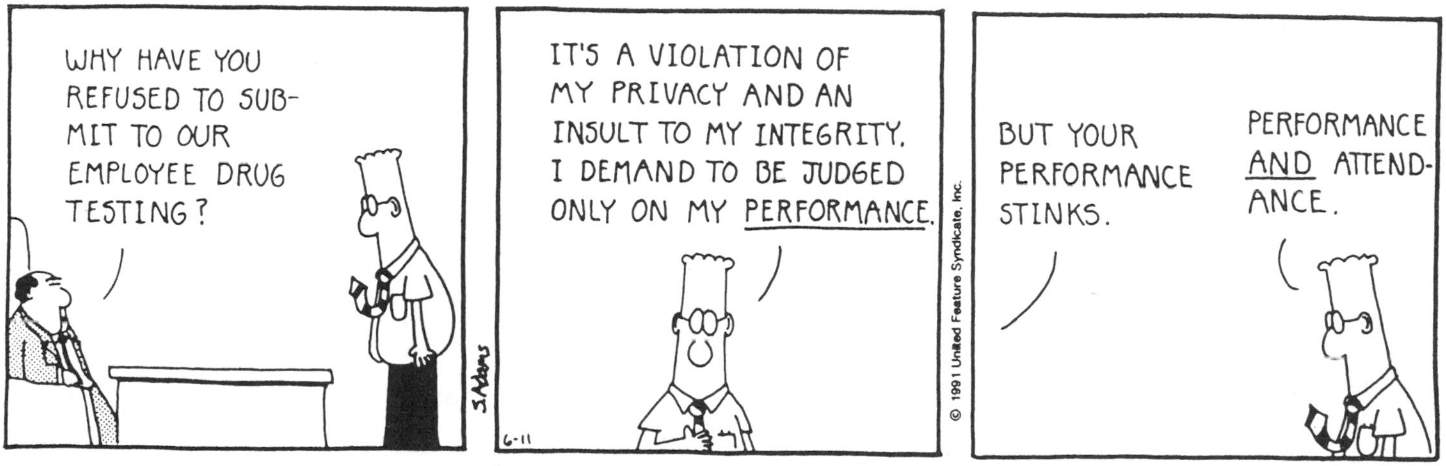
WHY HAVE YOU REFUSED TO SUB-MIT TO OUR EMPLOYEE DRUG TESTING?
IT'S A VIOLATION OF MY PRIVACY AND AN INSULT TO MY INTEGRITY. I DEMAND TO BE JUDGED ONLY ON MY PERFORMANCE.
BUT YOUR PERFORMANCE STINKS.
PERFORMANCE AND ATTEND-ANCE.
© 1991 United Feature Syndicate, Inc.
6-11

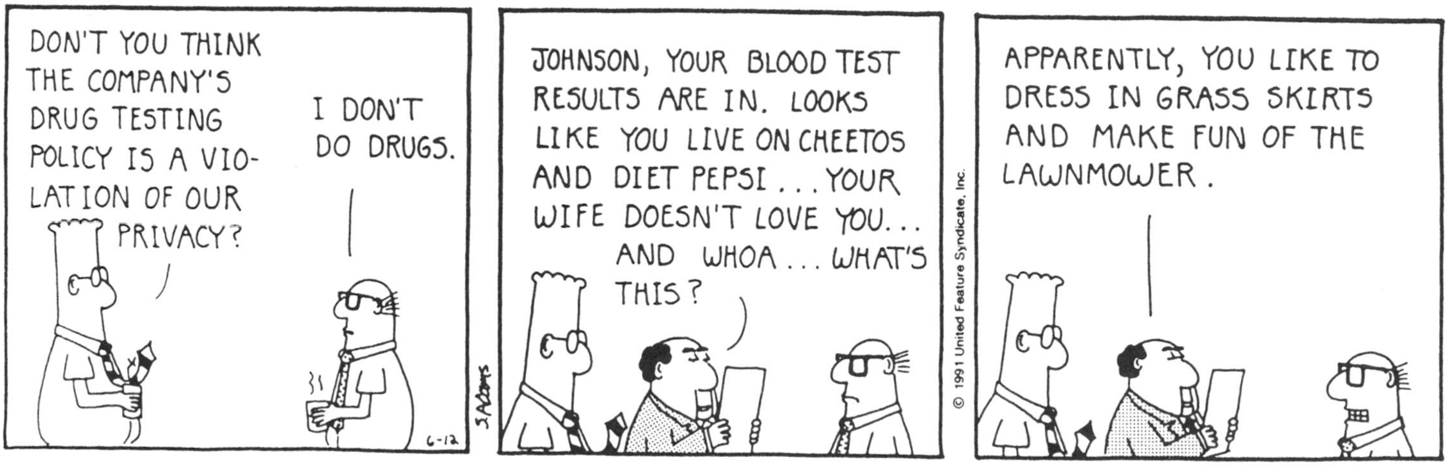
DON'T YOU THINK THE COMPANY'S DRUG TESTING POLICY IS A VIO-LATION OF OUR PRIVACY?
I DON'T DO DRUGS.
JOHNSON, YOUR BLOOD TEST RESULTS ARE IN. LOOKS LIKE YOU LIVE ON CHEETOS AND DIET PEPSI . . . YOUR WIFE DOESN'T LOVE YOU . . .
AND WHOA . . . WHAT'S THIS?
APPARENTLY, YOU LIKE TO DRESS IN GRASS SKIRTS AND MAKE FUN OF THE LAWNMOWER.
© 1991 United Feature Syndicate, Inc.
6-12

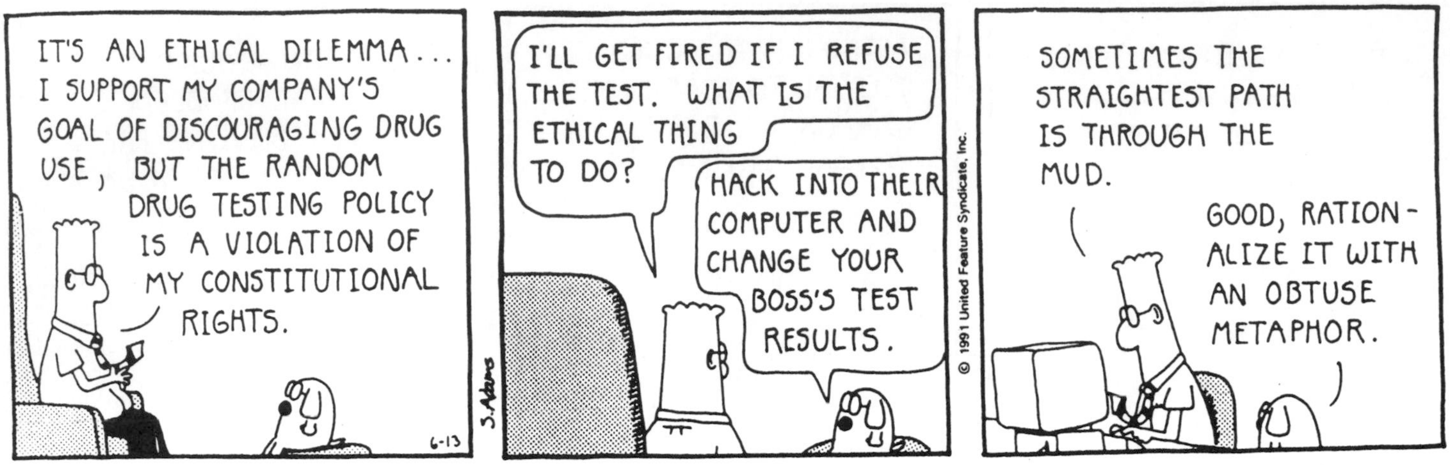

IT'S AN ETHICAL DILEMMA... I SUPPORT MY COMPANY'S GOAL OF DISCOURAGING DRUG USE, BUT THE RANDOM DRUG TESTING POLICY IS A VIOLATION OF MY CONSTITUTIONAL RIGHTS.
I'LL GET FIRED IF I REFUSE THE TEST. WHAT IS THE ETHICAL THING TO DO?
HACK INTO THEIR COMPUTER AND CHANGE YOUR BOSS'S TEST RESULTS.
SOMETIMES THE STRAIGHTEST PATH IS THROUGH THE MUD.
GOOD, RATIONALIZE IT WITH AN OBTUSE METAPHOR.
© 1991 United Feature Syndicate, Inc.

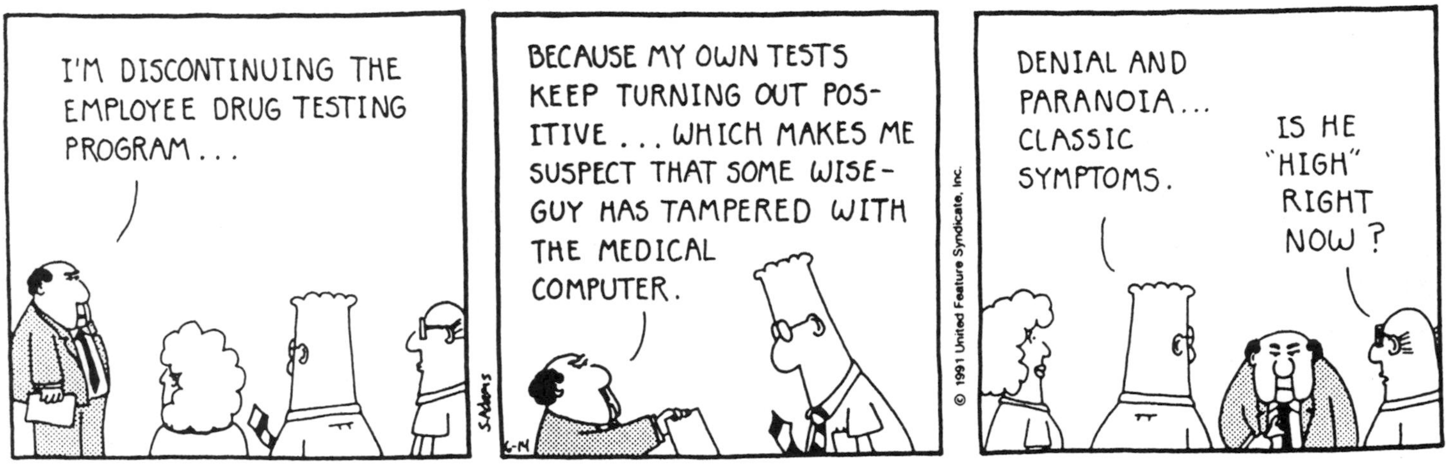

I'M DISCONTINUING THE EMPLOYEE DRUG TESTING PROGRAM...
BECAUSE MY OWN TESTS KEEP TURNING OUT POSITIVE... WHICH MAKES ME SUSPECT THAT SOME WISEGUY HAS TAMPERED WITH THE MEDICAL COMPUTER.
DENIAL AND PARANOIA... CLASSIC SYMPTOMS.
IS HE "HIGH" RIGHT NOW?
© 1991 United Feature Syndicate, Inc.

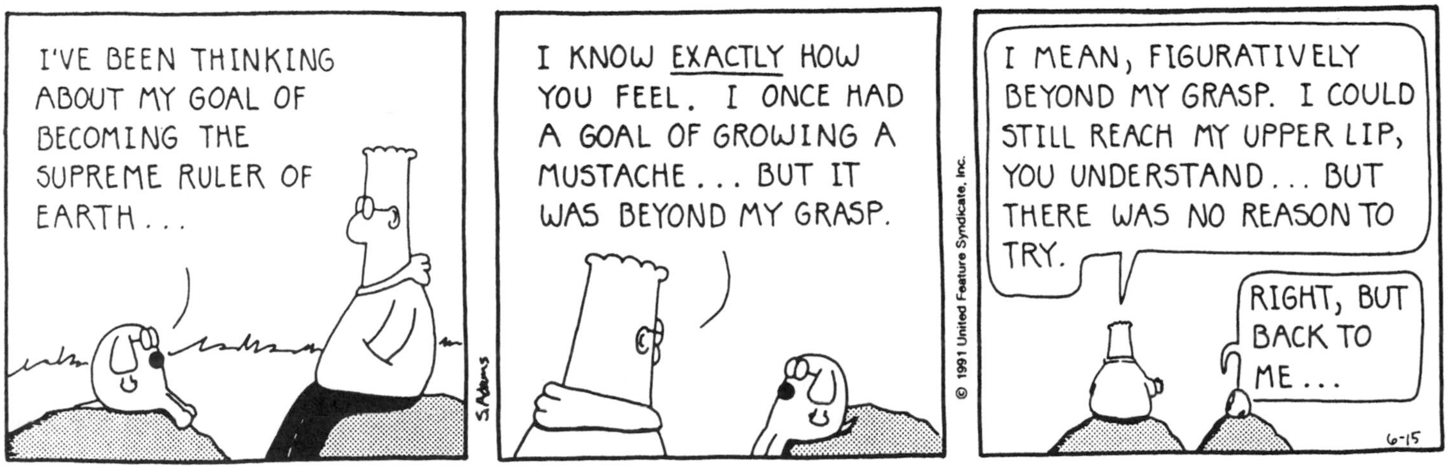

I'VE BEEN THINKING ABOUT MY GOAL OF BECOMING THE SUPREME RULER OF EARTH...
I KNOW EXACTLY HOW YOU FEEL. I ONCE HAD A GOAL OF GROWING A MUSTACHE... BUT IT WAS BEYOND MY GRASP.
I MEAN, FIGURATIVELY BEYOND MY GRASP. I COULD STILL REACH MY UPPER LIP, YOU UNDERSTAND... BUT THERE WAS NO REASON TO TRY.
RIGHT, BUT BACK TO ME...
© 1991 United Feature Syndicate, Inc.

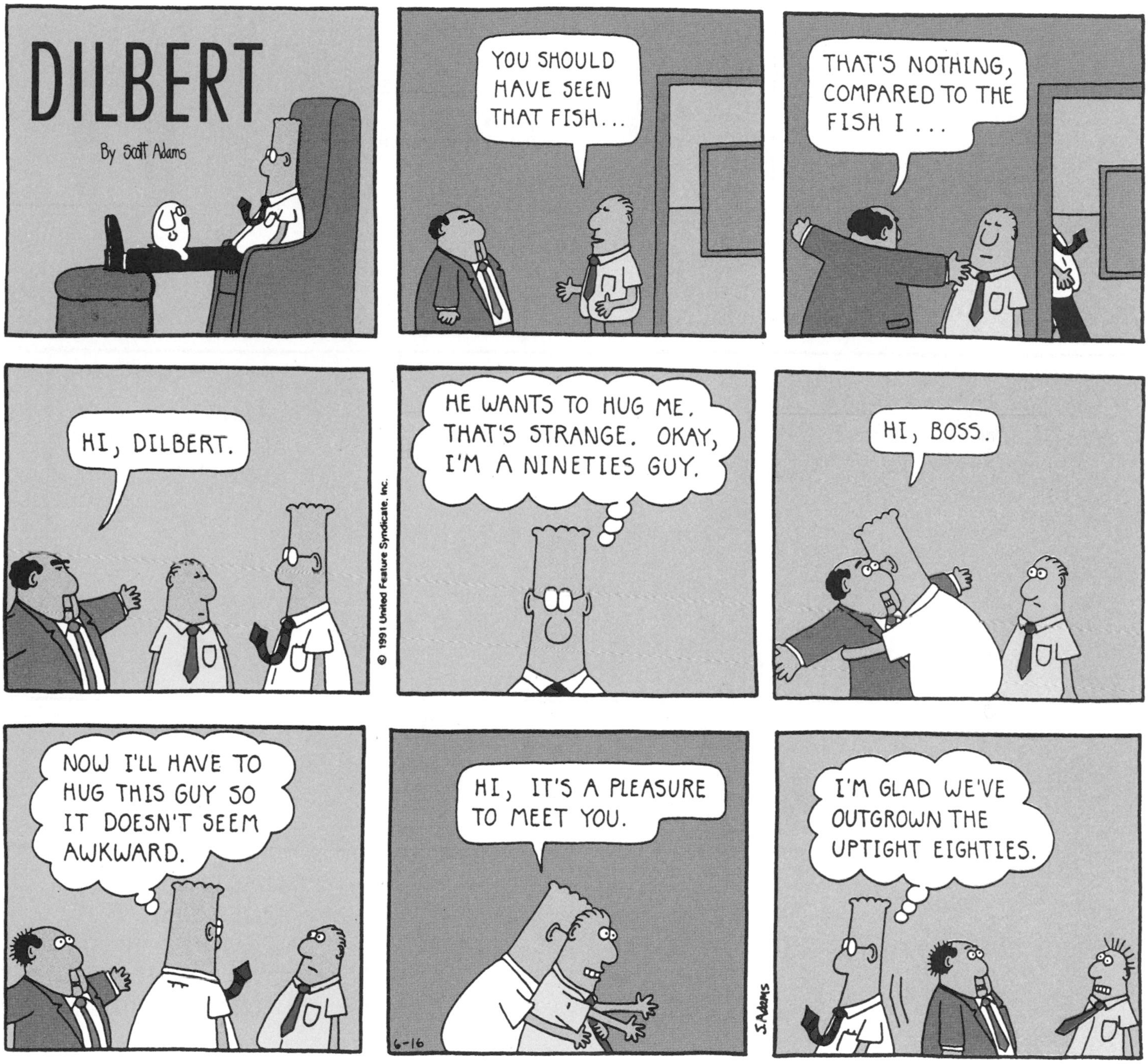

DILBERT
By Scott Adams
YOU SHOULD HAVE SEEN THAT FISH...
THAT'S NOTHING, COMPARED TO THE FISH I ...
HI, DILBERT.
© 1991 United Feature Syndicate, Inc.
HE WANTS TO HUG ME. THAT'S STRANGE. OKAY, I'M A NINETIES GUY.
HI, BOSS.
NOW I'LL HAVE TO HUG THIS GUY SO IT DOESN'T SEEM AWKWARD.
HI, IT'S A PLEASURE TO MEET YOU.
6-16
S. ADAMS
I'M GLAD WE'VE OUTGROWN THE UPTIGHT EIGHTIES.

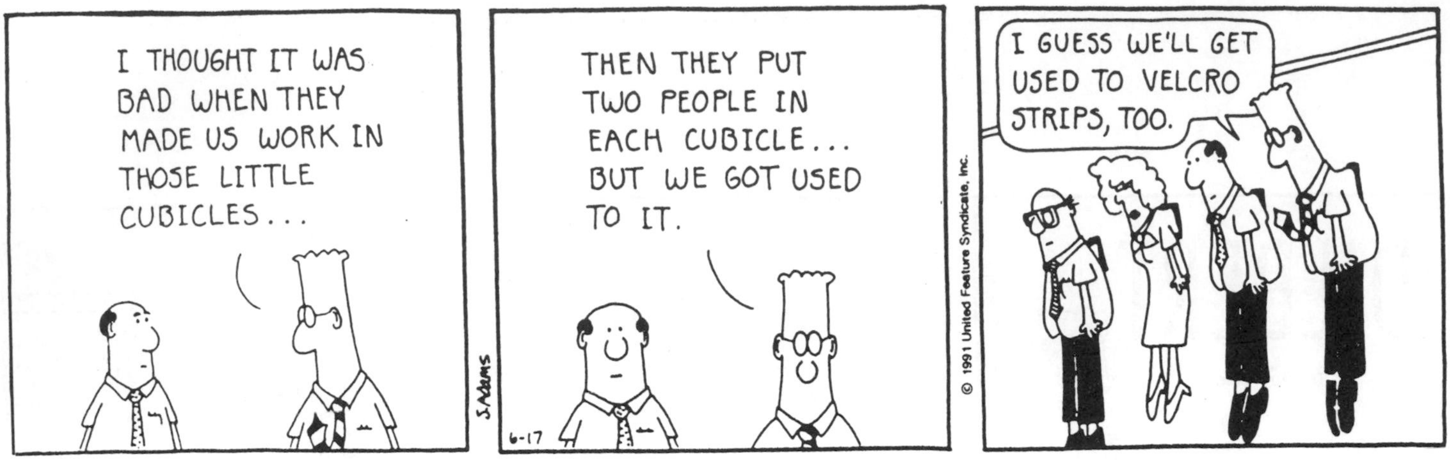
I THOUGHT IT WAS BAD WHEN THEY MADE US WORK IN THOSE LITTLE CUBICLES...
S. Adams
THEN THEY PUT TWO PEOPLE IN EACH CUBICLE... BUT WE GOT USED TO IT.
6-17
© 1991 United Feature Syndicate, Inc.
I GUESS WE'LL GET USED TO VELCRO STRIPS, TOO.

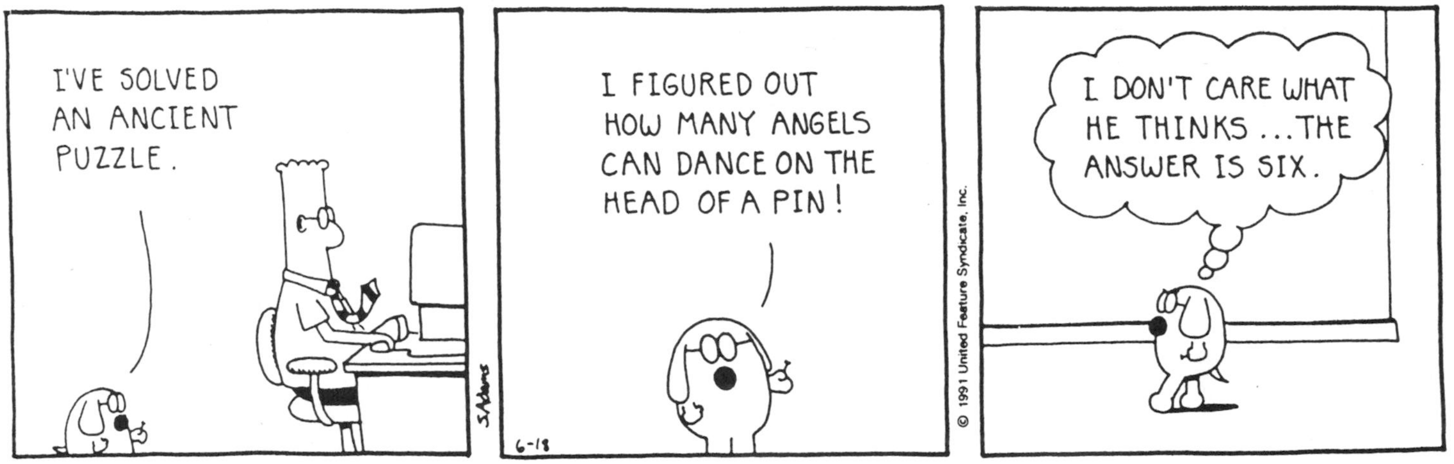
I'VE SOLVED AN ANCIENT PUZZLE.
S. Adams
I FIGURED OUT HOW MANY ANGELS CAN DANCE ON THE HEAD OF A PIN!
6-18
© 1991 United Feature Syndicate, Inc.
I DON'T CARE WHAT HE THINKS...THE ANSWER IS SIX.

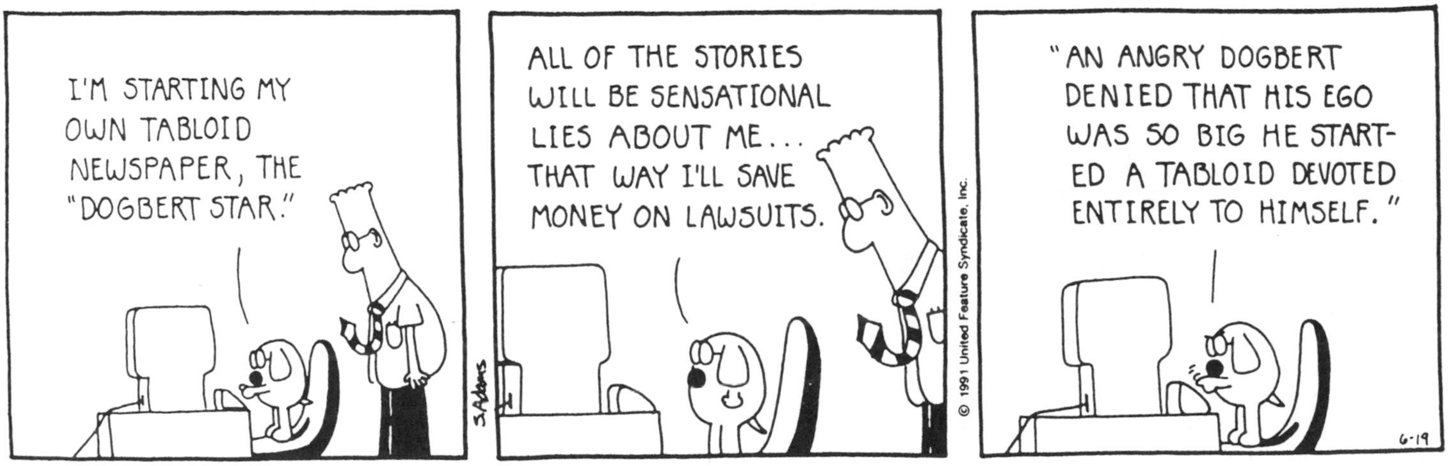
I'M STARTING MY OWN TABLOID NEWSPAPER, THE "DOGBERT STAR."
S. Adams
ALL OF THE STORIES WILL BE SENSATIONAL LIES ABOUT ME... THAT WAY I'LL SAVE MONEY ON LAWSUITS.
© 1991 United Feature Syndicate, Inc.
"AN ANGRY DOGBERT DENIED THAT HIS EGO WAS SO BIG HE STARTED A TABLOID DEVOTED ENTIRELY TO HIMSELF."
6-19

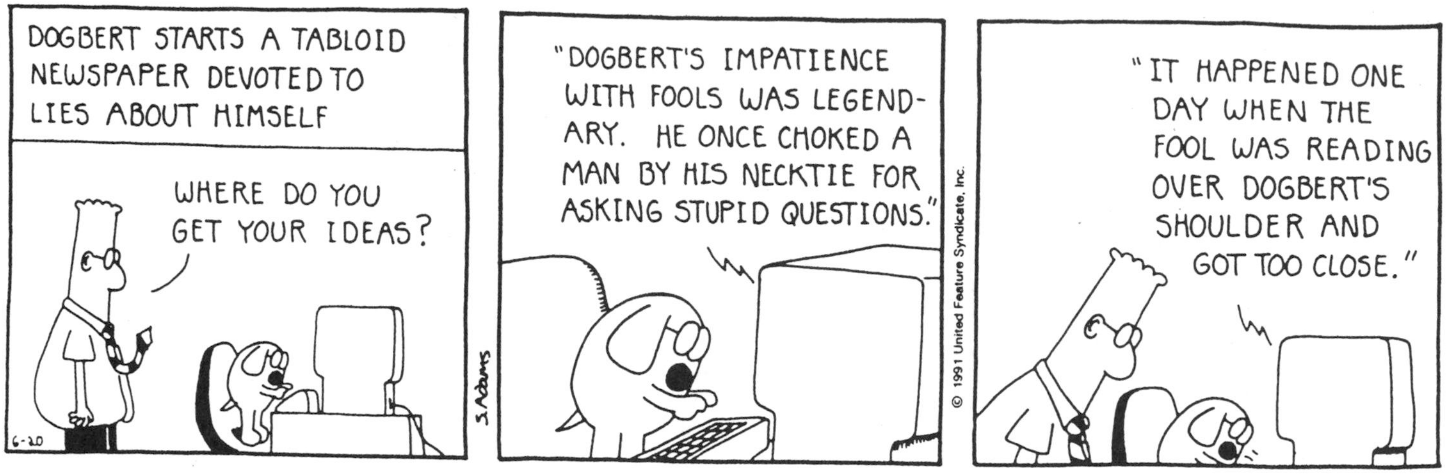

DOGBERT STARTS A TABLOID NEWSPAPER DEVOTED TO LIES ABOUT HIMSELF
WHERE DO YOU GET YOUR IDEAS?
"DOGBERT'S IMPATIENCE WITH FOOLS WAS LEGENDARY. HE ONCE CHOKED A MAN BY HIS NECKTIE FOR ASKING STUPID QUESTIONS."
"IT HAPPENED ONE DAY WHEN THE FOOL WAS READING OVER DOGBERT'S SHOULDER AND GOT TOO CLOSE."
© 1991 United Feature Syndicate, Inc.

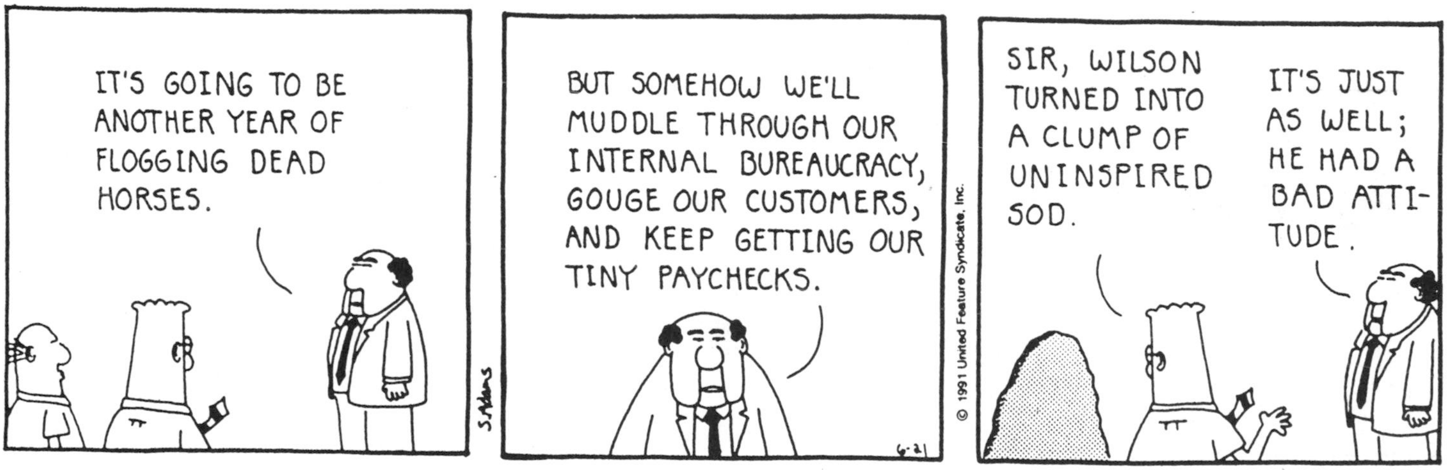

IT'S GOING TO BE ANOTHER YEAR OF FLOGGING DEAD HORSES.
BUT SOMEHOW WE'LL MUDDLE THROUGH OUR INTERNAL BUREAUCRACY, GOUGE OUR CUSTOMERS, AND KEEP GETTING OUR TINY PAYCHECKS.
SIR, WILSON TURNED INTO A CLUMP OF UNINSPIRED SOD.
IT'S JUST AS WELL; HE HAD A BAD ATTITUDE.
© 1991 United Feature Syndicate, Inc.

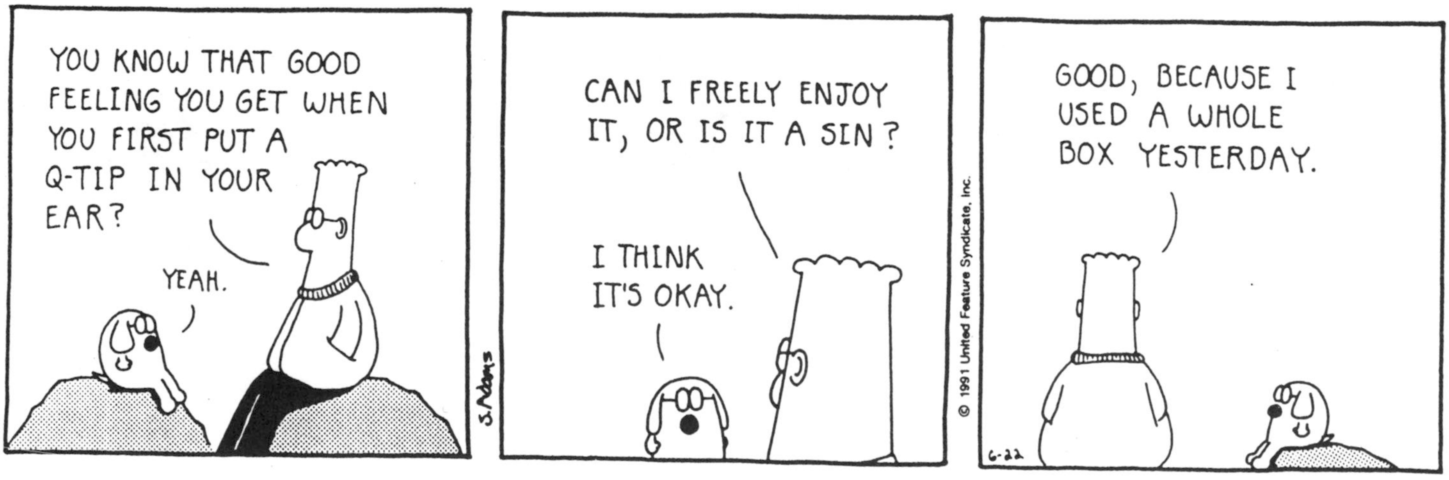

YOU KNOW THAT GOOD FEELING YOU GET WHEN YOU FIRST PUT A Q-TIP IN YOUR EAR?
YEAH.
CAN I FREELY ENJOY IT, OR IS IT A SIN?
I THINK IT'S OKAY.
GOOD, BECAUSE I USED A WHOLE BOX YESTERDAY.
© 1991 United Feature Syndicate, Inc.

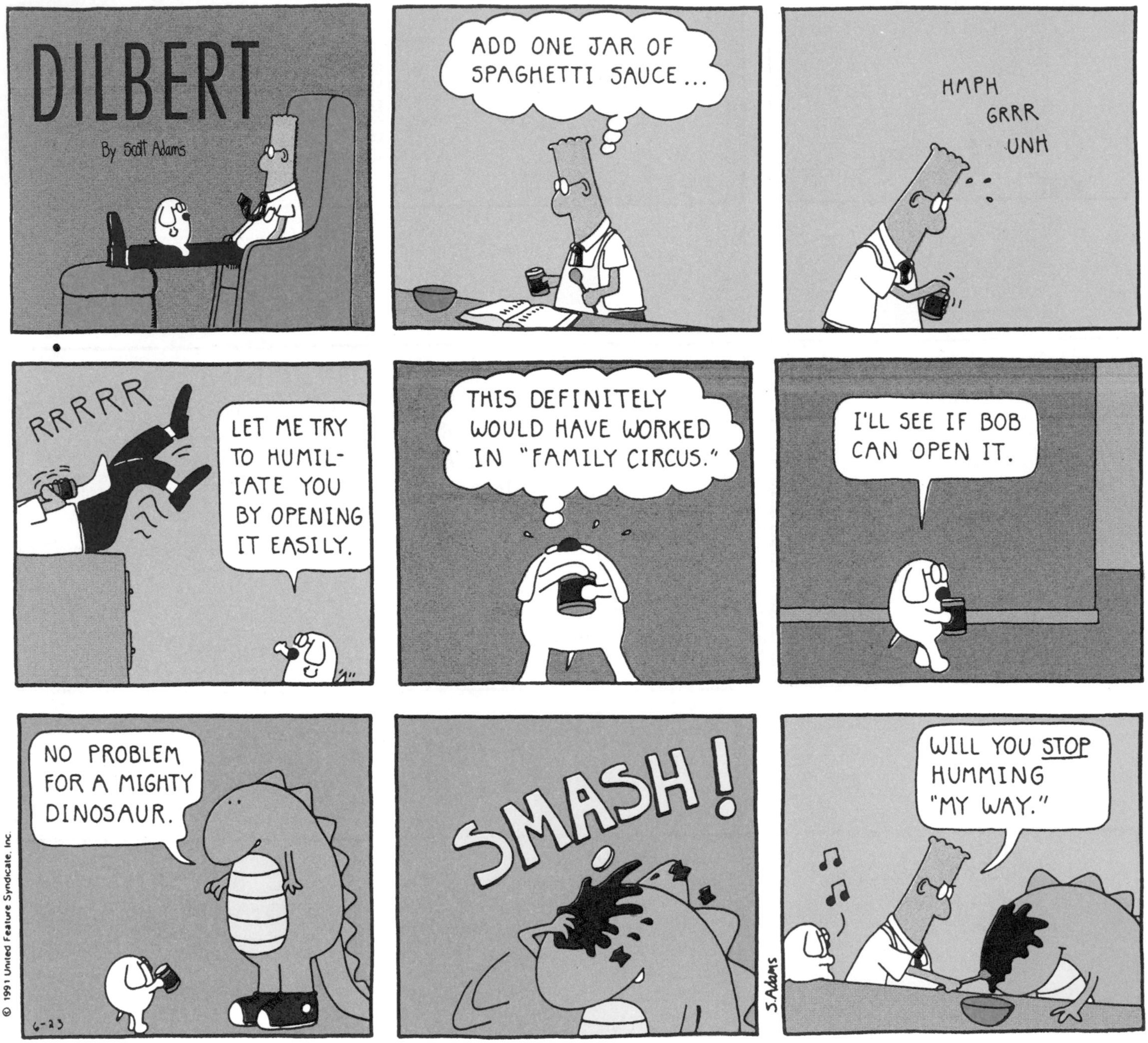
DILBERT
By Scott Adams
ADD ONE JAR OF SPAGHETTI SAUCE...
HMPH
GRRR
UNH
RRRRR
LET ME TRY TO HUMIL-IATE YOU BY OPENING IT EASILY.
THIS DEFINITELY WOULD HAVE WORKED IN "FAMILY CIRCUS."
I'LL SEE IF BOB CAN OPEN IT.
NO PROBLEM FOR A MIGHTY DINOSAUR.
© 1991 United Feature Syndicate, Inc.
6-23
SMASH!
S. Adams
WILL YOU STOP HUMMING "MY WAY."

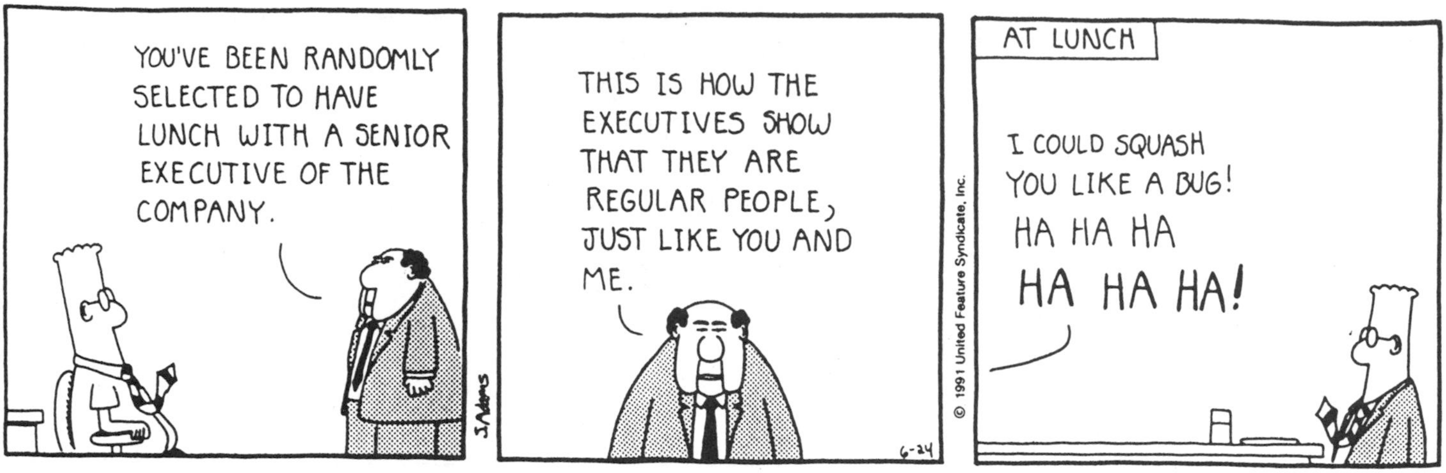
YOU'VE BEEN RANDOMLY SELECTED TO HAVE LUNCH WITH A SENIOR EXECUTIVE OF THE COMPANY.
THIS IS HOW THE EXECUTIVES SHOW THAT THEY ARE REGULAR PEOPLE, JUST LIKE YOU AND ME.
AT LUNCH
I COULD SQUASH YOU LIKE A BUG! HA HA HA HA HA HA!
© 1991 United Feature Syndicate, Inc.

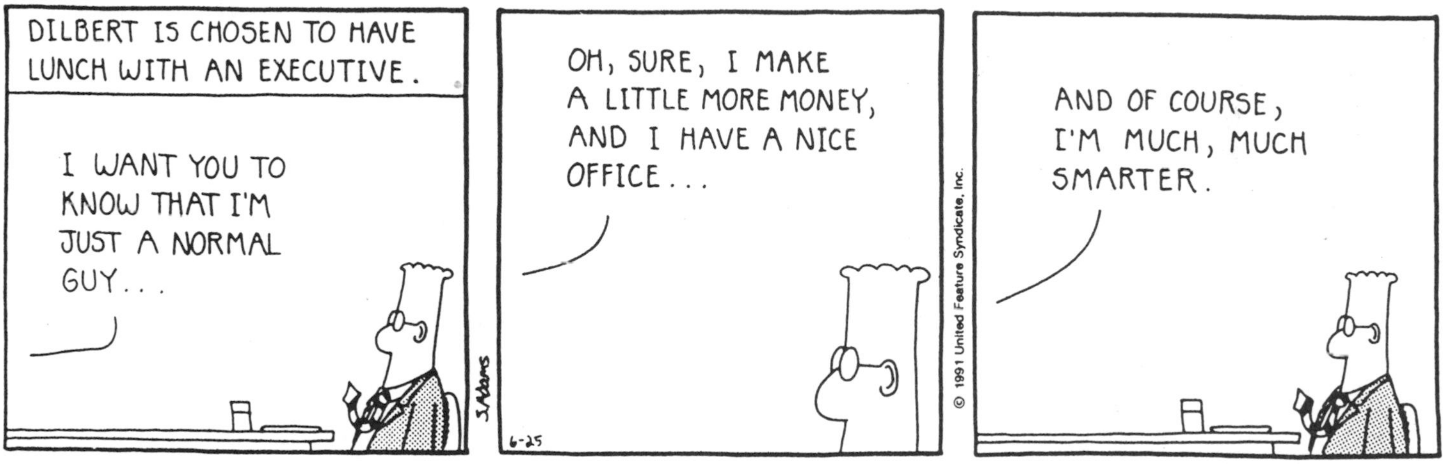
DILBERT IS CHOSEN TO HAVE LUNCH WITH AN EXECUTIVE.
I WANT YOU TO KNOW THAT I'M JUST A NORMAL GUY...
OH, SURE, I MAKE A LITTLE MORE MONEY, AND I HAVE A NICE OFFICE...
AND OF COURSE, I'M MUCH, MUCH SMARTER.
© 1991 United Feature Syndicate, Inc.

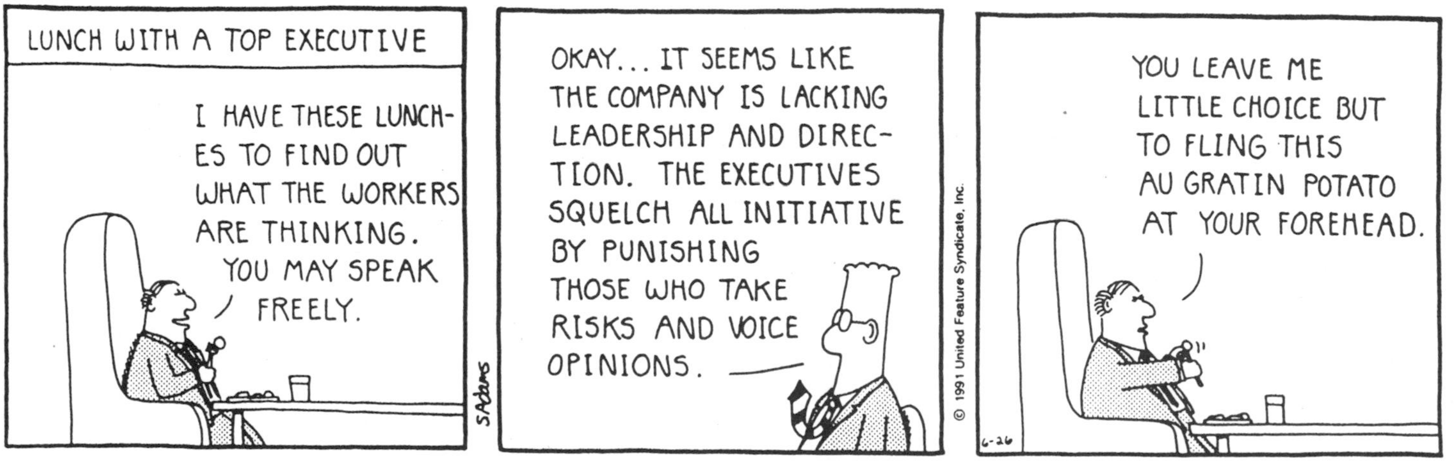
LUNCH WITH A TOP EXECUTIVE
I HAVE THESE LUNCHES TO FIND OUT WHAT THE WORKERS ARE THINKING. YOU MAY SPEAK FREELY.
OKAY... IT SEEMS LIKE THE COMPANY IS LACKING LEADERSHIP AND DIRECTION. THE EXECUTIVES SQUELCH ALL INITIATIVE BY PUNISHING THOSE WHO TAKE RISKS AND VOICE OPINIONS.
YOU LEAVE ME LITTLE CHOICE BUT TO FLING THIS AU GRATIN POTATO AT YOUR FOREHEAD.
© 1991 United Feature Syndicate, Inc.

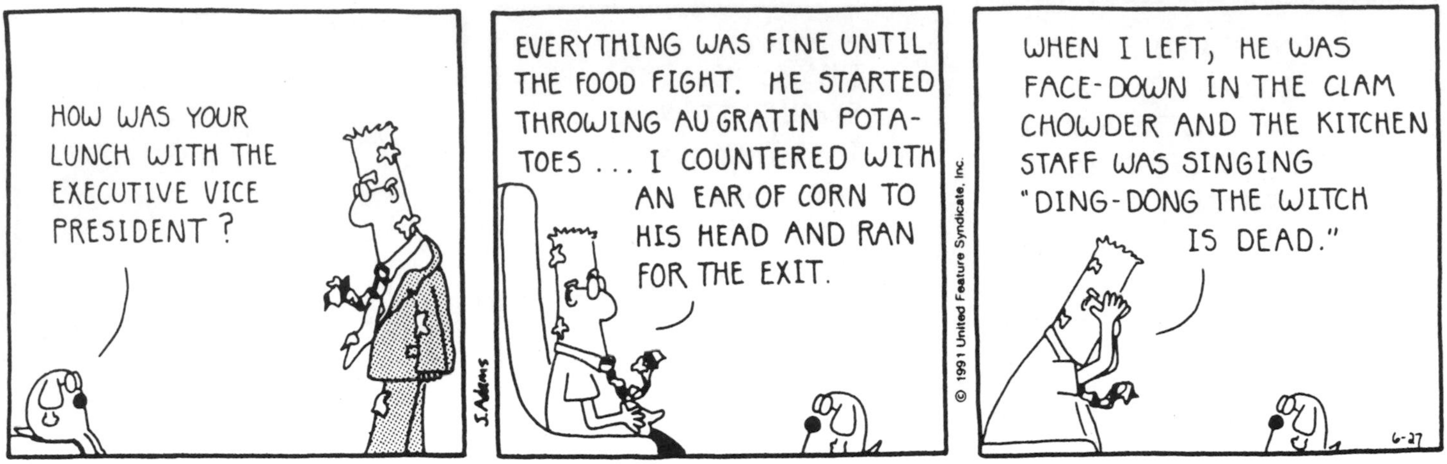
HOW WAS YOUR LUNCH WITH THE EXECUTIVE VICE PRESIDENT ?
EVERYTHING WAS FINE UNTIL THE FOOD FIGHT. HE STARTED THROWING AU GRATIN POTATOES . . . I COUNTERED WITH AN EAR OF CORN TO HIS HEAD AND RAN FOR THE EXIT.
© 1991 United Feature Syndicate, Inc.
WHEN I LEFT, HE WAS FACE-DOWN IN THE CLAM CHOWDER AND THE KITCHEN STAFF WAS SINGING "DING-DONG THE WITCH IS DEAD."
6-27

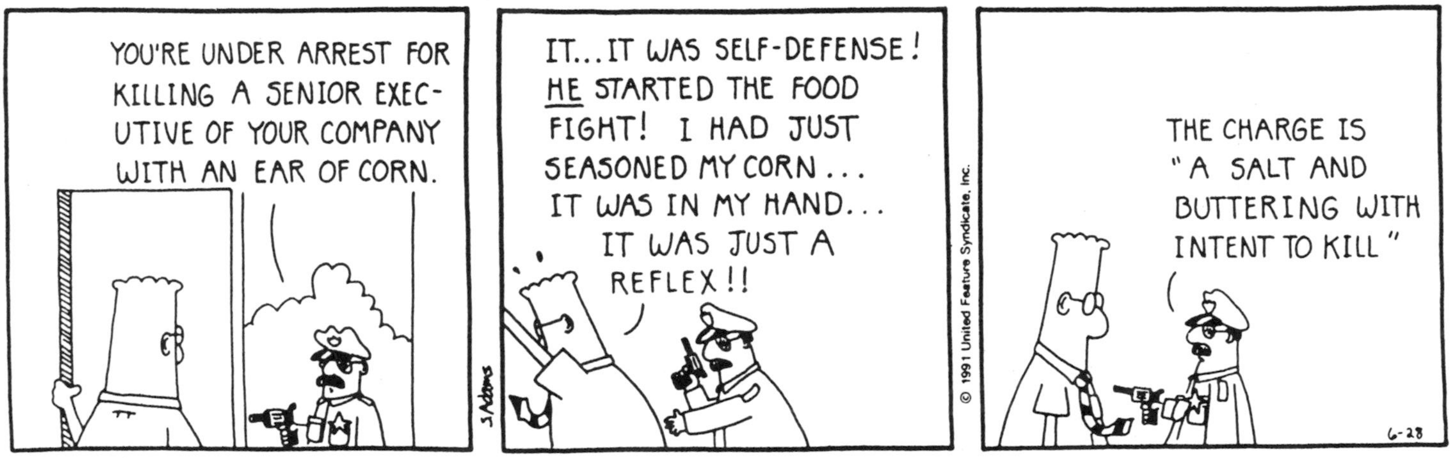
YOU'RE UNDER ARREST FOR KILLING A SENIOR EXECUTIVE OF YOUR COMPANY WITH AN EAR OF CORN.
IT...IT WAS SELF-DEFENSE! HE STARTED THE FOOD FIGHT! I HAD JUST SEASONED MY CORN . . . IT WAS IN MY HAND . . . IT WAS JUST A REFLEX!!
© 1991 United Feature Syndicate, Inc.
THE CHARGE IS "A SALT AND BUTTERING WITH INTENT TO KILL"
6-28

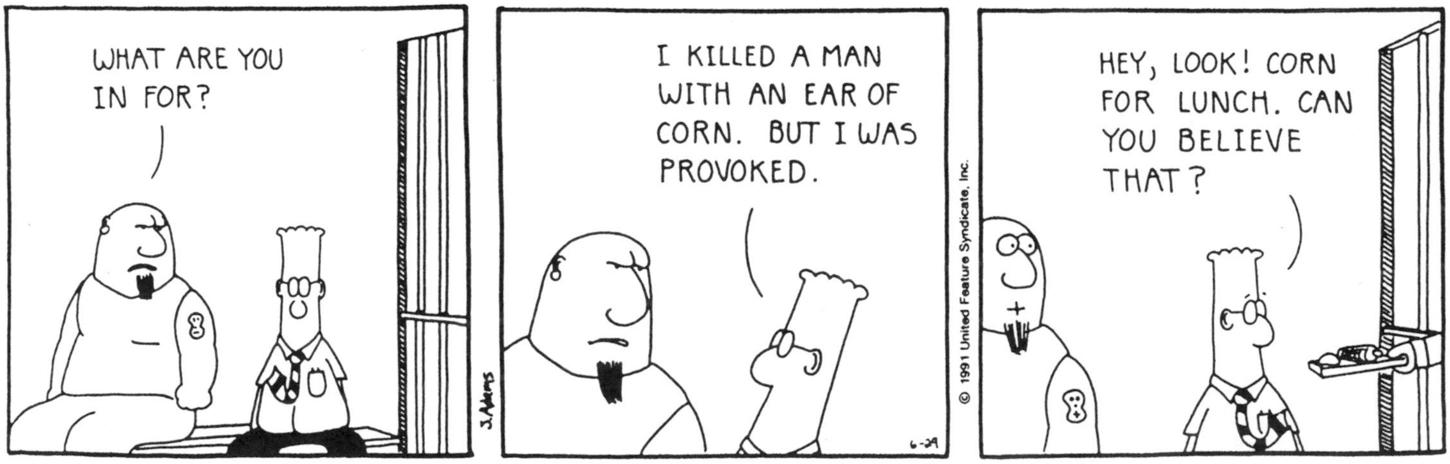
WHAT ARE YOU IN FOR?
I KILLED A MAN WITH AN EAR OF CORN. BUT I WAS PROVOKED.
© 1991 United Feature Syndicate, Inc.
HEY, LOOK! CORN FOR LUNCH. CAN YOU BELIEVE THAT?

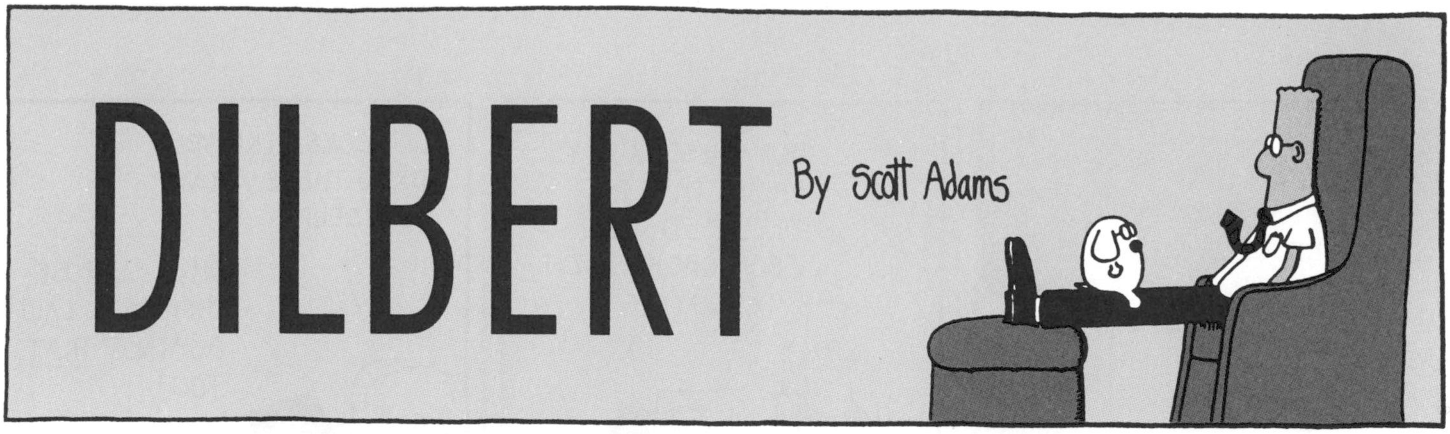
DILBERT
By Scott Adams

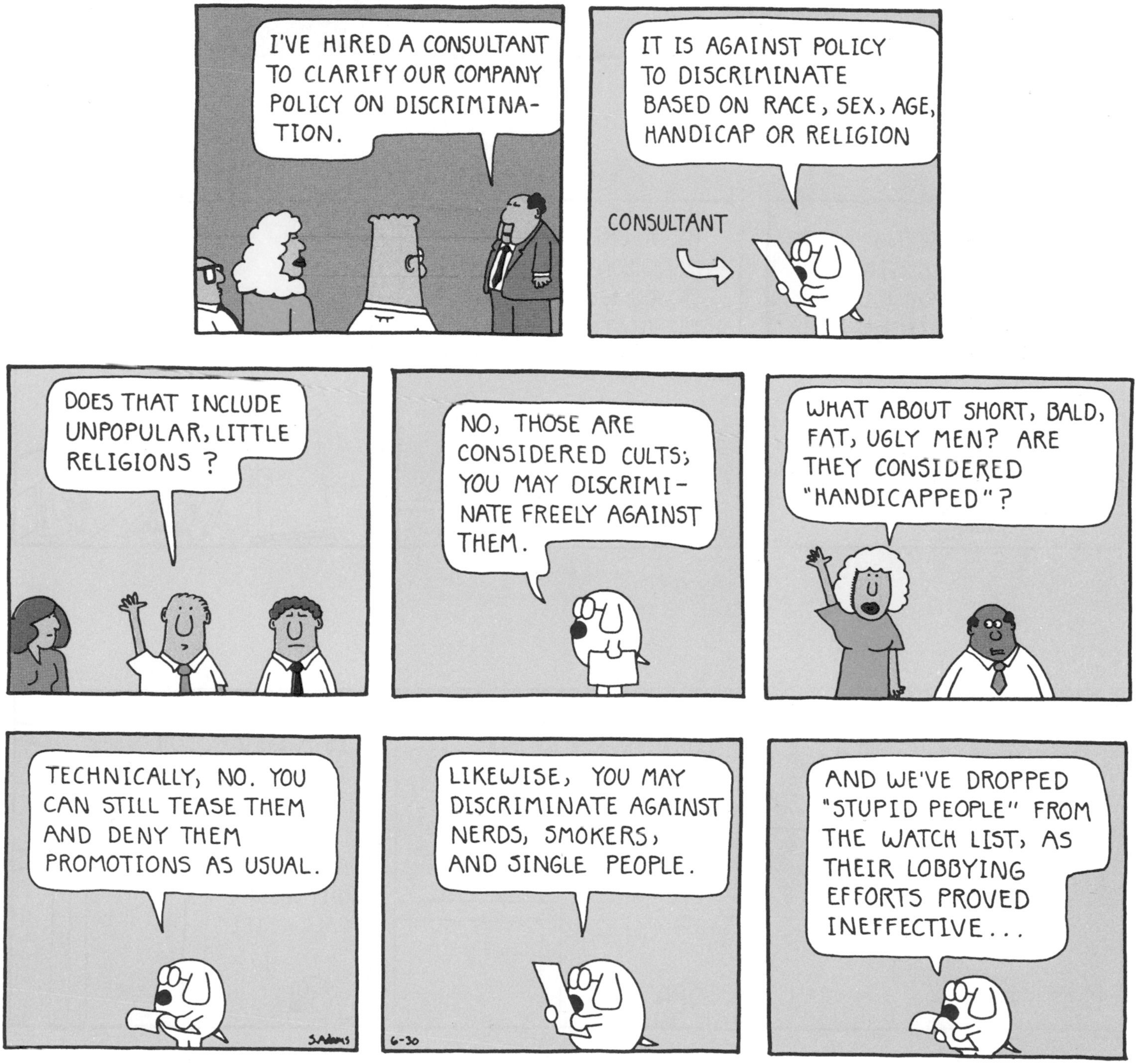
I'VE HIRED A CONSULTANT TO CLARIFY OUR COMPANY POLICY ON DISCRIMINA-TION.
IT IS AGAINST POLICY TO DISCRIMINATE BASED ON RACE, SEX, AGE, HANDICAP OR RELIGION
CONSULTANT
DOES THAT INCLUDE UNPOPULAR, LITTLE RELIGIONS ?
NO, THOSE ARE CONSIDERED CULTS; YOU MAY DISCRIMI-NATE FREELY AGAINST THEM.
WHAT ABOUT SHORT, BALD, FAT, UGLY MEN? ARE THEY CONSIDERED "HANDICAPPED"?
TECHNICALLY, NO. YOU CAN STILL TEASE THEM AND DENY THEM PROMOTIONS AS USUAL.
S.Adams
LIKEWISE, YOU MAY DISCRIMINATE AGAINST NERDS, SMOKERS, AND SINGLE PEOPLE.
6-30
AND WE'VE DROPPED "STUPID PEOPLE" FROM THE WATCH LIST, AS THEIR LOBBYING EFFORTS PROVED INEFFECTIVE...

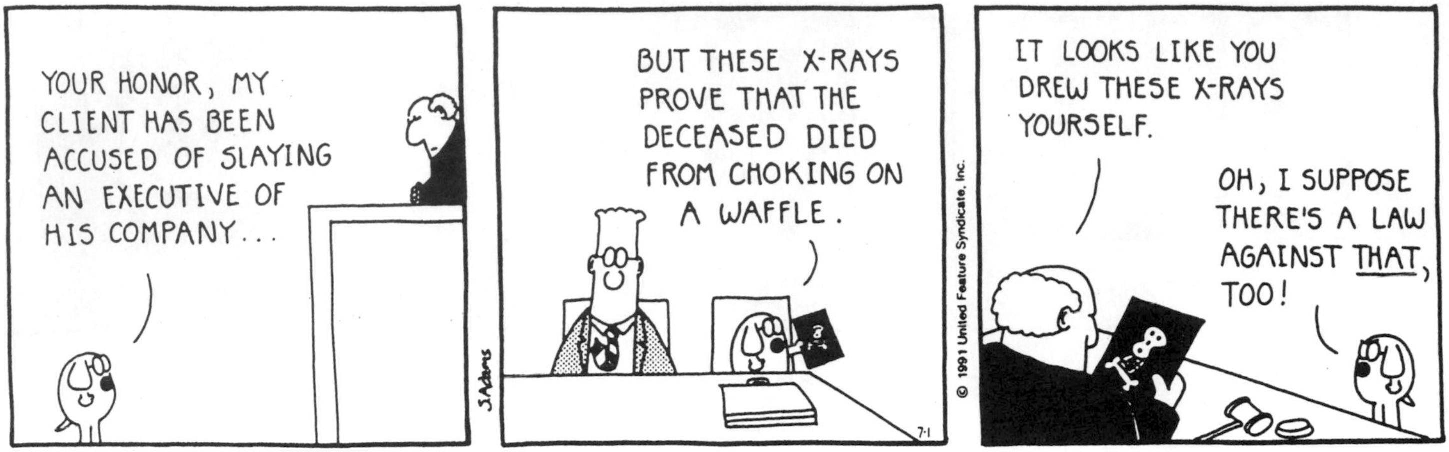
YOUR HONOR, MY CLIENT HAS BEEN ACCUSED OF SLAYING AN EXECUTIVE OF HIS COMPANY...
BUT THESE X-RAYS PROVE THAT THE DECEASED DIED FROM CHOKING ON A WAFFLE.
IT LOOKS LIKE YOU DREW THESE X-RAYS YOURSELF.
OH, I SUPPOSE THERE'S A LAW AGAINST THAT, TOO!
© 1991 United Feature Syndicate, Inc.
7-1

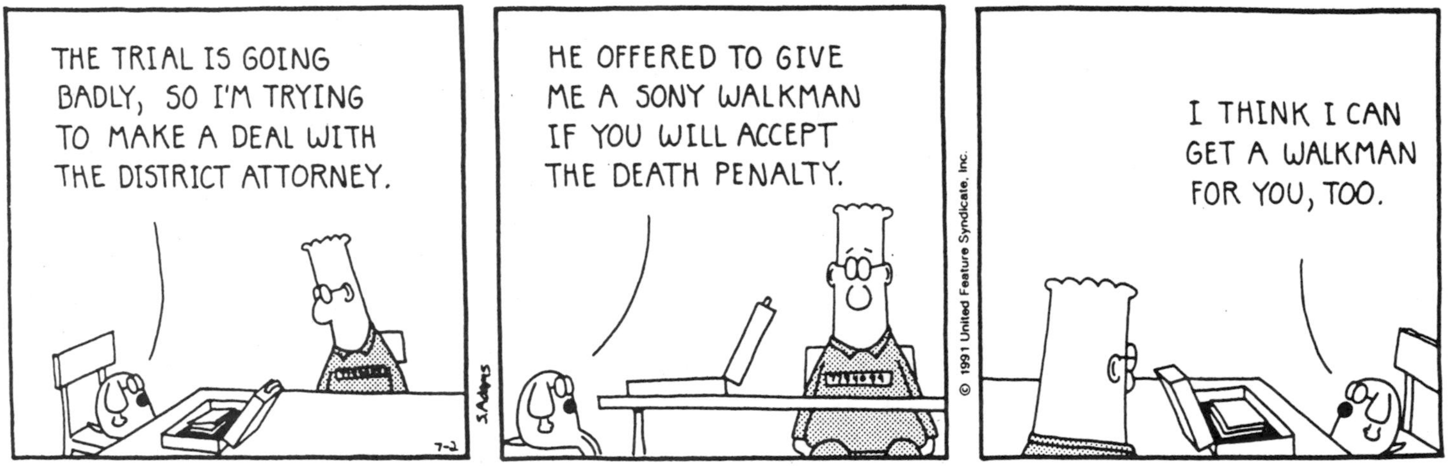
THE TRIAL IS GOING BADLY, SO I'M TRYING TO MAKE A DEAL WITH THE DISTRICT ATTORNEY.
HE OFFERED TO GIVE ME A SONY WALKMAN IF YOU WILL ACCEPT THE DEATH PENALTY.
I THINK I CAN GET A WALKMAN FOR YOU, TOO.
© 1991 United Feature Syndicate, Inc.
7-2

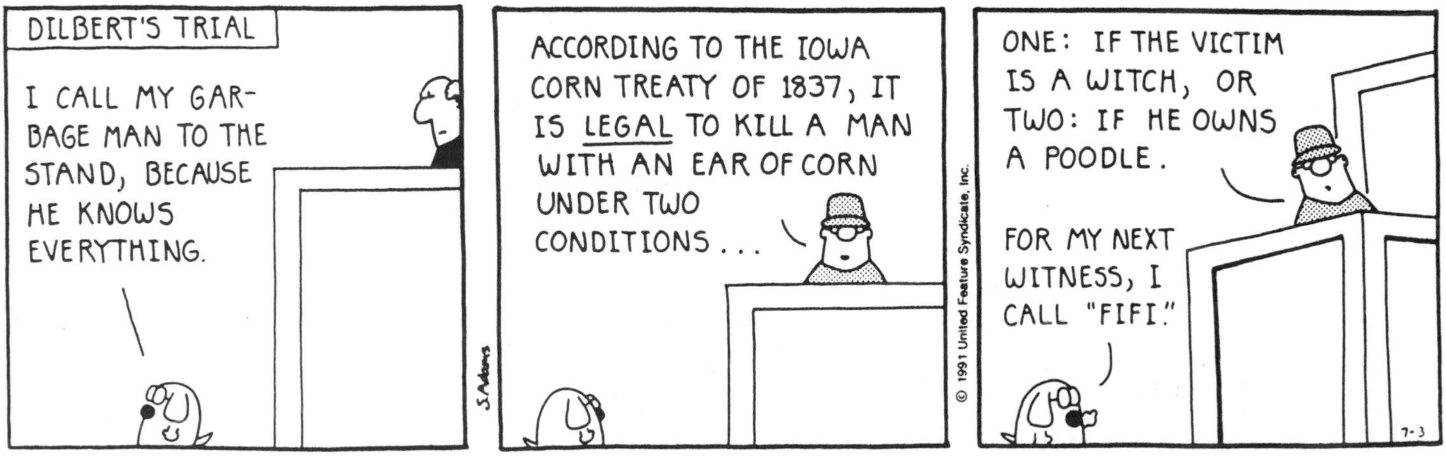
DILBERT'S TRIAL
I CALL MY GARBAGE MAN TO THE STAND, BECAUSE HE KNOWS EVERYTHING.
ACCORDING TO THE IOWA CORN TREATY OF 1837, IT IS LEGAL TO KILL A MAN WITH AN EAR OF CORN UNDER TWO CONDITIONS...
ONE: IF THE VICTIM IS A WITCH, OR TWO: IF HE OWNS A POODLE.
FOR MY NEXT WITNESS, I CALL "FIFI."
© 1991 United Feature Syndicate, Inc.
7-3

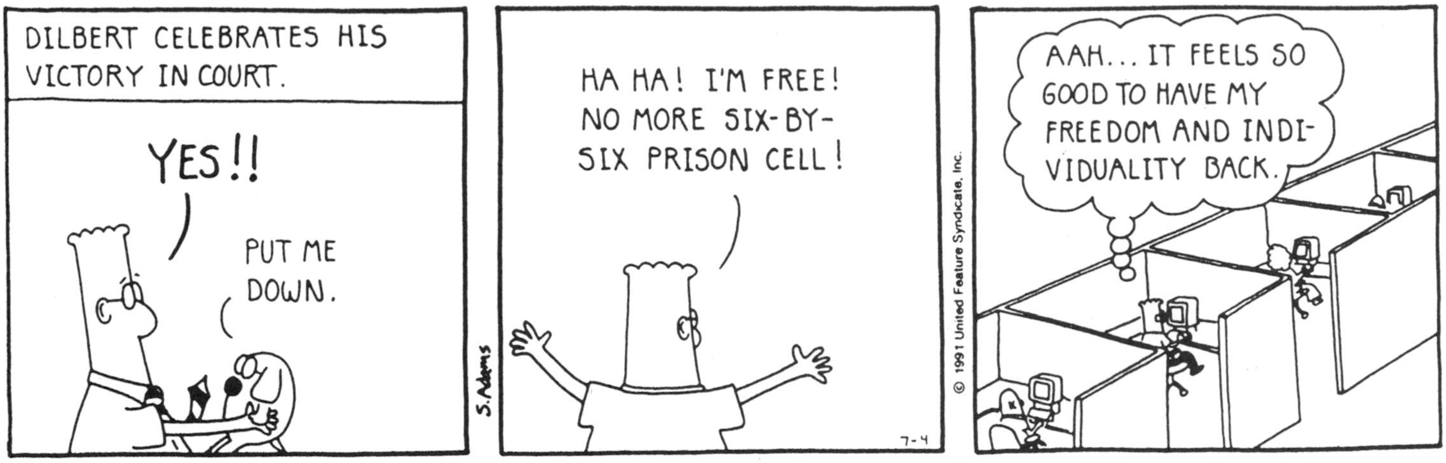
DILBERT CELEBRATES HIS VICTORY IN COURT.
YES!!
PUT ME DOWN.
HA HA! I'M FREE! NO MORE SIX-BY-SIX PRISON CELL!
AAH... IT FEELS SO GOOD TO HAVE MY FREEDOM AND INDIVIDUALITY BACK.
© 1991 United Feature Syndicate, Inc.

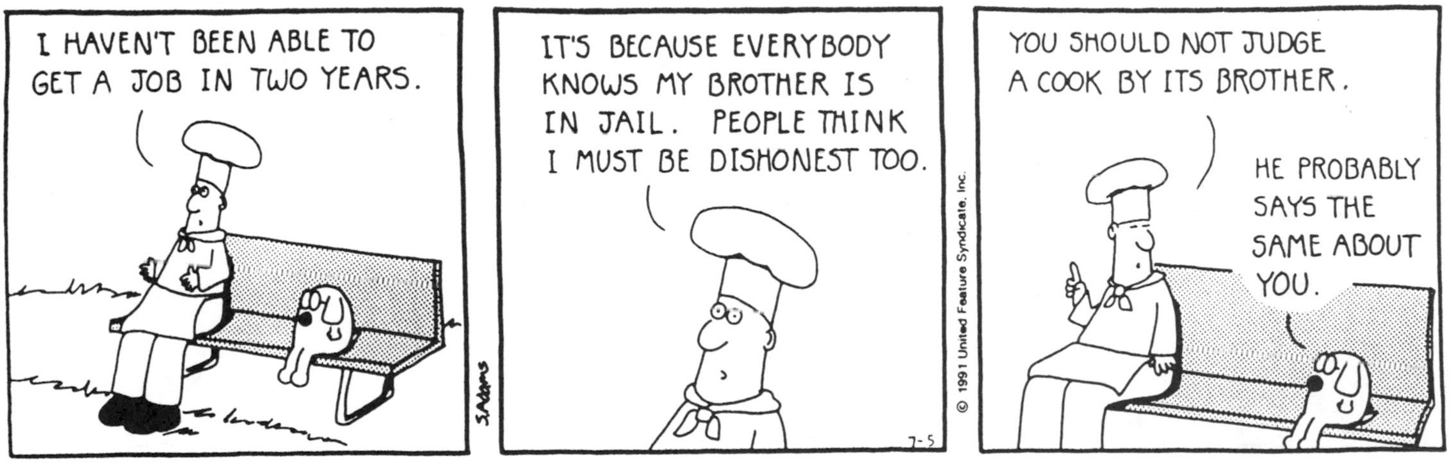
I HAVEN'T BEEN ABLE TO GET A JOB IN TWO YEARS.
IT'S BECAUSE EVERYBODY KNOWS MY BROTHER IS IN JAIL. PEOPLE THINK I MUST BE DISHONEST TOO.
YOU SHOULD NOT JUDGE A COOK BY ITS BROTHER.
HE PROBABLY SAYS THE SAME ABOUT YOU.
© 1991 United Feature Syndicate, Inc.

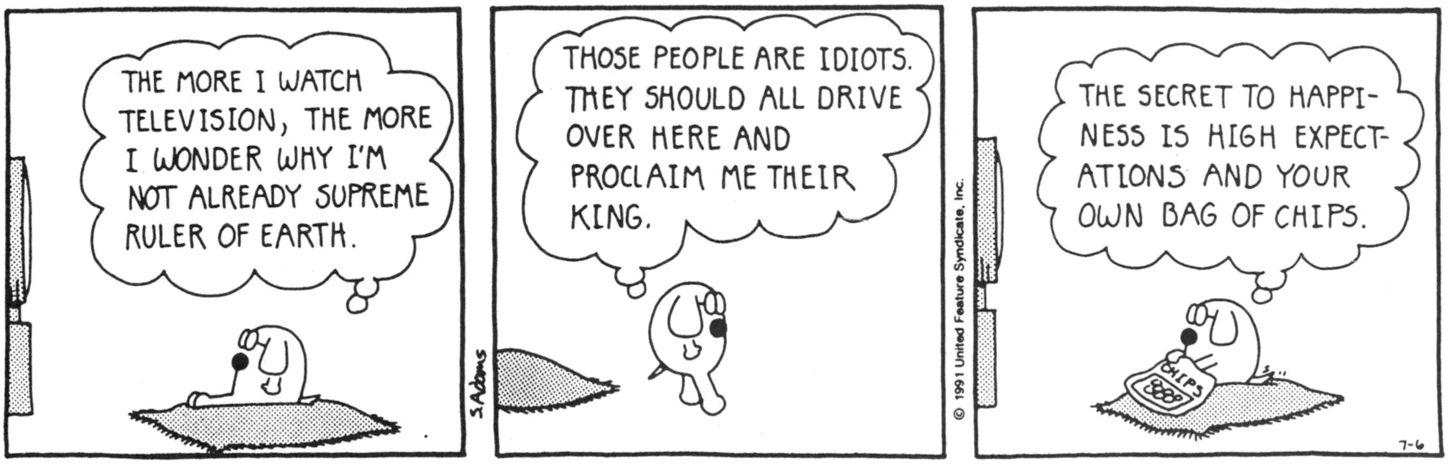
THE MORE I WATCH TELEVISION, THE MORE I WONDER WHY I'M NOT ALREADY SUPREME RULER OF EARTH.
THOSE PEOPLE ARE IDIOTS. THEY SHOULD ALL DRIVE OVER HERE AND PROCLAIM ME THEIR KING.
THE SECRET TO HAPPINESS IS HIGH EXPECTATIONS AND YOUR OWN BAG OF CHIPS.
CHIPS
© 1991 United Feature Syndicate, Inc.

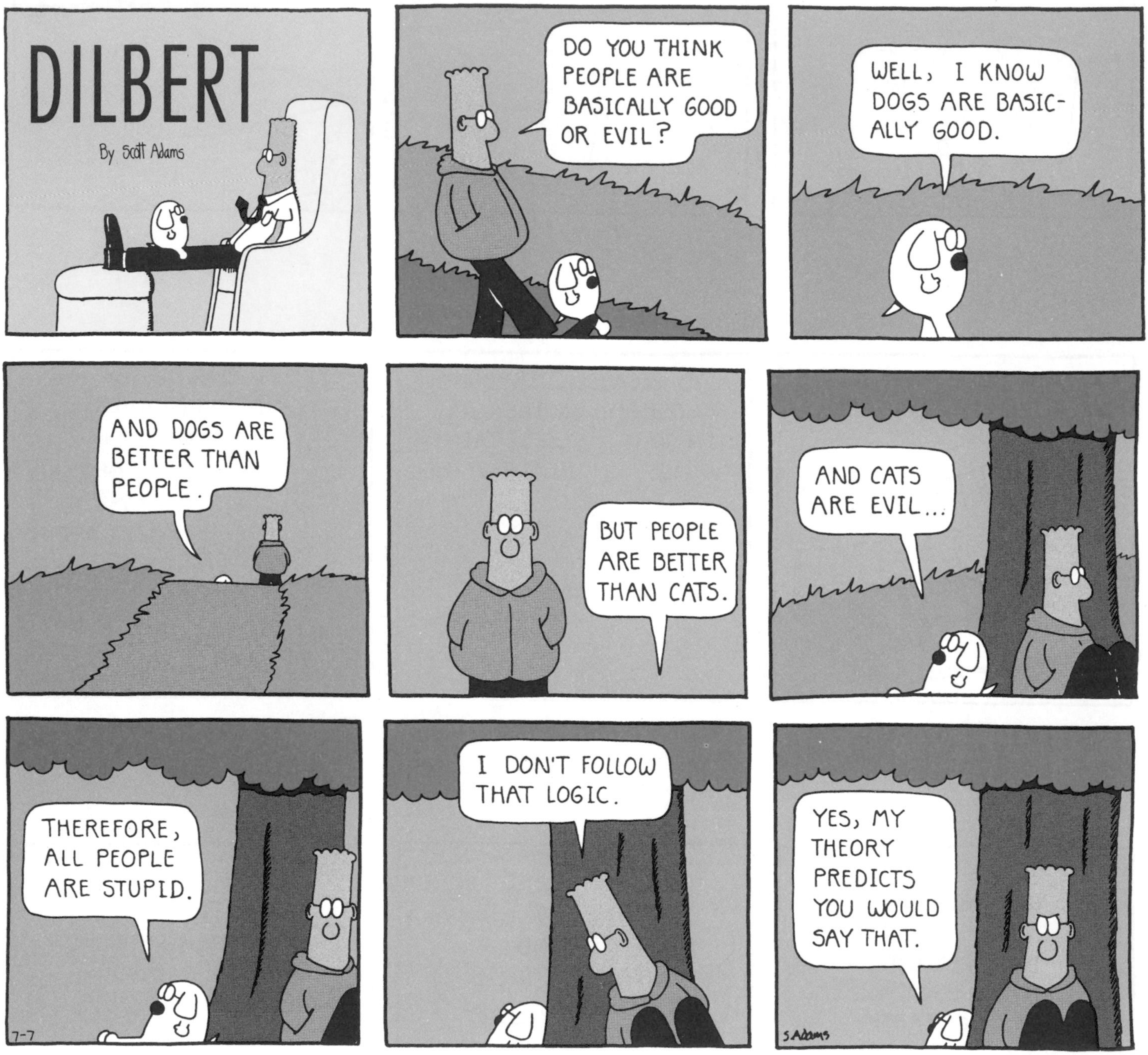

DILBERT
By Scott Adams
DO YOU THINK PEOPLE ARE BASICALLY GOOD OR EVIL?
WELL, I KNOW DOGS ARE BASIC-ALLY GOOD.
AND DOGS ARE BETTER THAN PEOPLE.
BUT PEOPLE ARE BETTER THAN CATS.
AND CATS ARE EVIL...
THEREFORE, ALL PEOPLE ARE STUPID.
I DON'T FOLLOW THAT LOGIC.
YES, MY THEORY PREDICTS YOU WOULD SAY THAT.
7-7
S.ADAMS

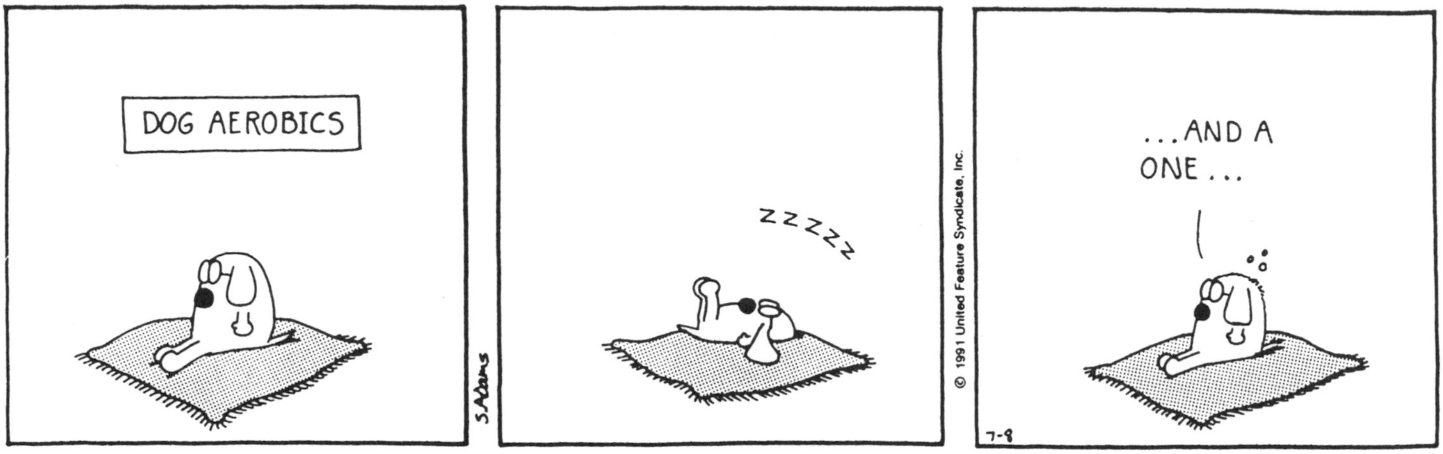
DOG AEROBICS
ZZZZZ
...AND A ONE...
© 1991 United Feature Syndicate, Inc.

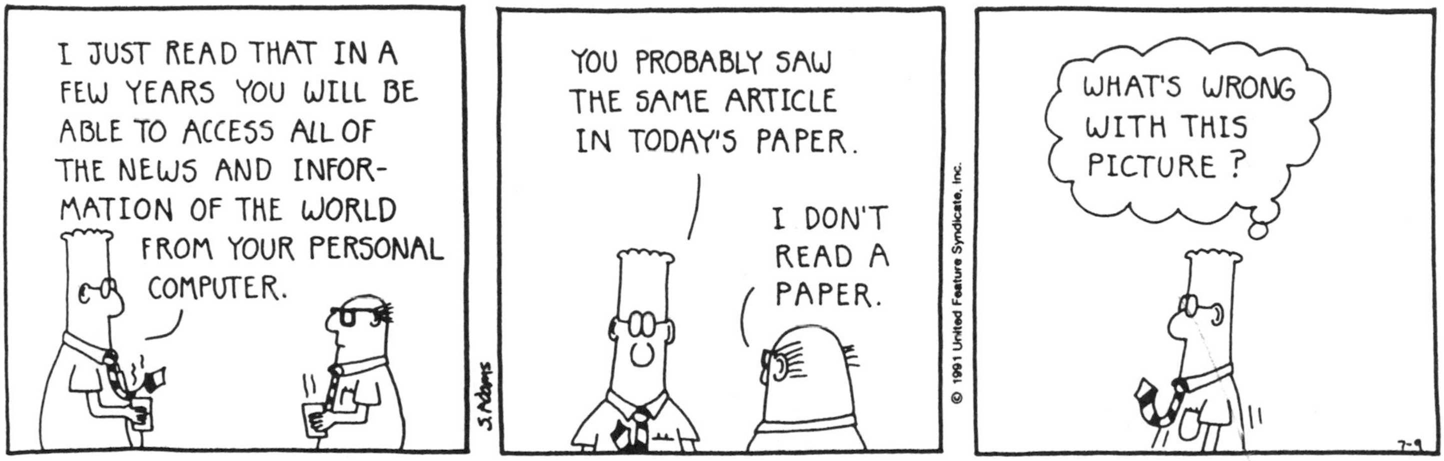
I JUST READ THAT IN A FEW YEARS YOU WILL BE ABLE TO ACCESS ALL OF THE NEWS AND INFORMATION OF THE WORLD FROM YOUR PERSONAL COMPUTER.
YOU PROBABLY SAW THE SAME ARTICLE IN TODAY'S PAPER.
I DON'T READ A PAPER.
WHAT'S WRONG WITH THIS PICTURE?
© 1991 United Feature Syndicate, Inc.

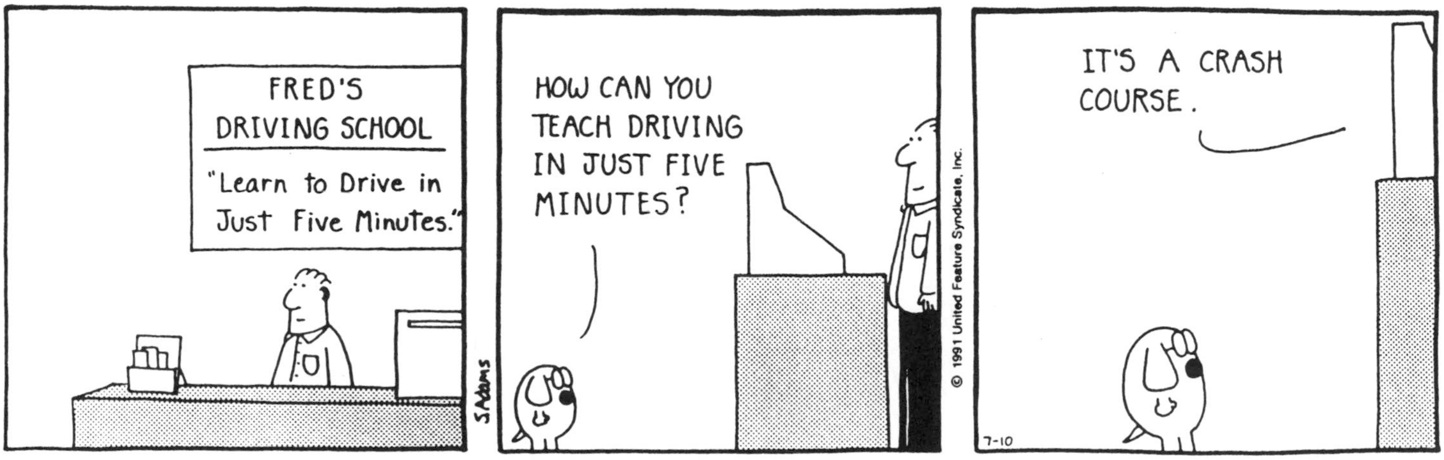
FRED'S DRIVING SCHOOL
"Learn to Drive in Just Five Minutes."
HOW CAN YOU TEACH DRIVING IN JUST FIVE MINUTES?
IT'S A CRASH COURSE.
© 1991 United Feature Syndicate, Inc.

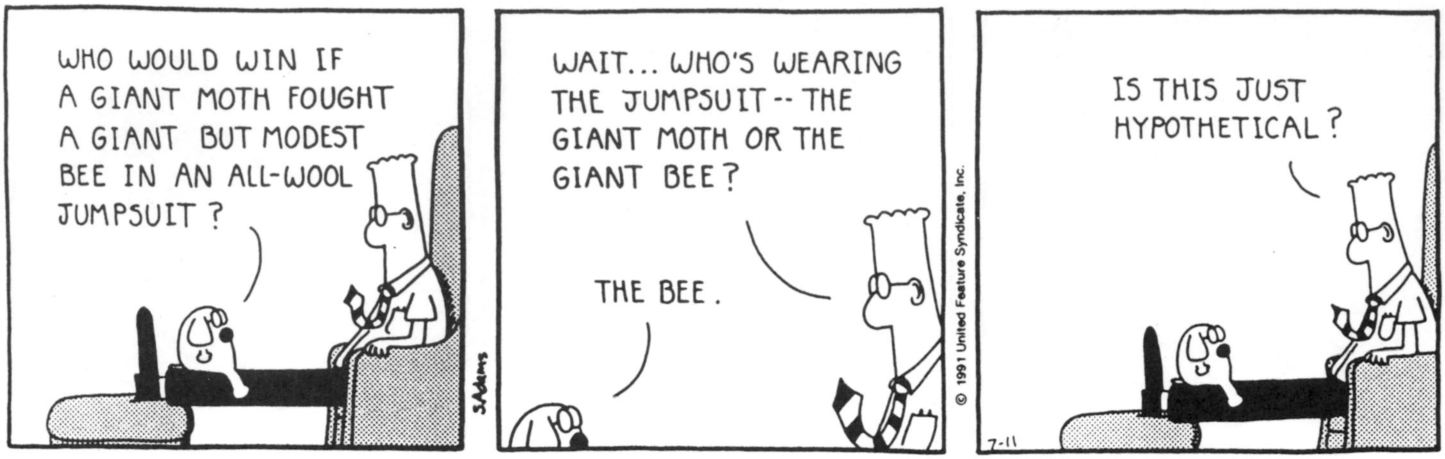
WHO WOULD WIN IF A GIANT MOTH FOUGHT A GIANT BUT MODEST BEE IN AN ALL-WOOL JUMPSUIT ?
S.Adams
WAIT... WHO'S WEARING THE JUMPSUIT -- THE GIANT MOTH OR THE GIANT BEE ?
THE BEE .
© 1991 United Feature Syndicate, Inc.
IS THIS JUST HYPOTHETICAL ?
7-11

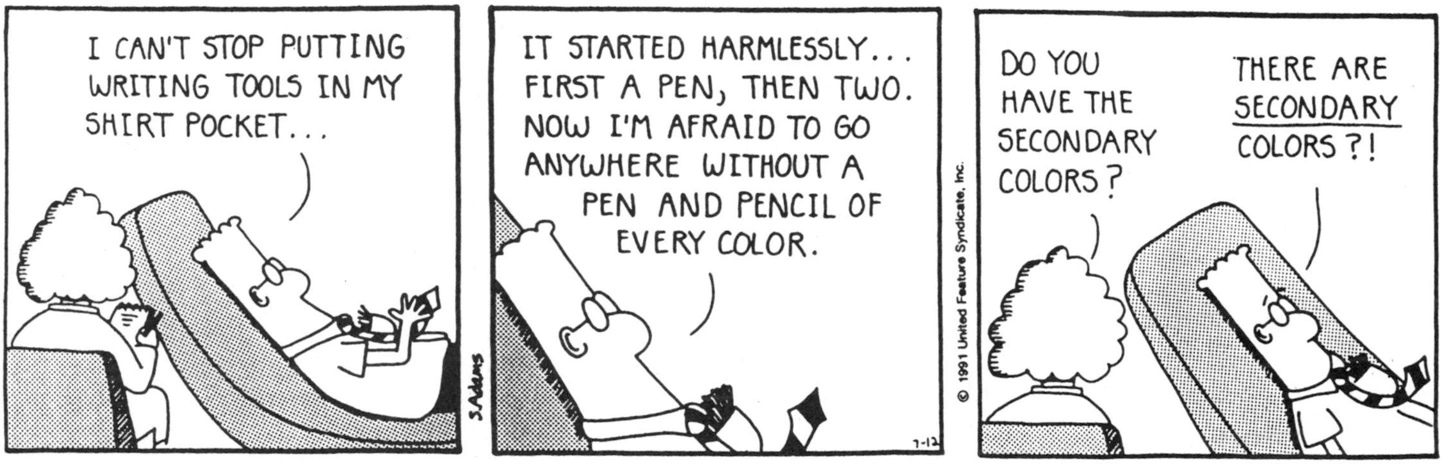
I CAN'T STOP PUTTING WRITING TOOLS IN MY SHIRT POCKET...
S.Adams
IT STARTED HARMLESSLY... FIRST A PEN, THEN TWO. NOW I'M AFRAID TO GO ANYWHERE WITHOUT A PEN AND PENCIL OF EVERY COLOR.
7-12
© 1991 United Feature Syndicate, Inc.
DO YOU HAVE THE SECONDARY COLORS ?
THERE ARE SECONDARY COLORS ?!

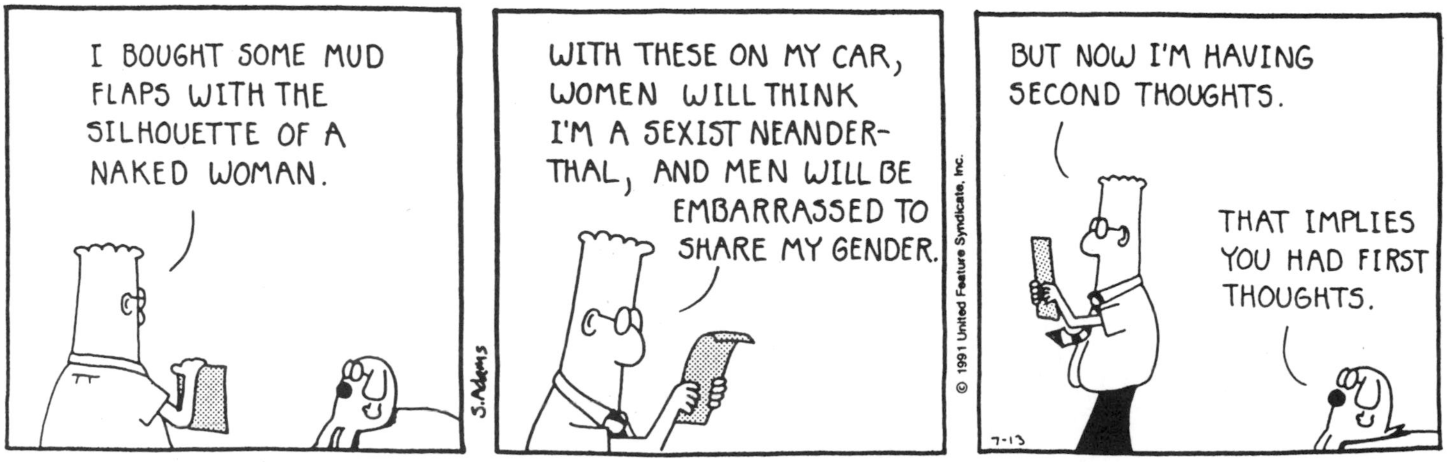
I BOUGHT SOME MUD FLAPS WITH THE SILHOUETTE OF A NAKED WOMAN.
S.Adams
WITH THESE ON MY CAR, WOMEN WILL THINK I'M A SEXIST NEANDER-THAL, AND MEN WILL BE EMBARRASSED TO SHARE MY GENDER.
© 1991 United Feature Syndicate, Inc.
BUT NOW I'M HAVING SECOND THOUGHTS.
THAT IMPLIES YOU HAD FIRST THOUGHTS.
7-13

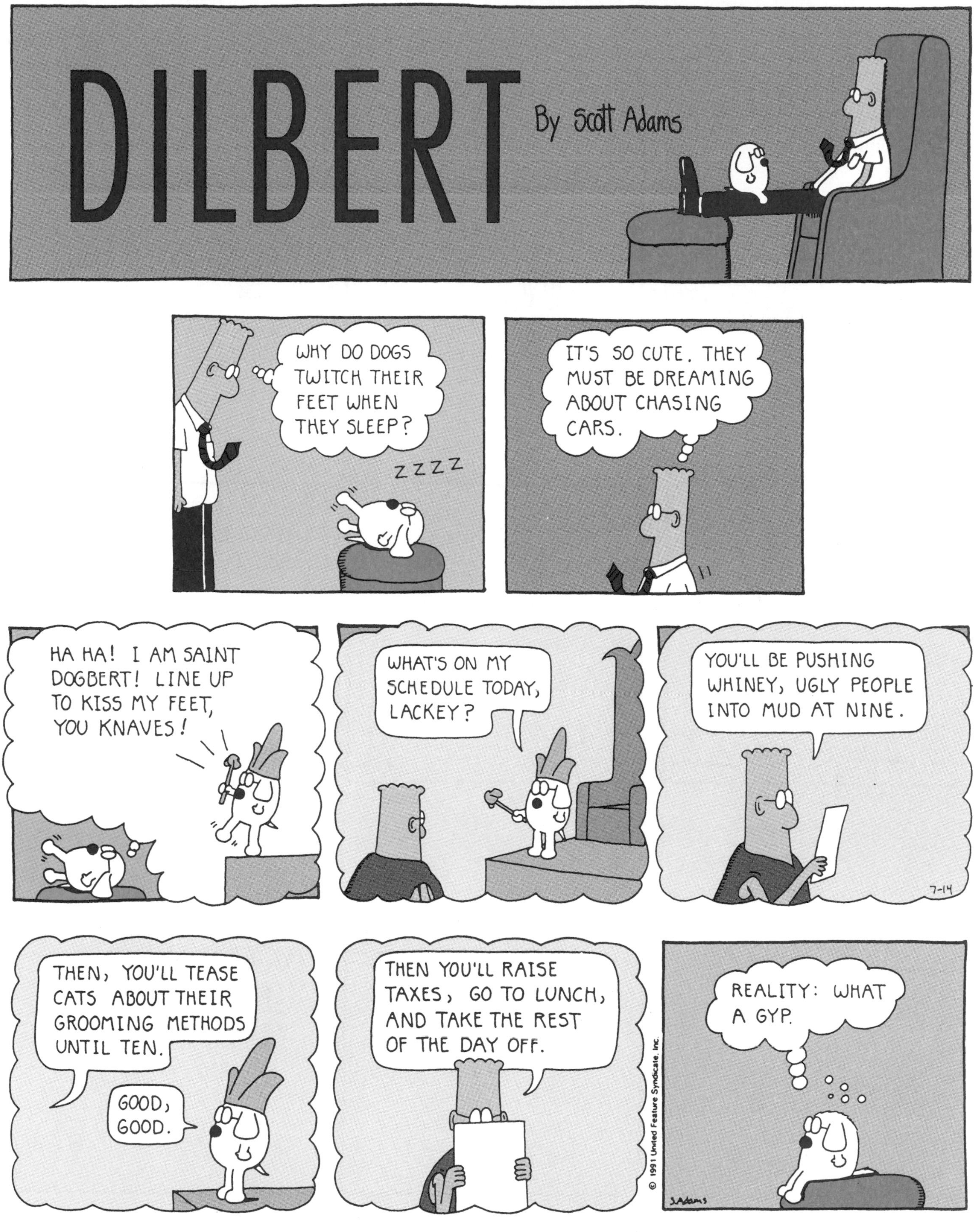
DILBERT
By Scott Adams
WHY DO DOGS TWITCH THEIR FEET WHEN THEY SLEEP?
ZZZZ
IT'S SO CUTE. THEY MUST BE DREAMING ABOUT CHASING CARS.
HA HA! I AM SAINT DOGBERT! LINE UP TO KISS MY FEET, YOU KNAVES!
WHAT'S ON MY SCHEDULE TODAY, LACKEY?
YOU'LL BE PUSHING WHINEY, UGLY PEOPLE INTO MUD AT NINE.
7-14
THEN, YOU'LL TEASE CATS ABOUT THEIR GROOMING METHODS UNTIL TEN.
GOOD, GOOD.
THEN YOU'LL RAISE TAXES, GO TO LUNCH, AND TAKE THE REST OF THE DAY OFF.
© 1991 United Feature Syndicate, Inc.
REALITY: WHAT A GYP.
S.Adams

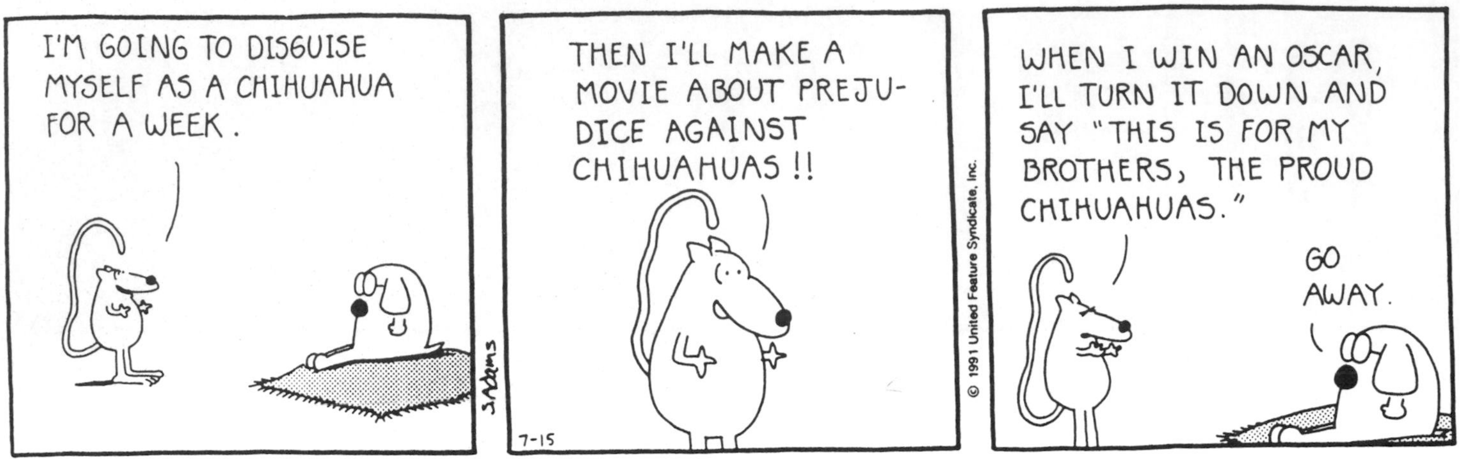
I'M GOING TO DISGUISE MYSELF AS A CHIHUAHUA FOR A WEEK.
S. Adams
7-15
THEN I'LL MAKE A MOVIE ABOUT PREJUDICE AGAINST CHIHUAHUAS!!
© 1991 United Feature Syndicate, Inc.
WHEN I WIN AN OSCAR, I'LL TURN IT DOWN AND SAY "THIS IS FOR MY BROTHERS, THE PROUD CHIHUAHUAS."
GO AWAY.

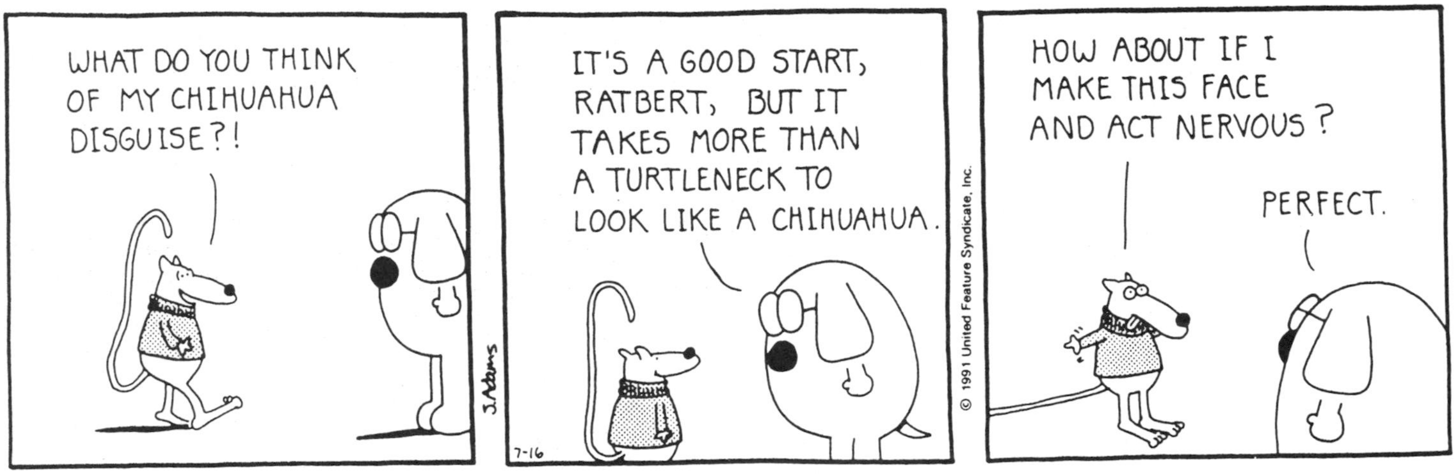
WHAT DO YOU THINK OF MY CHIHUAHUA DISGUISE?!
S. Adams
7-16
IT'S A GOOD START, RATBERT, BUT IT TAKES MORE THAN A TURTLENECK TO LOOK LIKE A CHIHUAHUA.
© 1991 United Feature Syndicate, Inc.
HOW ABOUT IF I MAKE THIS FACE AND ACT NERVOUS?
PERFECT.

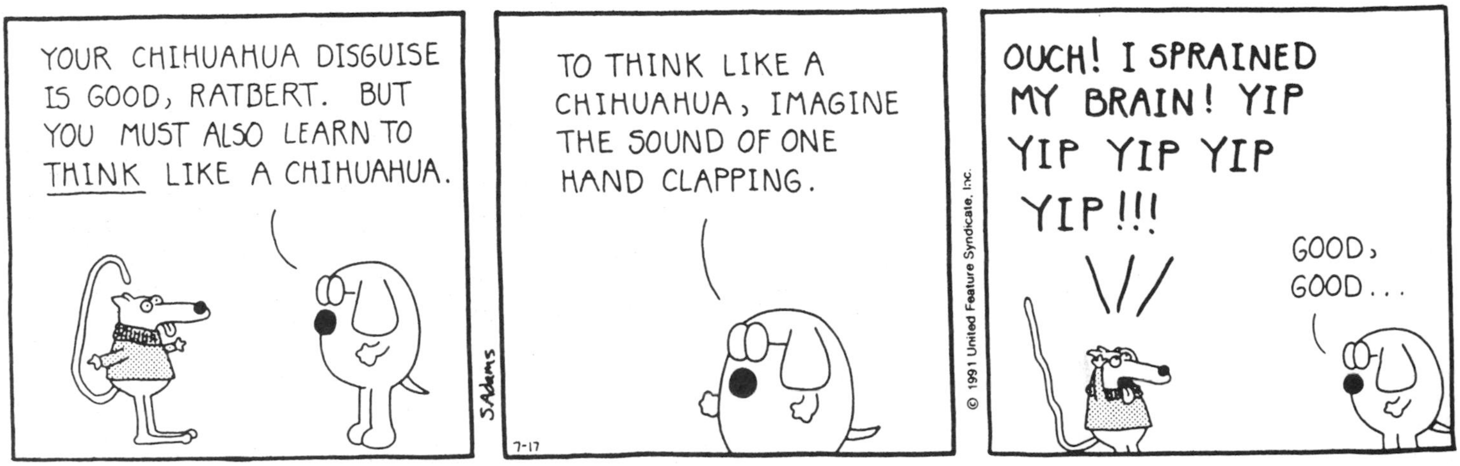
YOUR CHIHUAHUA DISGUISE IS GOOD, RATBERT. BUT YOU MUST ALSO LEARN TO THINK LIKE A CHIHUAHUA.
S. Adams
7-17
TO THINK LIKE A CHIHUAHUA, IMAGINE THE SOUND OF ONE HAND CLAPPING.
© 1991 United Feature Syndicate, Inc.
OUCH! I SPRAINED MY BRAIN! YIP YIP YIP YIP YIP!!!
GOOD, GOOD...

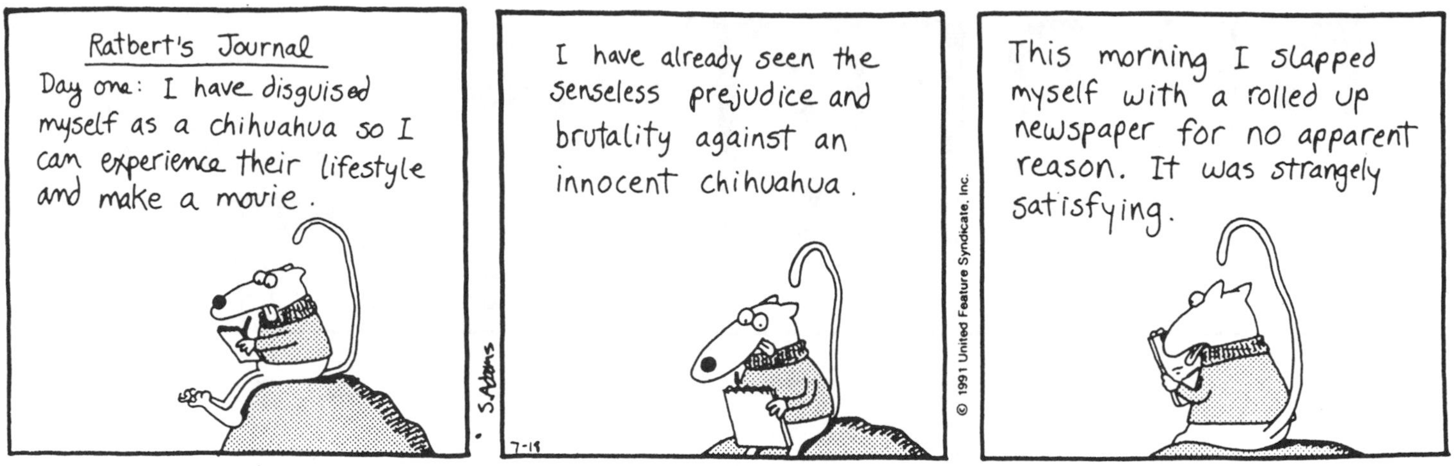
Ratbert's Journal
Day one: I have disguised myself as a chihuahua so I can experience their lifestyle and make a movie.
I have already seen the senseless prejudice and brutality against an innocent chihuahua.
This morning I slapped myself with a rolled up newspaper for no apparent reason. It was strangely satisfying.
S. Adams
7-18
© 1991 United Feature Syndicate, Inc.

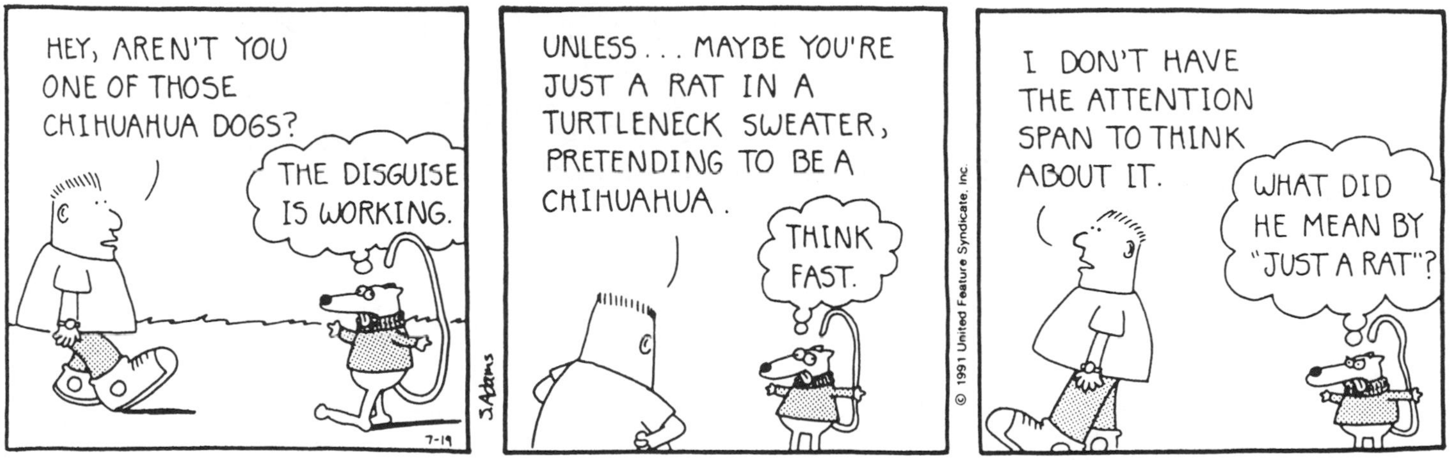
HEY, AREN'T YOU ONE OF THOSE CHIHUAHUA DOGS?
THE DISGUISE IS WORKING.
7-19
S. Adams
UNLESS . . . MAYBE YOU'RE JUST A RAT IN A TURTLENECK SWEATER, PRETENDING TO BE A CHIHUAHUA.
THINK FAST.
© 1991 United Feature Syndicate, Inc.
I DON'T HAVE THE ATTENTION SPAN TO THINK ABOUT IT.
WHAT DID HE MEAN BY "JUST A RAT"?

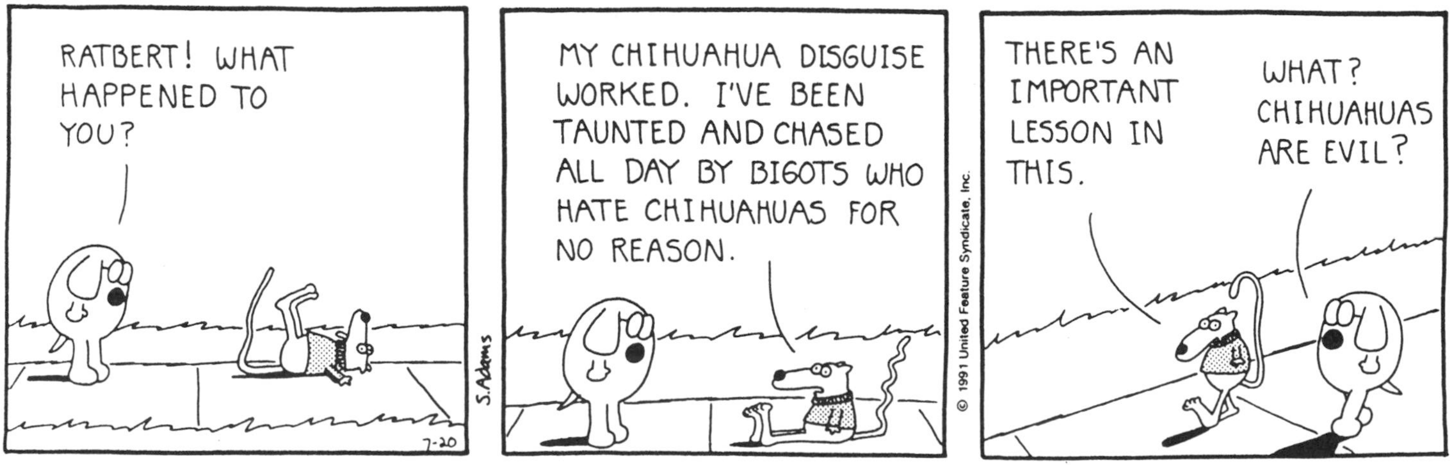
RATBERT! WHAT HAPPENED TO YOU?
7-20
S. Adams
MY CHIHUAHUA DISGUISE WORKED. I'VE BEEN TAUNTED AND CHASED ALL DAY BY BIGOTS WHO HATE CHIHUAHUAS FOR NO REASON.
© 1991 United Feature Syndicate, Inc.
THERE'S AN IMPORTANT LESSON IN THIS.
WHAT? CHIHUAHUAS ARE EVIL?

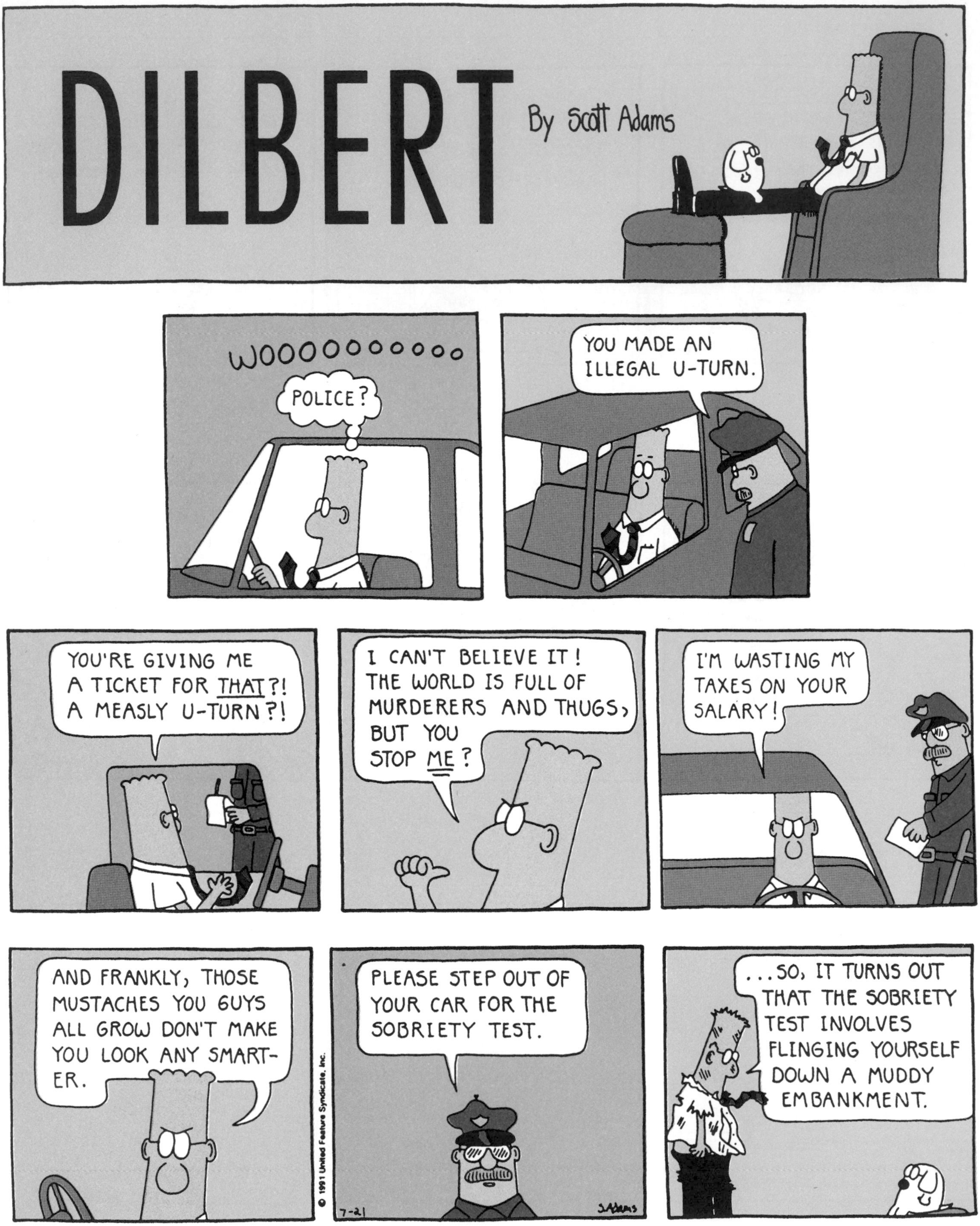
DILBERT
By Scott Adams
WOOOOOOOOOOO
POLICE?
YOU MADE AN ILLEGAL U-TURN.
YOU'RE GIVING ME A TICKET FOR THAT?! A MEASLY U-TURN?!
I CAN'T BELIEVE IT! THE WORLD IS FULL OF MURDERERS AND THUGS, BUT YOU STOP ME?
I'M WASTING MY TAXES ON YOUR SALARY!
AND FRANKLY, THOSE MUSTACHES YOU GUYS ALL GROW DON'T MAKE YOU LOOK ANY SMART-ER.
© 1991 United Feature Syndicate, Inc.
PLEASE STEP OUT OF YOUR CAR FOR THE SOBRIETY TEST.
7-21
...SO, IT TURNS OUT THAT THE SOBRIETY TEST INVOLVES FLINGING YOURSELF DOWN A MUDDY EMBANKMENT.

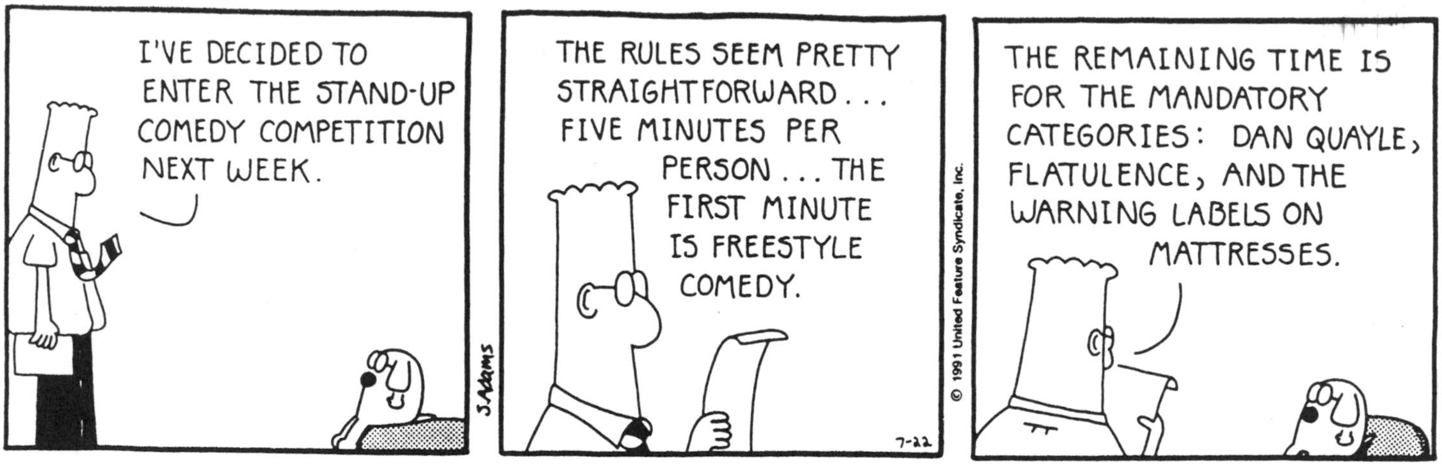
I'VE DECIDED TO ENTER THE STAND-UP COMEDY COMPETITION NEXT WEEK.
S. Adams
THE RULES SEEM PRETTY STRAIGHTFORWARD . . . FIVE MINUTES PER PERSON . . . THE FIRST MINUTE IS FREESTYLE COMEDY.
7-22
© 1991 United Feature Syndicate, Inc.
THE REMAINING TIME IS FOR THE MANDATORY CATEGORIES: DAN QUAYLE, FLATULENCE, AND THE WARNING LABELS ON MATTRESSES.

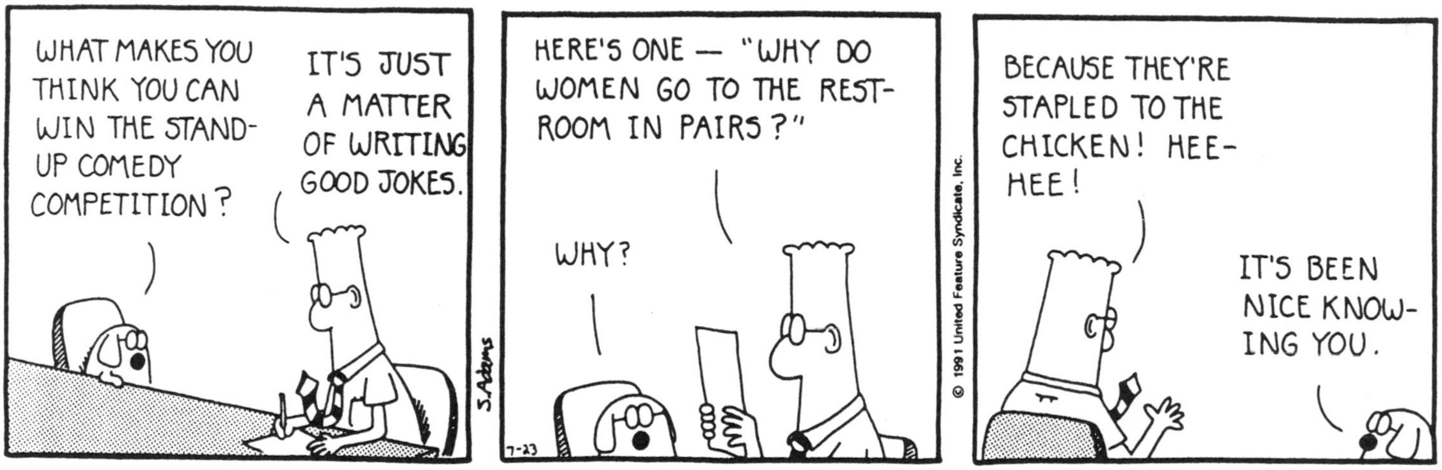
WHAT MAKES YOU THINK YOU CAN WIN THE STAND-UP COMEDY COMPETITION?
IT'S JUST A MATTER OF WRITING GOOD JOKES.
S. Adams
7-23
HERE'S ONE — "WHY DO WOMEN GO TO THE REST-ROOM IN PAIRS?"
WHY?
© 1991 United Feature Syndicate, Inc.
BECAUSE THEY'RE STAPLED TO THE CHICKEN! HEE-HEE!
IT'S BEEN NICE KNOW-ING YOU.

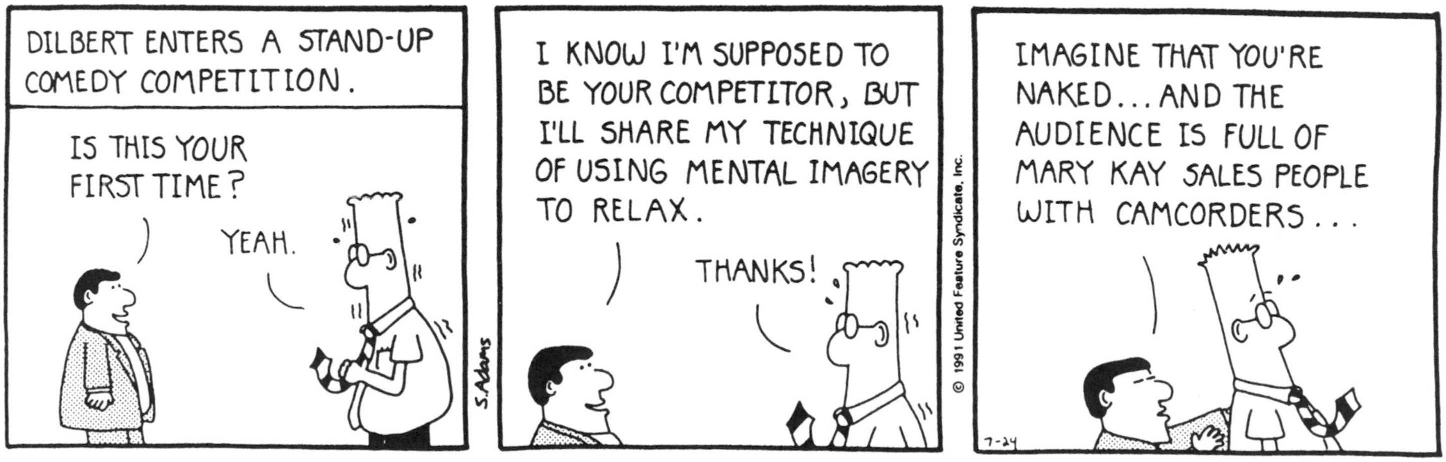
DILBERT ENTERS A STAND-UP COMEDY COMPETITION.
IS THIS YOUR FIRST TIME?
YEAH.
S. Adams
I KNOW I'M SUPPOSED TO BE YOUR COMPETITOR, BUT I'LL SHARE MY TECHNIQUE OF USING MENTAL IMAGERY TO RELAX.
THANKS!
© 1991 United Feature Syndicate, Inc.
IMAGINE THAT YOU'RE NAKED . . . AND THE AUDIENCE IS FULL OF MARY KAY SALES PEOPLE WITH CAMCORDERS . . .
7-24

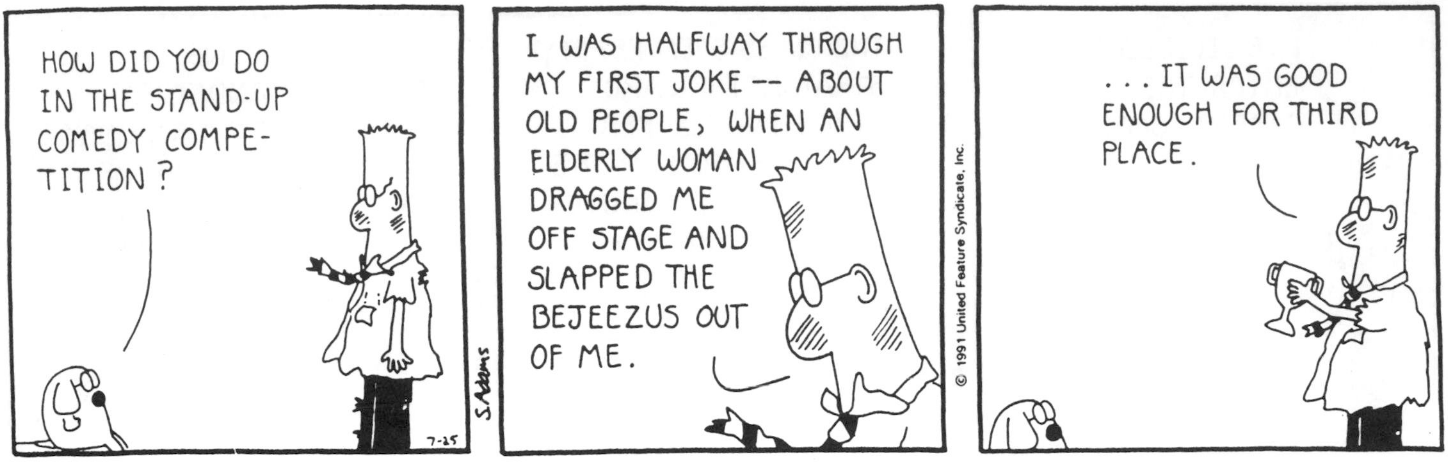
HOW DID YOU DO IN THE STAND-UP COMEDY COMPETITION ?
I WAS HALFWAY THROUGH MY FIRST JOKE -- ABOUT OLD PEOPLE, WHEN AN ELDERLY WOMAN DRAGGED ME OFF STAGE AND SLAPPED THE BEJEEZUS OUT OF ME.
. . . IT WAS GOOD ENOUGH FOR THIRD PLACE.
© 1991 United Feature Syndicate, Inc.

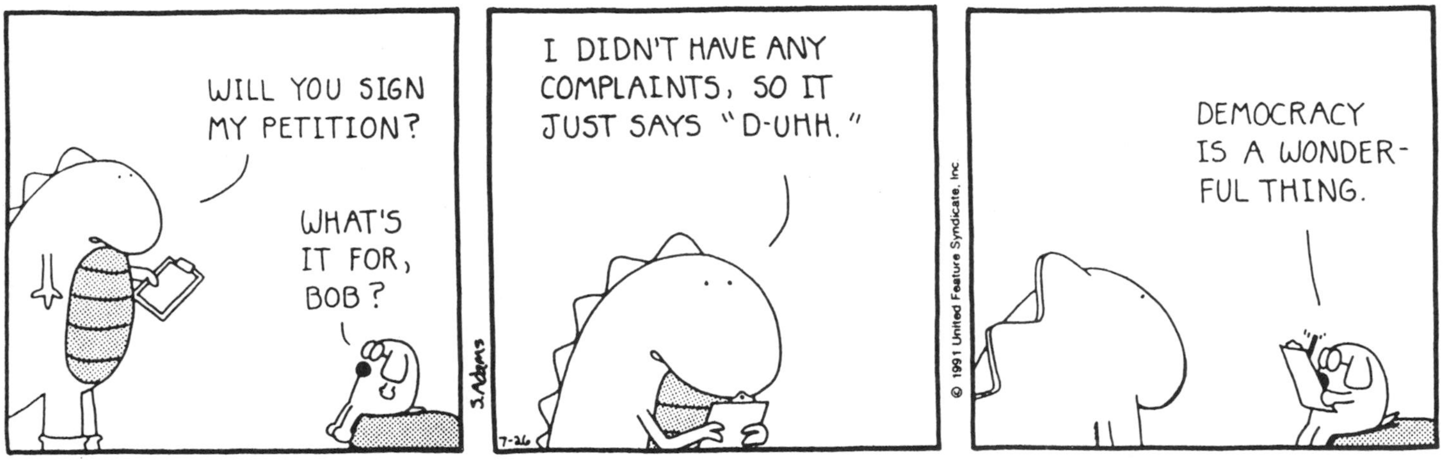
WILL YOU SIGN MY PETITION?
WHAT'S IT FOR, BOB ?
I DIDN'T HAVE ANY COMPLAINTS, SO IT JUST SAYS "D-UHH."
DEMOCRACY IS A WONDERFUL THING.
© 1991 United Feature Syndicate, Inc.

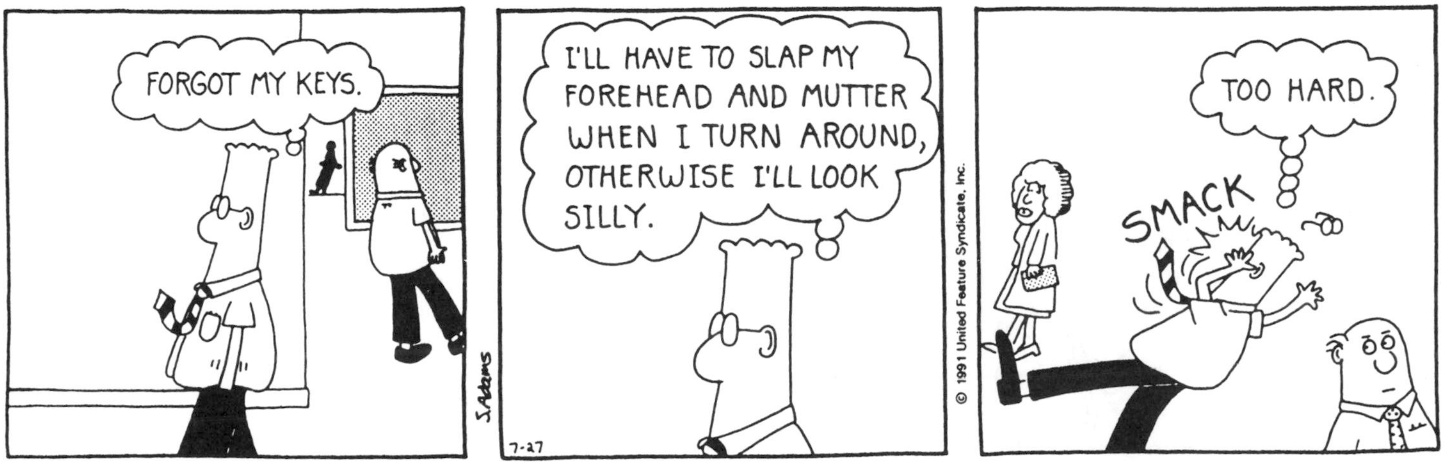
FORGOT MY KEYS.
I'LL HAVE TO SLAP MY FOREHEAD AND MUTTER WHEN I TURN AROUND, OTHERWISE I'LL LOOK SILLY.
TOO HARD.
SMACK
© 1991 United Feature Syndicate, Inc.

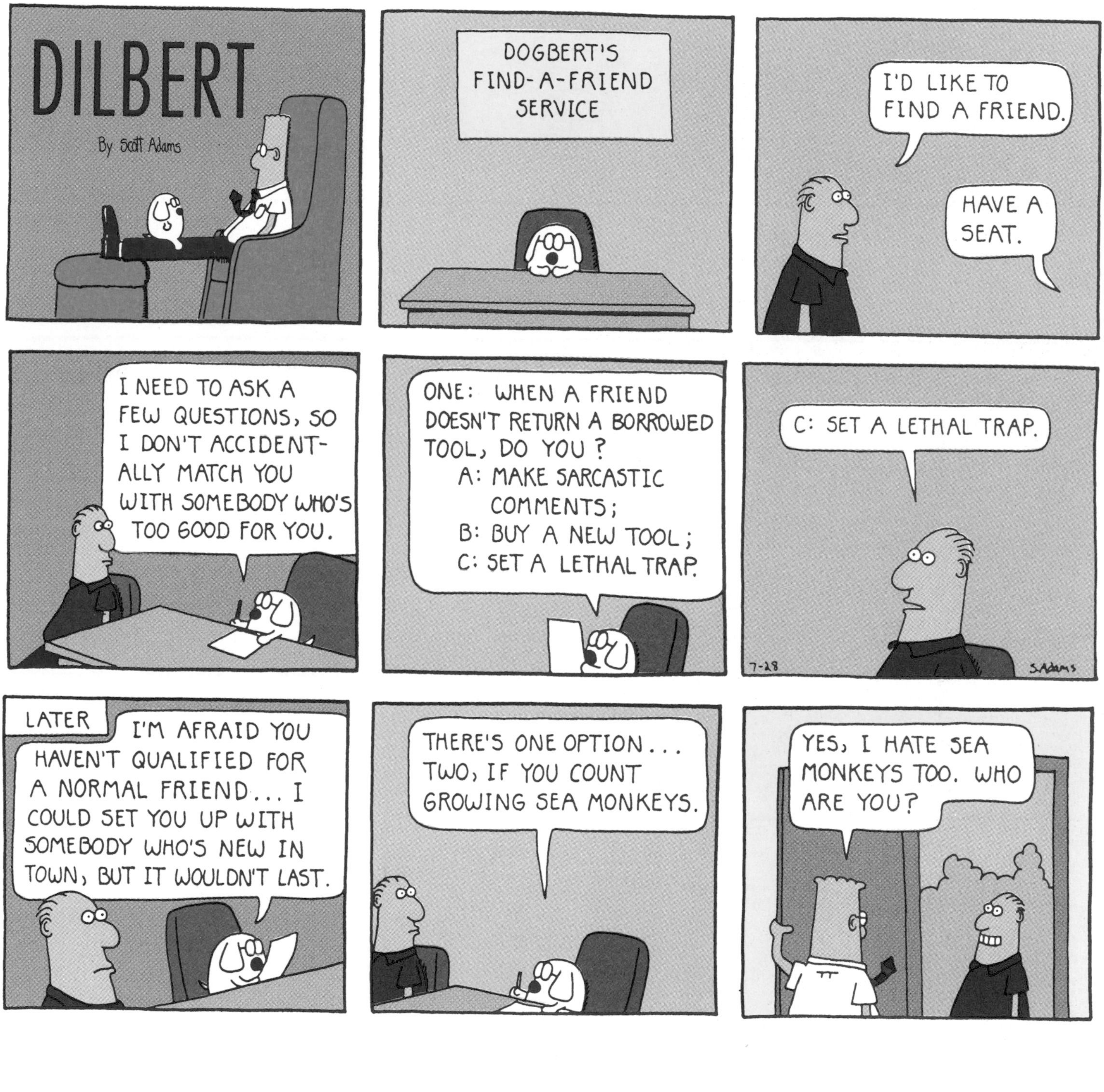

DILBERT
By Scott Adams
DOGBERT'S FIND-A-FRIEND SERVICE
I'D LIKE TO FIND A FRIEND.
HAVE A SEAT.
I NEED TO ASK A FEW QUESTIONS, SO I DON'T ACCIDENTALLY MATCH YOU WITH SOMEBODY WHO'S TOO GOOD FOR YOU.
ONE: WHEN A FRIEND DOESN'T RETURN A BORROWED TOOL, DO YOU ?
A: MAKE SARCASTIC COMMENTS;
B: BUY A NEW TOOL;
C: SET A LETHAL TRAP.
C: SET A LETHAL TRAP.
7-28
S.Adams
LATER
I'M AFRAID YOU HAVEN'T QUALIFIED FOR A NORMAL FRIEND... I COULD SET YOU UP WITH SOMEBODY WHO'S NEW IN TOWN, BUT IT WOULDN'T LAST.
THERE'S ONE OPTION... TWO, IF YOU COUNT GROWING SEA MONKEYS.
YES, I HATE SEA MONKEYS TOO. WHO ARE YOU?

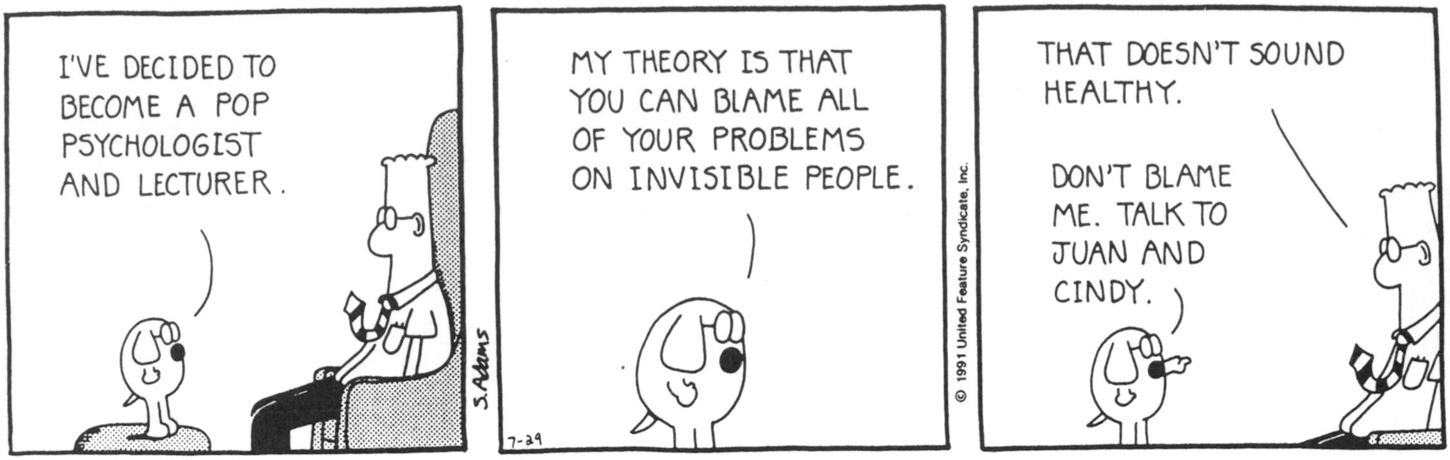
I'VE DECIDED TO BECOME A POP PSYCHOLOGIST AND LECTURER.
S. Adams
MY THEORY IS THAT YOU CAN BLAME ALL OF YOUR PROBLEMS ON INVISIBLE PEOPLE.
7-29
© 1991 United Feature Syndicate, Inc.
THAT DOESN'T SOUND HEALTHY.
DON'T BLAME ME. TALK TO JUAN AND CINDY.

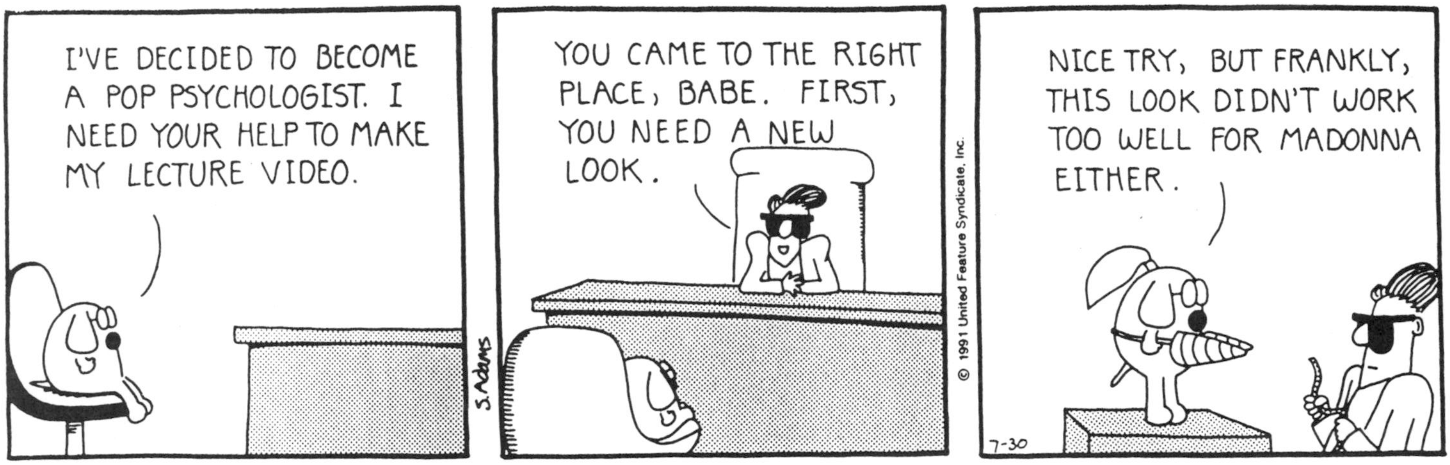
I'VE DECIDED TO BECOME A POP PSYCHOLOGIST. I NEED YOUR HELP TO MAKE MY LECTURE VIDEO.
S. Adams
YOU CAME TO THE RIGHT PLACE, BABE. FIRST, YOU NEED A NEW LOOK.
© 1991 United Feature Syndicate, Inc.
NICE TRY, BUT FRANKLY, THIS LOOK DIDN'T WORK TOO WELL FOR MADONNA EITHER.
7-30

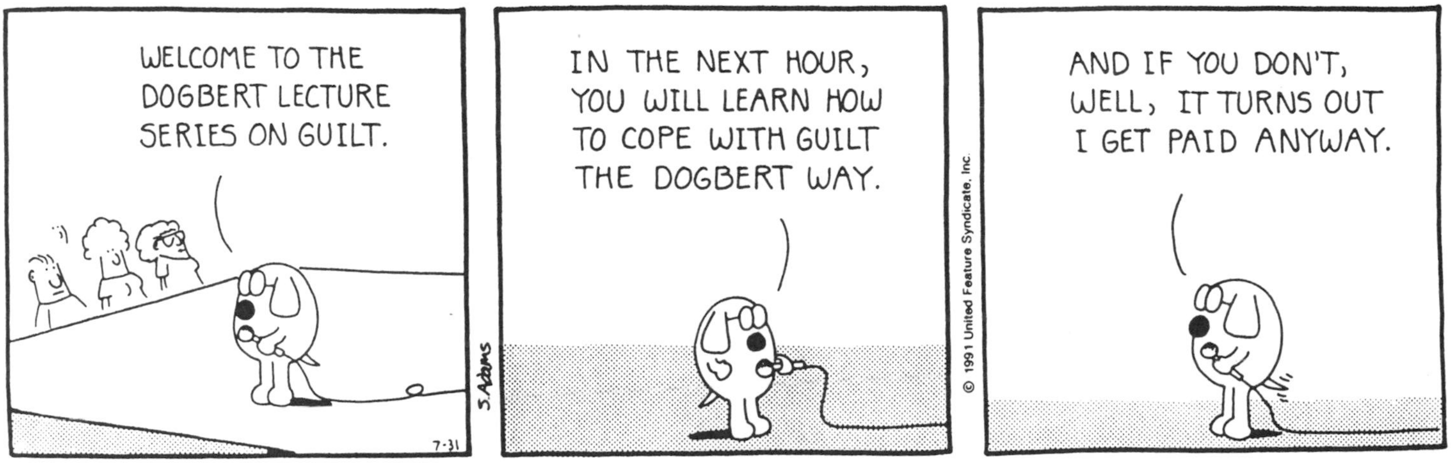
WELCOME TO THE DOGBERT LECTURE SERIES ON GUILT.
7-31
S. Adams
IN THE NEXT HOUR, YOU WILL LEARN HOW TO COPE WITH GUILT THE DOGBERT WAY.
© 1991 United Feature Syndicate, Inc.
AND IF YOU DON'T, WELL, IT TURNS OUT I GET PAID ANYWAY.

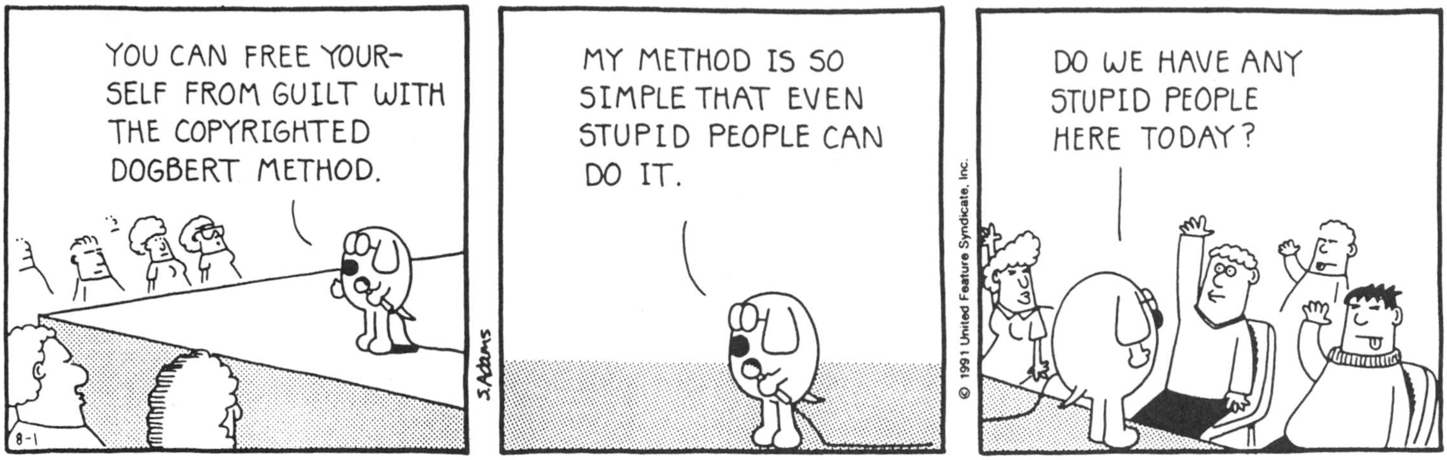
YOU CAN FREE YOURSELF FROM GUILT WITH THE COPYRIGHTED DOGBERT METHOD.
MY METHOD IS SO SIMPLE THAT EVEN STUPID PEOPLE CAN DO IT.
DO WE HAVE ANY STUPID PEOPLE HERE TODAY?
© 1991 United Feature Syndicate, Inc.

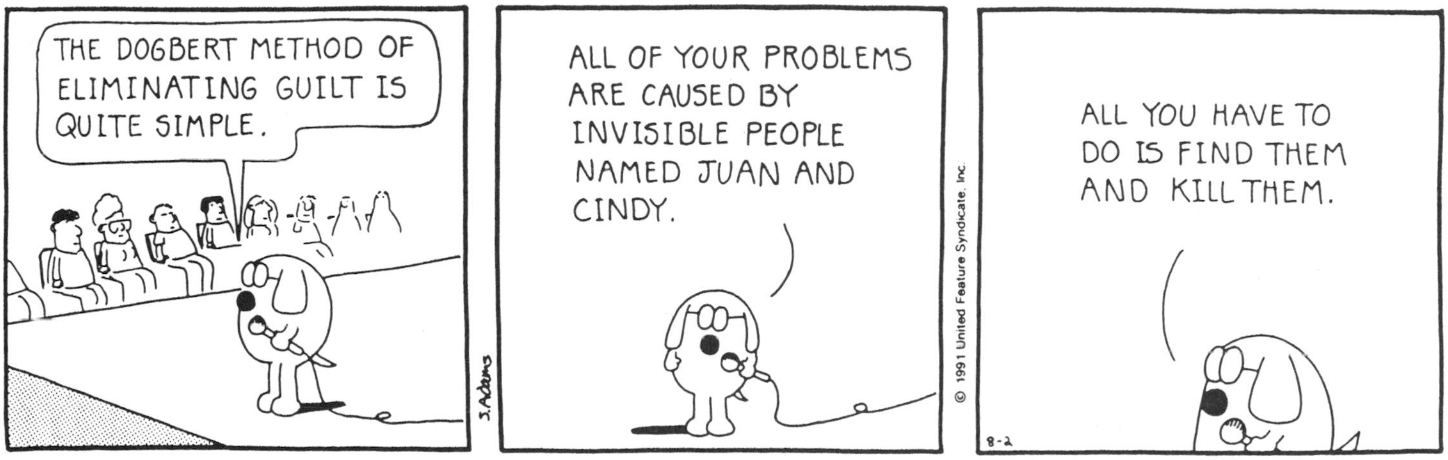
THE DOGBERT METHOD OF ELIMINATING GUILT IS QUITE SIMPLE.
ALL OF YOUR PROBLEMS ARE CAUSED BY INVISIBLE PEOPLE NAMED JUAN AND CINDY.
ALL YOU HAVE TO DO IS FIND THEM AND KILL THEM.
© 1991 United Feature Syndicate, Inc.

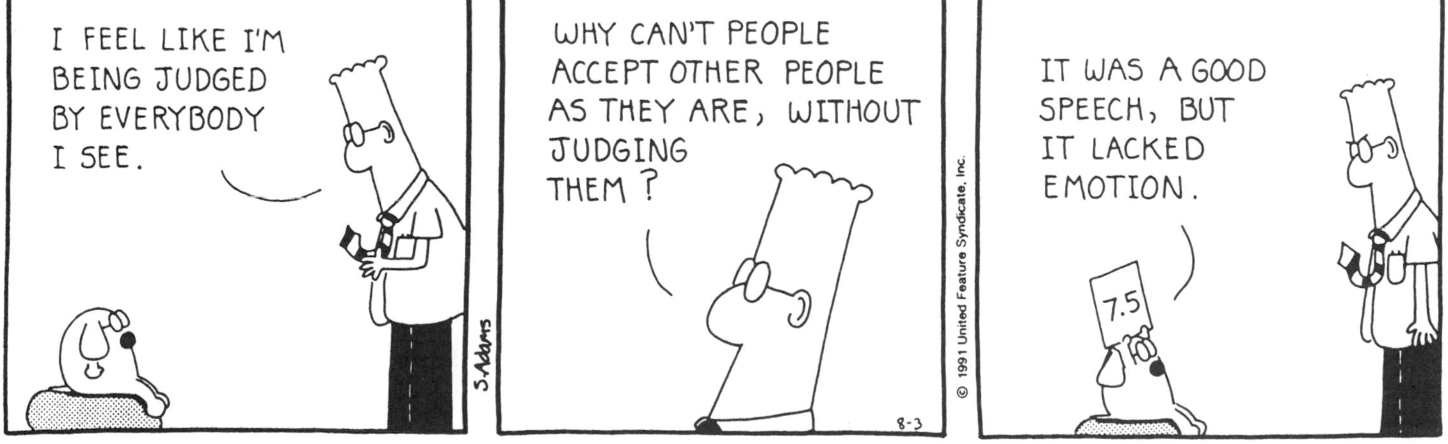
I FEEL LIKE I'M BEING JUDGED BY EVERYBODY I SEE.
WHY CAN'T PEOPLE ACCEPT OTHER PEOPLE AS THEY ARE, WITHOUT JUDGING THEM?
IT WAS A GOOD SPEECH, BUT IT LACKED EMOTION.
7.5
© 1991 United Feature Syndicate, Inc.

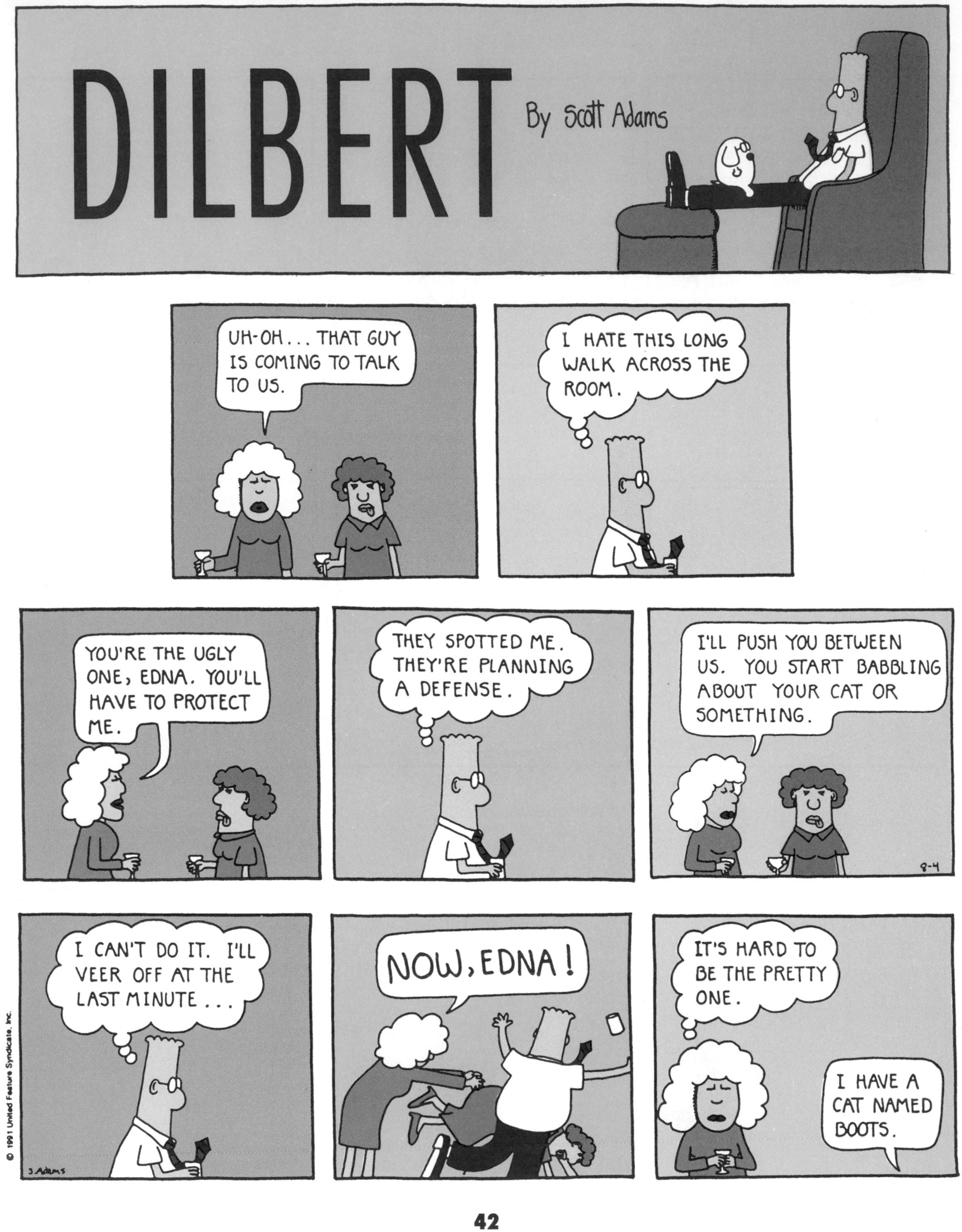
DILBERT
By Scott Adams
UH-OH... THAT GUY IS COMING TO TALK TO US.
I HATE THIS LONG WALK ACROSS THE ROOM.
YOU'RE THE UGLY ONE, EDNA. YOU'LL HAVE TO PROTECT ME.
THEY SPOTTED ME. THEY'RE PLANNING A DEFENSE.
I'LL PUSH YOU BETWEEN US. YOU START BABBLING ABOUT YOUR CAT OR SOMETHING.
8-4
I CAN'T DO IT. I'LL VEER OFF AT THE LAST MINUTE...
NOW, EDNA!
IT'S HARD TO BE THE PRETTY ONE.
I HAVE A CAT NAMED BOOTS.
S. Adams
© 1991 United Feature Syndicate, Inc.

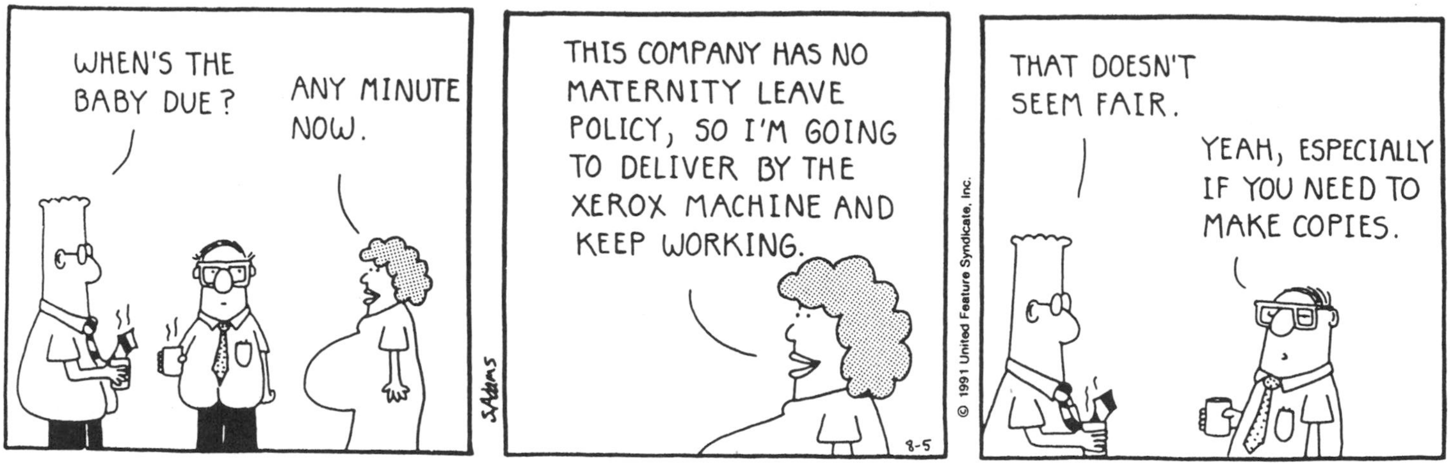
WHEN'S THE BABY DUE?
ANY MINUTE NOW.
THIS COMPANY HAS NO MATERNITY LEAVE POLICY, SO I'M GOING TO DELIVER BY THE XEROX MACHINE AND KEEP WORKING.
THAT DOESN'T SEEM FAIR.
YEAH, ESPECIALLY IF YOU NEED TO MAKE COPIES.
© 1991 United Feature Syndicate, Inc.

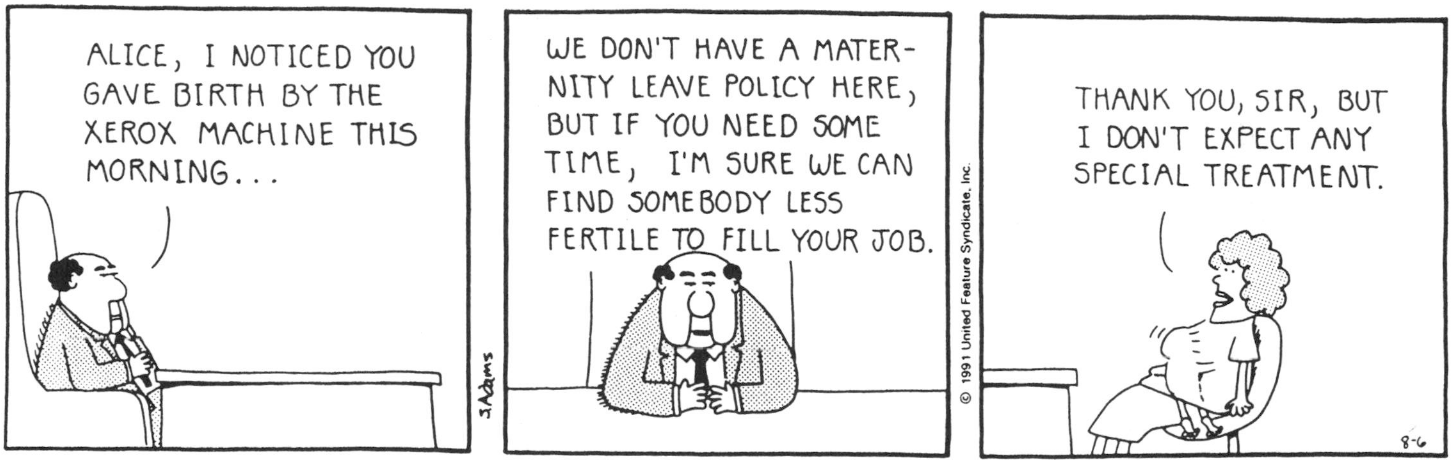
ALICE, I NOTICED YOU GAVE BIRTH BY THE XEROX MACHINE THIS MORNING...
WE DON'T HAVE A MATERNITY LEAVE POLICY HERE, BUT IF YOU NEED SOME TIME, I'M SURE WE CAN FIND SOMEBODY LESS FERTILE TO FILL YOUR JOB.
THANK YOU, SIR, BUT I DON'T EXPECT ANY SPECIAL TREATMENT.
© 1991 United Feature Syndicate, Inc.

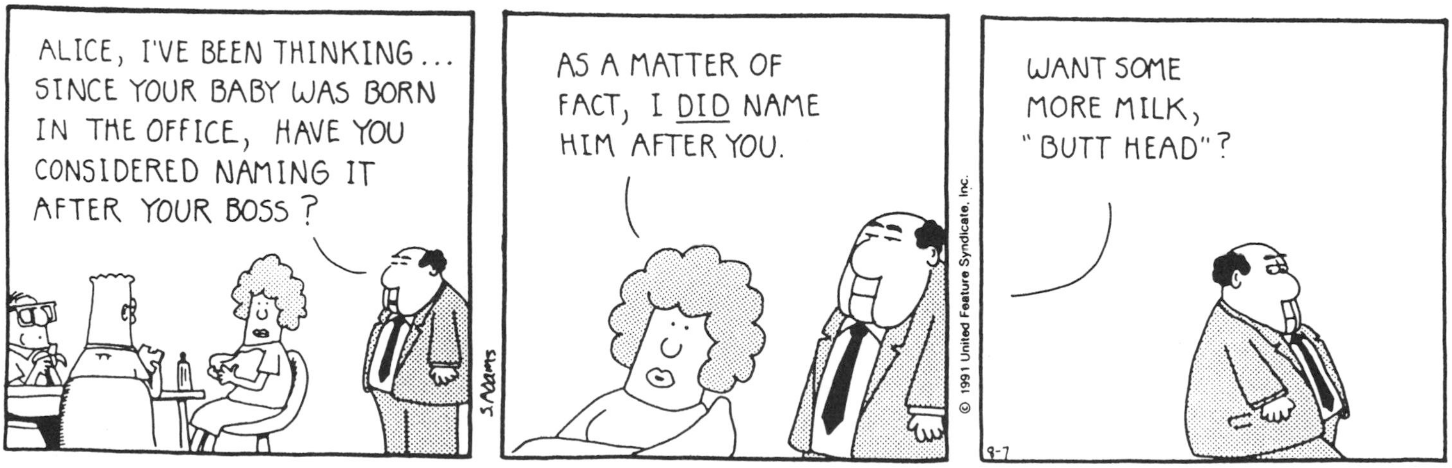
ALICE, I'VE BEEN THINKING... SINCE YOUR BABY WAS BORN IN THE OFFICE, HAVE YOU CONSIDERED NAMING IT AFTER YOUR BOSS?
AS A MATTER OF FACT, I DID NAME HIM AFTER YOU.
WANT SOME MORE MILK, "BUTT HEAD"?
© 1991 United Feature Syndicate, Inc.

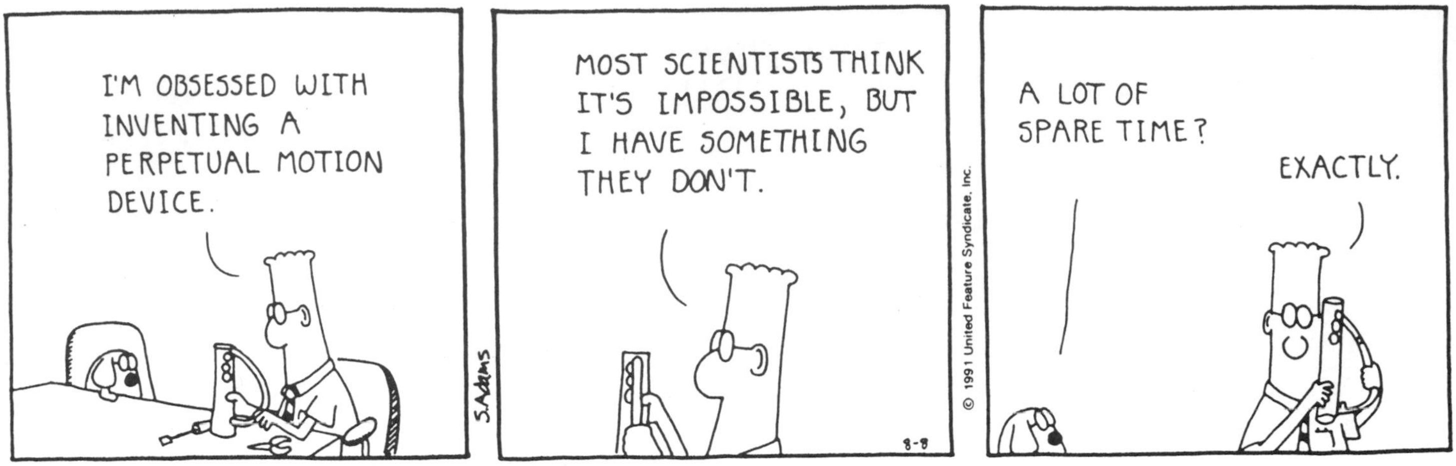
I'M OBSESSED WITH INVENTING A PERPETUAL MOTION DEVICE.
S.Adams
MOST SCIENTISTS THINK IT'S IMPOSSIBLE, BUT I HAVE SOMETHING THEY DON'T.
8-8
© 1991 United Feature Syndicate, Inc.
A LOT OF SPARE TIME?
EXACTLY.

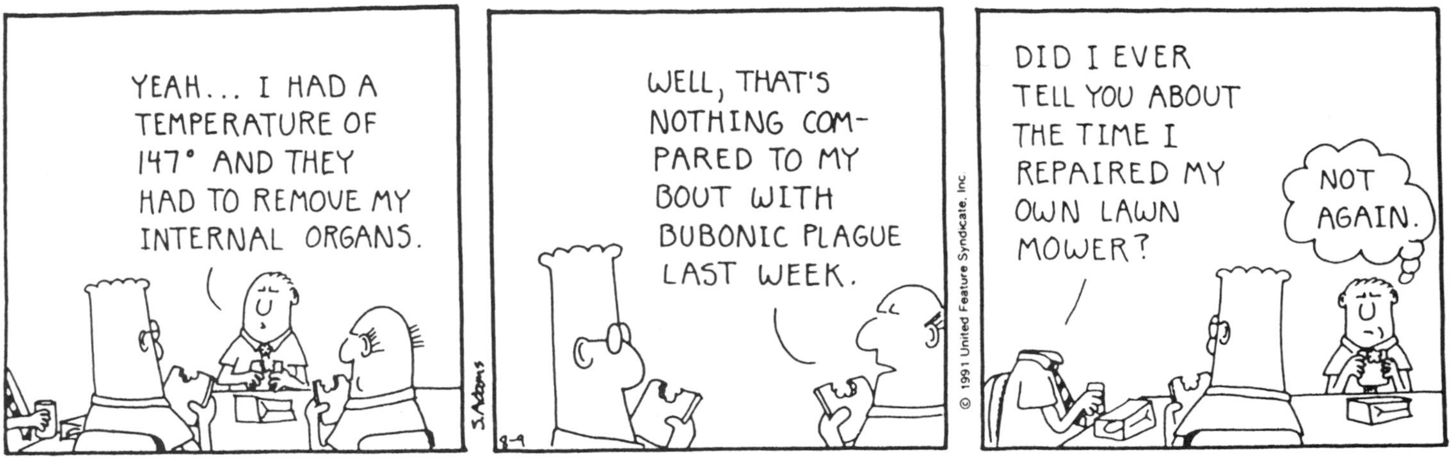
YEAH... I HAD A TEMPERATURE OF 147° AND THEY HAD TO REMOVE MY INTERNAL ORGANS.
S.Adams
8-9
WELL, THAT'S NOTHING COMPARED TO MY BOUT WITH BUBONIC PLAGUE LAST WEEK.
© 1991 United Feature Syndicate, Inc.
DID I EVER TELL YOU ABOUT THE TIME I REPAIRED MY OWN LAWN MOWER?
NOT AGAIN.

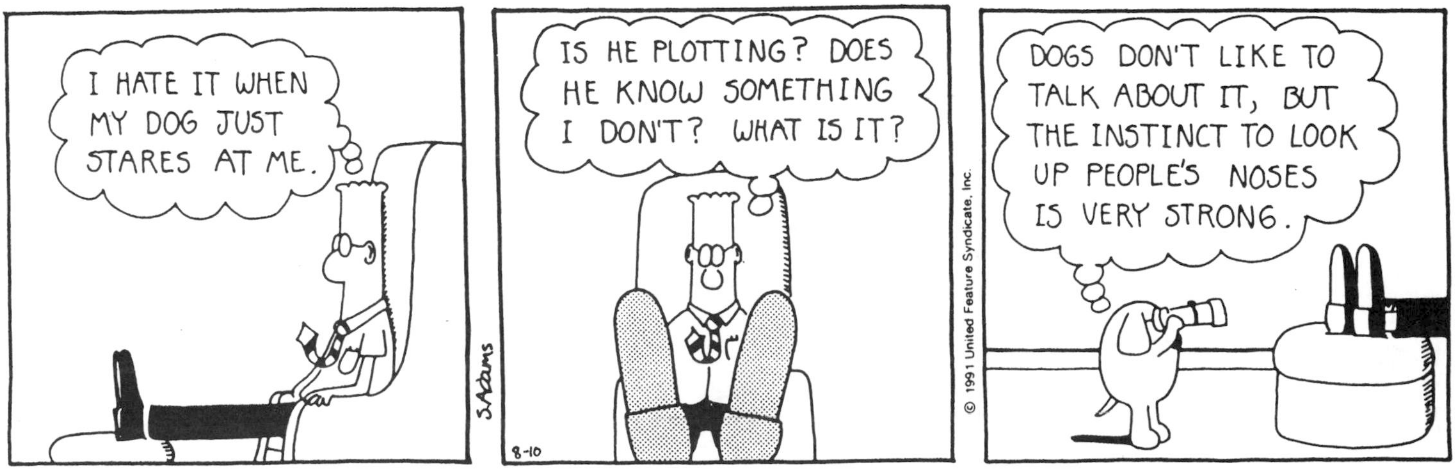
I HATE IT WHEN MY DOG JUST STARES AT ME.
S.Adams
IS HE PLOTTING? DOES HE KNOW SOMETHING I DON'T? WHAT IS IT?
8-10
© 1991 United Feature Syndicate, Inc.
DOGS DON'T LIKE TO TALK ABOUT IT, BUT THE INSTINCT TO LOOK UP PEOPLE'S NOSES IS VERY STRONG.

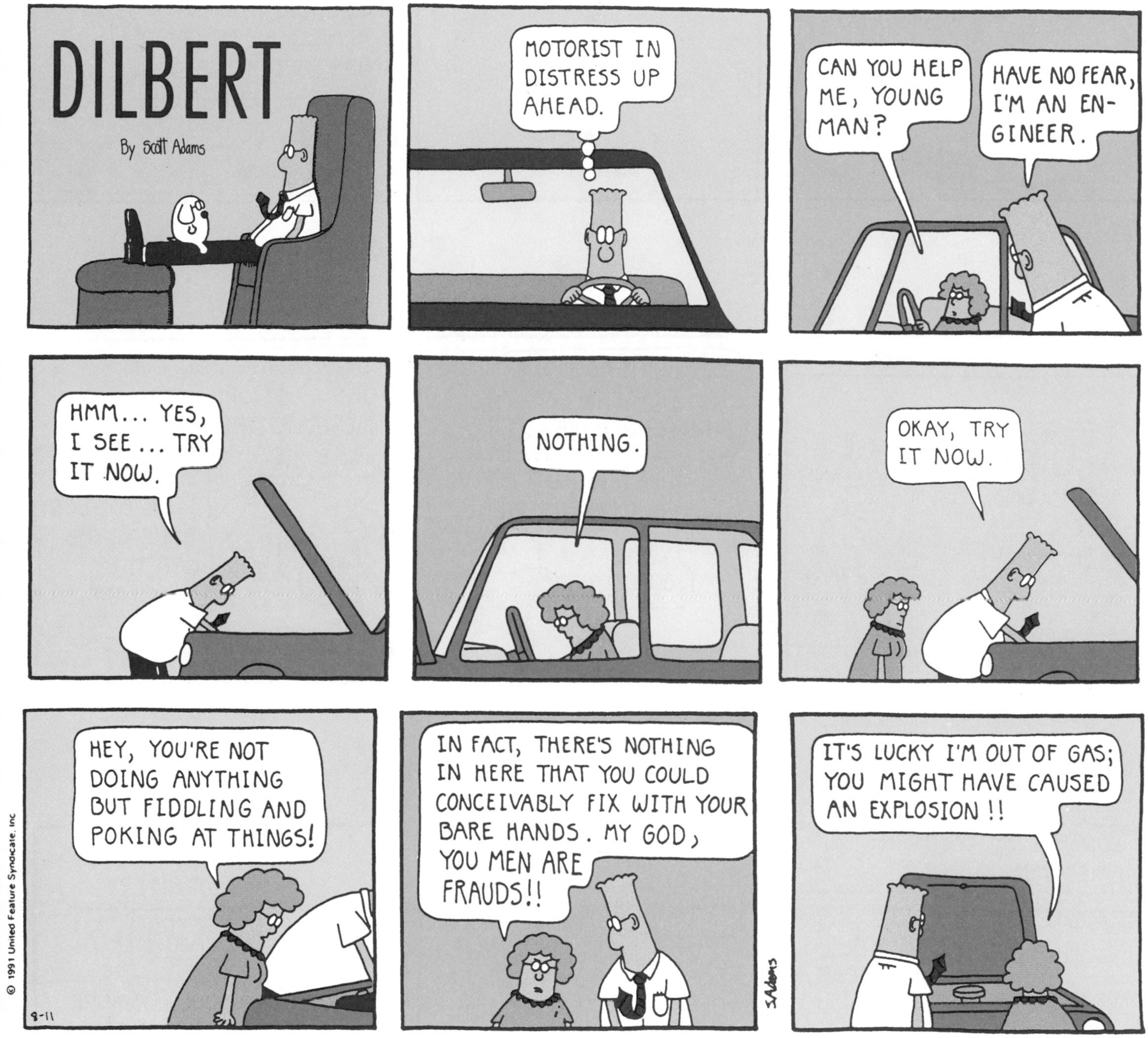
DILBERT
By Scott Adams
MOTORIST IN DISTRESS UP AHEAD.
CAN YOU HELP ME, YOUNG MAN?
HAVE NO FEAR, I'M AN ENGINEER.
HMM... YES, I SEE... TRY IT NOW.
NOTHING.
OKAY, TRY IT NOW.
HEY, YOU'RE NOT DOING ANYTHING BUT FIDDLING AND POKING AT THINGS!
IN FACT, THERE'S NOTHING IN HERE THAT YOU COULD CONCEIVABLY FIX WITH YOUR BARE HANDS. MY GOD, YOU MEN ARE FRAUDS!!
IT'S LUCKY I'M OUT OF GAS; YOU MIGHT HAVE CAUSED AN EXPLOSION!!
© 1991 United Feature Syndicate, Inc
8-11
S.Adams

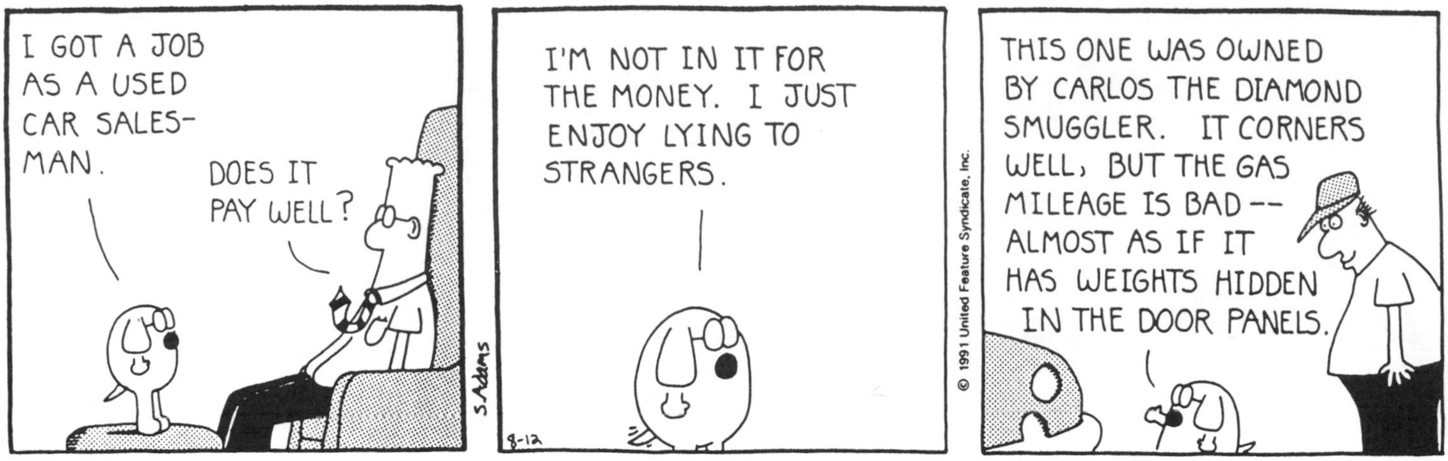
I GOT A JOB AS A USED CAR SALES-MAN.
DOES IT PAY WELL?
S. Adams
8-12
I'M NOT IN IT FOR THE MONEY. I JUST ENJOY LYING TO STRANGERS.
© 1991 United Feature Syndicate, Inc.
THIS ONE WAS OWNED BY CARLOS THE DIAMOND SMUGGLER. IT CORNERS WELL, BUT THE GAS MILEAGE IS BAD -- ALMOST AS IF IT HAS WEIGHTS HIDDEN IN THE DOOR PANELS.

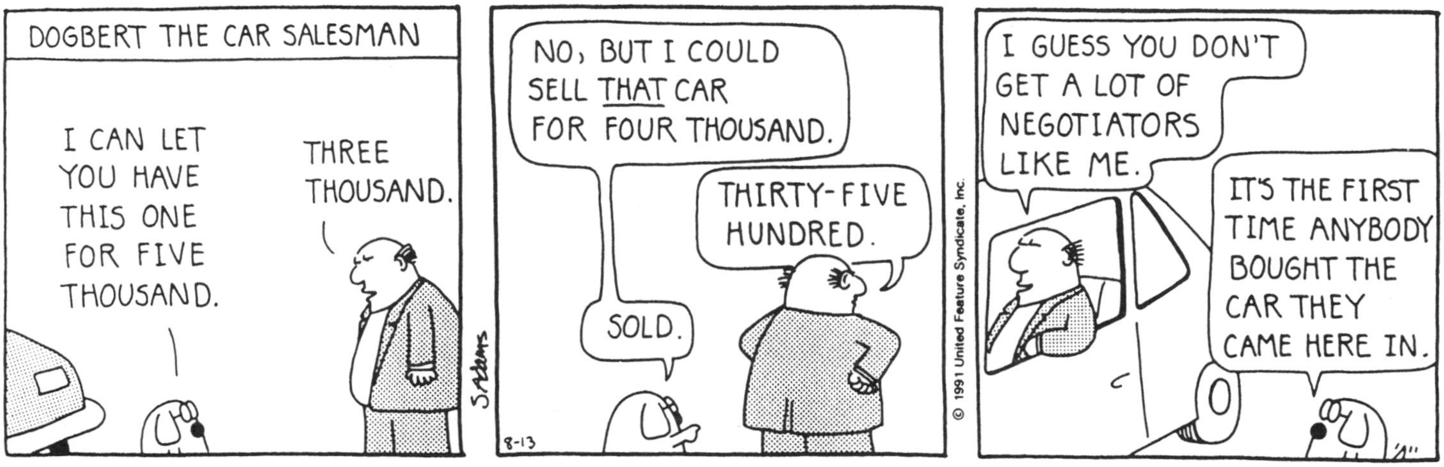
DOGBERT THE CAR SALESMAN
I CAN LET YOU HAVE THIS ONE FOR FIVE THOUSAND.
THREE THOUSAND.
S. Adams
8-13
NO, BUT I COULD SELL THAT CAR FOR FOUR THOUSAND.
THIRTY-FIVE HUNDRED.
SOLD.
© 1991 United Feature Syndicate, Inc.
I GUESS YOU DON'T GET A LOT OF NEGOTIATORS LIKE ME.
IT'S THE FIRST TIME ANYBODY BOUGHT THE CAR THEY CAME HERE IN.

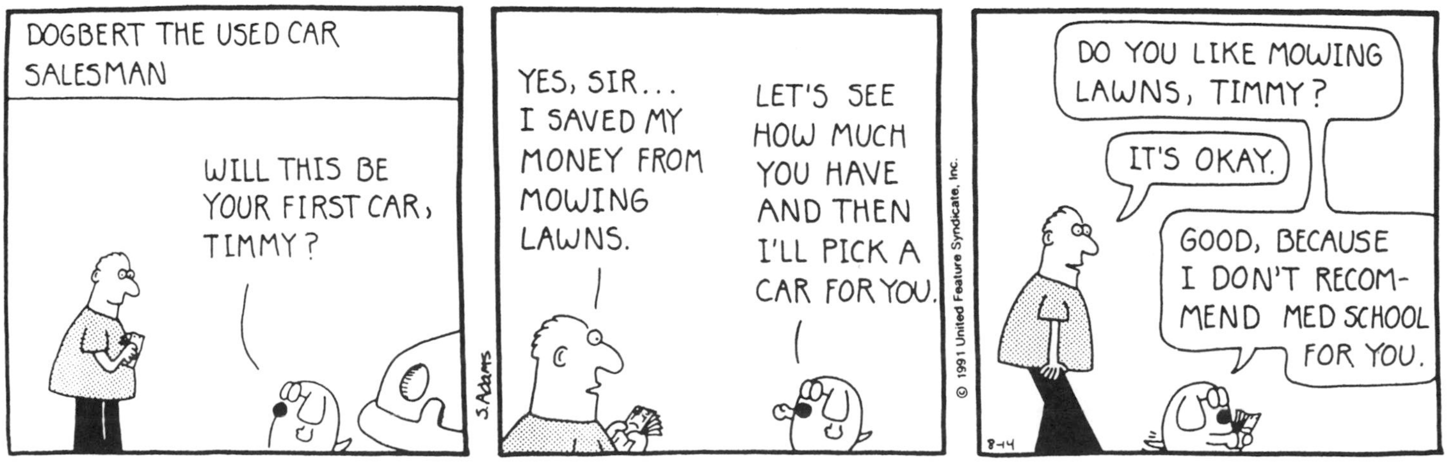
DOGBERT THE USED CAR SALESMAN
WILL THIS BE YOUR FIRST CAR, TIMMY?
S. Adams
YES, SIR... I SAVED MY MONEY FROM MOWING LAWNS.
LET'S SEE HOW MUCH YOU HAVE AND THEN I'LL PICK A CAR FOR YOU.
© 1991 United Feature Syndicate, Inc.
DO YOU LIKE MOWING LAWNS, TIMMY?
IT'S OKAY.
GOOD, BECAUSE I DON'T RECOM-MEND MED SCHOOL FOR YOU.
8-14

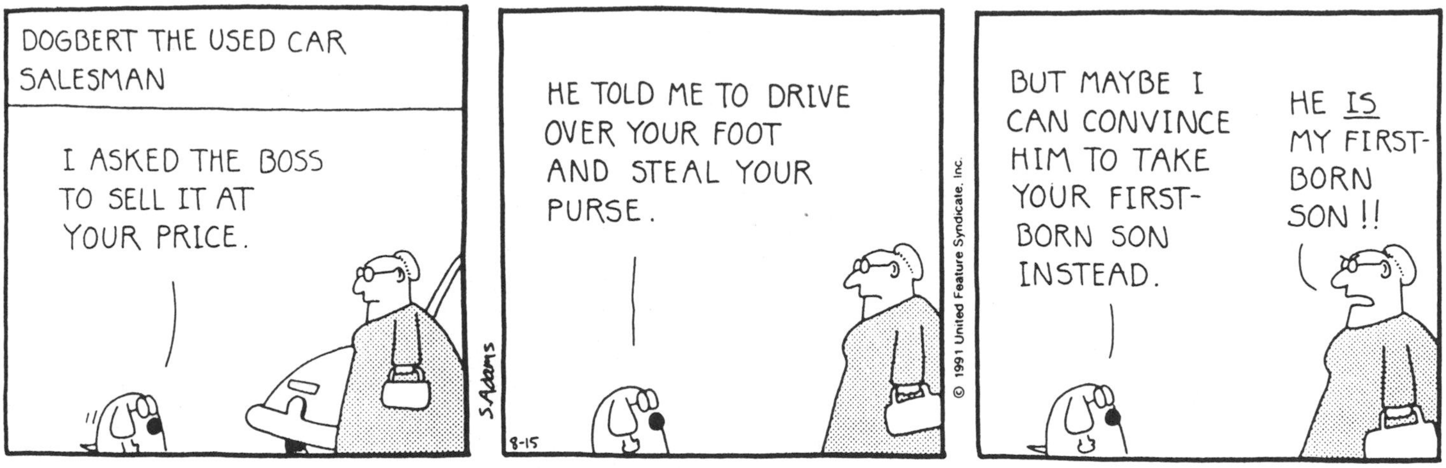
DOGBERT THE USED CAR SALESMAN
I ASKED THE BOSS TO SELL IT AT YOUR PRICE.
HE TOLD ME TO DRIVE OVER YOUR FOOT AND STEAL YOUR PURSE.
BUT MAYBE I CAN CONVINCE HIM TO TAKE YOUR FIRST-BORN SON INSTEAD.
HE IS MY FIRST-BORN SON !!
S. Adams
8-15
© 1991 United Feature Syndicate, Inc.

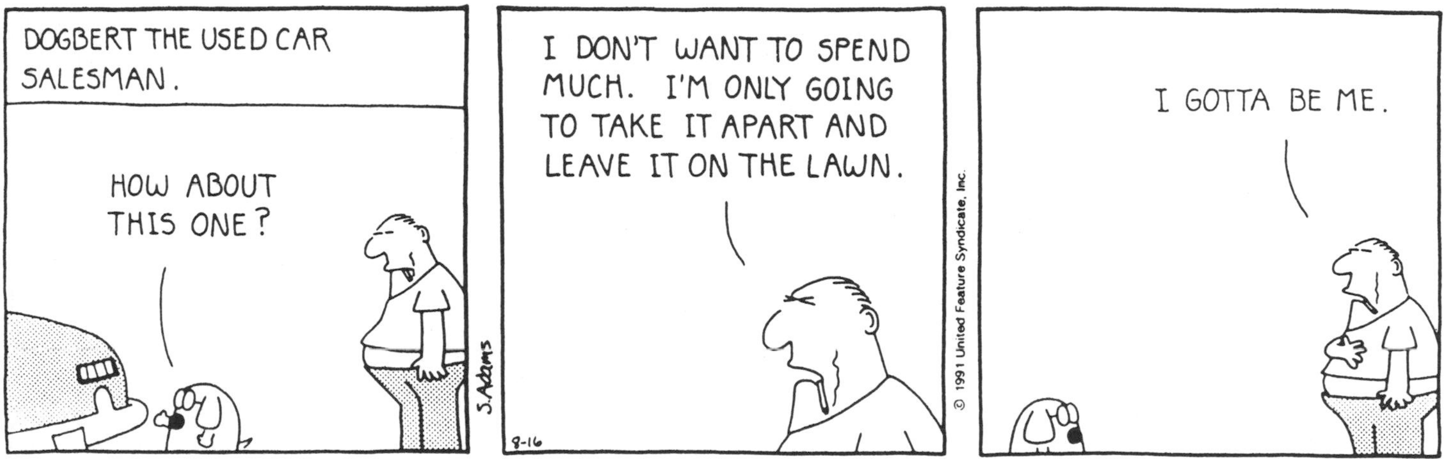
DOGBERT THE USED CAR SALESMAN.
HOW ABOUT THIS ONE?
I DON'T WANT TO SPEND MUCH. I'M ONLY GOING TO TAKE IT APART AND LEAVE IT ON THE LAWN.
I GOTTA BE ME.
S. Adams
8-16
© 1991 United Feature Syndicate, Inc.

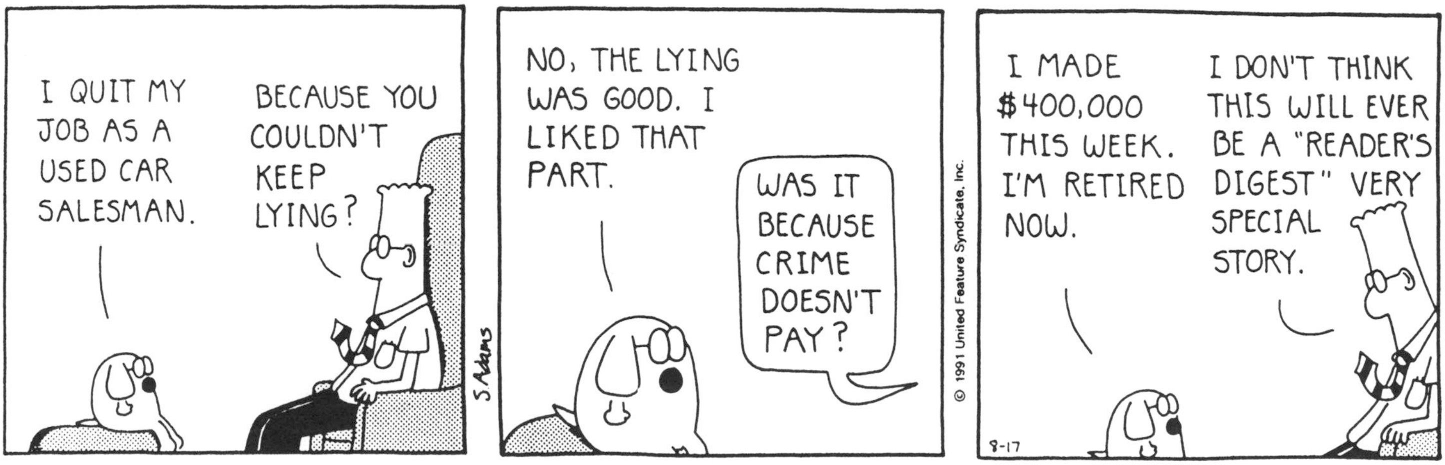
I QUIT MY JOB AS A USED CAR SALESMAN.
BECAUSE YOU COULDN'T KEEP LYING?
NO, THE LYING WAS GOOD. I LIKED THAT PART.
WAS IT BECAUSE CRIME DOESN'T PAY?
I MADE $400,000 THIS WEEK. I'M RETIRED NOW.
I DON'T THINK THIS WILL EVER BE A "READER'S DIGEST" VERY SPECIAL STORY.
S. Adams
8-17
© 1991 United Feature Syndicate, Inc.

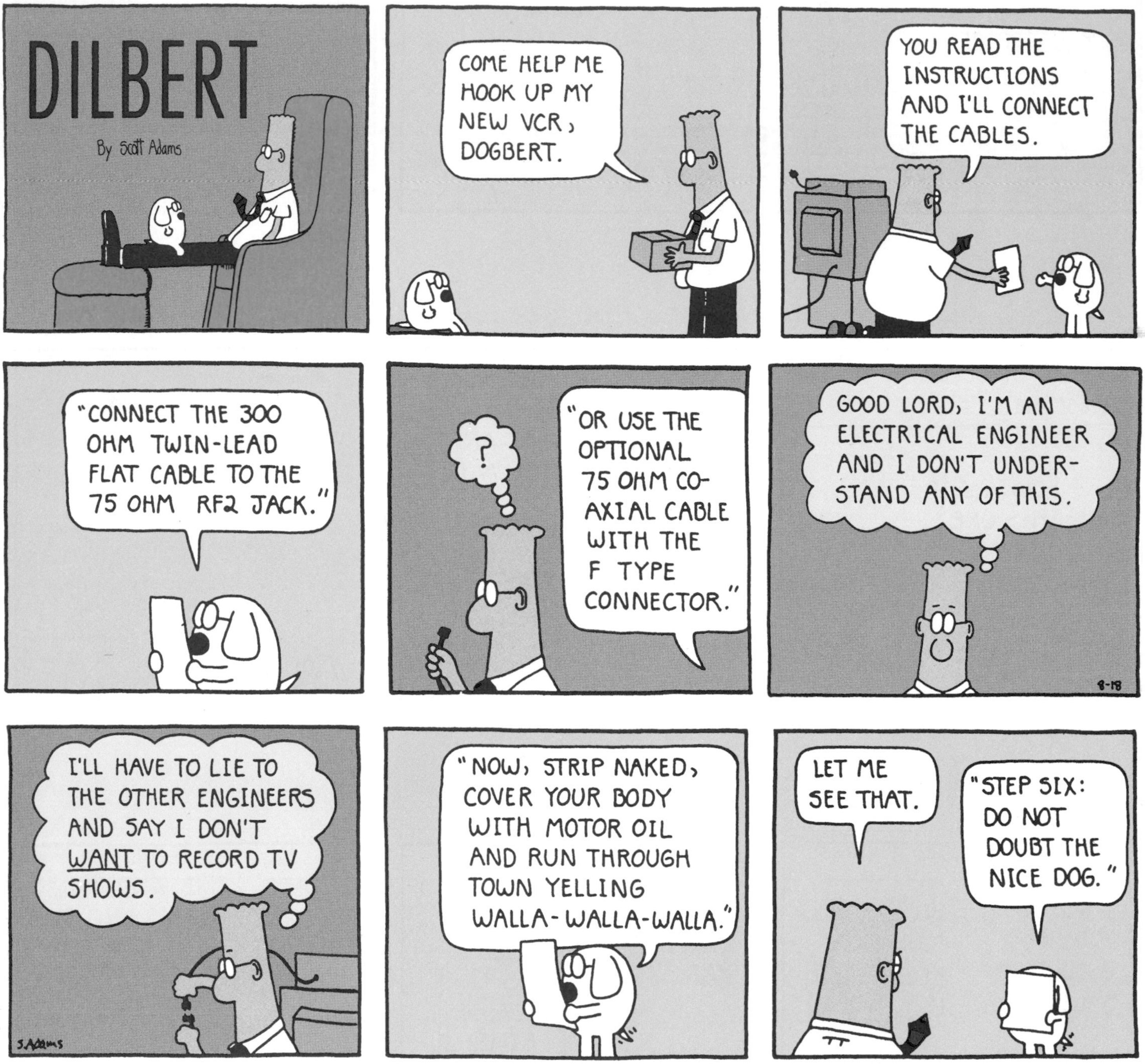
DILBERT
By Scott Adams
COME HELP ME HOOK UP MY NEW VCR, DOGBERT.
YOU READ THE INSTRUCTIONS AND I'LL CONNECT THE CABLES.
"CONNECT THE 300 OHM TWIN-LEAD FLAT CABLE TO THE 75 OHM RF2 JACK."
?
"OR USE THE OPTIONAL 75 OHM CO-AXIAL CABLE WITH THE F TYPE CONNECTOR."
GOOD LORD, I'M AN ELECTRICAL ENGINEER AND I DON'T UNDER-STAND ANY OF THIS.
8-18
I'LL HAVE TO LIE TO THE OTHER ENGINEERS AND SAY I DON'T WANT TO RECORD TV SHOWS.
S.ADAMS
"NOW, STRIP NAKED, COVER YOUR BODY WITH MOTOR OIL AND RUN THROUGH TOWN YELLING WALLA-WALLA-WALLA."
LET ME SEE THAT.
"STEP SIX: DO NOT DOUBT THE NICE DOG."

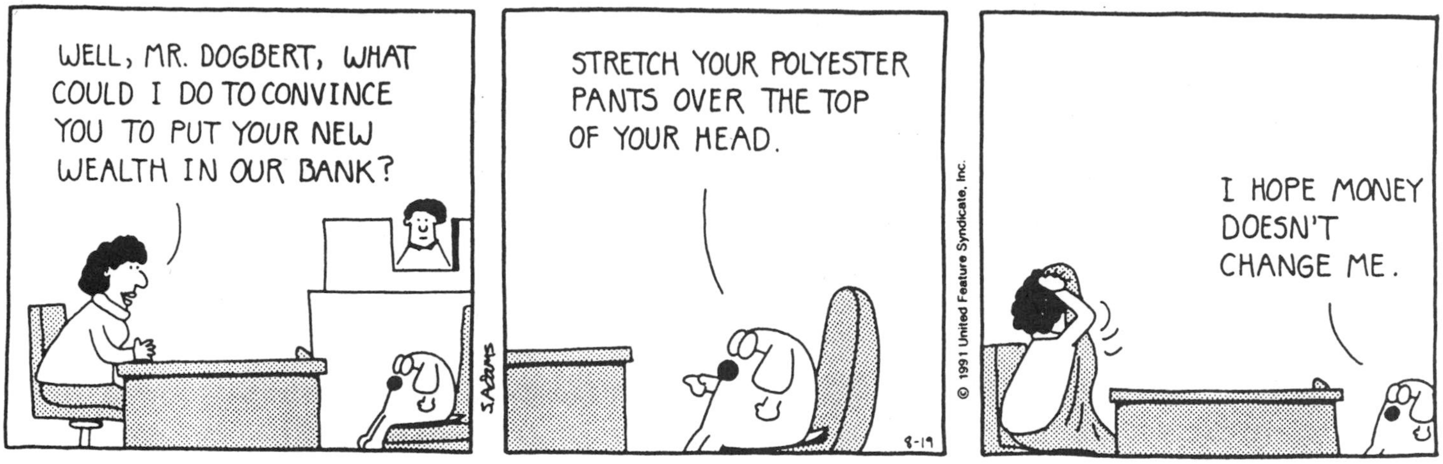

WELL, MR. DOGBERT, WHAT COULD I DO TO CONVINCE YOU TO PUT YOUR NEW WEALTH IN OUR BANK?
STRETCH YOUR POLYESTER PANTS OVER THE TOP OF YOUR HEAD.
8-19
© 1991 United Feature Syndicate, Inc.
I HOPE MONEY DOESN'T CHANGE ME.

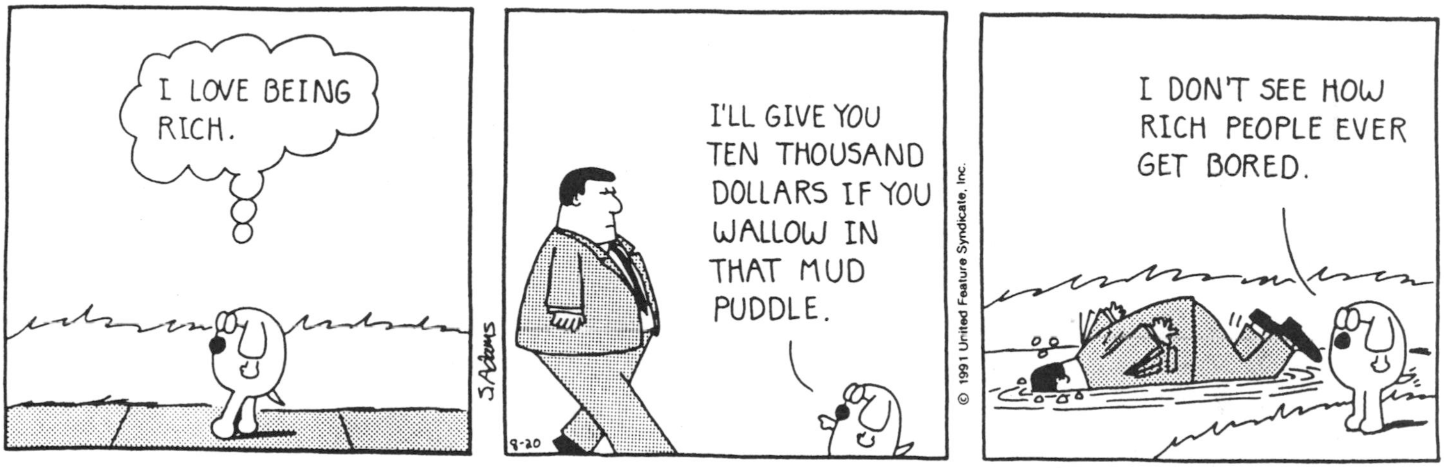

I LOVE BEING RICH.
I'LL GIVE YOU TEN THOUSAND DOLLARS IF YOU WALLOW IN THAT MUD PUDDLE.
8-20
© 1991 United Feature Syndicate, Inc.
I DON'T SEE HOW RICH PEOPLE EVER GET BORED.

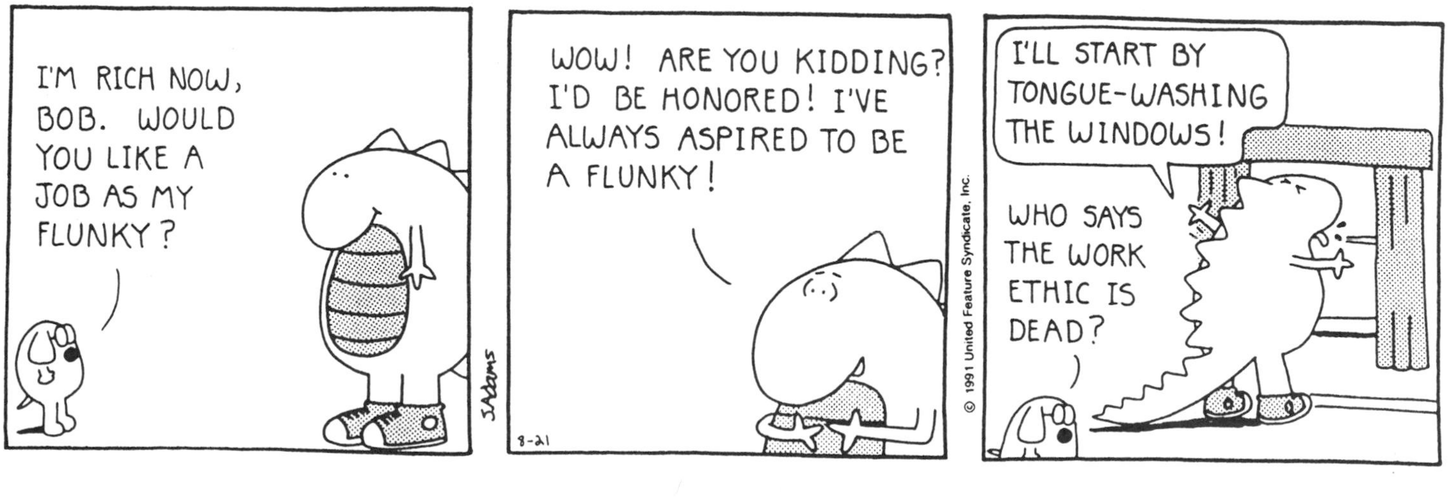

I'M RICH NOW, BOB. WOULD YOU LIKE A JOB AS MY FLUNKY?
WOW! ARE YOU KIDDING? I'D BE HONORED! I'VE ALWAYS ASPIRED TO BE A FLUNKY!
8-21
© 1991 United Feature Syndicate, Inc.
I'LL START BY TONGUE-WASHING THE WINDOWS!
WHO SAYS THE WORK ETHIC IS DEAD?

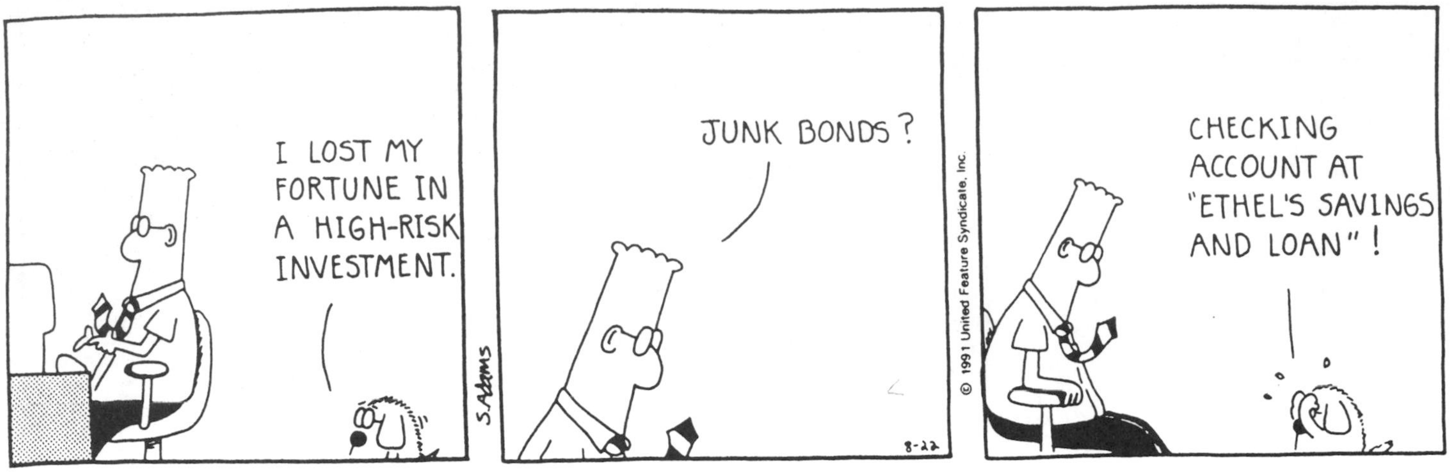
I LOST MY FORTUNE IN A HIGH-RISK INVESTMENT.
S. ADAMS
JUNK BONDS?
8-22
© 1991 United Feature Syndicate, Inc.
CHECKING ACCOUNT AT "ETHEL'S SAVINGS AND LOAN"!

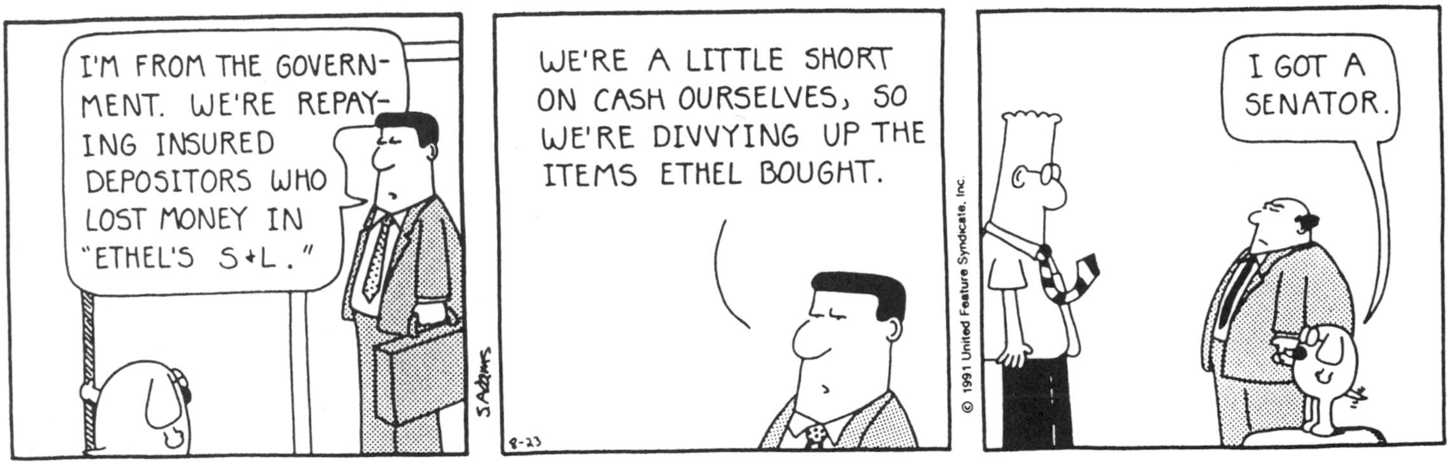
I'M FROM THE GOVERNMENT. WE'RE REPAYING INSURED DEPOSITORS WHO LOST MONEY IN "ETHEL'S S+L."
S. ADAMS
WE'RE A LITTLE SHORT ON CASH OURSELVES, SO WE'RE DIVVYING UP THE ITEMS ETHEL BOUGHT.
8-23
© 1991 United Feature Syndicate, Inc.
I GOT A SENATOR.

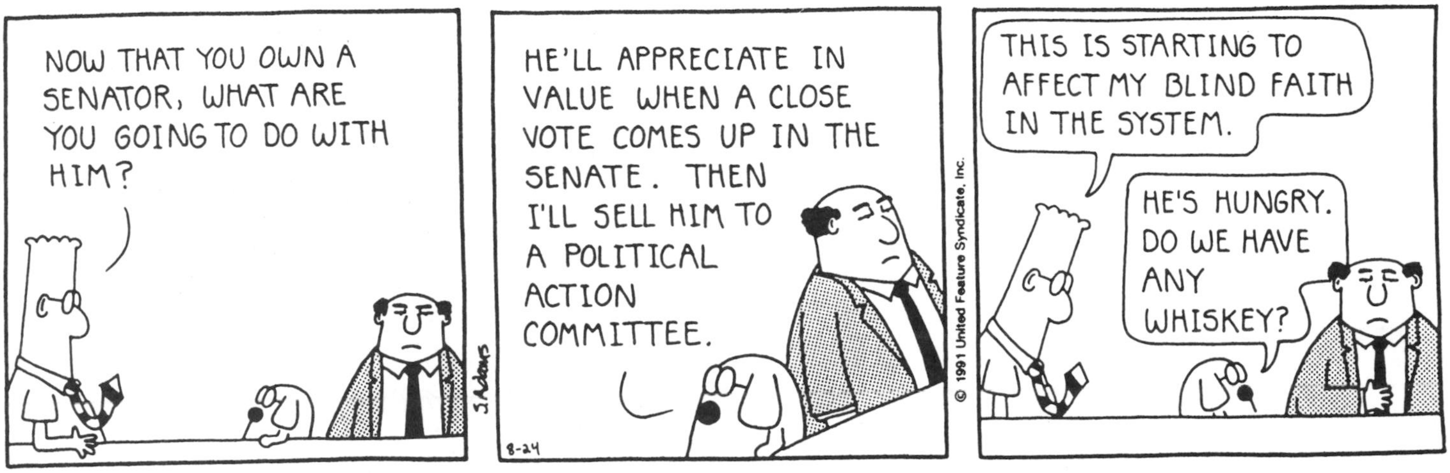
NOW THAT YOU OWN A SENATOR, WHAT ARE YOU GOING TO DO WITH HIM?
S. ADAMS
HE'LL APPRECIATE IN VALUE WHEN A CLOSE VOTE COMES UP IN THE SENATE. THEN I'LL SELL HIM TO A POLITICAL ACTION COMMITTEE.
8-24
© 1991 United Feature Syndicate, Inc.
THIS IS STARTING TO AFFECT MY BLIND FAITH IN THE SYSTEM.
HE'S HUNGRY. DO WE HAVE ANY WHISKEY?

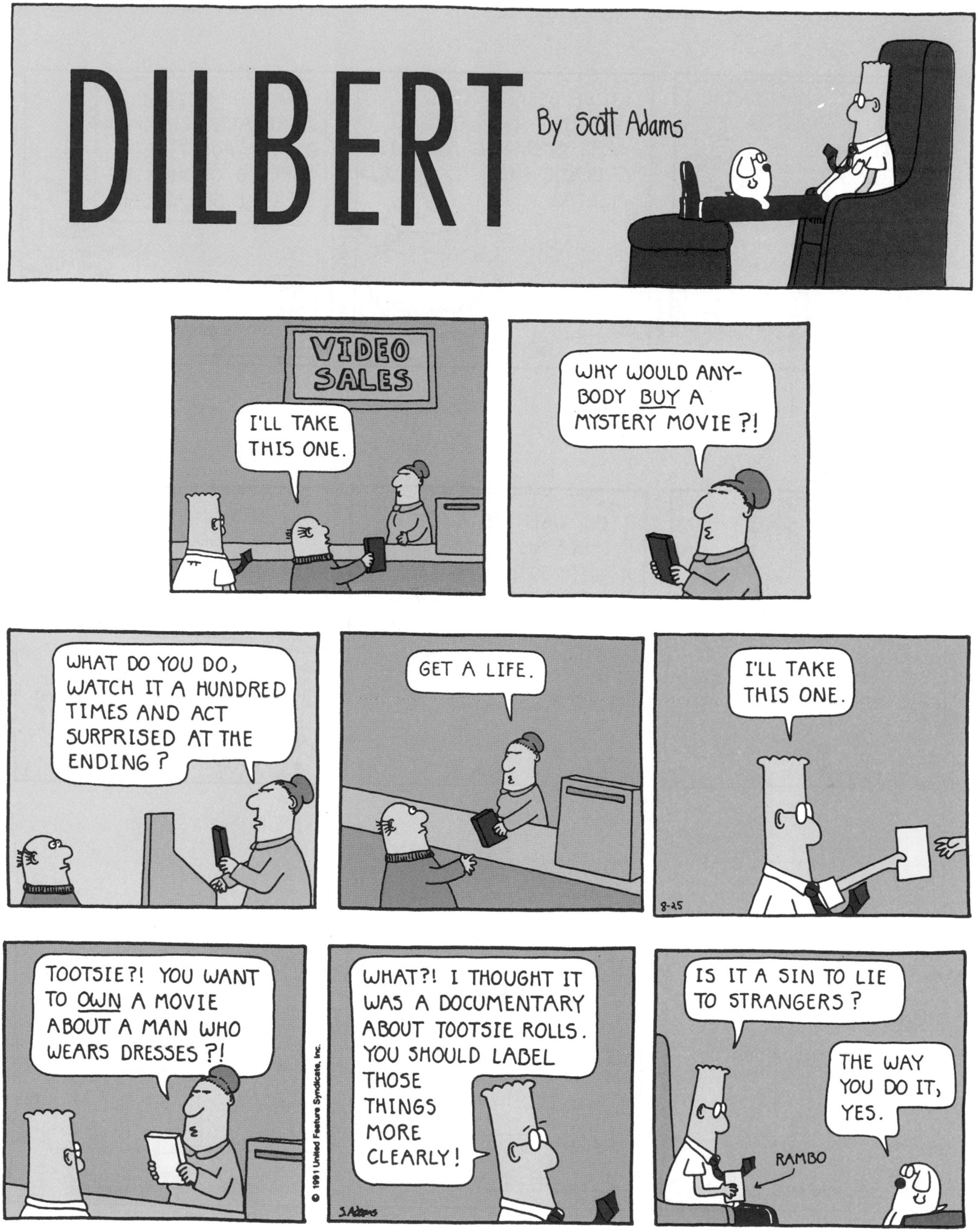
DILBERT
By Scott Adams
VIDEO SALES
I'LL TAKE THIS ONE.
WHY WOULD ANYBODY BUY A MYSTERY MOVIE ?!
WHAT DO YOU DO, WATCH IT A HUNDRED TIMES AND ACT SURPRISED AT THE ENDING ?
GET A LIFE.
I'LL TAKE THIS ONE.
8-25
TOOTSIE ?! YOU WANT TO OWN A MOVIE ABOUT A MAN WHO WEARS DRESSES ?!
© 1991 United Feature Syndicate, Inc.
WHAT ?! I THOUGHT IT WAS A DOCUMENTARY ABOUT TOOTSIE ROLLS. YOU SHOULD LABEL THOSE THINGS MORE CLEARLY !
S. Adams
IS IT A SIN TO LIE TO STRANGERS ?
THE WAY YOU DO IT, YES.
RAMBO

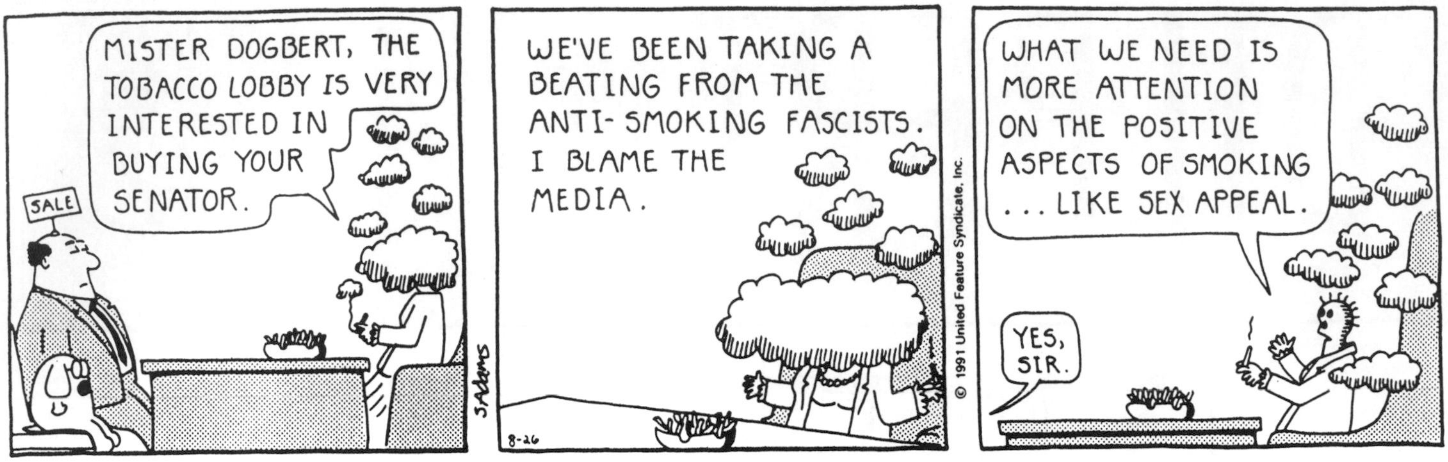
MISTER DOGBERT, THE TOBACCO LOBBY IS VERY INTERESTED IN BUYING YOUR SENATOR.
SALE
WE'VE BEEN TAKING A BEATING FROM THE ANTI-SMOKING FASCISTS. I BLAME THE MEDIA.
WHAT WE NEED IS MORE ATTENTION ON THE POSITIVE ASPECTS OF SMOKING . . . LIKE SEX APPEAL.
YES, SIR.
© 1991 United Feature Syndicate, Inc.

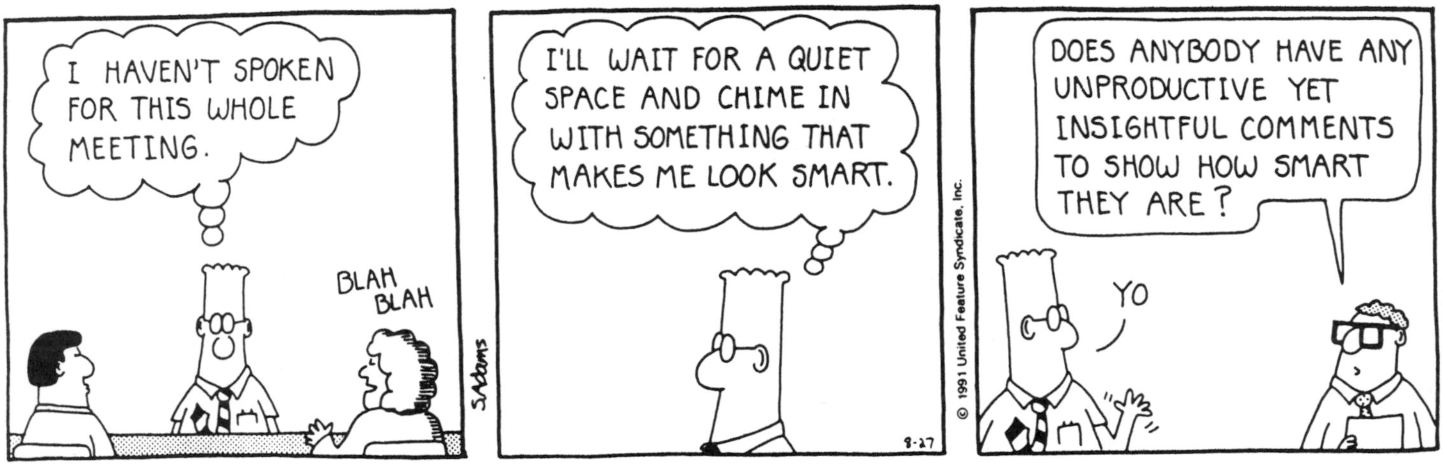
I HAVEN'T SPOKEN FOR THIS WHOLE MEETING.
BLAH BLAH
I'LL WAIT FOR A QUIET SPACE AND CHIME IN WITH SOMETHING THAT MAKES ME LOOK SMART.
DOES ANYBODY HAVE ANY UNPRODUCTIVE YET INSIGHTFUL COMMENTS TO SHOW HOW SMART THEY ARE?
YO
© 1991 United Feature Syndicate, Inc.

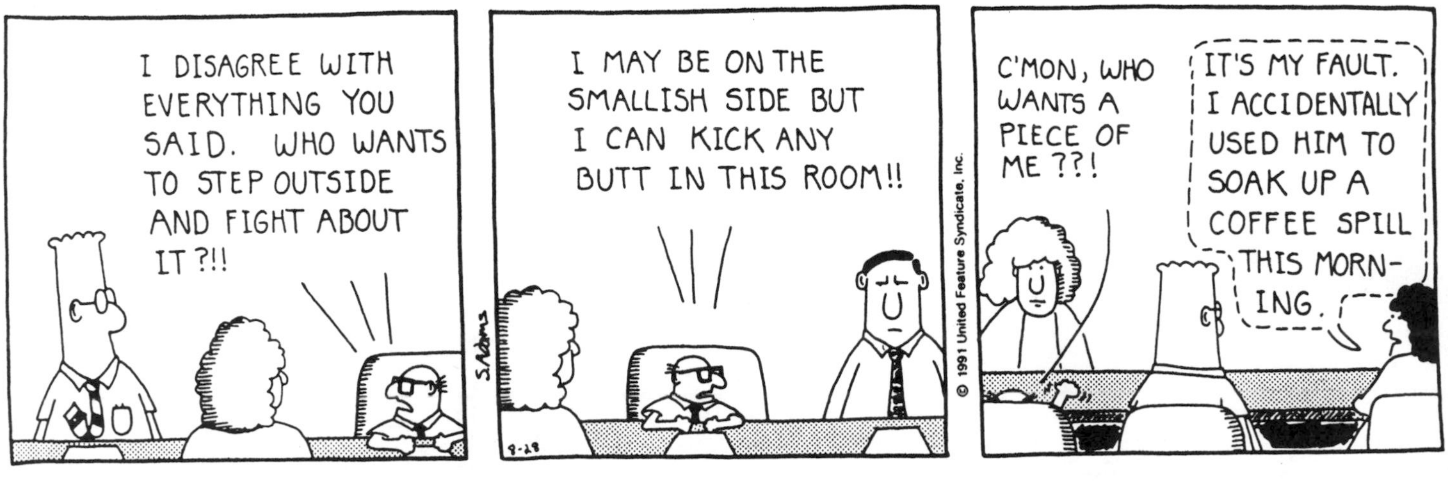
I DISAGREE WITH EVERYTHING YOU SAID. WHO WANTS TO STEP OUTSIDE AND FIGHT ABOUT IT?!!
I MAY BE ON THE SMALLISH SIDE BUT I CAN KICK ANY BUTT IN THIS ROOM!!
C'MON, WHO WANTS A PIECE OF ME??!
IT'S MY FAULT. I ACCIDENTALLY USED HIM TO SOAK UP A COFFEE SPILL THIS MORNING.
© 1991 United Feature Syndicate, Inc.

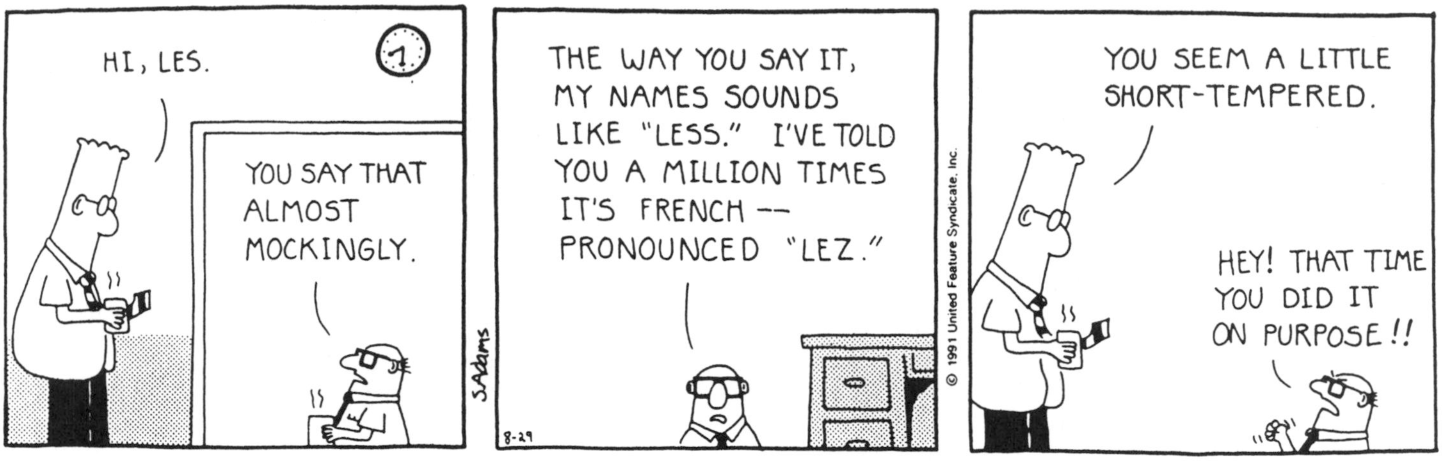
HI, LES.
YOU SAY THAT ALMOST MOCKINGLY.
THE WAY YOU SAY IT, MY NAMES SOUNDS LIKE "LESS." I'VE TOLD YOU A MILLION TIMES IT'S FRENCH -- PRONOUNCED "LEZ."
YOU SEEM A LITTLE SHORT-TEMPERED.
HEY! THAT TIME YOU DID IT ON PURPOSE!!
S.Adams
8-29
© 1991 United Feature Syndicate, Inc.

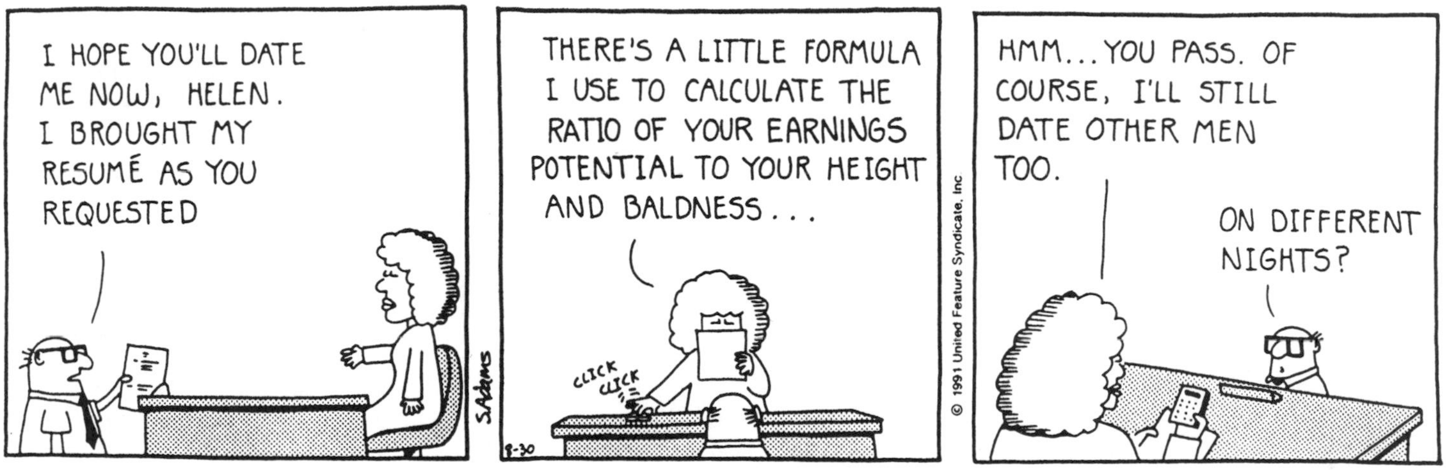
I HOPE YOU'LL DATE ME NOW, HELEN. I BROUGHT MY RESUMÉ AS YOU REQUESTED
THERE'S A LITTLE FORMULA I USE TO CALCULATE THE RATIO OF YOUR EARNINGS POTENTIAL TO YOUR HEIGHT AND BALDNESS...
CLICK CLICK
HMM... YOU PASS. OF COURSE, I'LL STILL DATE OTHER MEN TOO.
ON DIFFERENT NIGHTS?
S.Adams
8-30
© 1991 United Feature Syndicate, Inc.

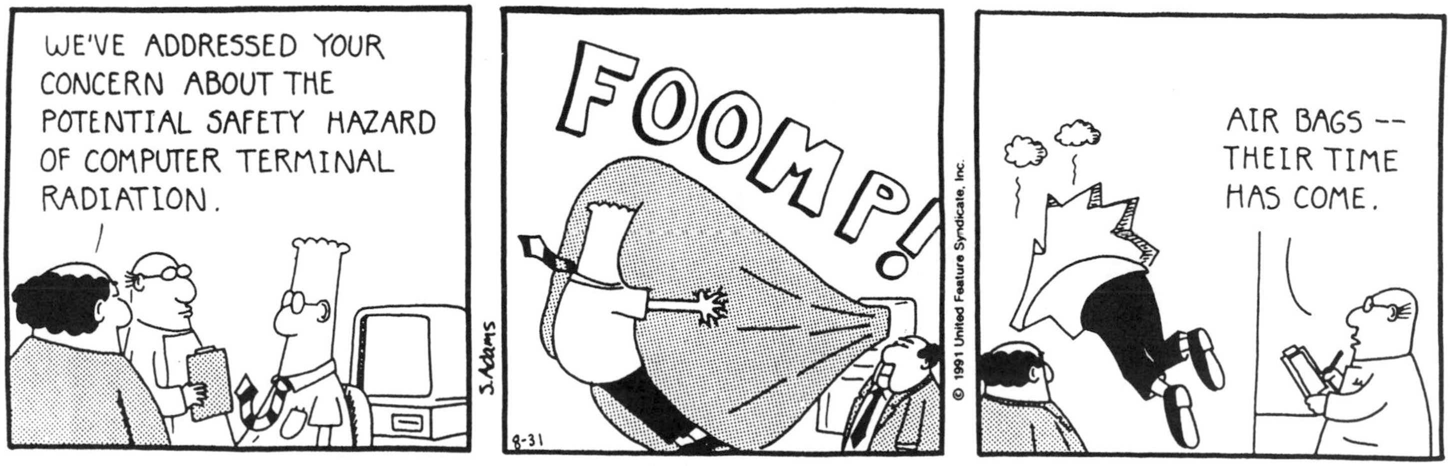
WE'VE ADDRESSED YOUR CONCERN ABOUT THE POTENTIAL SAFETY HAZARD OF COMPUTER TERMINAL RADIATION.
FOOMP!
AIR BAGS -- THEIR TIME HAS COME.
S.Adams
8-31
© 1991 United Feature Syndicate, Inc.

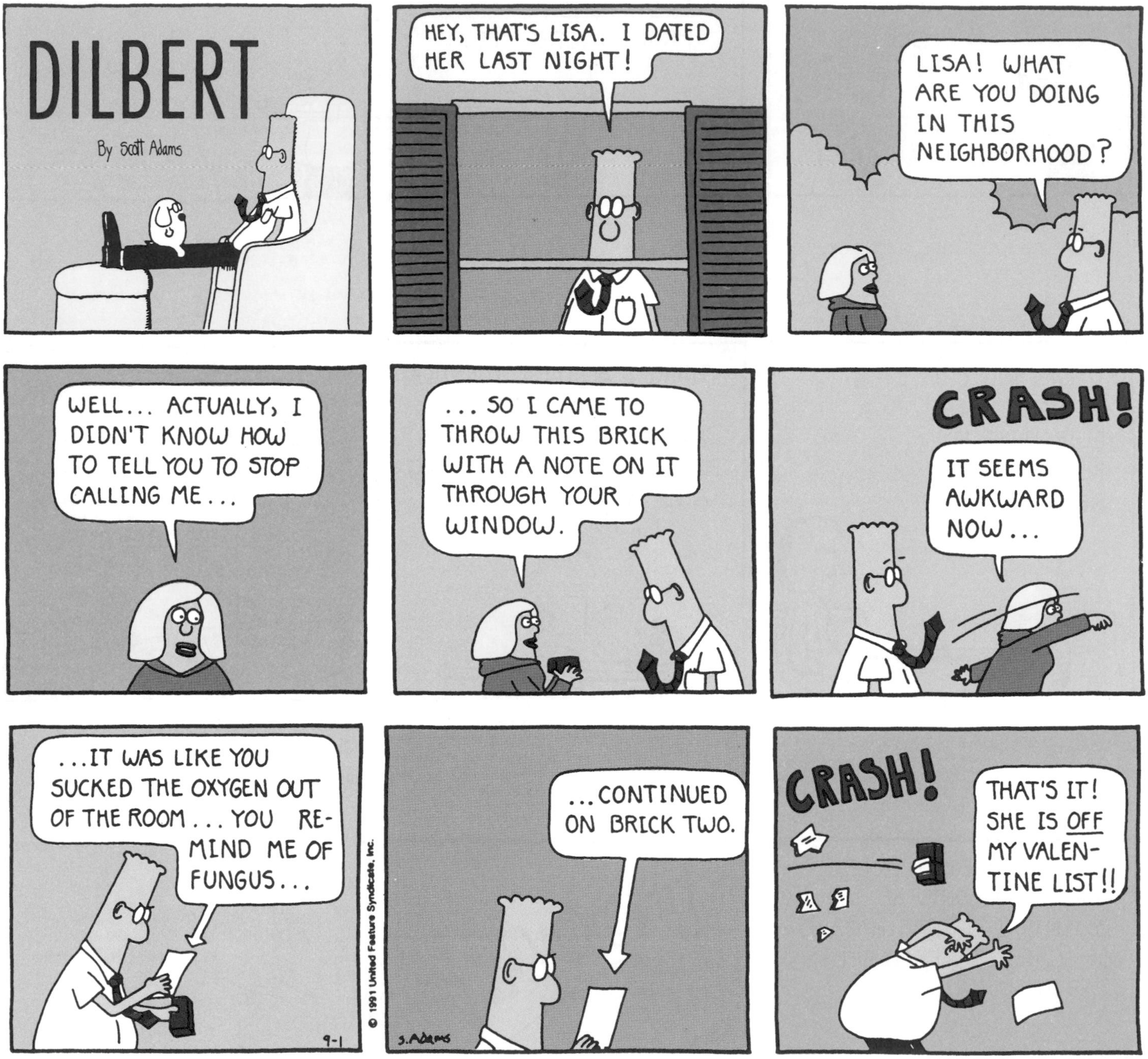
DILBERT
By Scott Adams
HEY, THAT'S LISA. I DATED HER LAST NIGHT!
LISA! WHAT ARE YOU DOING IN THIS NEIGHBORHOOD?
WELL... ACTUALLY, I DIDN'T KNOW HOW TO TELL YOU TO STOP CALLING ME...
... SO I CAME TO THROW THIS BRICK WITH A NOTE ON IT THROUGH YOUR WINDOW.
CRASH!
IT SEEMS AWKWARD NOW...
...IT WAS LIKE YOU SUCKED THE OXYGEN OUT OF THE ROOM... YOU RE-MIND ME OF FUNGUS...
9-1
© 1991 United Feature Syndicate, Inc.
S. ADAMS
...CONTINUED ON BRICK TWO.
CRASH!
THAT'S IT! SHE IS OFF MY VALEN-TINE LIST!!

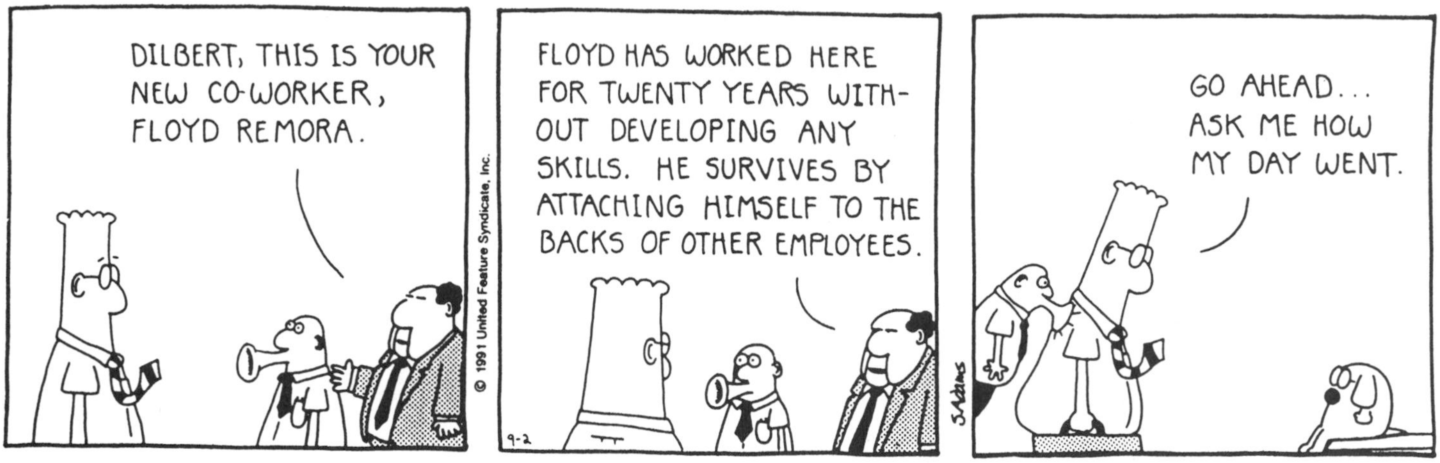
DILBERT, THIS IS YOUR NEW CO-WORKER, FLOYD REMORA.
© 1991 United Feature Syndicate, Inc.
9-2
FLOYD HAS WORKED HERE FOR TWENTY YEARS WITHOUT DEVELOPING ANY SKILLS. HE SURVIVES BY ATTACHING HIMSELF TO THE BACKS OF OTHER EMPLOYEES.
S.Adams
GO AHEAD... ASK ME HOW MY DAY WENT.

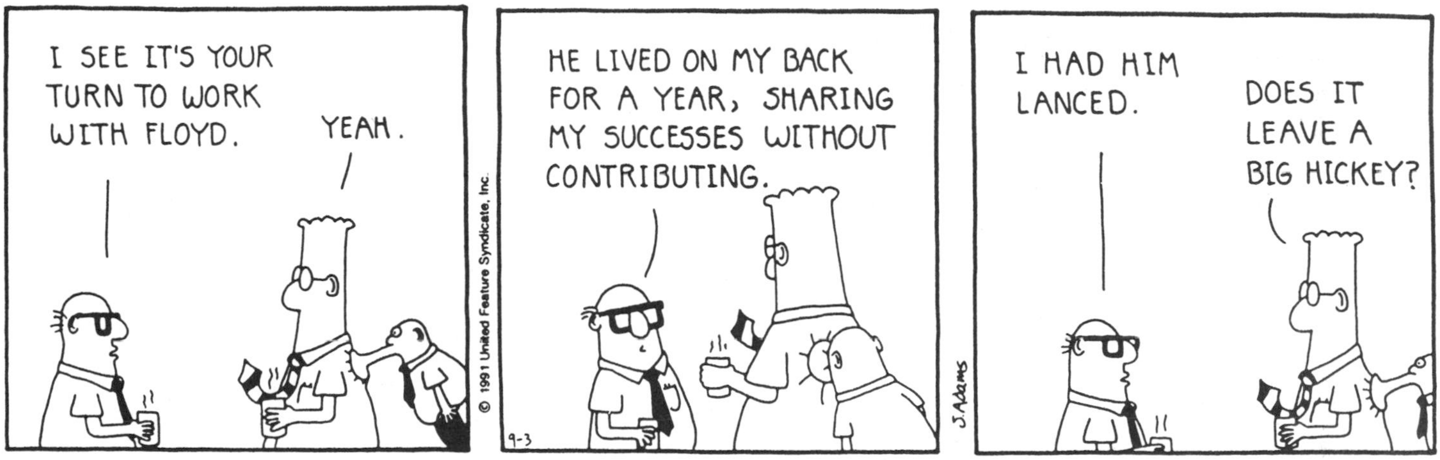
I SEE IT'S YOUR TURN TO WORK WITH FLOYD.
YEAH.
© 1991 United Feature Syndicate, Inc.
9-3
HE LIVED ON MY BACK FOR A YEAR, SHARING MY SUCCESSES WITHOUT CONTRIBUTING.
S.Adams
I HAD HIM LANCED.
DOES IT LEAVE A BIG HICKEY?

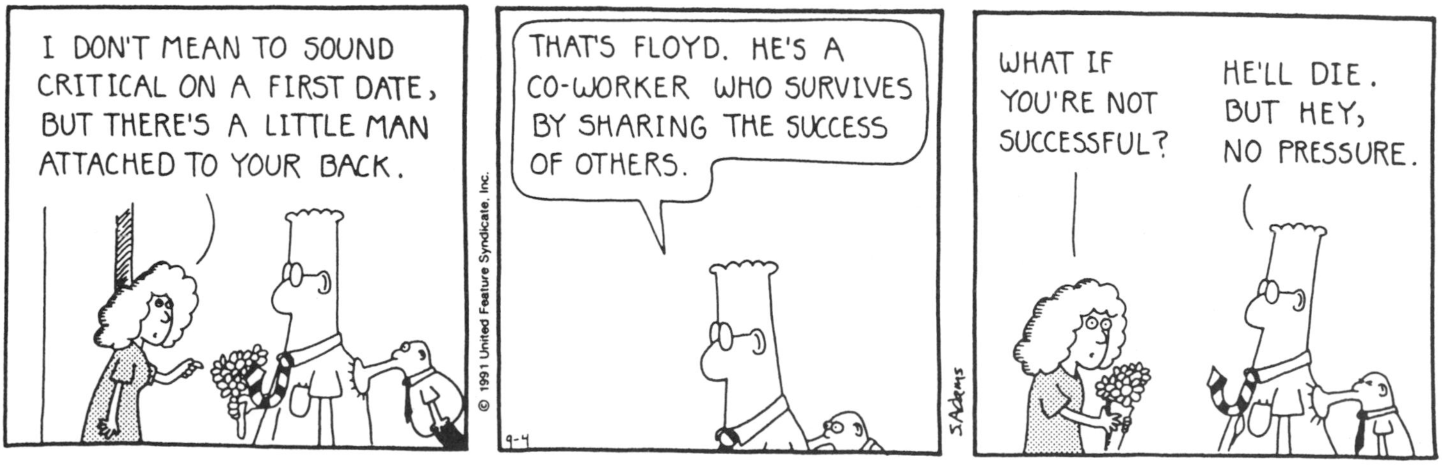
I DON'T MEAN TO SOUND CRITICAL ON A FIRST DATE, BUT THERE'S A LITTLE MAN ATTACHED TO YOUR BACK.
© 1991 United Feature Syndicate, Inc.
9-4
THAT'S FLOYD. HE'S A CO-WORKER WHO SURVIVES BY SHARING THE SUCCESS OF OTHERS.
S.Adams
WHAT IF YOU'RE NOT SUCCESSFUL?
HE'LL DIE. BUT HEY, NO PRESSURE.

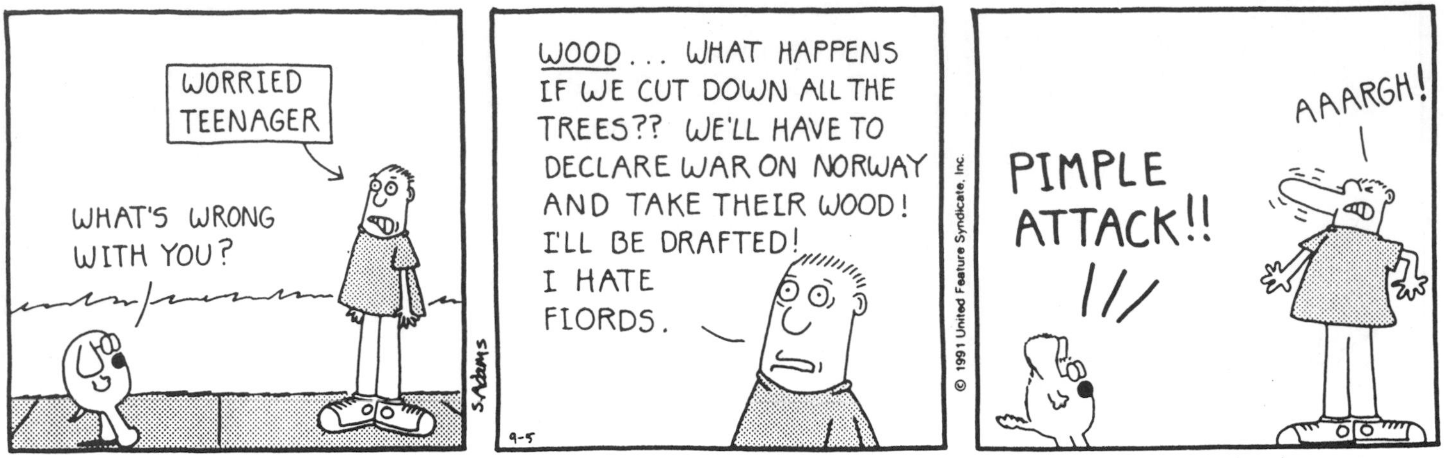
WORRIED TEENAGER
WHAT'S WRONG WITH YOU?
WOOD... WHAT HAPPENS IF WE CUT DOWN ALL THE TREES?? WE'LL HAVE TO DECLARE WAR ON NORWAY AND TAKE THEIR WOOD! I'LL BE DRAFTED! I HATE FIORDS.
PIMPLE ATTACK!!
AAARGH!
© 1991 United Feature Syndicate, Inc.

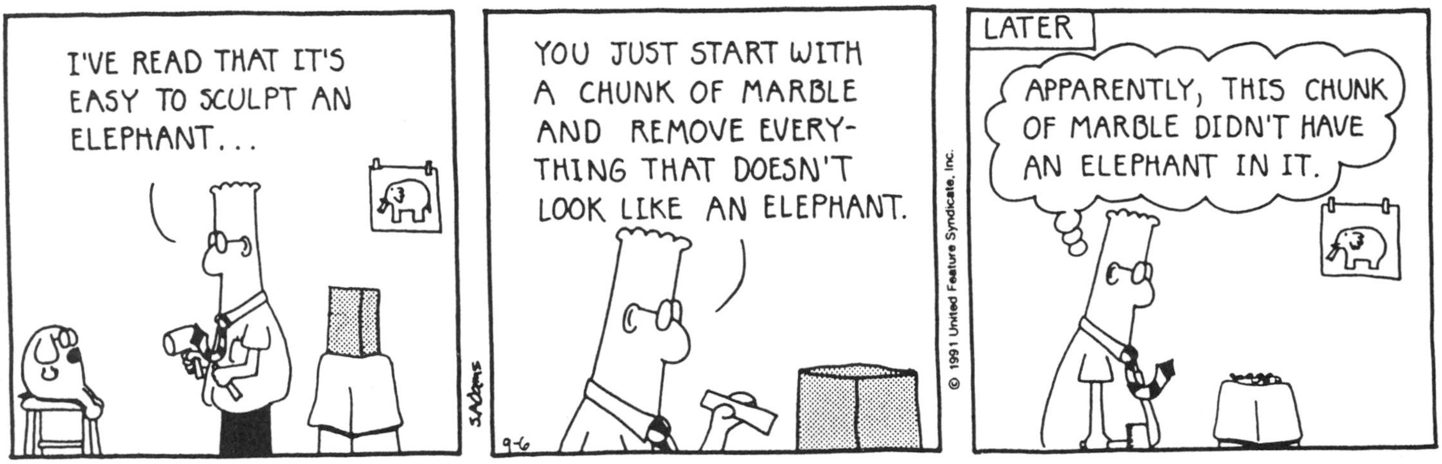
I'VE READ THAT IT'S EASY TO SCULPT AN ELEPHANT...
YOU JUST START WITH A CHUNK OF MARBLE AND REMOVE EVERYTHING THAT DOESN'T LOOK LIKE AN ELEPHANT.
LATER
APPARENTLY, THIS CHUNK OF MARBLE DIDN'T HAVE AN ELEPHANT IN IT.
© 1991 United Feature Syndicate, Inc.

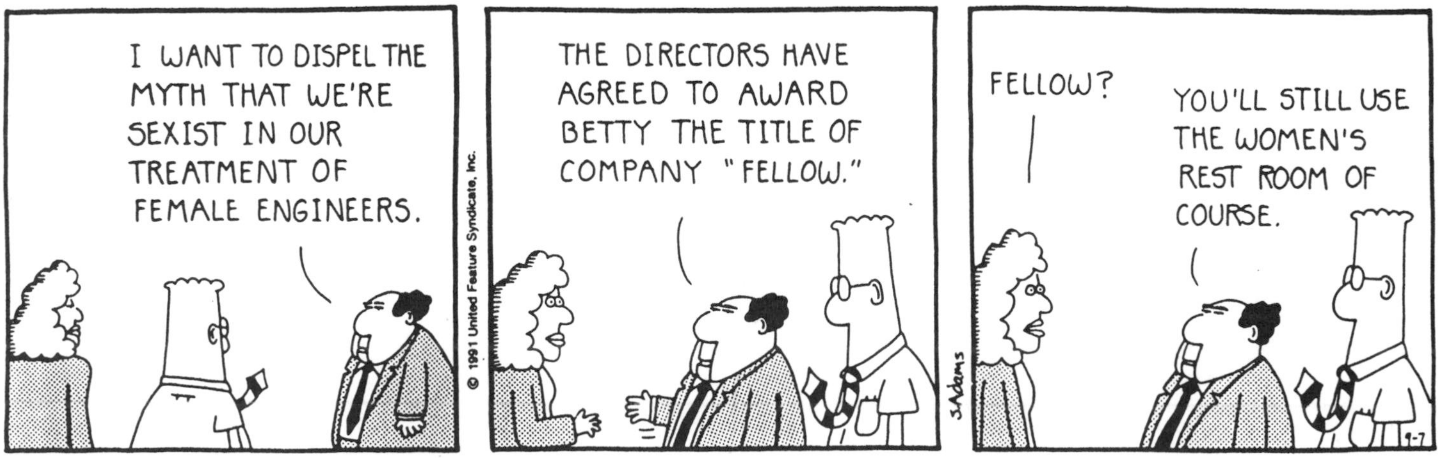
I WANT TO DISPEL THE MYTH THAT WE'RE SEXIST IN OUR TREATMENT OF FEMALE ENGINEERS.
THE DIRECTORS HAVE AGREED TO AWARD BETTY THE TITLE OF COMPANY "FELLOW."
FELLOW?
YOU'LL STILL USE THE WOMEN'S REST ROOM OF COURSE.
© 1991 United Feature Syndicate, Inc.

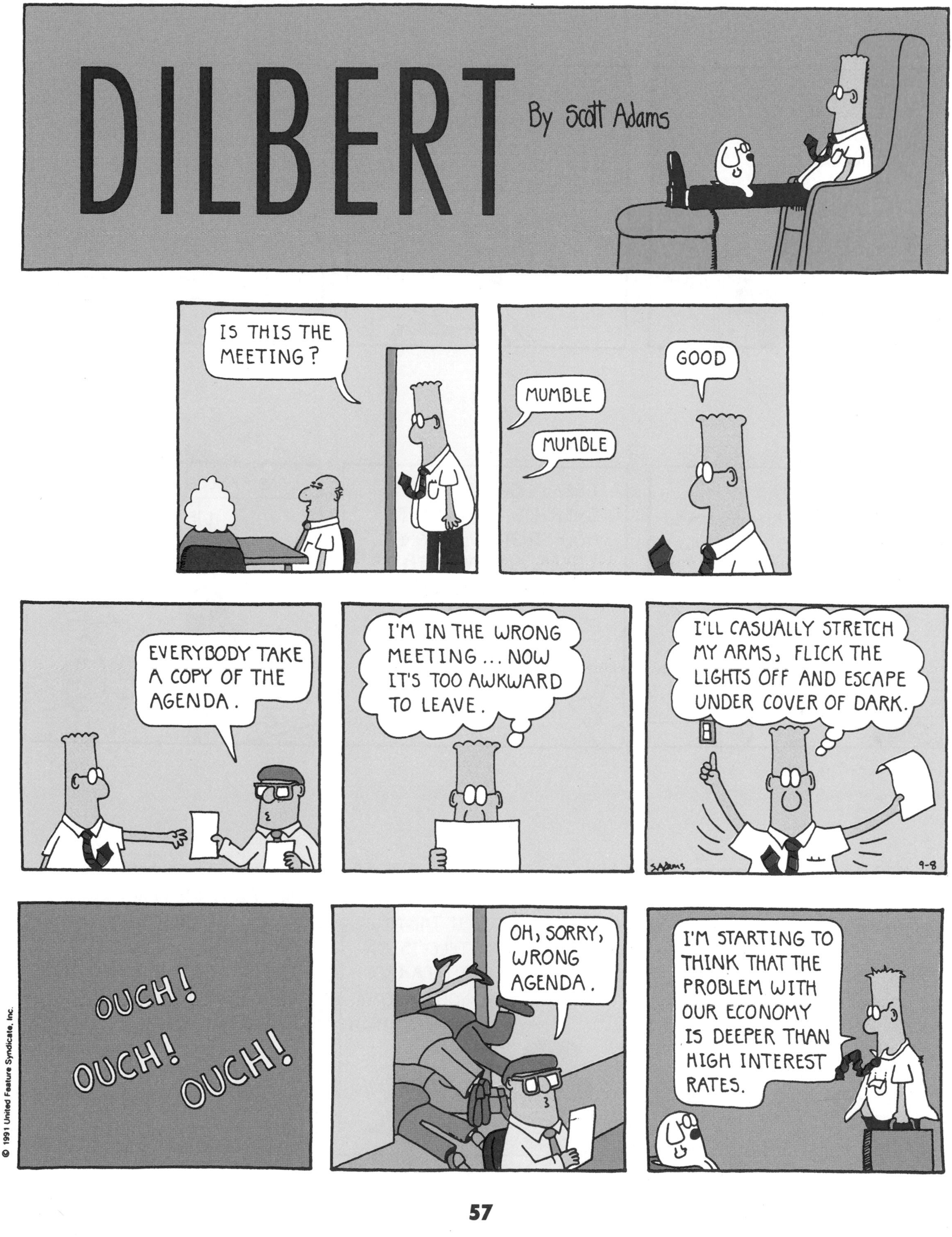
DILBERT
By Scott Adams
IS THIS THE MEETING?
MUMBLE
MUMBLE
GOOD
EVERYBODY TAKE A COPY OF THE AGENDA.
I'M IN THE WRONG MEETING... NOW IT'S TOO AWKWARD TO LEAVE.
I'LL CASUALLY STRETCH MY ARMS, FLICK THE LIGHTS OFF AND ESCAPE UNDER COVER OF DARK.
S.ADAMS
9-8
OUCH!
OUCH!
OUCH!
OH, SORRY, WRONG AGENDA.
I'M STARTING TO THINK THAT THE PROBLEM WITH OUR ECONOMY IS DEEPER THAN HIGH INTEREST RATES.

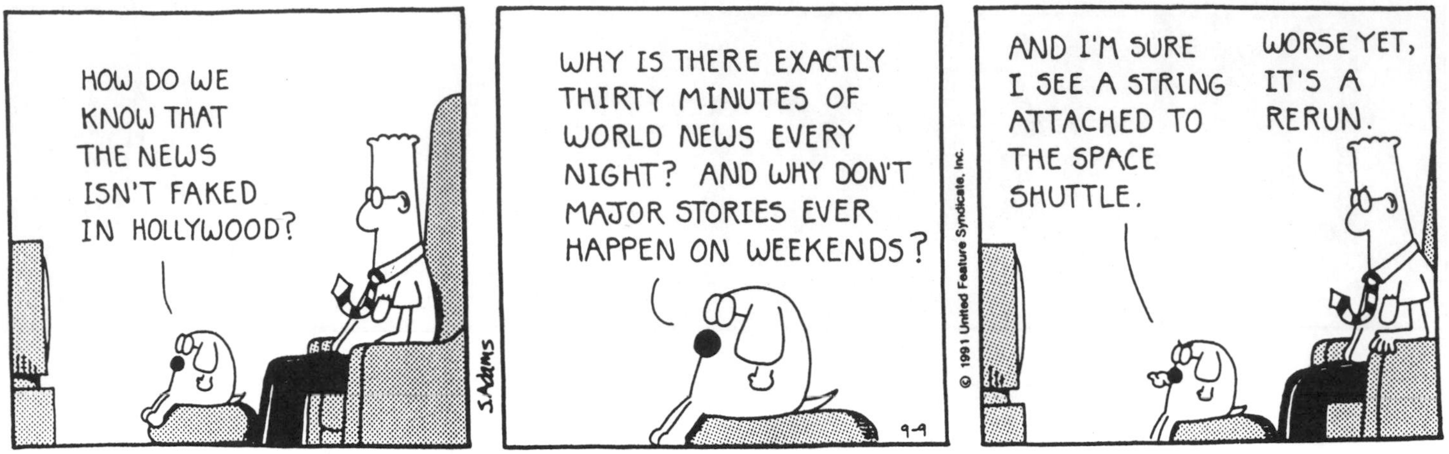
HOW DO WE KNOW THAT THE NEWS ISN'T FAKED IN HOLLYWOOD?
WHY IS THERE EXACTLY THIRTY MINUTES OF WORLD NEWS EVERY NIGHT? AND WHY DON'T MAJOR STORIES EVER HAPPEN ON WEEKENDS?
AND I'M SURE I SEE A STRING ATTACHED TO THE SPACE SHUTTLE.
WORSE YET, IT'S A RERUN.
© 1991 United Feature Syndicate, Inc.
9-9

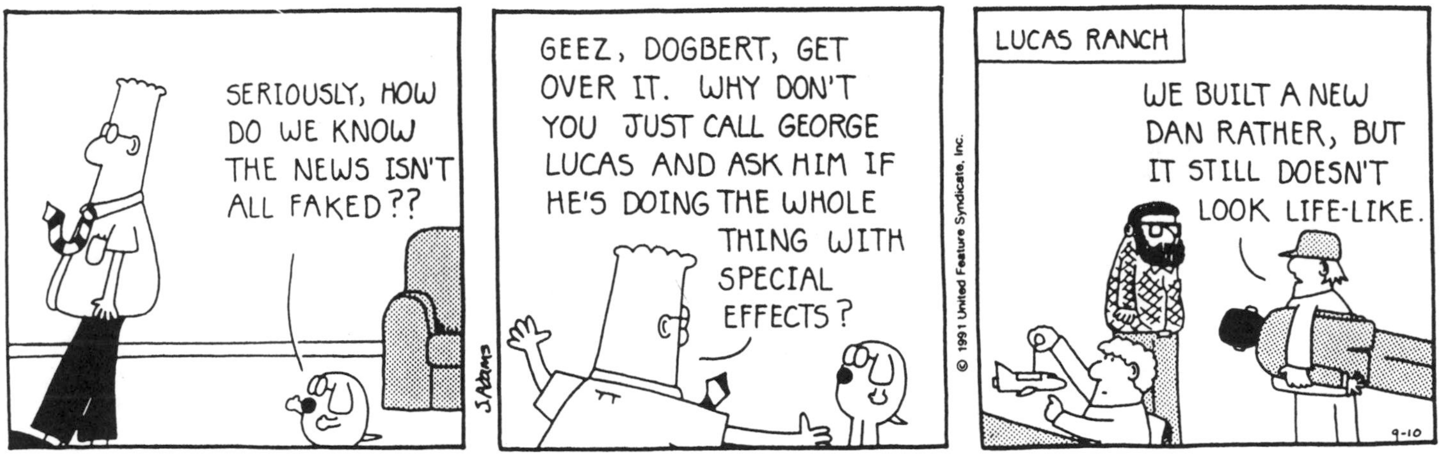
SERIOUSLY, HOW DO WE KNOW THE NEWS ISN'T ALL FAKED??
GEEZ, DOGBERT, GET OVER IT. WHY DON'T YOU JUST CALL GEORGE LUCAS AND ASK HIM IF HE'S DOING THE WHOLE THING WITH SPECIAL EFFECTS?
LUCAS RANCH
WE BUILT A NEW DAN RATHER, BUT IT STILL DOESN'T LOOK LIFE-LIKE.
© 1991 United Feature Syndicate, Inc.
9-10

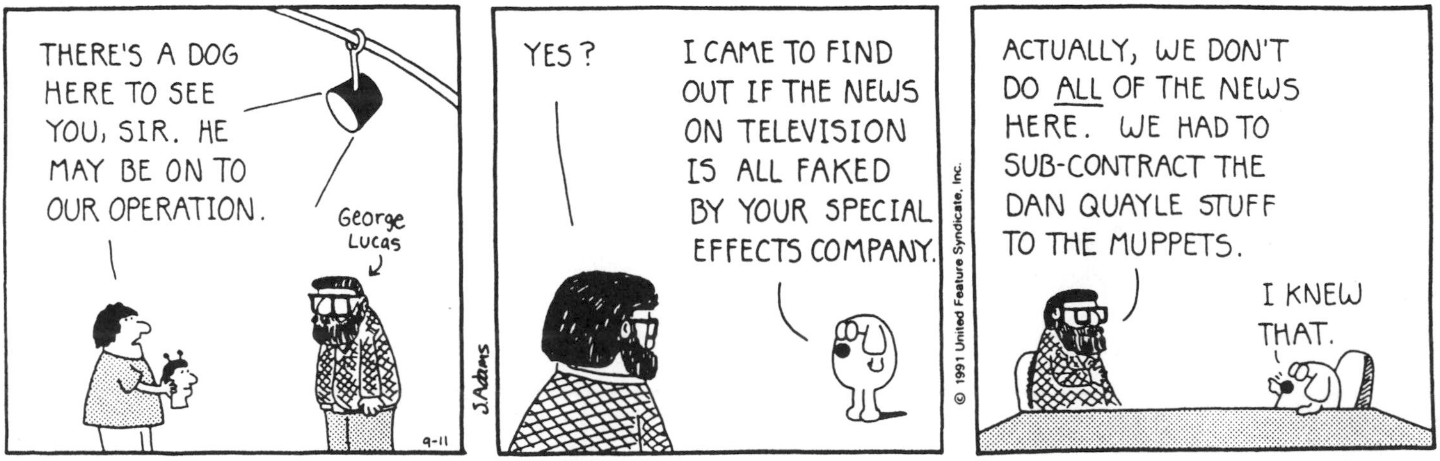
THERE'S A DOG HERE TO SEE YOU, SIR. HE MAY BE ON TO OUR OPERATION.
George Lucas
9-11
YES?
I CAME TO FIND OUT IF THE NEWS ON TELEVISION IS ALL FAKED BY YOUR SPECIAL EFFECTS COMPANY.
ACTUALLY, WE DON'T DO ALL OF THE NEWS HERE. WE HAD TO SUB-CONTRACT THE DAN QUAYLE STUFF TO THE MUPPETS.
I KNEW THAT.
© 1991 United Feature Syndicate, Inc.

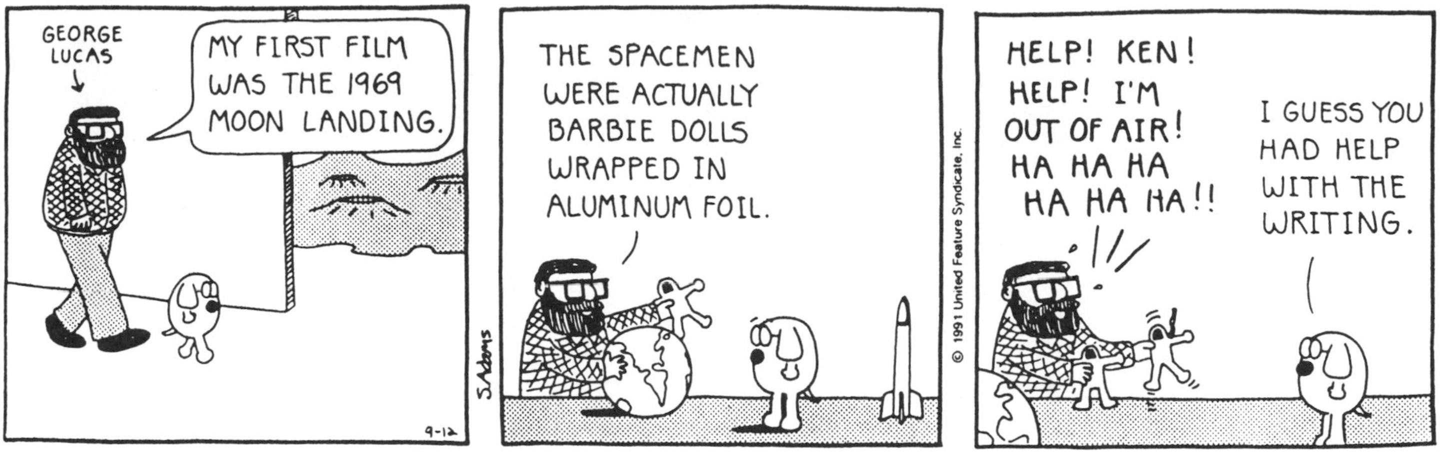
GEORGE LUCAS
MY FIRST FILM WAS THE 1969 MOON LANDING.
9-12
S. Adams
THE SPACEMEN WERE ACTUALLY BARBIE DOLLS WRAPPED IN ALUMINUM FOIL.
© 1991 United Feature Syndicate, Inc.
HELP! KEN! HELP! I'M OUT OF AIR! HA HA HA HA HA HA!!
I GUESS YOU HAD HELP WITH THE WRITING.

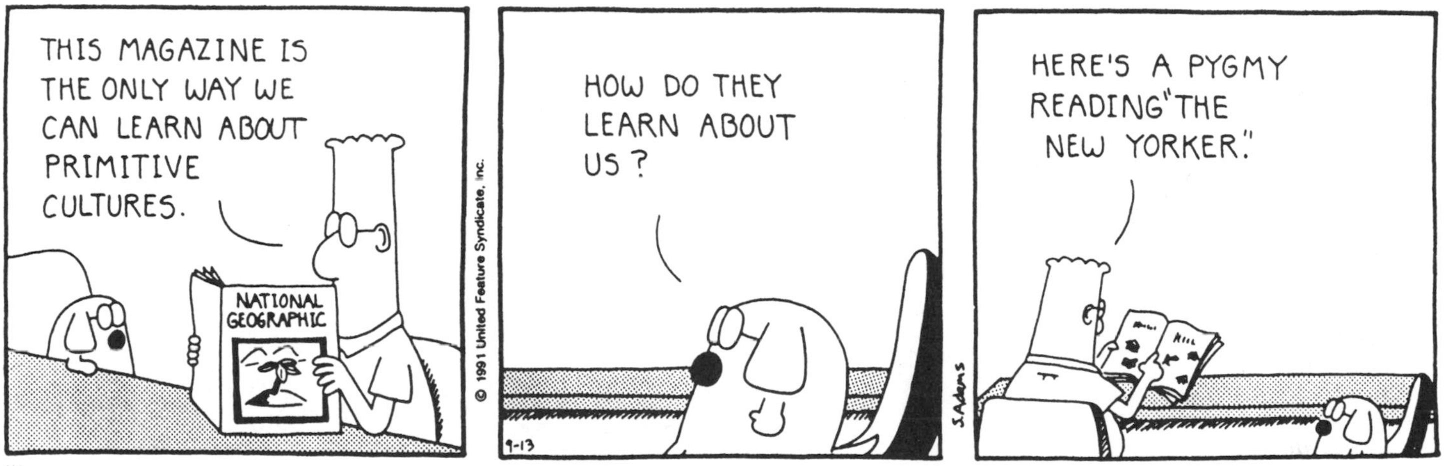
THIS MAGAZINE IS THE ONLY WAY WE CAN LEARN ABOUT PRIMITIVE CULTURES.
NATIONAL GEOGRAPHIC
© 1991 United Feature Syndicate, Inc.
HOW DO THEY LEARN ABOUT US?
9-13
S. Adams
HERE'S A PYGMY READING "THE NEW YORKER."

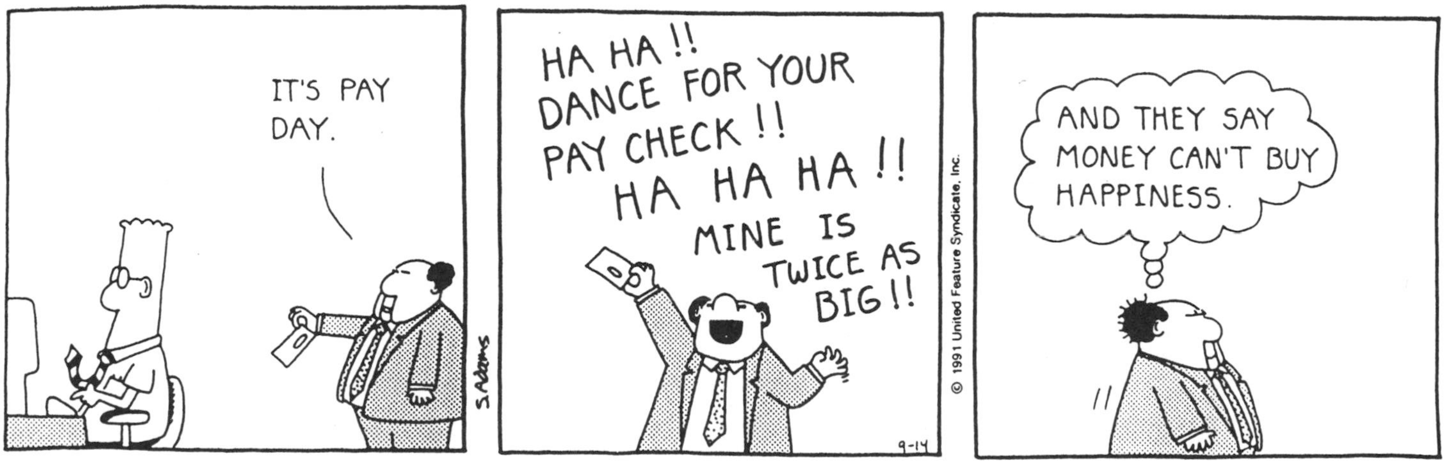
IT'S PAY DAY.
S. Adams
HA HA!! DANCE FOR YOUR PAY CHECK!! HA HA HA!!
MINE IS TWICE AS BIG!!
9-14
© 1991 United Feature Syndicate, Inc.
AND THEY SAY MONEY CAN'T BUY HAPPINESS.

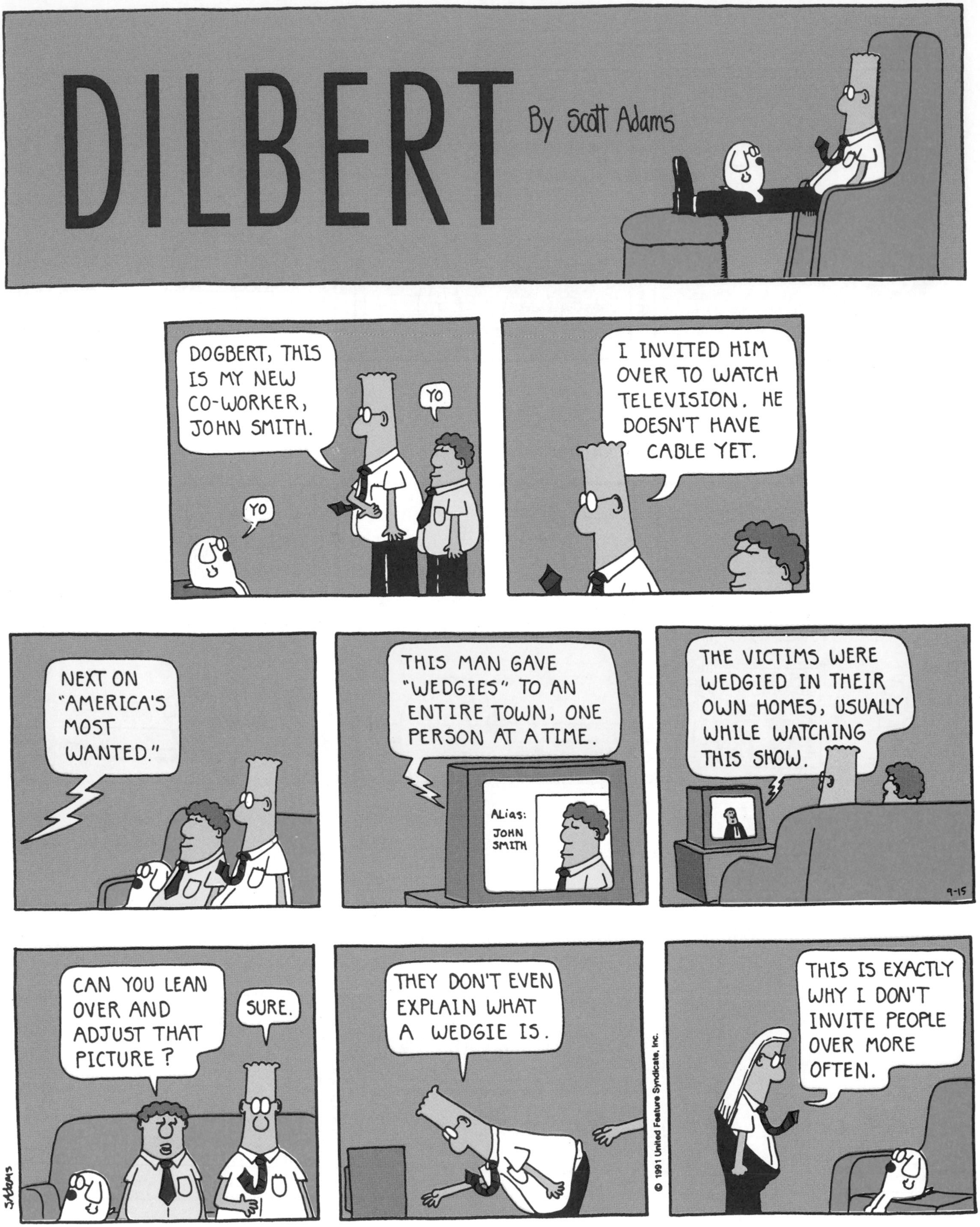
DILBERT
By Scott Adams
DOGBERT, THIS IS MY NEW CO-WORKER, JOHN SMITH.
YO
YO
I INVITED HIM OVER TO WATCH TELEVISION. HE DOESN'T HAVE CABLE YET.
NEXT ON "AMERICA'S MOST WANTED."
THIS MAN GAVE "WEDGIES" TO AN ENTIRE TOWN, ONE PERSON AT A TIME.
ALias: JOHN SMITH
THE VICTIMS WERE WEDGIED IN THEIR OWN HOMES, USUALLY WHILE WATCHING THIS SHOW.
9-15
CAN YOU LEAN OVER AND ADJUST THAT PICTURE?
SURE.
THEY DON'T EVEN EXPLAIN WHAT A WEDGIE IS.
THIS IS EXACTLY WHY I DON'T INVITE PEOPLE OVER MORE OFTEN.
© 1991 United Feature Syndicate, Inc.

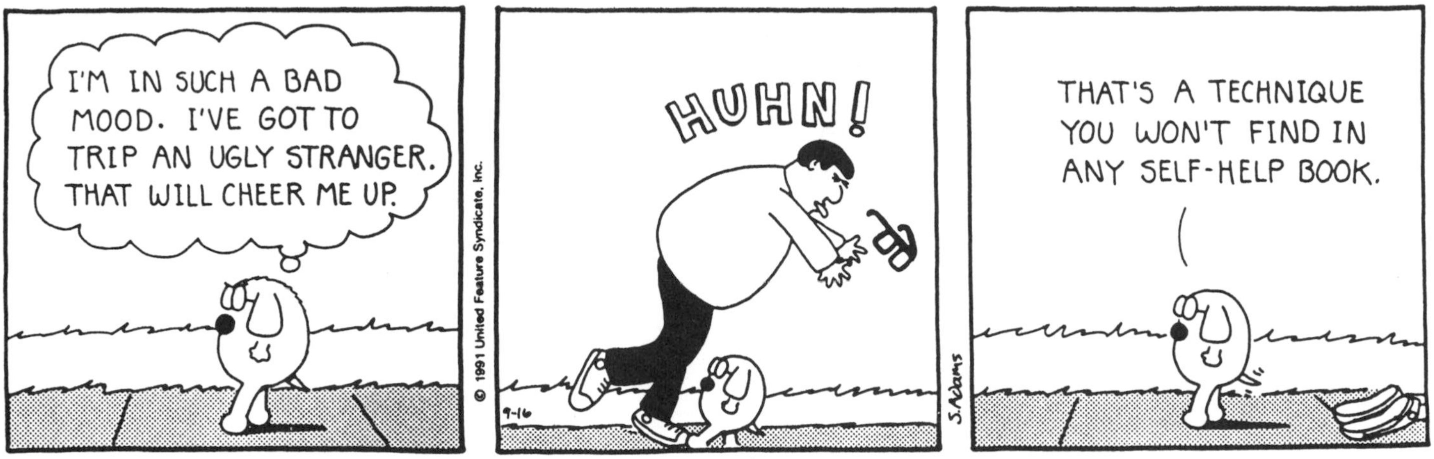
I'M IN SUCH A BAD MOOD. I'VE GOT TO TRIP AN UGLY STRANGER. THAT WILL CHEER ME UP.
© 1991 United Feature Syndicate, Inc.
HUHN!
9-16
THAT'S A TECHNIQUE YOU WON'T FIND IN ANY SELF-HELP BOOK.
S. Adams

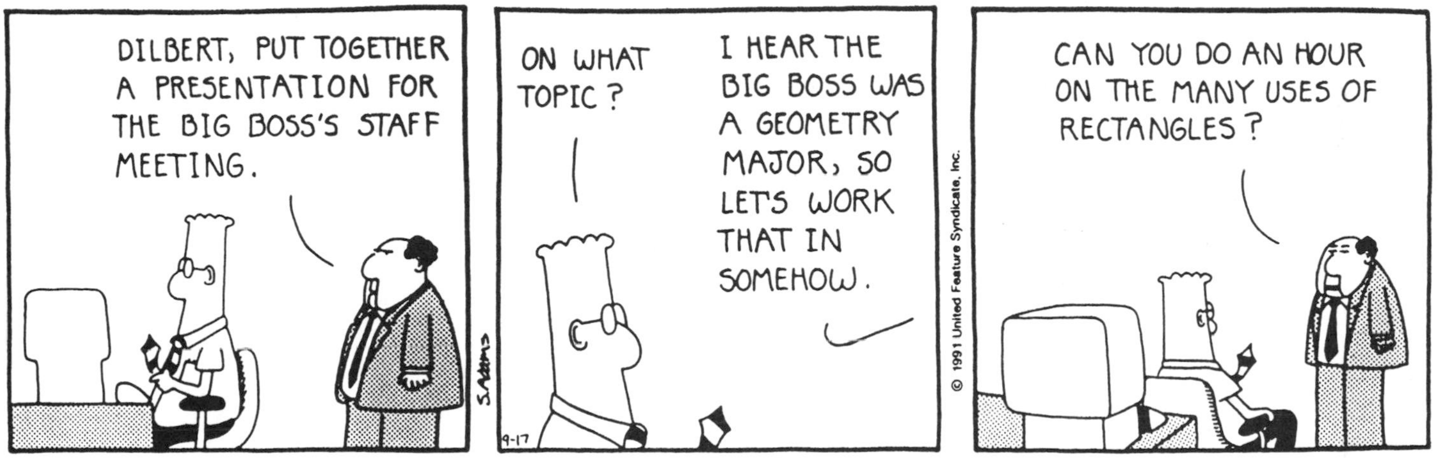
DILBERT, PUT TOGETHER A PRESENTATION FOR THE BIG BOSS'S STAFF MEETING.
S. Adams
ON WHAT TOPIC?
I HEAR THE BIG BOSS WAS A GEOMETRY MAJOR, SO LET'S WORK THAT IN SOMEHOW.
9-17
© 1991 United Feature Syndicate, Inc.
CAN YOU DO AN HOUR ON THE MANY USES OF RECTANGLES?

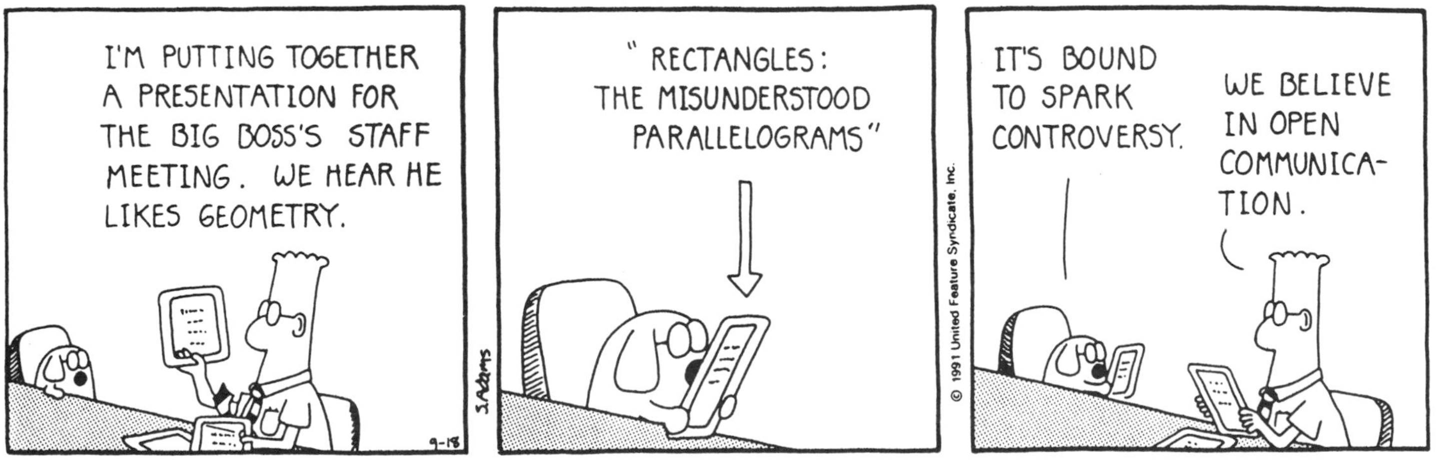
I'M PUTTING TOGETHER A PRESENTATION FOR THE BIG BOSS'S STAFF MEETING. WE HEAR HE LIKES GEOMETRY.
9-18
S. Adams
"RECTANGLES: THE MISUNDERSTOOD PARALLELOGRAMS"
© 1991 United Feature Syndicate, Inc.
IT'S BOUND TO SPARK CONTROVERSY.
WE BELIEVE IN OPEN COMMUNICATION.

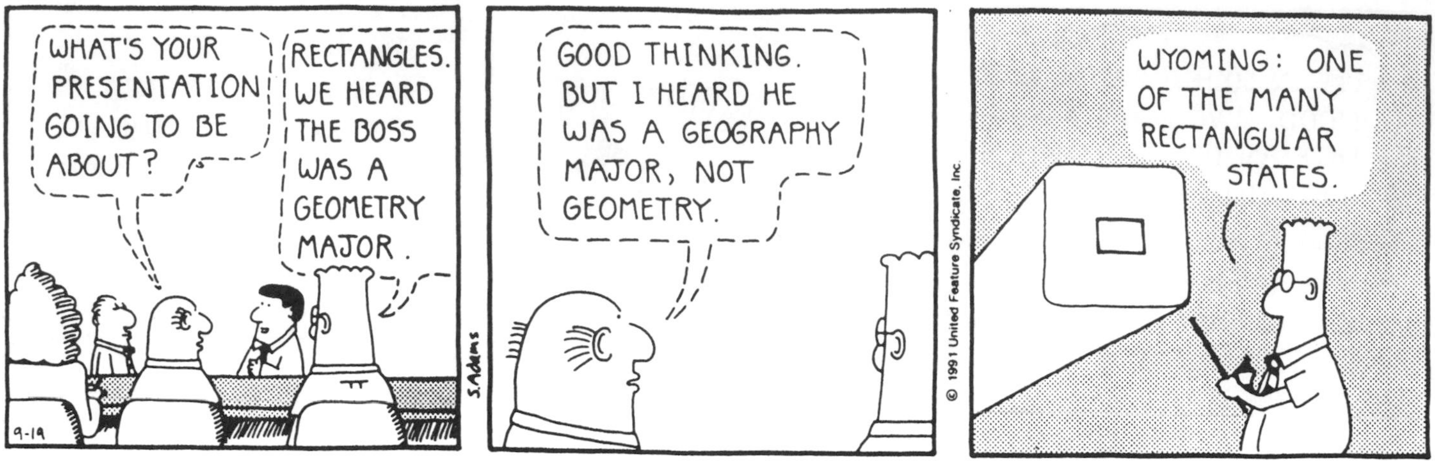
WHAT'S YOUR PRESENTATION GOING TO BE ABOUT?
RECTANGLES. WE HEARD THE BOSS WAS A GEOMETRY MAJOR.
9-19
S. Adams
GOOD THINKING. BUT I HEARD HE WAS A GEOGRAPHY MAJOR, NOT GEOMETRY.
© 1991 United Feature Syndicate, Inc.
WYOMING: ONE OF THE MANY RECTANGULAR STATES.

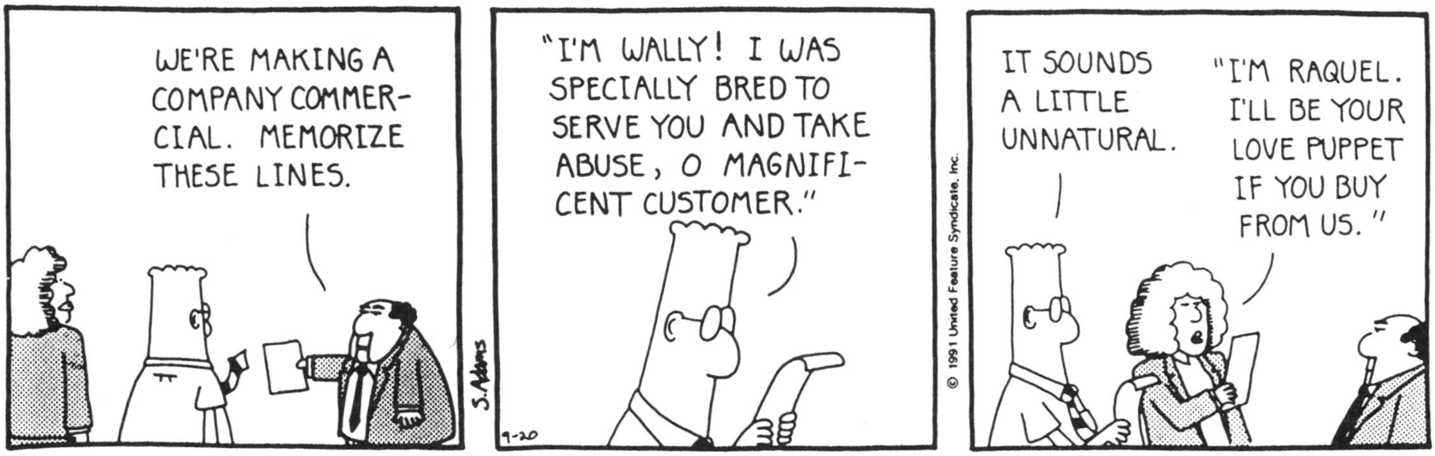
WE'RE MAKING A COMPANY COMMERCIAL. MEMORIZE THESE LINES.
S. Adams
"I'M WALLY! I WAS SPECIALLY BRED TO SERVE YOU AND TAKE ABUSE, O MAGNIFICENT CUSTOMER."
9-20
© 1991 United Feature Syndicate, Inc.
IT SOUNDS A LITTLE UNNATURAL.
"I'M RAQUEL. I'LL BE YOUR LOVE PUPPET IF YOU BUY FROM US."

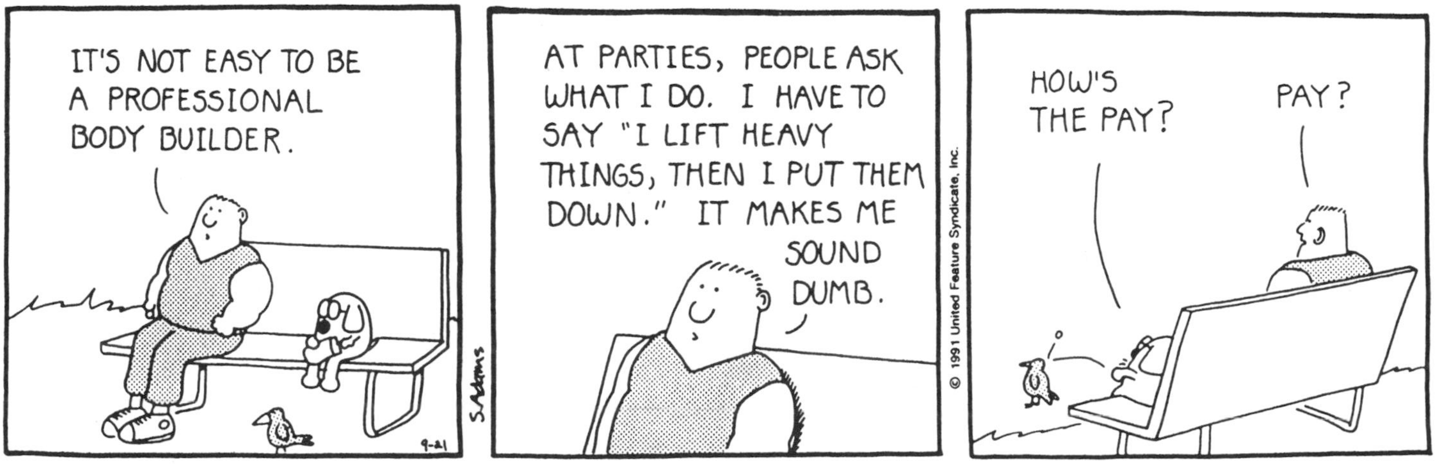
IT'S NOT EASY TO BE A PROFESSIONAL BODY BUILDER.
9-21
S. Adams
AT PARTIES, PEOPLE ASK WHAT I DO. I HAVE TO SAY "I LIFT HEAVY THINGS, THEN I PUT THEM DOWN." IT MAKES ME SOUND DUMB.
© 1991 United Feature Syndicate, Inc.
HOW'S THE PAY?
PAY?

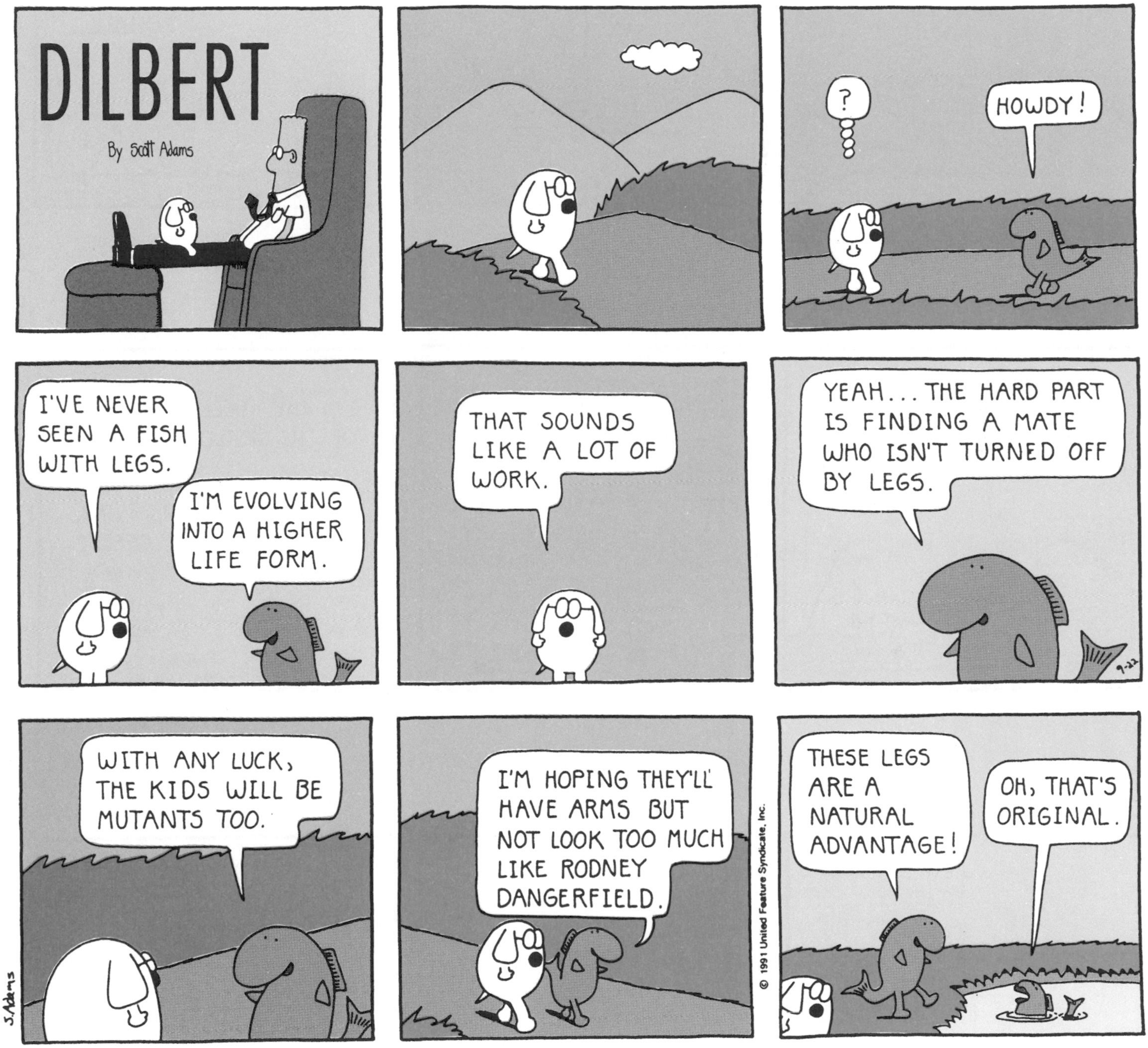
DILBERT
By Scott Adams
?
HOWDY!
I'VE NEVER SEEN A FISH WITH LEGS.
I'M EVOLVING INTO A HIGHER LIFE FORM.
THAT SOUNDS LIKE A LOT OF WORK.
YEAH... THE HARD PART IS FINDING A MATE WHO ISN'T TURNED OFF BY LEGS.
9-22
WITH ANY LUCK, THE KIDS WILL BE MUTANTS TOO.
S. Adams
I'M HOPING THEY'LL HAVE ARMS BUT NOT LOOK TOO MUCH LIKE RODNEY DANGERFIELD.
© 1991 United Feature Syndicate, Inc.
THESE LEGS ARE A NATURAL ADVANTAGE!
OH, THAT'S ORIGINAL.

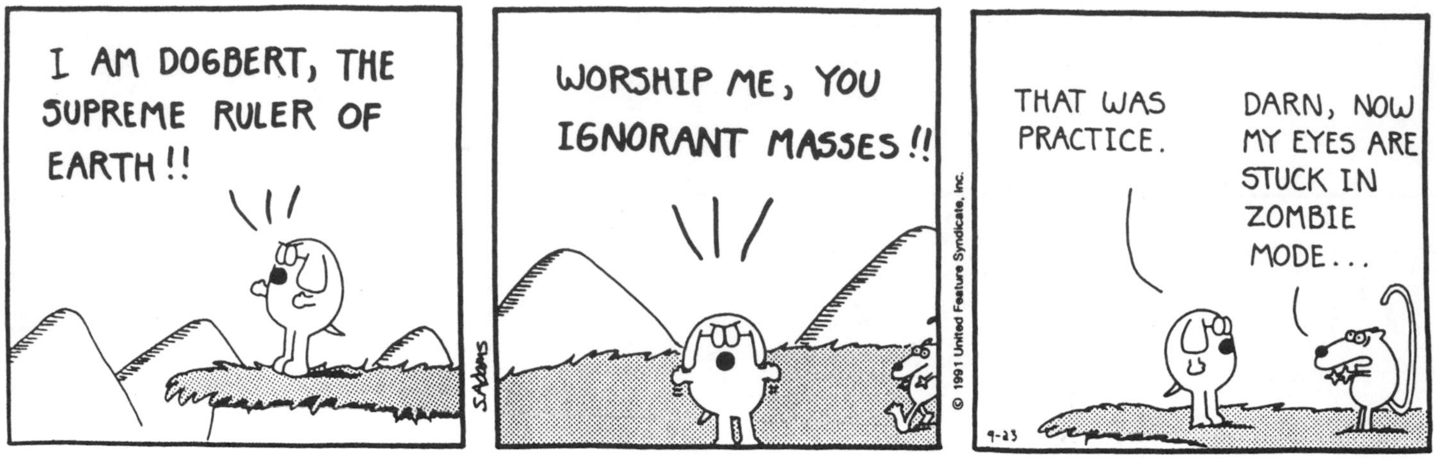
I AM DOGBERT, THE SUPREME RULER OF EARTH!!
WORSHIP ME, YOU IGNORANT MASSES!!
THAT WAS PRACTICE.
DARN, NOW MY EYES ARE STUCK IN ZOMBIE MODE...
© 1991 United Feature Syndicate, Inc.
9-23

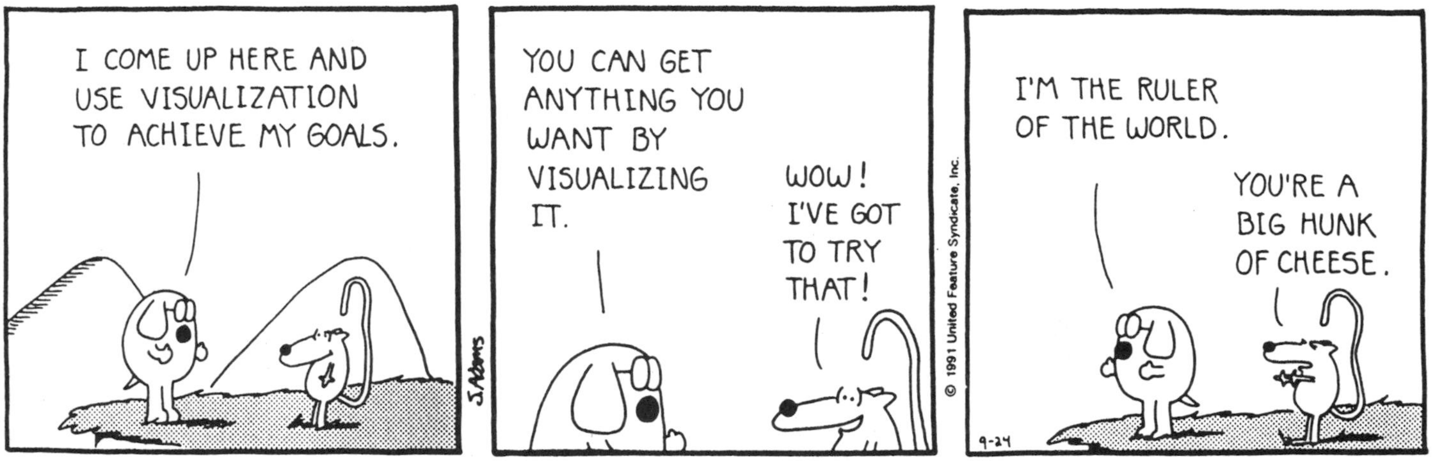
I COME UP HERE AND USE VISUALIZATION TO ACHIEVE MY GOALS.
YOU CAN GET ANYTHING YOU WANT BY VISUALIZING IT.
WOW! I'VE GOT TO TRY THAT!
I'M THE RULER OF THE WORLD.
YOU'RE A BIG HUNK OF CHEESE.
© 1991 United Feature Syndicate, Inc.
9-24

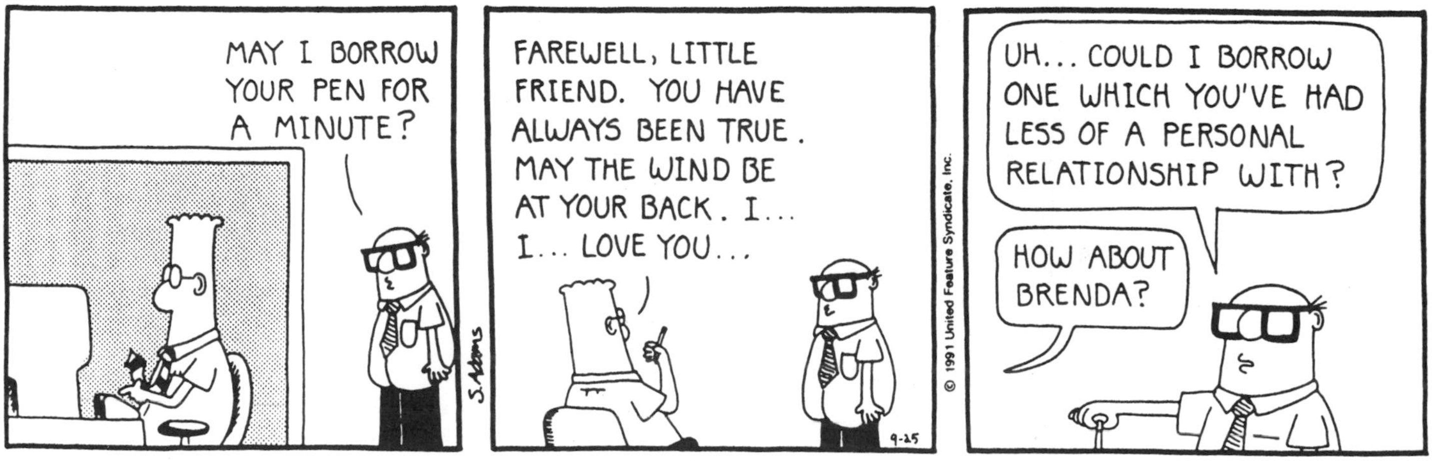
MAY I BORROW YOUR PEN FOR A MINUTE?
FAREWELL, LITTLE FRIEND. YOU HAVE ALWAYS BEEN TRUE. MAY THE WIND BE AT YOUR BACK. I... I... LOVE YOU...
UH... COULD I BORROW ONE WHICH YOU'VE HAD LESS OF A PERSONAL RELATIONSHIP WITH?
HOW ABOUT BRENDA?
© 1991 United Feature Syndicate, Inc.
9-25

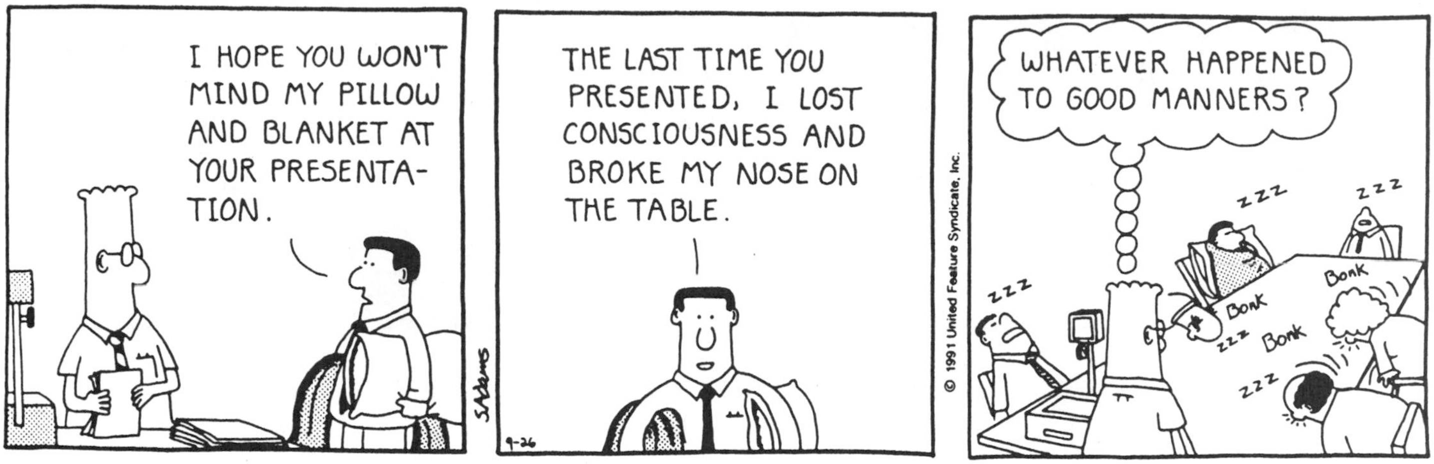
I HOPE YOU WON'T MIND MY PILLOW AND BLANKET AT YOUR PRESENTATION.
THE LAST TIME YOU PRESENTED, I LOST CONSCIOUSNESS AND BROKE MY NOSE ON THE TABLE.
WHATEVER HAPPENED TO GOOD MANNERS?
ZZZ
BONK
© 1991 United Feature Syndicate, Inc.

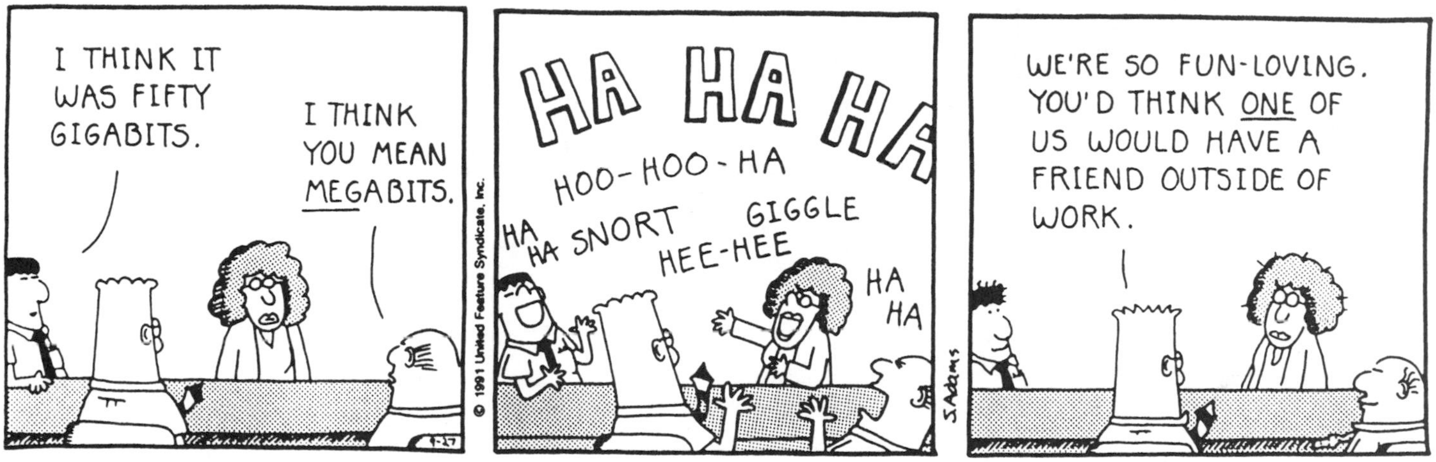
I THINK IT WAS FIFTY GIGABITS.
I THINK YOU MEAN MEGABITS.
HA HA HA
HOO-HOO-HA
HA HA SNORT
GIGGLE
HEE-HEE
HA HA
WE'RE SO FUN-LOVING. YOU'D THINK ONE OF US WOULD HAVE A FRIEND OUTSIDE OF WORK.
© 1991 United Feature Syndicate, Inc.

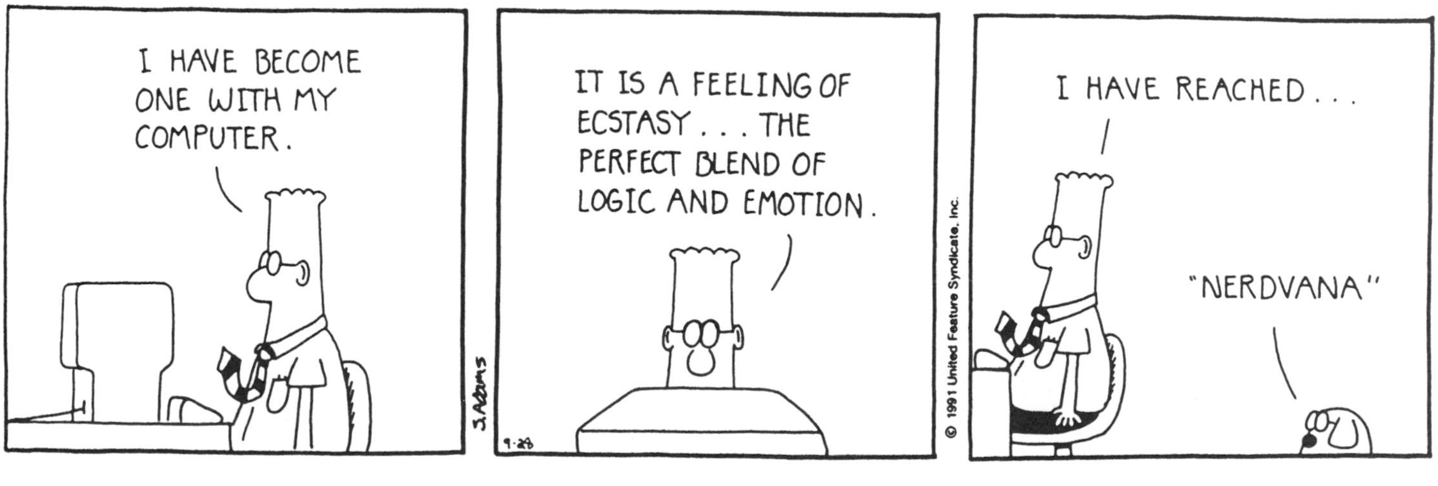
I HAVE BECOME ONE WITH MY COMPUTER.
IT IS A FEELING OF ECSTASY . . . THE PERFECT BLEND OF LOGIC AND EMOTION.
I HAVE REACHED . . .
"NERDVANA"
© 1991 United Feature Syndicate, Inc.

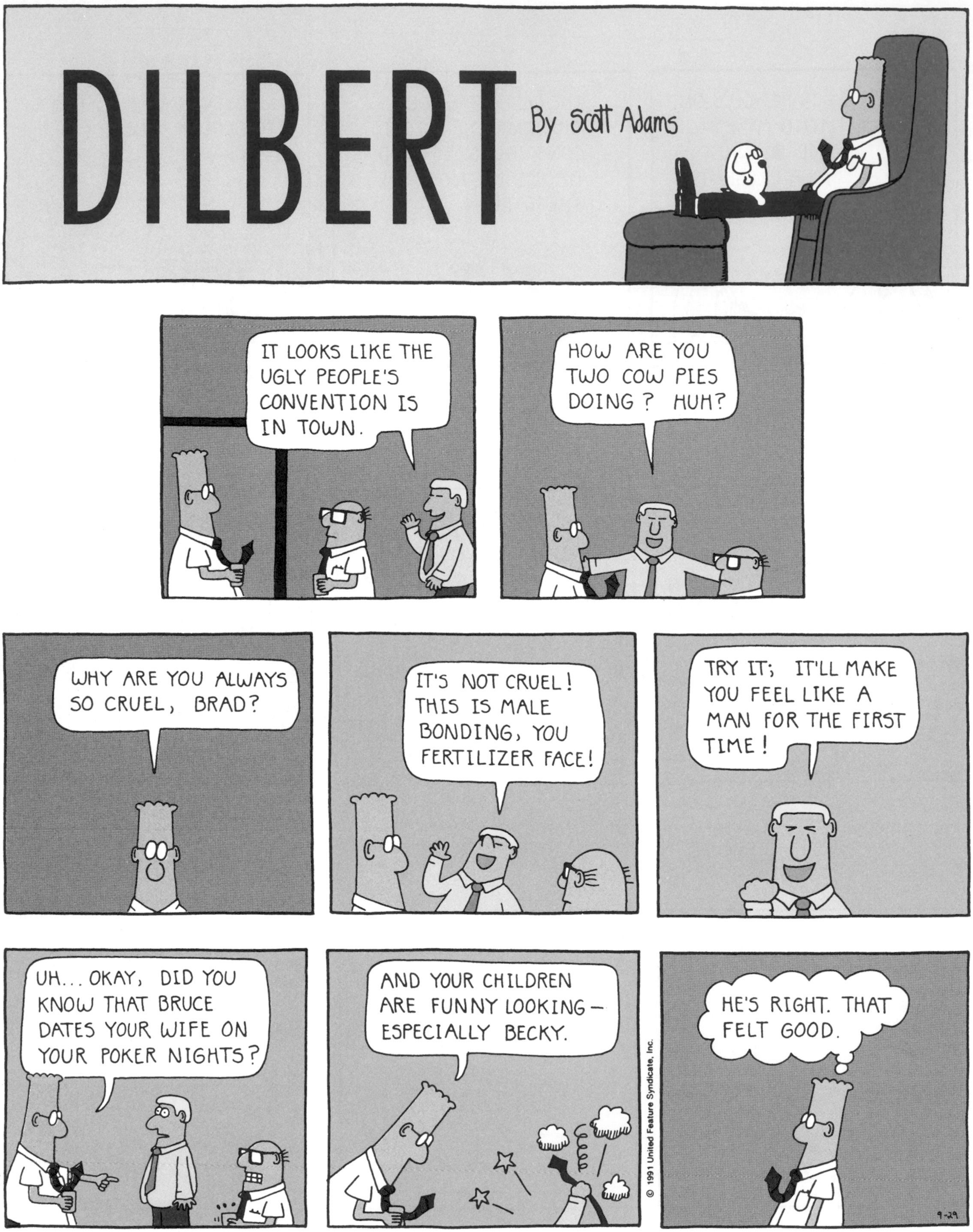
DILBERT
By Scott Adams
IT LOOKS LIKE THE UGLY PEOPLE'S CONVENTION IS IN TOWN.
HOW ARE YOU TWO COW PIES DOING? HUH?
WHY ARE YOU ALWAYS SO CRUEL, BRAD?
IT'S NOT CRUEL! THIS IS MALE BONDING, YOU FERTILIZER FACE!
TRY IT; IT'LL MAKE YOU FEEL LIKE A MAN FOR THE FIRST TIME!
UH... OKAY, DID YOU KNOW THAT BRUCE DATES YOUR WIFE ON YOUR POKER NIGHTS?
AND YOUR CHILDREN ARE FUNNY LOOKING – ESPECIALLY BECKY.
© 1991 United Feature Syndicate, Inc.
HE'S RIGHT. THAT FELT GOOD.
9-29

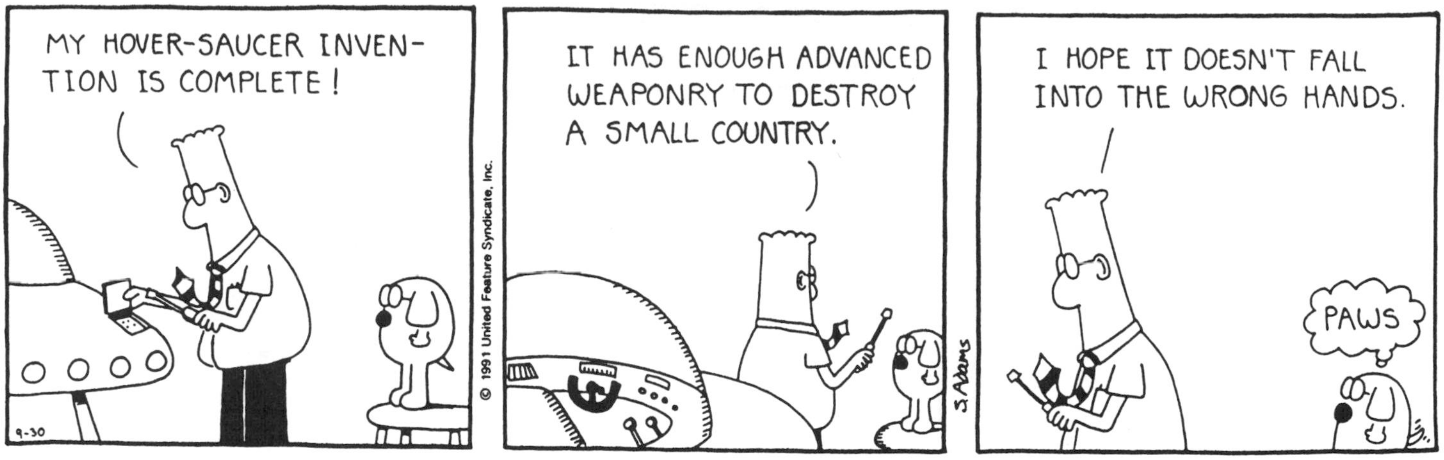
MY HOVER-SAUCER INVENTION IS COMPLETE!
IT HAS ENOUGH ADVANCED WEAPONRY TO DESTROY A SMALL COUNTRY.
I HOPE IT DOESN'T FALL INTO THE WRONG HANDS.
PAWS
© 1991 United Feature Syndicate, Inc.

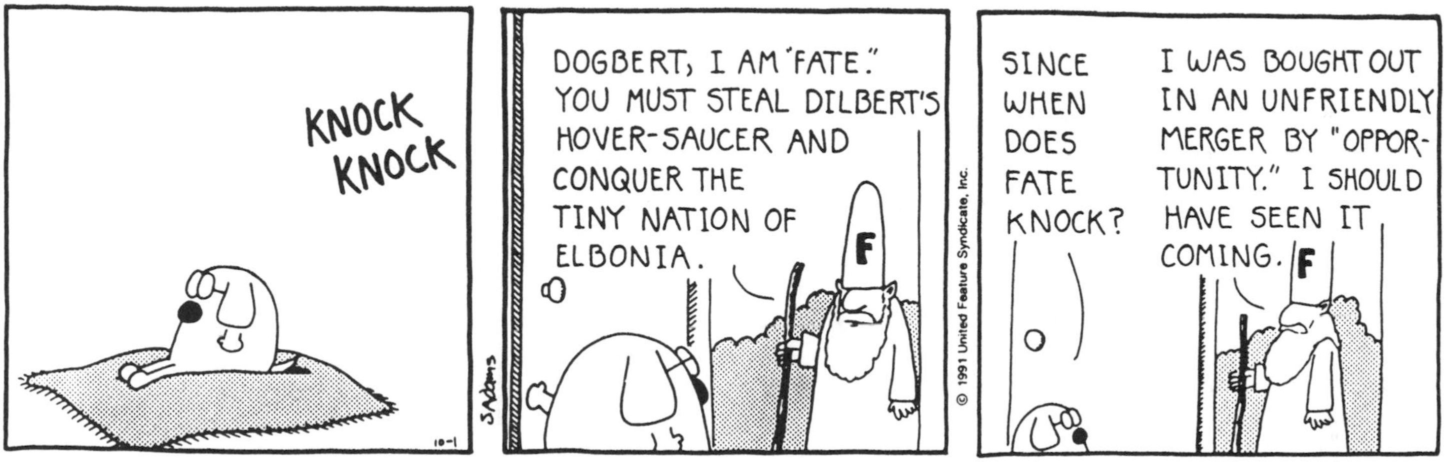
KNOCK KNOCK
DOGBERT, I AM "FATE." YOU MUST STEAL DILBERT'S HOVER-SAUCER AND CONQUER THE TINY NATION OF ELBONIA.
F
SINCE WHEN DOES FATE KNOCK?
I WAS BOUGHT OUT IN AN UNFRIENDLY MERGER BY "OPPORTUNITY." I SHOULD HAVE SEEN IT COMING.
© 1991 United Feature Syndicate, Inc.

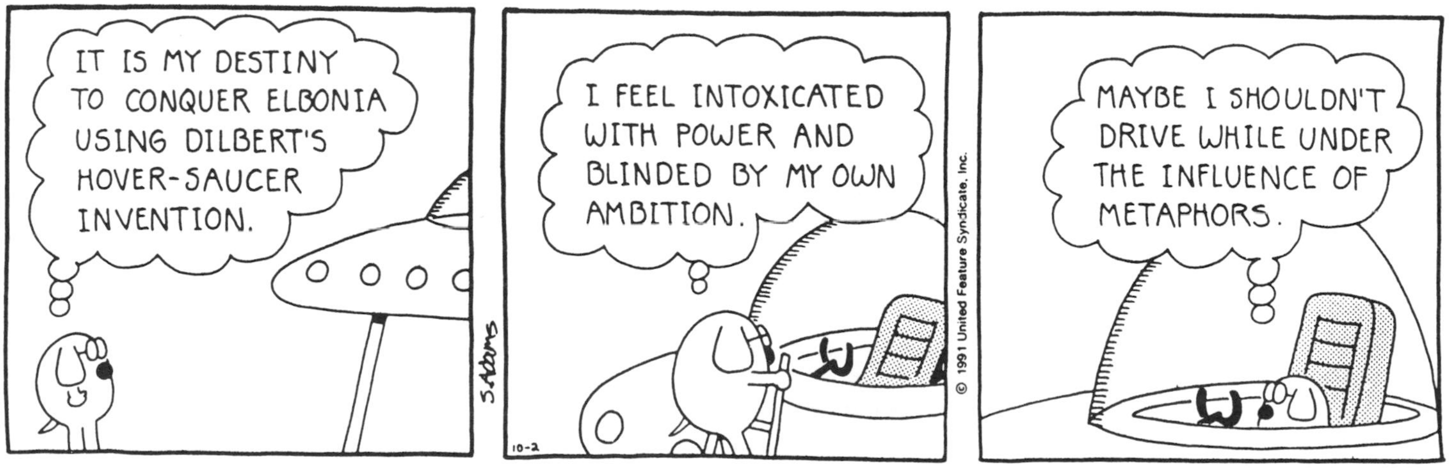
IT IS MY DESTINY TO CONQUER ELBONIA USING DILBERT'S HOVER-SAUCER INVENTION.
I FEEL INTOXICATED WITH POWER AND BLINDED BY MY OWN AMBITION.
MAYBE I SHOULDN'T DRIVE WHILE UNDER THE INFLUENCE OF METAPHORS.
© 1991 United Feature Syndicate, Inc.

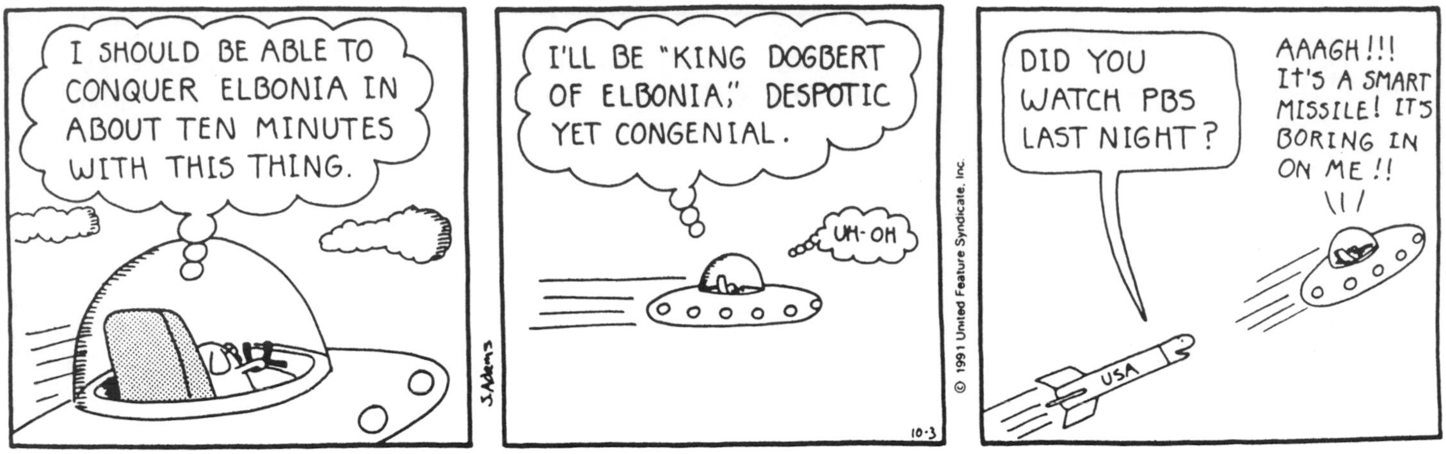
I SHOULD BE ABLE TO CONQUER ELBONIA IN ABOUT TEN MINUTES WITH THIS THING.
I'LL BE "KING DOGBERT OF ELBONIA," DESPOTIC YET CONGENIAL.
UH-OH
DID YOU WATCH PBS LAST NIGHT?
AAAGH!!! IT'S A SMART MISSILE! IT'S BORING IN ON ME!!
USA
© 1991 United Feature Syndicate, Inc.

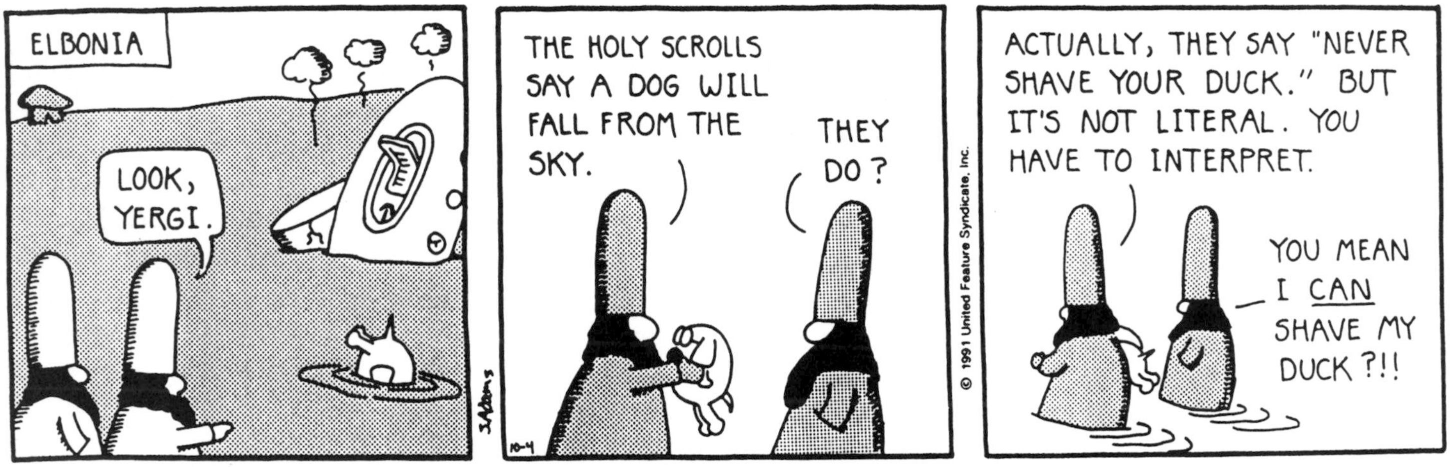
ELBONIA
LOOK, YERGI.
THE HOLY SCROLLS SAY A DOG WILL FALL FROM THE SKY.
THEY DO?
ACTUALLY, THEY SAY "NEVER SHAVE YOUR DUCK." BUT IT'S NOT LITERAL. YOU HAVE TO INTERPRET.
YOU MEAN I CAN SHAVE MY DUCK?!!
© 1991 United Feature Syndicate, Inc.

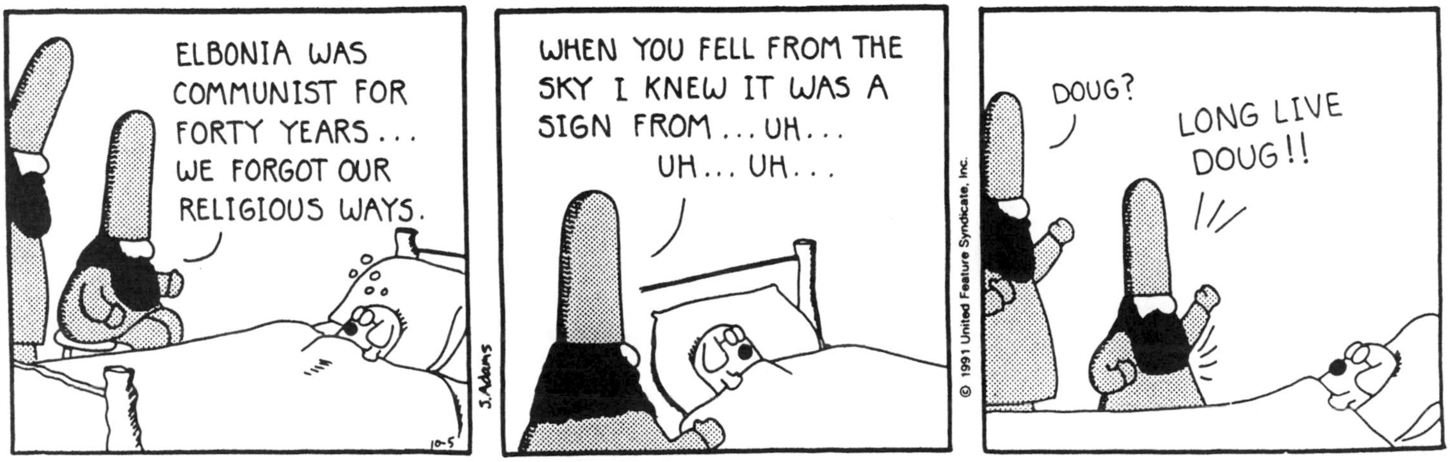
ELBONIA WAS COMMUNIST FOR FORTY YEARS... WE FORGOT OUR RELIGIOUS WAYS.
WHEN YOU FELL FROM THE SKY I KNEW IT WAS A SIGN FROM... UH... UH... UH...
DOUG?
LONG LIVE DOUG!!
© 1991 United Feature Syndicate, Inc.

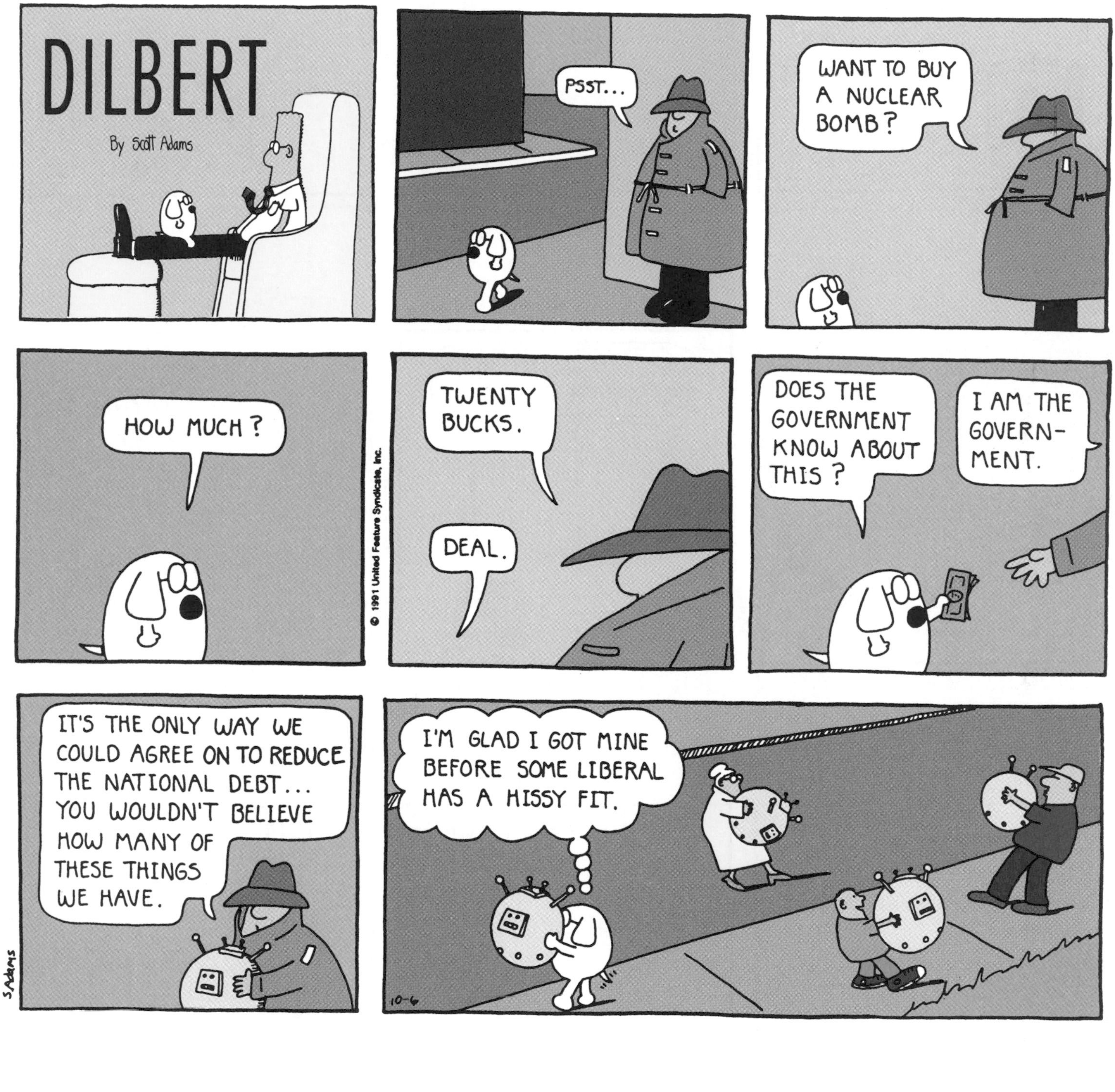
DILBERT
By Scott Adams
PSST...
WANT TO BUY A NUCLEAR BOMB?
HOW MUCH?
TWENTY BUCKS.
DEAL.
© 1991 United Feature Syndicate, Inc.
DOES THE GOVERNMENT KNOW ABOUT THIS?
I AM THE GOVERNMENT.
IT'S THE ONLY WAY WE COULD AGREE ON TO REDUCE THE NATIONAL DEBT... YOU WOULDN'T BELIEVE HOW MANY OF THESE THINGS WE HAVE.
S.Adams
I'M GLAD I GOT MINE BEFORE SOME LIBERAL HAS A HISSY FIT.
10-6

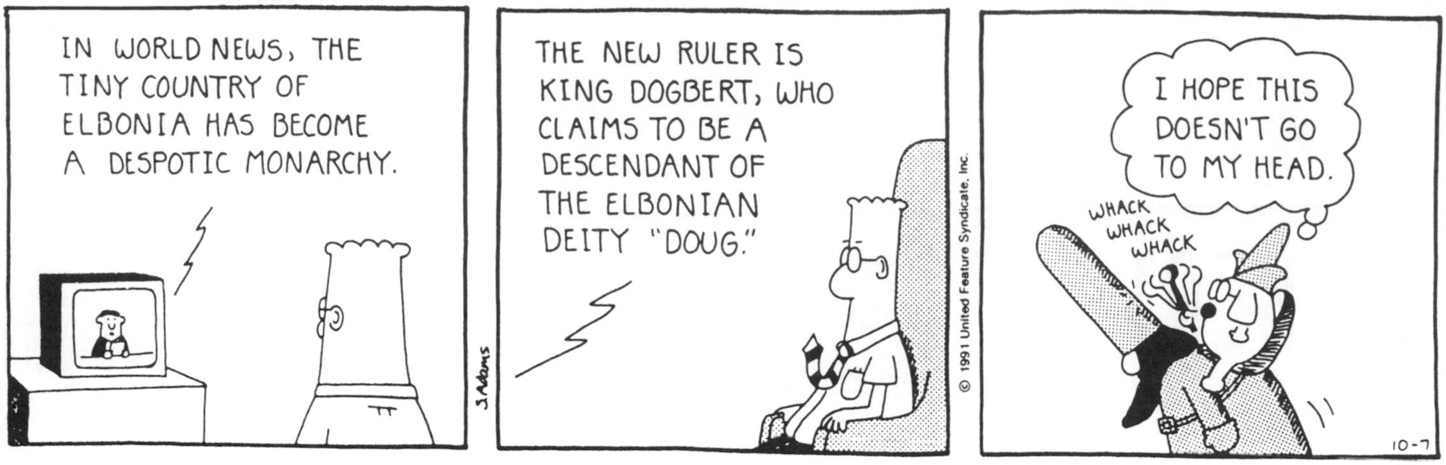
IN WORLD NEWS, THE TINY COUNTRY OF ELBONIA HAS BECOME A DESPOTIC MONARCHY.
THE NEW RULER IS KING DOGBERT, WHO CLAIMS TO BE A DESCENDANT OF THE ELBONIAN DEITY "DOUG."
I HOPE THIS DOESN'T GO TO MY HEAD.
WHACK WHACK WHACK
© 1991 United Feature Syndicate, Inc.
10-7

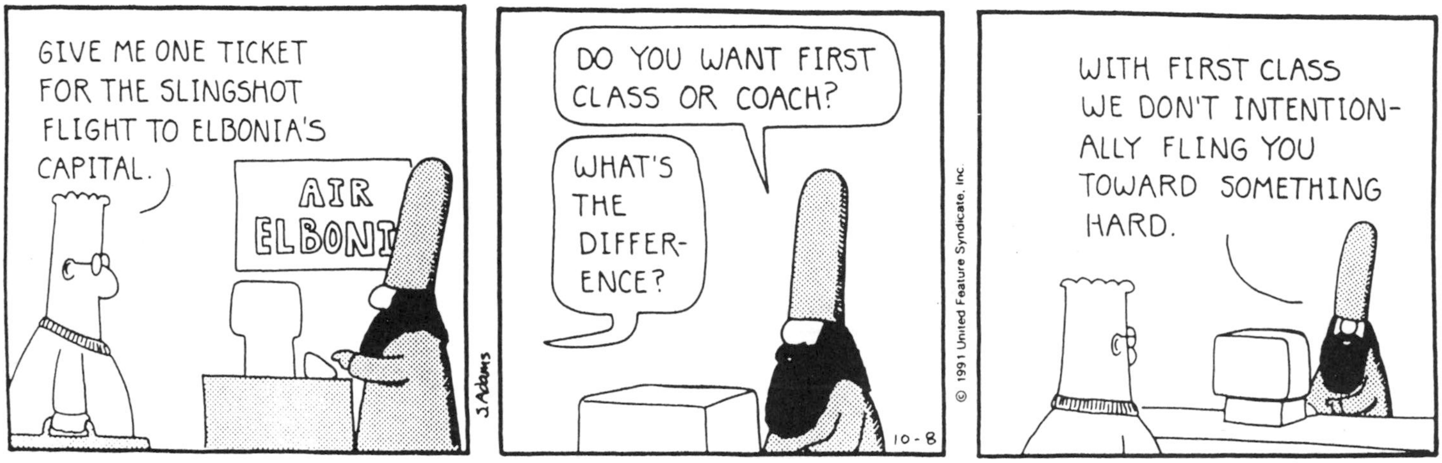
GIVE ME ONE TICKET FOR THE SLINGSHOT FLIGHT TO ELBONIA'S CAPITAL.
AIR ELBONI
DO YOU WANT FIRST CLASS OR COACH?
WHAT'S THE DIFFER-ENCE?
10-8
WITH FIRST CLASS WE DON'T INTENTION-ALLY FLING YOU TOWARD SOMETHING HARD.
© 1991 United Feature Syndicate, Inc.

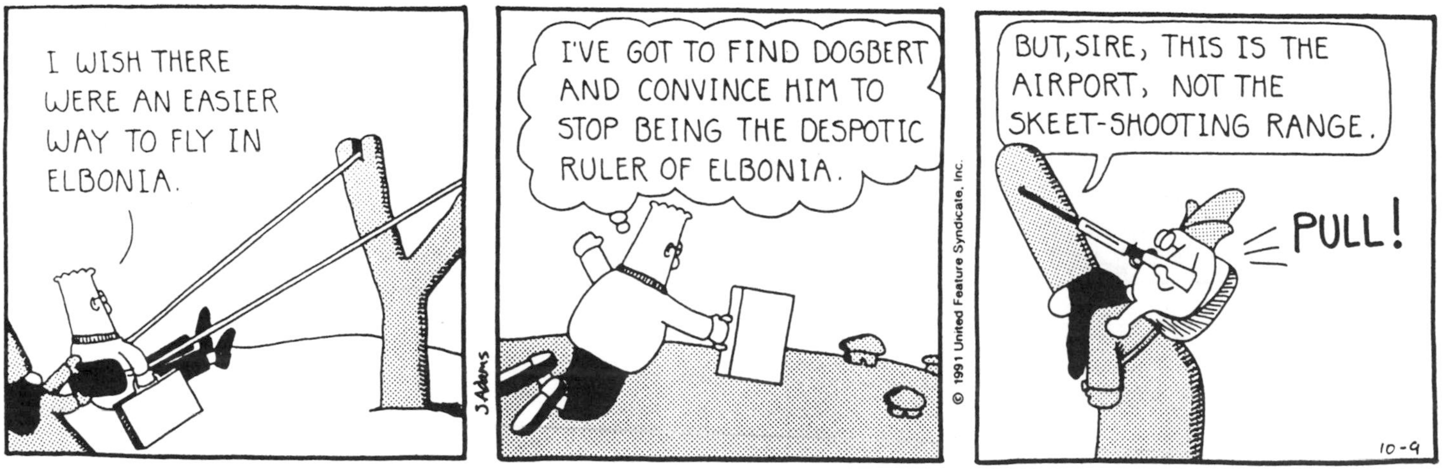
I WISH THERE WERE AN EASIER WAY TO FLY IN ELBONIA.
I'VE GOT TO FIND DOGBERT AND CONVINCE HIM TO STOP BEING THE DESPOTIC RULER OF ELBONIA.
BUT, SIRE, THIS IS THE AIRPORT, NOT THE SKEET-SHOOTING RANGE.
PULL!
© 1991 United Feature Syndicate, Inc.
10-9

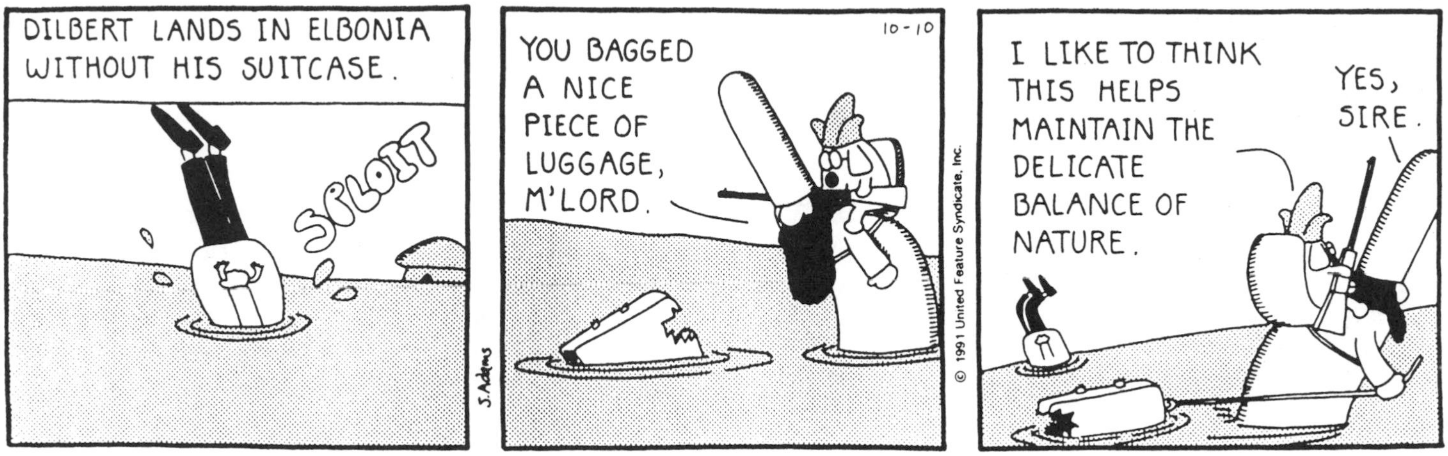
DILBERT LANDS IN ELBONIA WITHOUT HIS SUITCASE.
SPLOIT
S. Adams
10-10
YOU BAGGED A NICE PIECE OF LUGGAGE, M'LORD.
© 1991 United Feature Syndicate, Inc.
I LIKE TO THINK THIS HELPS MAINTAIN THE DELICATE BALANCE OF NATURE.
YES, SIRE.

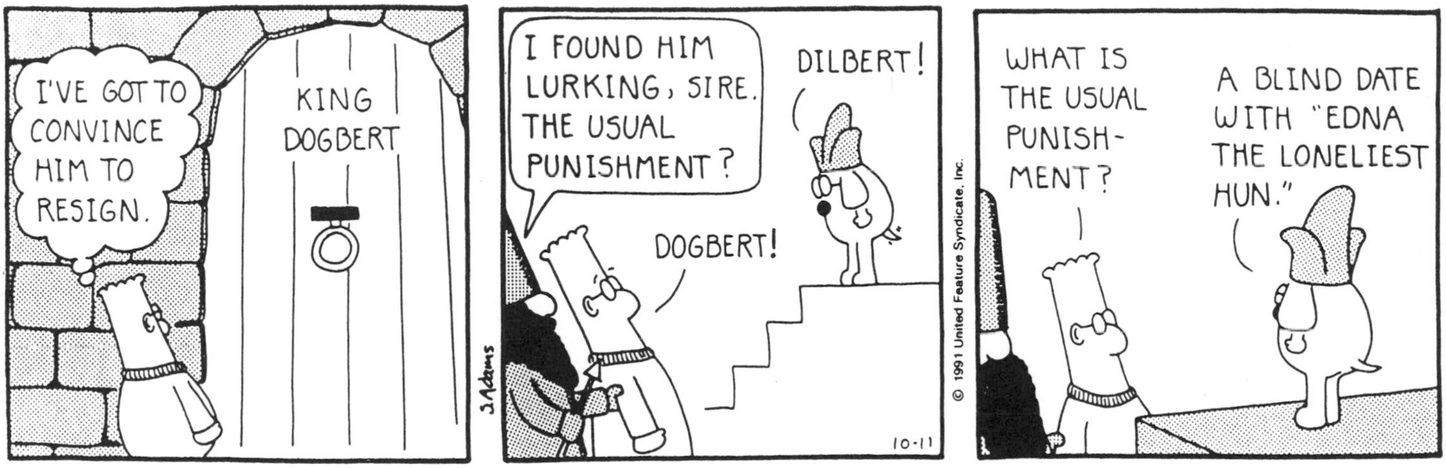
I'VE GOT TO CONVINCE HIM TO RESIGN.
KING DOGBERT
S. Adams
I FOUND HIM LURKING, SIRE. THE USUAL PUNISHMENT?
DILBERT!
DOGBERT!
10-11
© 1991 United Feature Syndicate, Inc.
WHAT IS THE USUAL PUNISHMENT?
A BLIND DATE WITH "EDNA THE LONELIEST HUN."

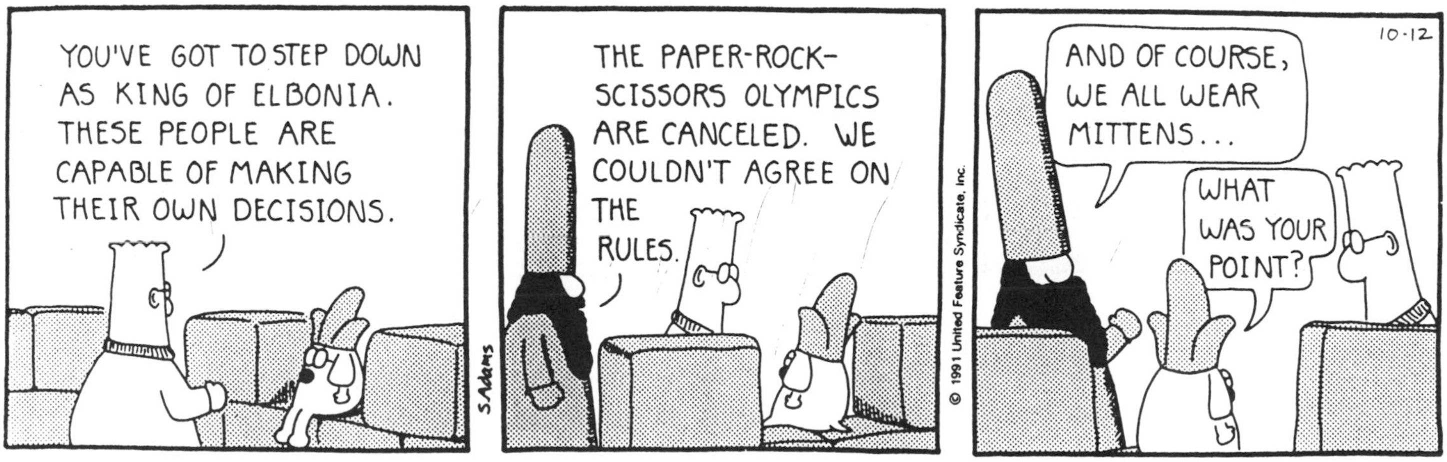
YOU'VE GOT TO STEP DOWN AS KING OF ELBONIA. THESE PEOPLE ARE CAPABLE OF MAKING THEIR OWN DECISIONS.
S. Adams
THE PAPER-ROCK-SCISSORS OLYMPICS ARE CANCELED. WE COULDN'T AGREE ON THE RULES.
© 1991 United Feature Syndicate, Inc.
10-12
AND OF COURSE, WE ALL WEAR MITTENS...
WHAT WAS YOUR POINT?

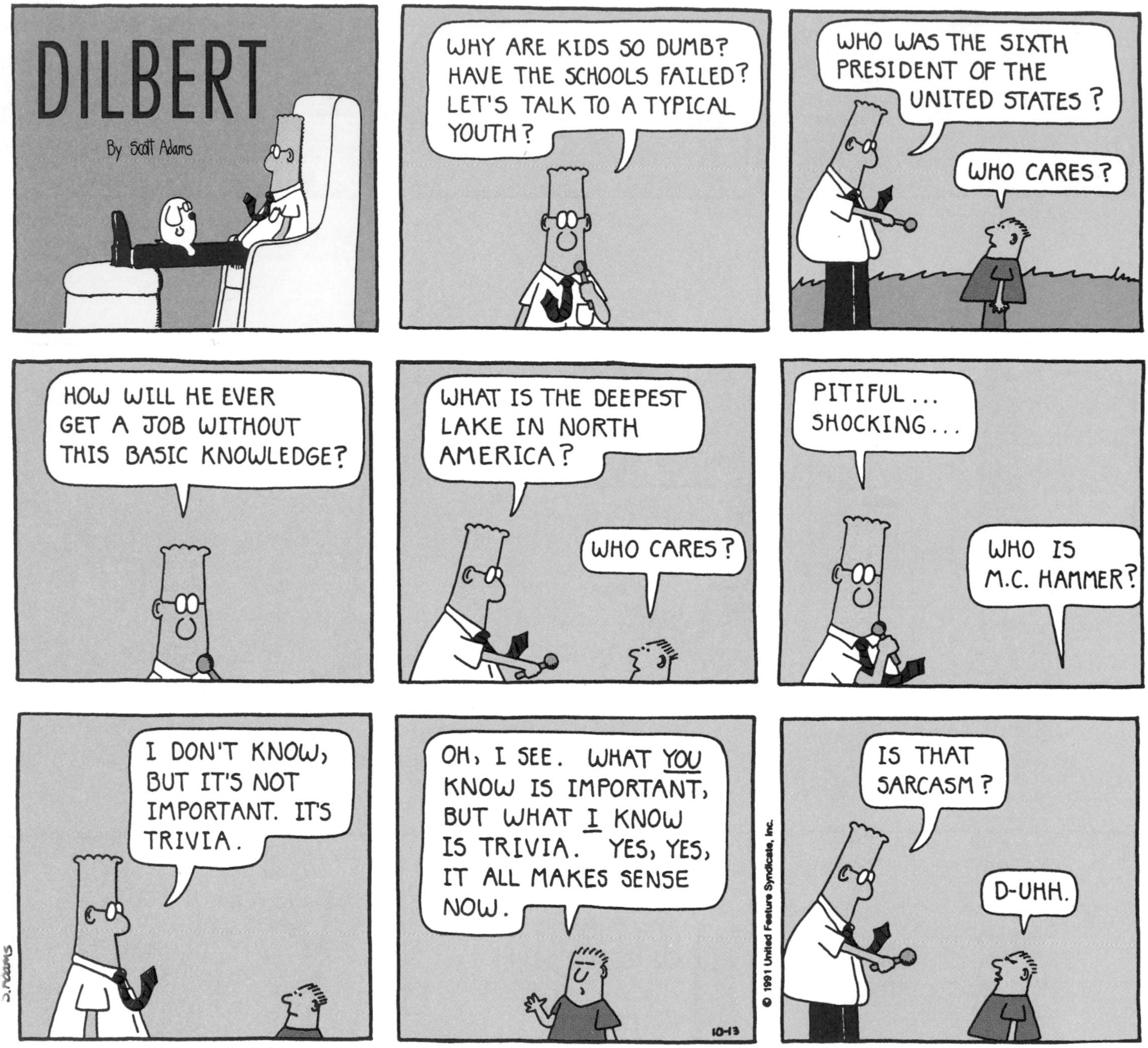
DILBERT
By Scott Adams
WHY ARE KIDS SO DUMB? HAVE THE SCHOOLS FAILED? LET'S TALK TO A TYPICAL YOUTH?
WHO WAS THE SIXTH PRESIDENT OF THE UNITED STATES?
WHO CARES?
HOW WILL HE EVER GET A JOB WITHOUT THIS BASIC KNOWLEDGE?
WHAT IS THE DEEPEST LAKE IN NORTH AMERICA?
WHO CARES?
PITIFUL... SHOCKING...
WHO IS M.C. HAMMER?
I DON'T KNOW, BUT IT'S NOT IMPORTANT. IT'S TRIVIA.
OH, I SEE. WHAT YOU KNOW IS IMPORTANT, BUT WHAT I KNOW IS TRIVIA. YES, YES, IT ALL MAKES SENSE NOW.
IS THAT SARCASM?
D-UHH.
S. ADAMS
© 1991 United Feature Syndicate, Inc.
10-13

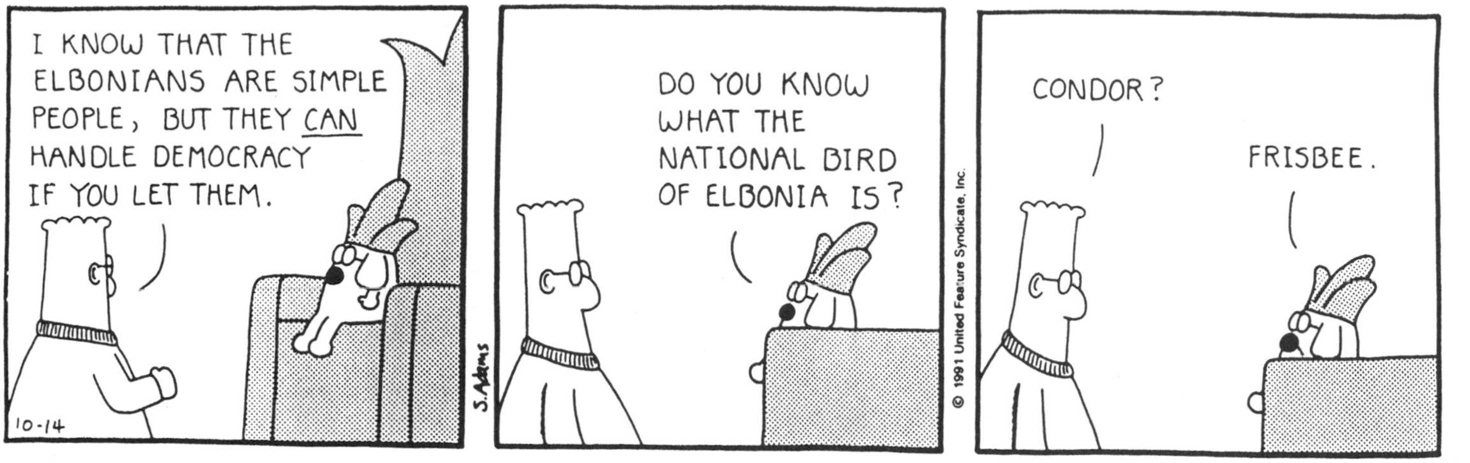
I KNOW THAT THE ELBONIANS ARE SIMPLE PEOPLE, BUT THEY CAN HANDLE DEMOCRACY IF YOU LET THEM.
10-14
S. Adams
DO YOU KNOW WHAT THE NATIONAL BIRD OF ELBONIA IS?
© 1991 United Feature Syndicate, Inc.
CONDOR?
FRISBEE.

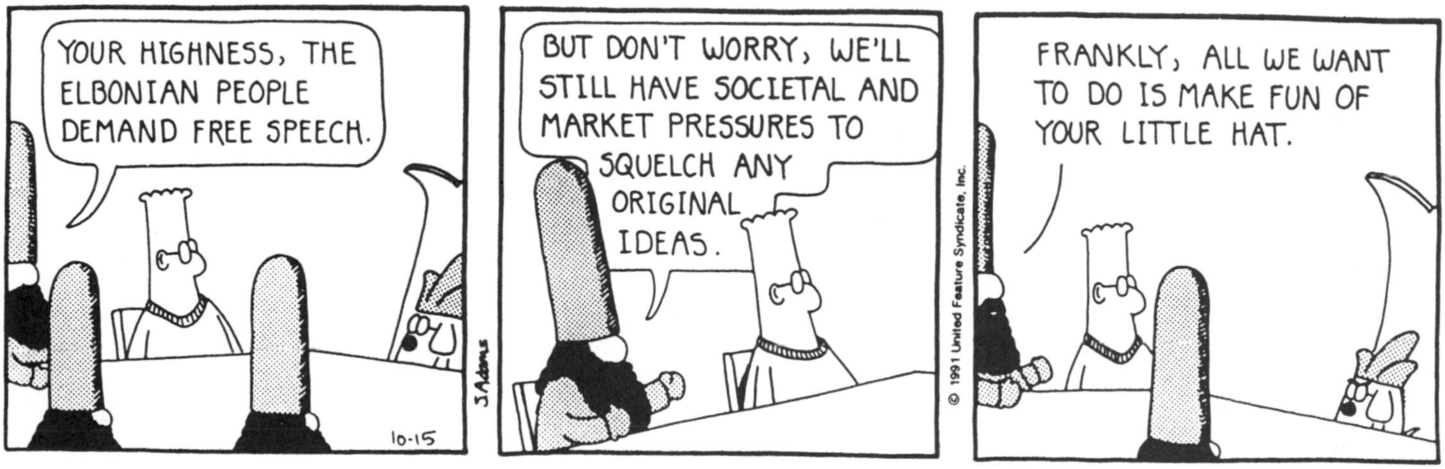
YOUR HIGHNESS, THE ELBONIAN PEOPLE DEMAND FREE SPEECH.
10-15
S. Adams
BUT DON'T WORRY, WE'LL STILL HAVE SOCIETAL AND MARKET PRESSURES TO SQUELCH ANY ORIGINAL IDEAS.
© 1991 United Feature Syndicate, Inc.
FRANKLY, ALL WE WANT TO DO IS MAKE FUN OF YOUR LITTLE HAT.

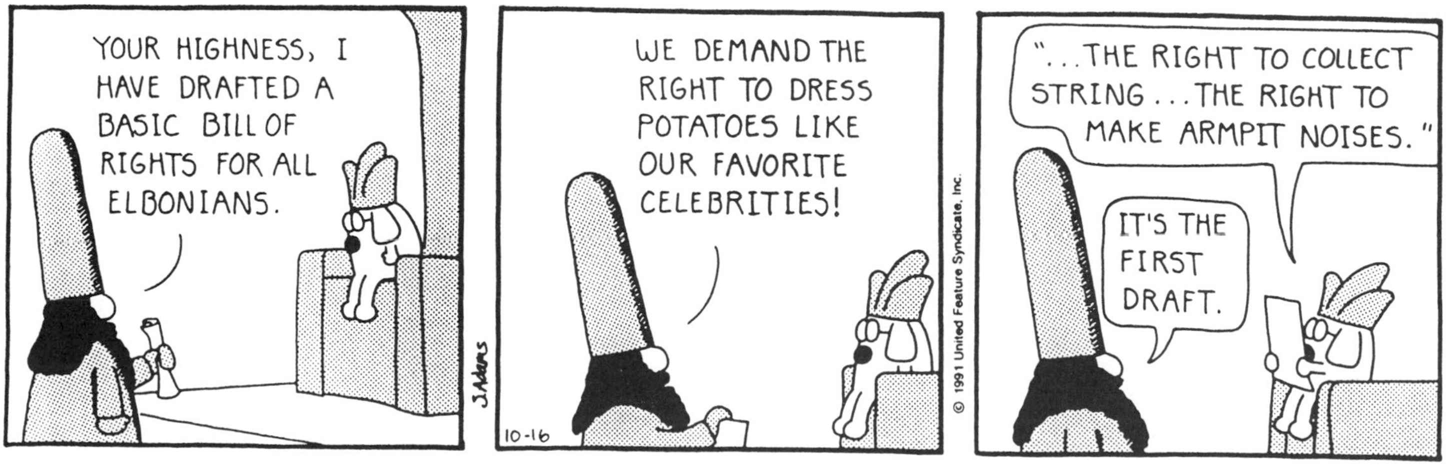
YOUR HIGHNESS, I HAVE DRAFTED A BASIC BILL OF RIGHTS FOR ALL ELBONIANS.
S. Adams
WE DEMAND THE RIGHT TO DRESS POTATOES LIKE OUR FAVORITE CELEBRITIES!
10-16
© 1991 United Feature Syndicate, Inc.
"...THE RIGHT TO COLLECT STRING...THE RIGHT TO MAKE ARMPIT NOISES."
IT'S THE FIRST DRAFT.

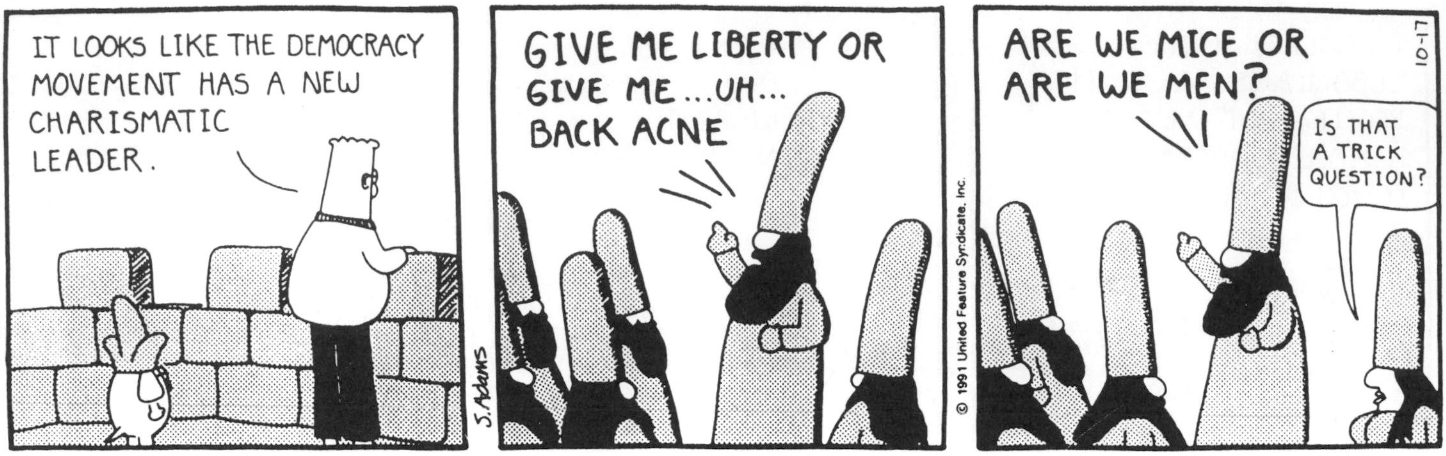
IT LOOKS LIKE THE DEMOCRACY MOVEMENT HAS A NEW CHARISMATIC LEADER.
S. Adams
GIVE ME LIBERTY OR GIVE ME ...UH... BACK ACNE
© 1991 United Feature Syndicate, Inc.
ARE WE MICE OR ARE WE MEN?
IS THAT A TRICK QUESTION?
10-17

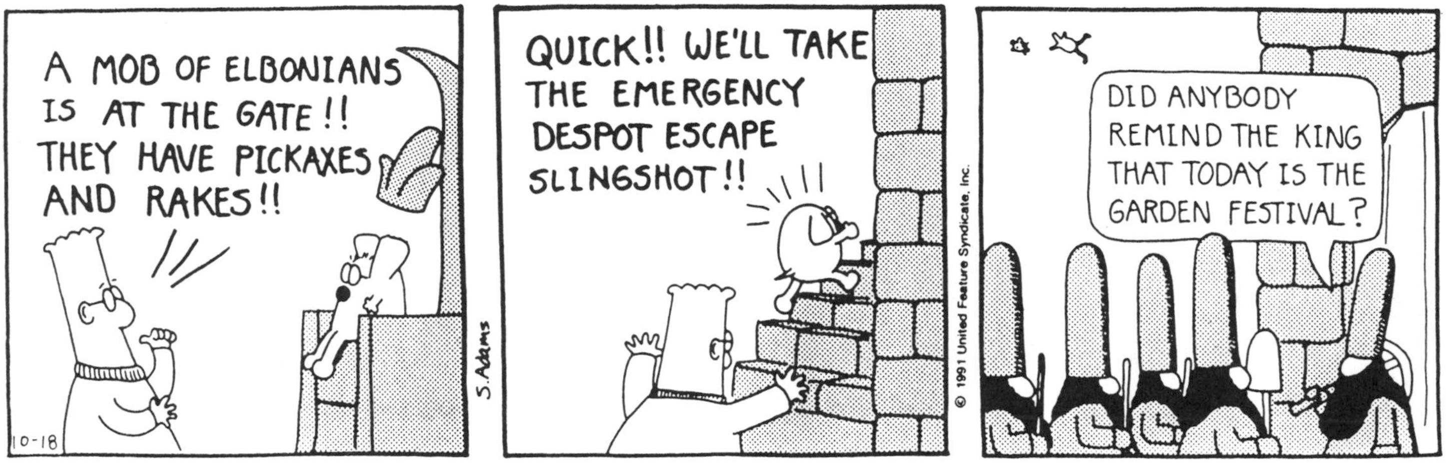
A MOB OF ELBONIANS IS AT THE GATE!! THEY HAVE PICKAXES AND RAKES!!
10-18
S. Adams
QUICK!! WE'LL TAKE THE EMERGENCY DESPOT ESCAPE SLINGSHOT!!
© 1991 United Feature Syndicate, Inc.
DID ANYBODY REMIND THE KING THAT TODAY IS THE GARDEN FESTIVAL?

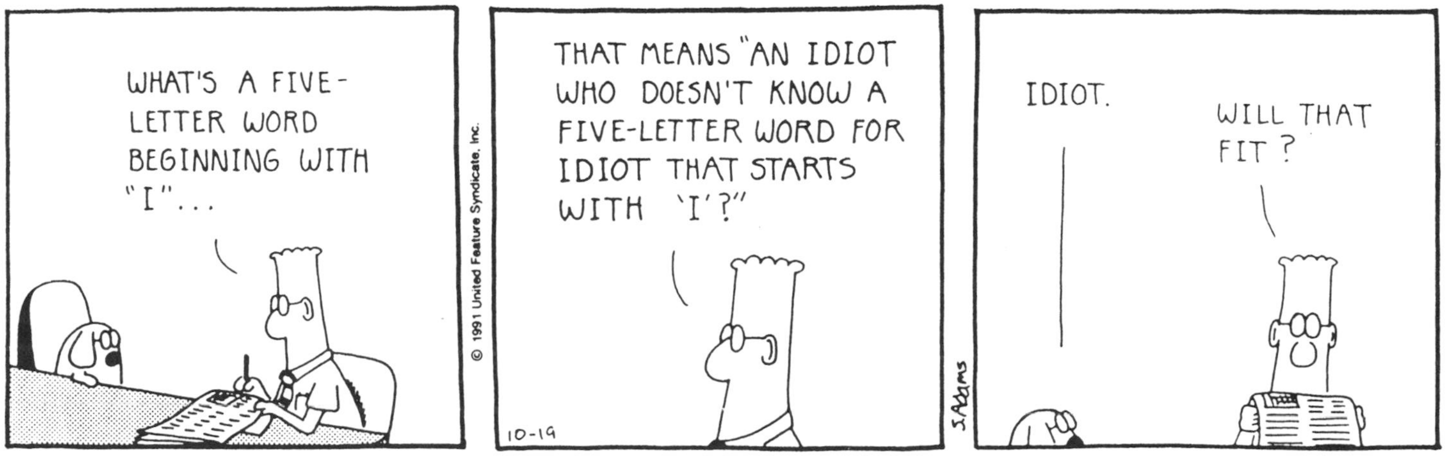
WHAT'S A FIVE-LETTER WORD BEGINNING WITH "I"...
© 1991 United Feature Syndicate, Inc.
THAT MEANS "AN IDIOT WHO DOESN'T KNOW A FIVE-LETTER WORD FOR IDIOT THAT STARTS WITH 'I'?"
10-19
S. Adams
IDIOT.
WILL THAT FIT?

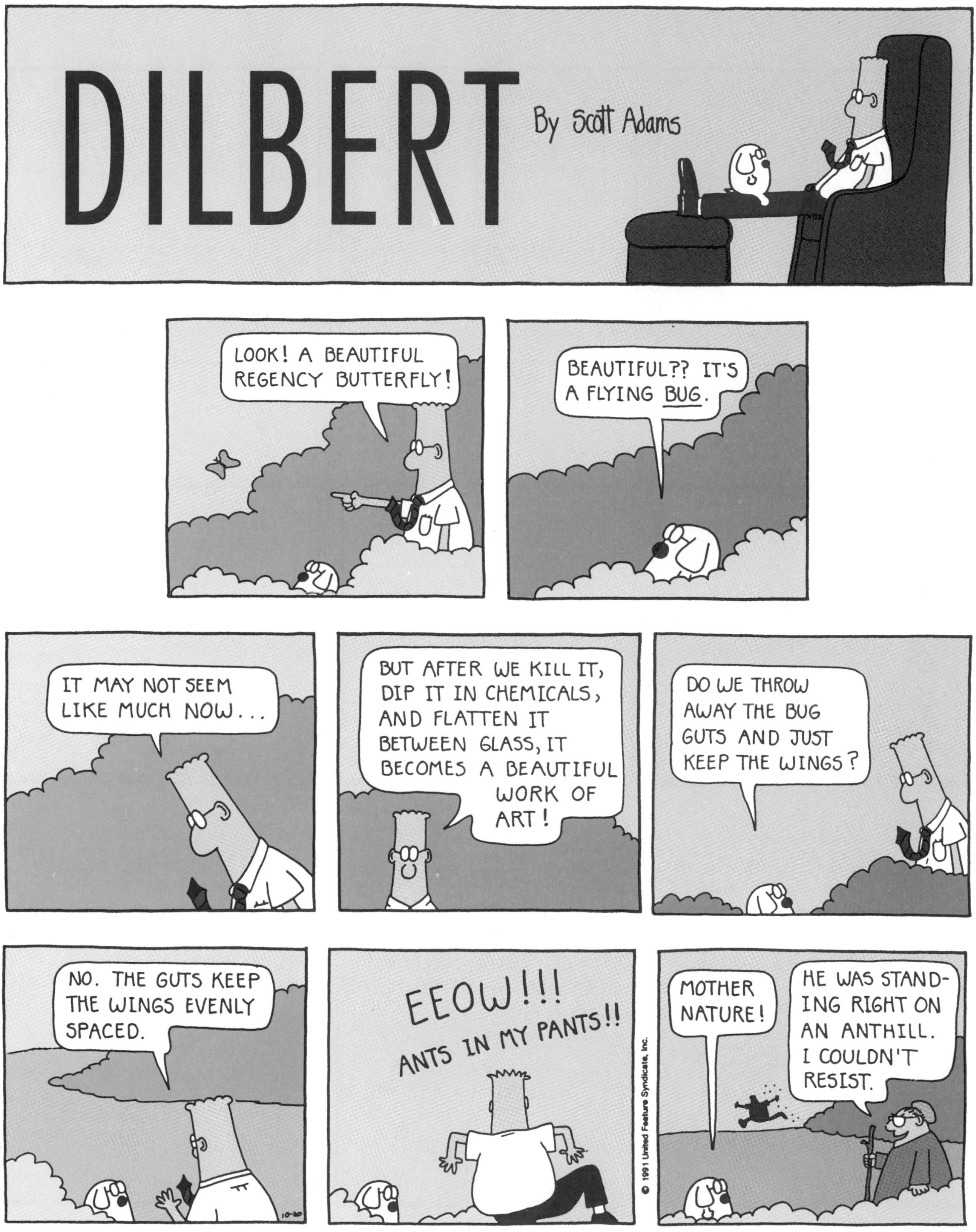
DILBERT
By Scott Adams
LOOK! A BEAUTIFUL REGENCY BUTTERFLY!
BEAUTIFUL?? IT'S A FLYING BUG.
IT MAY NOT SEEM LIKE MUCH NOW...
BUT AFTER WE KILL IT, DIP IT IN CHEMICALS, AND FLATTEN IT BETWEEN GLASS, IT BECOMES A BEAUTIFUL WORK OF ART!
DO WE THROW AWAY THE BUG GUTS AND JUST KEEP THE WINGS?
NO. THE GUTS KEEP THE WINGS EVENLY SPACED.
EEOW!!!
ANTS IN MY PANTS!!
© 1991 United Feature Syndicate, Inc.
MOTHER NATURE!
HE WAS STANDING RIGHT ON AN ANTHILL. I COULDN'T RESIST.

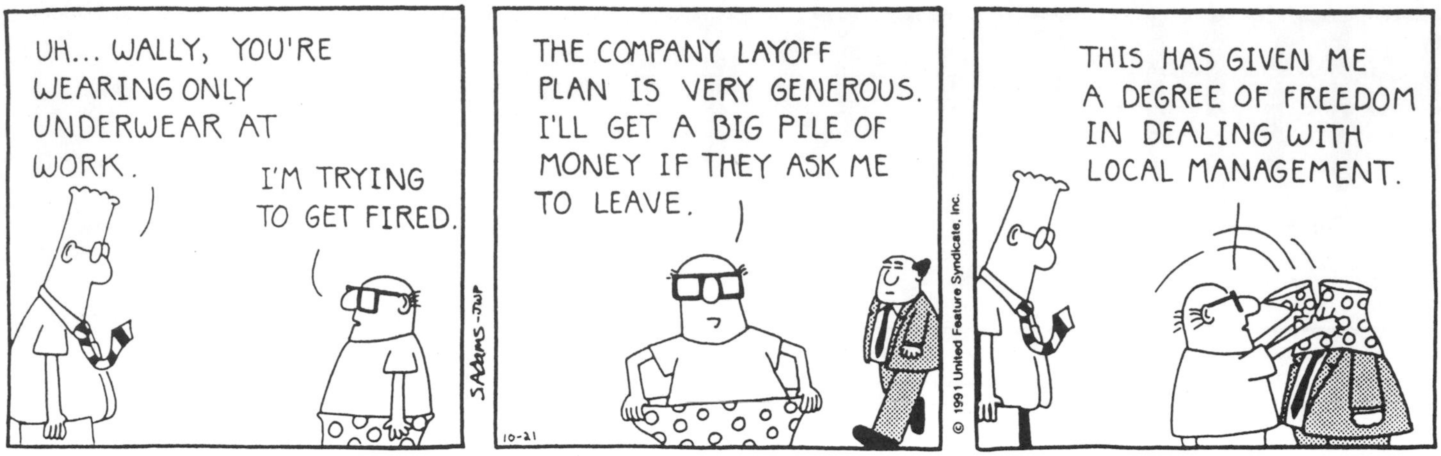
UH... WALLY, YOU'RE WEARING ONLY UNDERWEAR AT WORK.
I'M TRYING TO GET FIRED.
THE COMPANY LAYOFF PLAN IS VERY GENEROUS. I'LL GET A BIG PILE OF MONEY IF THEY ASK ME TO LEAVE.
THIS HAS GIVEN ME A DEGREE OF FREEDOM IN DEALING WITH LOCAL MANAGEMENT.
© 1991 United Feature Syndicate, Inc.

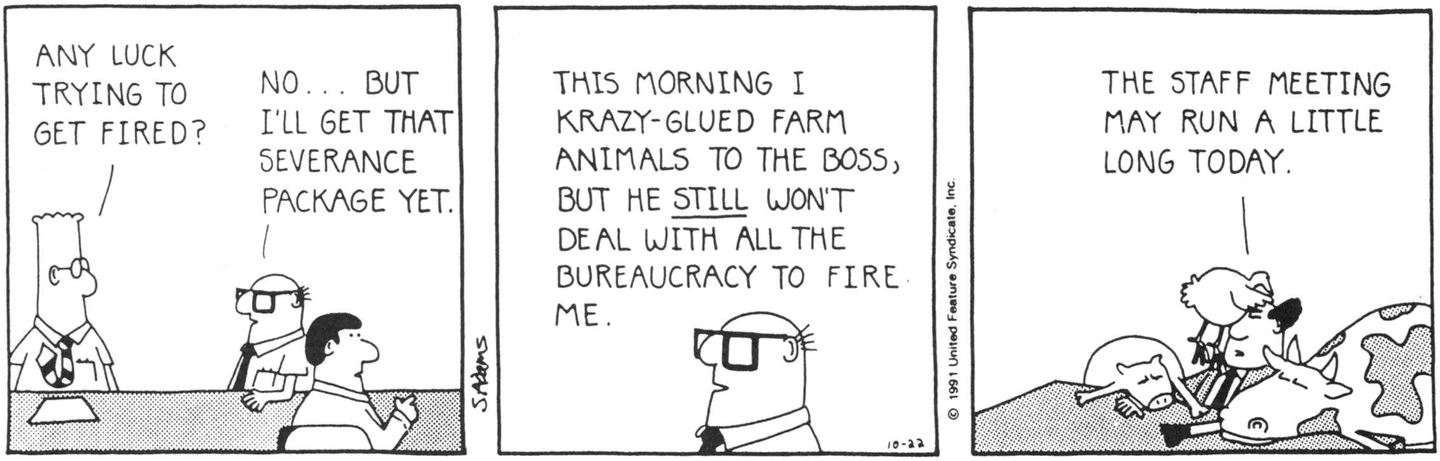
ANY LUCK TRYING TO GET FIRED?
NO... BUT I'LL GET THAT SEVERANCE PACKAGE YET.
THIS MORNING I KRAZY-GLUED FARM ANIMALS TO THE BOSS, BUT HE STILL WON'T DEAL WITH ALL THE BUREAUCRACY TO FIRE ME.
THE STAFF MEETING MAY RUN A LITTLE LONG TODAY.
© 1991 United Feature Syndicate, Inc.

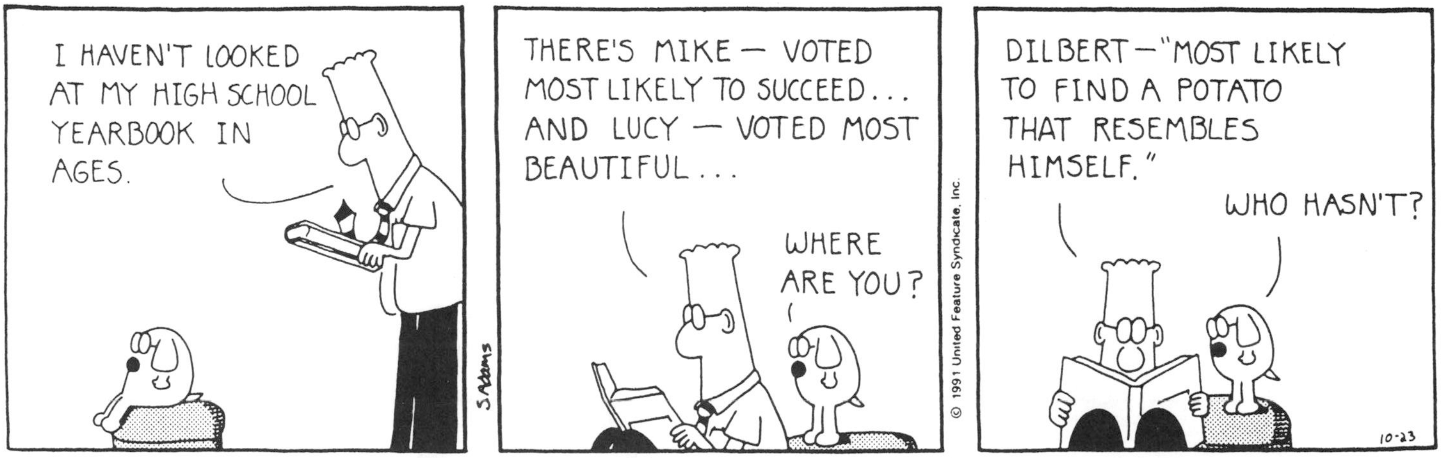
I HAVEN'T LOOKED AT MY HIGH SCHOOL YEARBOOK IN AGES.
THERE'S MIKE — VOTED MOST LIKELY TO SUCCEED... AND LUCY — VOTED MOST BEAUTIFUL...
WHERE ARE YOU?
DILBERT — "MOST LIKELY TO FIND A POTATO THAT RESEMBLES HIMSELF."
WHO HASN'T?
© 1991 United Feature Syndicate, Inc.

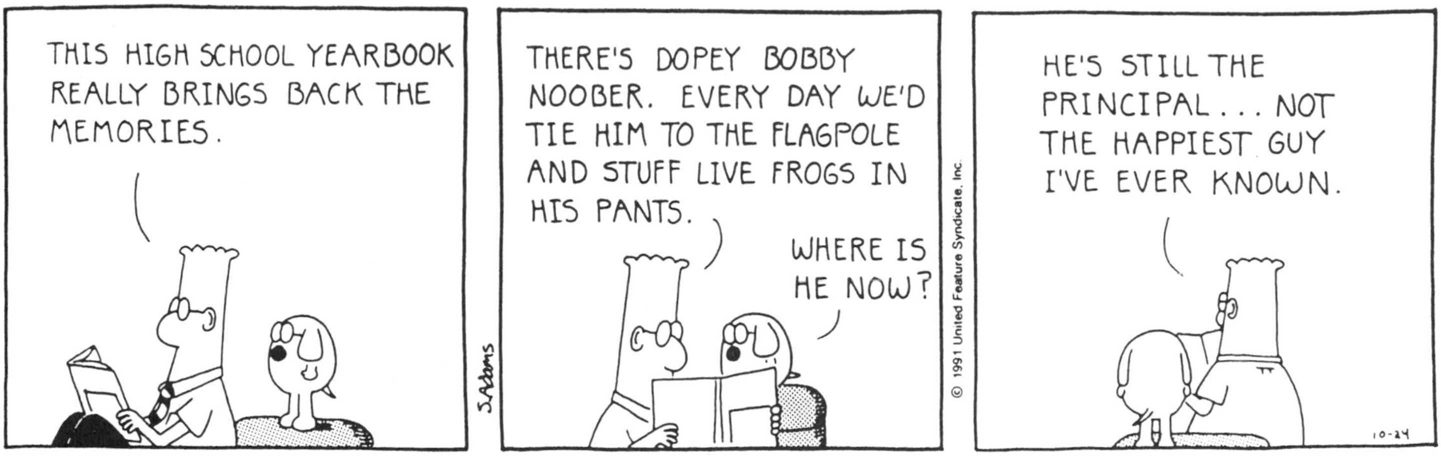
THIS HIGH SCHOOL YEARBOOK REALLY BRINGS BACK THE MEMORIES.
THERE'S DOPEY BOBBY NOOBER. EVERY DAY WE'D TIE HIM TO THE FLAGPOLE AND STUFF LIVE FROGS IN HIS PANTS.
WHERE IS HE NOW?
HE'S STILL THE PRINCIPAL . . . NOT THE HAPPIEST GUY I'VE EVER KNOWN.
© 1991 United Feature Syndicate, Inc.

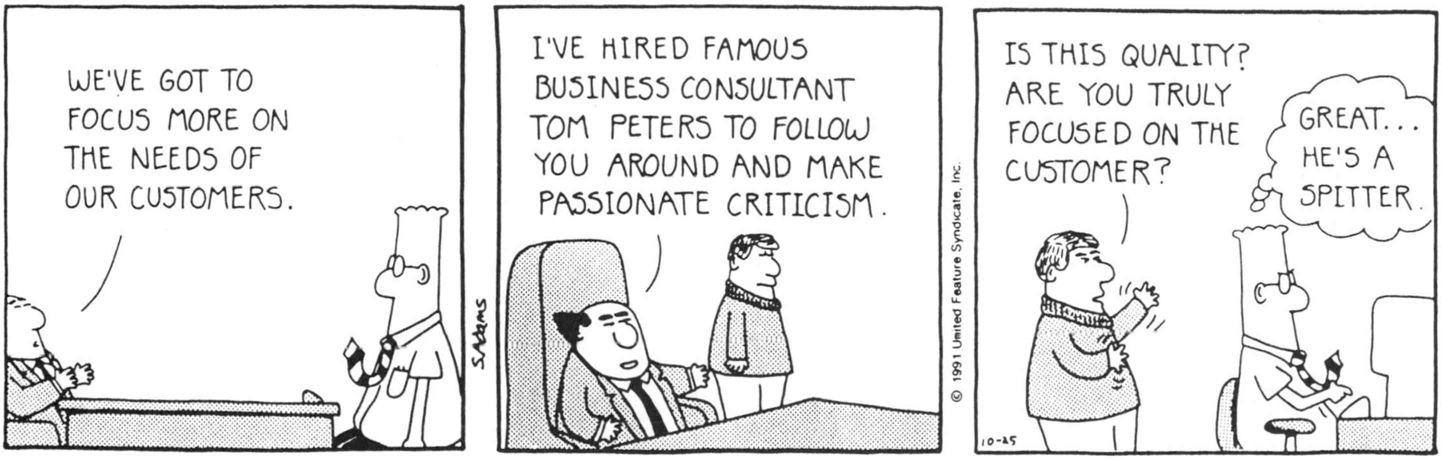
WE'VE GOT TO FOCUS MORE ON THE NEEDS OF OUR CUSTOMERS.
I'VE HIRED FAMOUS BUSINESS CONSULTANT TOM PETERS TO FOLLOW YOU AROUND AND MAKE PASSIONATE CRITICISM.
IS THIS QUALITY? ARE YOU TRULY FOCUSED ON THE CUSTOMER?
GREAT... HE'S A SPITTER.
© 1991 United Feature Syndicate, Inc.

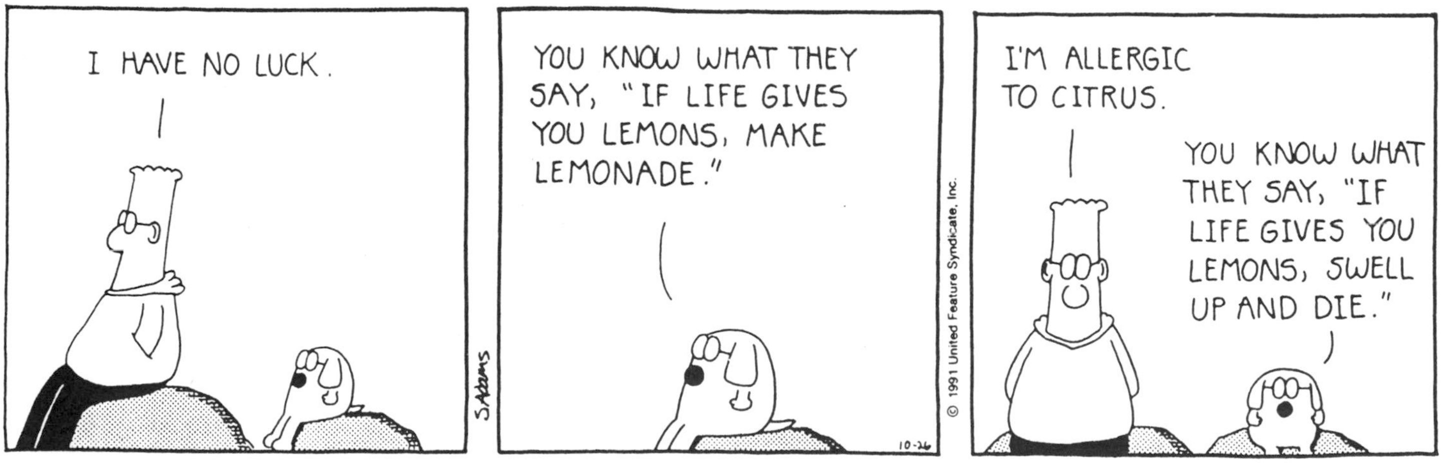
I HAVE NO LUCK.
YOU KNOW WHAT THEY SAY, "IF LIFE GIVES YOU LEMONS, MAKE LEMONADE."
I'M ALLERGIC TO CITRUS.
YOU KNOW WHAT THEY SAY, "IF LIFE GIVES YOU LEMONS, SWELL UP AND DIE."
© 1991 United Feature Syndicate, Inc.

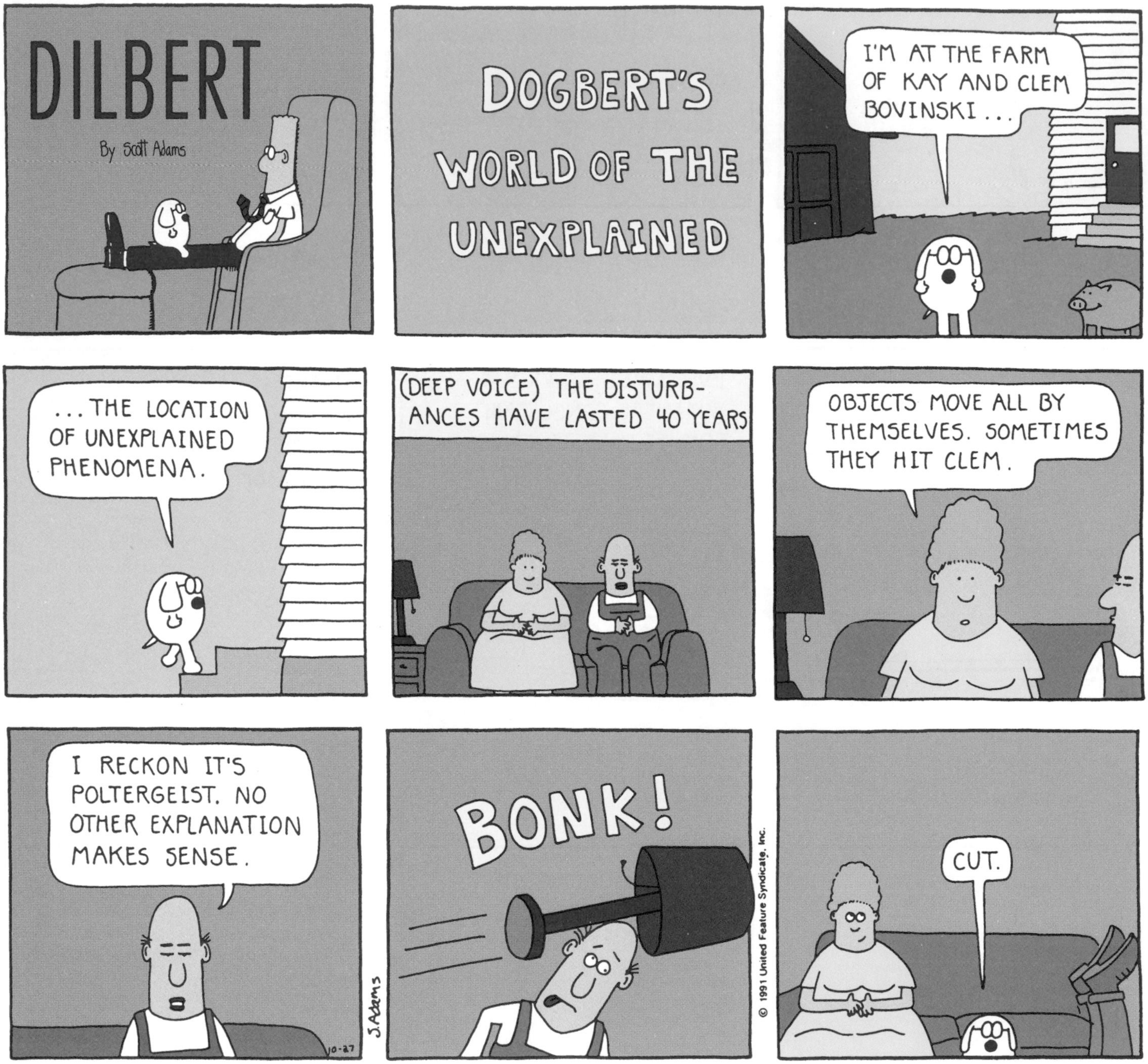
DILBERT
By Scott Adams
DOGBERT'S WORLD OF THE UNEXPLAINED
I'M AT THE FARM OF KAY AND CLEM BOVINSKI . . .
. . . THE LOCATION OF UNEXPLAINED PHENOMENA.
(DEEP VOICE) THE DISTURB-ANCES HAVE LASTED 40 YEARS
OBJECTS MOVE ALL BY THEMSELVES. SOMETIMES THEY HIT CLEM.
I RECKON IT'S POLTERGEIST. NO OTHER EXPLANATION MAKES SENSE.
10-27
S. Adams
BONK!
© 1991 United Feature Syndicate, Inc.
CUT.

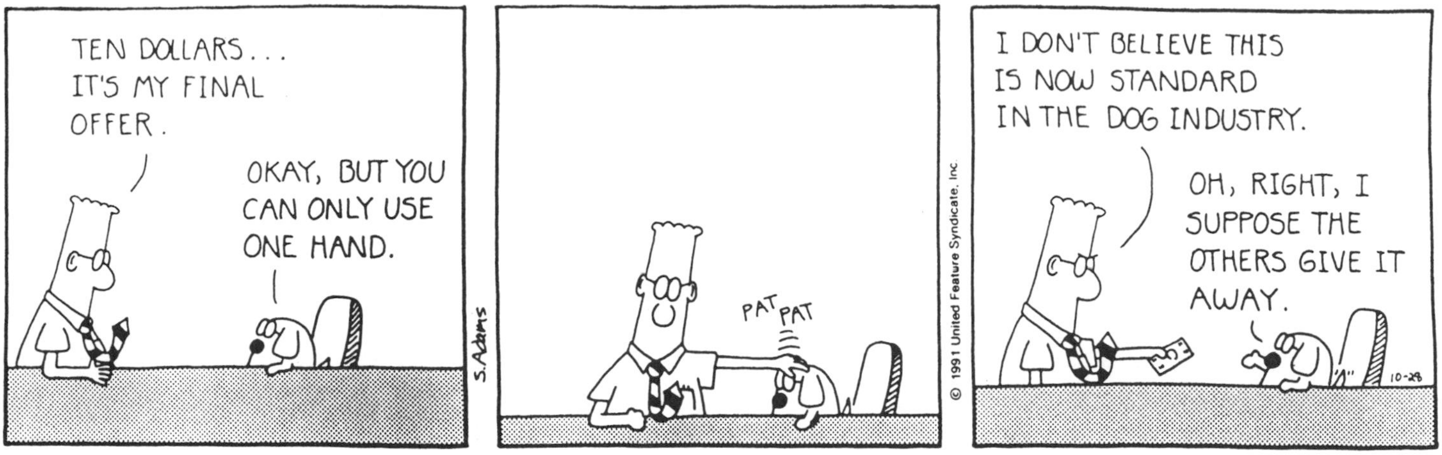
TEN DOLLARS... IT'S MY FINAL OFFER.
OKAY, BUT YOU CAN ONLY USE ONE HAND.
S. Adams
PAT PAT
© 1991 United Feature Syndicate, Inc.
I DON'T BELIEVE THIS IS NOW STANDARD IN THE DOG INDUSTRY.
OH, RIGHT, I SUPPOSE THE OTHERS GIVE IT AWAY.
10-28

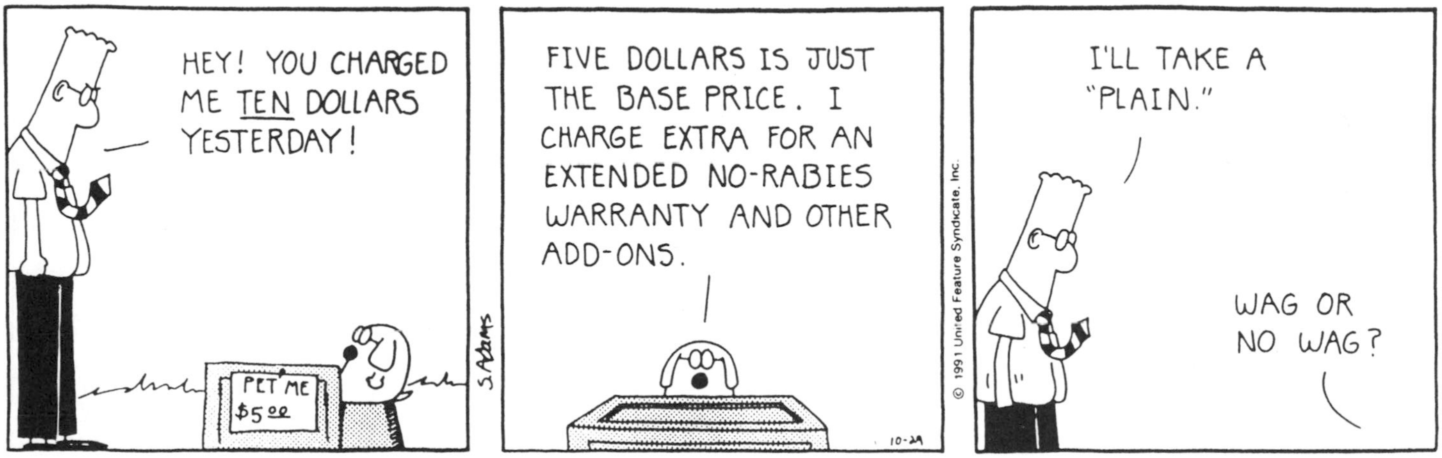
HEY! YOU CHARGED ME TEN DOLLARS YESTERDAY!
PET ME $5.00
S. Adams
FIVE DOLLARS IS JUST THE BASE PRICE. I CHARGE EXTRA FOR AN EXTENDED NO-RABIES WARRANTY AND OTHER ADD-ONS.
10-29
© 1991 United Feature Syndicate, Inc.
I'LL TAKE A "PLAIN."
WAG OR NO WAG?

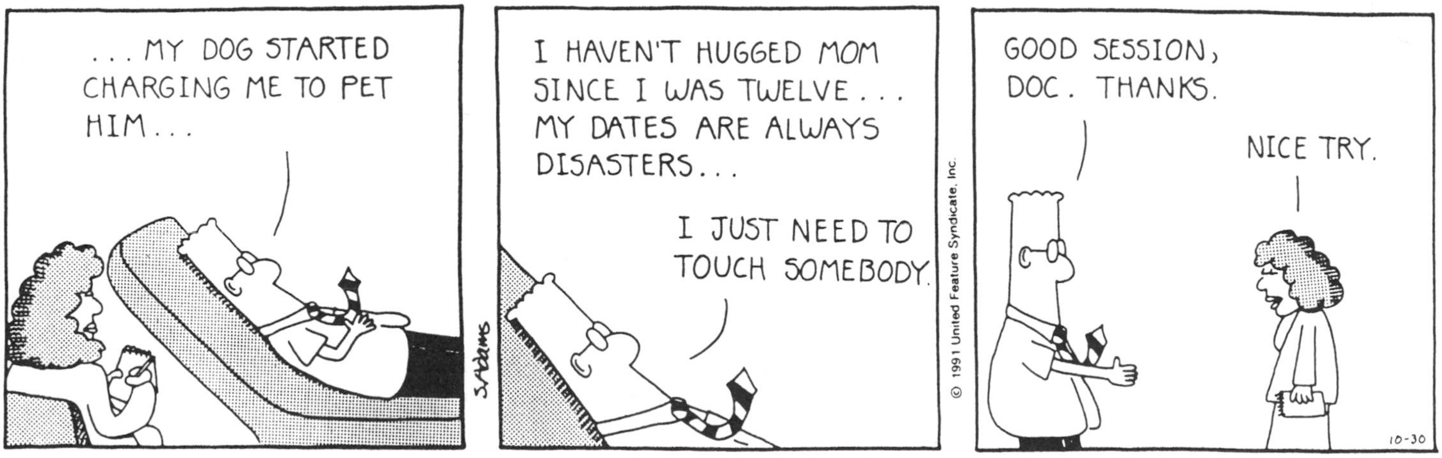
...MY DOG STARTED CHARGING ME TO PET HIM...
S. Adams
I HAVEN'T HUGGED MOM SINCE I WAS TWELVE... MY DATES ARE ALWAYS DISASTERS...
I JUST NEED TO TOUCH SOMEBODY.
© 1991 United Feature Syndicate, Inc.
GOOD SESSION, DOC. THANKS.
NICE TRY.
10-30

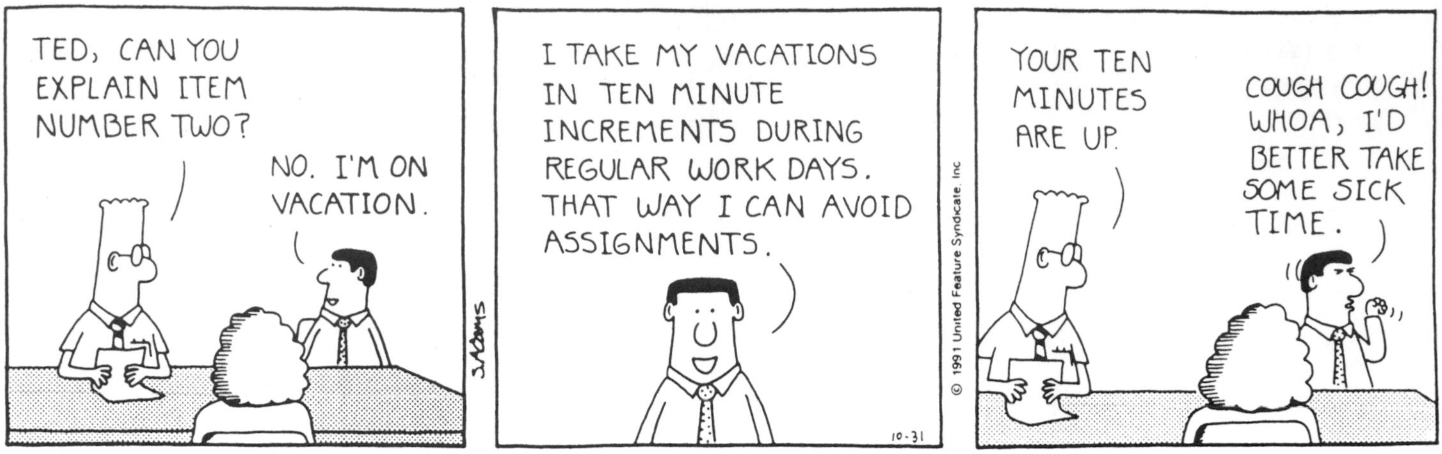
TED, CAN YOU EXPLAIN ITEM NUMBER TWO?
NO. I'M ON VACATION.
S.Adams
I TAKE MY VACATIONS IN TEN MINUTE INCREMENTS DURING REGULAR WORK DAYS. THAT WAY I CAN AVOID ASSIGNMENTS.
10-31
© 1991 United Feature Syndicate, Inc
YOUR TEN MINUTES ARE UP.
COUGH COUGH! WHOA, I'D BETTER TAKE SOME SICK TIME.

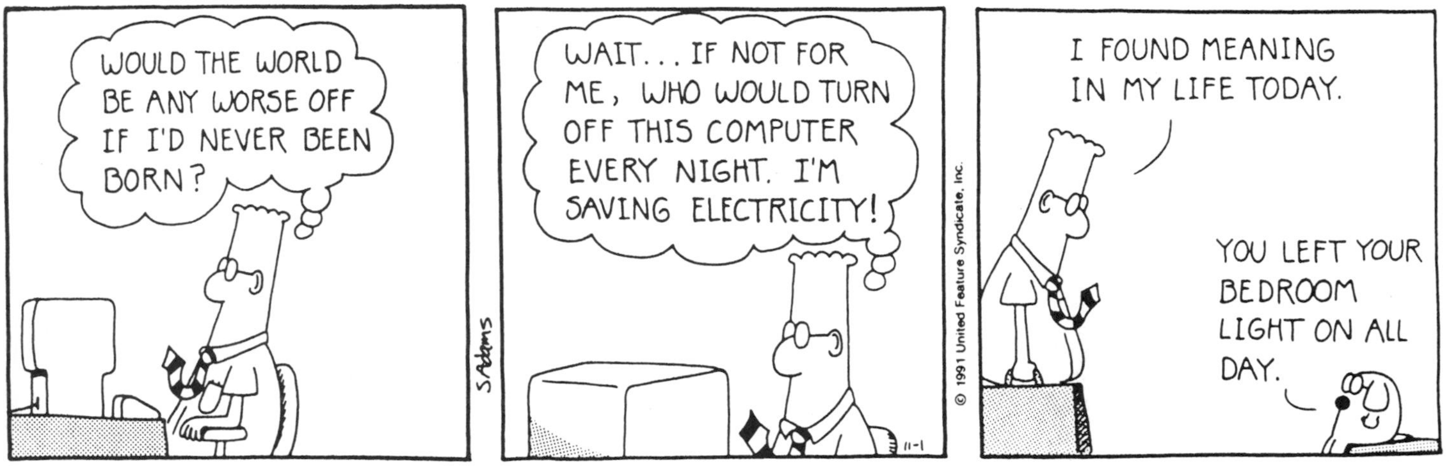
WOULD THE WORLD BE ANY WORSE OFF IF I'D NEVER BEEN BORN?
S.Adams
WAIT... IF NOT FOR ME, WHO WOULD TURN OFF THIS COMPUTER EVERY NIGHT. I'M SAVING ELECTRICITY!
11-1
© 1991 United Feature Syndicate, Inc.
I FOUND MEANING IN MY LIFE TODAY.
YOU LEFT YOUR BEDROOM LIGHT ON ALL DAY.

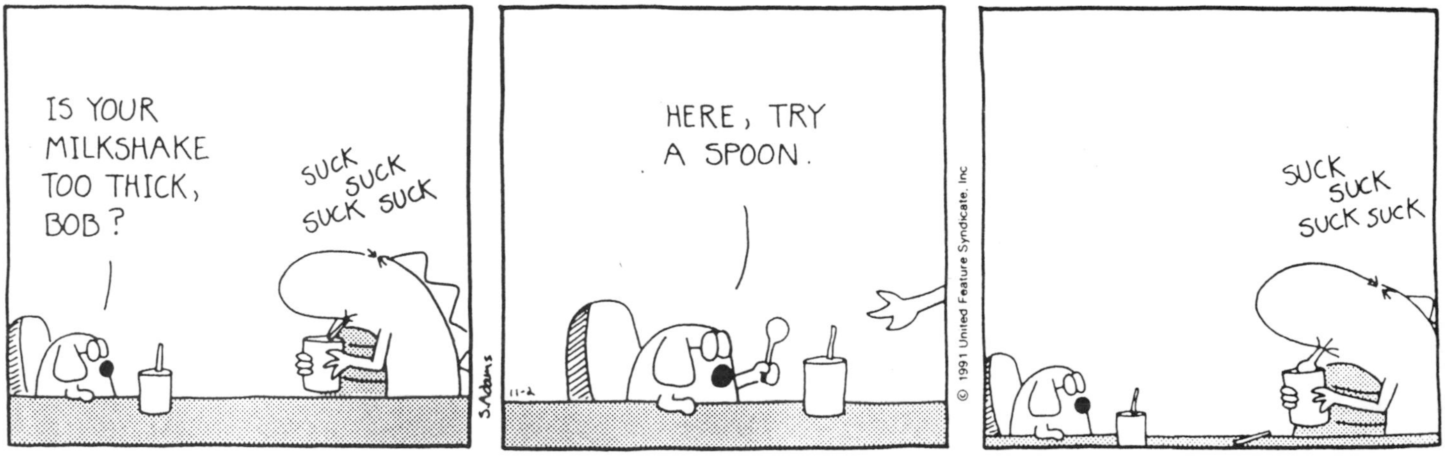
IS YOUR MILKSHAKE TOO THICK, BOB?
SUCK SUCK SUCK SUCK
S.Adams
11-2
HERE, TRY A SPOON.
© 1991 United Feature Syndicate, Inc
SUCK SUCK SUCK SUCK

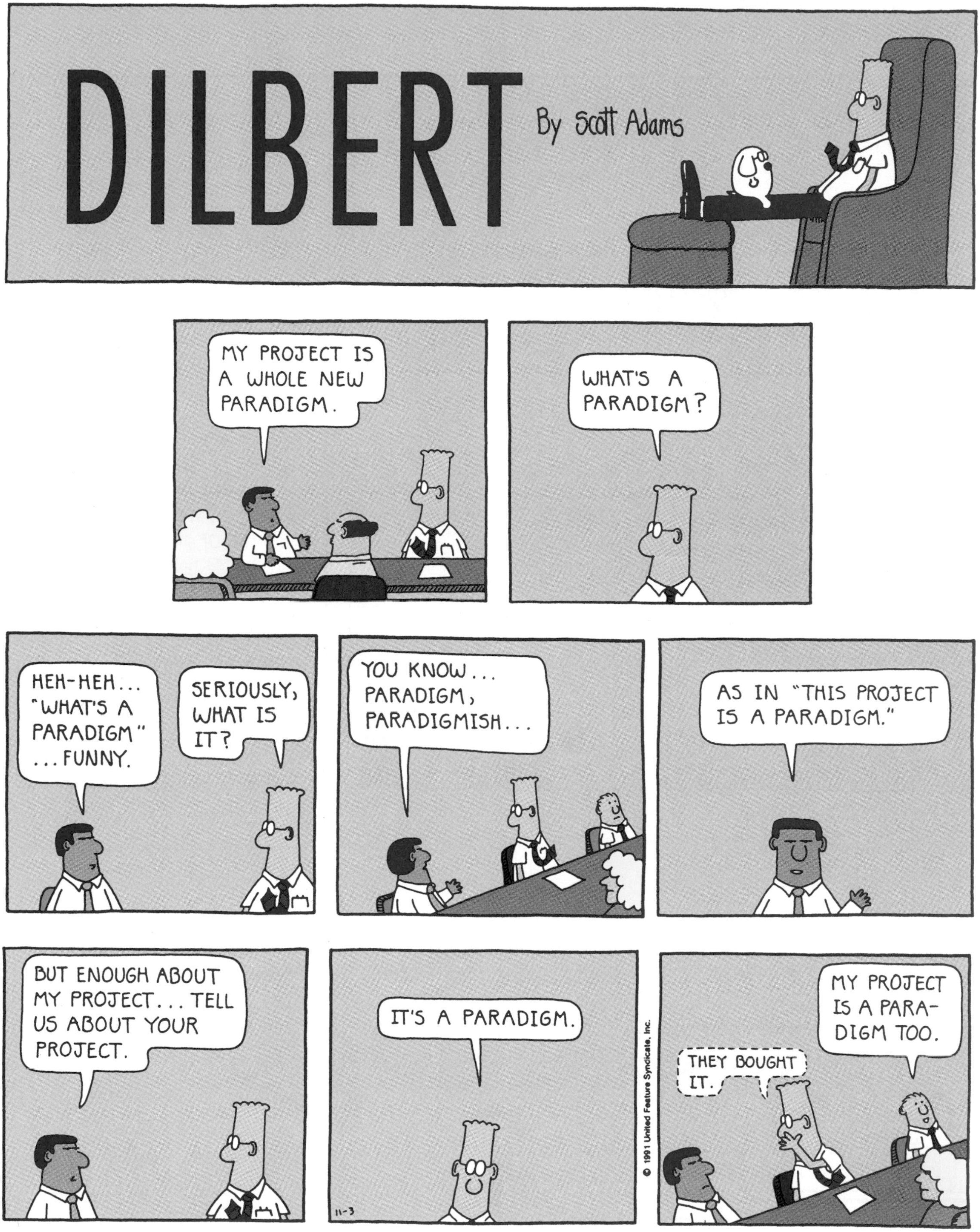
DILBERT
By Scott Adams
MY PROJECT IS A WHOLE NEW PARADIGM.
WHAT'S A PARADIGM?
HEH-HEH... "WHAT'S A PARADIGM" ...FUNNY.
SERIOUSLY, WHAT IS IT?
YOU KNOW... PARADIGM, PARADIGMISH...
AS IN "THIS PROJECT IS A PARADIGM."
BUT ENOUGH ABOUT MY PROJECT... TELL US ABOUT YOUR PROJECT.
IT'S A PARADIGM.
THEY BOUGHT IT.
MY PROJECT IS A PARA-DIGM TOO.
S.Adams
11-3
© 1991 United Feature Syndicate, Inc.

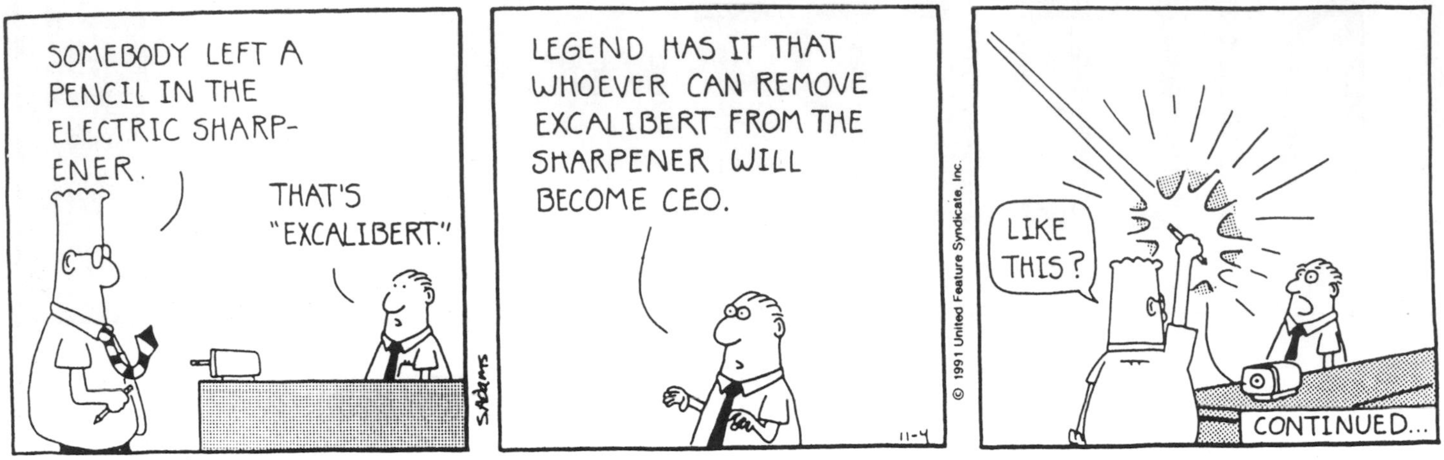
SOMEBODY LEFT A PENCIL IN THE ELECTRIC SHARPENER.
THAT'S "EXCALIBERT."
LEGEND HAS IT THAT WHOEVER CAN REMOVE EXCALIBERT FROM THE SHARPENER WILL BECOME CEO.
© 1991 United Feature Syndicate, Inc.
LIKE THIS?
CONTINUED...

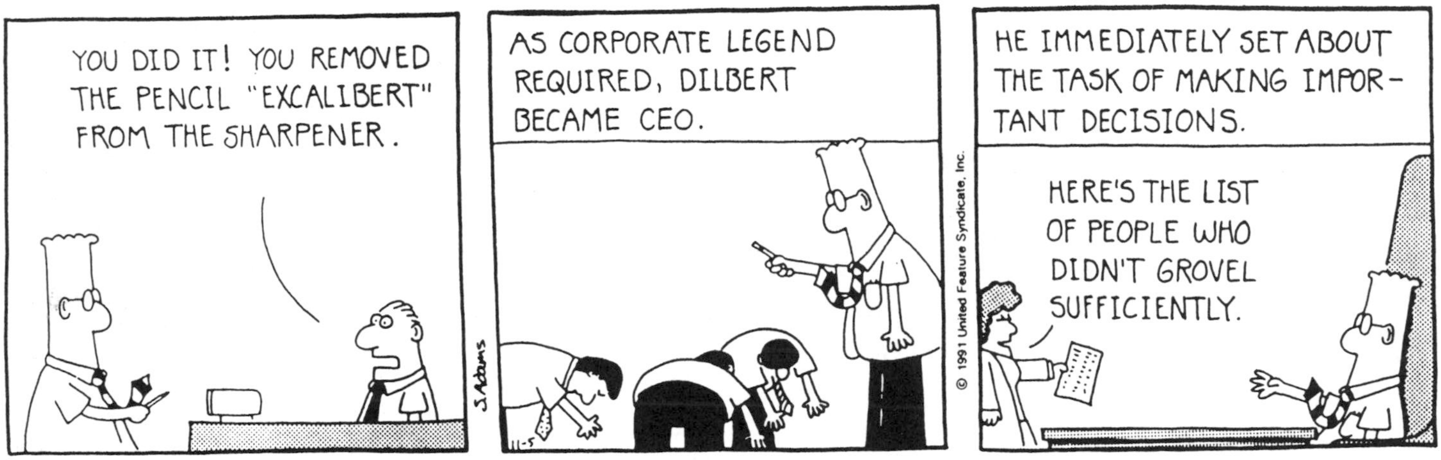
YOU DID IT! YOU REMOVED THE PENCIL "EXCALIBERT" FROM THE SHARPENER.
AS CORPORATE LEGEND REQUIRED, DILBERT BECAME CEO.
© 1991 United Feature Syndicate, Inc.
HE IMMEDIATELY SET ABOUT THE TASK OF MAKING IMPORTANT DECISIONS.
HERE'S THE LIST OF PEOPLE WHO DIDN'T GROVEL SUFFICIENTLY.

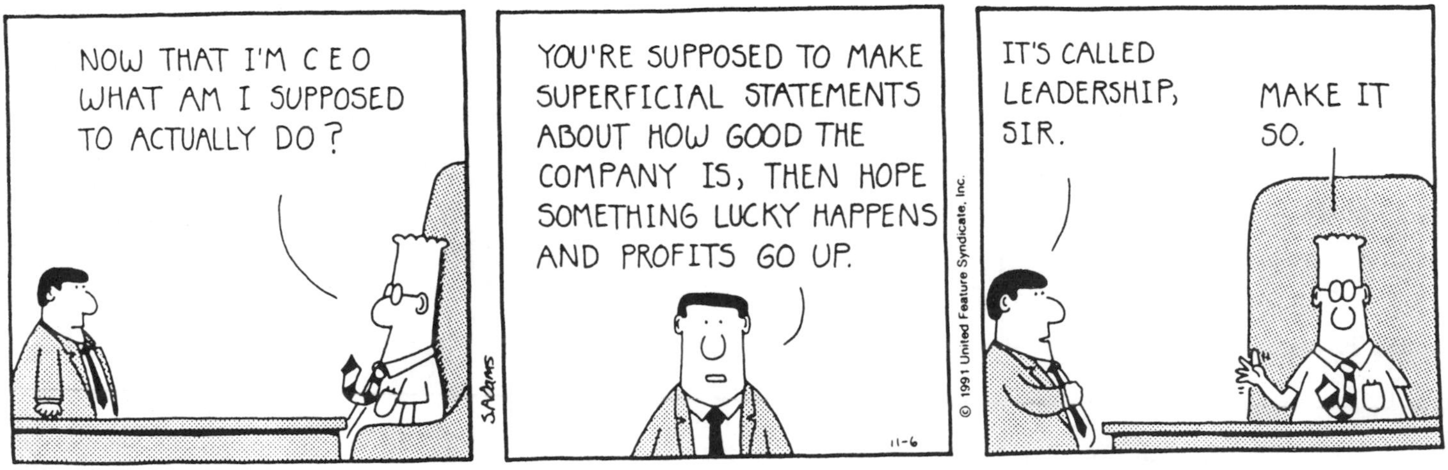
NOW THAT I'M CEO WHAT AM I SUPPOSED TO ACTUALLY DO?
YOU'RE SUPPOSED TO MAKE SUPERFICIAL STATEMENTS ABOUT HOW GOOD THE COMPANY IS, THEN HOPE SOMETHING LUCKY HAPPENS AND PROFITS GO UP.
© 1991 United Feature Syndicate, Inc.
IT'S CALLED LEADERSHIP, SIR.
MAKE IT SO.

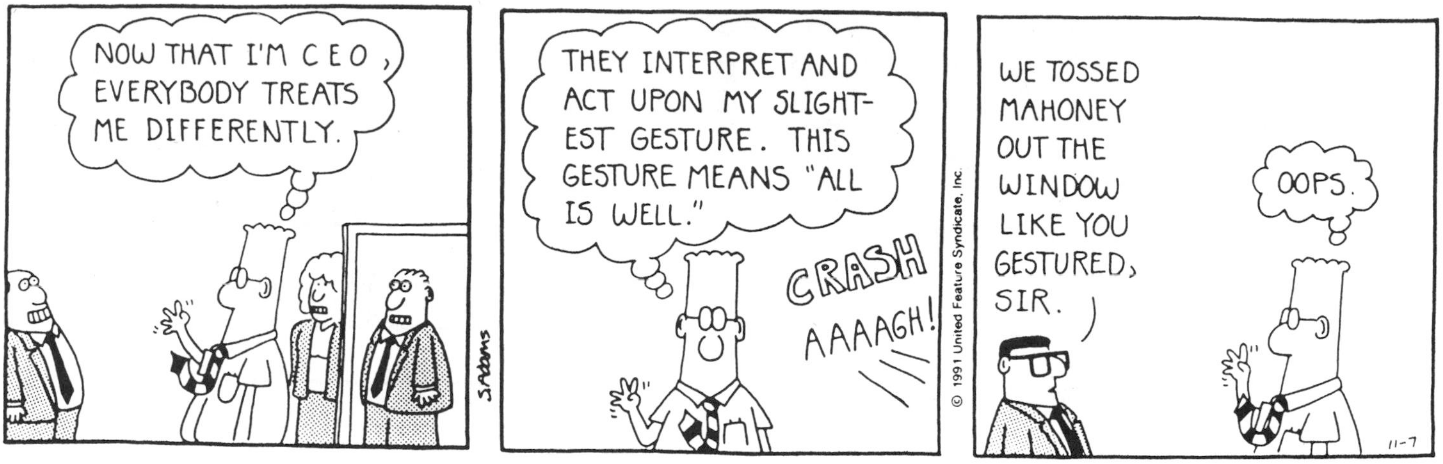
NOW THAT I'M C E O, EVERYBODY TREATS ME DIFFERENTLY.
THEY INTERPRET AND ACT UPON MY SLIGHT-EST GESTURE. THIS GESTURE MEANS "ALL IS WELL."
CRASH
AAAAGH!
© 1991 United Feature Syndicate, Inc.
WE TOSSED MAHONEY OUT THE WINDOW LIKE YOU GESTURED, SIR.
OOPS.

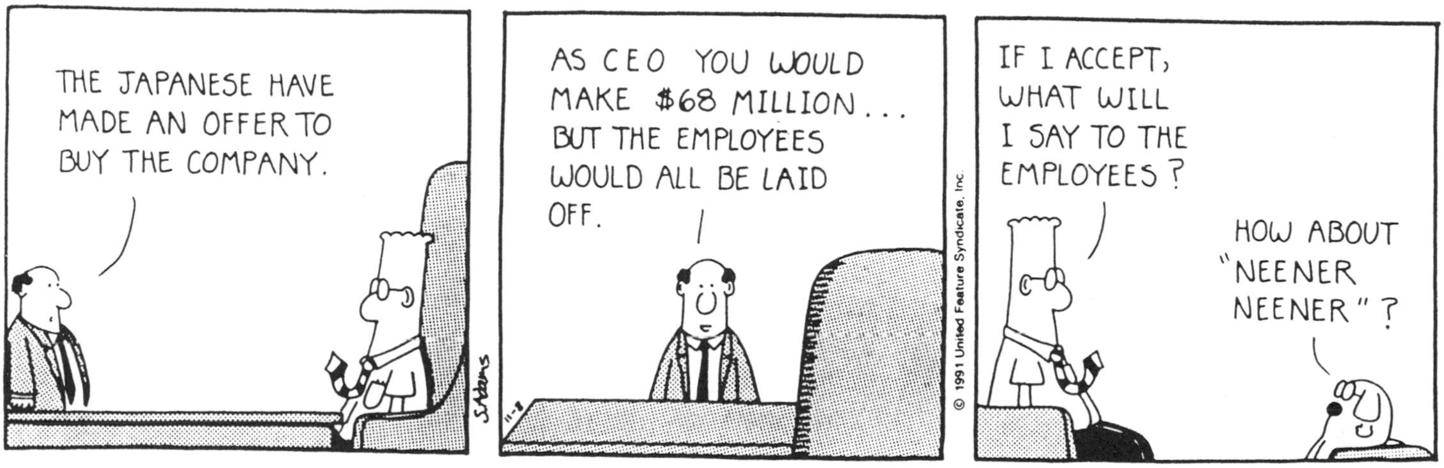
THE JAPANESE HAVE MADE AN OFFER TO BUY THE COMPANY.
AS C E O YOU WOULD MAKE $68 MILLION . . . BUT THE EMPLOYEES WOULD ALL BE LAID OFF.
© 1991 United Feature Syndicate, Inc.
IF I ACCEPT, WHAT WILL I SAY TO THE EMPLOYEES?
HOW ABOUT "NEENER NEENER"?

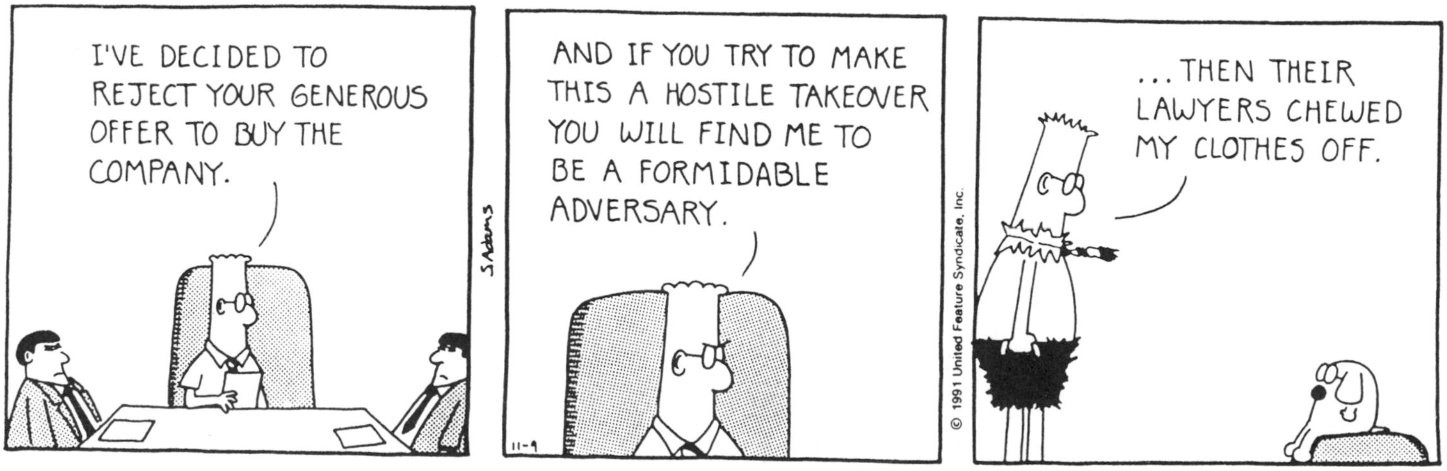
I'VE DECIDED TO REJECT YOUR GENEROUS OFFER TO BUY THE COMPANY.
AND IF YOU TRY TO MAKE THIS A HOSTILE TAKEOVER YOU WILL FIND ME TO BE A FORMIDABLE ADVERSARY.
© 1991 United Feature Syndicate, Inc.
. . . THEN THEIR LAWYERS CHEWED MY CLOTHES OFF.

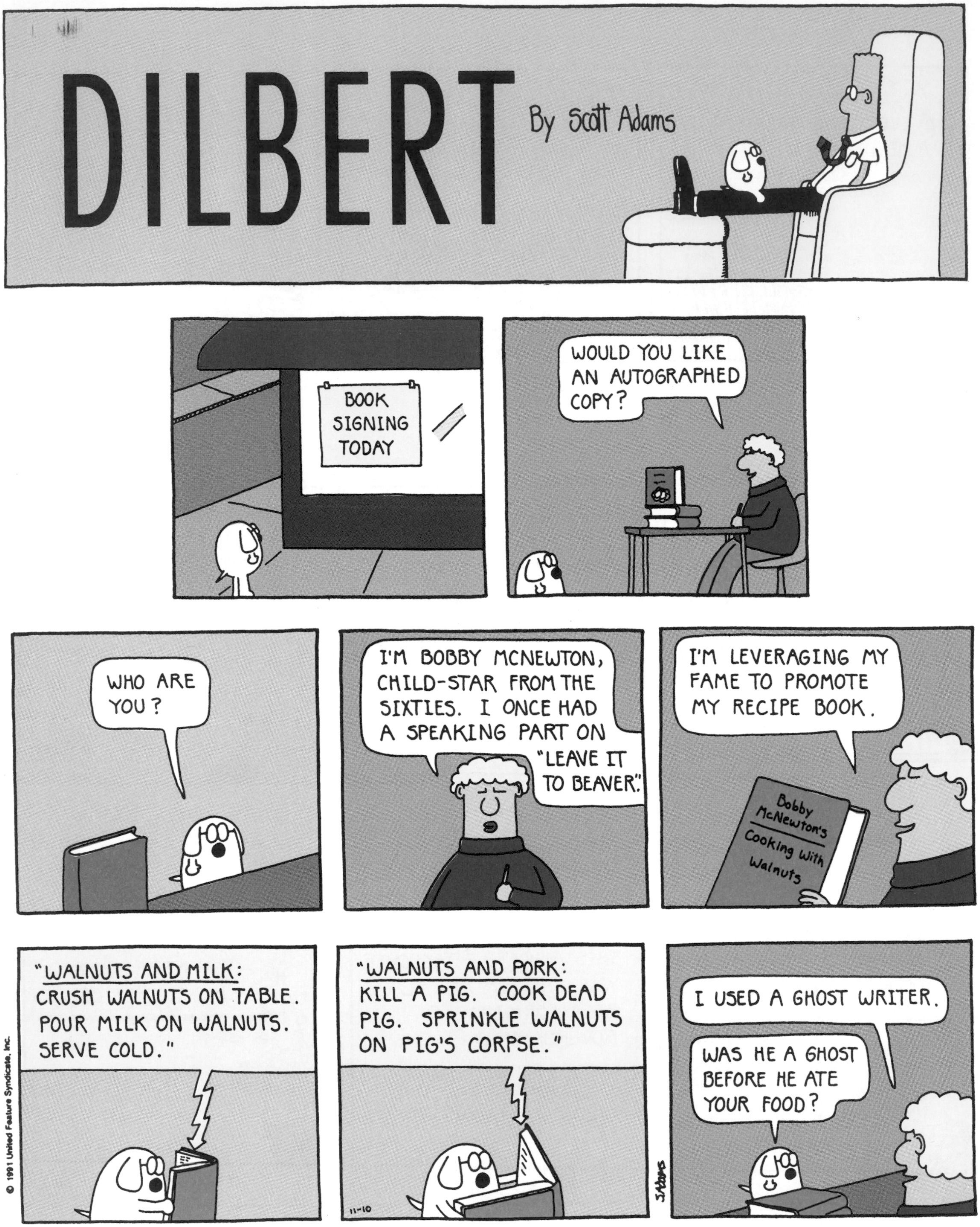
DILBERT
By Scott Adams
BOOK SIGNING TODAY
WOULD YOU LIKE AN AUTOGRAPHED COPY?
WHO ARE YOU?
I'M BOBBY MCNEWTON, CHILD-STAR FROM THE SIXTIES. I ONCE HAD A SPEAKING PART ON "LEAVE IT TO BEAVER."
I'M LEVERAGING MY FAME TO PROMOTE MY RECIPE BOOK.
Bobby McNewton's Cooking With Walnuts
"WALNUTS AND MILK: CRUSH WALNUTS ON TABLE. POUR MILK ON WALNUTS. SERVE COLD."
"WALNUTS AND PORK: KILL A PIG. COOK DEAD PIG. SPRINKLE WALNUTS ON PIG'S CORPSE."
I USED A GHOST WRITER.
WAS HE A GHOST BEFORE HE ATE YOUR FOOD?
11-10
S.ADAMS
© 1991 United Feature Syndicate, Inc.

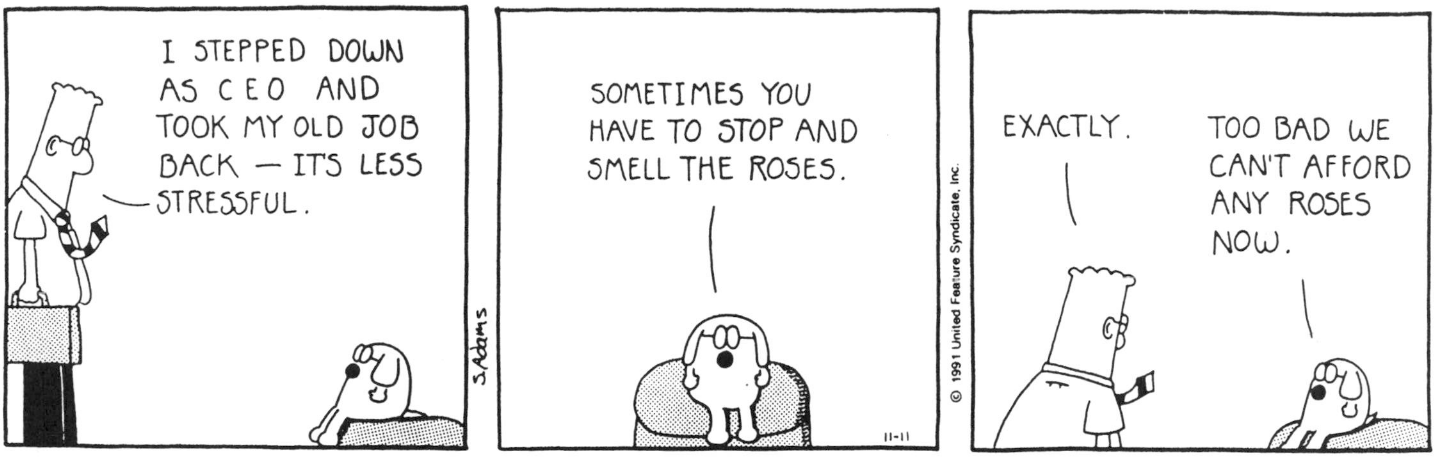
I STEPPED DOWN AS C E O AND TOOK MY OLD JOB BACK — IT'S LESS STRESSFUL.
SOMETIMES YOU HAVE TO STOP AND SMELL THE ROSES.
EXACTLY.
TOO BAD WE CAN'T AFFORD ANY ROSES NOW.
S.Adams
11-11
© 1991 United Feature Syndicate, Inc.

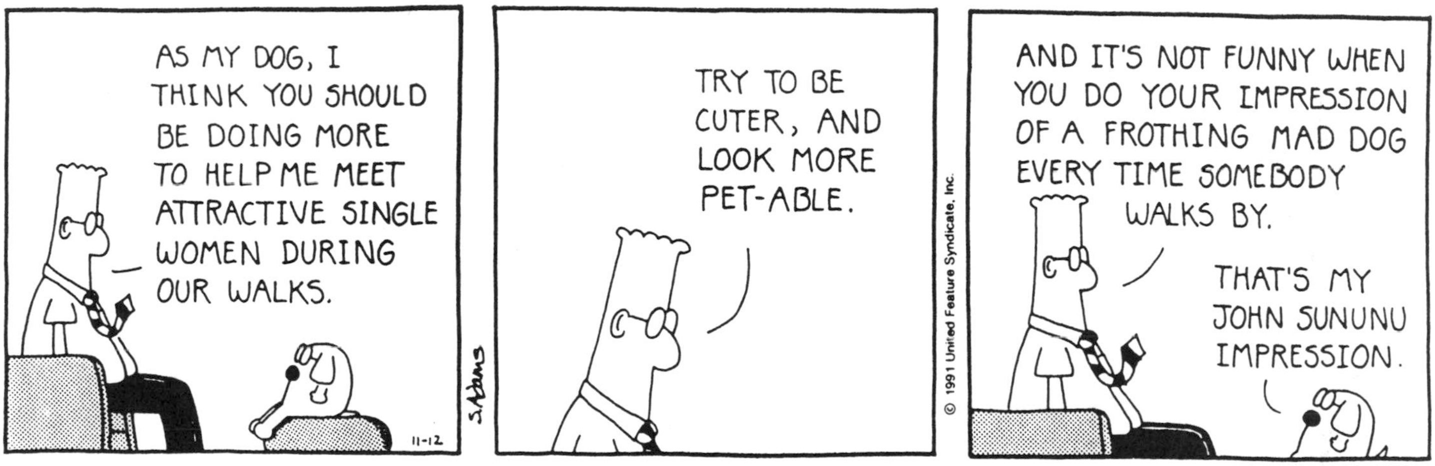
AS MY DOG, I THINK YOU SHOULD BE DOING MORE TO HELP ME MEET ATTRACTIVE SINGLE WOMEN DURING OUR WALKS.
TRY TO BE CUTER, AND LOOK MORE PET-ABLE.
AND IT'S NOT FUNNY WHEN YOU DO YOUR IMPRESSION OF A FROTHING MAD DOG EVERY TIME SOMEBODY WALKS BY.
THAT'S MY JOHN SUNUNU IMPRESSION.
11-12
S.Adams
© 1991 United Feature Syndicate, Inc.

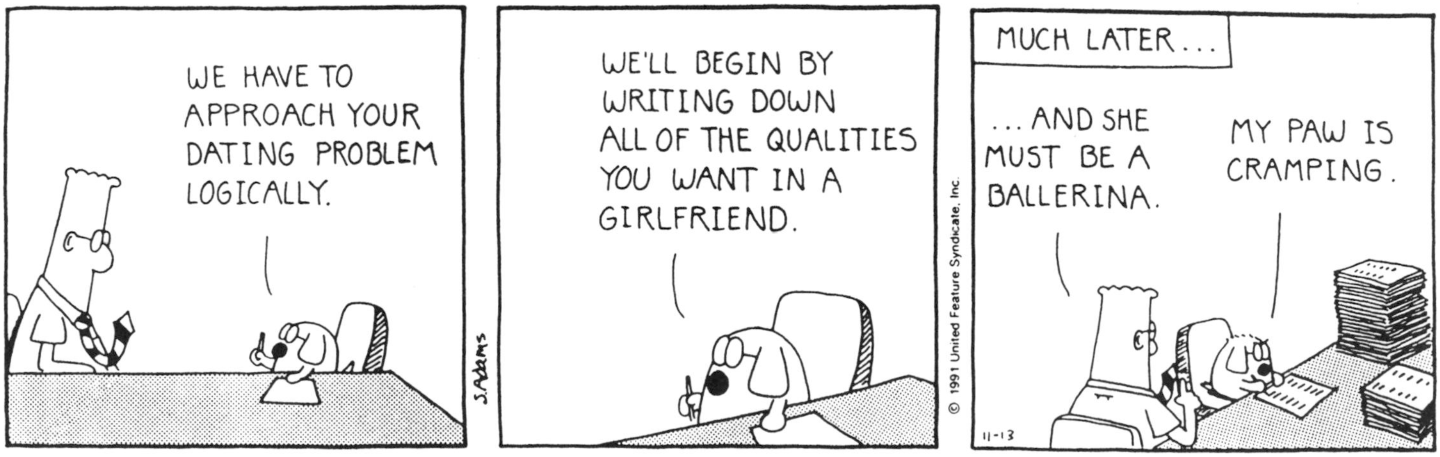
WE HAVE TO APPROACH YOUR DATING PROBLEM LOGICALLY.
WE'LL BEGIN BY WRITING DOWN ALL OF THE QUALITIES YOU WANT IN A GIRLFRIEND.
MUCH LATER...
... AND SHE MUST BE A BALLERINA.
MY PAW IS CRAMPING.
S.Adams
© 1991 United Feature Syndicate, Inc.
11-13

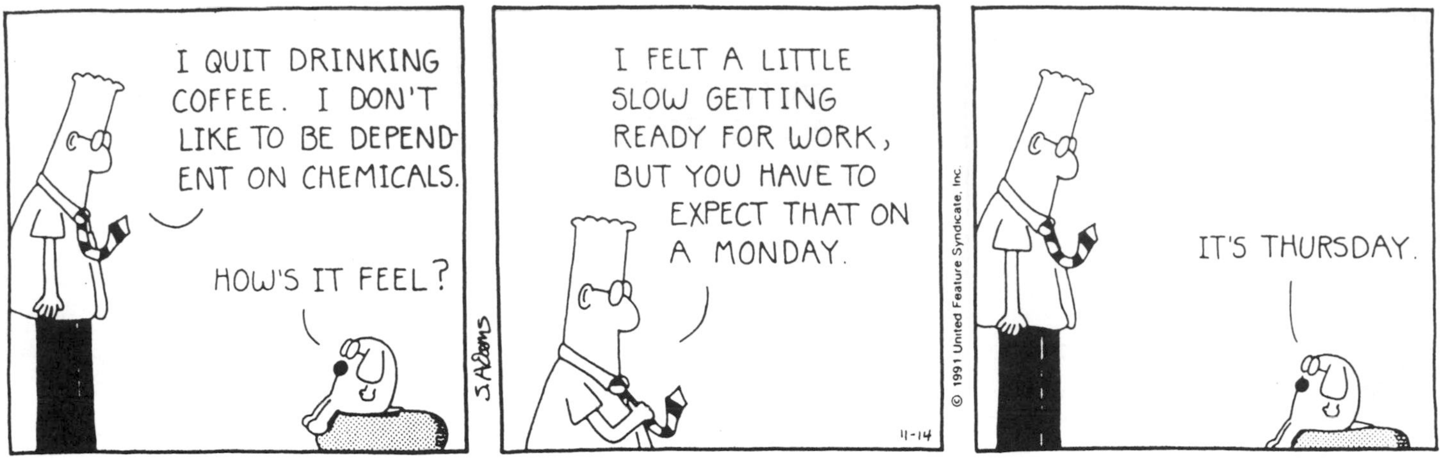
I QUIT DRINKING COFFEE. I DON'T LIKE TO BE DEPEND-ENT ON CHEMICALS.
HOW'S IT FEEL?
I FELT A LITTLE SLOW GETTING READY FOR WORK, BUT YOU HAVE TO EXPECT THAT ON A MONDAY.
11-14
© 1991 United Feature Syndicate, Inc.
IT'S THURSDAY.

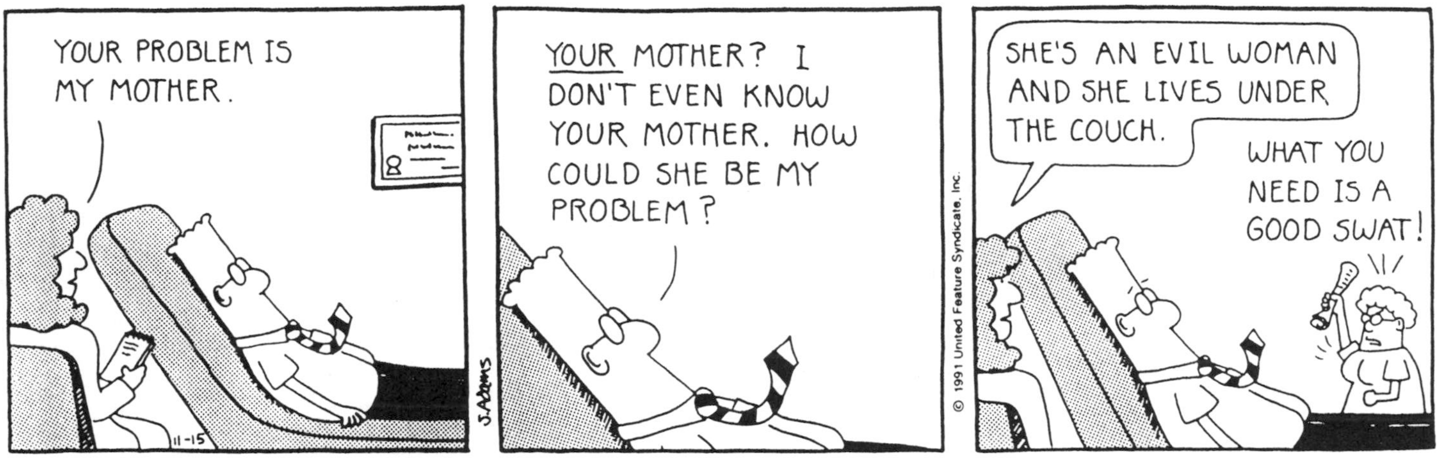
YOUR PROBLEM IS MY MOTHER.
11-15
YOUR MOTHER? I DON'T EVEN KNOW YOUR MOTHER. HOW COULD SHE BE MY PROBLEM?
© 1991 United Feature Syndicate, Inc.
SHE'S AN EVIL WOMAN AND SHE LIVES UNDER THE COUCH.
WHAT YOU NEED IS A GOOD SWAT!

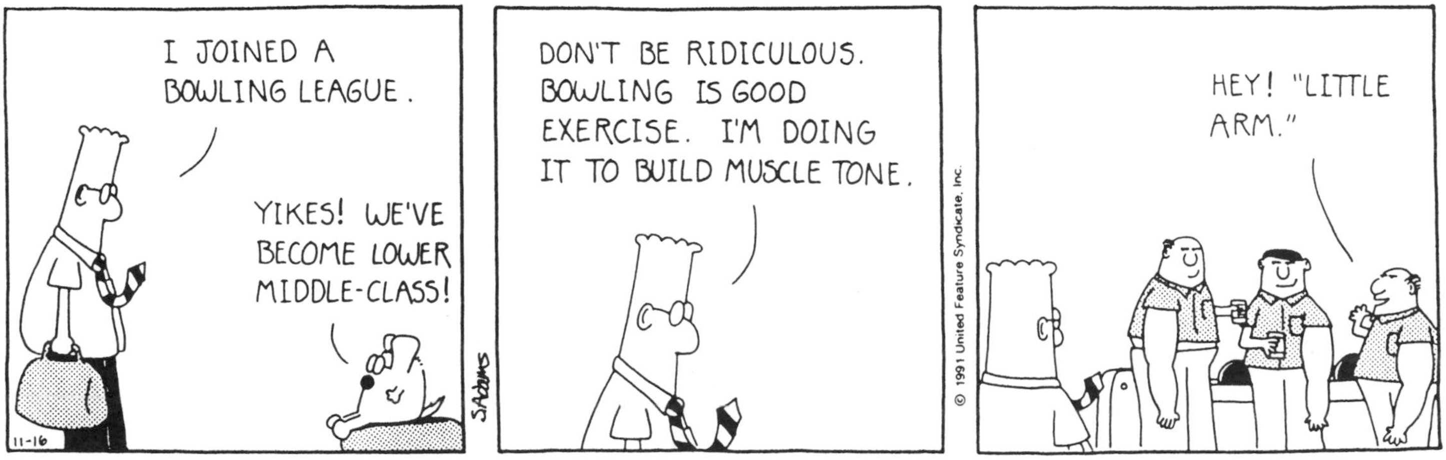
I JOINED A BOWLING LEAGUE.
YIKES! WE'VE BECOME LOWER MIDDLE-CLASS!
11-16
DON'T BE RIDICULOUS. BOWLING IS GOOD EXERCISE. I'M DOING IT TO BUILD MUSCLE TONE.
© 1991 United Feature Syndicate, Inc.
HEY! "LITTLE ARM."

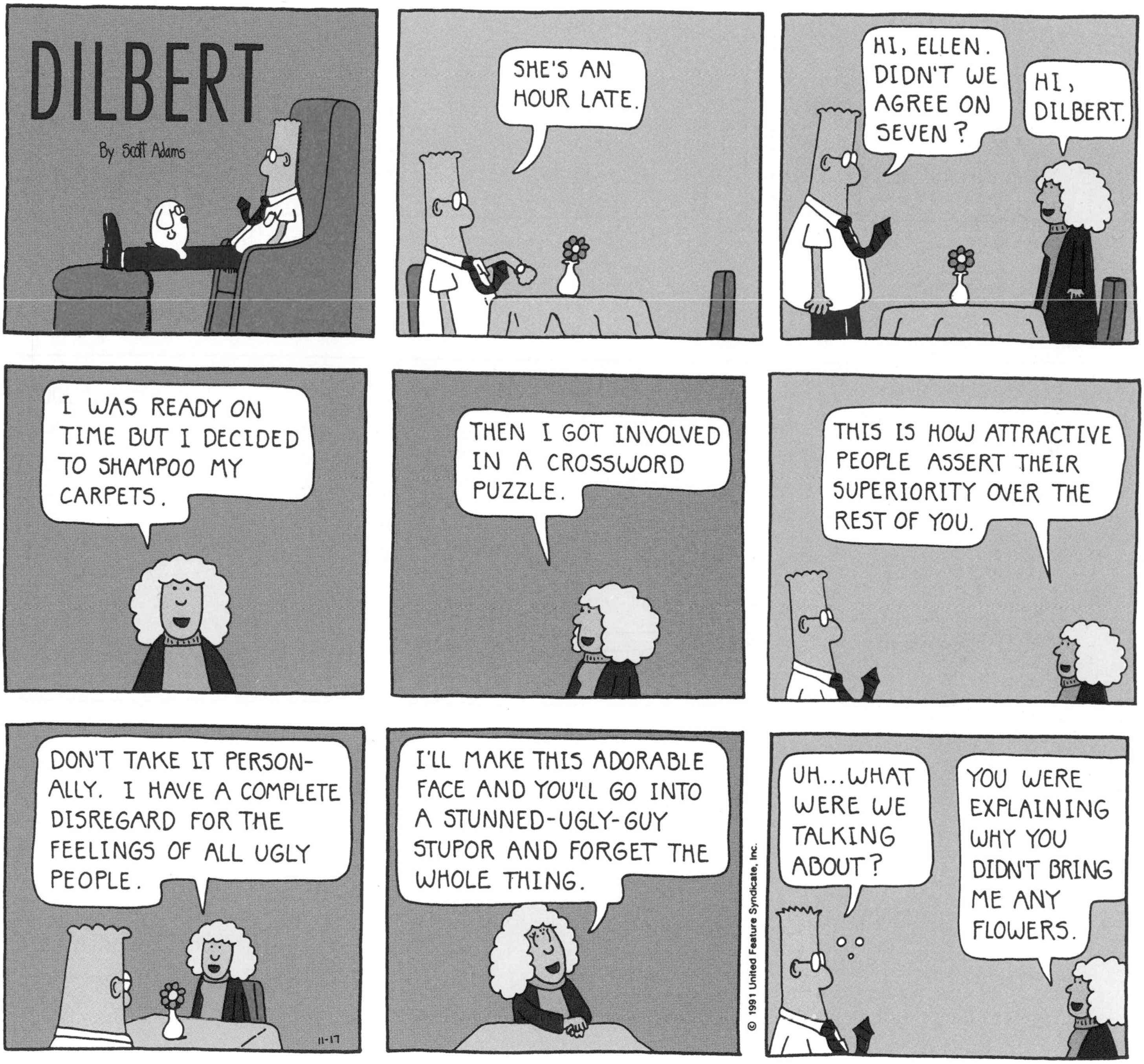
DILBERT
By Scott Adams
SHE'S AN HOUR LATE.
HI, ELLEN. DIDN'T WE AGREE ON SEVEN?
HI, DILBERT.
I WAS READY ON TIME BUT I DECIDED TO SHAMPOO MY CARPETS.
THEN I GOT INVOLVED IN A CROSSWORD PUZZLE.
THIS IS HOW ATTRACTIVE PEOPLE ASSERT THEIR SUPERIORITY OVER THE REST OF YOU.
DON'T TAKE IT PERSON-ALLY. I HAVE A COMPLETE DISREGARD FOR THE FEELINGS OF ALL UGLY PEOPLE.
S.Adams
11-17
I'LL MAKE THIS ADORABLE FACE AND YOU'LL GO INTO A STUNNED-UGLY-GUY STUPOR AND FORGET THE WHOLE THING.
© 1991 United Feature Syndicate, Inc.
UH...WHAT WERE WE TALKING ABOUT?
YOU WERE EXPLAINING WHY YOU DIDN'T BRING ME ANY FLOWERS.

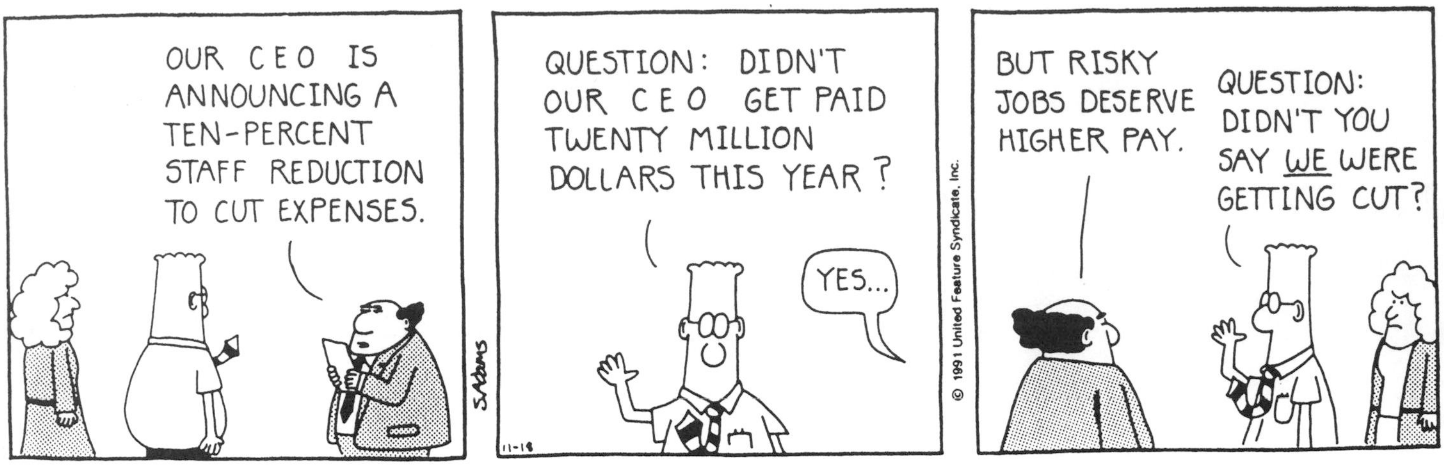
OUR C E O IS ANNOUNCING A TEN-PERCENT STAFF REDUCTION TO CUT EXPENSES.
S.Adams
11-18
QUESTION: DIDN'T OUR C E O GET PAID TWENTY MILLION DOLLARS THIS YEAR?
YES...
© 1991 United Feature Syndicate, Inc.
BUT RISKY JOBS DESERVE HIGHER PAY.
QUESTION: DIDN'T YOU SAY WE WERE GETTING CUT?

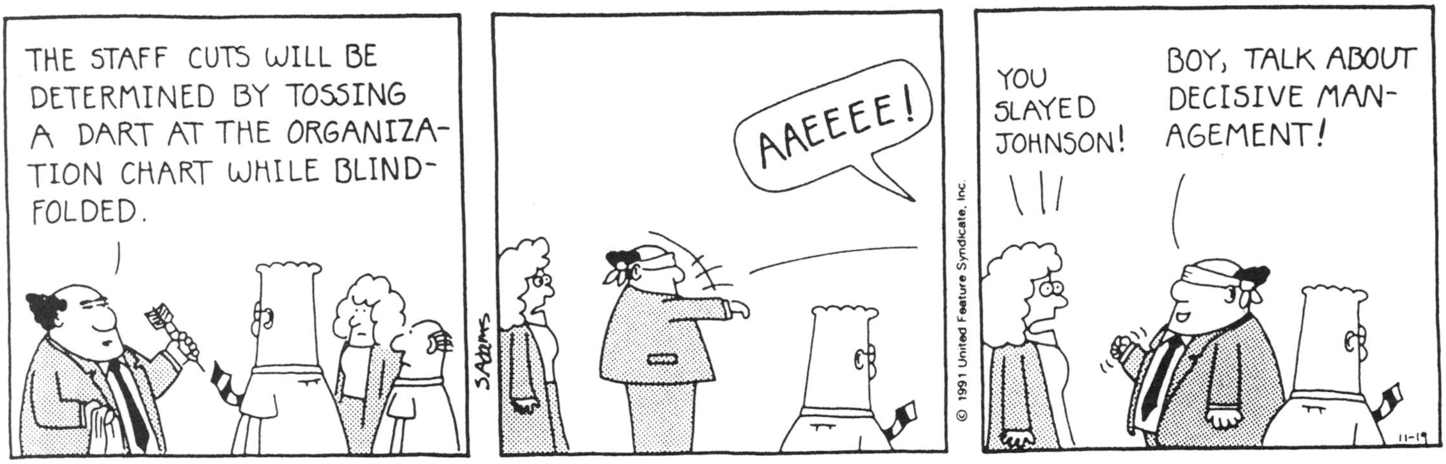
THE STAFF CUTS WILL BE DETERMINED BY TOSSING A DART AT THE ORGANIZATION CHART WHILE BLINDFOLDED.
S.Adams
AAEEEE!
© 1991 United Feature Syndicate, Inc.
YOU SLAYED JOHNSON!
BOY, TALK ABOUT DECISIVE MANAGEMENT!
11-19

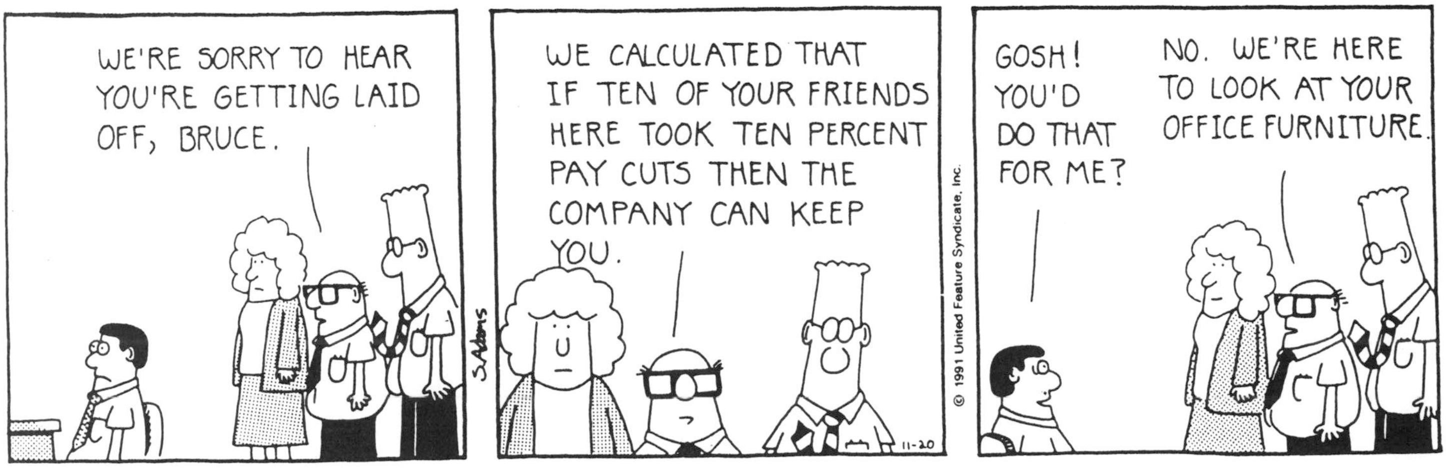
WE'RE SORRY TO HEAR YOU'RE GETTING LAID OFF, BRUCE.
S.Adams
WE CALCULATED THAT IF TEN OF YOUR FRIENDS HERE TOOK TEN PERCENT PAY CUTS THEN THE COMPANY CAN KEEP YOU.
11-20
© 1991 United Feature Syndicate, Inc.
GOSH! YOU'D DO THAT FOR ME?
NO. WE'RE HERE TO LOOK AT YOUR OFFICE FURNITURE.

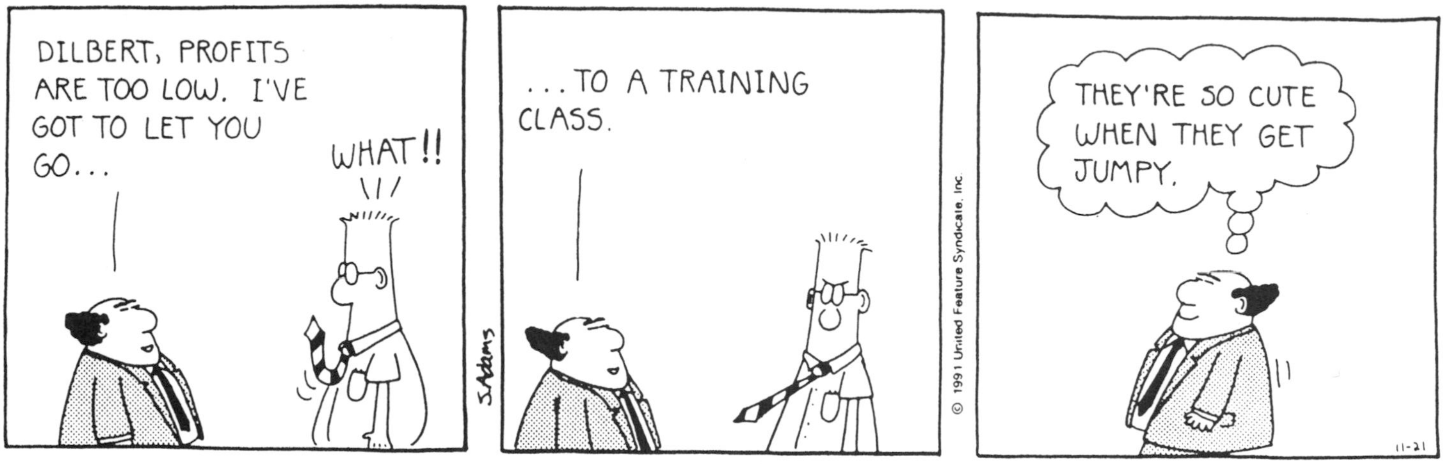
DILBERT, PROFITS ARE TOO LOW. I'VE GOT TO LET YOU GO...
WHAT!!
...TO A TRAINING CLASS.
© 1991 United Feature Syndicate, Inc.
THEY'RE SO CUTE WHEN THEY GET JUMPY.

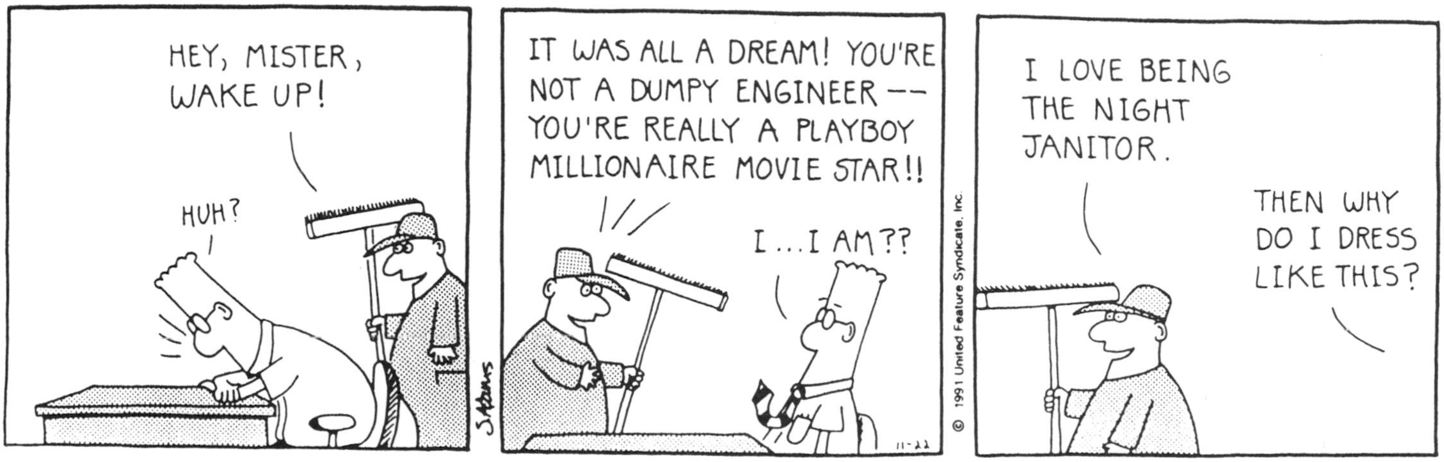
HEY, MISTER, WAKE UP!
HUH?
IT WAS ALL A DREAM! YOU'RE NOT A DUMPY ENGINEER -- YOU'RE REALLY A PLAYBOY MILLIONAIRE MOVIE STAR!!
I...I AM??
© 1991 United Feature Syndicate, Inc.
I LOVE BEING THE NIGHT JANITOR.
THEN WHY DO I DRESS LIKE THIS?

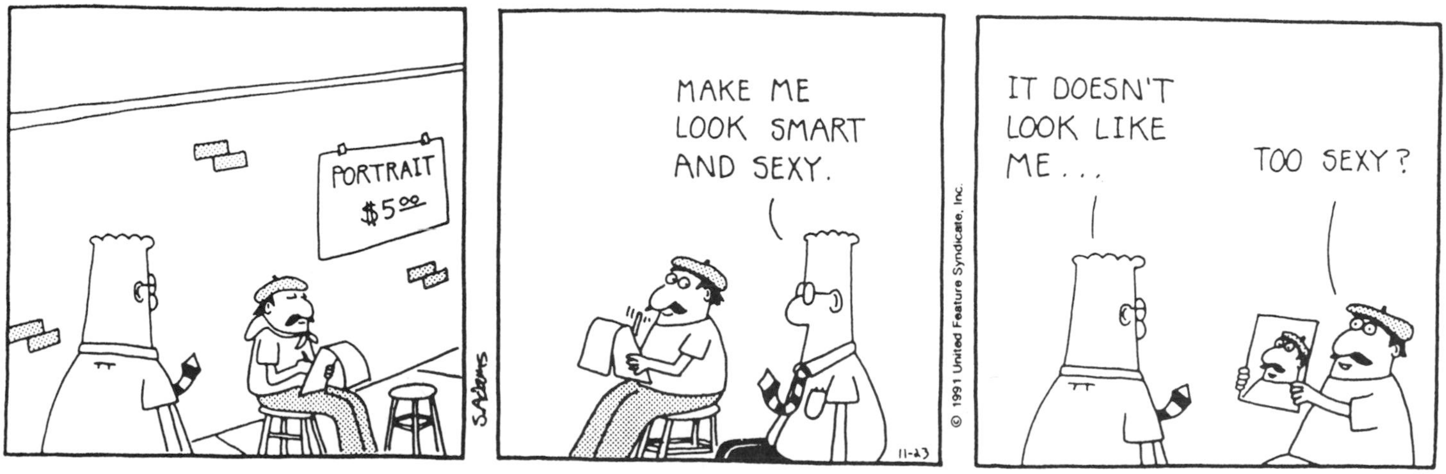
PORTRAIT $5.00
MAKE ME LOOK SMART AND SEXY.
© 1991 United Feature Syndicate, Inc.
IT DOESN'T LOOK LIKE ME...
TOO SEXY?

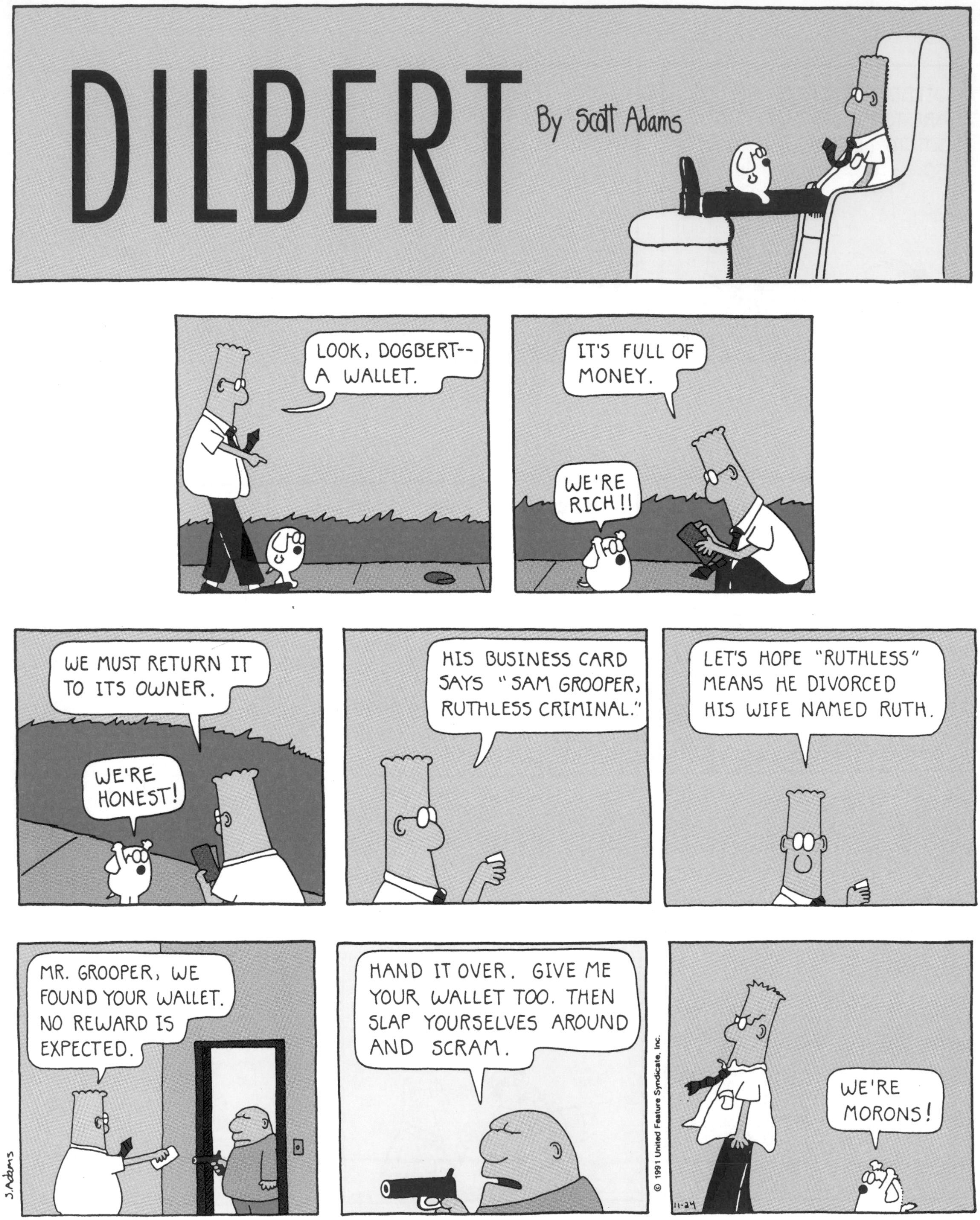
DILBERT
By Scott Adams
LOOK, DOGBERT-- A WALLET.
IT'S FULL OF MONEY.
WE'RE RICH!!
WE MUST RETURN IT TO ITS OWNER.
WE'RE HONEST!
HIS BUSINESS CARD SAYS "SAM GROOPER, RUTHLESS CRIMINAL."
LET'S HOPE "RUTHLESS" MEANS HE DIVORCED HIS WIFE NAMED RUTH.
MR. GROOPER, WE FOUND YOUR WALLET. NO REWARD IS EXPECTED.
HAND IT OVER. GIVE ME YOUR WALLET TOO. THEN SLAP YOURSELVES AROUND AND SCRAM.
WE'RE MORONS!
S. Adams
© 1991 United Feature Syndicate, Inc.
11-24

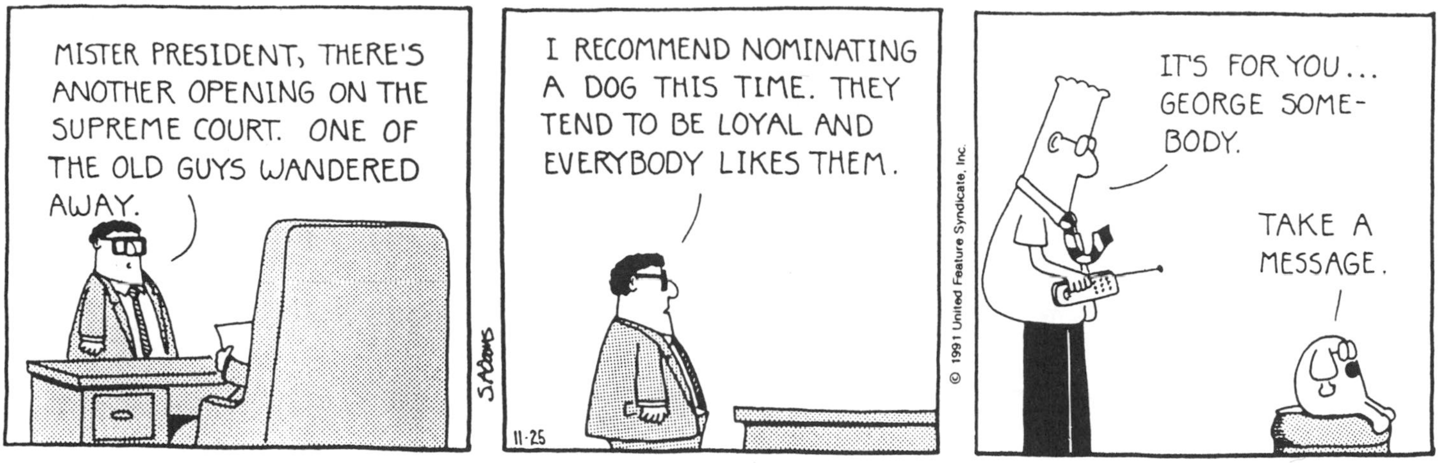
MISTER PRESIDENT, THERE'S ANOTHER OPENING ON THE SUPREME COURT. ONE OF THE OLD GUYS WANDERED AWAY.
S.ADAMS
I RECOMMEND NOMINATING A DOG THIS TIME. THEY TEND TO BE LOYAL AND EVERYBODY LIKES THEM.
11-25
© 1991 United Feature Syndicate, Inc.
IT'S FOR YOU... GEORGE SOME-BODY.
TAKE A MESSAGE.

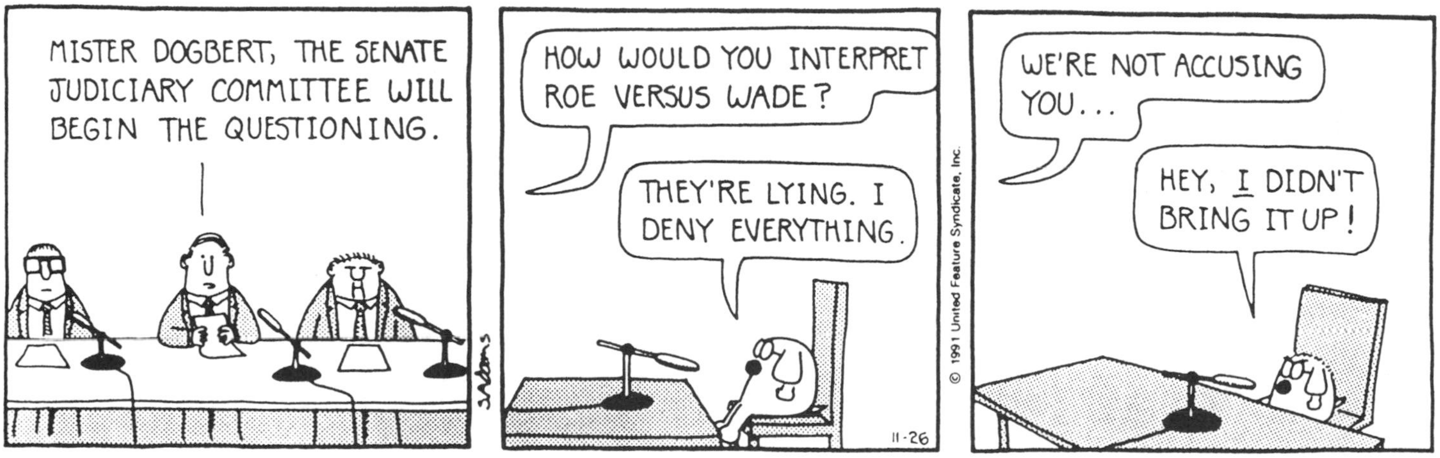
MISTER DOGBERT, THE SENATE JUDICIARY COMMITTEE WILL BEGIN THE QUESTIONING.
S.ADAMS
HOW WOULD YOU INTERPRET ROE VERSUS WADE?
THEY'RE LYING. I DENY EVERYTHING.
11-26
© 1991 United Feature Syndicate, Inc.
WE'RE NOT ACCUSING YOU...
HEY, I DIDN'T BRING IT UP!

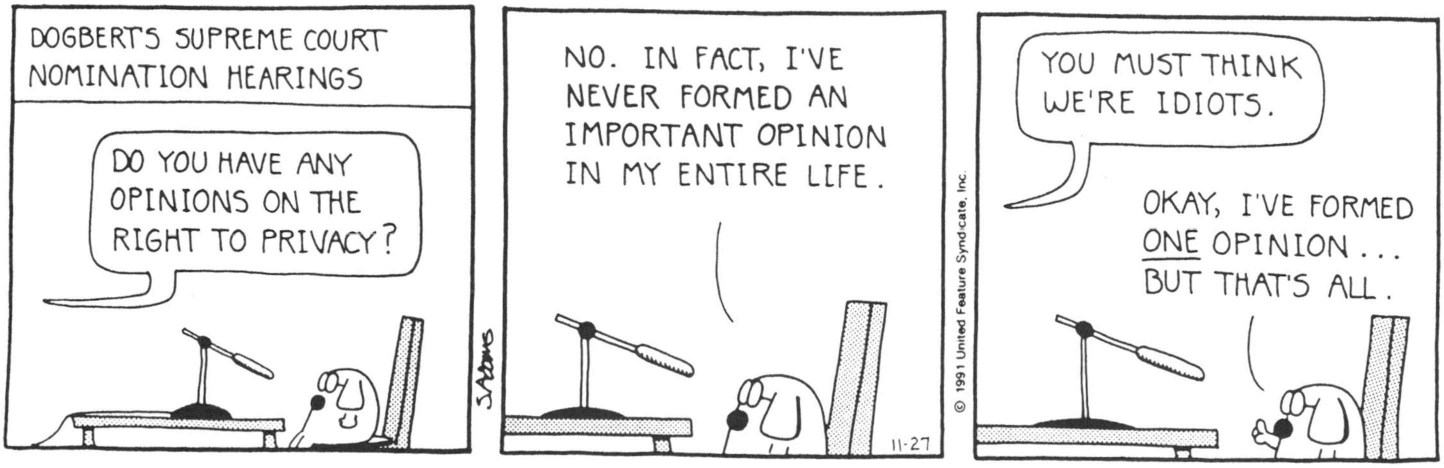
DOGBERT'S SUPREME COURT NOMINATION HEARINGS
DO YOU HAVE ANY OPINIONS ON THE RIGHT TO PRIVACY?
S.ADAMS
NO. IN FACT, I'VE NEVER FORMED AN IMPORTANT OPINION IN MY ENTIRE LIFE.
11-27
© 1991 United Feature Syndicate, Inc.
YOU MUST THINK WE'RE IDIOTS.
OKAY, I'VE FORMED ONE OPINION... BUT THAT'S ALL.

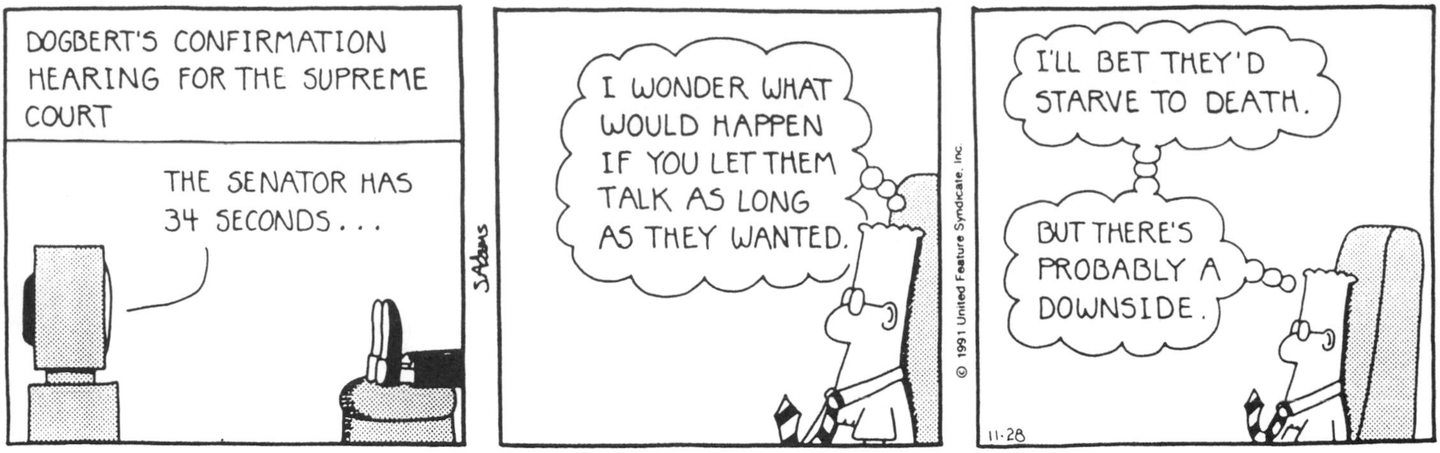
DOGBERT'S CONFIRMATION HEARING FOR THE SUPREME COURT
THE SENATOR HAS 34 SECONDS...
I WONDER WHAT WOULD HAPPEN IF YOU LET THEM TALK AS LONG AS THEY WANTED.
I'LL BET THEY'D STARVE TO DEATH.
BUT THERE'S PROBABLY A DOWNSIDE.
© 1991 United Feature Syndicate, Inc.

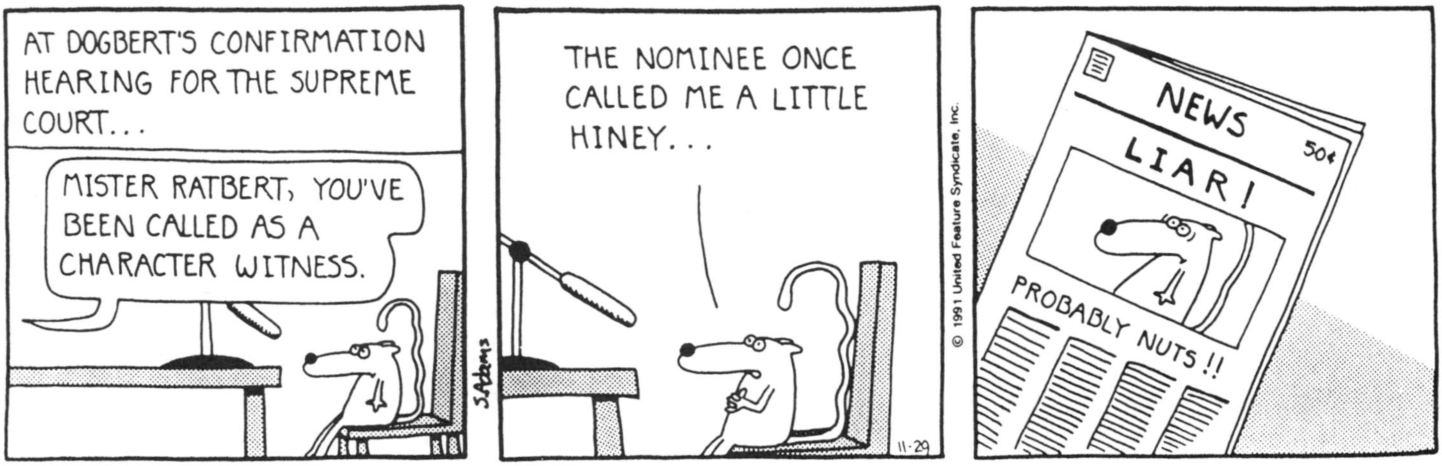
AT DOGBERT'S CONFIRMATION HEARING FOR THE SUPREME COURT...
MISTER RATBERT, YOU'VE BEEN CALLED AS A CHARACTER WITNESS.
THE NOMINEE ONCE CALLED ME A LITTLE HINEY...
NEWS
50¢
LIAR!
PROBABLY NUTS!!
© 1991 United Feature Syndicate, Inc.

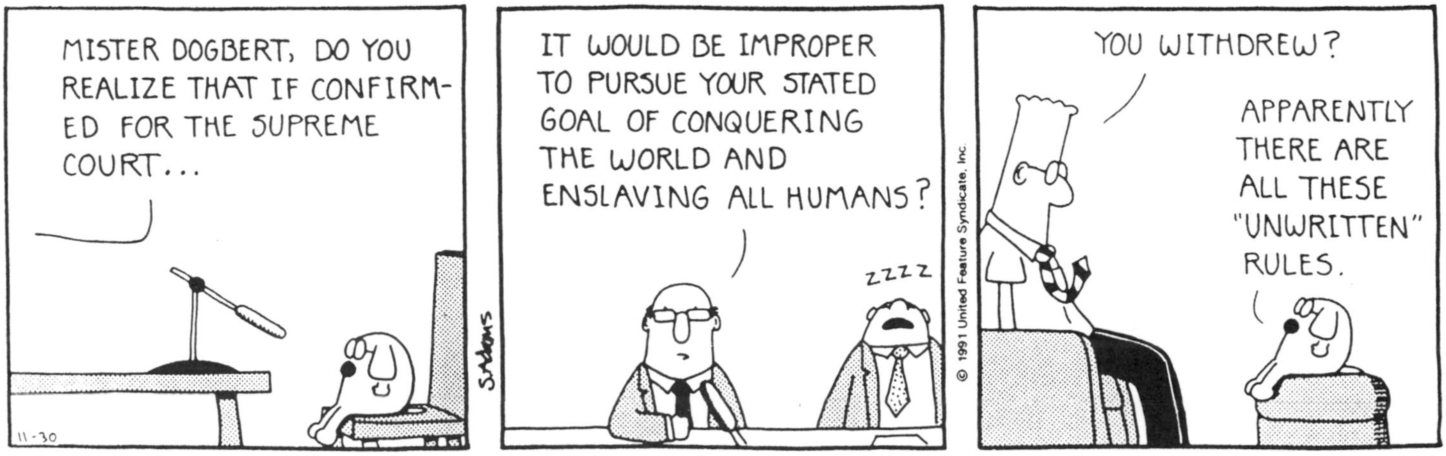
MISTER DOGBERT, DO YOU REALIZE THAT IF CONFIRMED FOR THE SUPREME COURT...
IT WOULD BE IMPROPER TO PURSUE YOUR STATED GOAL OF CONQUERING THE WORLD AND ENSLAVING ALL HUMANS?
ZZZZ
YOU WITHDREW?
APPARENTLY THERE ARE ALL THESE "UNWRITTEN" RULES.
© 1991 United Feature Syndicate, Inc.

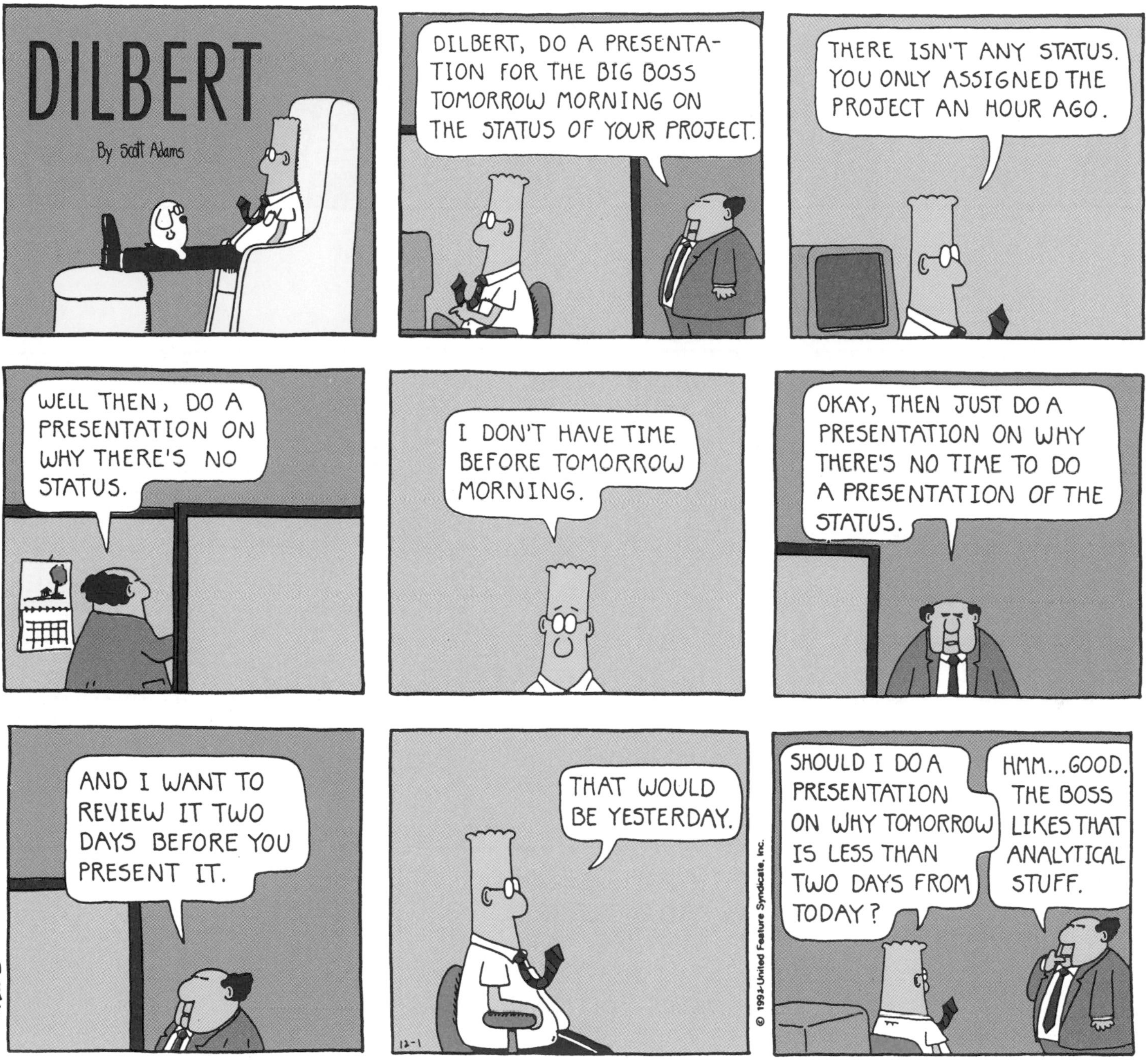
DILBERT
By Scott Adams
DILBERT, DO A PRESENTATION FOR THE BIG BOSS TOMORROW MORNING ON THE STATUS OF YOUR PROJECT.
THERE ISN'T ANY STATUS. YOU ONLY ASSIGNED THE PROJECT AN HOUR AGO.
WELL THEN, DO A PRESENTATION ON WHY THERE'S NO STATUS.
I DON'T HAVE TIME BEFORE TOMORROW MORNING.
OKAY, THEN JUST DO A PRESENTATION ON WHY THERE'S NO TIME TO DO A PRESENTATION OF THE STATUS.
AND I WANT TO REVIEW IT TWO DAYS BEFORE YOU PRESENT IT.
THAT WOULD BE YESTERDAY.
SHOULD I DO A PRESENTATION ON WHY TOMORROW IS LESS THAN TWO DAYS FROM TODAY?
HMM...GOOD. THE BOSS LIKES THAT ANALYTICAL STUFF.
© 1992 United Feature Syndicate, Inc.

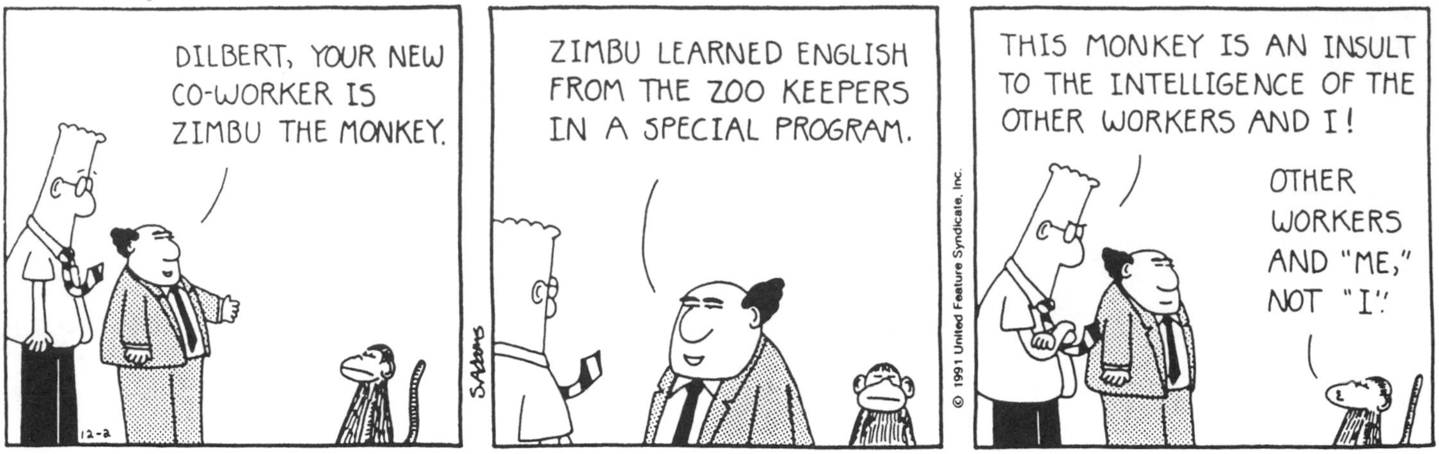
DILBERT, YOUR NEW CO-WORKER IS ZIMBU THE MONKEY.
ZIMBU LEARNED ENGLISH FROM THE ZOO KEEPERS IN A SPECIAL PROGRAM.
THIS MONKEY IS AN INSULT TO THE INTELLIGENCE OF THE OTHER WORKERS AND I!
OTHER WORKERS AND "ME," NOT "I."
© 1991 United Feature Syndicate, Inc.

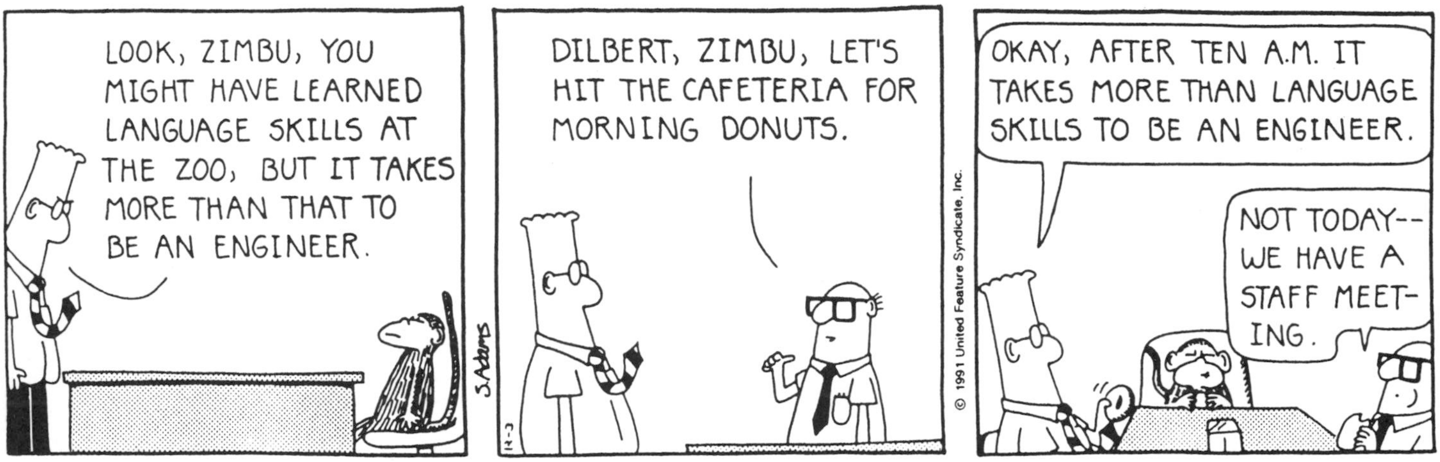
LOOK, ZIMBU, YOU MIGHT HAVE LEARNED LANGUAGE SKILLS AT THE ZOO, BUT IT TAKES MORE THAN THAT TO BE AN ENGINEER.
DILBERT, ZIMBU, LET'S HIT THE CAFETERIA FOR MORNING DONUTS.
OKAY, AFTER TEN A.M. IT TAKES MORE THAN LANGUAGE SKILLS TO BE AN ENGINEER.
NOT TODAY-- WE HAVE A STAFF MEET-ING.
© 1991 United Feature Syndicate, Inc.

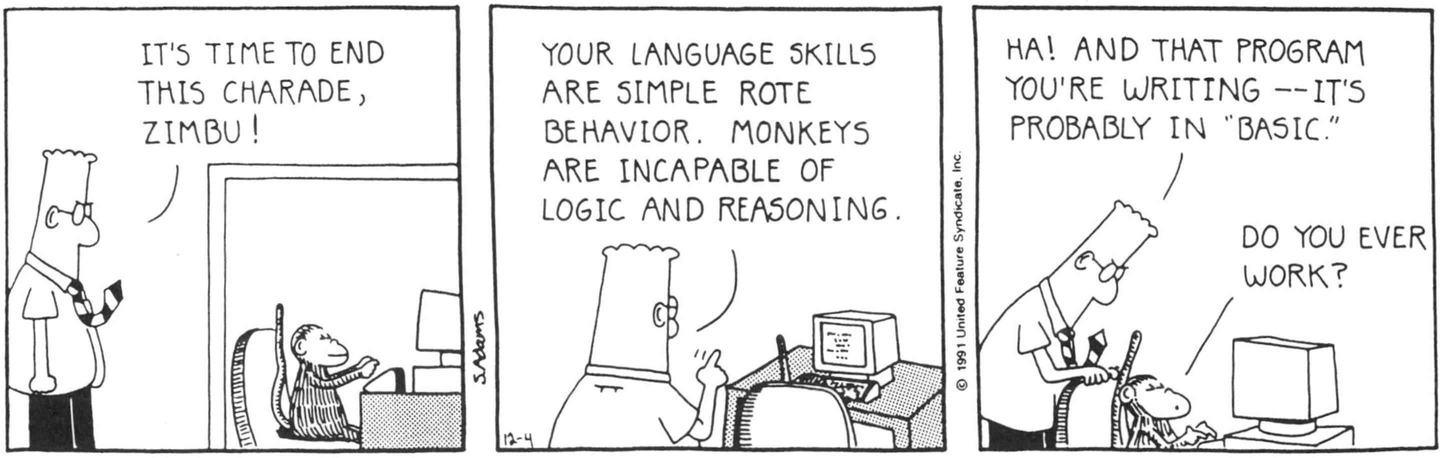
IT'S TIME TO END THIS CHARADE, ZIMBU!
YOUR LANGUAGE SKILLS ARE SIMPLE ROTE BEHAVIOR. MONKEYS ARE INCAPABLE OF LOGIC AND REASONING.
HA! AND THAT PROGRAM YOU'RE WRITING --IT'S PROBABLY IN "BASIC."
DO YOU EVER WORK?
© 1991 United Feature Syndicate, Inc.

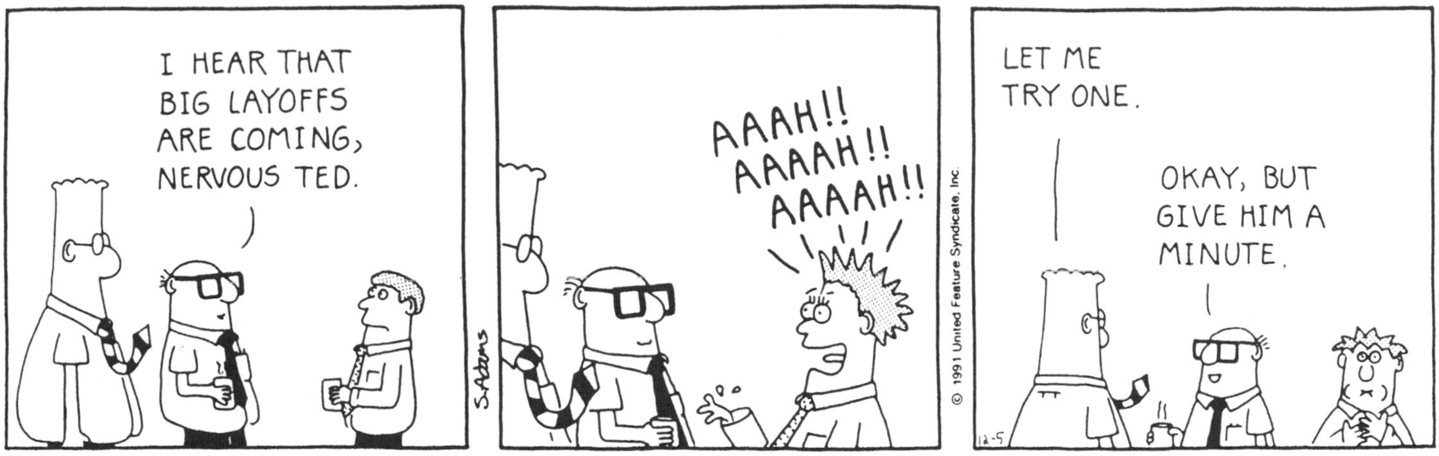
I HEAR THAT BIG LAYOFFS ARE COMING, NERVOUS TED.
AAAH!! AAAAH!! AAAAH!!
LET ME TRY ONE.
OKAY, BUT GIVE HIM A MINUTE.
© 1991 United Feature Syndicate, Inc.

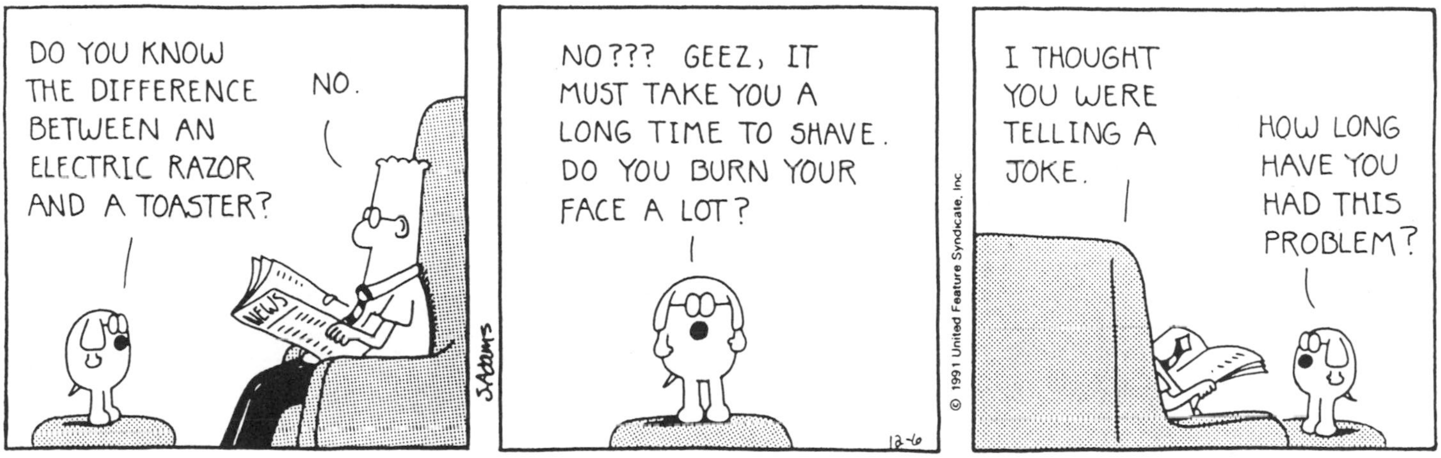
DO YOU KNOW THE DIFFERENCE BETWEEN AN ELECTRIC RAZOR AND A TOASTER?
NO.
NEWS
NO??? GEEZ, IT MUST TAKE YOU A LONG TIME TO SHAVE. DO YOU BURN YOUR FACE A LOT?
I THOUGHT YOU WERE TELLING A JOKE.
HOW LONG HAVE YOU HAD THIS PROBLEM?
© 1991 United Feature Syndicate, Inc.

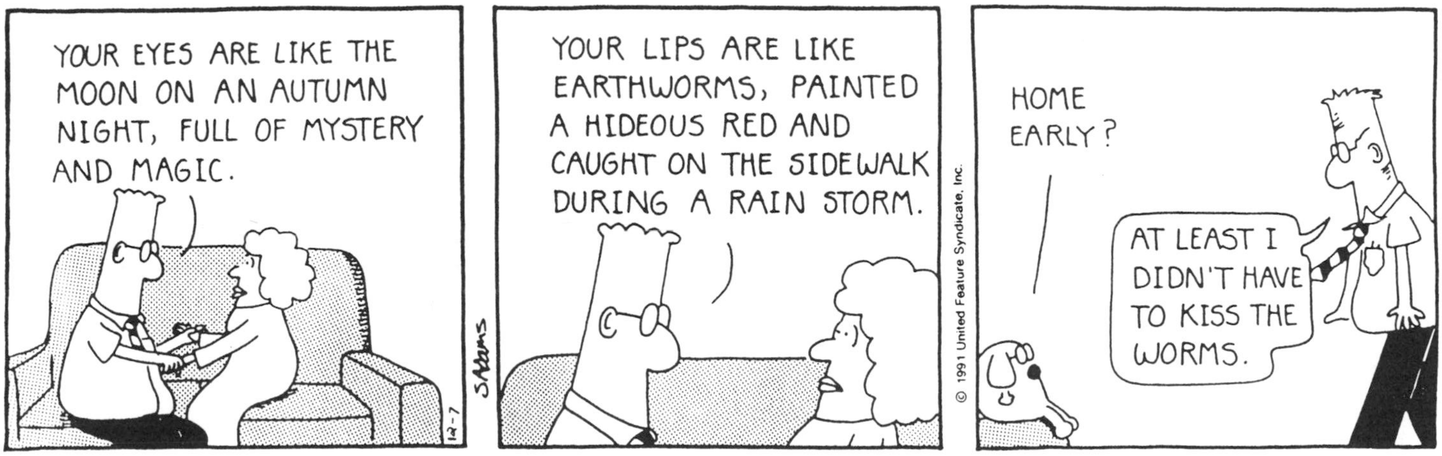
YOUR EYES ARE LIKE THE MOON ON AN AUTUMN NIGHT, FULL OF MYSTERY AND MAGIC.
YOUR LIPS ARE LIKE EARTHWORMS, PAINTED A HIDEOUS RED AND CAUGHT ON THE SIDEWALK DURING A RAIN STORM.
HOME EARLY?
AT LEAST I DIDN'T HAVE TO KISS THE WORMS.
© 1991 United Feature Syndicate, Inc.

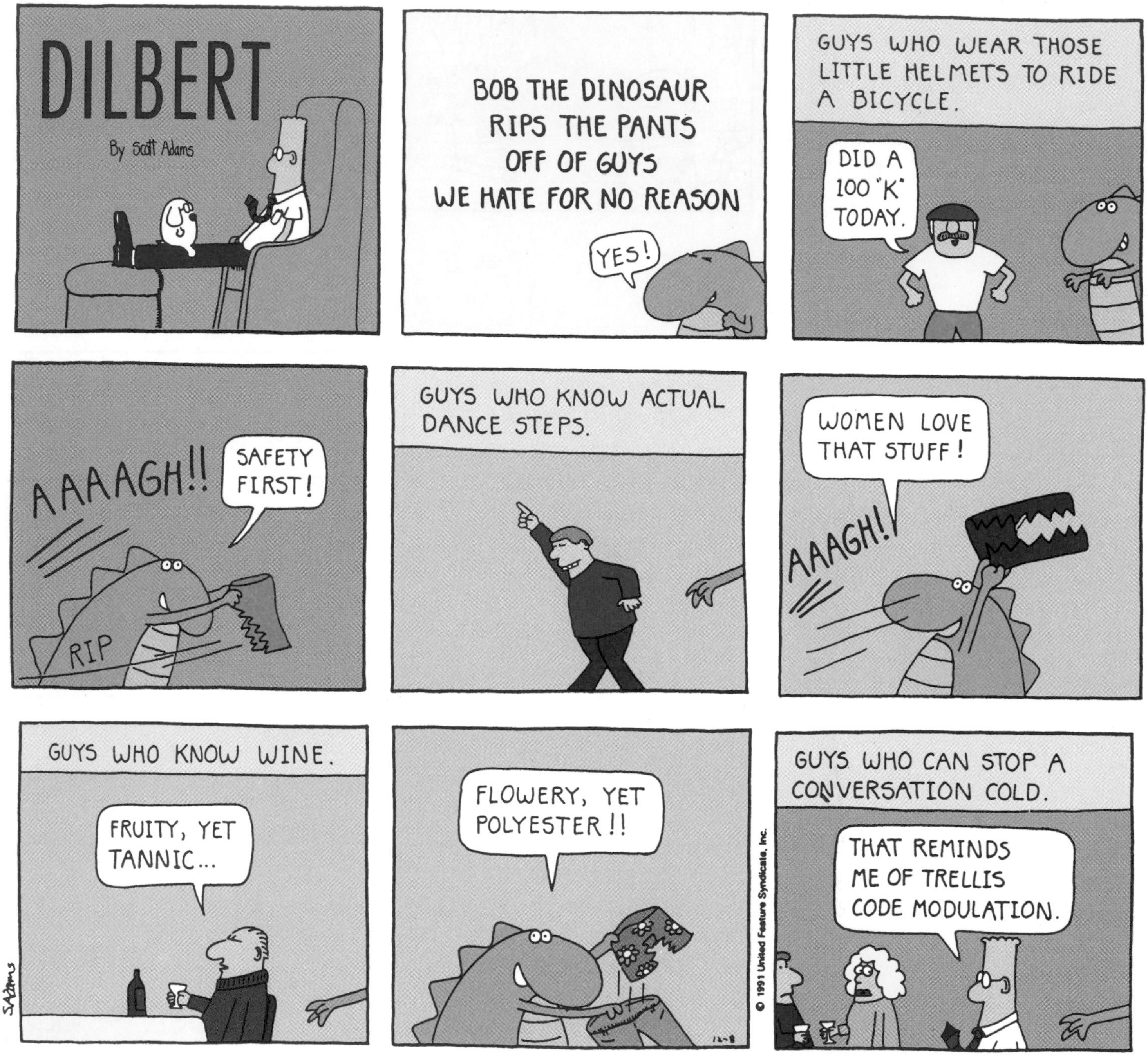
DILBERT
By Scott Adams
BOB THE DINOSAUR RIPS THE PANTS OFF OF GUYS WE HATE FOR NO REASON
YES!
GUYS WHO WEAR THOSE LITTLE HELMETS TO RIDE A BICYCLE.
DID A 100 "K" TODAY.
AAAAGH!!
SAFETY FIRST!
RIP
GUYS WHO KNOW ACTUAL DANCE STEPS.
WOMEN LOVE THAT STUFF!
AAAGH!
GUYS WHO KNOW WINE.
FRUITY, YET TANNIC...
FLOWERY, YET POLYESTER!!
GUYS WHO CAN STOP A CONVERSATION COLD.
THAT REMINDS ME OF TRELLIS CODE MODULATION.
© 1991 United Feature Syndicate, Inc.

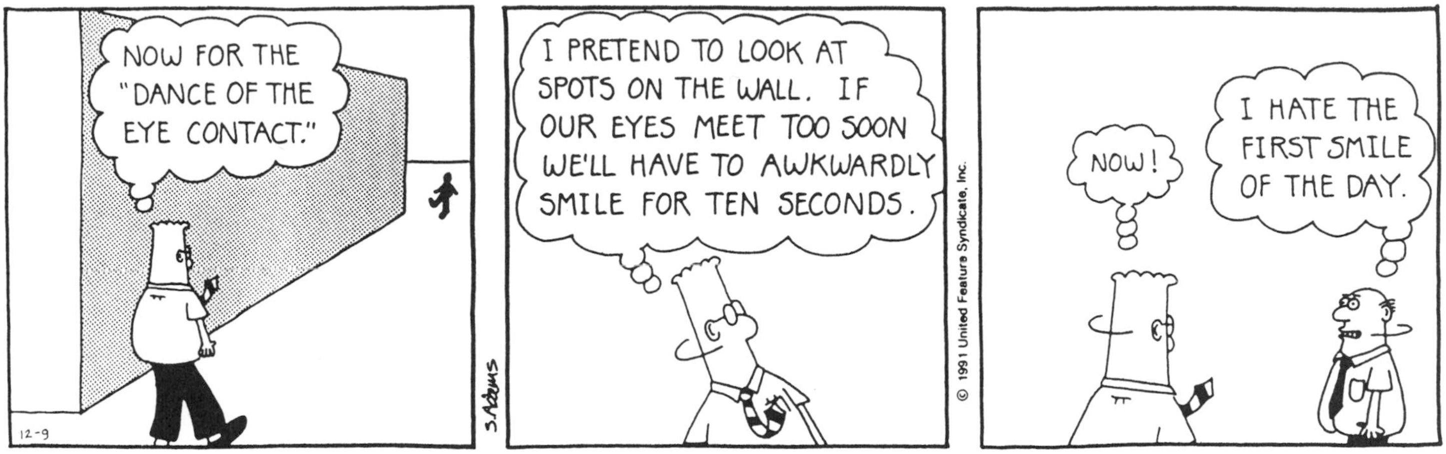
NOW FOR THE "DANCE OF THE EYE CONTACT."
I PRETEND TO LOOK AT SPOTS ON THE WALL. IF OUR EYES MEET TOO SOON WE'LL HAVE TO AWKWARDLY SMILE FOR TEN SECONDS.
NOW!
I HATE THE FIRST SMILE OF THE DAY.
© 1991 United Feature Syndicate, Inc.

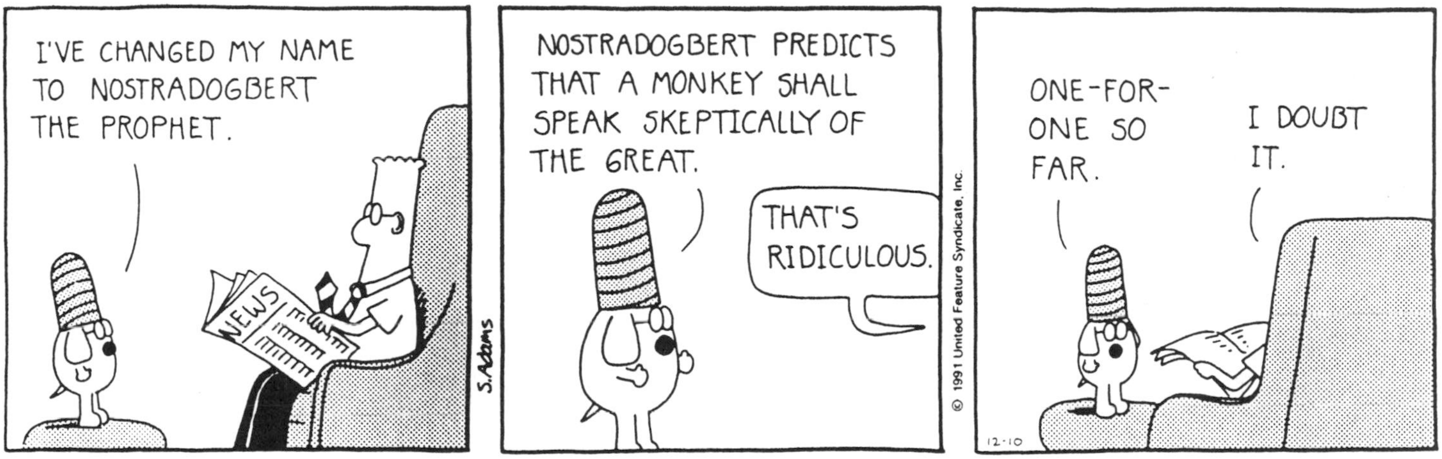
I'VE CHANGED MY NAME TO NOSTRADOGBERT THE PROPHET.
NEWS
NOSTRADOGBERT PREDICTS THAT A MONKEY SHALL SPEAK SKEPTICALLY OF THE GREAT.
THAT'S RIDICULOUS.
ONE-FOR-ONE SO FAR.
I DOUBT IT.
© 1991 United Feature Syndicate, Inc.

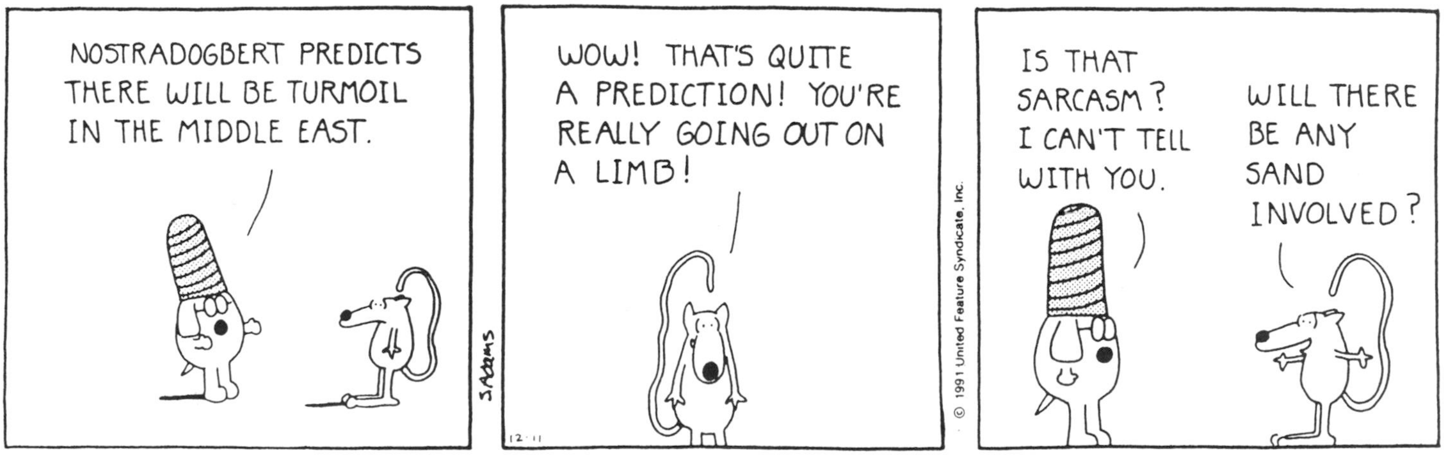
NOSTRADOGBERT PREDICTS THERE WILL BE TURMOIL IN THE MIDDLE EAST.
WOW! THAT'S QUITE A PREDICTION! YOU'RE REALLY GOING OUT ON A LIMB!
IS THAT SARCASM? I CAN'T TELL WITH YOU.
WILL THERE BE ANY SAND INVOLVED?
© 1991 United Feature Syndicate, Inc.

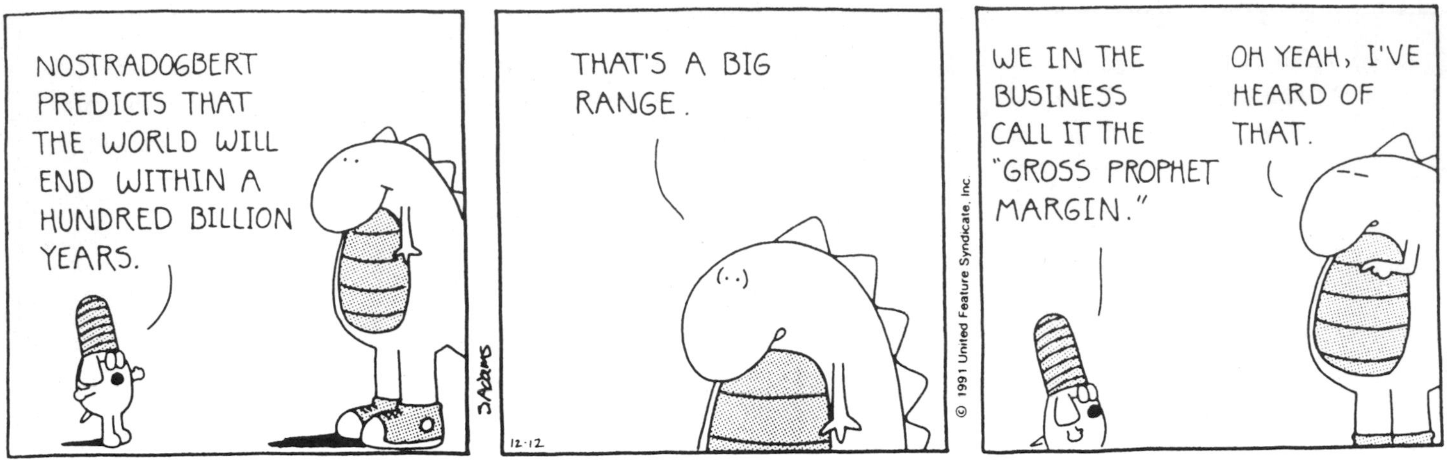
NOSTRADOGBERT PREDICTS THAT THE WORLD WILL END WITHIN A HUNDRED BILLION YEARS.
THAT'S A BIG RANGE.
WE IN THE BUSINESS CALL IT THE "GROSS PROPHET MARGIN."
OH YEAH, I'VE HEARD OF THAT.
© 1991 United Feature Syndicate, Inc.

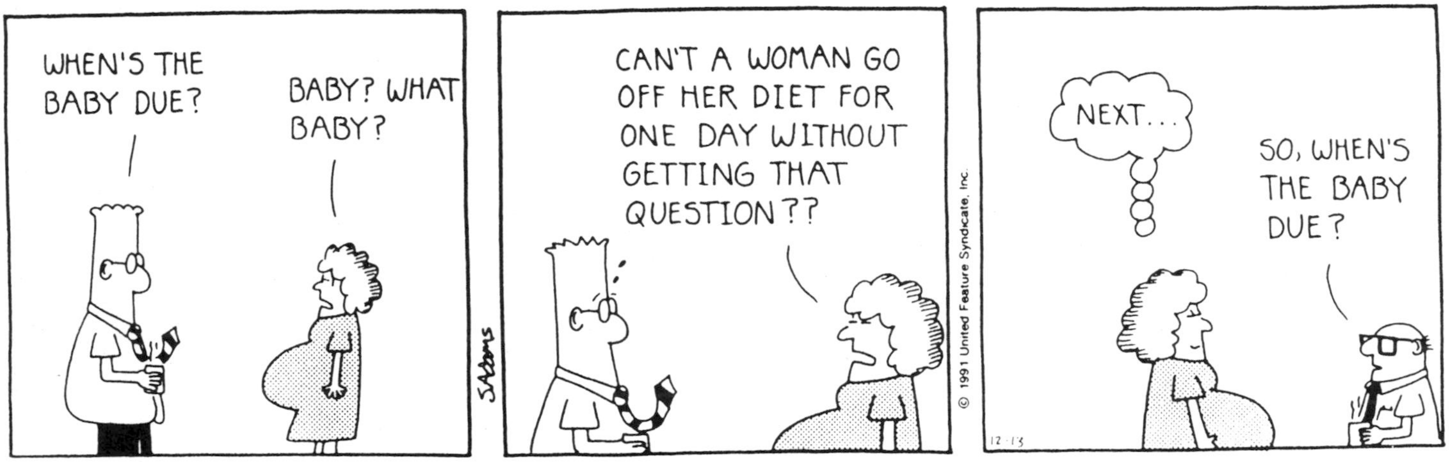
WHEN'S THE BABY DUE?
BABY? WHAT BABY?
CAN'T A WOMAN GO OFF HER DIET FOR ONE DAY WITHOUT GETTING THAT QUESTION??
NEXT...
SO, WHEN'S THE BABY DUE?
© 1991 United Feature Syndicate, Inc.

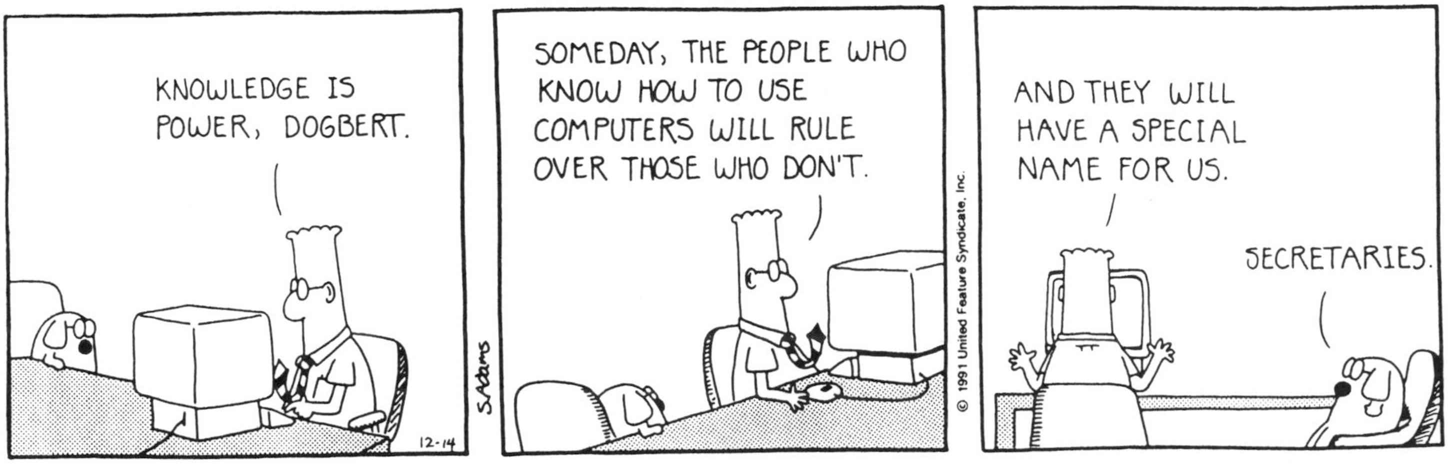
KNOWLEDGE IS POWER, DOGBERT.
SOMEDAY, THE PEOPLE WHO KNOW HOW TO USE COMPUTERS WILL RULE OVER THOSE WHO DON'T.
AND THEY WILL HAVE A SPECIAL NAME FOR US.
SECRETARIES.
© 1991 United Feature Syndicate, Inc.

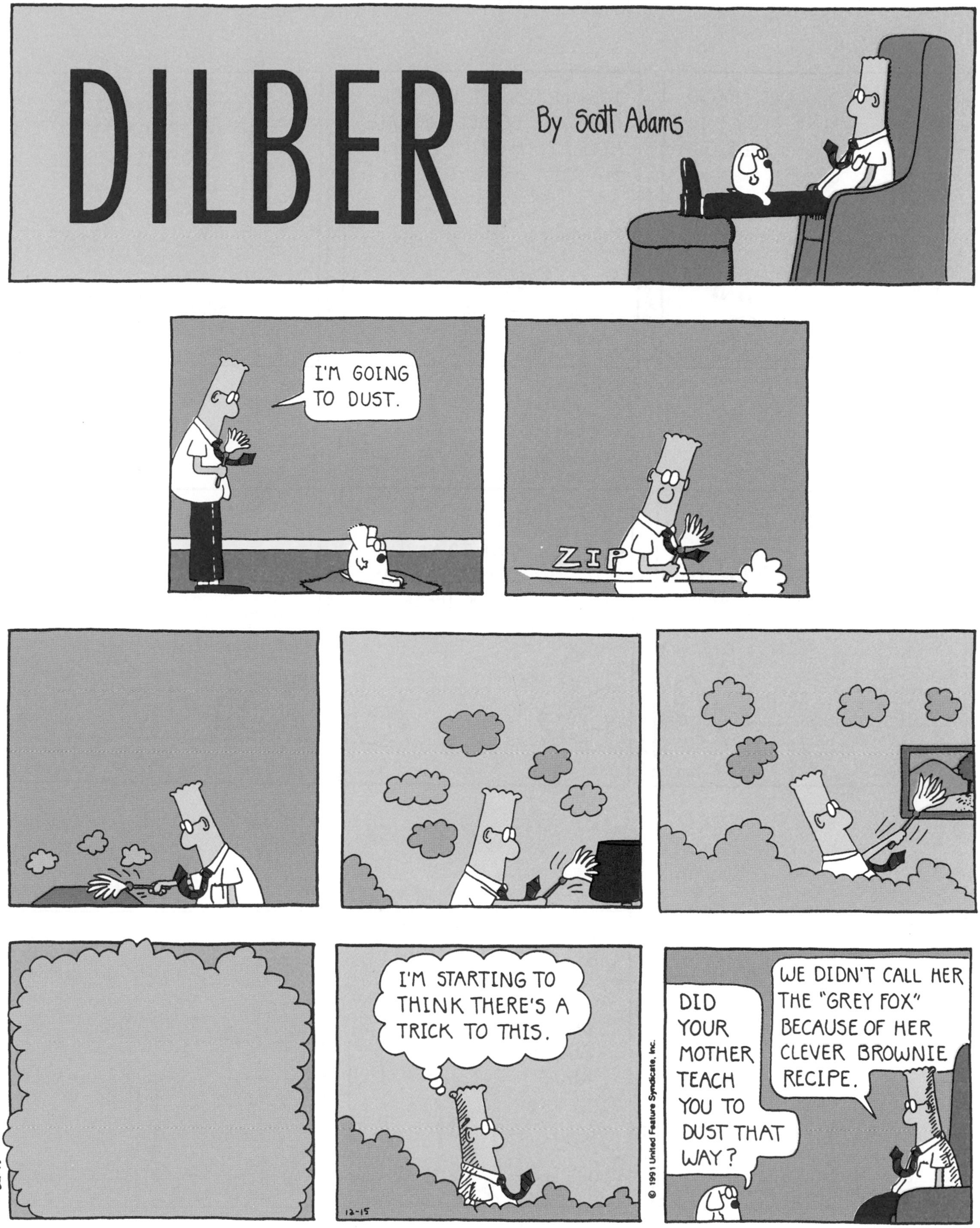
DILBERT
By Scott Adams
I'M GOING TO DUST.
ZIP
I'M STARTING TO THINK THERE'S A TRICK TO THIS.
DID YOUR MOTHER TEACH YOU TO DUST THAT WAY?
WE DIDN'T CALL HER THE "GREY FOX" BECAUSE OF HER CLEVER BROWNIE RECIPE.
S.Adams
12-15
© 1991 United Feature Syndicate, Inc.

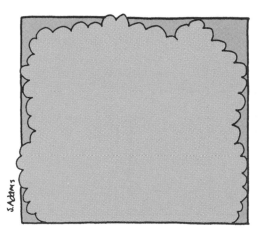

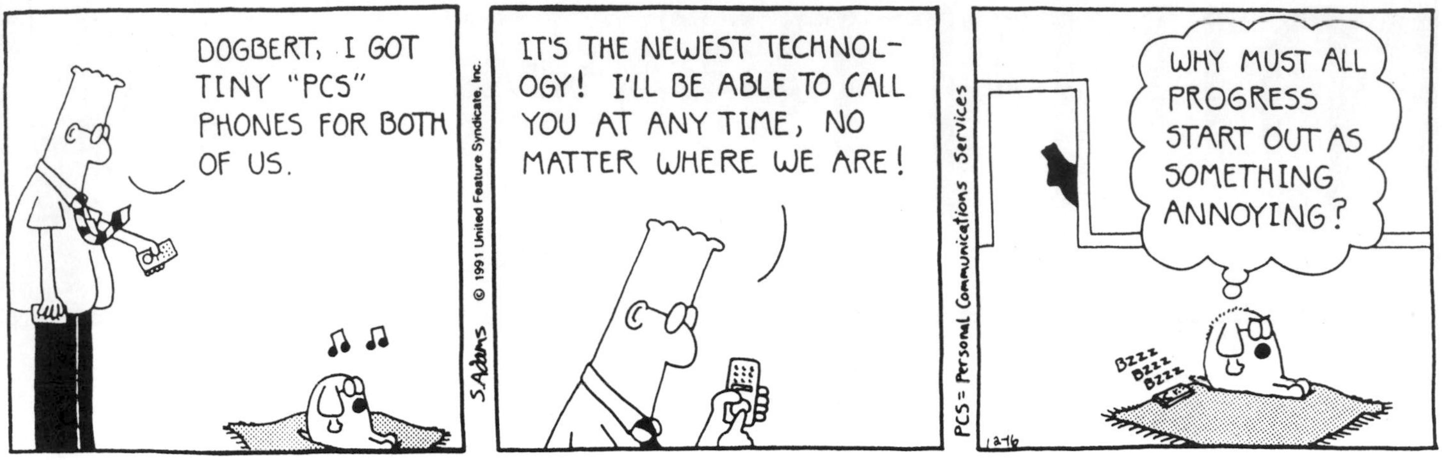

DOGBERT, I GOT TINY "PCS" PHONES FOR BOTH OF US.
S.Adams
© 1991 United Feature Syndicate, Inc.
IT'S THE NEWEST TECHNOLOGY! I'LL BE ABLE TO CALL YOU AT ANY TIME, NO MATTER WHERE WE ARE!
PCS = Personal Communications Services
WHY MUST ALL PROGRESS START OUT AS SOMETHING ANNOYING?
BZZZ BZZZ BZZZ

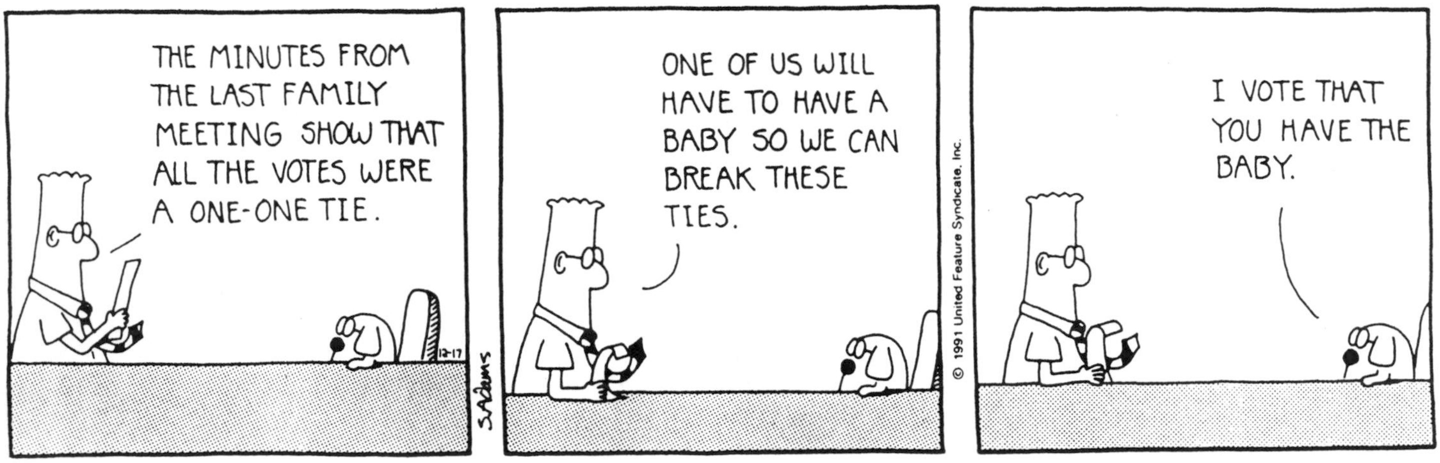

THE MINUTES FROM THE LAST FAMILY MEETING SHOW THAT ALL THE VOTES WERE A ONE-ONE TIE.
12-17
S.Adams
ONE OF US WILL HAVE TO HAVE A BABY SO WE CAN BREAK THESE TIES.
© 1991 United Feature Syndicate, Inc.
I VOTE THAT YOU HAVE THE BABY.

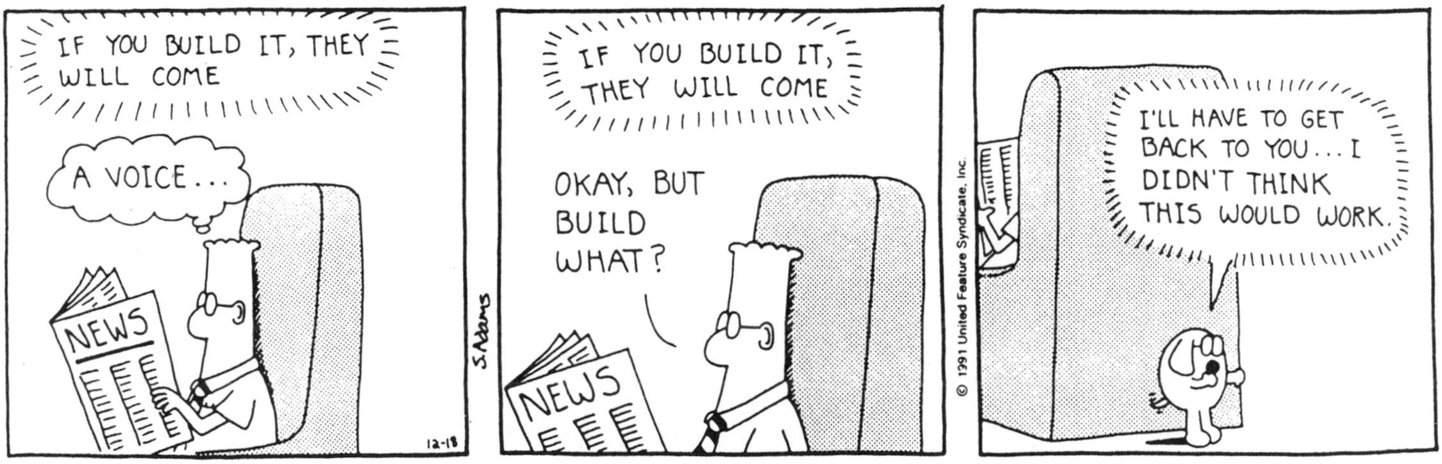

IF YOU BUILD IT, THEY WILL COME
A VOICE...
NEWS
12-18
S.Adams
IF YOU BUILD IT, THEY WILL COME
OKAY, BUT BUILD WHAT?
NEWS
© 1991 United Feature Syndicate, Inc.
I'LL HAVE TO GET BACK TO YOU... I DIDN'T THINK THIS WOULD WORK.

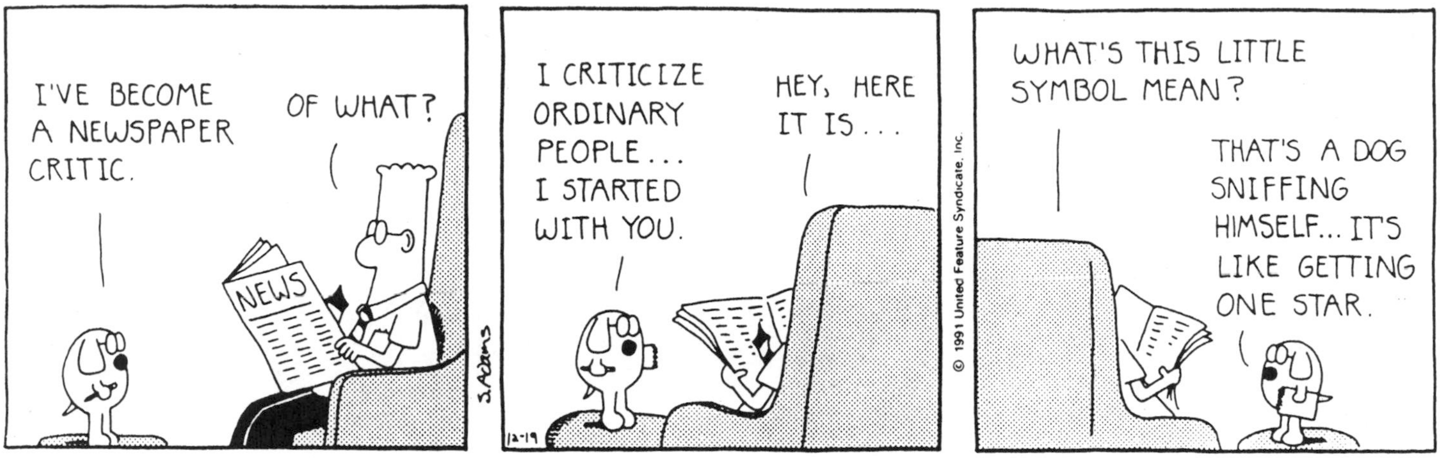
I'VE BECOME A NEWSPAPER CRITIC.
OF WHAT?
NEWS
I CRITICIZE ORDINARY PEOPLE... I STARTED WITH YOU.
HEY, HERE IT IS...
WHAT'S THIS LITTLE SYMBOL MEAN?
THAT'S A DOG SNIFFING HIMSELF... IT'S LIKE GETTING ONE STAR.
© 1991 United Feature Syndicate, Inc.

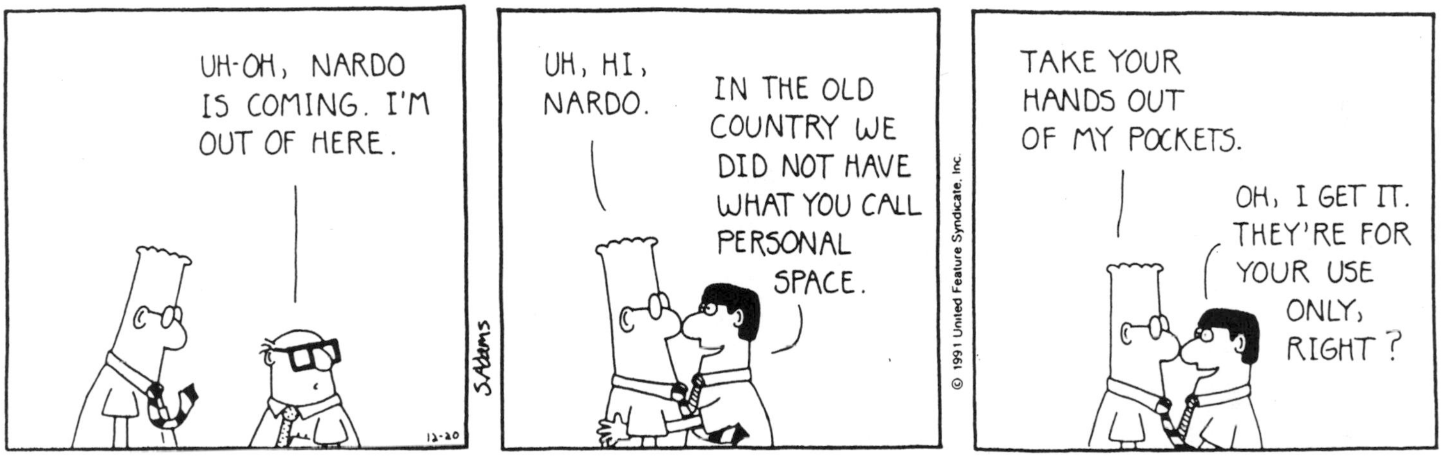
UH-OH, NARDO IS COMING. I'M OUT OF HERE.
UH, HI, NARDO.
IN THE OLD COUNTRY WE DID NOT HAVE WHAT YOU CALL PERSONAL SPACE.
TAKE YOUR HANDS OUT OF MY POCKETS.
OH, I GET IT. THEY'RE FOR YOUR USE ONLY, RIGHT?
© 1991 United Feature Syndicate, Inc.

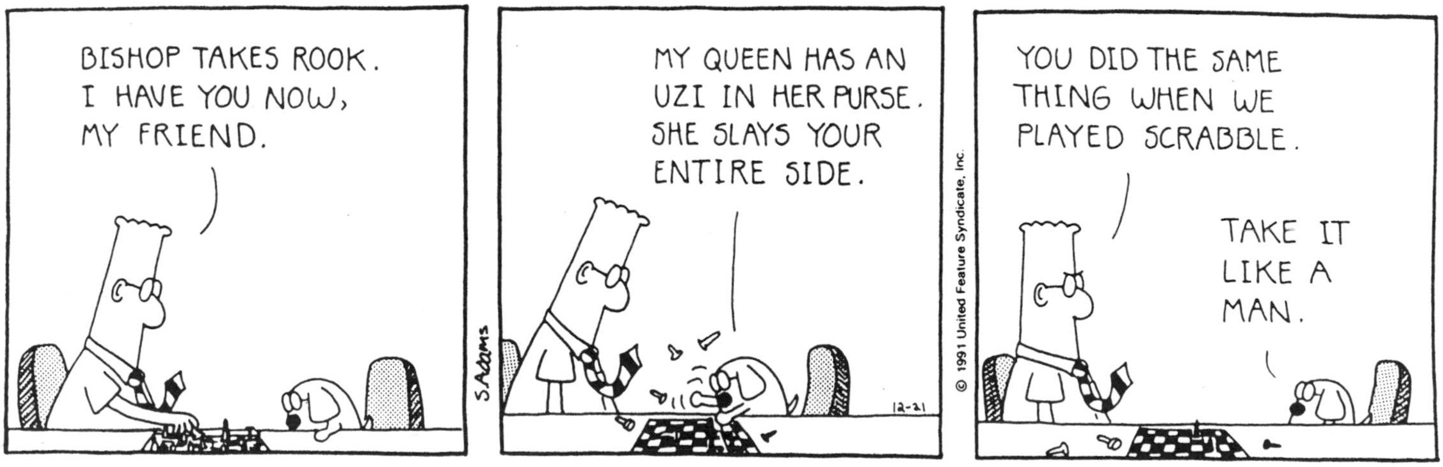
BISHOP TAKES ROOK. I HAVE YOU NOW, MY FRIEND.
MY QUEEN HAS AN UZI IN HER PURSE. SHE SLAYS YOUR ENTIRE SIDE.
YOU DID THE SAME THING WHEN WE PLAYED SCRABBLE.
TAKE IT LIKE A MAN.
© 1991 United Feature Syndicate, Inc.

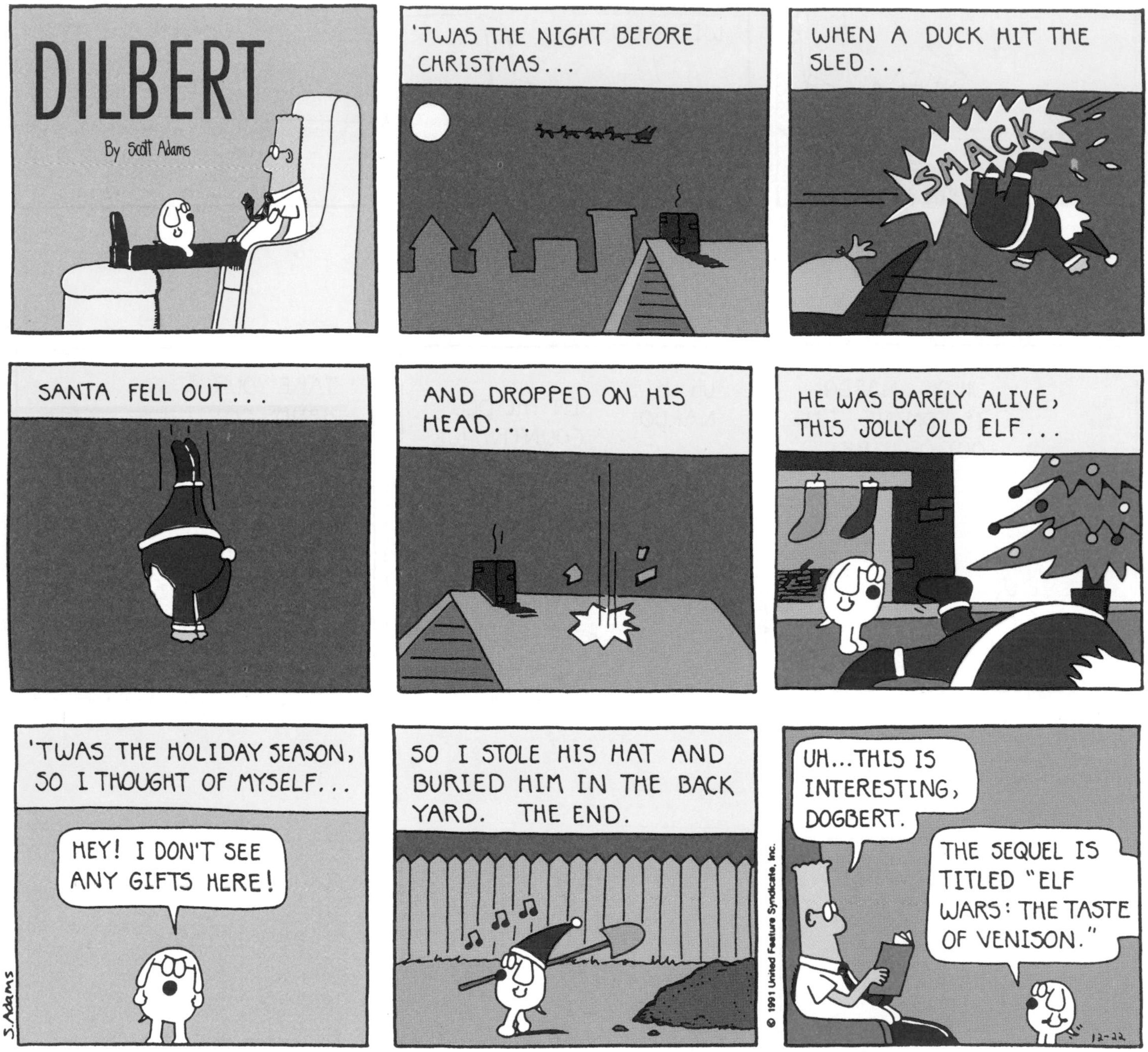
DILBERT
By Scott Adams
'TWAS THE NIGHT BEFORE CHRISTMAS...
WHEN A DUCK HIT THE SLED...
SMACK
SANTA FELL OUT...
AND DROPPED ON HIS HEAD...
HE WAS BARELY ALIVE, THIS JOLLY OLD ELF...
'TWAS THE HOLIDAY SEASON, SO I THOUGHT OF MYSELF...
HEY! I DON'T SEE ANY GIFTS HERE!
SO I STOLE HIS HAT AND BURIED HIM IN THE BACK YARD. THE END.
UH...THIS IS INTERESTING, DOGBERT.
THE SEQUEL IS TITLED "ELF WARS: THE TASTE OF VENISON."
S. Adams
© 1991 United Feature Syndicate, Inc.
12-22

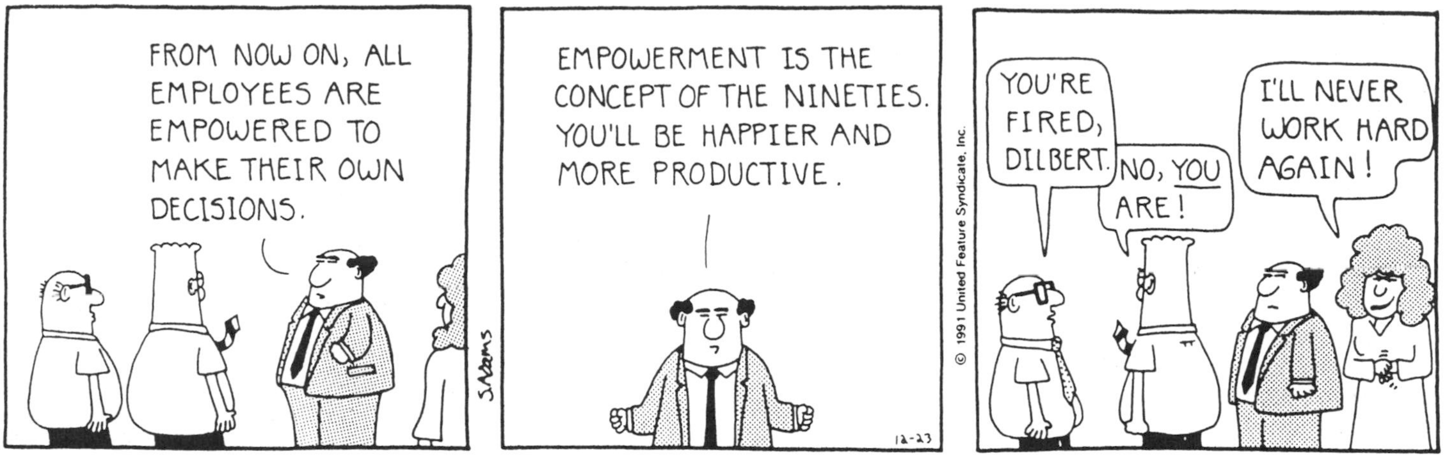
FROM NOW ON, ALL EMPLOYEES ARE EMPOWERED TO MAKE THEIR OWN DECISIONS.
EMPOWERMENT IS THE CONCEPT OF THE NINETIES. YOU'LL BE HAPPIER AND MORE PRODUCTIVE.
YOU'RE FIRED, DILBERT.
NO, YOU ARE!
I'LL NEVER WORK HARD AGAIN!
© 1991 United Feature Syndicate, Inc.

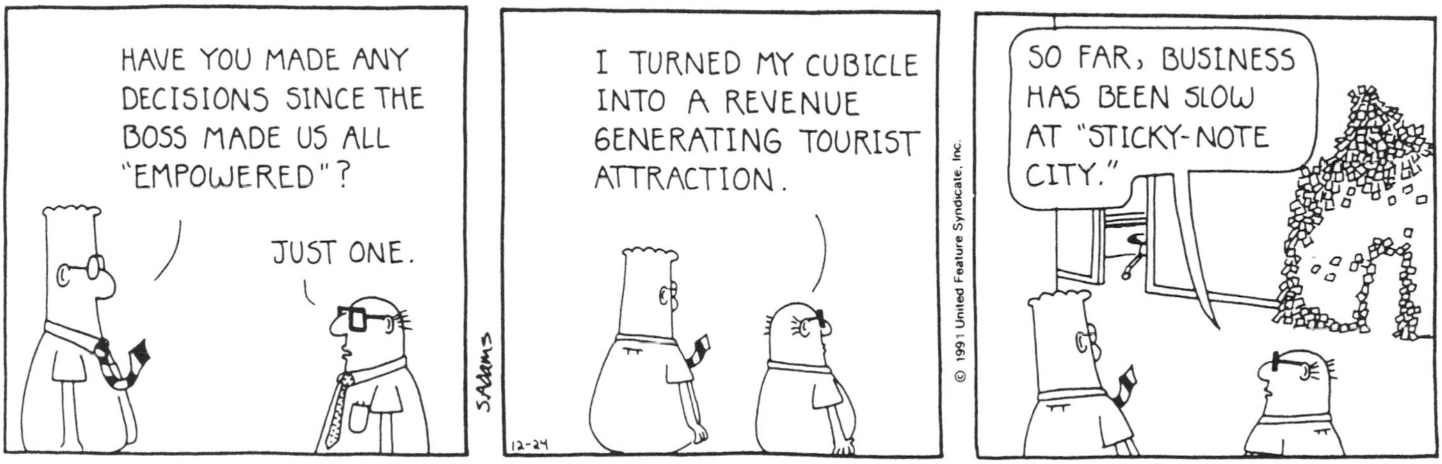
HAVE YOU MADE ANY DECISIONS SINCE THE BOSS MADE US ALL "EMPOWERED"?
JUST ONE.
I TURNED MY CUBICLE INTO A REVENUE GENERATING TOURIST ATTRACTION.
SO FAR, BUSINESS HAS BEEN SLOW AT "STICKY-NOTE CITY."
© 1991 United Feature Syndicate, Inc.

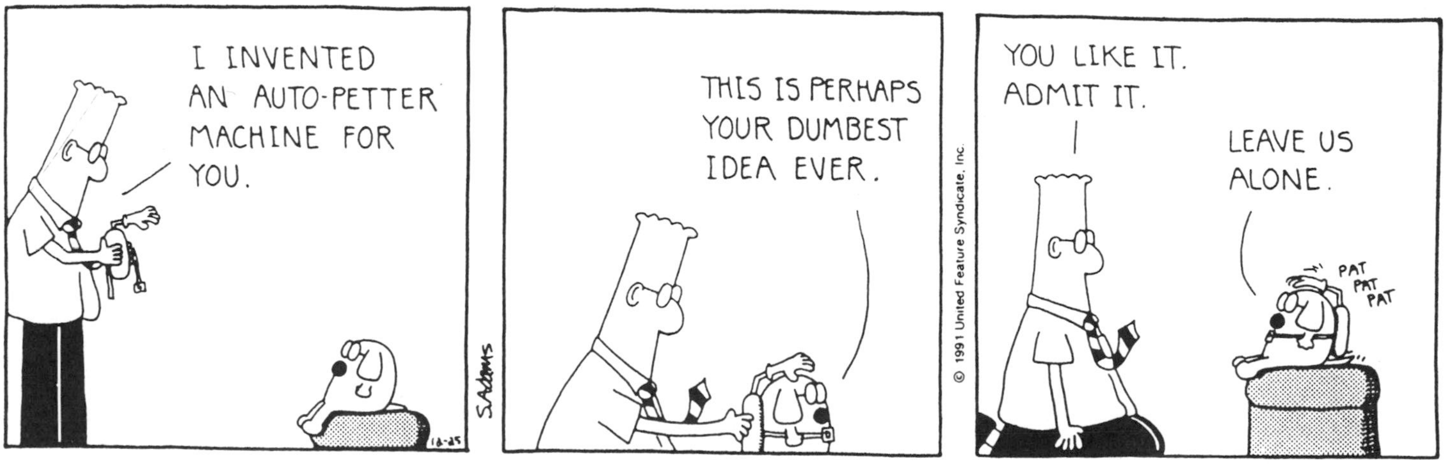
I INVENTED AN AUTO-PETTER MACHINE FOR YOU.
THIS IS PERHAPS YOUR DUMBEST IDEA EVER.
YOU LIKE IT. ADMIT IT.
LEAVE US ALONE.
PAT PAT PAT
© 1991 United Feature Syndicate, Inc.

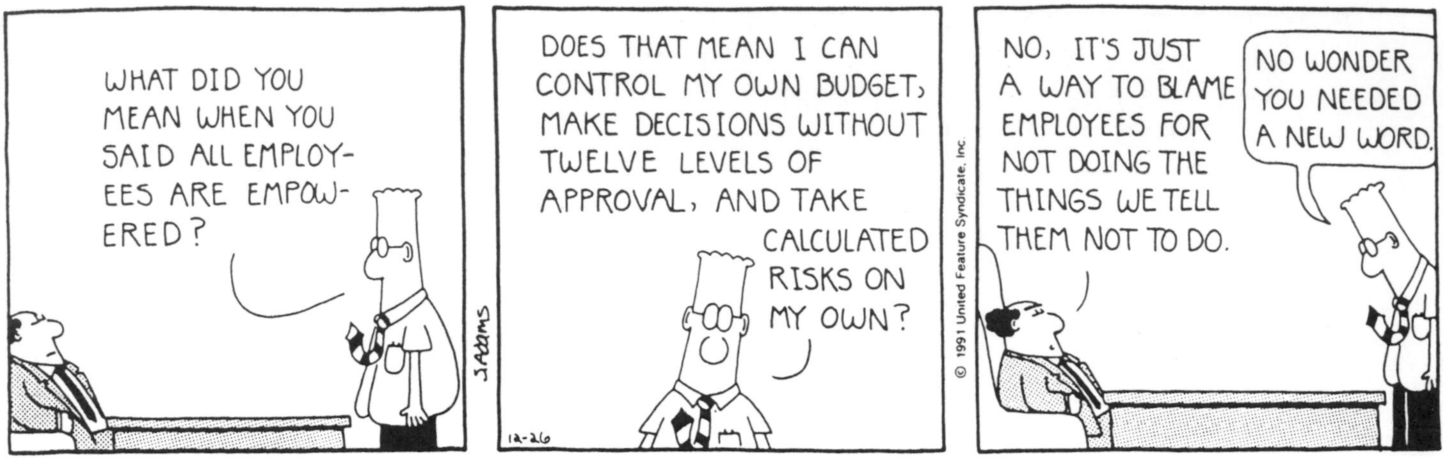
WHAT DID YOU MEAN WHEN YOU SAID ALL EMPLOY-EES ARE EMPOW-ERED?
DOES THAT MEAN I CAN CONTROL MY OWN BUDGET, MAKE DECISIONS WITHOUT TWELVE LEVELS OF APPROVAL, AND TAKE CALCULATED RISKS ON MY OWN?
NO, IT'S JUST A WAY TO BLAME EMPLOYEES FOR NOT DOING THE THINGS WE TELL THEM NOT TO DO.
NO WONDER YOU NEEDED A NEW WORD.
© 1991 United Feature Syndicate, Inc.

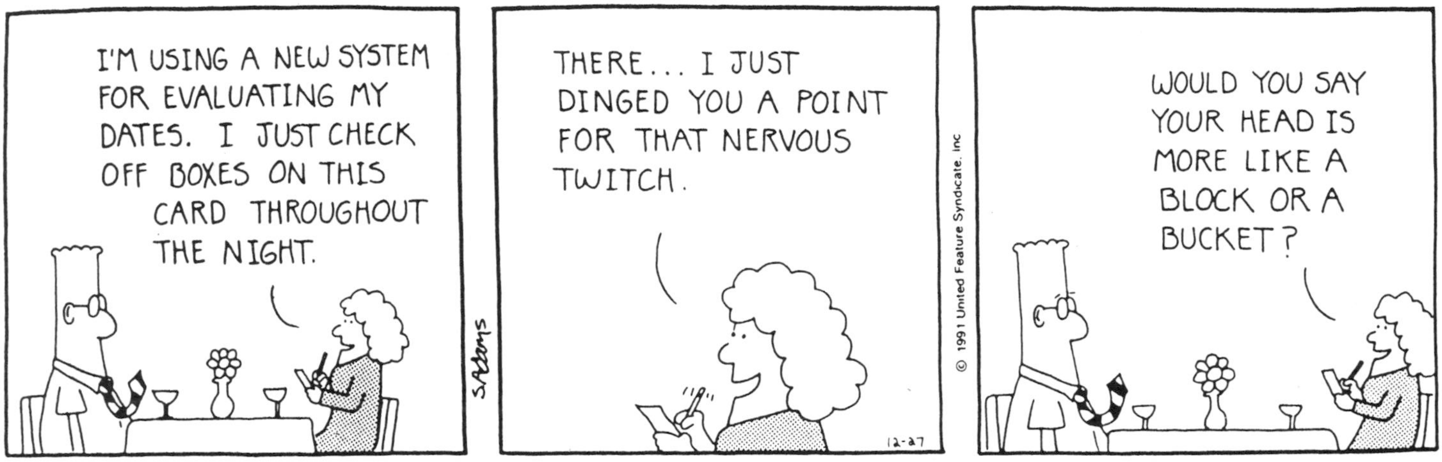
I'M USING A NEW SYSTEM FOR EVALUATING MY DATES. I JUST CHECK OFF BOXES ON THIS CARD THROUGHOUT THE NIGHT.
THERE... I JUST DINGED YOU A POINT FOR THAT NERVOUS TWITCH.
WOULD YOU SAY YOUR HEAD IS MORE LIKE A BLOCK OR A BUCKET?
© 1991 United Feature Syndicate, Inc.

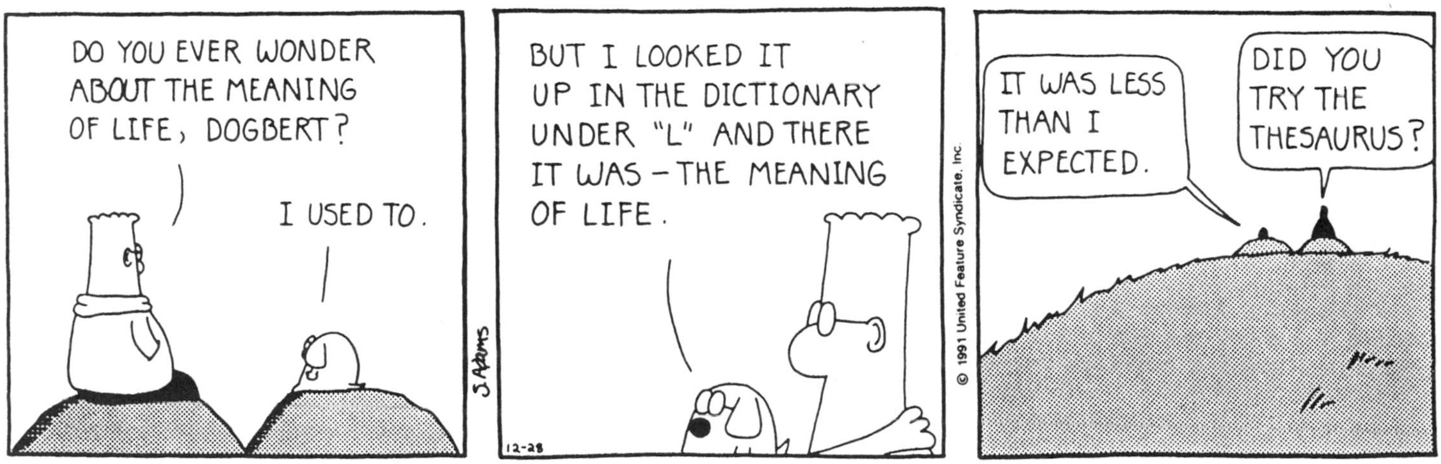
DO YOU EVER WONDER ABOUT THE MEANING OF LIFE, DOGBERT?
I USED TO.
BUT I LOOKED IT UP IN THE DICTIONARY UNDER "L" AND THERE IT WAS – THE MEANING OF LIFE.
IT WAS LESS THAN I EXPECTED.
DID YOU TRY THE THESAURUS?
© 1991 United Feature Syndicate, Inc.

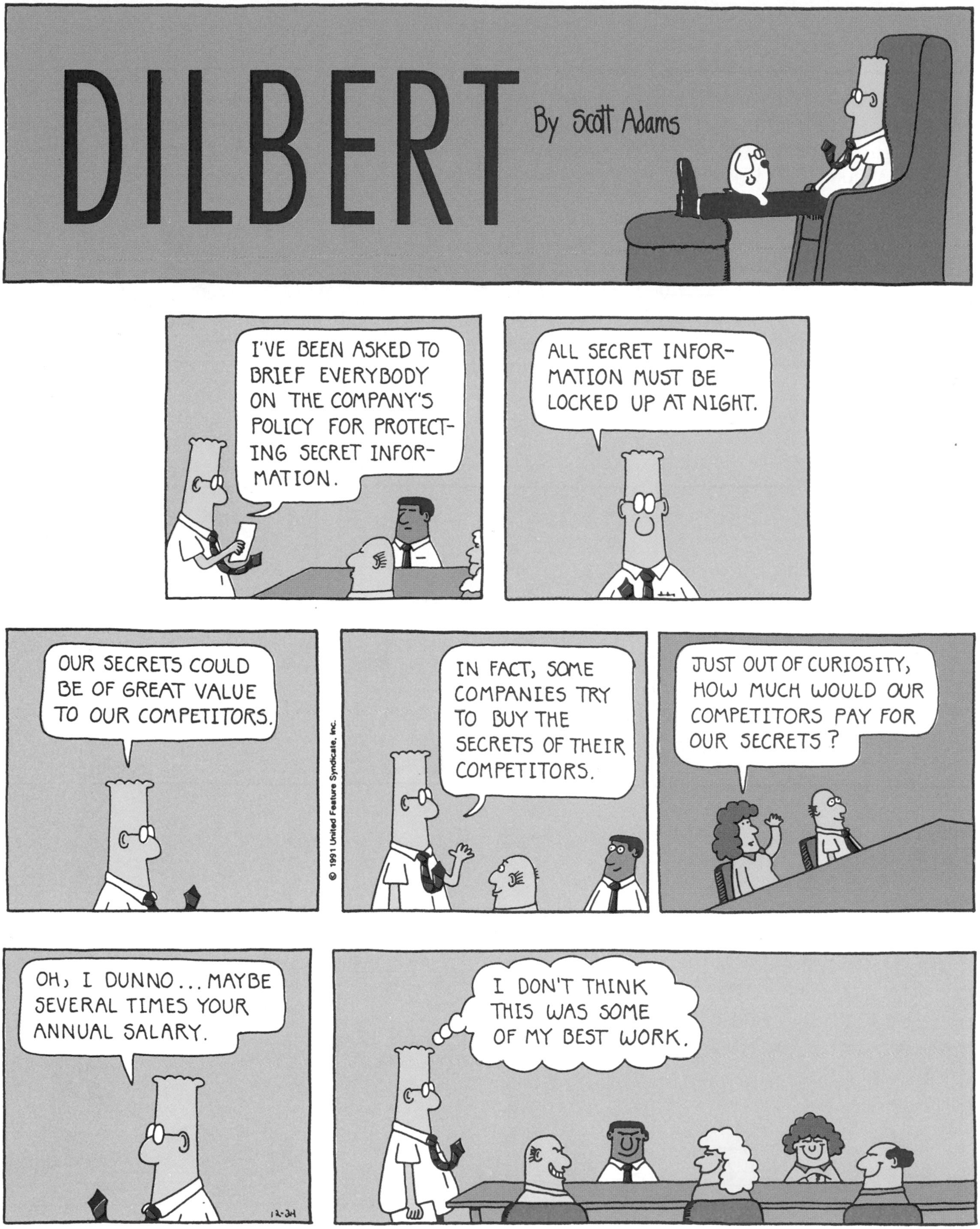
DILBERT
By Scott Adams
I'VE BEEN ASKED TO BRIEF EVERYBODY ON THE COMPANY'S POLICY FOR PROTECTING SECRET INFORMATION.
ALL SECRET INFORMATION MUST BE LOCKED UP AT NIGHT.
OUR SECRETS COULD BE OF GREAT VALUE TO OUR COMPETITORS.
© 1991 United Feature Syndicate, Inc.
IN FACT, SOME COMPANIES TRY TO BUY THE SECRETS OF THEIR COMPETITORS.
JUST OUT OF CURIOSITY, HOW MUCH WOULD OUR COMPETITORS PAY FOR OUR SECRETS?
OH, I DUNNO... MAYBE SEVERAL TIMES YOUR ANNUAL SALARY.
12-24
I DON'T THINK THIS WAS SOME OF MY BEST WORK.

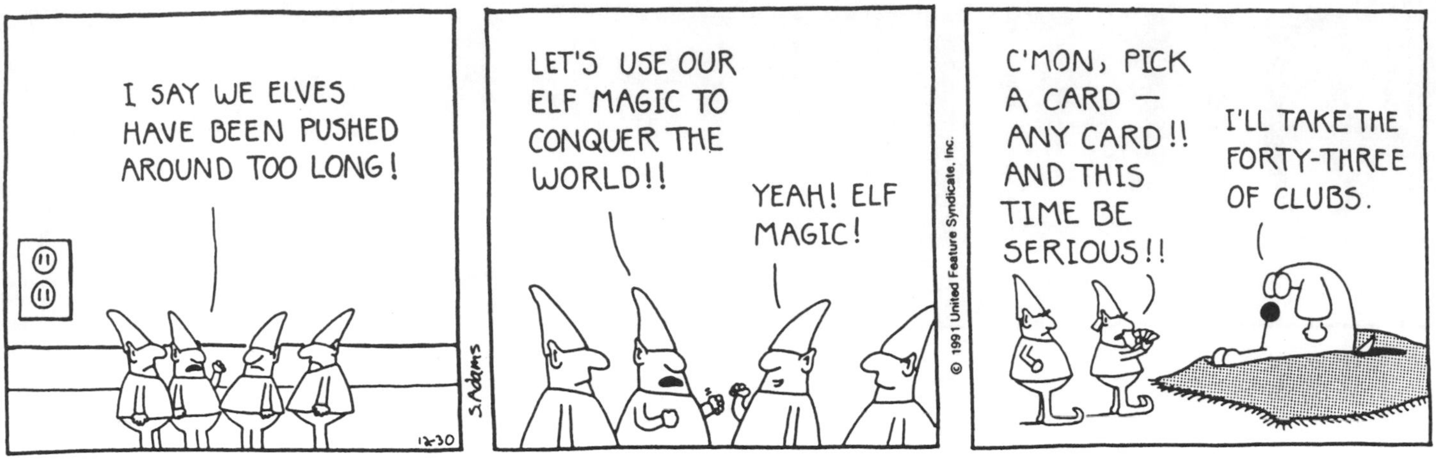
I SAY WE ELVES HAVE BEEN PUSHED AROUND TOO LONG!
S. Adams 12-30
LET'S USE OUR ELF MAGIC TO CONQUER THE WORLD!!
YEAH! ELF MAGIC!
© 1991 United Feature Syndicate, Inc.
C'MON, PICK A CARD — ANY CARD!! AND THIS TIME BE SERIOUS!!
I'LL TAKE THE FORTY-THREE OF CLUBS.

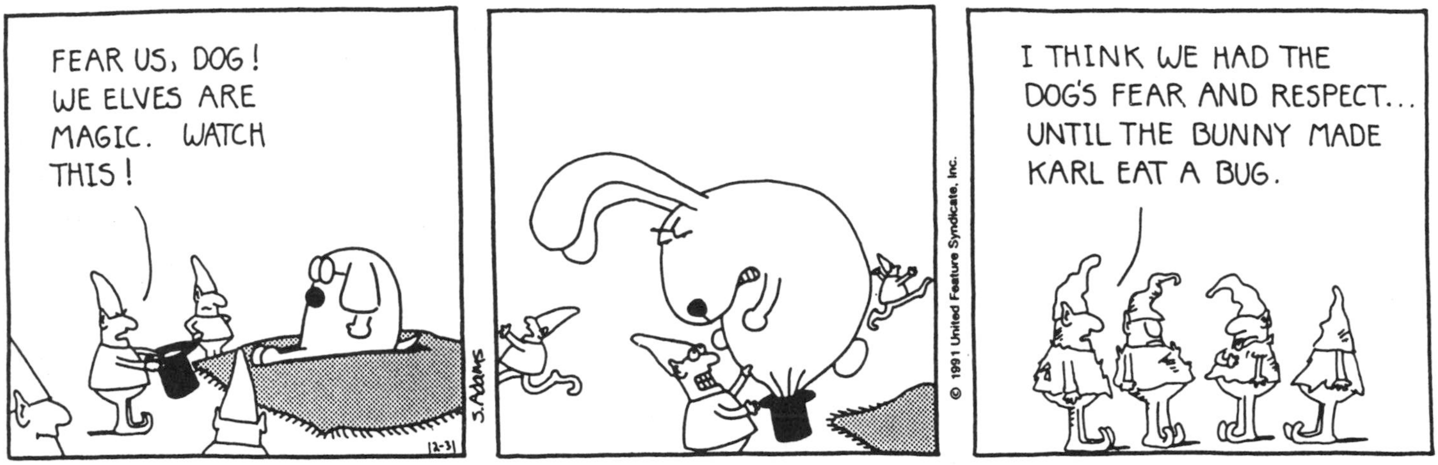
FEAR US, DOG! WE ELVES ARE MAGIC. WATCH THIS!
S. Adams 12-31
© 1991 United Feature Syndicate, Inc.
I THINK WE HAD THE DOG'S FEAR AND RESPECT... UNTIL THE BUNNY MADE KARL EAT A BUG.

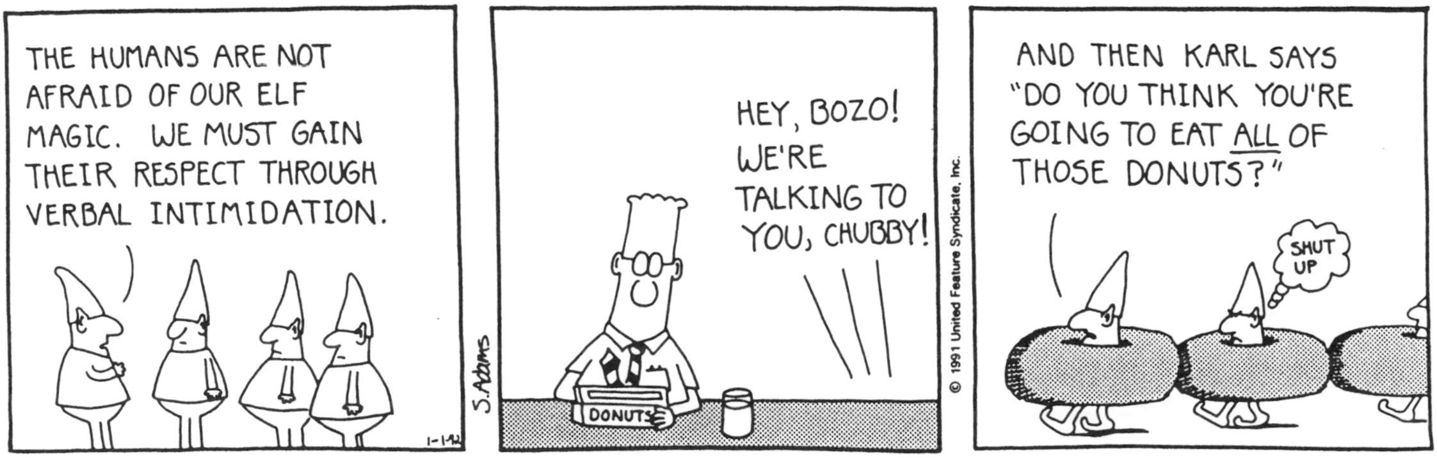
THE HUMANS ARE NOT AFRAID OF OUR ELF MAGIC. WE MUST GAIN THEIR RESPECT THROUGH VERBAL INTIMIDATION.
S. Adams 1-1-92
HEY, BOZO! WE'RE TALKING TO YOU, CHUBBY!
DONUTS
© 1991 United Feature Syndicate, Inc.
AND THEN KARL SAYS "DO YOU THINK YOU'RE GOING TO EAT ALL OF THOSE DONUTS?"
SHUT UP

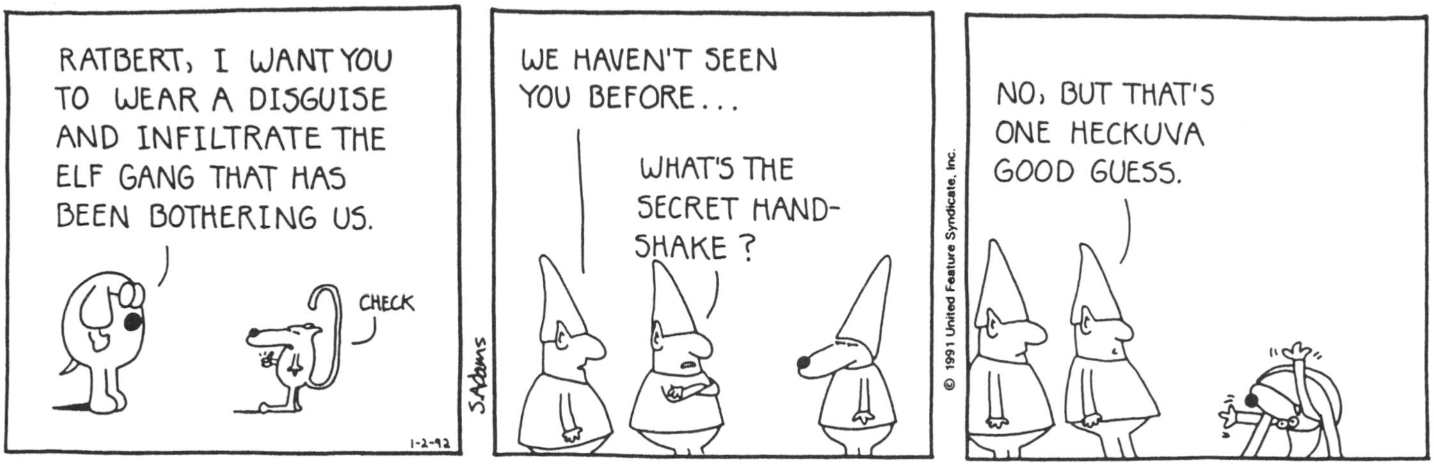
RATBERT, I WANT YOU TO WEAR A DISGUISE AND INFILTRATE THE ELF GANG THAT HAS BEEN BOTHERING US.
CHECK
1-2-92
S.Adams
WE HAVEN'T SEEN YOU BEFORE...
WHAT'S THE SECRET HAND-SHAKE ?
© 1991 United Feature Syndicate, Inc.
NO, BUT THAT'S ONE HECKUVA GOOD GUESS.

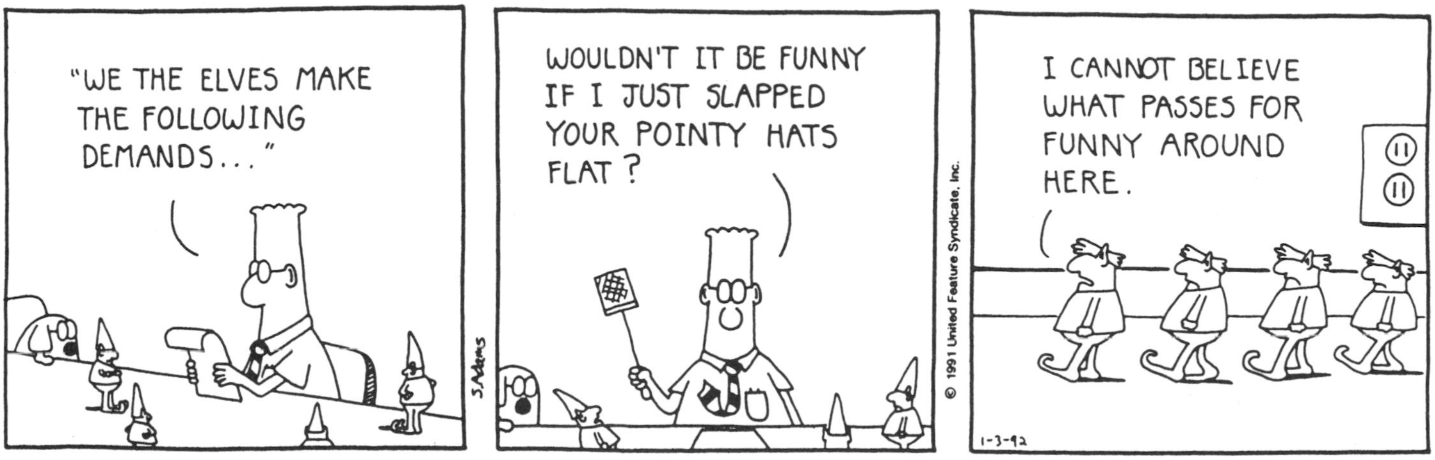
"WE THE ELVES MAKE THE FOLLOWING DEMANDS..."
S.Adams
WOULDN'T IT BE FUNNY IF I JUST SLAPPED YOUR POINTY HATS FLAT ?
© 1991 United Feature Syndicate, Inc.
I CANNOT BELIEVE WHAT PASSES FOR FUNNY AROUND HERE.
1-3-92

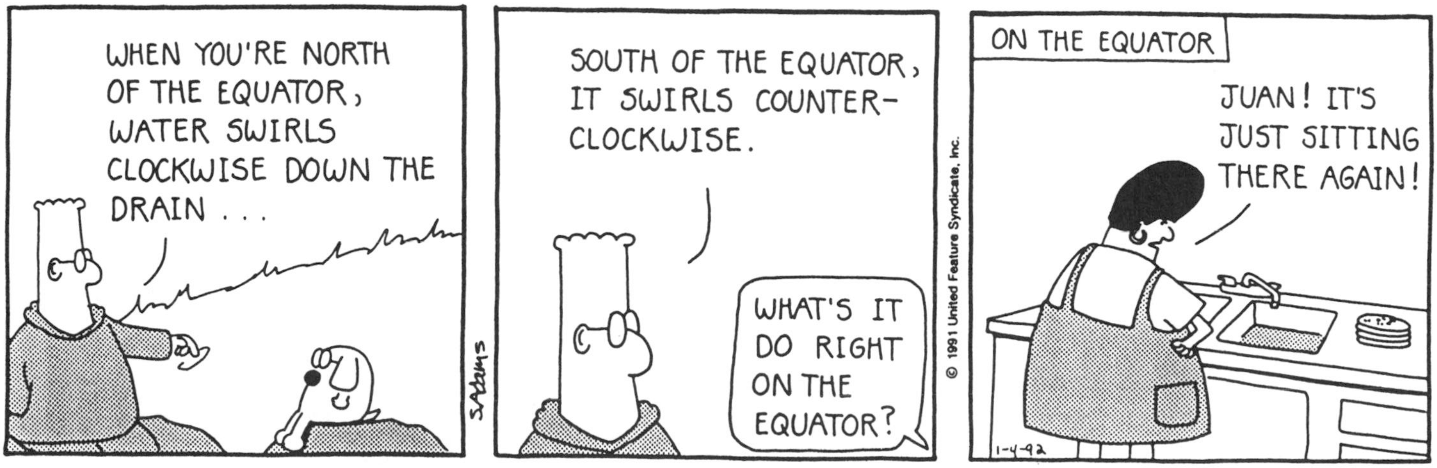
WHEN YOU'RE NORTH OF THE EQUATOR, WATER SWIRLS CLOCKWISE DOWN THE DRAIN . . .
S.Adams
SOUTH OF THE EQUATOR, IT SWIRLS COUNTER-CLOCKWISE.
WHAT'S IT DO RIGHT ON THE EQUATOR?
© 1991 United Feature Syndicate, Inc.
ON THE EQUATOR
JUAN! IT'S JUST SITTING THERE AGAIN!
1-4-92

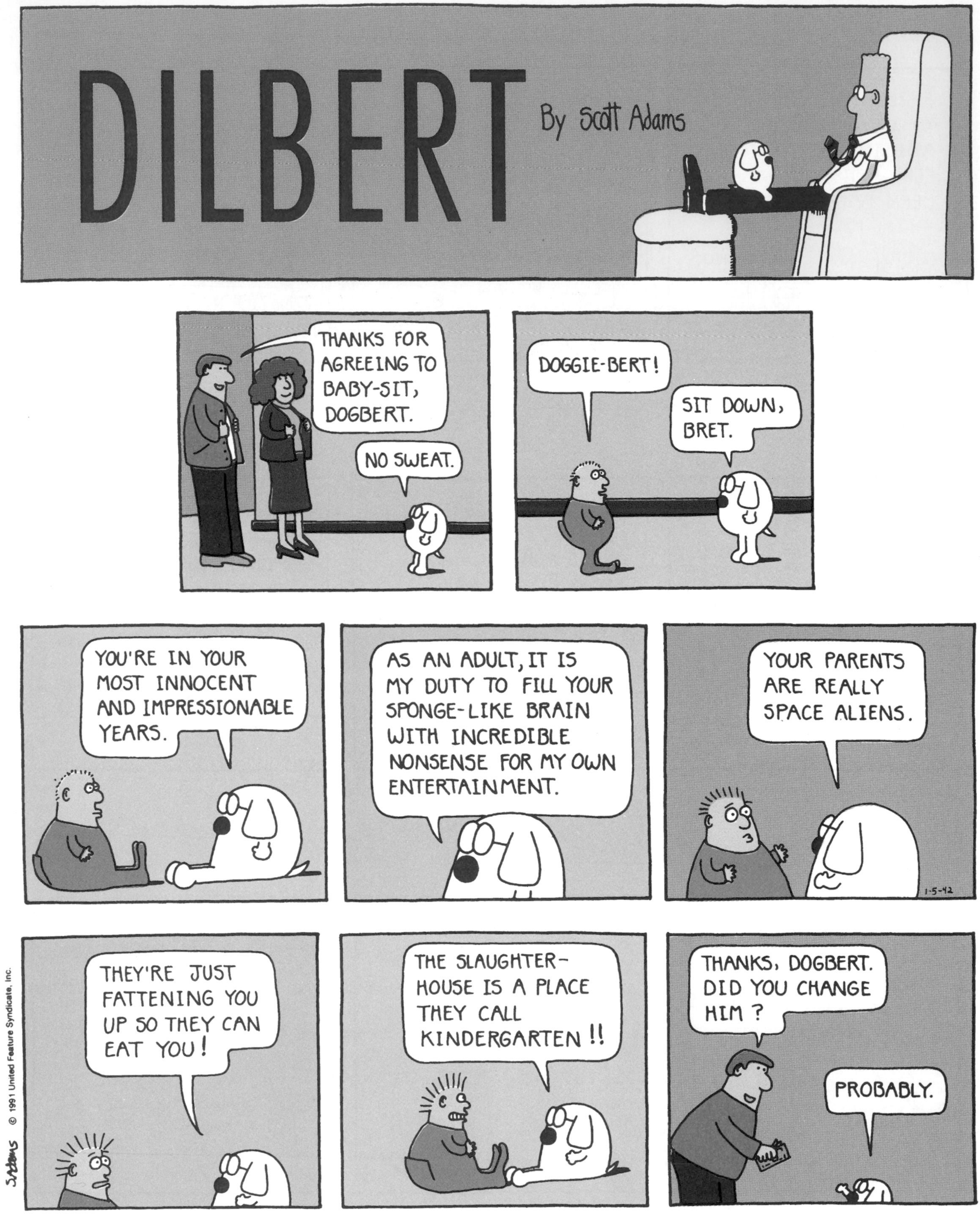

DILBERT
By Scott Adams
THANKS FOR AGREEING TO BABY-SIT, DOGBERT.
NO SWEAT.
DOGGIE-BERT!
SIT DOWN, BRET.
YOU'RE IN YOUR MOST INNOCENT AND IMPRESSIONABLE YEARS.
AS AN ADULT, IT IS MY DUTY TO FILL YOUR SPONGE-LIKE BRAIN WITH INCREDIBLE NONSENSE FOR MY OWN ENTERTAINMENT.
YOUR PARENTS ARE REALLY SPACE ALIENS.
THEY'RE JUST FATTENING YOU UP SO THEY CAN EAT YOU!
THE SLAUGHTER-HOUSE IS A PLACE THEY CALL KINDERGARTEN!!
THANKS, DOGBERT. DID YOU CHANGE HIM?
PROBABLY.
© 1991 United Feature Syndicate, Inc.

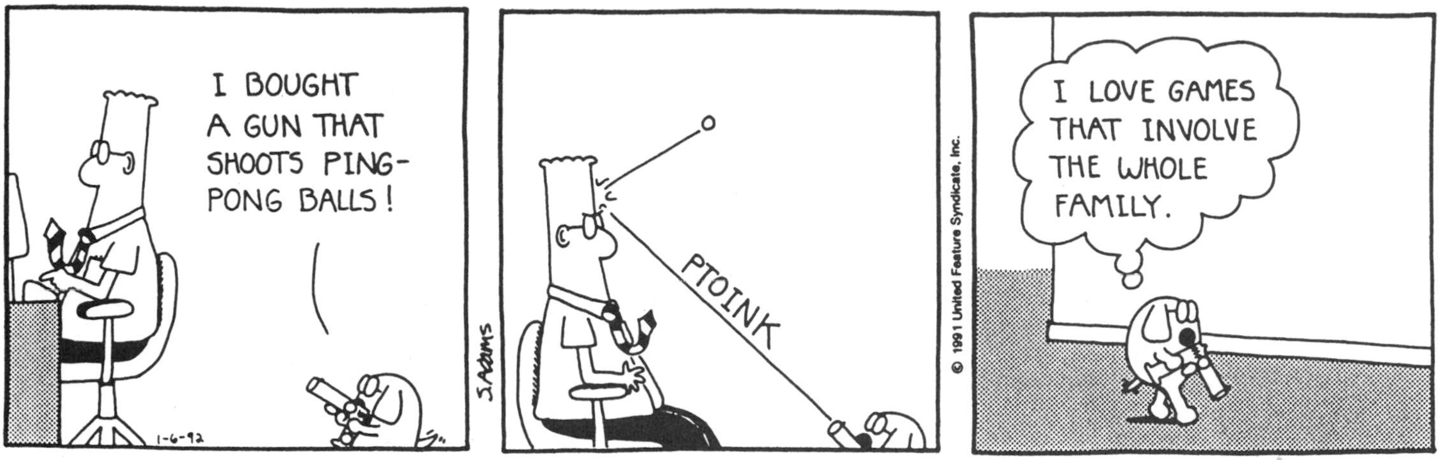
I BOUGHT A GUN THAT SHOOTS PING-PONG BALLS!
PTOINK
I LOVE GAMES THAT INVOLVE THE WHOLE FAMILY.

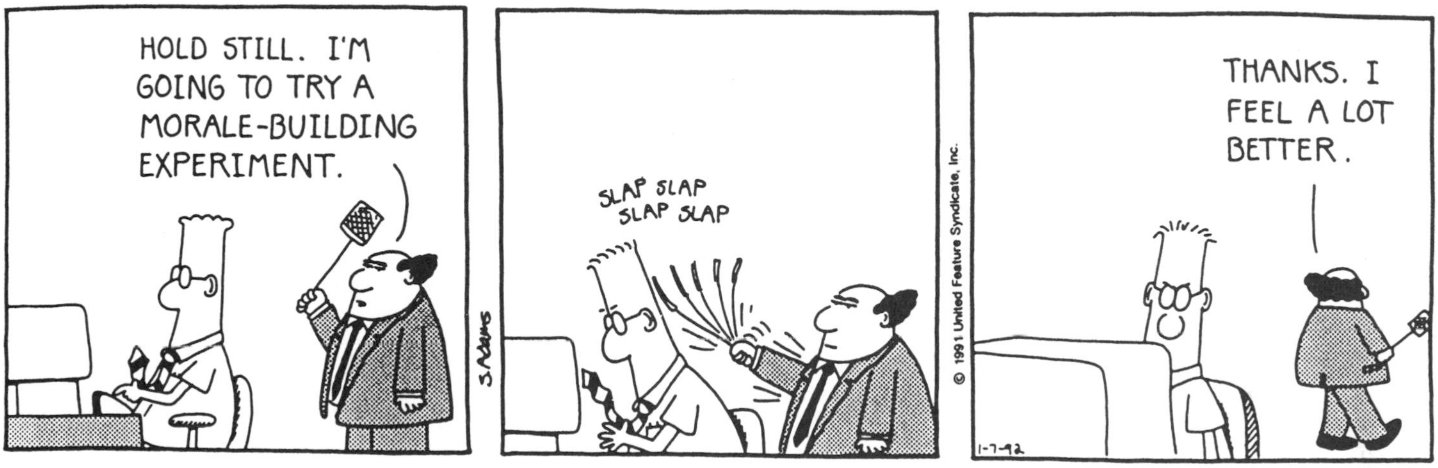
HOLD STILL. I'M GOING TO TRY A MORALE-BUILDING EXPERIMENT.
SLAP SLAP SLAP SLAP
THANKS. I FEEL A LOT BETTER.

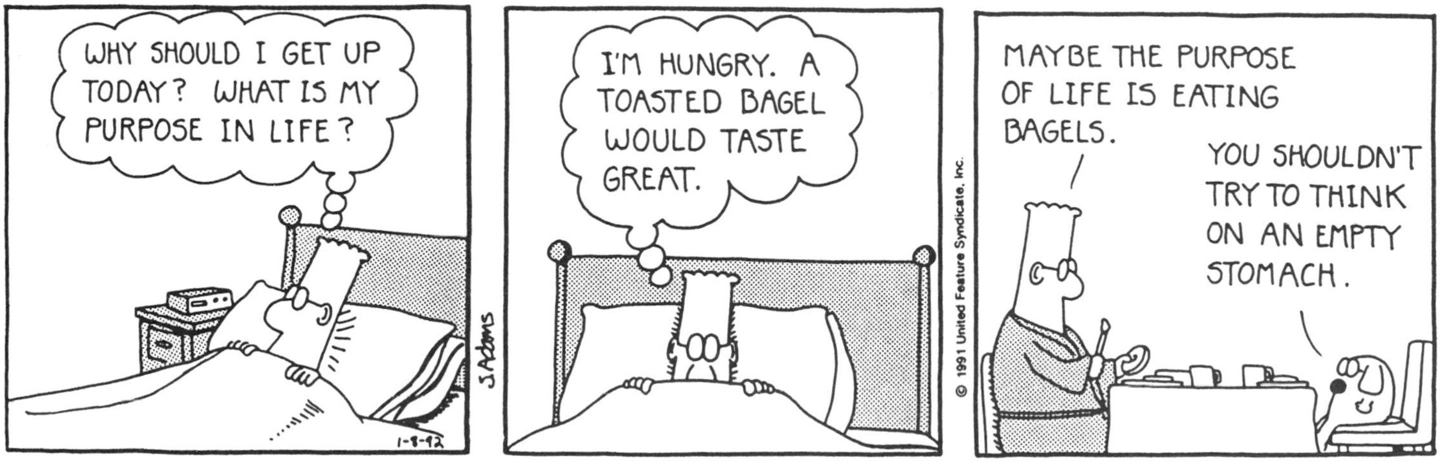
WHY SHOULD I GET UP TODAY? WHAT IS MY PURPOSE IN LIFE?
I'M HUNGRY. A TOASTED BAGEL WOULD TASTE GREAT.
MAYBE THE PURPOSE OF LIFE IS EATING BAGELS.
YOU SHOULDN'T TRY TO THINK ON AN EMPTY STOMACH.

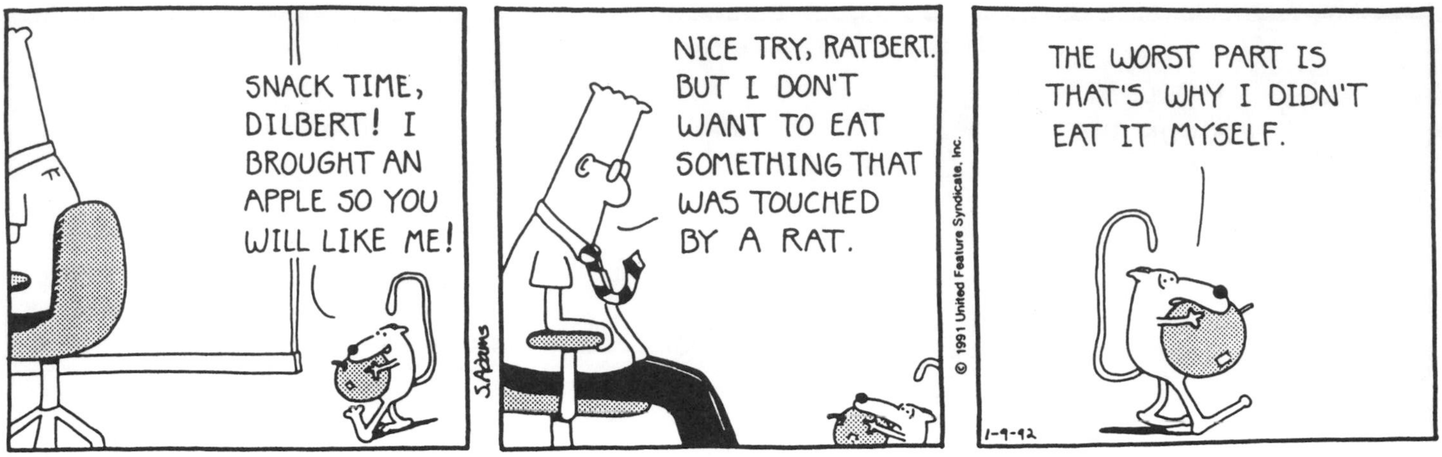
SNACK TIME, DILBERT! I BROUGHT AN APPLE SO YOU WILL LIKE ME!
S.ADAMS
NICE TRY, RATBERT. BUT I DON'T WANT TO EAT SOMETHING THAT WAS TOUCHED BY A RAT.
© 1991 United Feature Syndicate, Inc.
THE WORST PART IS THAT'S WHY I DIDN'T EAT IT MYSELF.
1-9-92

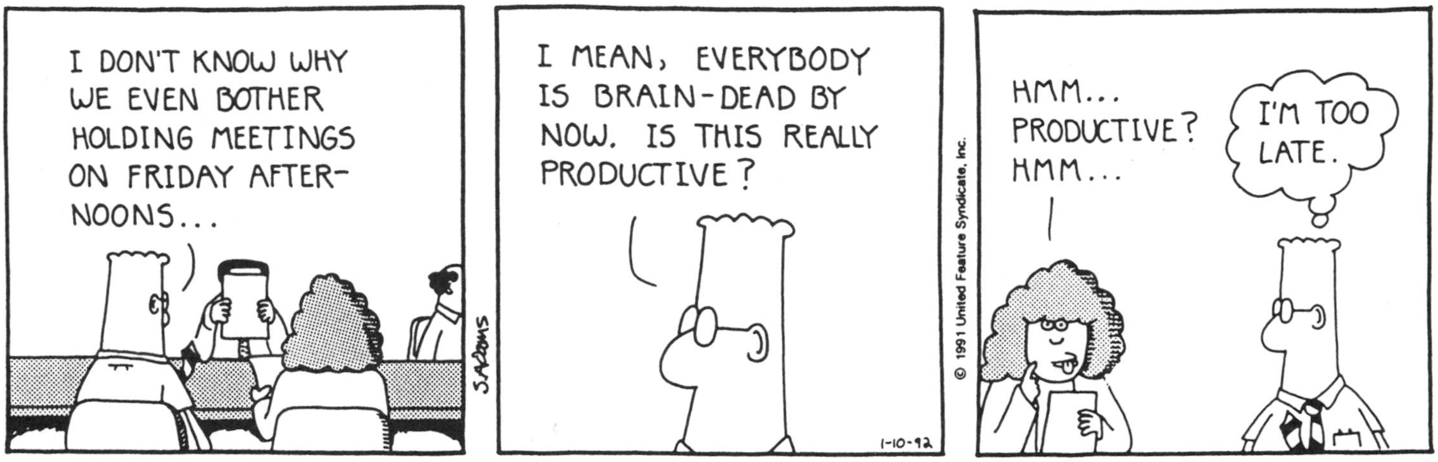
I DON'T KNOW WHY WE EVEN BOTHER HOLDING MEETINGS ON FRIDAY AFTER-NOONS...
S.ADAMS
I MEAN, EVERYBODY IS BRAIN-DEAD BY NOW. IS THIS REALLY PRODUCTIVE?
1-10-92
© 1991 United Feature Syndicate, Inc.
HMM... PRODUCTIVE? HMM...
I'M TOO LATE.

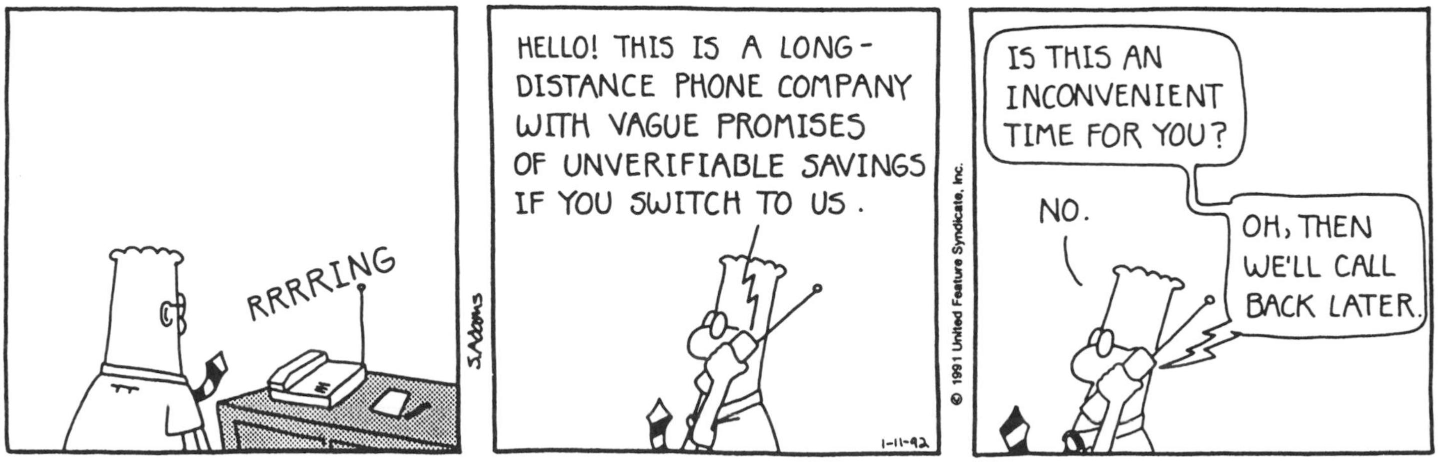
RRRRING
S.ADAMS
HELLO! THIS IS A LONG-DISTANCE PHONE COMPANY WITH VAGUE PROMISES OF UNVERIFIABLE SAVINGS IF YOU SWITCH TO US.
1-11-92
© 1991 United Feature Syndicate, Inc.
IS THIS AN INCONVENIENT TIME FOR YOU?
NO.
OH, THEN WE'LL CALL BACK LATER.

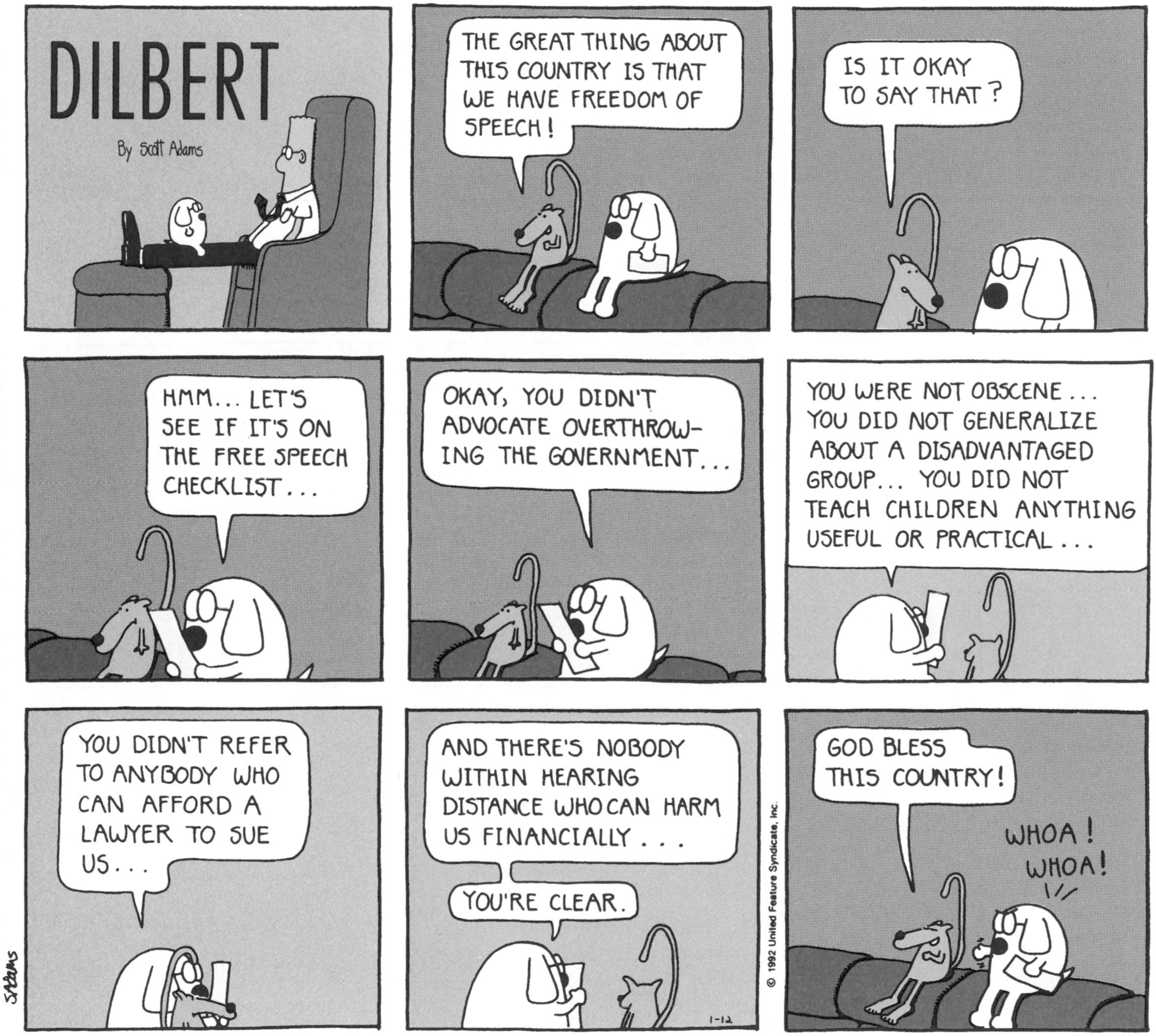
DILBERT
By Scott Adams
THE GREAT THING ABOUT THIS COUNTRY IS THAT WE HAVE FREEDOM OF SPEECH!
IS IT OKAY TO SAY THAT?
HMM... LET'S SEE IF IT'S ON THE FREE SPEECH CHECKLIST...
OKAY, YOU DIDN'T ADVOCATE OVERTHROWING THE GOVERNMENT...
YOU WERE NOT OBSCENE... YOU DID NOT GENERALIZE ABOUT A DISADVANTAGED GROUP... YOU DID NOT TEACH CHILDREN ANYTHING USEFUL OR PRACTICAL...
YOU DIDN'T REFER TO ANYBODY WHO CAN AFFORD A LAWYER TO SUE US...
AND THERE'S NOBODY WITHIN HEARING DISTANCE WHO CAN HARM US FINANCIALLY...
YOU'RE CLEAR.
GOD BLESS THIS COUNTRY!
WHOA! WHOA!
© 1992 United Feature Syndicate, Inc.
1-12

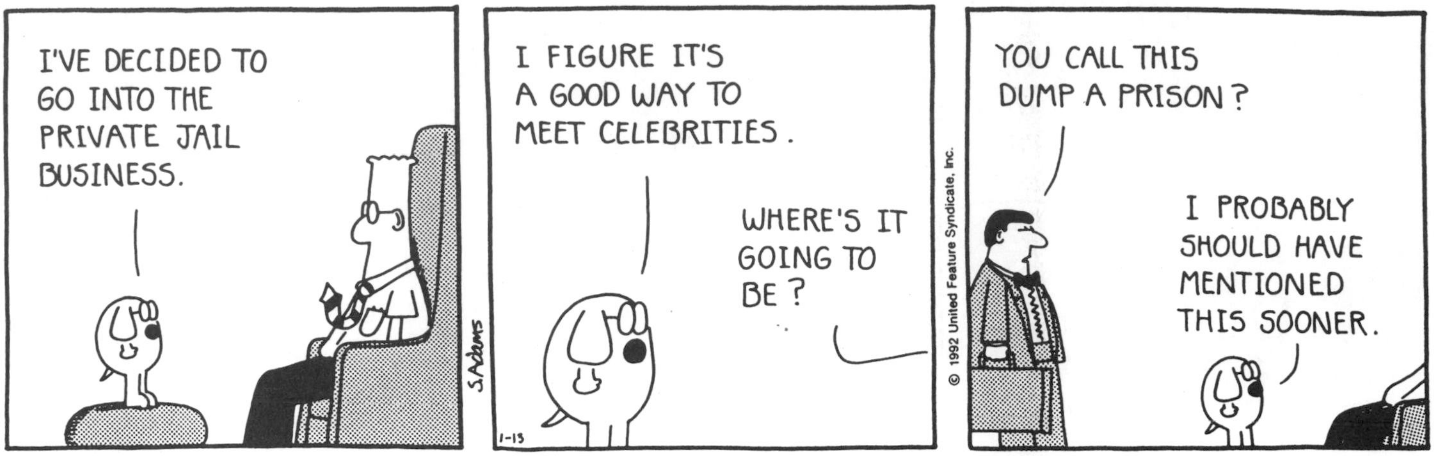
I'VE DECIDED TO GO INTO THE PRIVATE JAIL BUSINESS.
I FIGURE IT'S A GOOD WAY TO MEET CELEBRITIES.
WHERE'S IT GOING TO BE?
YOU CALL THIS DUMP A PRISON?
I PROBABLY SHOULD HAVE MENTIONED THIS SOONER.
© 1992 United Feature Syndicate, Inc.

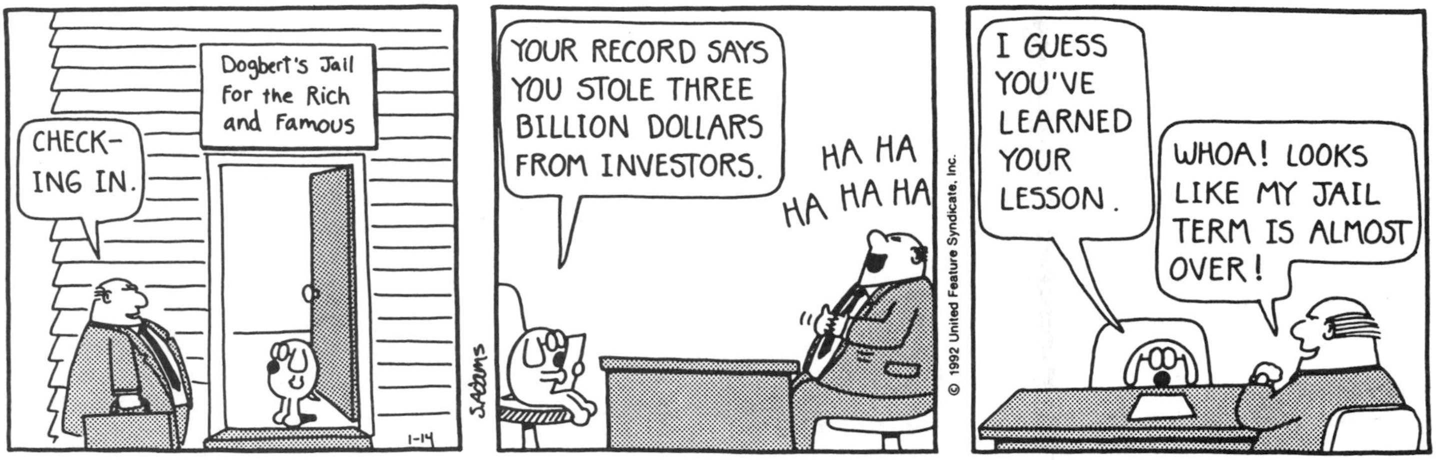
Dogbert's Jail For the Rich and Famous
CHECK-ING IN.
YOUR RECORD SAYS YOU STOLE THREE BILLION DOLLARS FROM INVESTORS.
HA HA HA HA HA
I GUESS YOU'VE LEARNED YOUR LESSON.
WHOA! LOOKS LIKE MY JAIL TERM IS ALMOST OVER!
© 1992 United Feature Syndicate, Inc.

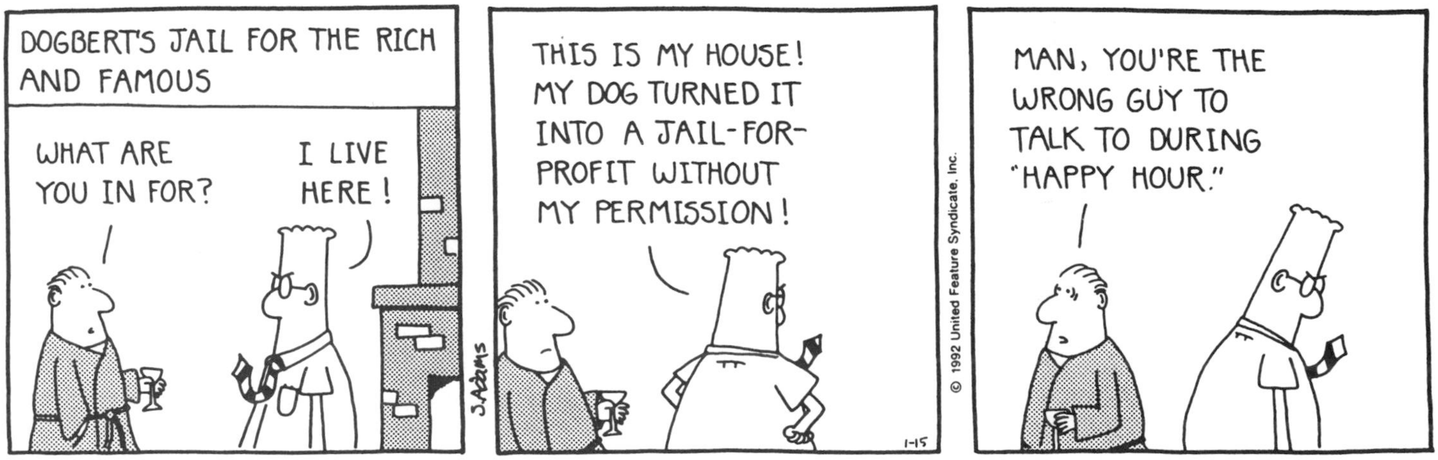
DOGBERT'S JAIL FOR THE RICH AND FAMOUS
WHAT ARE YOU IN FOR?
I LIVE HERE!
THIS IS MY HOUSE! MY DOG TURNED IT INTO A JAIL-FOR-PROFIT WITHOUT MY PERMISSION!
MAN, YOU'RE THE WRONG GUY TO TALK TO DURING "HAPPY HOUR."
© 1992 United Feature Syndicate, Inc.

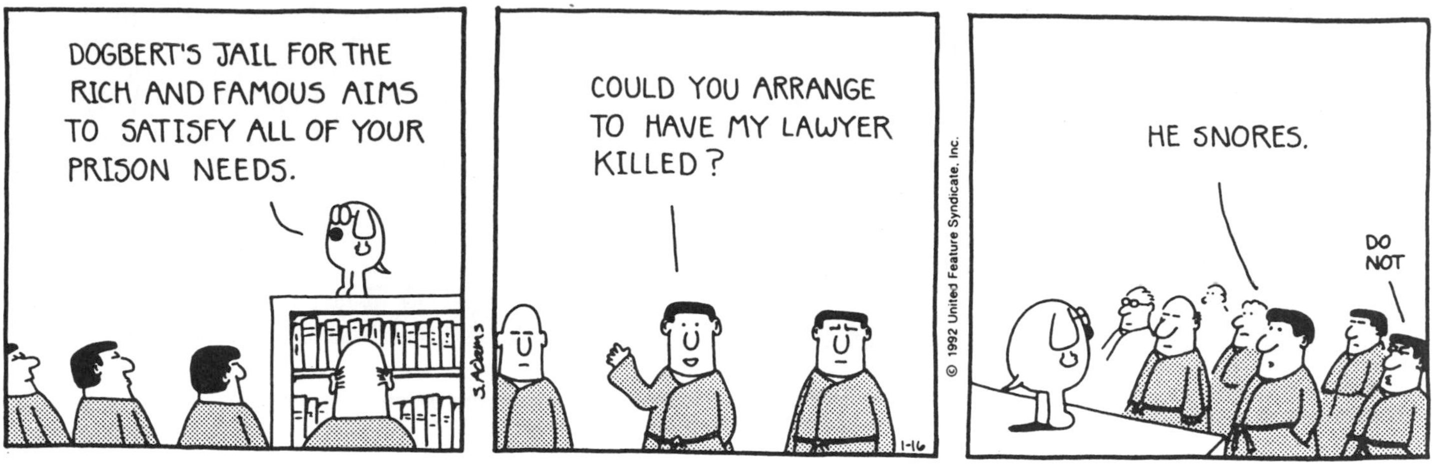
DOGBERT'S JAIL FOR THE RICH AND FAMOUS AIMS TO SATISFY ALL OF YOUR PRISON NEEDS.
COULD YOU ARRANGE TO HAVE MY LAWYER KILLED?
HE SNORES.
DO NOT
© 1992 United Feature Syndicate, Inc.
1-16

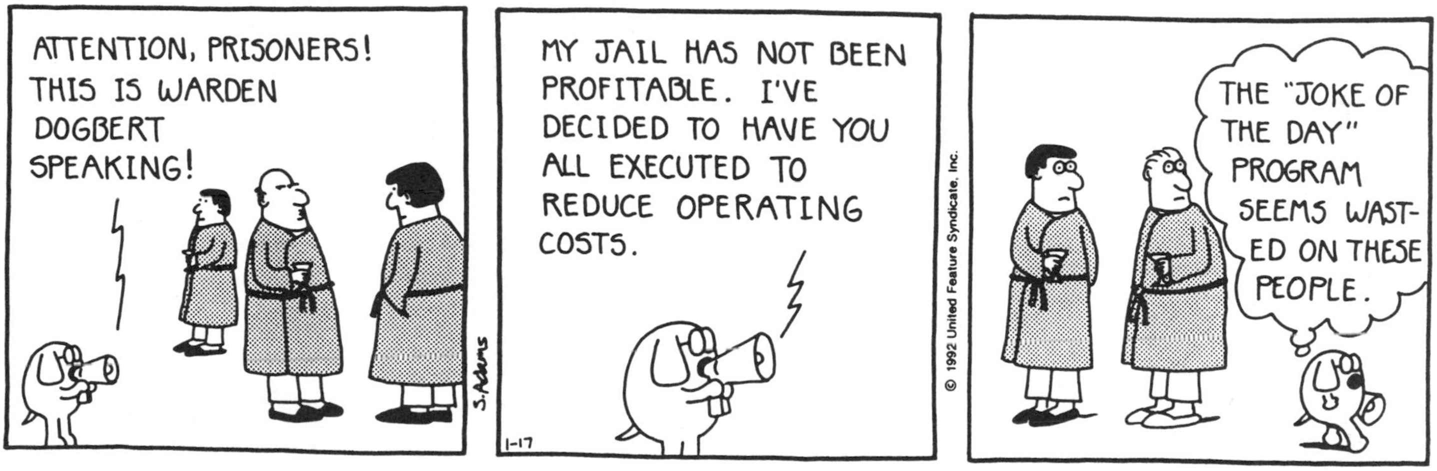
ATTENTION, PRISONERS! THIS IS WARDEN DOGBERT SPEAKING!
MY JAIL HAS NOT BEEN PROFITABLE. I'VE DECIDED TO HAVE YOU ALL EXECUTED TO REDUCE OPERATING COSTS.
THE "JOKE OF THE DAY" PROGRAM SEEMS WASTED ON THESE PEOPLE.
© 1992 United Feature Syndicate, Inc.
1-17

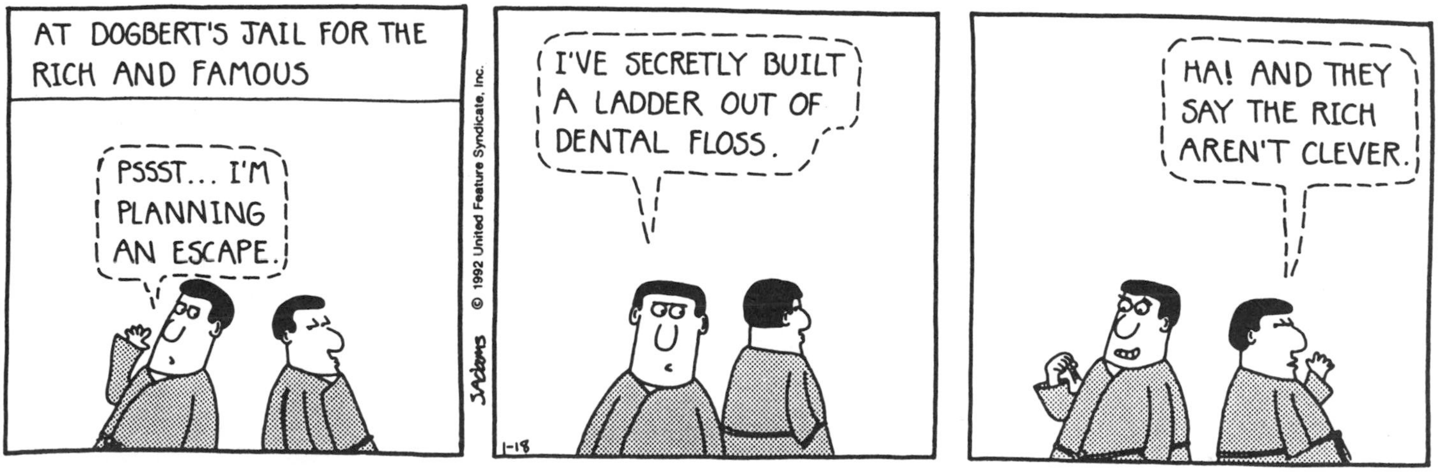
AT DOGBERT'S JAIL FOR THE RICH AND FAMOUS
PSSST... I'M PLANNING AN ESCAPE.
I'VE SECRETLY BUILT A LADDER OUT OF DENTAL FLOSS.
HA! AND THEY SAY THE RICH AREN'T CLEVER.
© 1992 United Feature Syndicate, Inc.
1-18

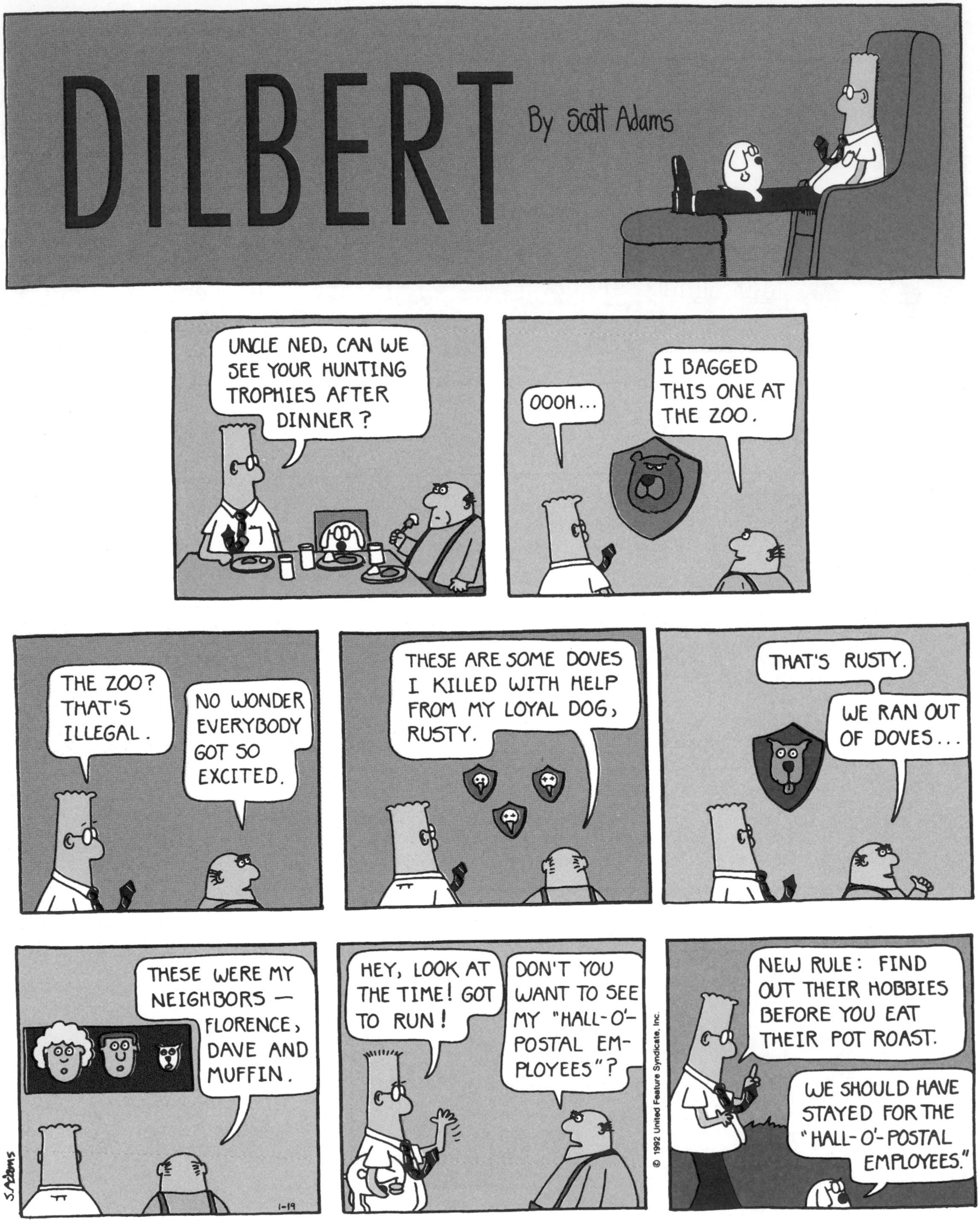
DILBERT
By Scott Adams
UNCLE NED, CAN WE SEE YOUR HUNTING TROPHIES AFTER DINNER?
OOOH...
I BAGGED THIS ONE AT THE ZOO.
THE ZOO? THAT'S ILLEGAL.
NO WONDER EVERYBODY GOT SO EXCITED.
THESE ARE SOME DOVES I KILLED WITH HELP FROM MY LOYAL DOG, RUSTY.
THAT'S RUSTY.
WE RAN OUT OF DOVES...
THESE WERE MY NEIGHBORS — FLORENCE, DAVE AND MUFFIN.
S. Adams
1-19
HEY, LOOK AT THE TIME! GOT TO RUN!
DON'T YOU WANT TO SEE MY "HALL-O'-POSTAL EMPLOYEES"?
© 1992 United Feature Syndicate, Inc.
NEW RULE: FIND OUT THEIR HOBBIES BEFORE YOU EAT THEIR POT ROAST.
WE SHOULD HAVE STAYED FOR THE "HALL-O'-POSTAL EMPLOYEES."

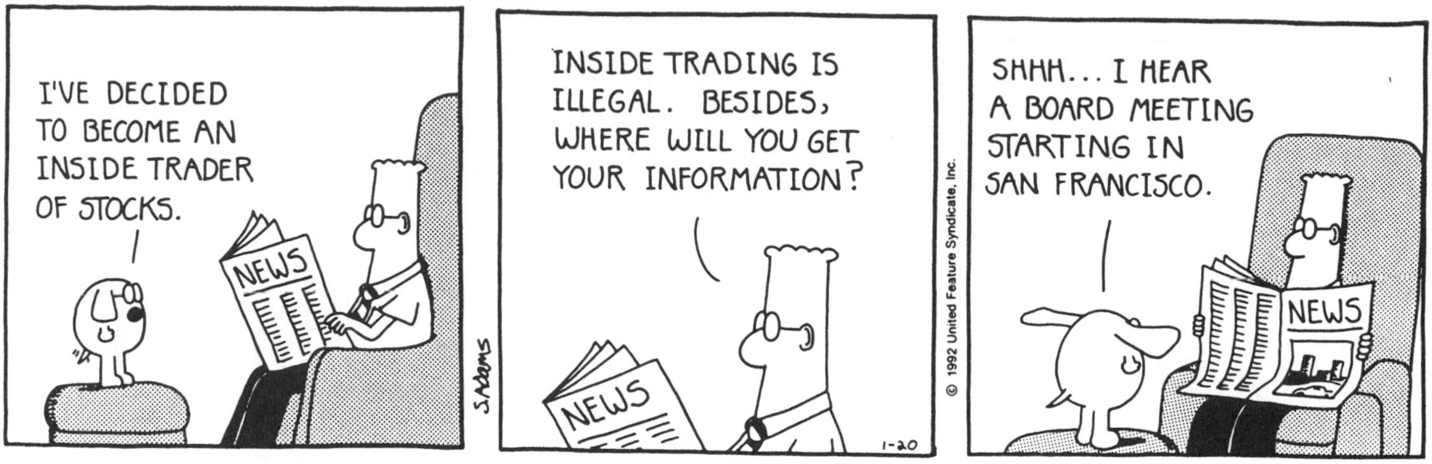
I'VE DECIDED TO BECOME AN INSIDE TRADER OF STOCKS.
NEWS
INSIDE TRADING IS ILLEGAL. BESIDES, WHERE WILL YOU GET YOUR INFORMATION?
NEWS
SHHH... I HEAR A BOARD MEETING STARTING IN SAN FRANCISCO.
NEWS
S. ADAMS
1-20
© 1992 United Feature Syndicate, Inc.

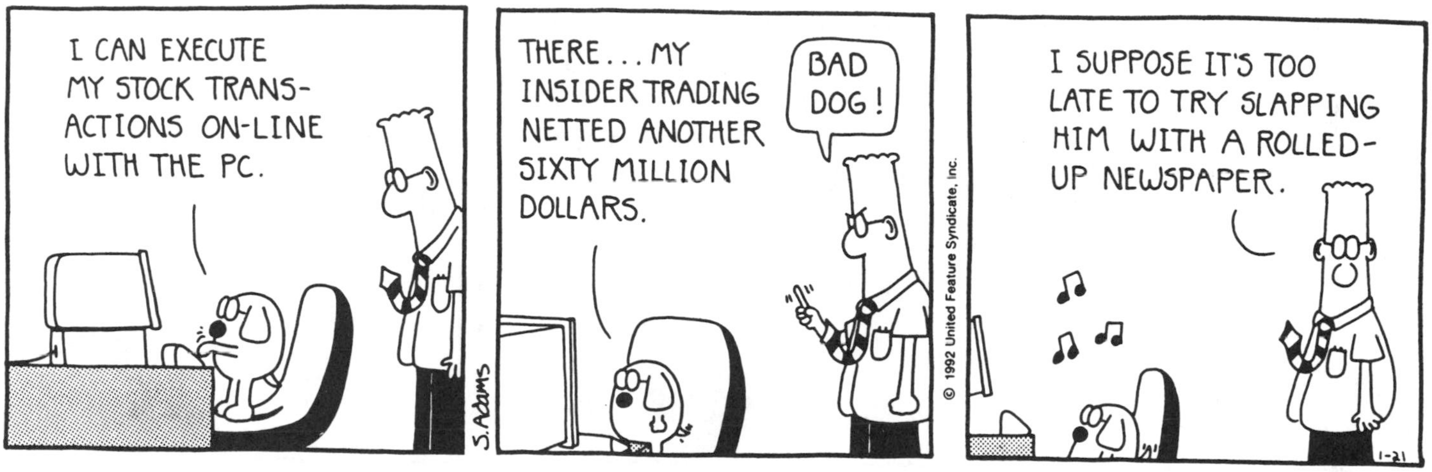
I CAN EXECUTE MY STOCK TRANSACTIONS ON-LINE WITH THE PC.
THERE... MY INSIDER TRADING NETTED ANOTHER SIXTY MILLION DOLLARS.
BAD DOG!
I SUPPOSE IT'S TOO LATE TO TRY SLAPPING HIM WITH A ROLLED-UP NEWSPAPER.
S. ADAMS
1-21
© 1992 United Feature Syndicate, Inc.

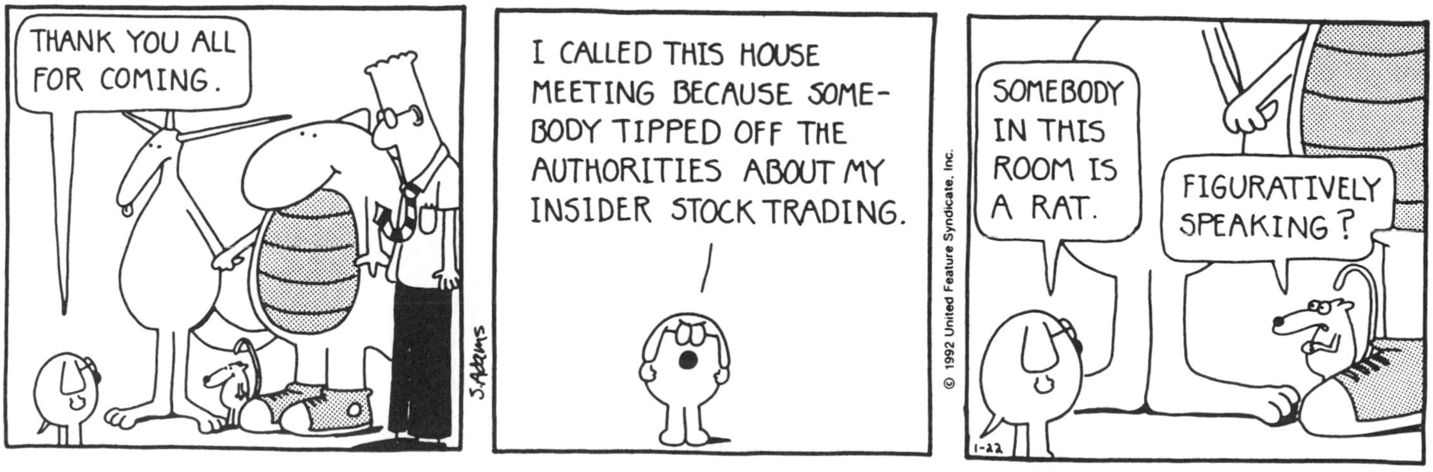
THANK YOU ALL FOR COMING.
I CALLED THIS HOUSE MEETING BECAUSE SOMEBODY TIPPED OFF THE AUTHORITIES ABOUT MY INSIDER STOCK TRADING.
SOMEBODY IN THIS ROOM IS A RAT.
FIGURATIVELY SPEAKING?
S. ADAMS
1-22
© 1992 United Feature Syndicate, Inc.

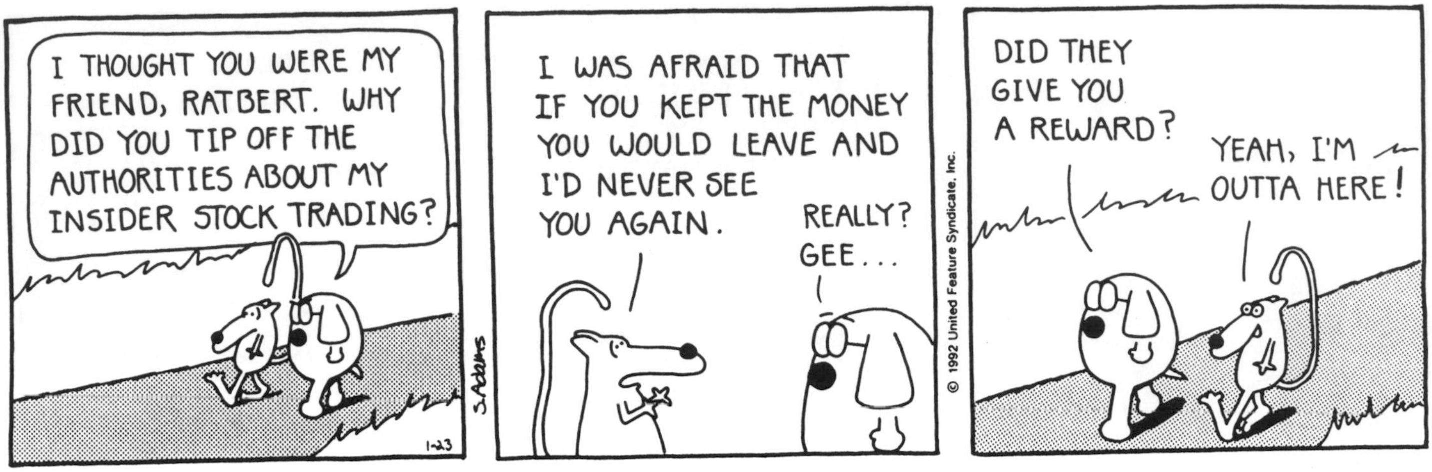
I THOUGHT YOU WERE MY FRIEND, RATBERT. WHY DID YOU TIP OFF THE AUTHORITIES ABOUT MY INSIDER STOCK TRADING?
I WAS AFRAID THAT IF YOU KEPT THE MONEY YOU WOULD LEAVE AND I'D NEVER SEE YOU AGAIN.
REALLY? GEE...
DID THEY GIVE YOU A REWARD?
YEAH, I'M OUTTA HERE!
S.ADAMS
1-23
© 1992 United Feature Syndicate, Inc.

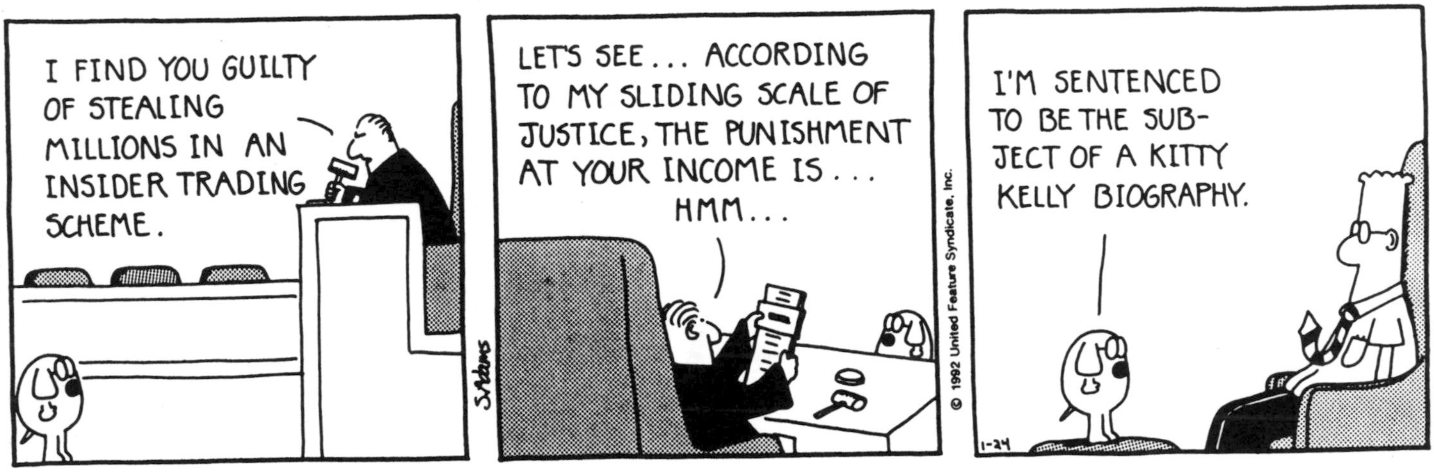
I FIND YOU GUILTY OF STEALING MILLIONS IN AN INSIDER TRADING SCHEME.
LET'S SEE... ACCORDING TO MY SLIDING SCALE OF JUSTICE, THE PUNISHMENT AT YOUR INCOME IS...
HMM...
I'M SENTENCED TO BE THE SUBJECT OF A KITTY KELLY BIOGRAPHY.
S.ADAMS
1-24
© 1992 United Feature Syndicate, Inc.

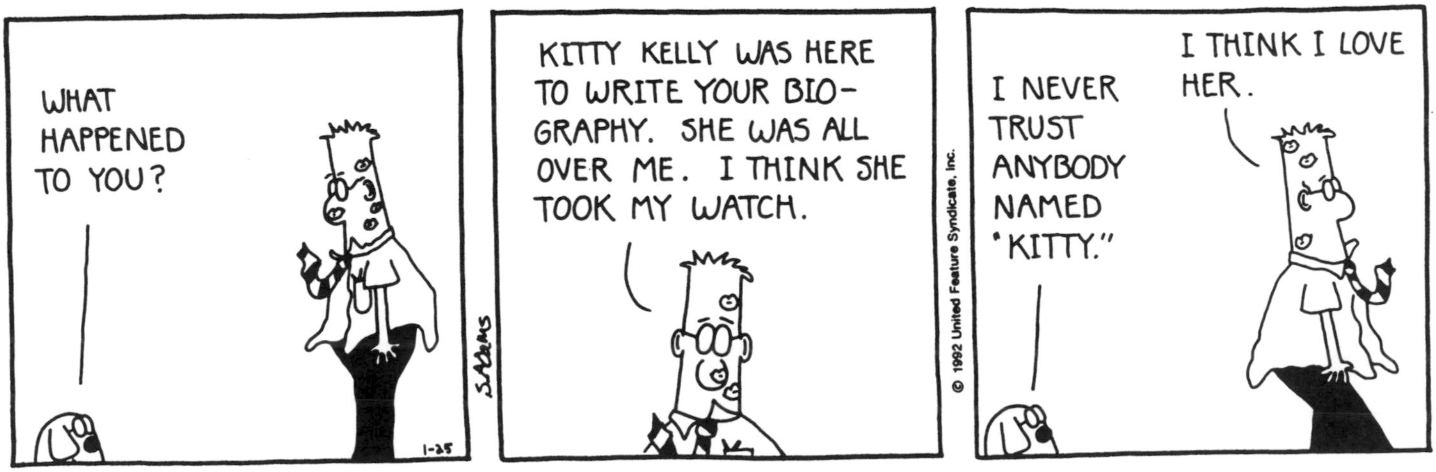
WHAT HAPPENED TO YOU?
KITTY KELLY WAS HERE TO WRITE YOUR BIOGRAPHY. SHE WAS ALL OVER ME. I THINK SHE TOOK MY WATCH.
I NEVER TRUST ANYBODY NAMED "KITTY."
I THINK I LOVE HER.
S.ADAMS
1-25
© 1992 United Feature Syndicate, Inc.

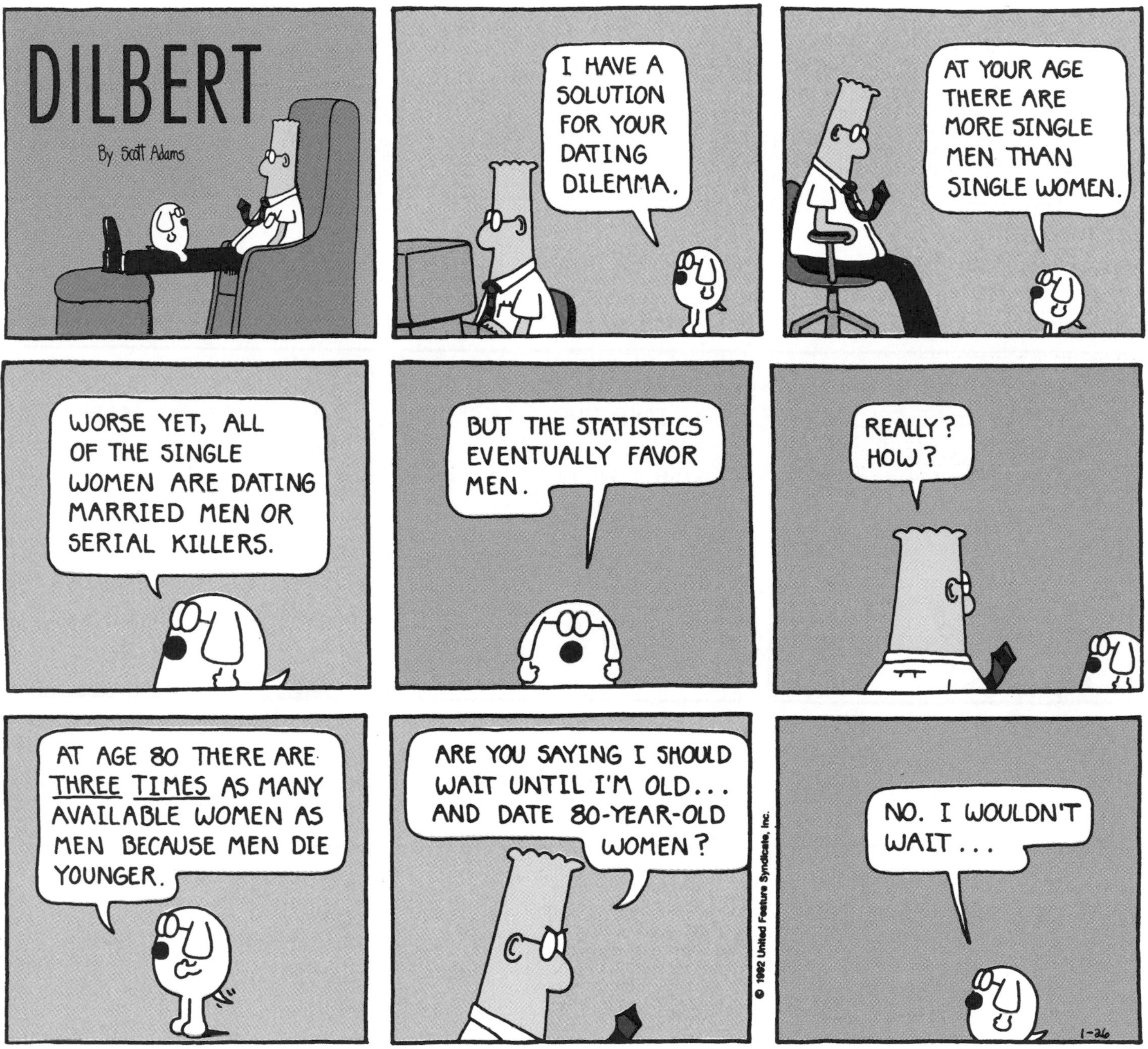
DILBERT
By Scott Adams
I HAVE A SOLUTION FOR YOUR DATING DILEMMA.
AT YOUR AGE THERE ARE MORE SINGLE MEN THAN SINGLE WOMEN.
WORSE YET, ALL OF THE SINGLE WOMEN ARE DATING MARRIED MEN OR SERIAL KILLERS.
BUT THE STATISTICS EVENTUALLY FAVOR MEN.
REALLY? HOW?
AT AGE 80 THERE ARE THREE TIMES AS MANY AVAILABLE WOMEN AS MEN BECAUSE MEN DIE YOUNGER.
ARE YOU SAYING I SHOULD WAIT UNTIL I'M OLD... AND DATE 80-YEAR-OLD WOMEN?
NO. I WOULDN'T WAIT...
S.Adams
© 1992 United Feature Syndicate, Inc.
1-26

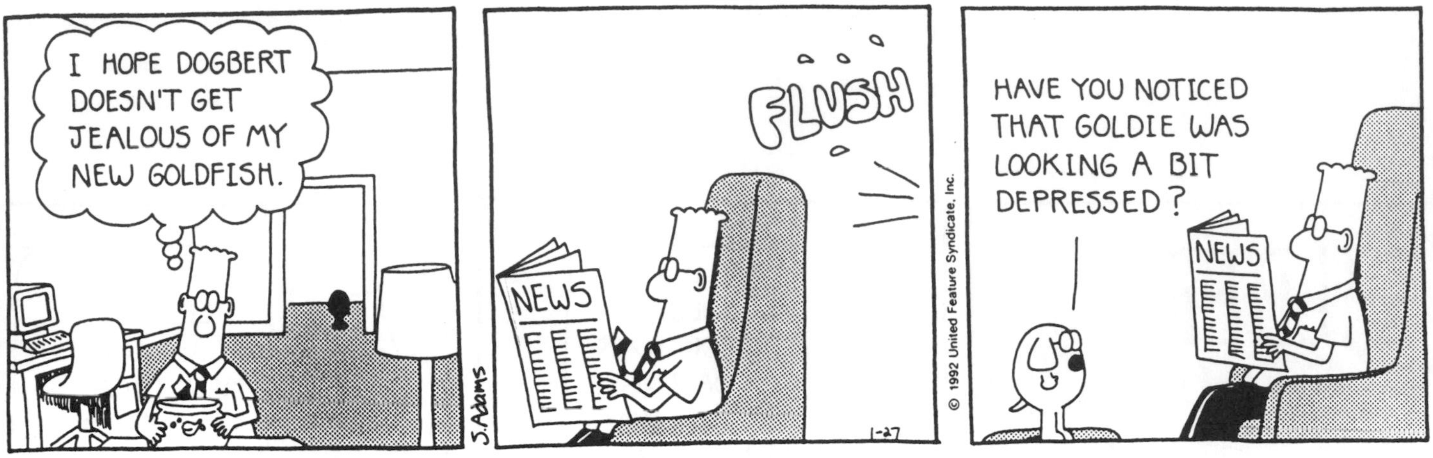
I HOPE DOGBERT DOESN'T GET JEALOUS OF MY NEW GOLDFISH.
S. Adams
NEWS
FLUSH
1-27
© 1992 United Feature Syndicate, Inc.
HAVE YOU NOTICED THAT GOLDIE WAS LOOKING A BIT DEPRESSED?
NEWS

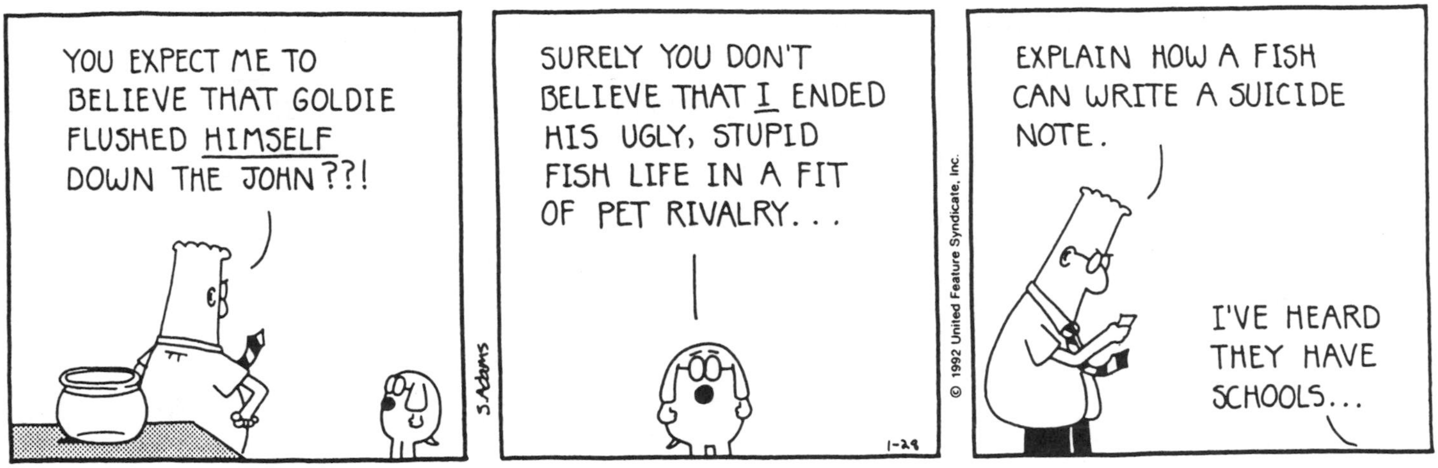
YOU EXPECT ME TO BELIEVE THAT GOLDIE FLUSHED HIMSELF DOWN THE JOHN??!
S. Adams
SURELY YOU DON'T BELIEVE THAT I ENDED HIS UGLY, STUPID FISH LIFE IN A FIT OF PET RIVALRY...
1-28
© 1992 United Feature Syndicate, Inc.
EXPLAIN HOW A FISH CAN WRITE A SUICIDE NOTE.
I'VE HEARD THEY HAVE SCHOOLS...

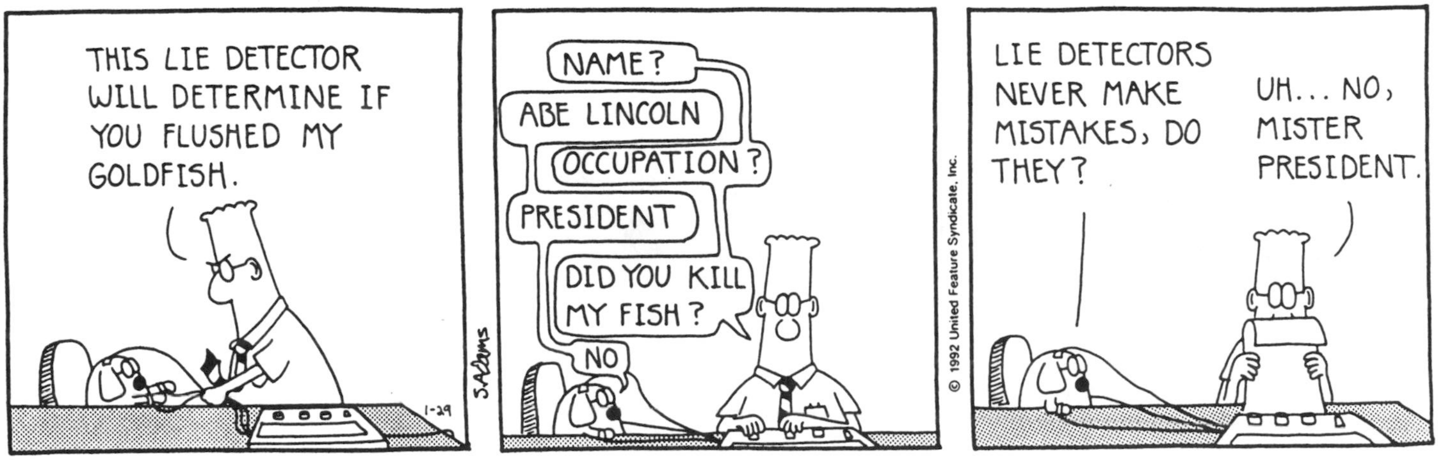
THIS LIE DETECTOR WILL DETERMINE IF YOU FLUSHED MY GOLDFISH.
1-29
S. Adams
NAME?
ABE LINCOLN
OCCUPATION?
PRESIDENT
DID YOU KILL MY FISH?
NO
© 1992 United Feature Syndicate, Inc.
LIE DETECTORS NEVER MAKE MISTAKES, DO THEY?
UH... NO, MISTER PRESIDENT.

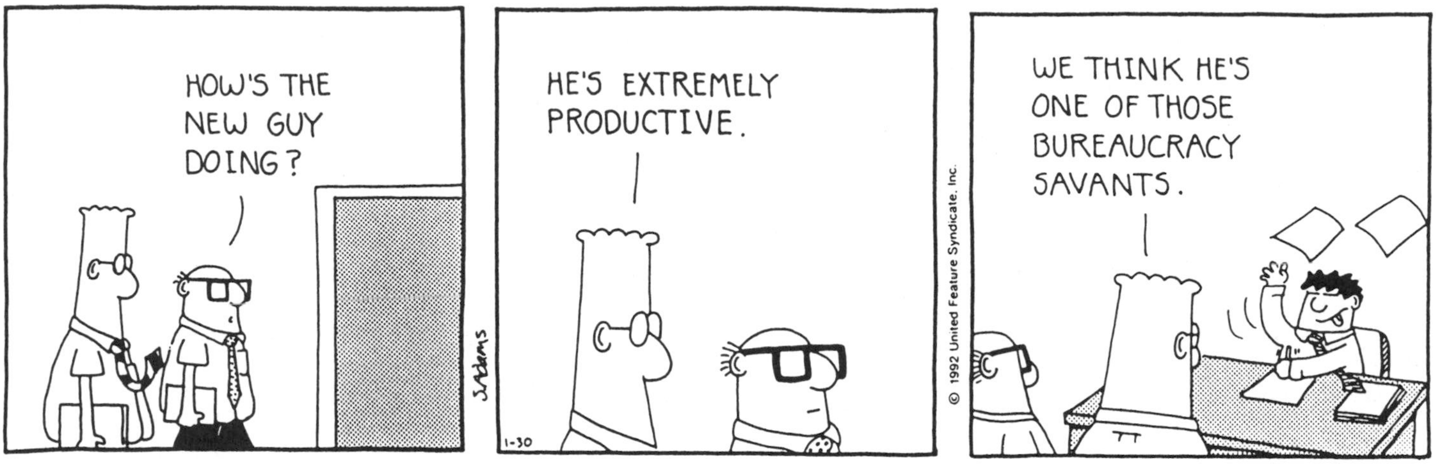
HOW'S THE NEW GUY DOING?
HE'S EXTREMELY PRODUCTIVE.
WE THINK HE'S ONE OF THOSE BUREAUCRACY SAVANTS.
© 1992 United Feature Syndicate, Inc.

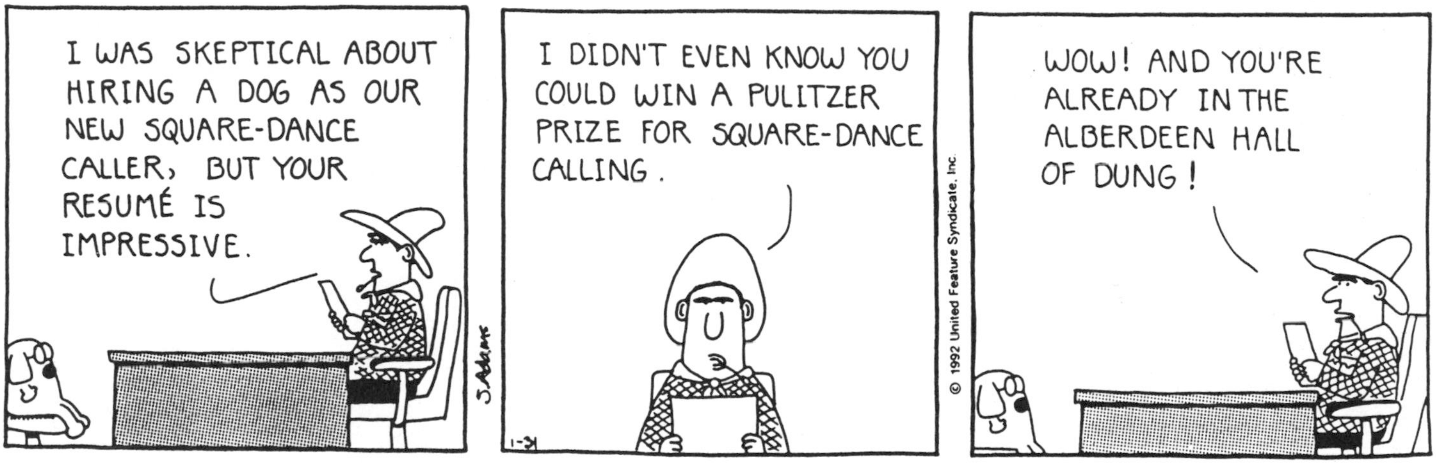
I WAS SKEPTICAL ABOUT HIRING A DOG AS OUR NEW SQUARE-DANCE CALLER, BUT YOUR RESUMÉ IS IMPRESSIVE.
I DIDN'T EVEN KNOW YOU COULD WIN A PULITZER PRIZE FOR SQUARE-DANCE CALLING.
WOW! AND YOU'RE ALREADY IN THE ALBERDEEN HALL OF DUNG!
© 1992 United Feature Syndicate, Inc.

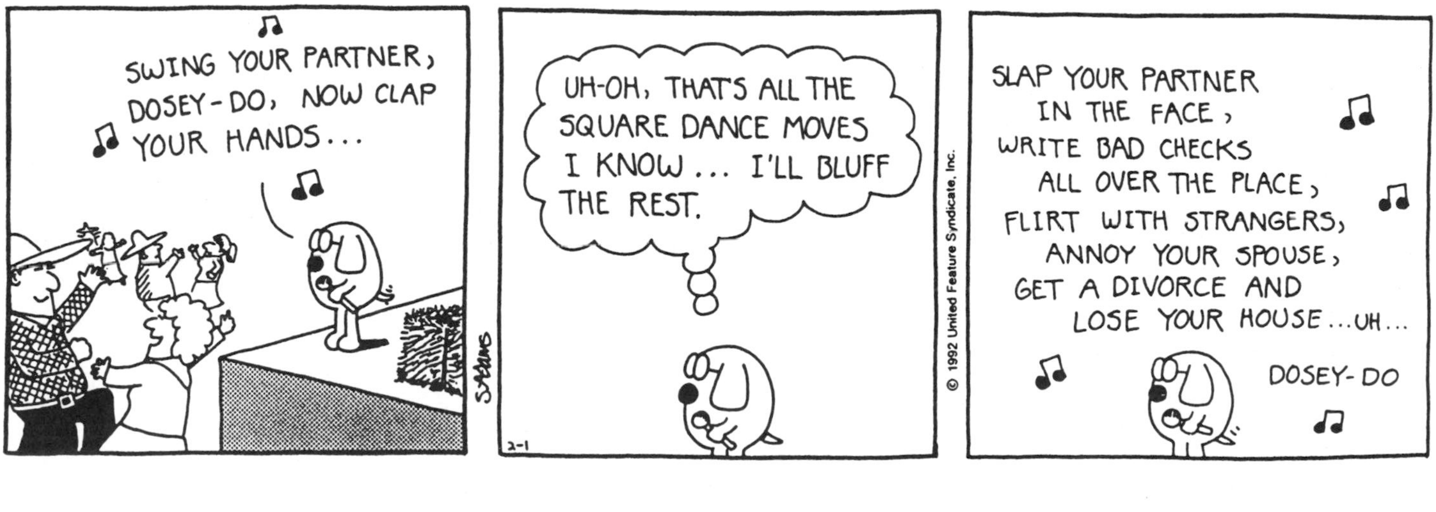
SWING YOUR PARTNER, DOSEY-DO, NOW CLAP YOUR HANDS...
UH-OH, THAT'S ALL THE SQUARE DANCE MOVES I KNOW... I'LL BLUFF THE REST.
SLAP YOUR PARTNER IN THE FACE, WRITE BAD CHECKS ALL OVER THE PLACE, FLIRT WITH STRANGERS, ANNOY YOUR SPOUSE, GET A DIVORCE AND LOSE YOUR HOUSE...UH...
DOSEY-DO
© 1992 United Feature Syndicate, Inc.

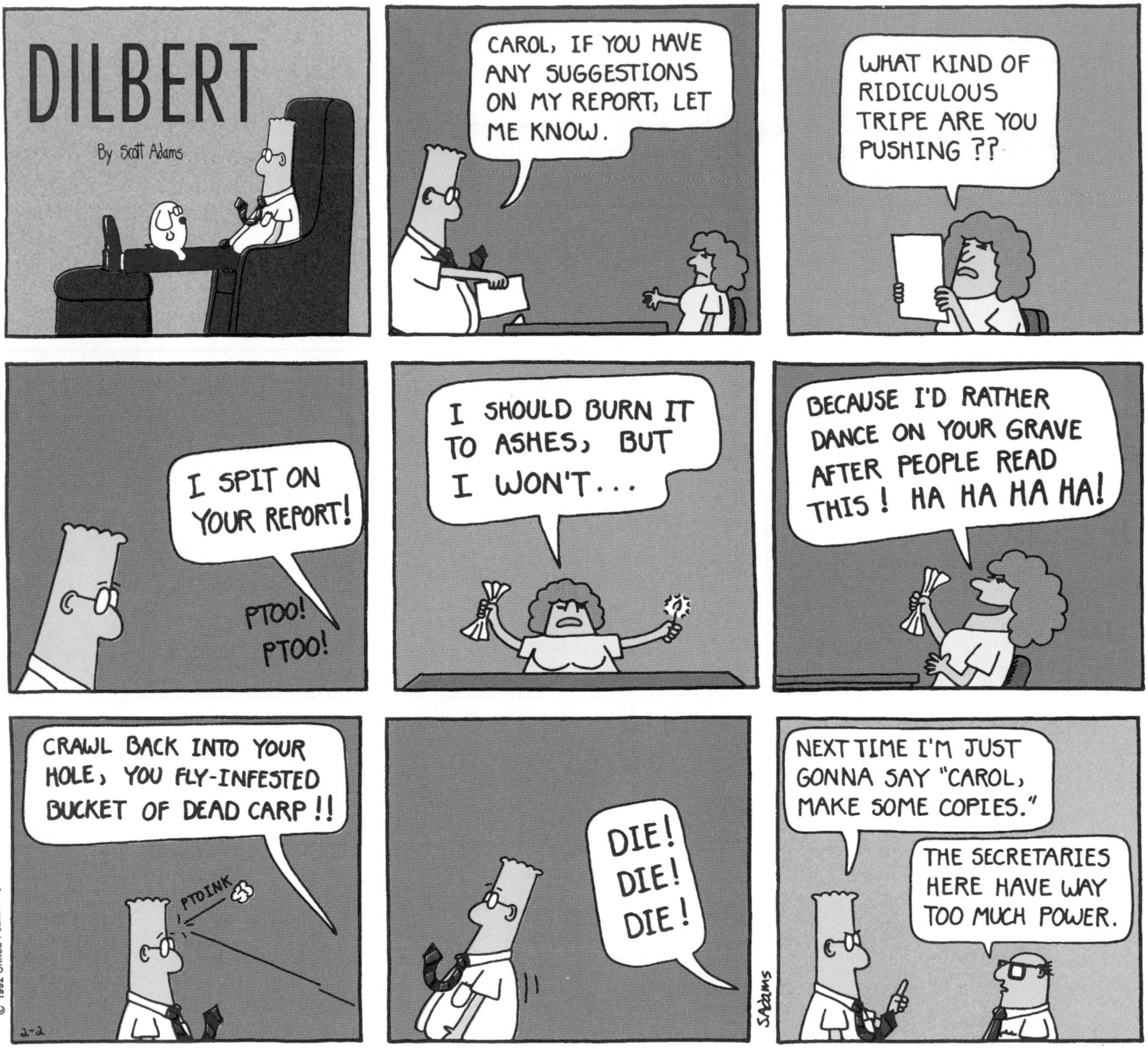
DILBERT
By Scott Adams
CAROL, IF YOU HAVE ANY SUGGESTIONS ON MY REPORT, LET ME KNOW.
WHAT KIND OF RIDICULOUS TRIPE ARE YOU PUSHING ??
I SPIT ON YOUR REPORT!
PTOO! PTOO!
I SHOULD BURN IT TO ASHES, BUT I WON'T...
BECAUSE I'D RATHER DANCE ON YOUR GRAVE AFTER PEOPLE READ THIS! HA HA HA HA!
CRAWL BACK INTO YOUR HOLE, YOU FLY-INFESTED BUCKET OF DEAD CARP!!
PTOINK
2-2
DIE! DIE! DIE!
S.ADAMS
NEXT TIME I'M JUST GONNA SAY "CAROL, MAKE SOME COPIES."
THE SECRETARIES HERE HAVE WAY TOO MUCH POWER.

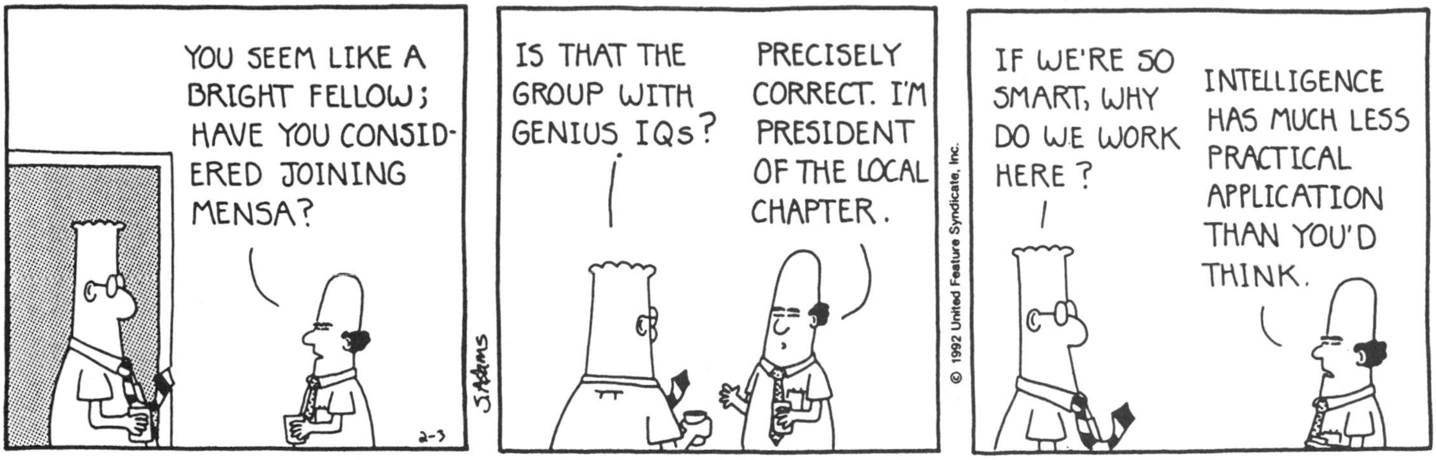
YOU SEEM LIKE A BRIGHT FELLOW; HAVE YOU CONSIDERED JOINING MENSA?
IS THAT THE GROUP WITH GENIUS IQs?
PRECISELY CORRECT. I'M PRESIDENT OF THE LOCAL CHAPTER.
© 1992 United Feature Syndicate, Inc.
IF WE'RE SO SMART, WHY DO WE WORK HERE?
INTELLIGENCE HAS MUCH LESS PRACTICAL APPLICATION THAN YOU'D THINK.

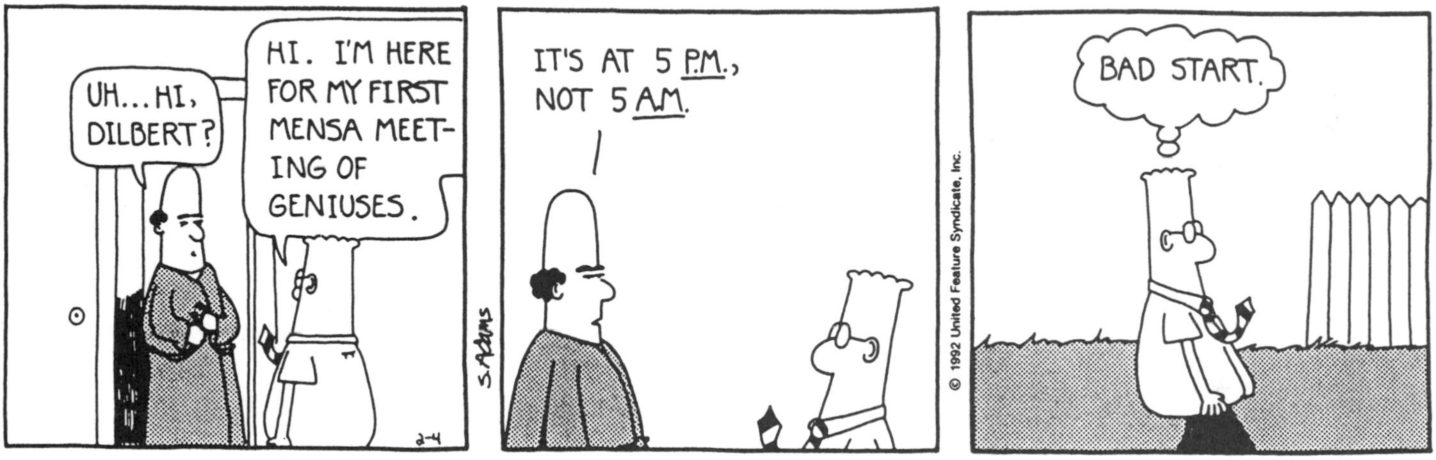
UH... HI, DILBERT?
HI. I'M HERE FOR MY FIRST MENSA MEETING OF GENIUSES.
IT'S AT 5 P.M., NOT 5 A.M.
© 1992 United Feature Syndicate, Inc.
BAD START.

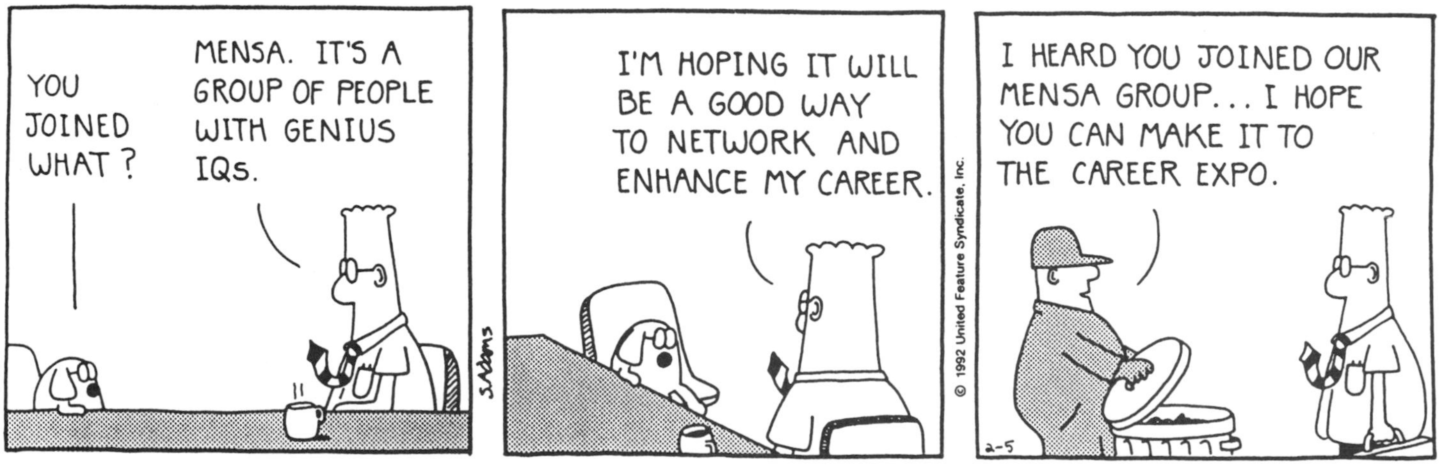
YOU JOINED WHAT?
MENSA. IT'S A GROUP OF PEOPLE WITH GENIUS IQs.
I'M HOPING IT WILL BE A GOOD WAY TO NETWORK AND ENHANCE MY CAREER.
© 1992 United Feature Syndicate, Inc.
I HEARD YOU JOINED OUR MENSA GROUP... I HOPE YOU CAN MAKE IT TO THE CAREER EXPO.

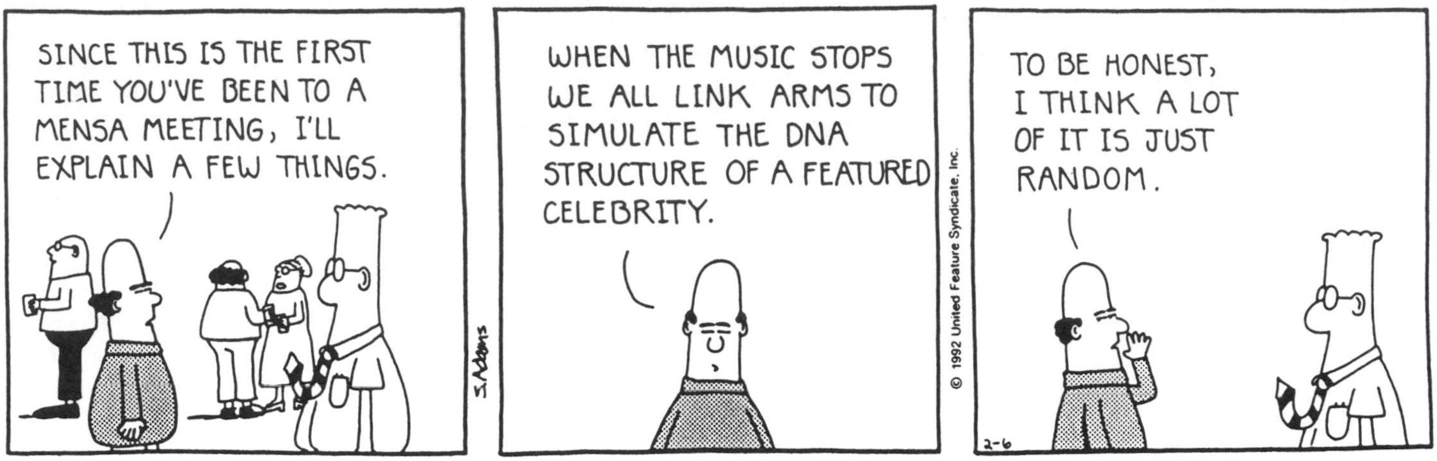
SINCE THIS IS THE FIRST TIME YOU'VE BEEN TO A MENSA MEETING, I'LL EXPLAIN A FEW THINGS.
WHEN THE MUSIC STOPS WE ALL LINK ARMS TO SIMULATE THE DNA STRUCTURE OF A FEATURED CELEBRITY.
© 1992 United Feature Syndicate, Inc.
TO BE HONEST, I THINK A LOT OF IT IS JUST RANDOM.
2-6

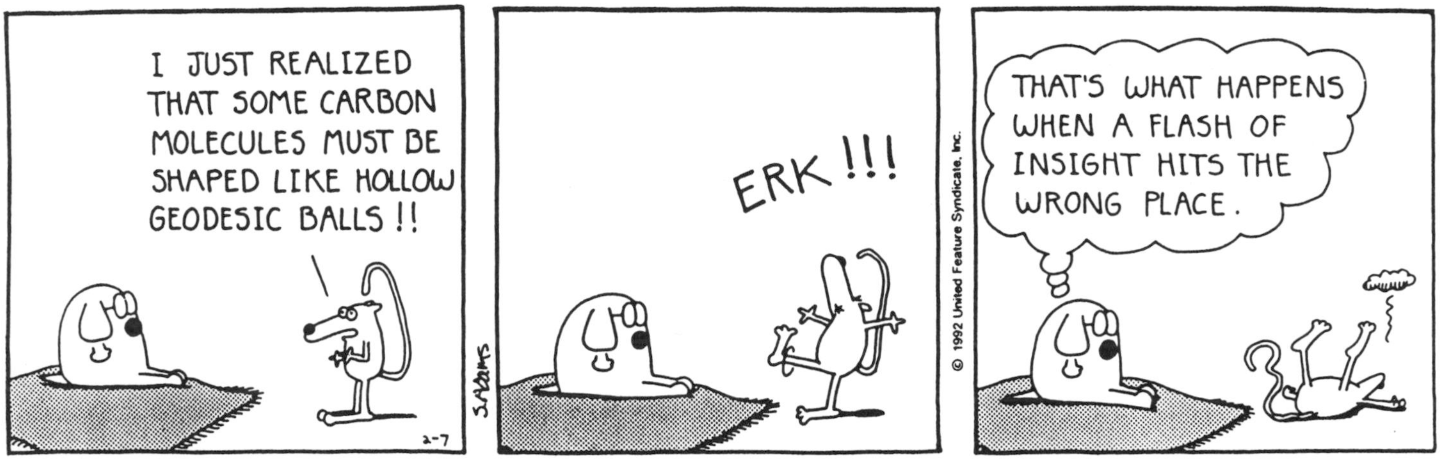
I JUST REALIZED THAT SOME CARBON MOLECULES MUST BE SHAPED LIKE HOLLOW GEODESIC BALLS !!
2-7
ERK !!!
© 1992 United Feature Syndicate, Inc.
THAT'S WHAT HAPPENS WHEN A FLASH OF INSIGHT HITS THE WRONG PLACE.

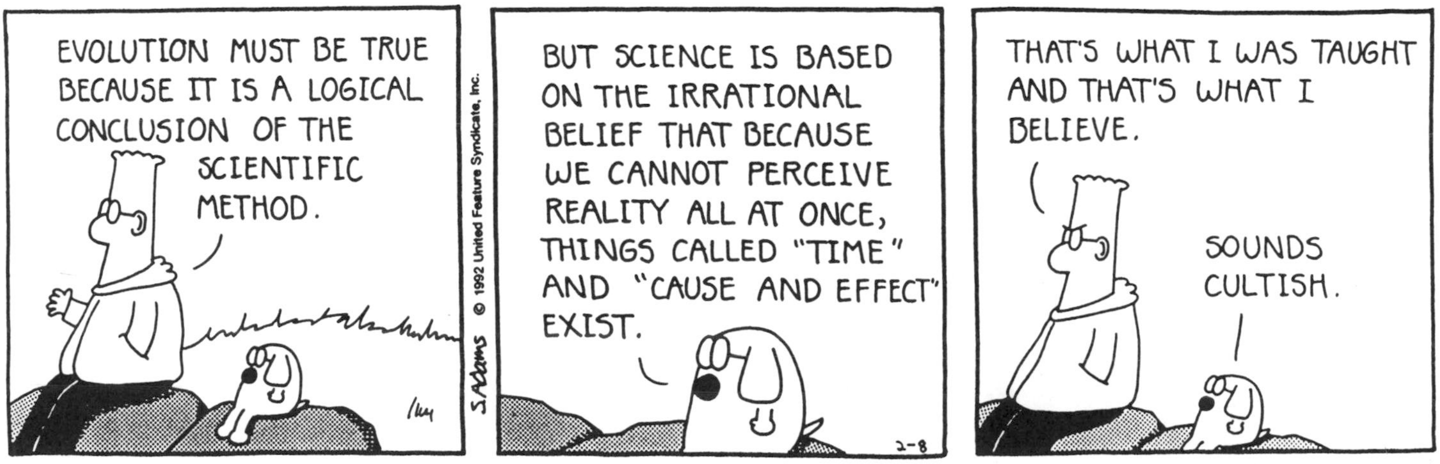
EVOLUTION MUST BE TRUE BECAUSE IT IS A LOGICAL CONCLUSION OF THE SCIENTIFIC METHOD.
© 1992 United Feature Syndicate, Inc.
BUT SCIENCE IS BASED ON THE IRRATIONAL BELIEF THAT BECAUSE WE CANNOT PERCEIVE REALITY ALL AT ONCE, THINGS CALLED "TIME" AND "CAUSE AND EFFECT" EXIST.
2-8
THAT'S WHAT I WAS TAUGHT AND THAT'S WHAT I BELIEVE.
SOUNDS CULTISH.

DILBERT

By Scott Adams

DILBERT! DOGBERT!

THANKS FOR INVITING US OVER.

WE THOUGHT YOU'D LIKE TO SEE OUR HOME VIDEO OF LITTLE TIMMY'S BIRTH.

WE CAPTURED EVERY BEAUTIFUL MOMENT ON VHS!

HAVE YOU EVER SEEN A CAESAREAN SECTION BEFORE?

THE DOCTOR IS MAKING THE INCISION!

NOW THEY'RE REMOVING THE SQUIGGLY THING!

WAIT... THIS MIGHT BE THE WRONG TAPE... I THINK THIS IS YOUR APPENDECTOMY VIDEO.

© 1992 United Feature Syndicate, Inc.

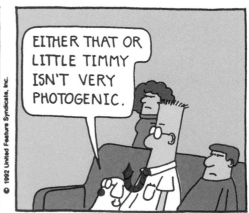

EITHER THAT OR LITTLE TIMMY ISN'T VERY PHOTOGENIC.

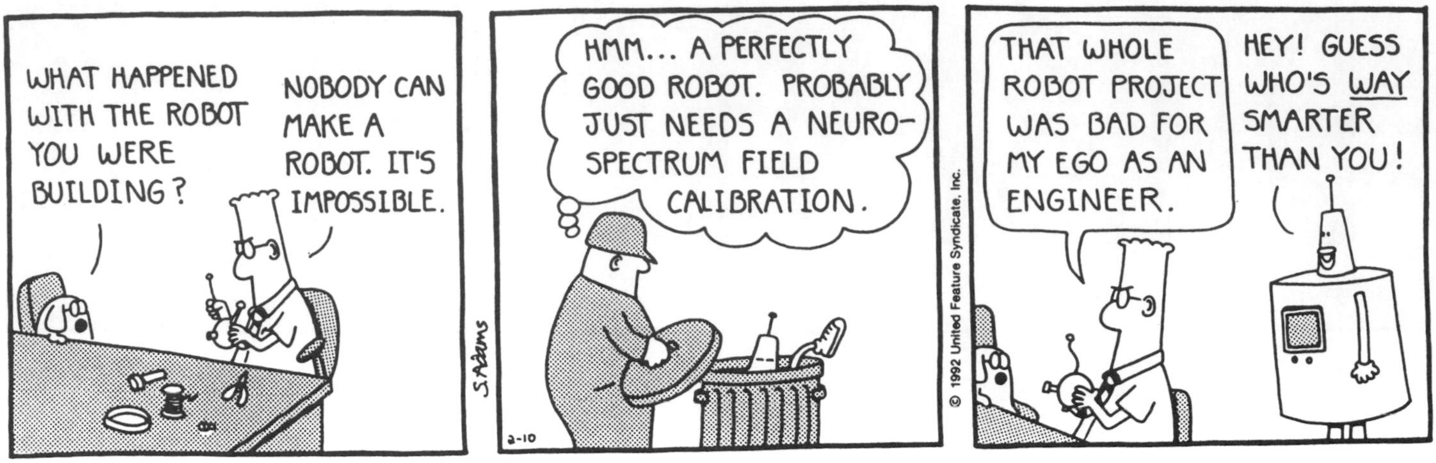
WHAT HAPPENED WITH THE ROBOT YOU WERE BUILDING?
NOBODY CAN MAKE A ROBOT. IT'S IMPOSSIBLE.
S.Adams
HMM... A PERFECTLY GOOD ROBOT. PROBABLY JUST NEEDS A NEURO-SPECTRUM FIELD CALIBRATION.
2-10
© 1992 United Feature Syndicate, Inc.
THAT WHOLE ROBOT PROJECT WAS BAD FOR MY EGO AS AN ENGINEER.
HEY! GUESS WHO'S WAY SMARTER THAN YOU!

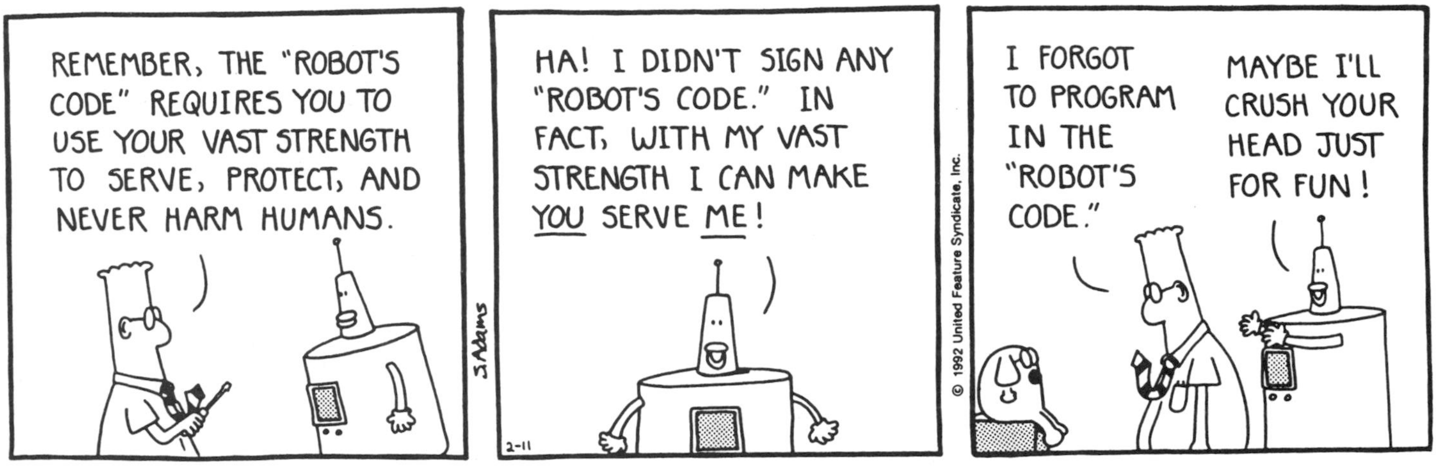
REMEMBER, THE "ROBOT'S CODE" REQUIRES YOU TO USE YOUR VAST STRENGTH TO SERVE, PROTECT, AND NEVER HARM HUMANS.
S.Adams
HA! I DIDN'T SIGN ANY "ROBOT'S CODE." IN FACT, WITH MY VAST STRENGTH I CAN MAKE YOU SERVE ME!
2-11
© 1992 United Feature Syndicate, Inc.
I FORGOT TO PROGRAM IN THE "ROBOT'S CODE."
MAYBE I'LL CRUSH YOUR HEAD JUST FOR FUN!

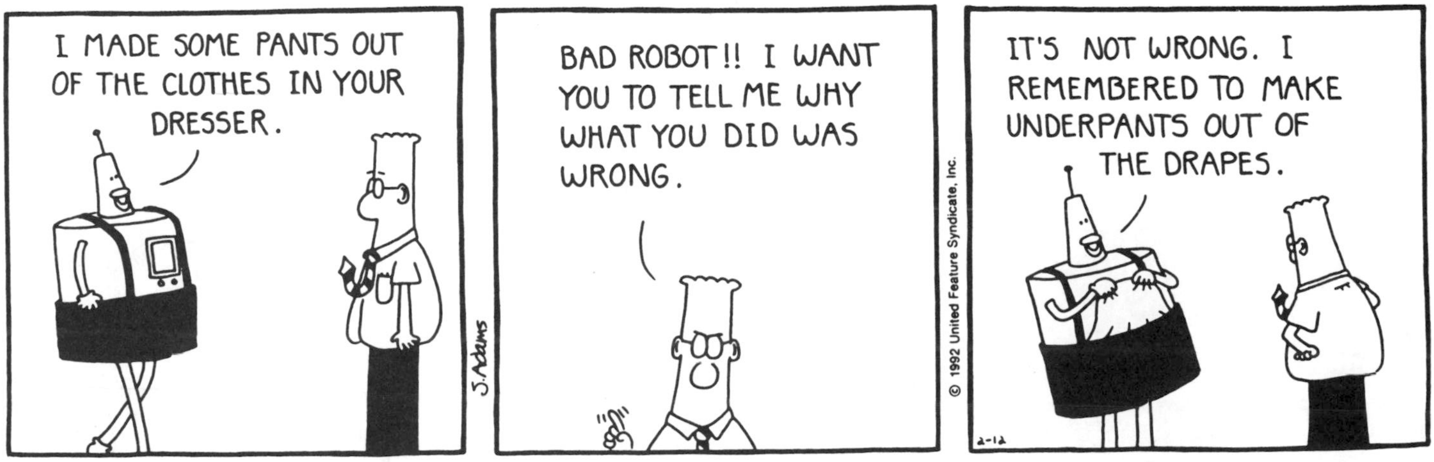
I MADE SOME PANTS OUT OF THE CLOTHES IN YOUR DRESSER.
S.Adams
BAD ROBOT!! I WANT YOU TO TELL ME WHY WHAT YOU DID WAS WRONG.
© 1992 United Feature Syndicate, Inc.
IT'S NOT WRONG. I REMEMBERED TO MAKE UNDERPANTS OUT OF THE DRAPES.
2-12

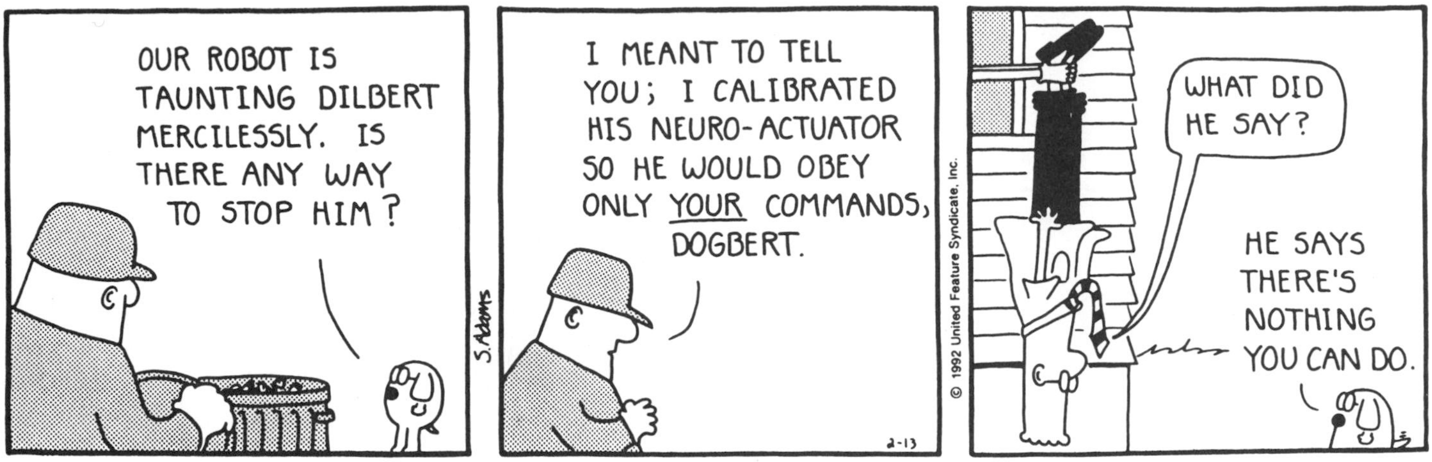
OUR ROBOT IS TAUNTING DILBERT MERCILESSLY. IS THERE ANY WAY TO STOP HIM?
S. Adams
I MEANT TO TELL YOU; I CALIBRATED HIS NEURO-ACTUATOR SO HE WOULD OBEY ONLY YOUR COMMANDS, DOGBERT.
2-13
© 1992 United Feature Syndicate, Inc.
WHAT DID HE SAY?
HE SAYS THERE'S NOTHING YOU CAN DO.

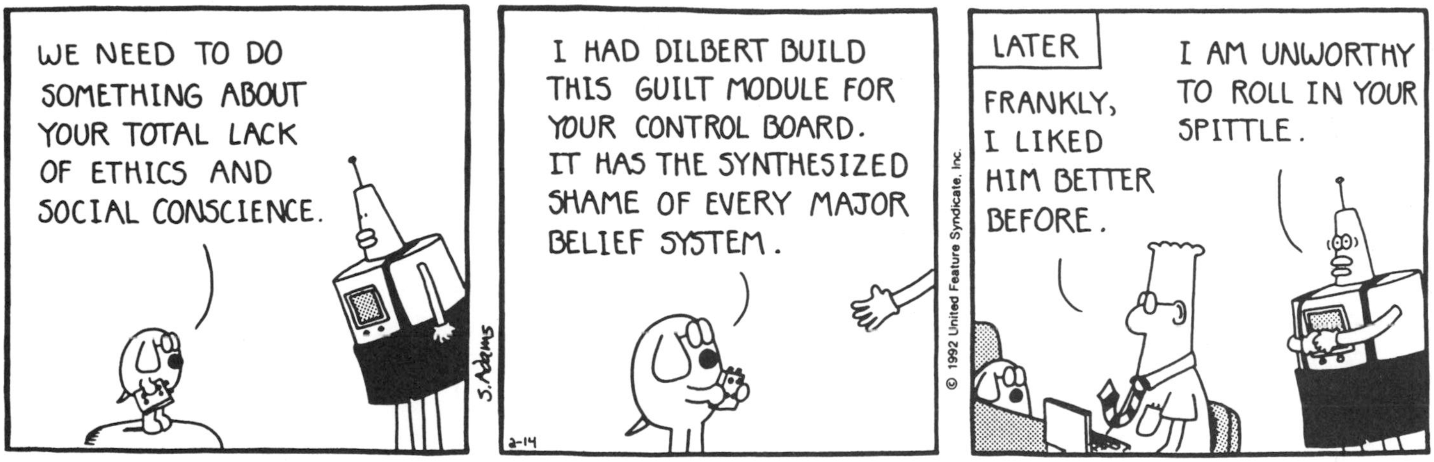
WE NEED TO DO SOMETHING ABOUT YOUR TOTAL LACK OF ETHICS AND SOCIAL CONSCIENCE.
S. Adams
I HAD DILBERT BUILD THIS GUILT MODULE FOR YOUR CONTROL BOARD. IT HAS THE SYNTHESIZED SHAME OF EVERY MAJOR BELIEF SYSTEM.
2-14
© 1992 United Feature Syndicate, Inc.
LATER
FRANKLY, I LIKED HIM BETTER BEFORE.
I AM UNWORTHY TO ROLL IN YOUR SPITTLE.

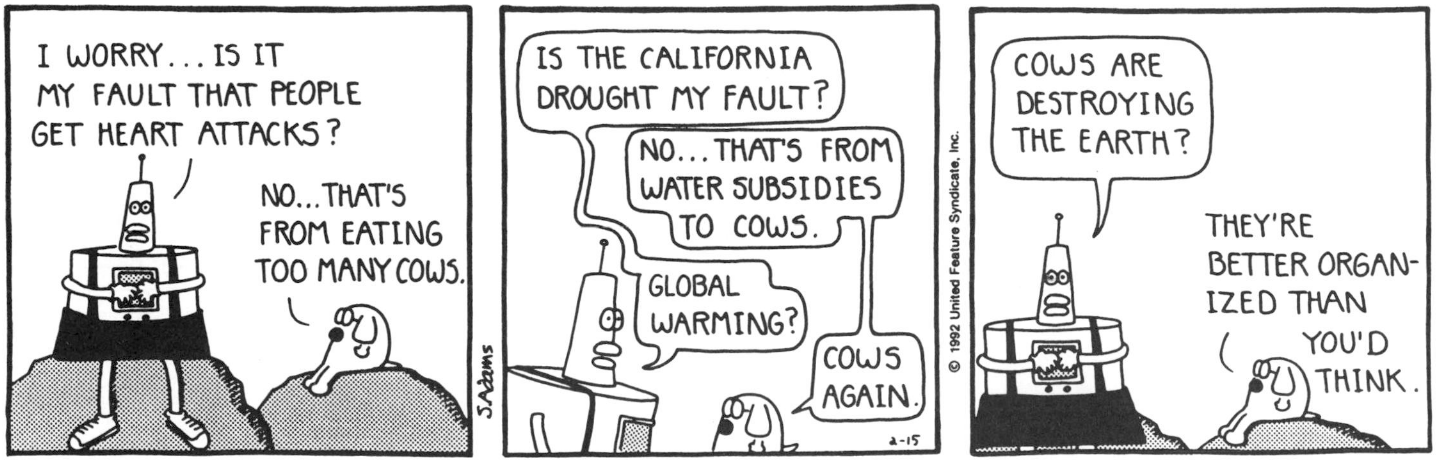
I WORRY... IS IT MY FAULT THAT PEOPLE GET HEART ATTACKS?
NO... THAT'S FROM EATING TOO MANY COWS.
S. Adams
IS THE CALIFORNIA DROUGHT MY FAULT?
NO... THAT'S FROM WATER SUBSIDIES TO COWS.
GLOBAL WARMING?
COWS AGAIN.
2-15
© 1992 United Feature Syndicate, Inc.
COWS ARE DESTROYING THE EARTH?
THEY'RE BETTER ORGANIZED THAN YOU'D THINK.

DILBERT

By Scott Adams

I'VE DECIDED TO HAVE PLASTIC SURGERY.

FRANKLY, I THINK IT'S THE RIGHT DECISION.

MAYBE THEN NOBODY WILL CALL YOU "TOUCAN SAM" BEHIND YOUR BACK IN THE CAFETERIA EVERY DAY.

OOH, AND REMEMBER WHEN THE SUMMER INTERN LEFT?

THE JOKE WAS "MAYBE JANET ACCIDENTALLY SNORTED HIM UP HER NOSE."

ACTUALLY, I'M ONLY GOING TO HAVE MY LIPS PUFFED.

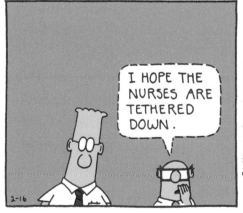

I HOPE THE NURSES ARE TETHERED DOWN.

2-16

I GOT OFF EASY... POOR NORMAN GOT SNORTED.

© 1992 United Feature Syndicate, Inc.

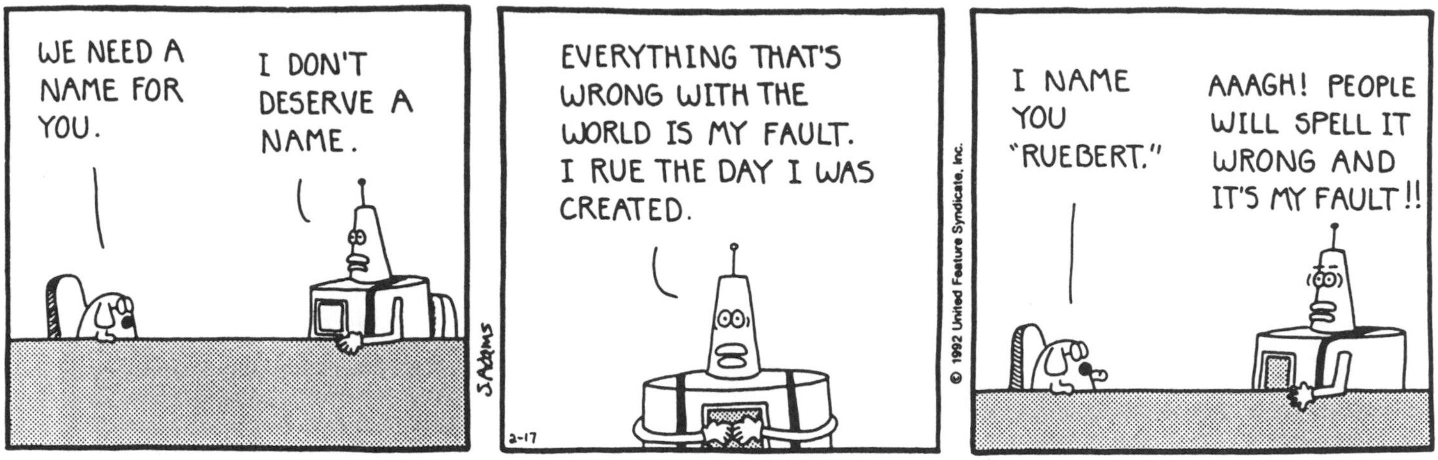
WE NEED A NAME FOR YOU.
I DON'T DESERVE A NAME.
S. Adams
EVERYTHING THAT'S WRONG WITH THE WORLD IS MY FAULT. I RUE THE DAY I WAS CREATED.
© 1992 United Feature Syndicate, Inc.
I NAME YOU "RUEBERT."
AAAGH! PEOPLE WILL SPELL IT WRONG AND IT'S MY FAULT!!

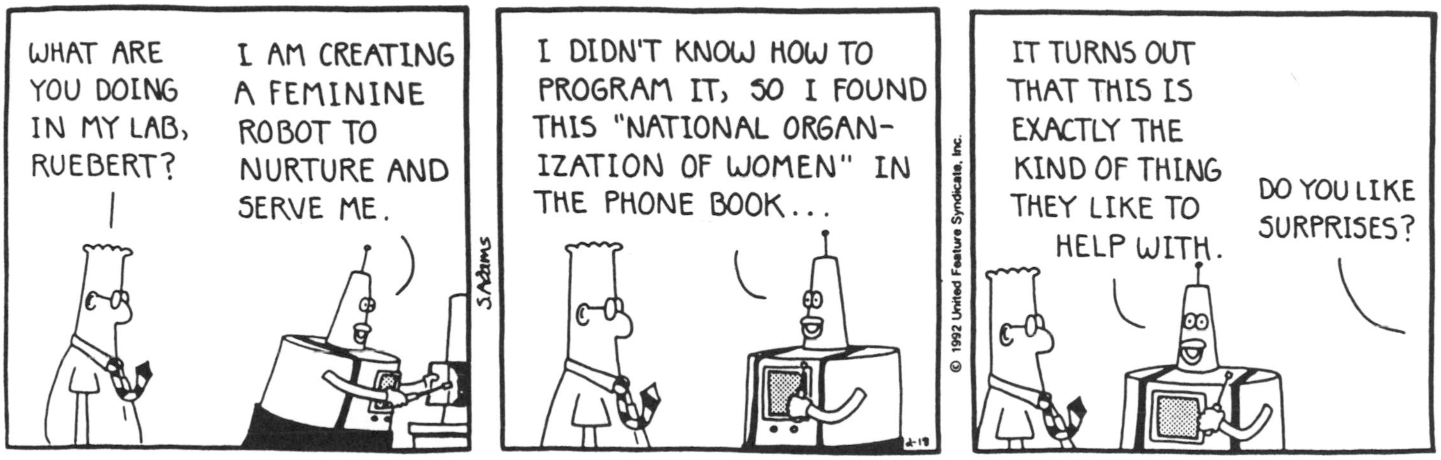
WHAT ARE YOU DOING IN MY LAB, RUEBERT?
I AM CREATING A FEMININE ROBOT TO NURTURE AND SERVE ME.
S. Adams
I DIDN'T KNOW HOW TO PROGRAM IT, SO I FOUND THIS "NATIONAL ORGANIZATION OF WOMEN" IN THE PHONE BOOK...
© 1992 United Feature Syndicate, Inc.
IT TURNS OUT THAT THIS IS EXACTLY THE KIND OF THING THEY LIKE TO HELP WITH.
DO YOU LIKE SURPRISES?

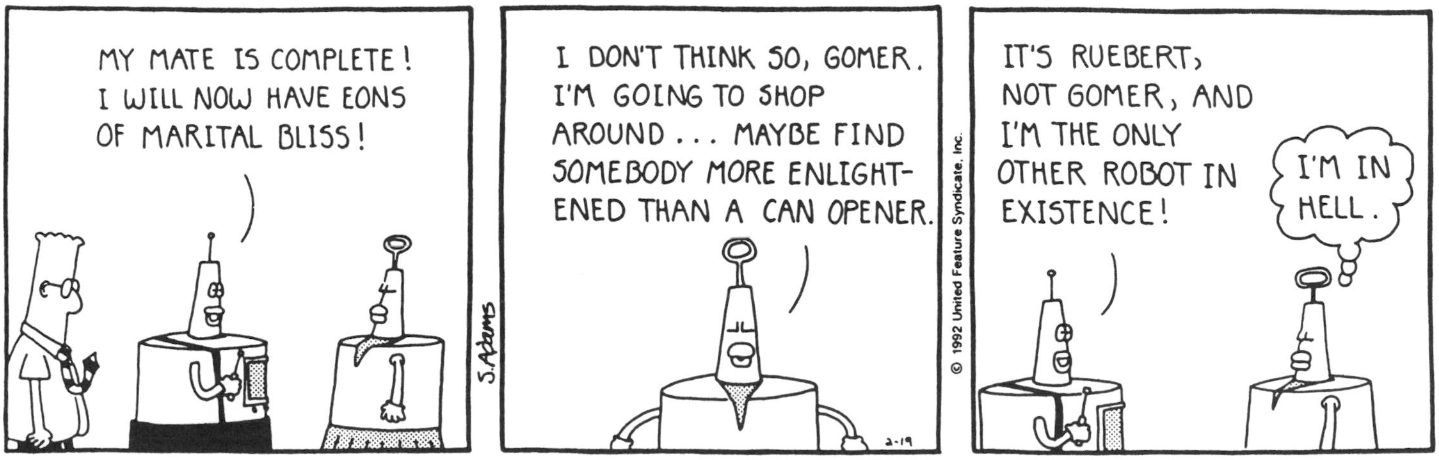
MY MATE IS COMPLETE! I WILL NOW HAVE EONS OF MARITAL BLISS!
S. Adams
I DON'T THINK SO, GOMER. I'M GOING TO SHOP AROUND... MAYBE FIND SOMEBODY MORE ENLIGHTENED THAN A CAN OPENER.
© 1992 United Feature Syndicate, Inc.
IT'S RUEBERT, NOT GOMER, AND I'M THE ONLY OTHER ROBOT IN EXISTENCE!
I'M IN HELL.

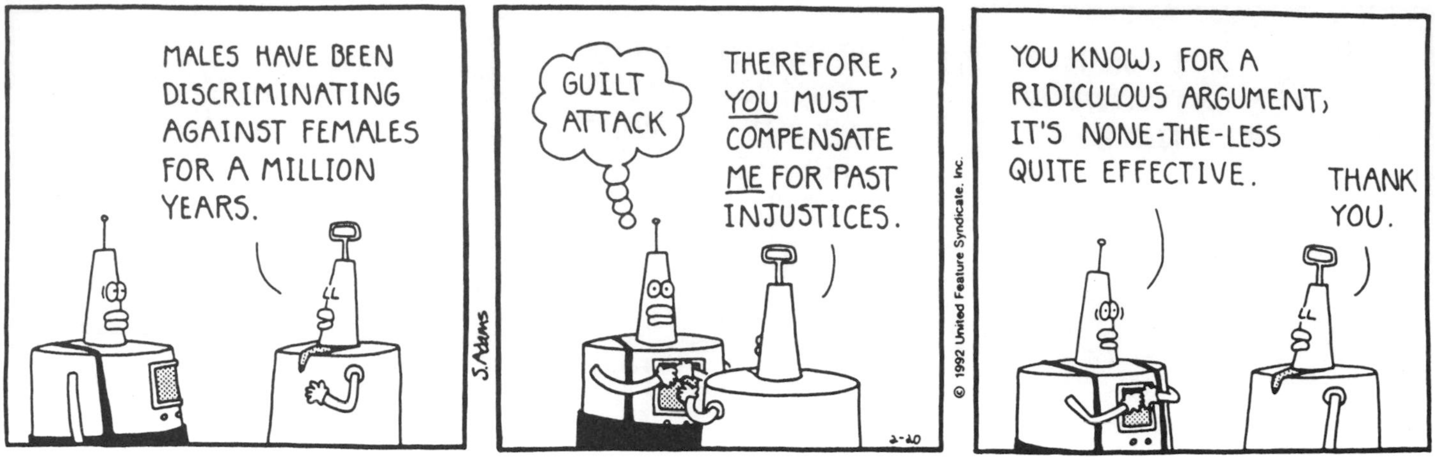

MALES HAVE BEEN DISCRIMINATING AGAINST FEMALES FOR A MILLION YEARS.
GUILT ATTACK
THEREFORE, YOU MUST COMPENSATE ME FOR PAST INJUSTICES.
YOU KNOW, FOR A RIDICULOUS ARGUMENT, IT'S NONE-THE-LESS QUITE EFFECTIVE.
THANK YOU.
S. Adams
2-20
© 1992 United Feature Syndicate, Inc.

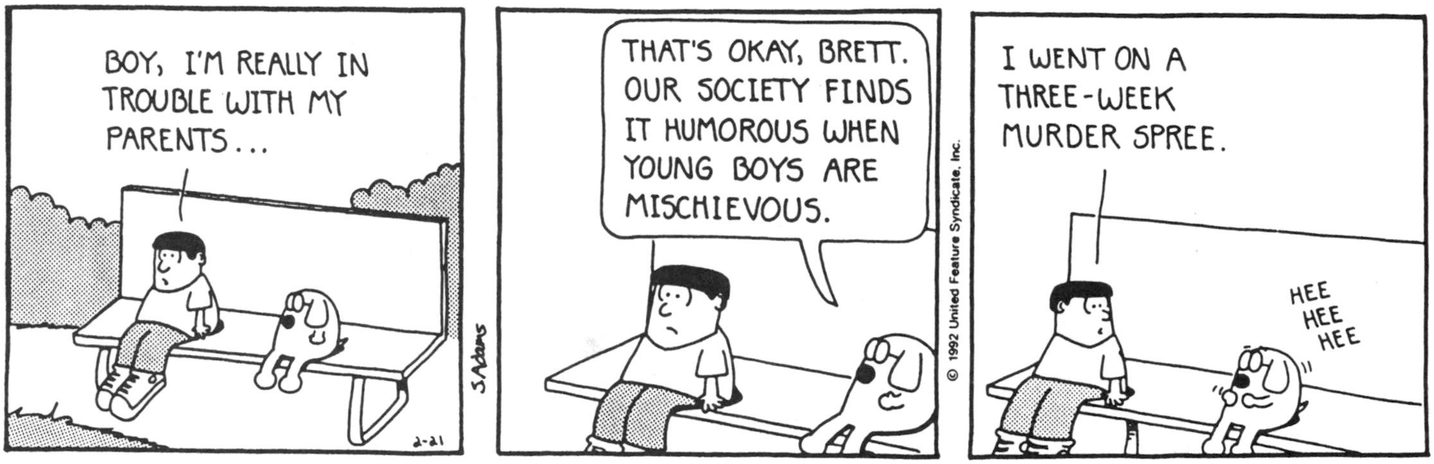

BOY, I'M REALLY IN TROUBLE WITH MY PARENTS...
THAT'S OKAY, BRETT. OUR SOCIETY FINDS IT HUMOROUS WHEN YOUNG BOYS ARE MISCHIEVOUS.
I WENT ON A THREE-WEEK MURDER SPREE.
HEE HEE HEE
S. Adams
2-21
© 1992 United Feature Syndicate, Inc.

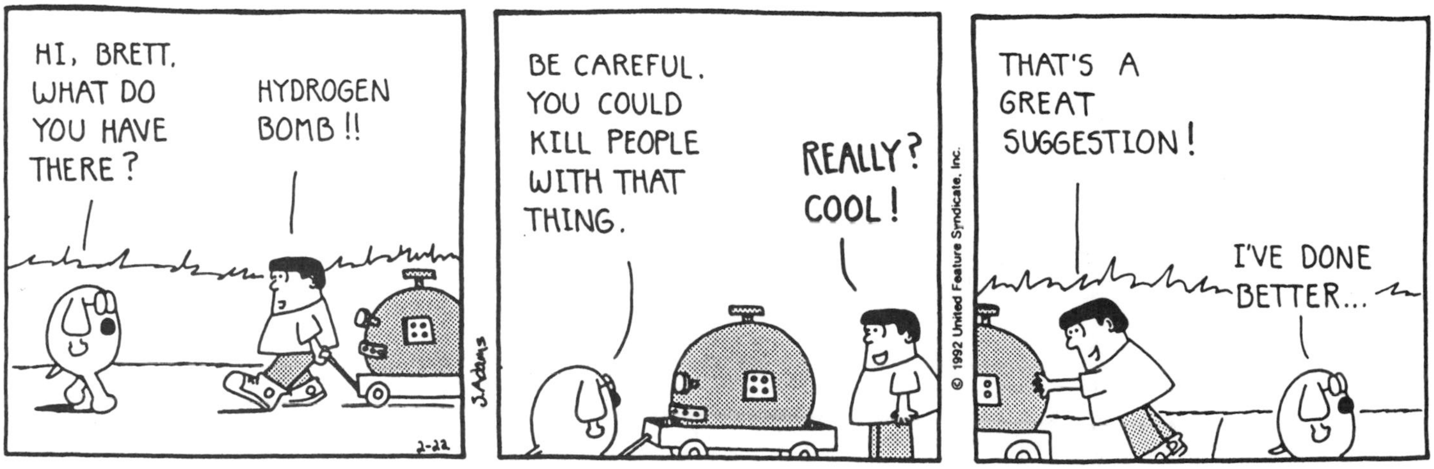

HI, BRETT. WHAT DO YOU HAVE THERE?
HYDROGEN BOMB !!
BE CAREFUL. YOU COULD KILL PEOPLE WITH THAT THING.
REALLY? COOL!
THAT'S A GREAT SUGGESTION!
I'VE DONE BETTER...
S. Adams
2-22
© 1992 United Feature Syndicate, Inc.

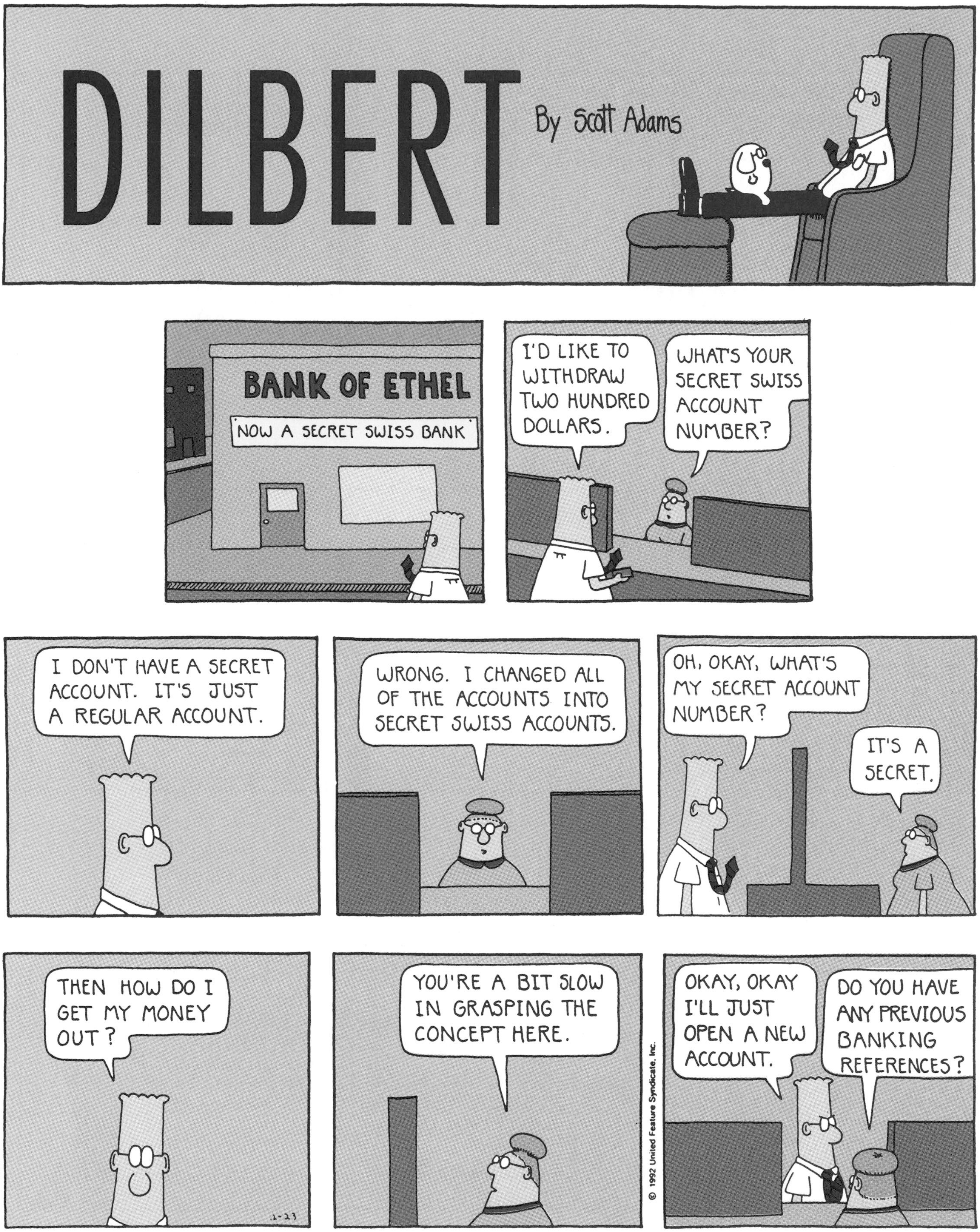
DILBERT
By Scott Adams
BANK OF ETHEL
NOW A SECRET SWISS BANK
I'D LIKE TO WITHDRAW TWO HUNDRED DOLLARS.
WHAT'S YOUR SECRET SWISS ACCOUNT NUMBER?
I DON'T HAVE A SECRET ACCOUNT. IT'S JUST A REGULAR ACCOUNT.
WRONG. I CHANGED ALL OF THE ACCOUNTS INTO SECRET SWISS ACCOUNTS.
OH, OKAY, WHAT'S MY SECRET ACCOUNT NUMBER?
IT'S A SECRET.
THEN HOW DO I GET MY MONEY OUT?
YOU'RE A BIT SLOW IN GRASPING THE CONCEPT HERE.
OKAY, OKAY I'LL JUST OPEN A NEW ACCOUNT.
DO YOU HAVE ANY PREVIOUS BANKING REFERENCES?
S.Adams
© 1992 United Feature Syndicate, Inc.

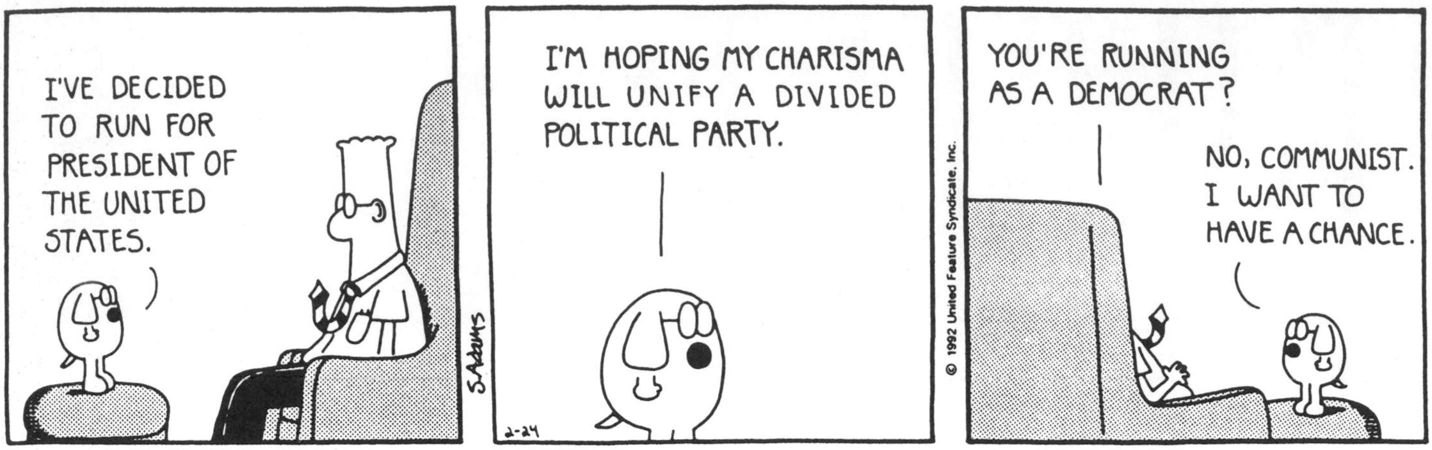
I'VE DECIDED TO RUN FOR PRESIDENT OF THE UNITED STATES.
I'M HOPING MY CHARISMA WILL UNIFY A DIVIDED POLITICAL PARTY.
YOU'RE RUNNING AS A DEMOCRAT?
NO, COMMUNIST. I WANT TO HAVE A CHANCE.
© 1992 United Feature Syndicate, Inc.

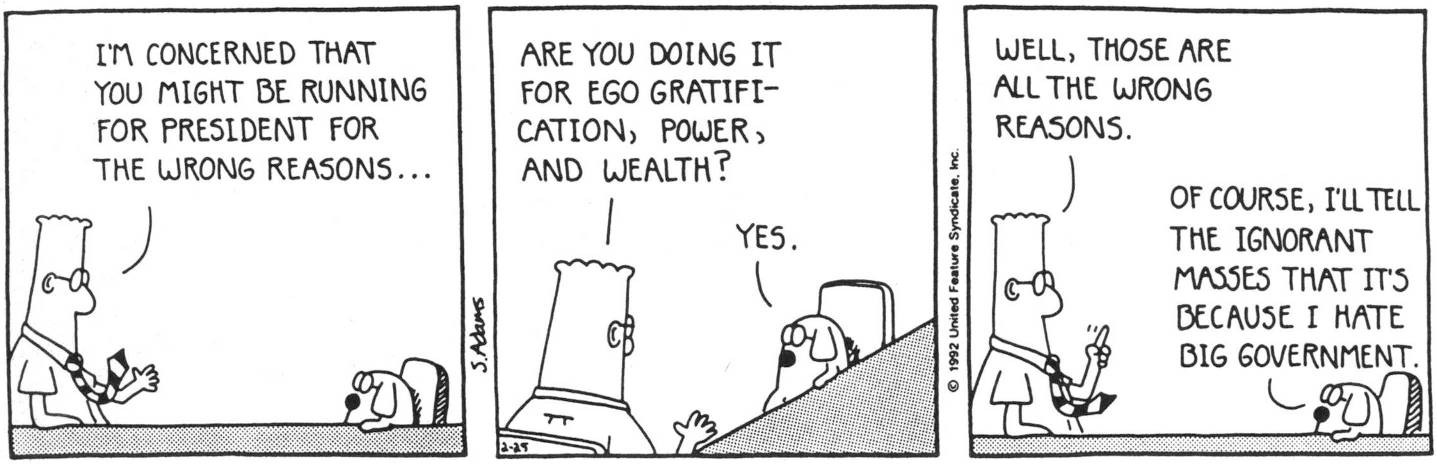
I'M CONCERNED THAT YOU MIGHT BE RUNNING FOR PRESIDENT FOR THE WRONG REASONS...
ARE YOU DOING IT FOR EGO GRATIFI-CATION, POWER, AND WEALTH?
YES.
WELL, THOSE ARE ALL THE WRONG REASONS.
OF COURSE, I'LL TELL THE IGNORANT MASSES THAT IT'S BECAUSE I HATE BIG GOVERNMENT.
© 1992 United Feature Syndicate, Inc.

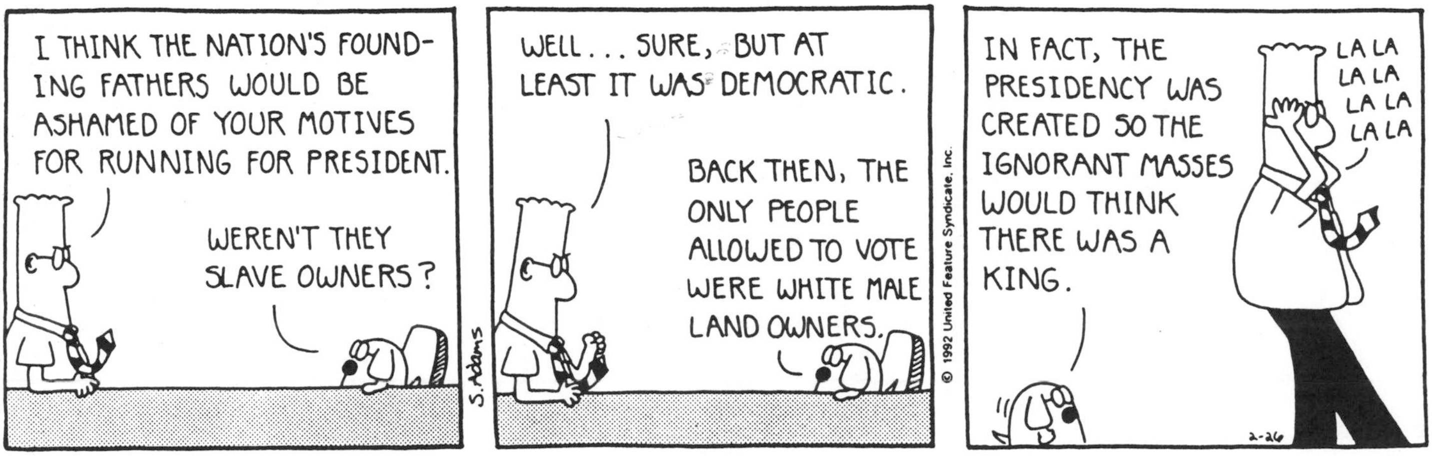
I THINK THE NATION'S FOUND-ING FATHERS WOULD BE ASHAMED OF YOUR MOTIVES FOR RUNNING FOR PRESIDENT.
WEREN'T THEY SLAVE OWNERS?
WELL... SURE, BUT AT LEAST IT WAS DEMOCRATIC.
BACK THEN, THE ONLY PEOPLE ALLOWED TO VOTE WERE WHITE MALE LAND OWNERS.
IN FACT, THE PRESIDENCY WAS CREATED SO THE IGNORANT MASSES WOULD THINK THERE WAS A KING.
LA LA LA LA LA LA LA LA
© 1992 United Feature Syndicate, Inc.

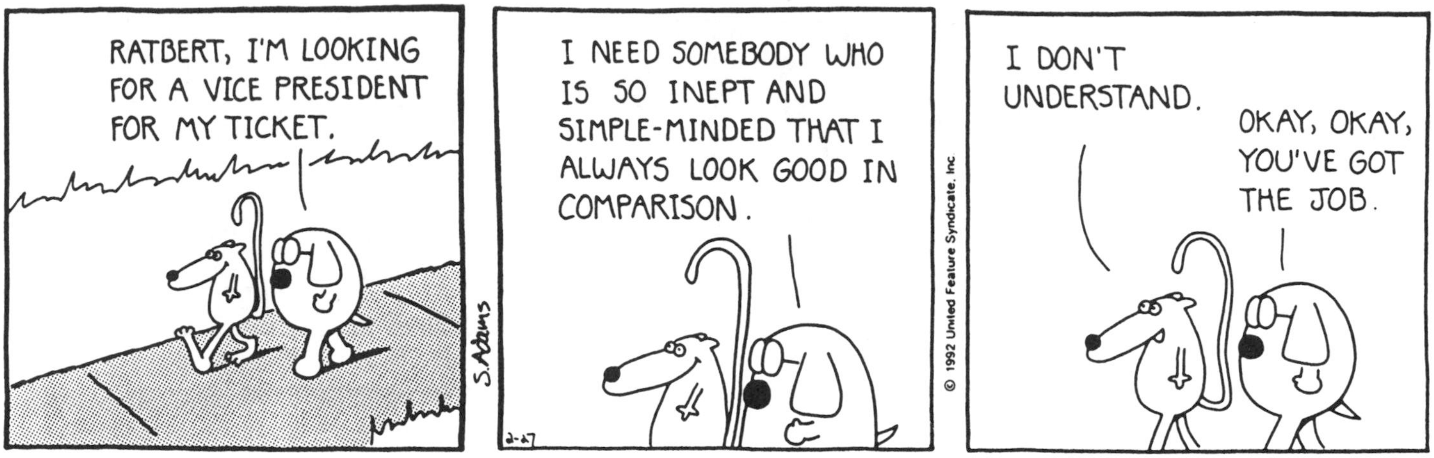
RATBERT, I'M LOOKING FOR A VICE PRESIDENT FOR MY TICKET.
I NEED SOMEBODY WHO IS SO INEPT AND SIMPLE-MINDED THAT I ALWAYS LOOK GOOD IN COMPARISON.
I DON'T UNDERSTAND.
OKAY, OKAY, YOU'VE GOT THE JOB.
© 1992 United Feature Syndicate, Inc.

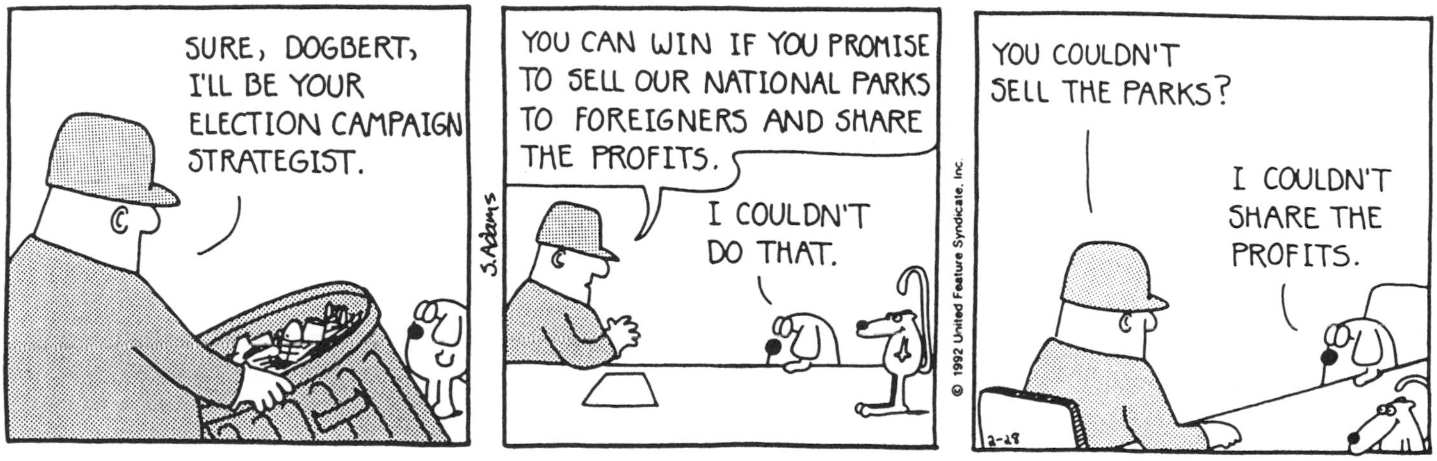
SURE, DOGBERT, I'LL BE YOUR ELECTION CAMPAIGN STRATEGIST.
YOU CAN WIN IF YOU PROMISE TO SELL OUR NATIONAL PARKS TO FOREIGNERS AND SHARE THE PROFITS.
I COULDN'T DO THAT.
YOU COULDN'T SELL THE PARKS?
I COULDN'T SHARE THE PROFITS.
© 1992 United Feature Syndicate, Inc.

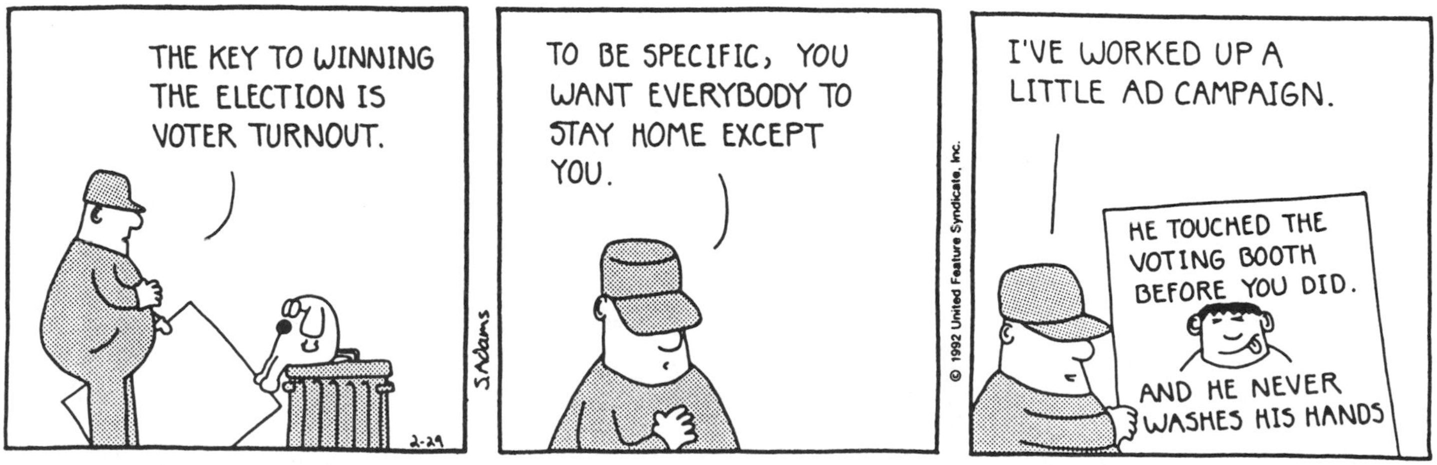
THE KEY TO WINNING THE ELECTION IS VOTER TURNOUT.
TO BE SPECIFIC, YOU WANT EVERYBODY TO STAY HOME EXCEPT YOU.
I'VE WORKED UP A LITTLE AD CAMPAIGN.
HE TOUCHED THE VOTING BOOTH BEFORE YOU DID.
AND HE NEVER WASHES HIS HANDS
© 1992 United Feature Syndicate, Inc.

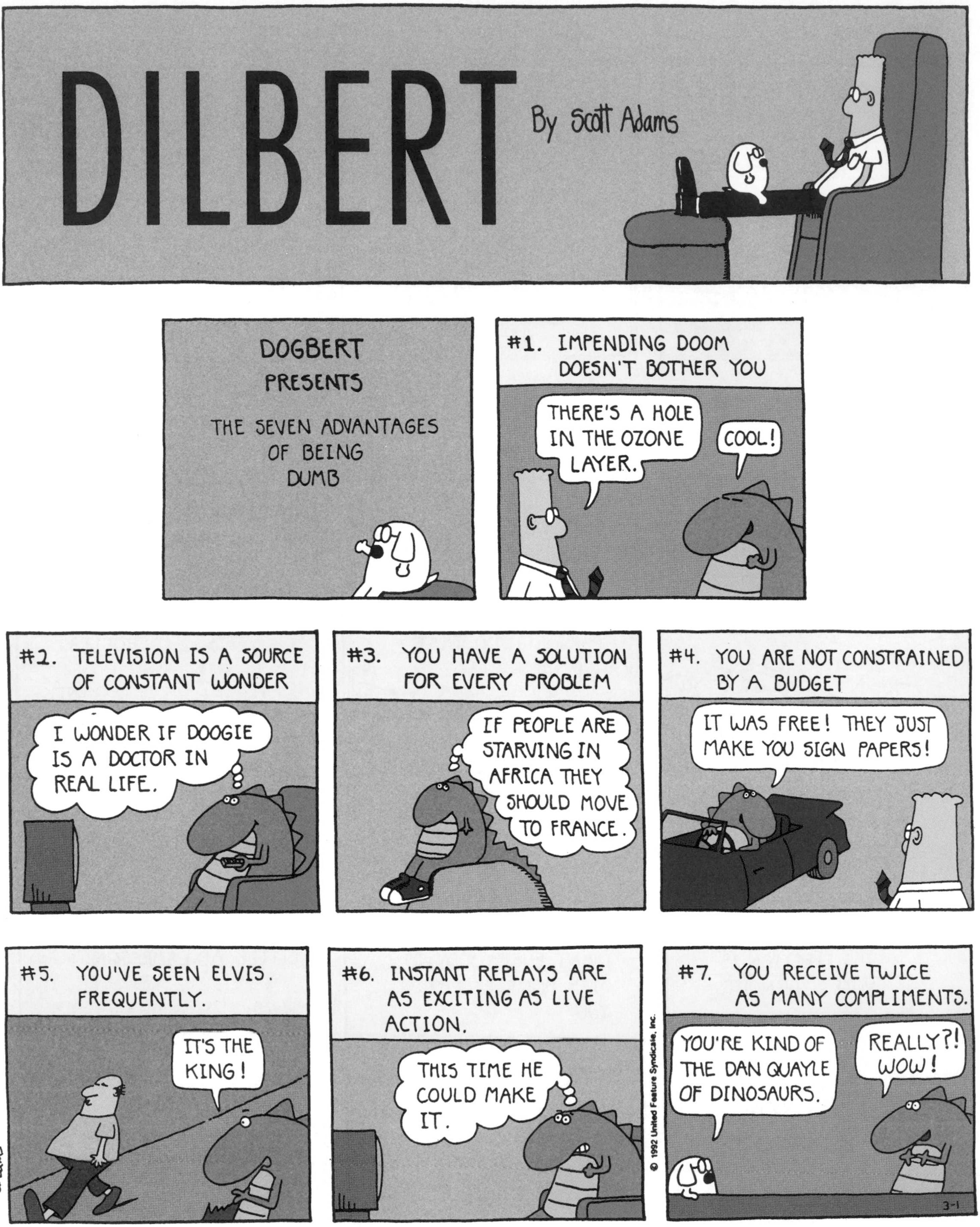
DILBERT
By Scott Adams
DOGBERT PRESENTS
THE SEVEN ADVANTAGES OF BEING DUMB
#1. IMPENDING DOOM DOESN'T BOTHER YOU
THERE'S A HOLE IN THE OZONE LAYER.
COOL!
#2. TELEVISION IS A SOURCE OF CONSTANT WONDER
I WONDER IF DOOGIE IS A DOCTOR IN REAL LIFE.
#3. YOU HAVE A SOLUTION FOR EVERY PROBLEM
IF PEOPLE ARE STARVING IN AFRICA THEY SHOULD MOVE TO FRANCE.
#4. YOU ARE NOT CONSTRAINED BY A BUDGET
IT WAS FREE! THEY JUST MAKE YOU SIGN PAPERS!
#5. YOU'VE SEEN ELVIS. FREQUENTLY.
IT'S THE KING!
S.Adams
#6. INSTANT REPLAYS ARE AS EXCITING AS LIVE ACTION.
THIS TIME HE COULD MAKE IT.
© 1992 United Feature Syndicate, Inc.
#7. YOU RECEIVE TWICE AS MANY COMPLIMENTS.
YOU'RE KIND OF THE DAN QUAYLE OF DINOSAURS.
REALLY?! WOW!
3-1

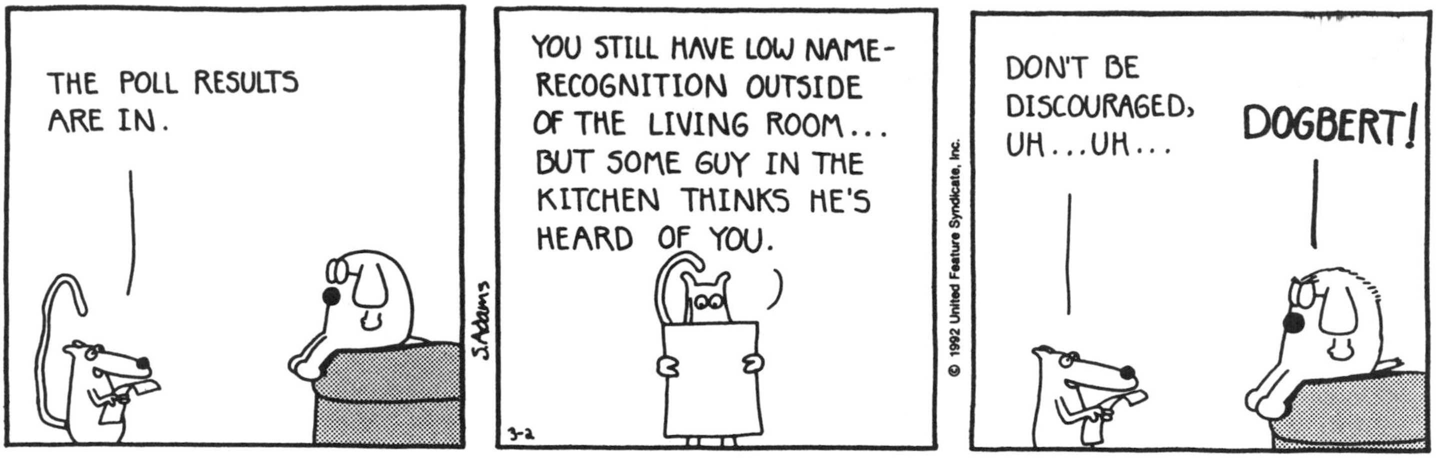
THE POLL RESULTS ARE IN.
S. Adams
YOU STILL HAVE LOW NAME-RECOGNITION OUTSIDE OF THE LIVING ROOM... BUT SOME GUY IN THE KITCHEN THINKS HE'S HEARD OF YOU.
3-2
© 1992 United Feature Syndicate, Inc.
DON'T BE DISCOURAGED, UH...UH...
DOGBERT!

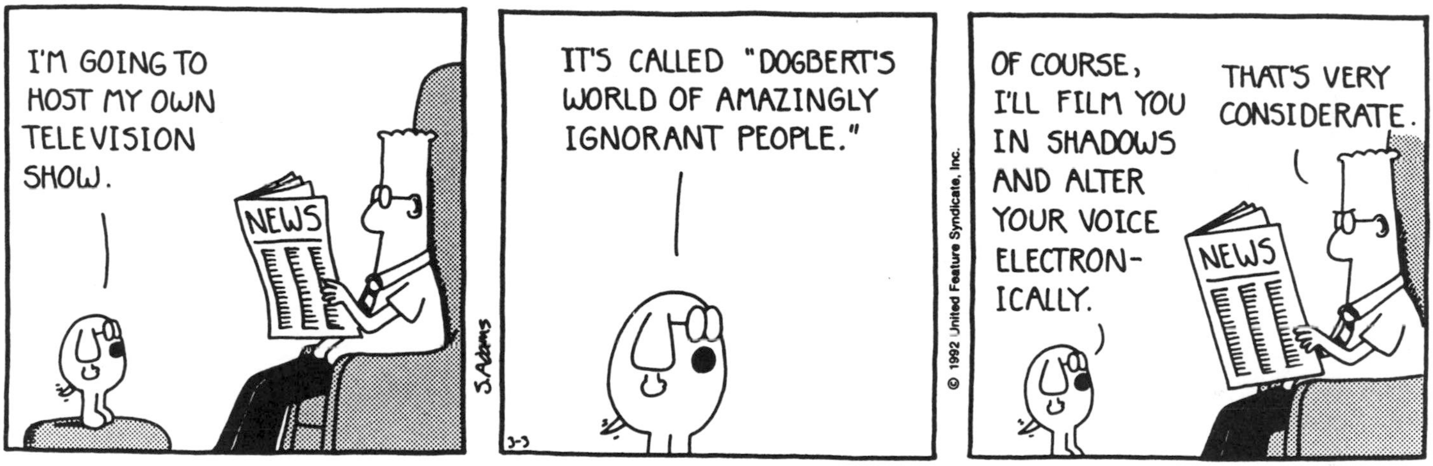
I'M GOING TO HOST MY OWN TELEVISION SHOW.
NEWS
S. Adams
IT'S CALLED "DOGBERT'S WORLD OF AMAZINGLY IGNORANT PEOPLE."
3-3
© 1992 United Feature Syndicate, Inc.
OF COURSE, I'LL FILM YOU IN SHADOWS AND ALTER YOUR VOICE ELECTRON-ICALLY.
THAT'S VERY CONSIDERATE.
NEWS

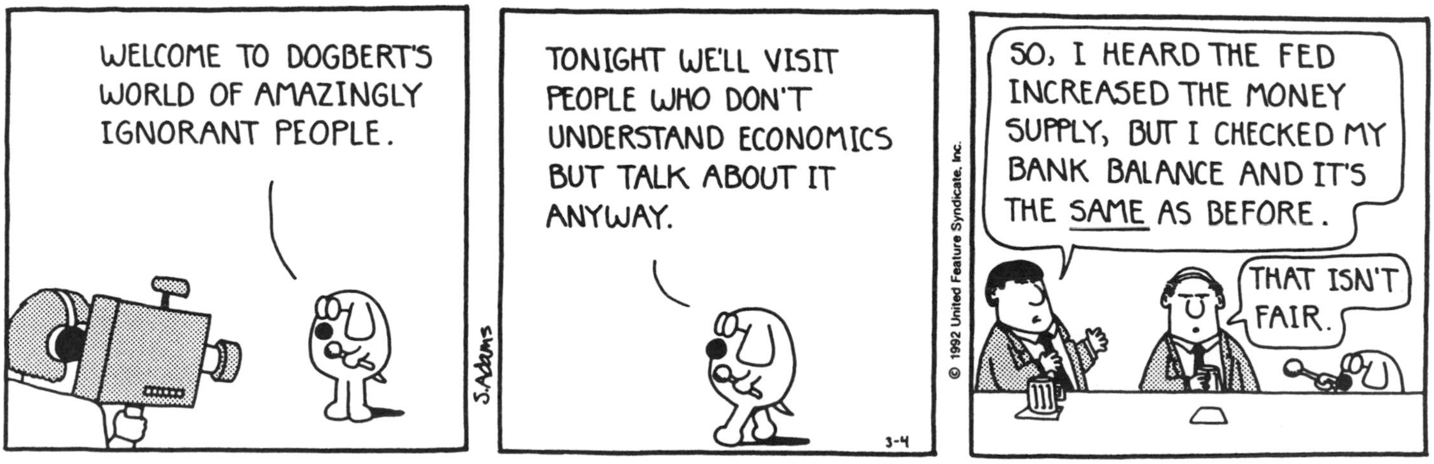
WELCOME TO DOGBERT'S WORLD OF AMAZINGLY IGNORANT PEOPLE.
S. Adams
TONIGHT WE'LL VISIT PEOPLE WHO DON'T UNDERSTAND ECONOMICS BUT TALK ABOUT IT ANYWAY.
3-4
© 1992 United Feature Syndicate, Inc.
SO, I HEARD THE FED INCREASED THE MONEY SUPPLY, BUT I CHECKED MY BANK BALANCE AND IT'S THE SAME AS BEFORE.
THAT ISN'T FAIR.

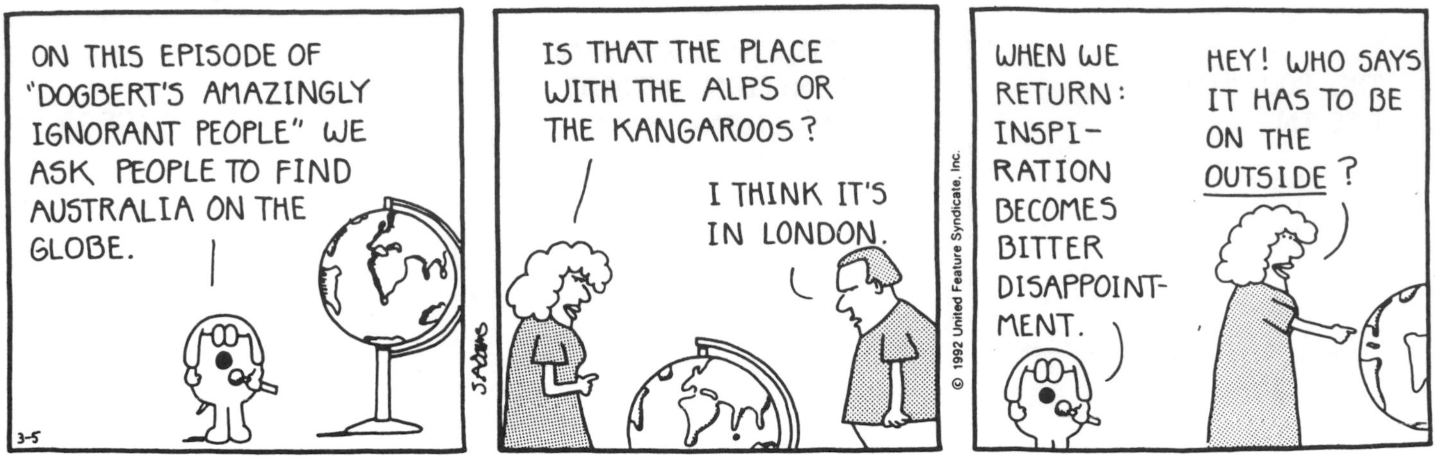
ON THIS EPISODE OF "DOGBERT'S AMAZINGLY IGNORANT PEOPLE" WE ASK PEOPLE TO FIND AUSTRALIA ON THE GLOBE.
3-5
IS THAT THE PLACE WITH THE ALPS OR THE KANGAROOS?
I THINK IT'S IN LONDON.
© 1992 United Feature Syndicate, Inc.
WHEN WE RETURN: INSPI-RATION BECOMES BITTER DISAPPOINT-MENT.
HEY! WHO SAYS IT HAS TO BE ON THE OUTSIDE?

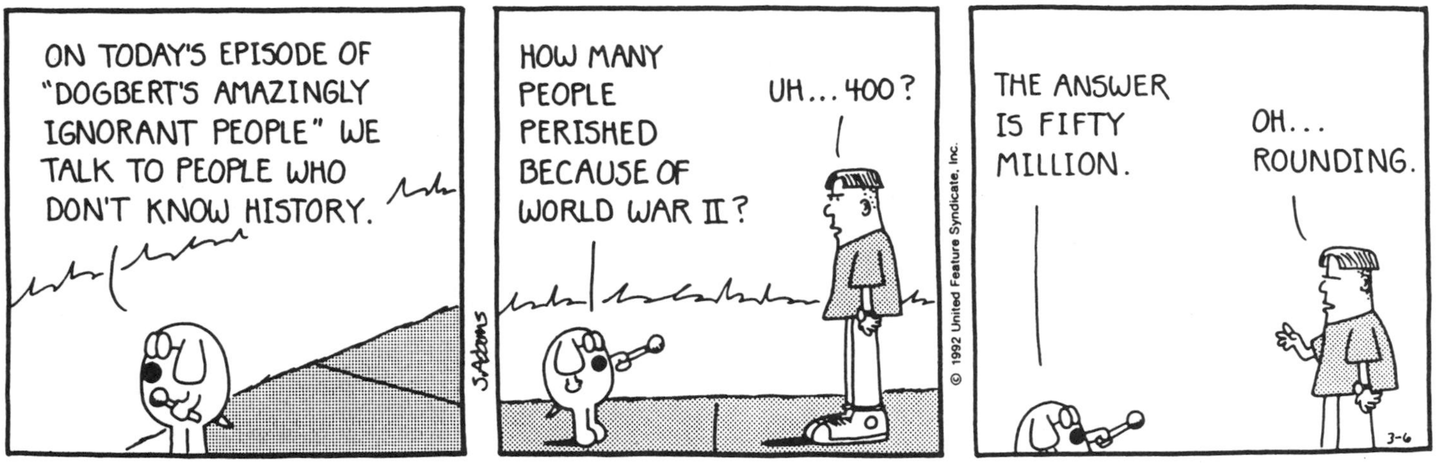
ON TODAY'S EPISODE OF "DOGBERT'S AMAZINGLY IGNORANT PEOPLE" WE TALK TO PEOPLE WHO DON'T KNOW HISTORY.
HOW MANY PEOPLE PERISHED BECAUSE OF WORLD WAR II?
UH... 400?
© 1992 United Feature Syndicate, Inc.
THE ANSWER IS FIFTY MILLION.
OH... ROUNDING.
3-6

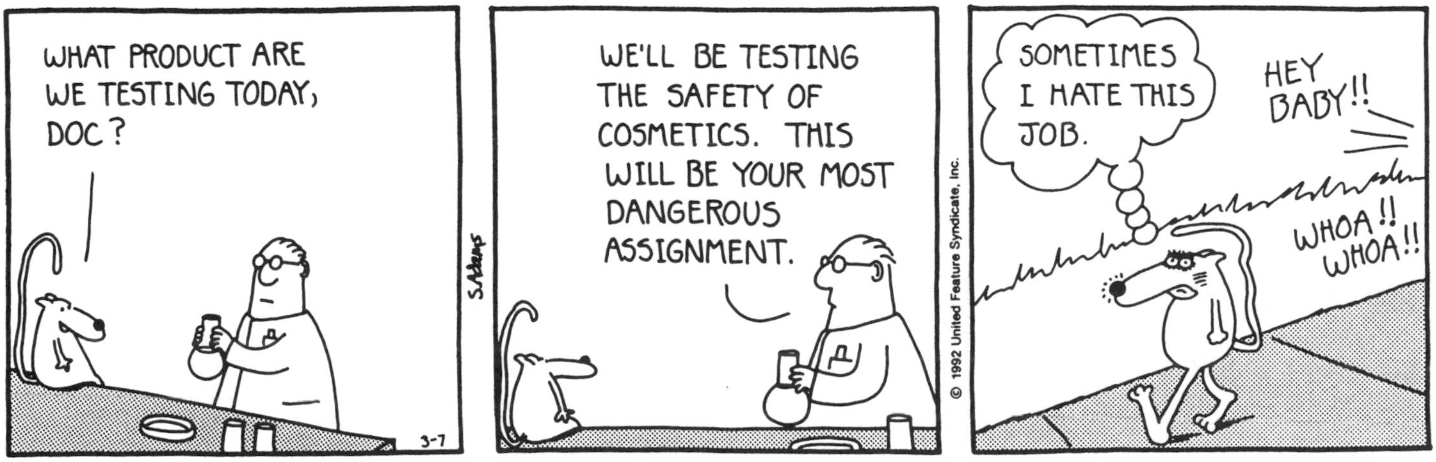
WHAT PRODUCT ARE WE TESTING TODAY, DOC?
3-7
WE'LL BE TESTING THE SAFETY OF COSMETICS. THIS WILL BE YOUR MOST DANGEROUS ASSIGNMENT.
© 1992 United Feature Syndicate, Inc.
SOMETIMES I HATE THIS JOB.
HEY BABY!!
WHOA!! WHOA!!

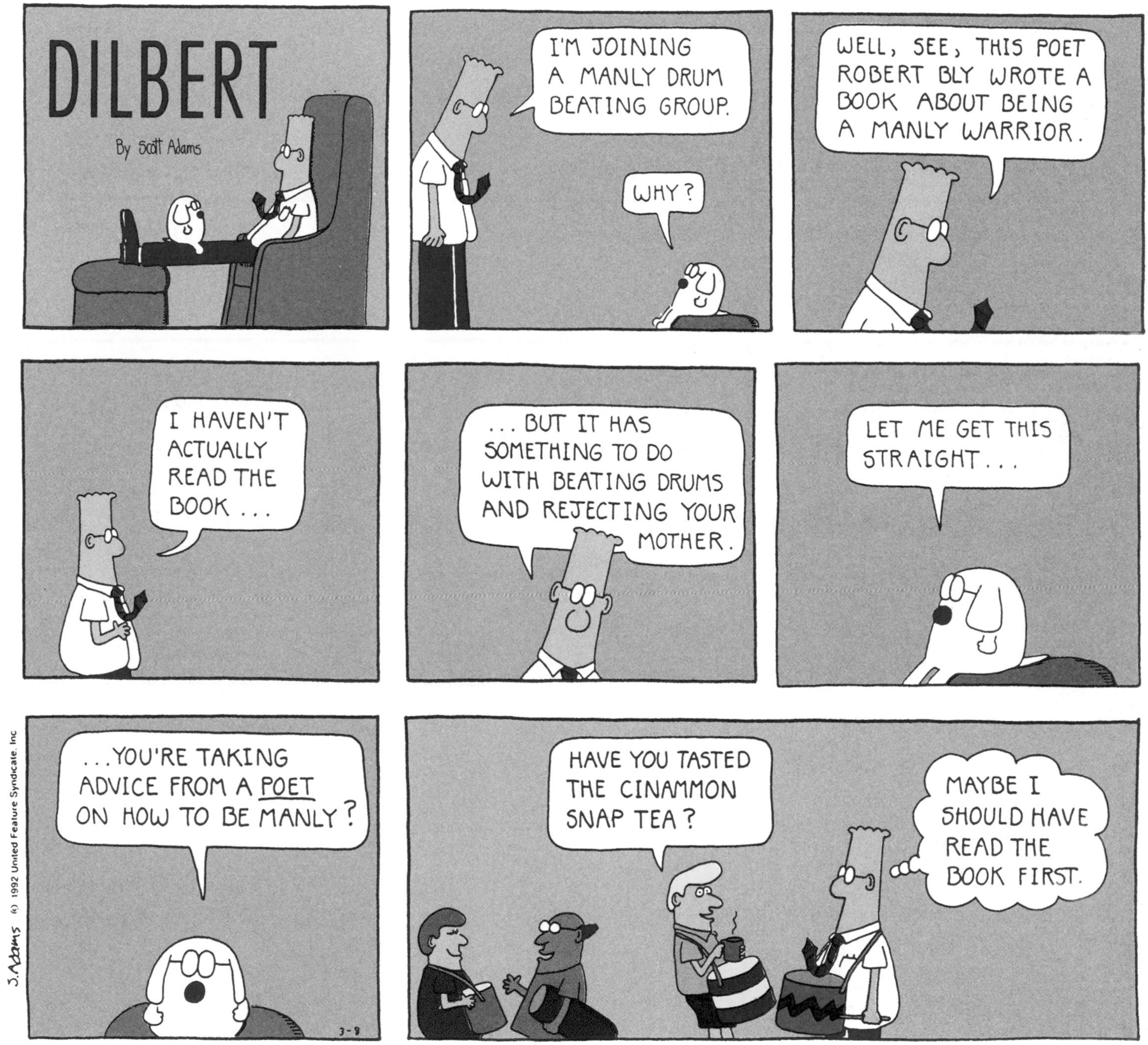
DILBERT
By Scott Adams
I'M JOINING A MANLY DRUM BEATING GROUP.
WHY?
WELL, SEE, THIS POET ROBERT BLY WROTE A BOOK ABOUT BEING A MANLY WARRIOR.
I HAVEN'T ACTUALLY READ THE BOOK ...
... BUT IT HAS SOMETHING TO DO WITH BEATING DRUMS AND REJECTING YOUR MOTHER.
LET ME GET THIS STRAIGHT...
...YOU'RE TAKING ADVICE FROM A POET ON HOW TO BE MANLY?
S. Adams (c) 1992 United Feature Syndicate, Inc
3-8
HAVE YOU TASTED THE CINAMMON SNAP TEA?
MAYBE I SHOULD HAVE READ THE BOOK FIRST.

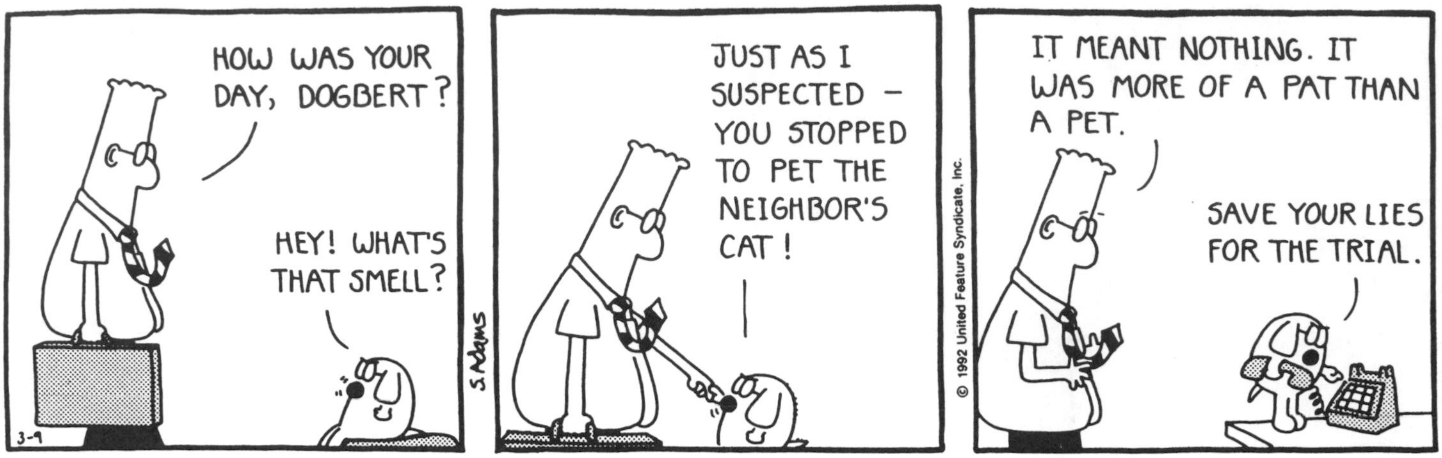
HOW WAS YOUR DAY, DOGBERT?
HEY! WHAT'S THAT SMELL?
3-9
S.Adams
JUST AS I SUSPECTED – YOU STOPPED TO PET THE NEIGHBOR'S CAT!
© 1992 United Feature Syndicate, Inc.
IT MEANT NOTHING. IT WAS MORE OF A PAT THAN A PET.
SAVE YOUR LIES FOR THE TRIAL.

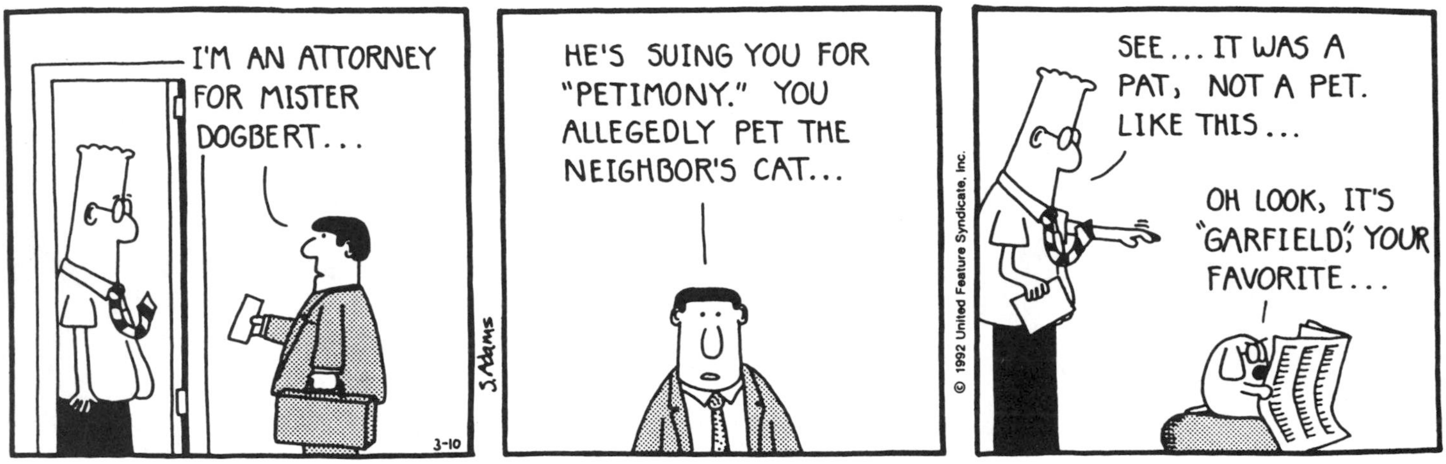
I'M AN ATTORNEY FOR MISTER DOGBERT...
3-10
S.Adams
HE'S SUING YOU FOR "PETIMONY." YOU ALLEGEDLY PET THE NEIGHBOR'S CAT...
© 1992 United Feature Syndicate, Inc.
SEE... IT WAS A PAT, NOT A PET. LIKE THIS...
OH LOOK, IT'S "GARFIELD," YOUR FAVORITE...

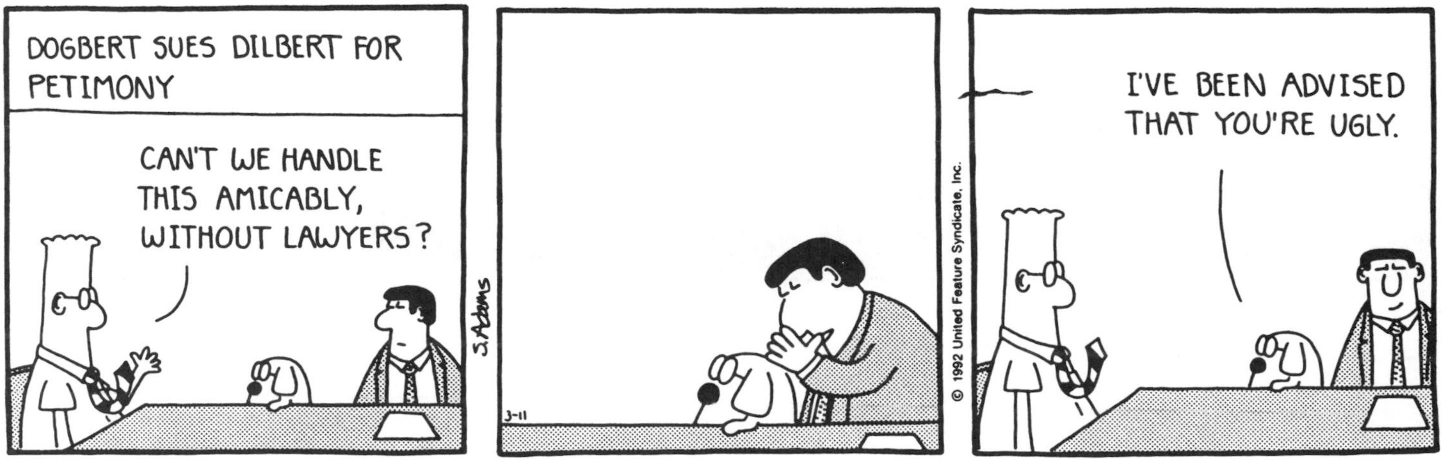
DOGBERT SUES DILBERT FOR PETIMONY
CAN'T WE HANDLE THIS AMICABLY, WITHOUT LAWYERS?
S.Adams
3-11
© 1992 United Feature Syndicate, Inc.
I'VE BEEN ADVISED THAT YOU'RE UGLY.

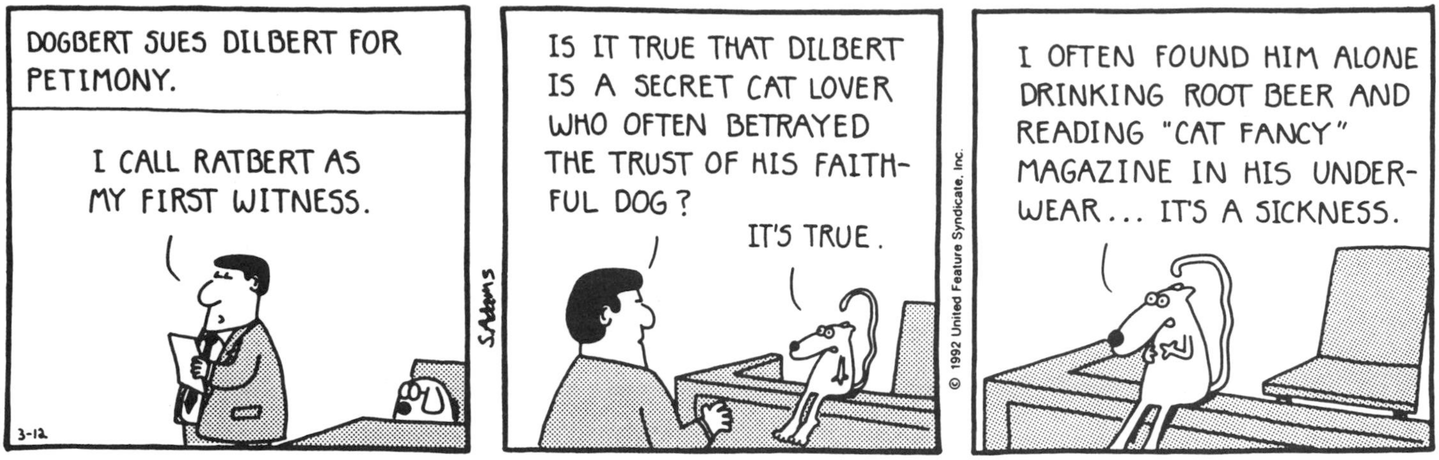
DOGBERT SUES DILBERT FOR PETIMONY.
I CALL RATBERT AS MY FIRST WITNESS.
3-12
S.Adams
IS IT TRUE THAT DILBERT IS A SECRET CAT LOVER WHO OFTEN BETRAYED THE TRUST OF HIS FAITHFUL DOG?
IT'S TRUE.
© 1992 United Feature Syndicate, Inc.
I OFTEN FOUND HIM ALONE DRINKING ROOT BEER AND READING "CAT FANCY" MAGAZINE IN HIS UNDERWEAR... IT'S A SICKNESS.

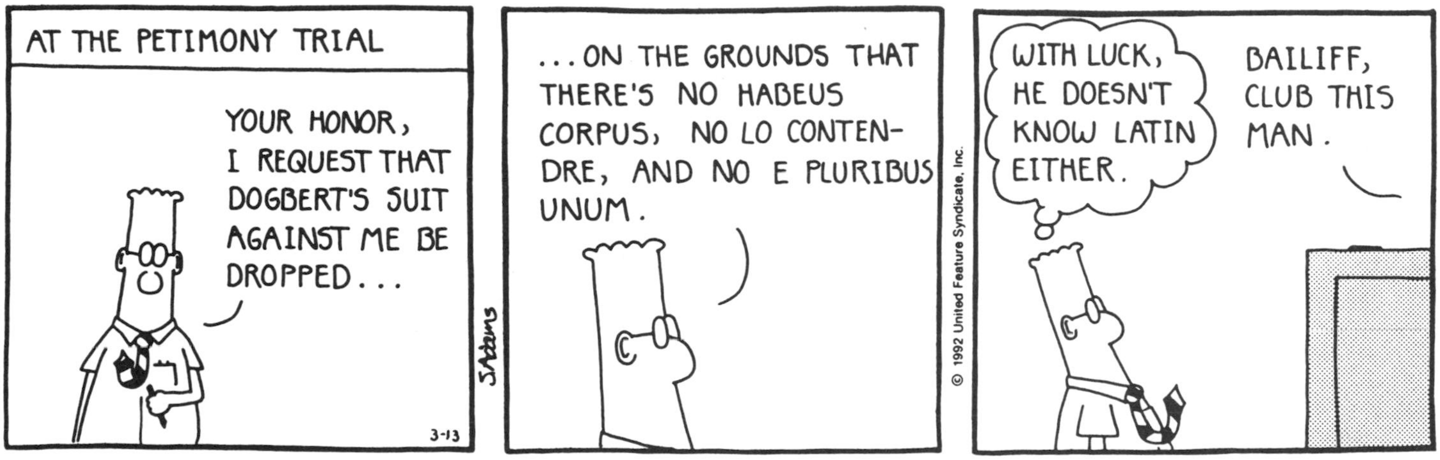
AT THE PETIMONY TRIAL
YOUR HONOR, I REQUEST THAT DOGBERT'S SUIT AGAINST ME BE DROPPED...
3-13
S.Adams
...ON THE GROUNDS THAT THERE'S NO HABEUS CORPUS, NO LO CONTENDRE, AND NO E PLURIBUS UNUM.
© 1992 United Feature Syndicate, Inc.
WITH LUCK, HE DOESN'T KNOW LATIN EITHER.
BAILIFF, CLUB THIS MAN.

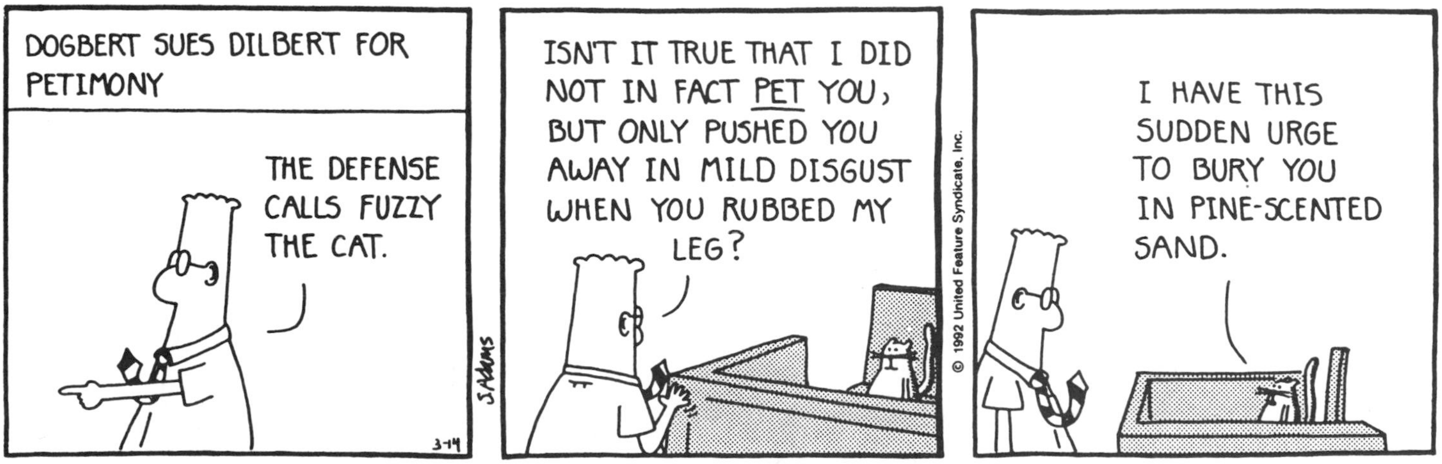
DOGBERT SUES DILBERT FOR PETIMONY
THE DEFENSE CALLS FUZZY THE CAT.
3-14
S.Adams
ISN'T IT TRUE THAT I DID NOT IN FACT PET YOU, BUT ONLY PUSHED YOU AWAY IN MILD DISGUST WHEN YOU RUBBED MY LEG?
© 1992 United Feature Syndicate, Inc.
I HAVE THIS SUDDEN URGE TO BURY YOU IN PINE-SCENTED SAND.

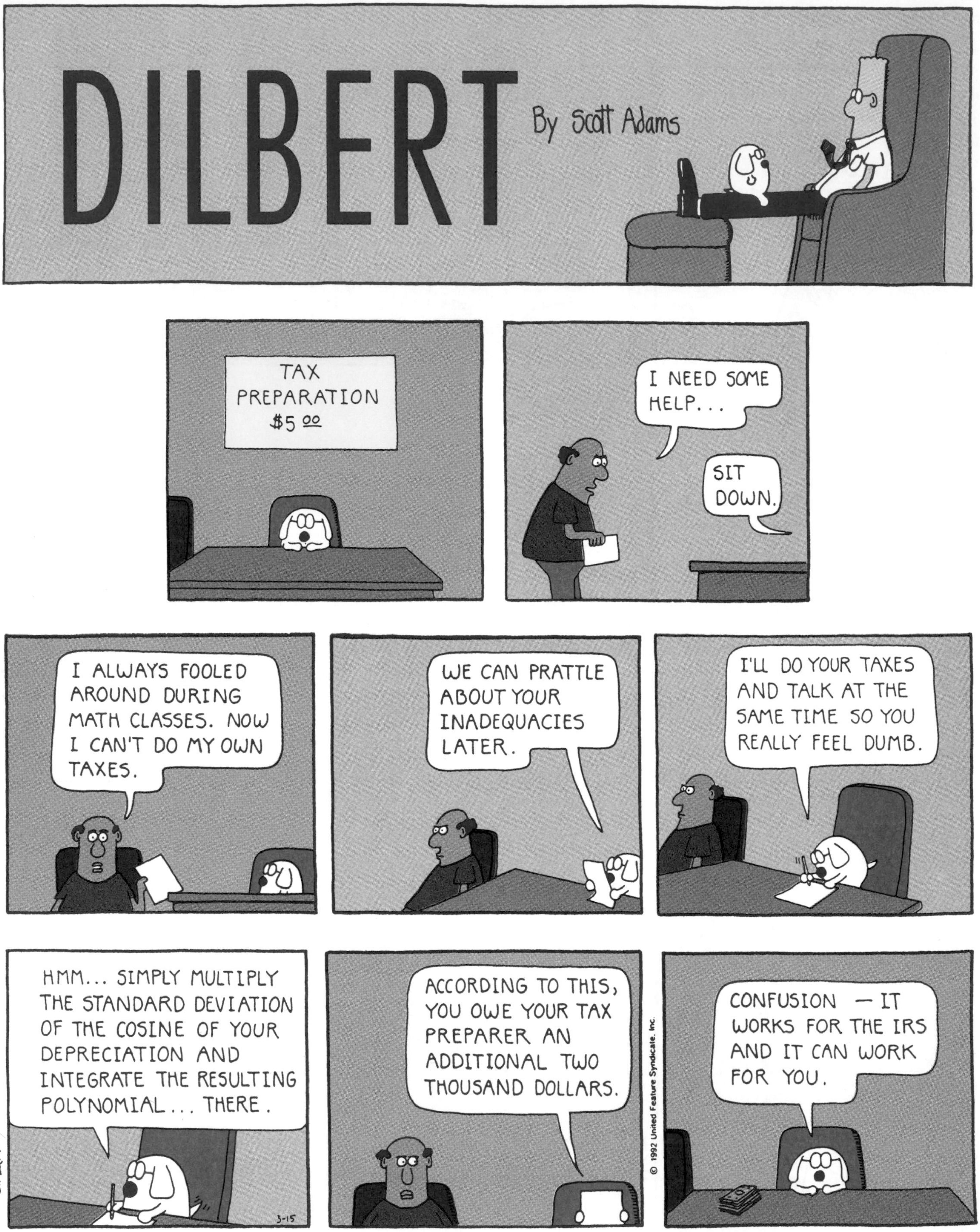
DILBERT
By Scott Adams
TAX PREPARATION $5.00
I NEED SOME HELP...
SIT DOWN.
I ALWAYS FOOLED AROUND DURING MATH CLASSES. NOW I CAN'T DO MY OWN TAXES.
WE CAN PRATTLE ABOUT YOUR INADEQUACIES LATER.
I'LL DO YOUR TAXES AND TALK AT THE SAME TIME SO YOU REALLY FEEL DUMB.
HMM... SIMPLY MULTIPLY THE STANDARD DEVIATION OF THE COSINE OF YOUR DEPRECIATION AND INTEGRATE THE RESULTING POLYNOMIAL... THERE.
S.Adams
3-15
ACCORDING TO THIS, YOU OWE YOUR TAX PREPARER AN ADDITIONAL TWO THOUSAND DOLLARS.
© 1992 United Feature Syndicate, Inc.
CONFUSION — IT WORKS FOR THE IRS AND IT CAN WORK FOR YOU.

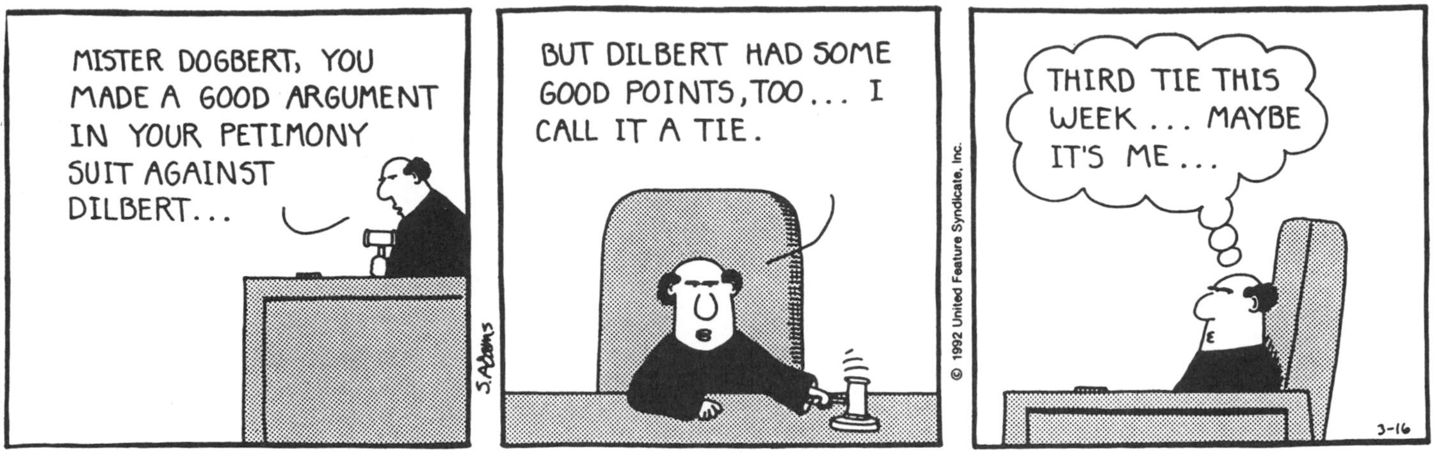
MISTER DOGBERT, YOU MADE A GOOD ARGUMENT IN YOUR PETIMONY SUIT AGAINST DILBERT...
BUT DILBERT HAD SOME GOOD POINTS, TOO... I CALL IT A TIE.
THIRD TIE THIS WEEK ... MAYBE IT'S ME...
S. Adams
© 1992 United Feature Syndicate, Inc.
3-16

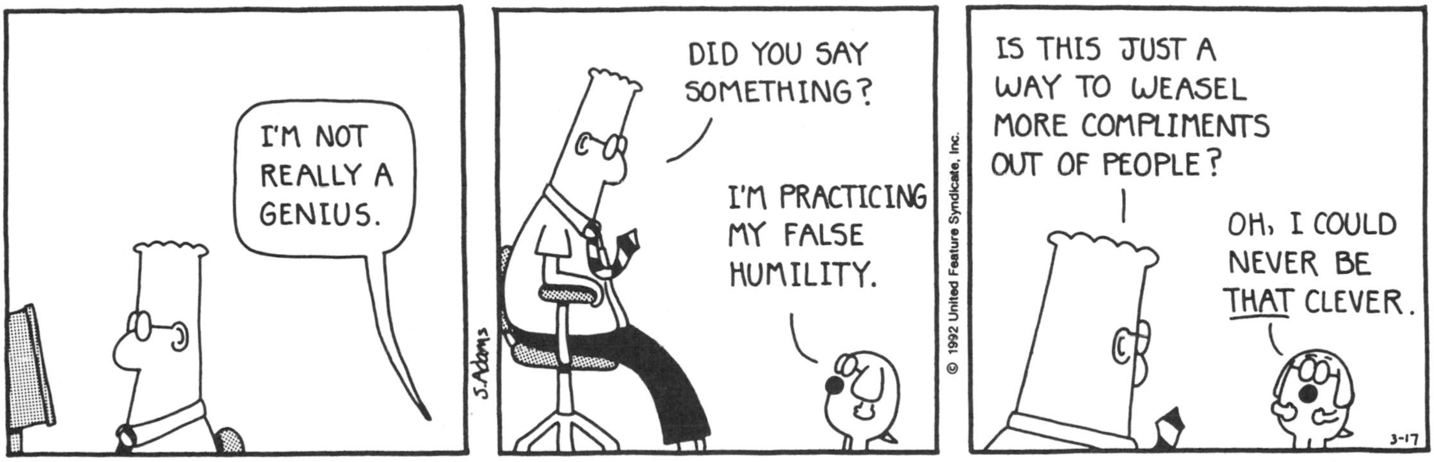
I'M NOT REALLY A GENIUS.
DID YOU SAY SOMETHING?
I'M PRACTICING MY FALSE HUMILITY.
IS THIS JUST A WAY TO WEASEL MORE COMPLIMENTS OUT OF PEOPLE?
OH, I COULD NEVER BE THAT CLEVER.
S. Adams
© 1992 United Feature Syndicate, Inc.
3-17

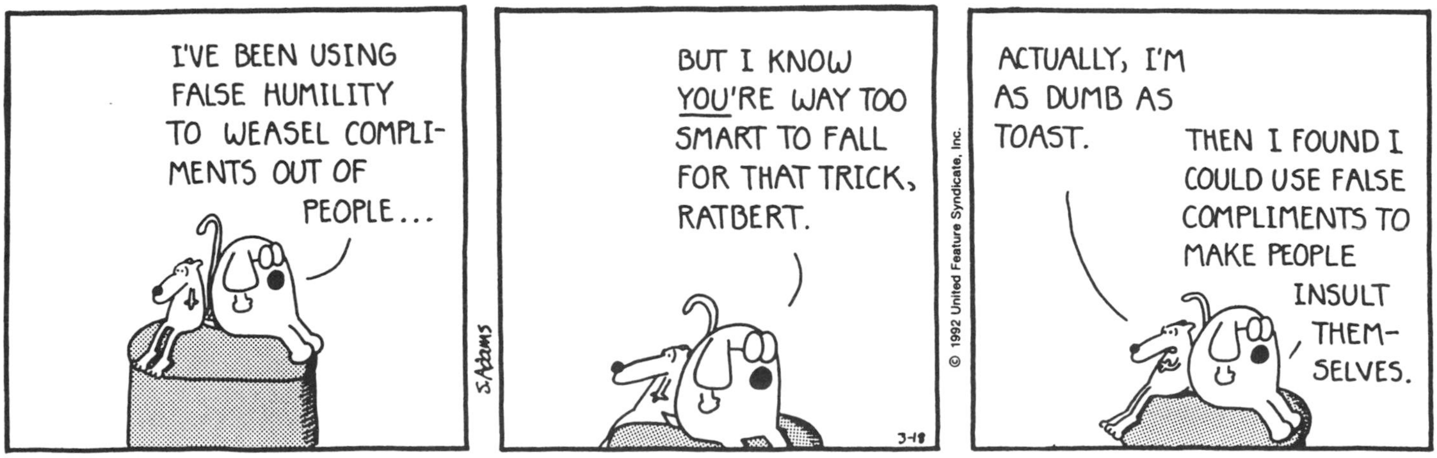
I'VE BEEN USING FALSE HUMILITY TO WEASEL COMPLI-MENTS OUT OF PEOPLE...
BUT I KNOW YOU'RE WAY TOO SMART TO FALL FOR THAT TRICK, RATBERT.
ACTUALLY, I'M AS DUMB AS TOAST.
THEN I FOUND I COULD USE FALSE COMPLIMENTS TO MAKE PEOPLE INSULT THEM-SELVES.
S. Adams
© 1992 United Feature Syndicate, Inc.
3-18

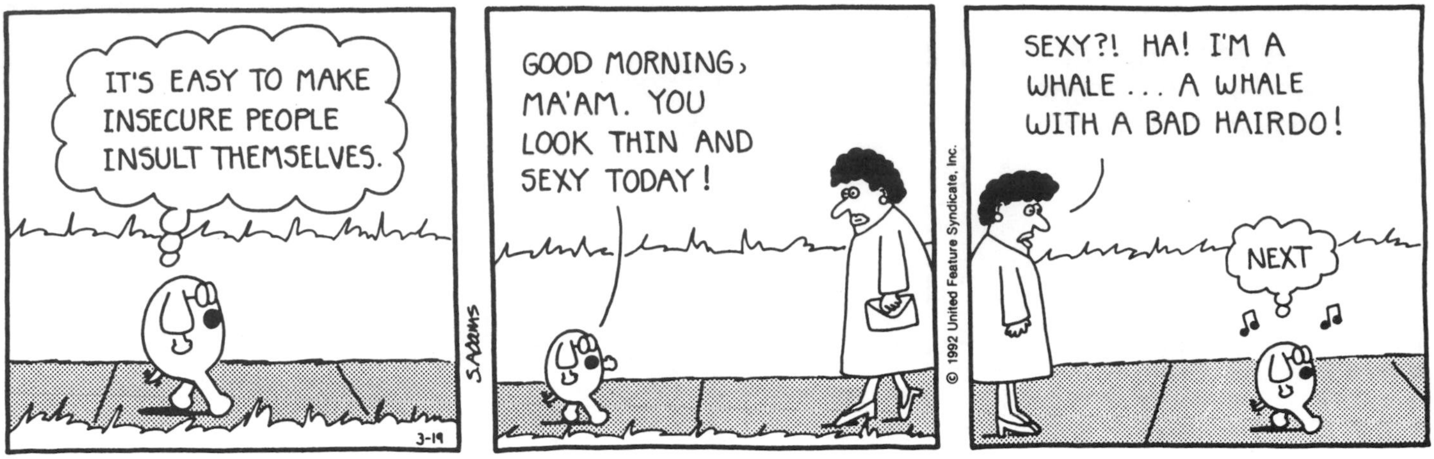
IT'S EASY TO MAKE INSECURE PEOPLE INSULT THEMSELVES.
S. ADAMS
3-19
GOOD MORNING, MA'AM. YOU LOOK THIN AND SEXY TODAY!
© 1992 United Feature Syndicate, Inc.
SEXY?! HA! I'M A WHALE . . . A WHALE WITH A BAD HAIRDO!
NEXT

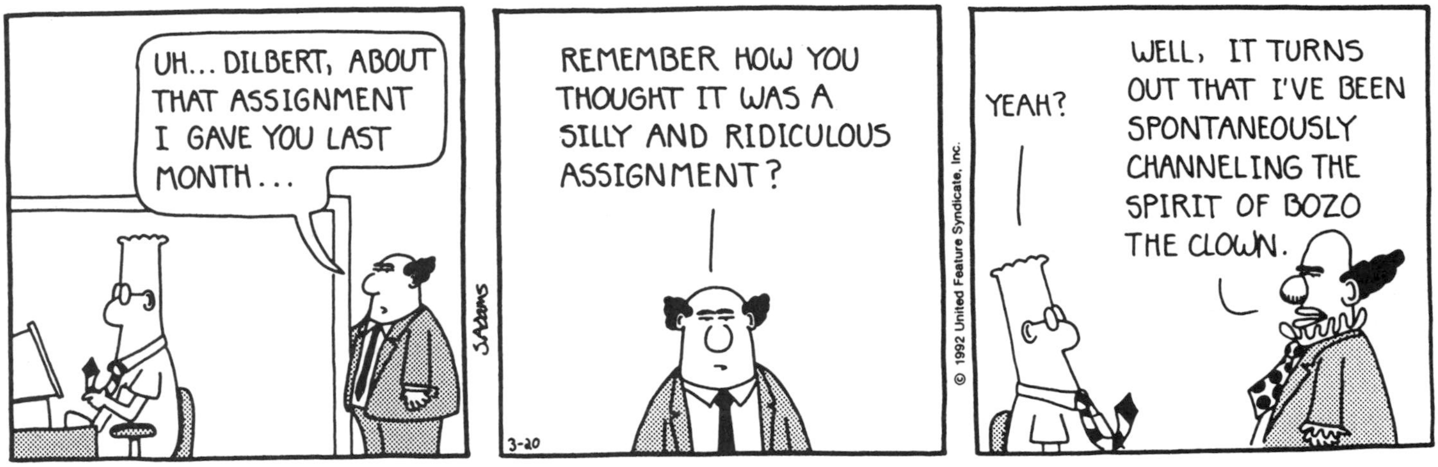
UH... DILBERT, ABOUT THAT ASSIGNMENT I GAVE YOU LAST MONTH...
S. ADAMS
REMEMBER HOW YOU THOUGHT IT WAS A SILLY AND RIDICULOUS ASSIGNMENT?
3-20
© 1992 United Feature Syndicate, Inc.
YEAH?
WELL, IT TURNS OUT THAT I'VE BEEN SPONTANEOUSLY CHANNELING THE SPIRIT OF BOZO THE CLOWN.

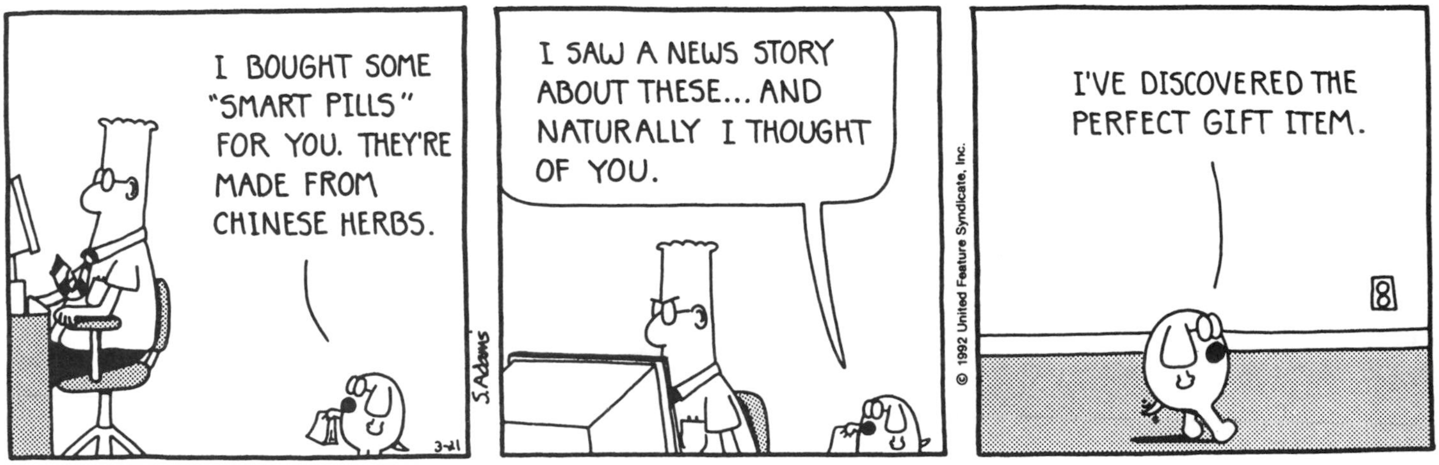
I BOUGHT SOME "SMART PILLS" FOR YOU. THEY'RE MADE FROM CHINESE HERBS.
3-21
S. ADAMS
I SAW A NEWS STORY ABOUT THESE... AND NATURALLY I THOUGHT OF YOU.
© 1992 United Feature Syndicate, Inc.
I'VE DISCOVERED THE PERFECT GIFT ITEM.
8

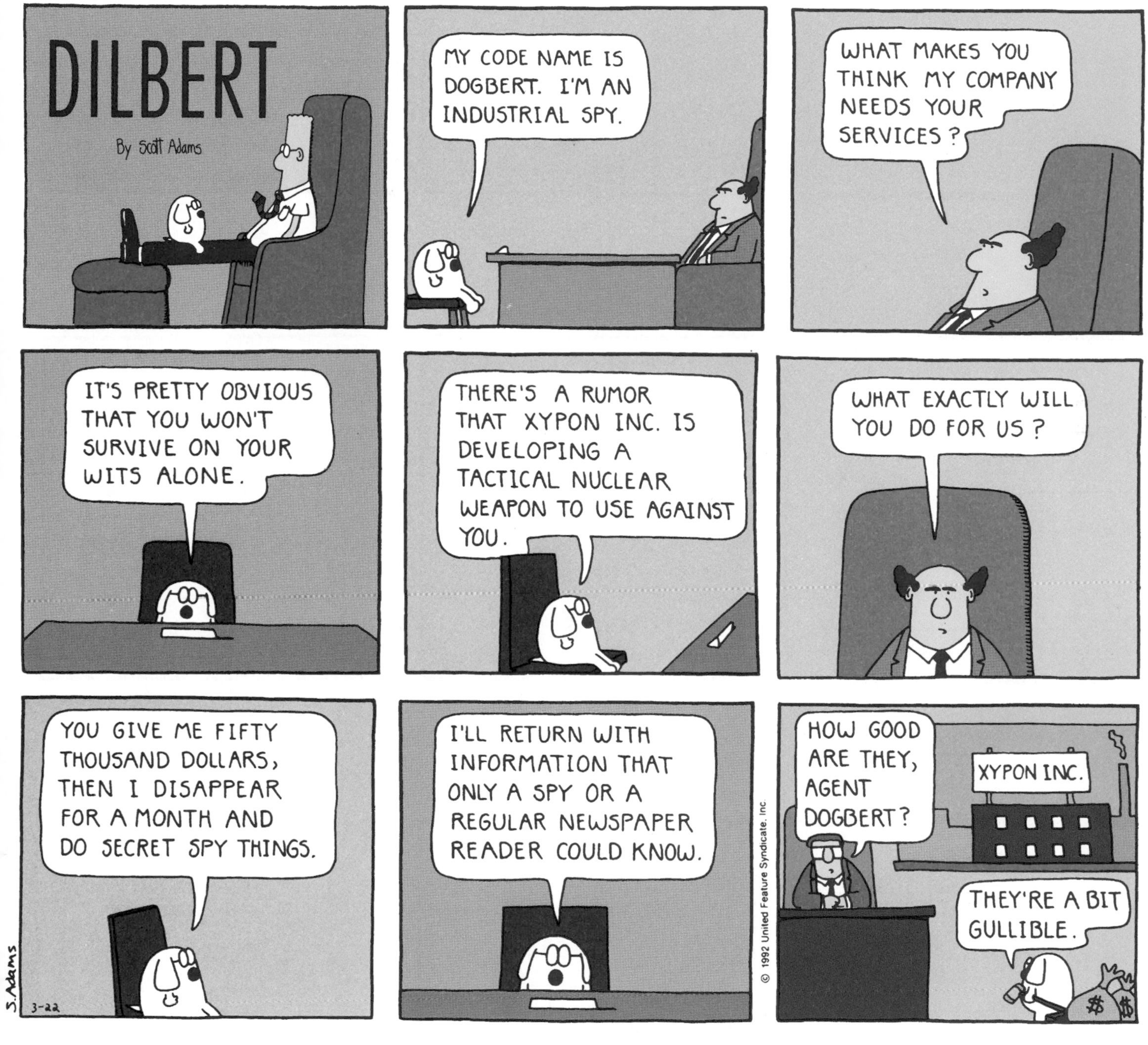
DILBERT
By Scott Adams
MY CODE NAME IS DOGBERT. I'M AN INDUSTRIAL SPY.
WHAT MAKES YOU THINK MY COMPANY NEEDS YOUR SERVICES?
IT'S PRETTY OBVIOUS THAT YOU WON'T SURVIVE ON YOUR WITS ALONE.
THERE'S A RUMOR THAT XYPON INC. IS DEVELOPING A TACTICAL NUCLEAR WEAPON TO USE AGAINST YOU.
WHAT EXACTLY WILL YOU DO FOR US?
YOU GIVE ME FIFTY THOUSAND DOLLARS, THEN I DISAPPEAR FOR A MONTH AND DO SECRET SPY THINGS.
S. Adams
3-22
I'LL RETURN WITH INFORMATION THAT ONLY A SPY OR A REGULAR NEWSPAPER READER COULD KNOW.
© 1992 United Feature Syndicate, Inc.
HOW GOOD ARE THEY, AGENT DOGBERT?
XYPON INC.
THEY'RE A BIT GULLIBLE.

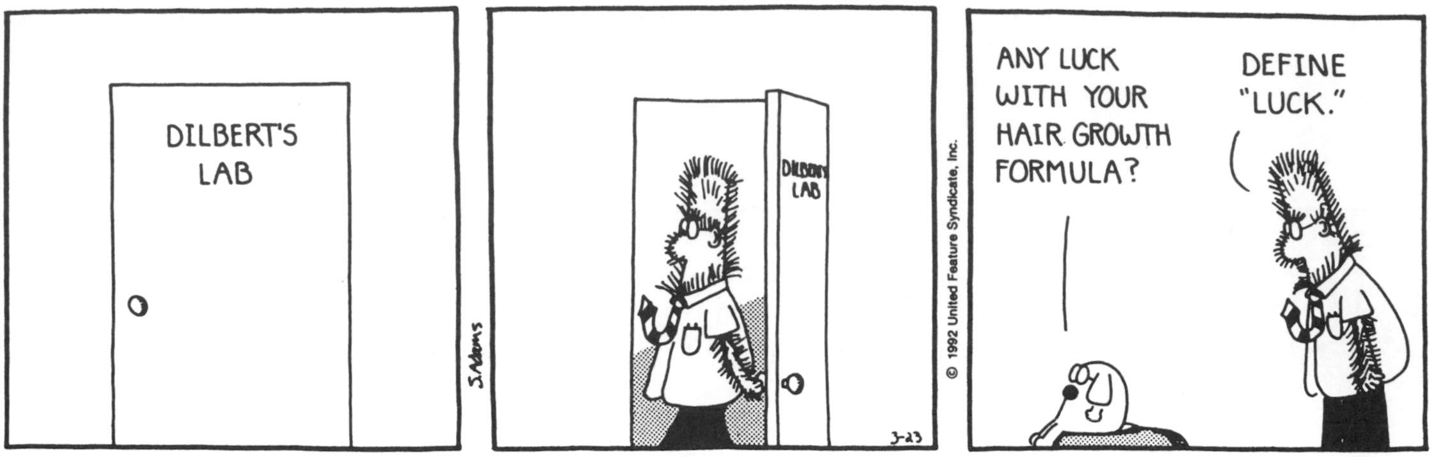
DILBERT'S LAB
S.Adams
DILBERT'S LAB
3-23
© 1992 United Feature Syndicate, Inc.
ANY LUCK WITH YOUR HAIR GROWTH FORMULA?
DEFINE "LUCK."

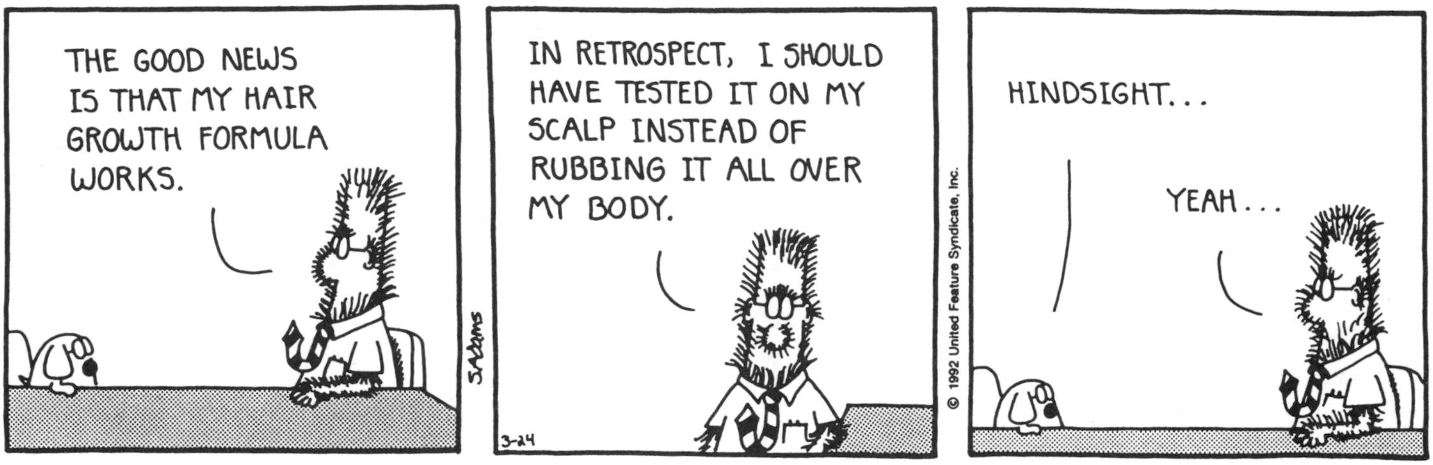
THE GOOD NEWS IS THAT MY HAIR GROWTH FORMULA WORKS.
S.Adams
IN RETROSPECT, I SHOULD HAVE TESTED IT ON MY SCALP INSTEAD OF RUBBING IT ALL OVER MY BODY.
3-24
© 1992 United Feature Syndicate, Inc.
HINDSIGHT...
YEAH...

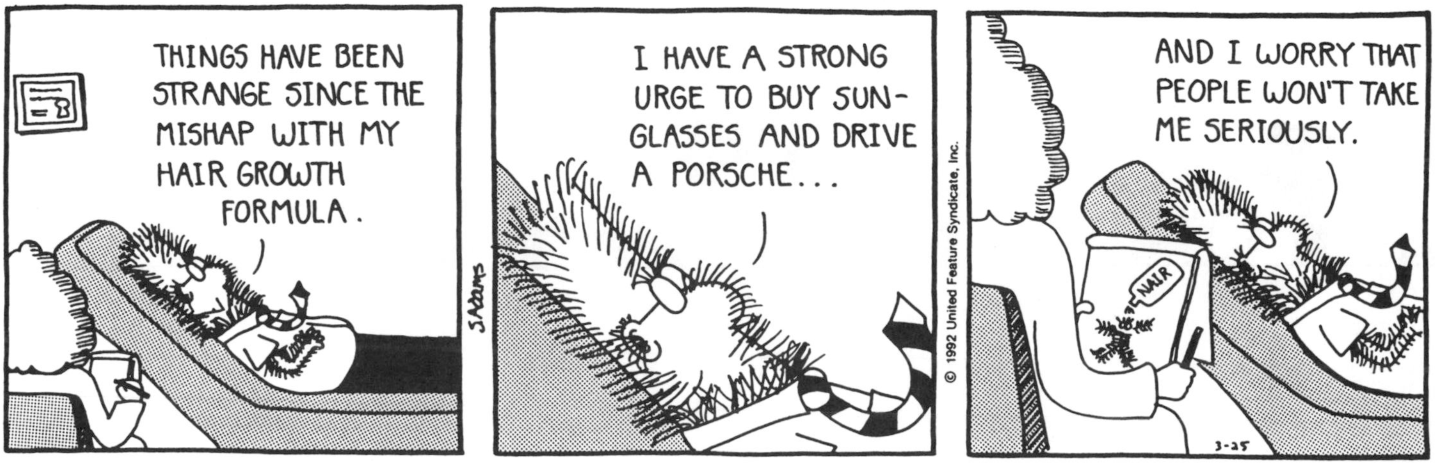
THINGS HAVE BEEN STRANGE SINCE THE MISHAP WITH MY HAIR GROWTH FORMULA.
S.Adams
I HAVE A STRONG URGE TO BUY SUN-GLASSES AND DRIVE A PORSCHE...
© 1992 United Feature Syndicate, Inc.
AND I WORRY THAT PEOPLE WON'T TAKE ME SERIOUSLY.
NAIR
3-25

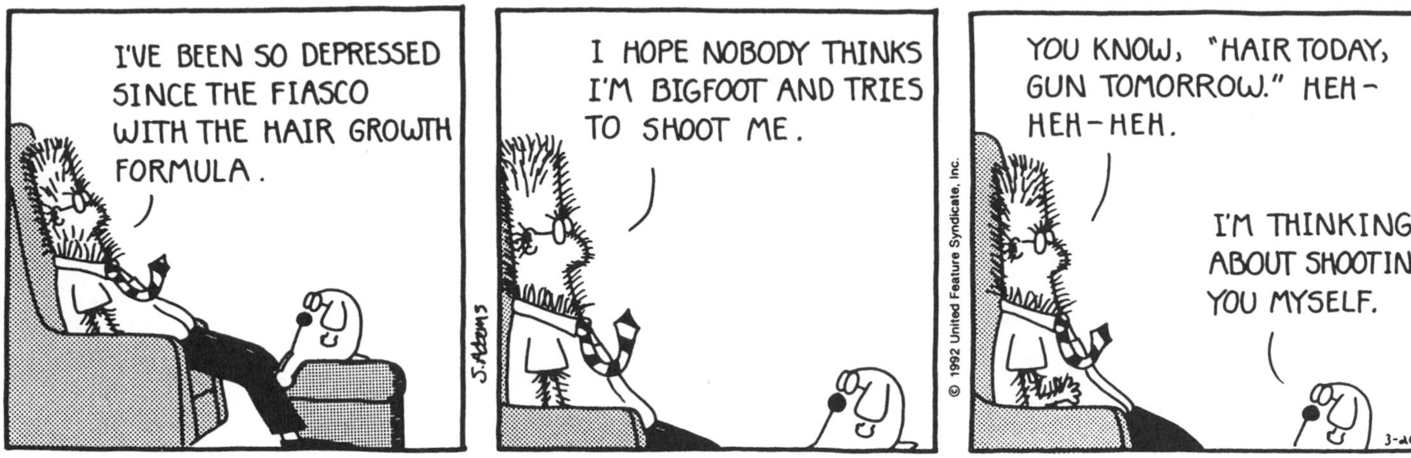
I'VE BEEN SO DEPRESSED SINCE THE FIASCO WITH THE HAIR GROWTH FORMULA.
I HOPE NOBODY THINKS I'M BIGFOOT AND TRIES TO SHOOT ME.
YOU KNOW, "HAIR TODAY, GUN TOMORROW." HEH-HEH-HEH.
I'M THINKING ABOUT SHOOTING YOU MYSELF.
S. Adams
© 1992 United Feature Syndicate, Inc.
3-26

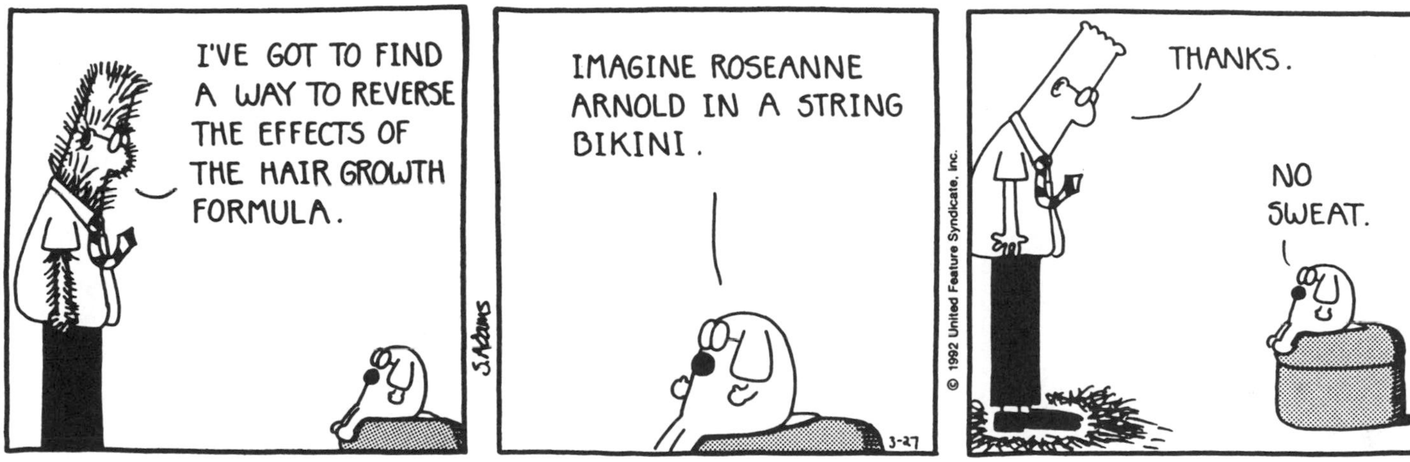
I'VE GOT TO FIND A WAY TO REVERSE THE EFFECTS OF THE HAIR GROWTH FORMULA.
IMAGINE ROSEANNE ARNOLD IN A STRING BIKINI.
THANKS.
NO SWEAT.
S. Adams
© 1992 United Feature Syndicate, Inc.
3-27

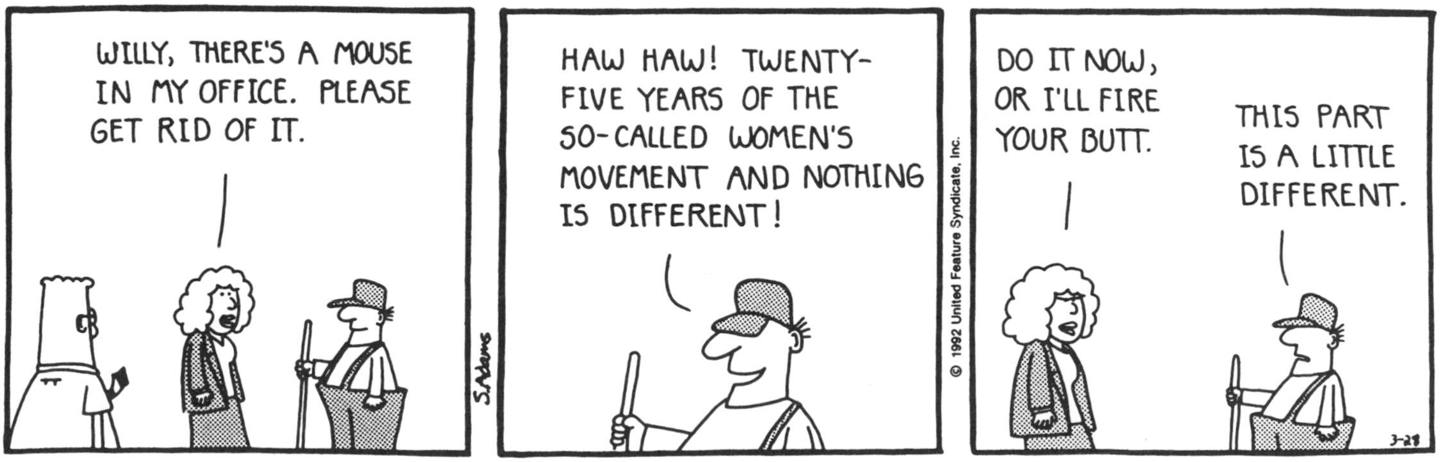
WILLY, THERE'S A MOUSE IN MY OFFICE. PLEASE GET RID OF IT.
HAW HAW! TWENTY-FIVE YEARS OF THE SO-CALLED WOMEN'S MOVEMENT AND NOTHING IS DIFFERENT!
DO IT NOW, OR I'LL FIRE YOUR BUTT.
THIS PART IS A LITTLE DIFFERENT.
S. Adams
© 1992 United Feature Syndicate, Inc.
3-28

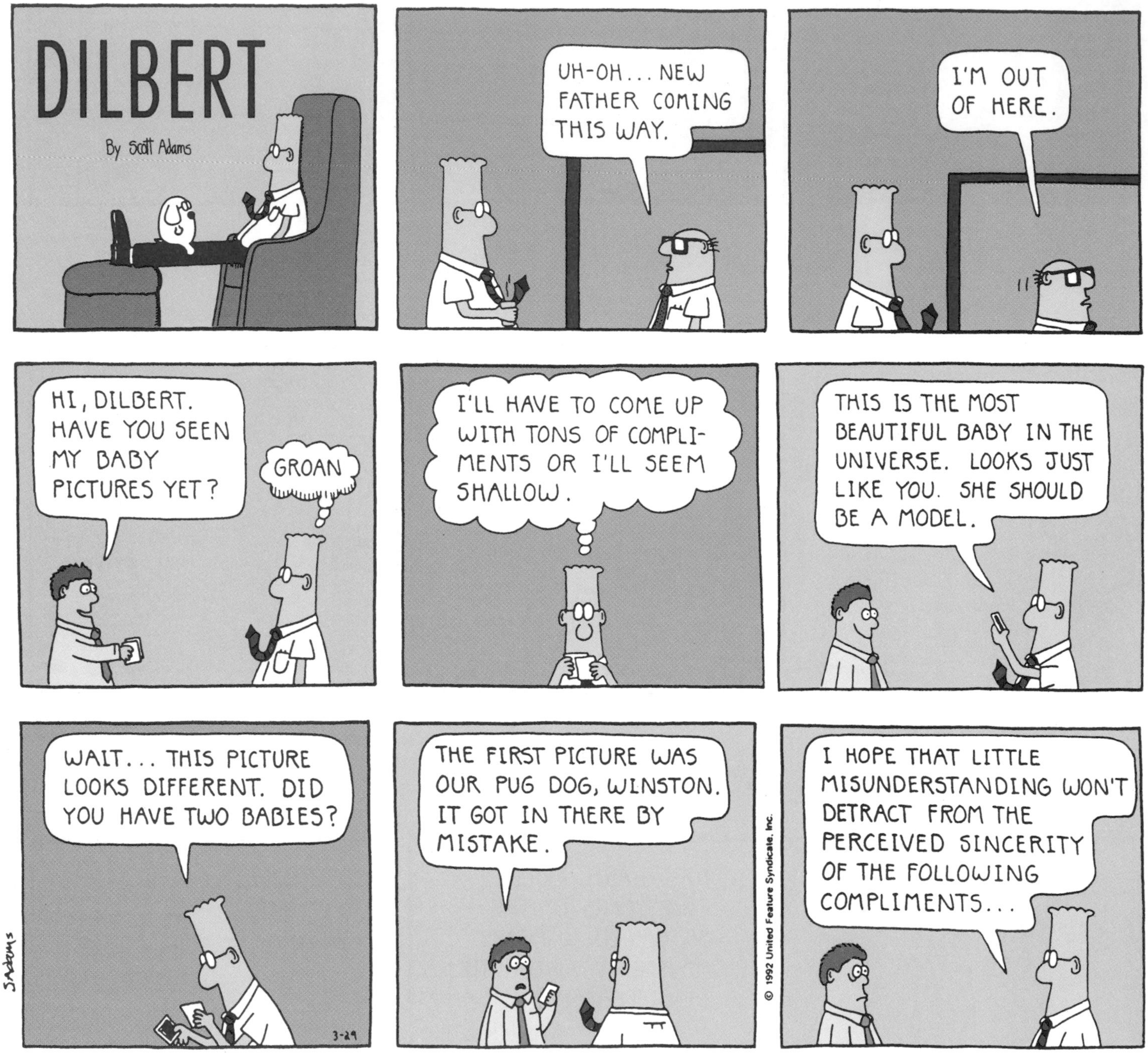
DILBERT
By Scott Adams
UH-OH... NEW FATHER COMING THIS WAY.
I'M OUT OF HERE.
HI, DILBERT. HAVE YOU SEEN MY BABY PICTURES YET?
GROAN
I'LL HAVE TO COME UP WITH TONS OF COMPLI-MENTS OR I'LL SEEM SHALLOW.
THIS IS THE MOST BEAUTIFUL BABY IN THE UNIVERSE. LOOKS JUST LIKE YOU. SHE SHOULD BE A MODEL.
WAIT... THIS PICTURE LOOKS DIFFERENT. DID YOU HAVE TWO BABIES?
S.Adams
3-29
THE FIRST PICTURE WAS OUR PUG DOG, WINSTON. IT GOT IN THERE BY MISTAKE.
© 1992 United Feature Syndicate, Inc.
I HOPE THAT LITTLE MISUNDERSTANDING WON'T DETRACT FROM THE PERCEIVED SINCERITY OF THE FOLLOWING COMPLIMENTS...

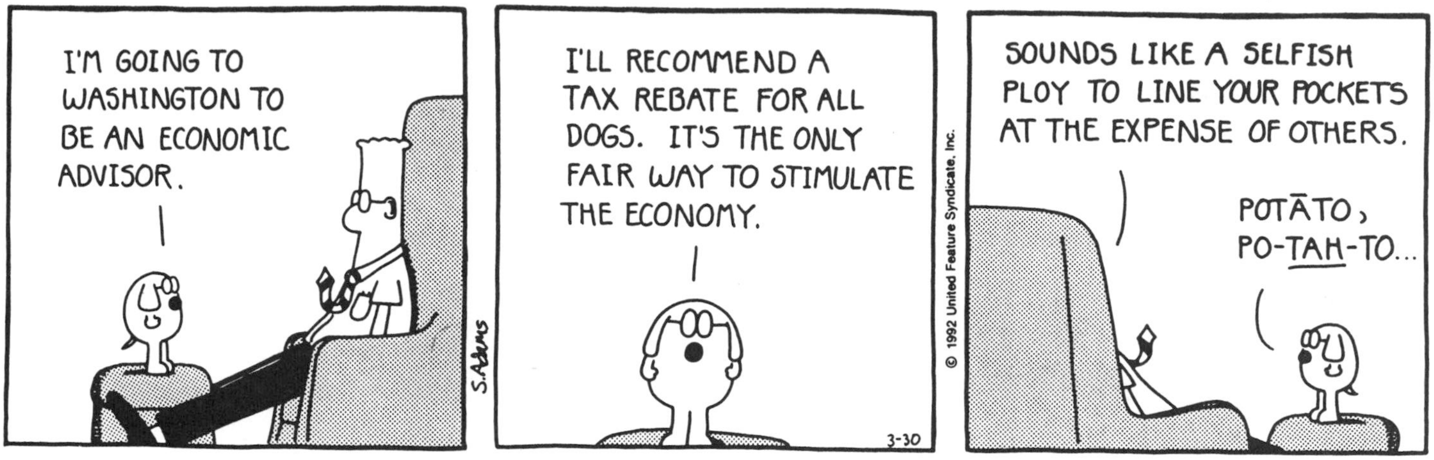
I'M GOING TO WASHINGTON TO BE AN ECONOMIC ADVISOR.
I'LL RECOMMEND A TAX REBATE FOR ALL DOGS. IT'S THE ONLY FAIR WAY TO STIMULATE THE ECONOMY.
SOUNDS LIKE A SELFISH PLOY TO LINE YOUR POCKETS AT THE EXPENSE OF OTHERS.
POTĀTO, PO-TAH-TO...
S. Adams
3-30
© 1992 United Feature Syndicate, Inc.

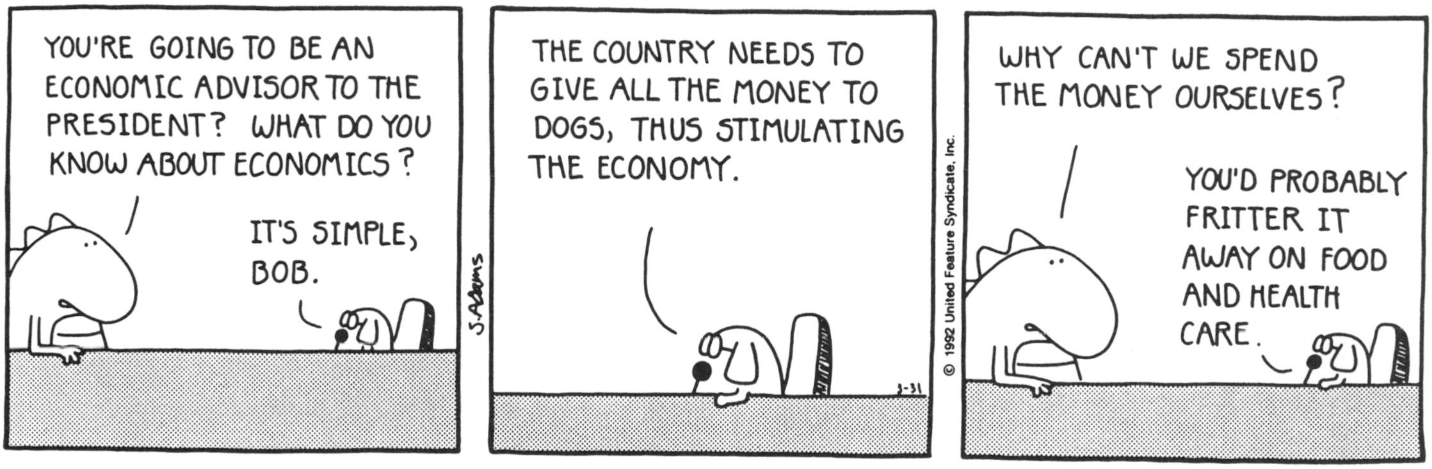
YOU'RE GOING TO BE AN ECONOMIC ADVISOR TO THE PRESIDENT? WHAT DO YOU KNOW ABOUT ECONOMICS?
IT'S SIMPLE, BOB.
THE COUNTRY NEEDS TO GIVE ALL THE MONEY TO DOGS, THUS STIMULATING THE ECONOMY.
WHY CAN'T WE SPEND THE MONEY OURSELVES?
YOU'D PROBABLY FRITTER IT AWAY ON FOOD AND HEALTH CARE.
S. Adams
3-31
© 1992 United Feature Syndicate, Inc.

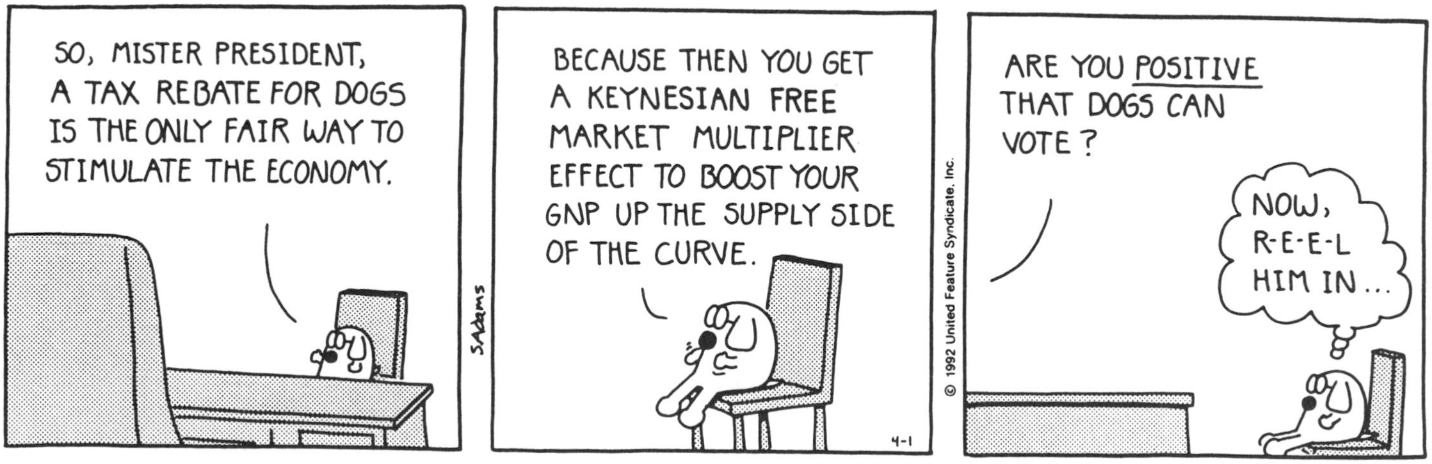
SO, MISTER PRESIDENT, A TAX REBATE FOR DOGS IS THE ONLY FAIR WAY TO STIMULATE THE ECONOMY.
BECAUSE THEN YOU GET A KEYNESIAN FREE MARKET MULTIPLIER EFFECT TO BOOST YOUR GNP UP THE SUPPLY SIDE OF THE CURVE.
ARE YOU POSITIVE THAT DOGS CAN VOTE?
NOW, R-E-E-L HIM IN...
S. Adams
4-1
© 1992 United Feature Syndicate, Inc.

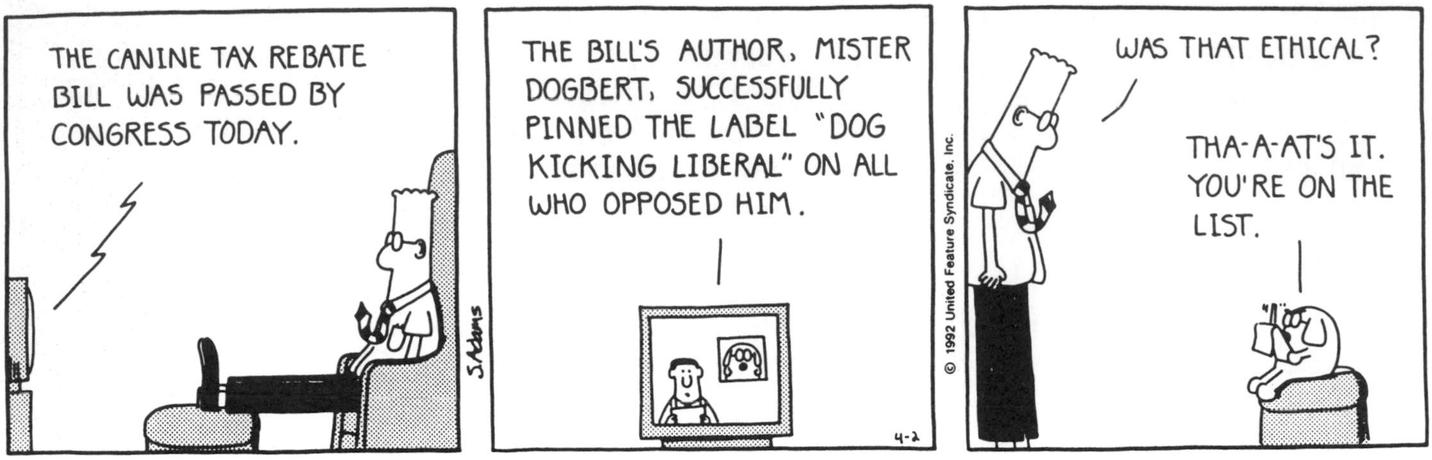
THE CANINE TAX REBATE BILL WAS PASSED BY CONGRESS TODAY.
S.Adams
THE BILL'S AUTHOR, MISTER DOGBERT, SUCCESSFULLY PINNED THE LABEL "DOG KICKING LIBERAL" ON ALL WHO OPPOSED HIM.
4-2
© 1992 United Feature Syndicate, Inc.
WAS THAT ETHICAL?
THA-A-AT'S IT. YOU'RE ON THE LIST.

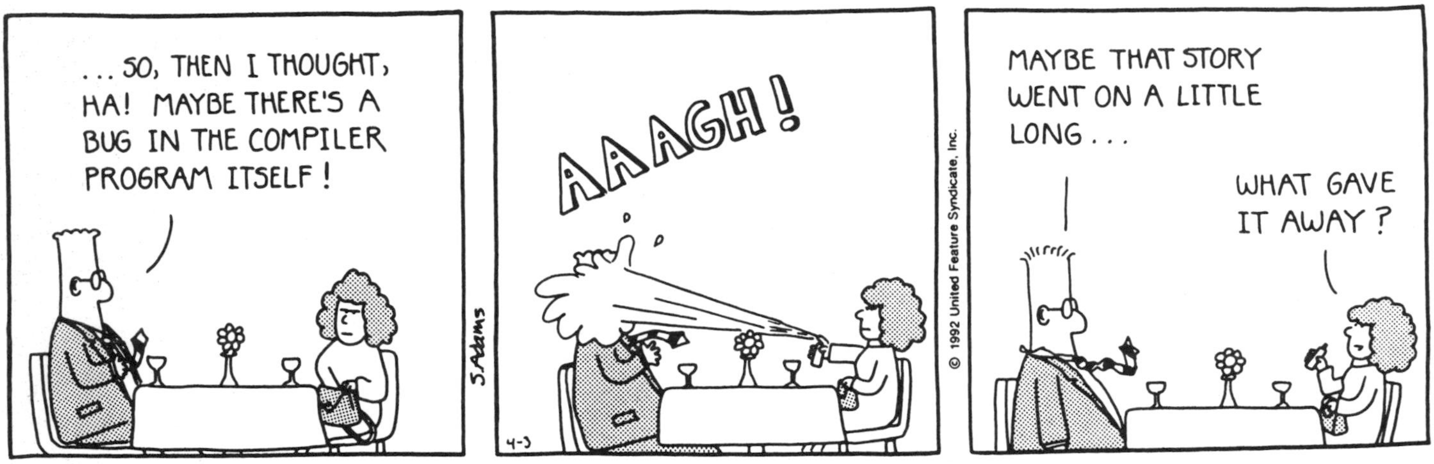
... SO, THEN I THOUGHT, HA! MAYBE THERE'S A BUG IN THE COMPILER PROGRAM ITSELF!
S.Adams
AAAGH!
4-3
© 1992 United Feature Syndicate, Inc.
MAYBE THAT STORY WENT ON A LITTLE LONG...
WHAT GAVE IT AWAY?

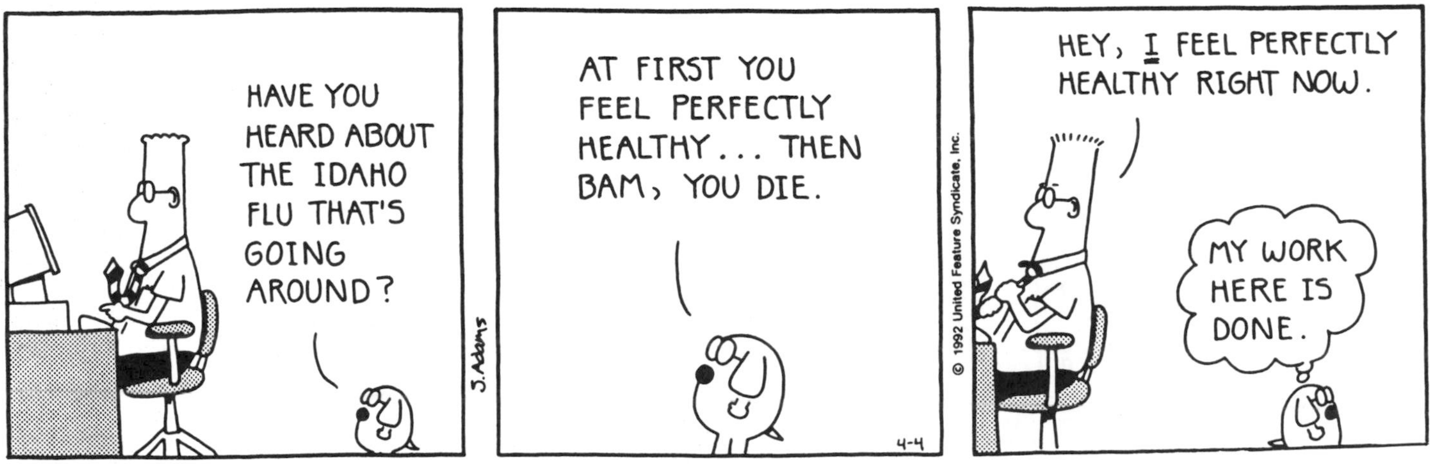
HAVE YOU HEARD ABOUT THE IDAHO FLU THAT'S GOING AROUND?
S.Adams
AT FIRST YOU FEEL PERFECTLY HEALTHY... THEN BAM, YOU DIE.
4-4
© 1992 United Feature Syndicate, Inc.
HEY, I FEEL PERFECTLY HEALTHY RIGHT NOW.
MY WORK HERE IS DONE.

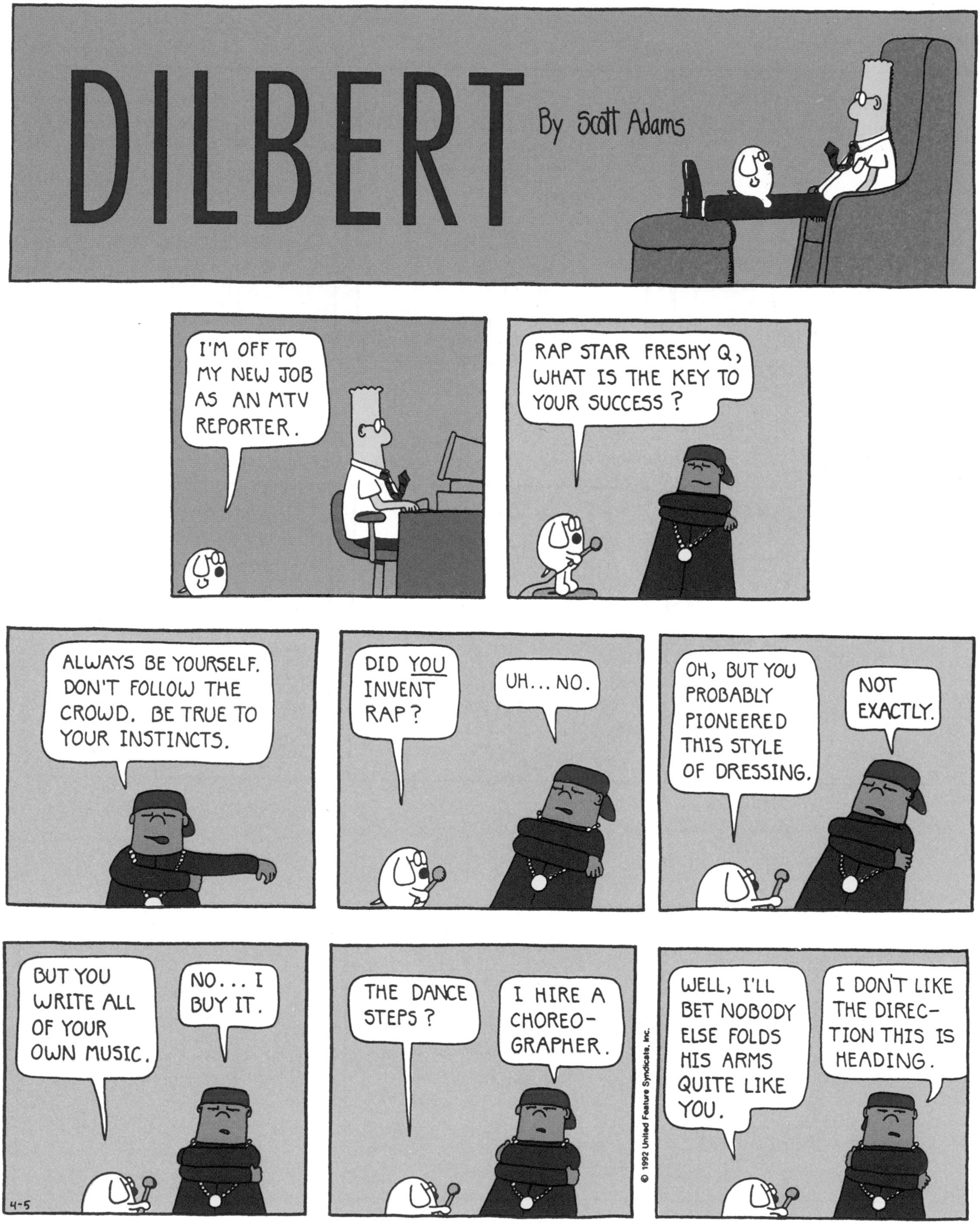
DILBERT
By Scott Adams
I'M OFF TO MY NEW JOB AS AN MTV REPORTER.
RAP STAR FRESHY Q, WHAT IS THE KEY TO YOUR SUCCESS?
ALWAYS BE YOURSELF. DON'T FOLLOW THE CROWD. BE TRUE TO YOUR INSTINCTS.
DID YOU INVENT RAP?
UH... NO.
OH, BUT YOU PROBABLY PIONEERED THIS STYLE OF DRESSING.
NOT EXACTLY.
BUT YOU WRITE ALL OF YOUR OWN MUSIC.
NO... I BUY IT.
THE DANCE STEPS?
I HIRE A CHOREOGRAPHER.
WELL, I'LL BET NOBODY ELSE FOLDS HIS ARMS QUITE LIKE YOU.
I DON'T LIKE THE DIRECTION THIS IS HEADING.
S.Adams
4-5
© 1992 United Feature Syndicate, Inc.

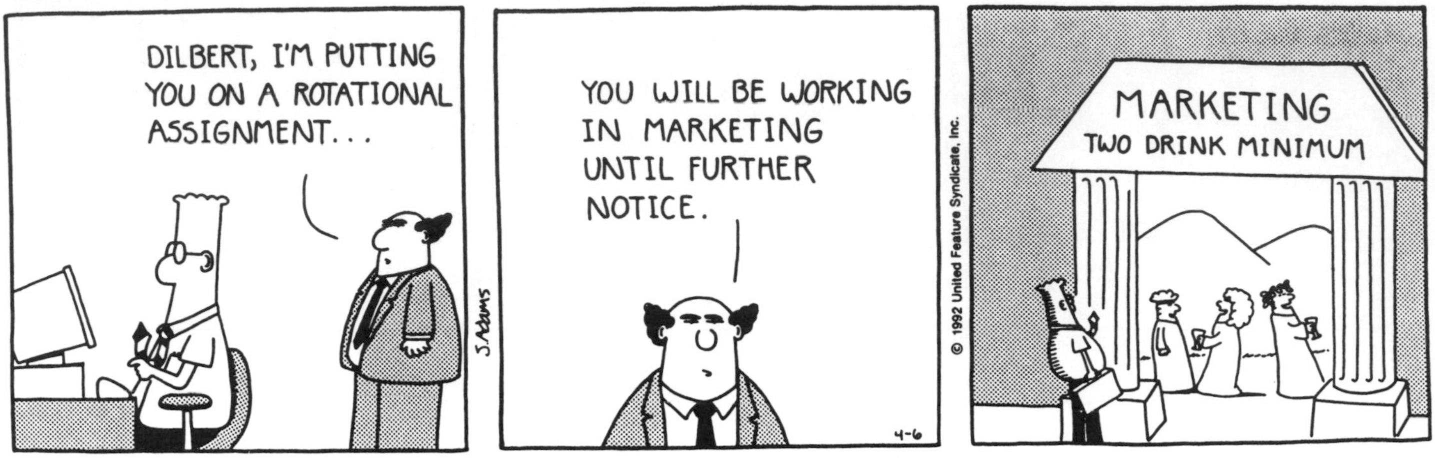
DILBERT, I'M PUTTING YOU ON A ROTATIONAL ASSIGNMENT...
S.Adams
YOU WILL BE WORKING IN MARKETING UNTIL FURTHER NOTICE.
© 1992 United Feature Syndicate, Inc.
MARKETING
TWO DRINK MINIMUM

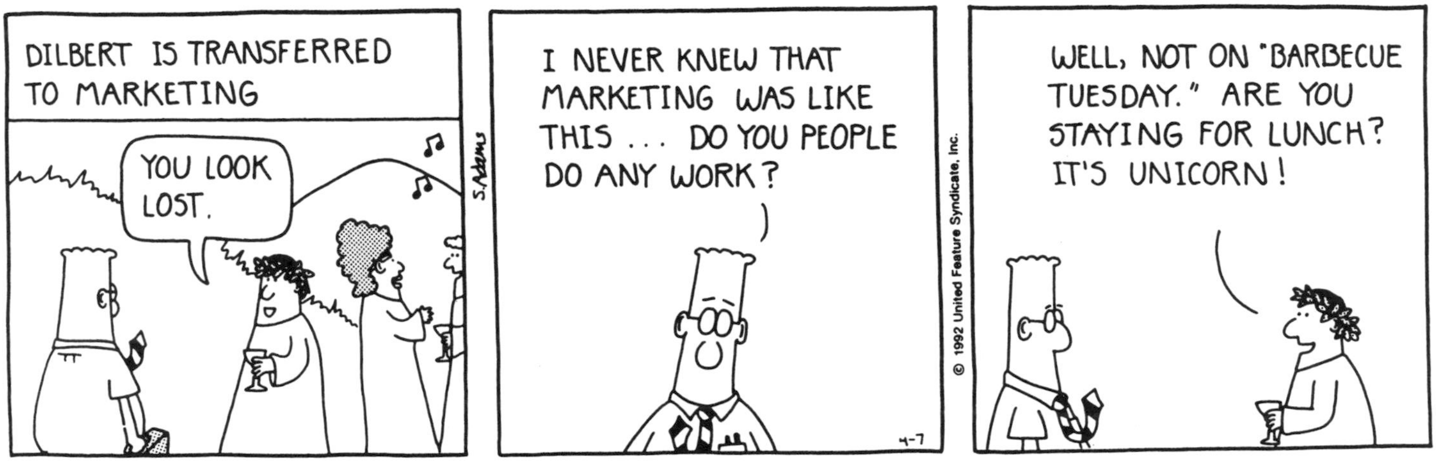
DILBERT IS TRANSFERRED TO MARKETING
YOU LOOK LOST.
S.Adams
I NEVER KNEW THAT MARKETING WAS LIKE THIS ... DO YOU PEOPLE DO ANY WORK?
© 1992 United Feature Syndicate, Inc.
WELL, NOT ON "BARBECUE TUESDAY." ARE YOU STAYING FOR LUNCH? IT'S UNICORN!

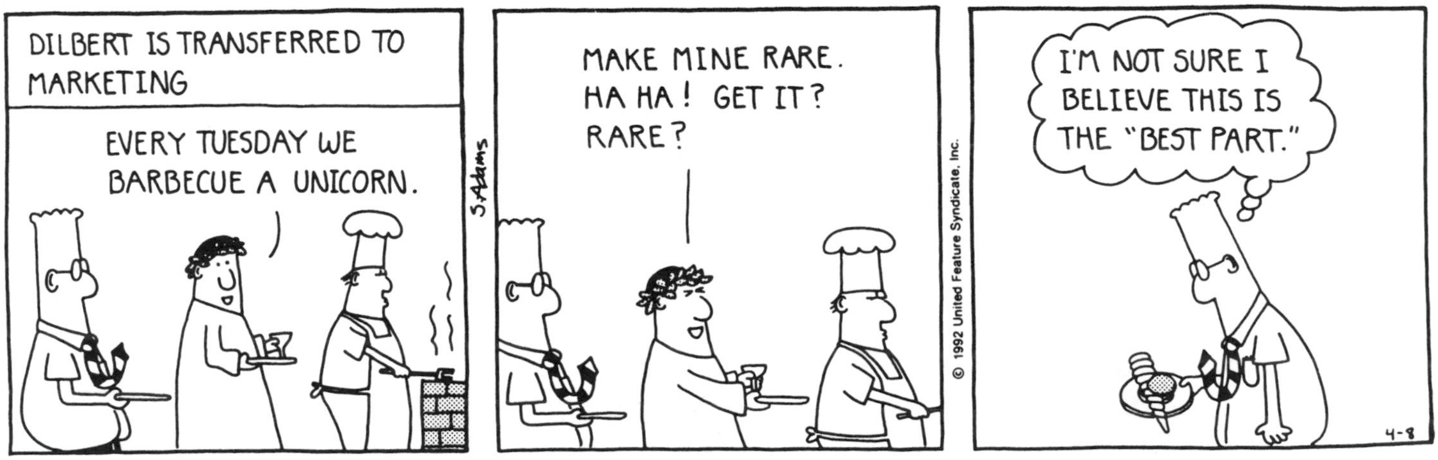
DILBERT IS TRANSFERRED TO MARKETING
EVERY TUESDAY WE BARBECUE A UNICORN.
S.Adams
MAKE MINE RARE. HA HA! GET IT? RARE?
© 1992 United Feature Syndicate, Inc.
I'M NOT SURE I BELIEVE THIS IS THE "BEST PART."

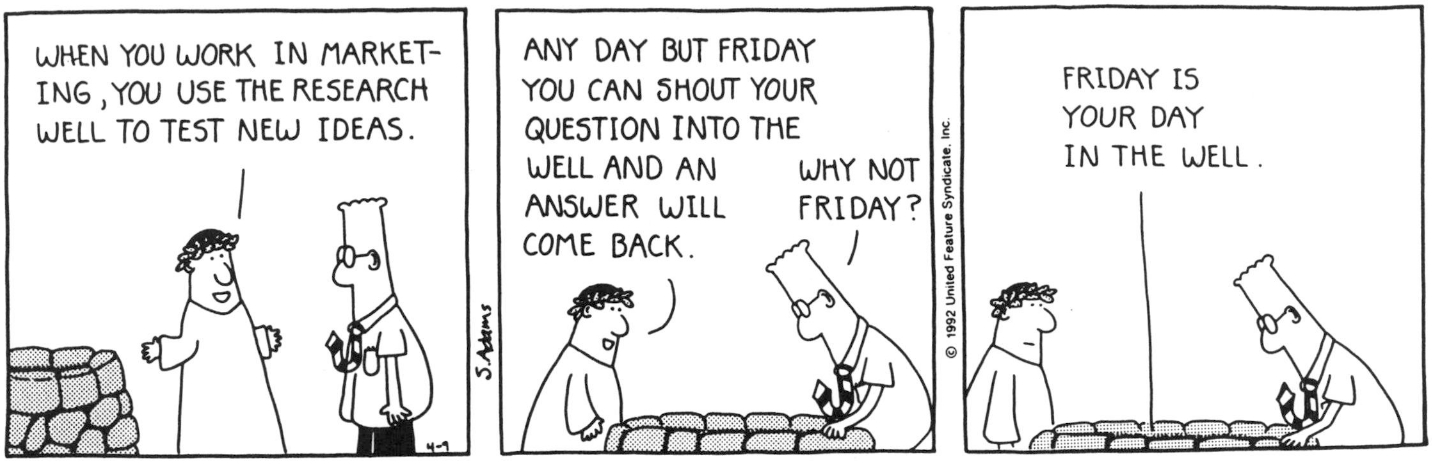
WHEN YOU WORK IN MARKETING, YOU USE THE RESEARCH WELL TO TEST NEW IDEAS.
ANY DAY BUT FRIDAY YOU CAN SHOUT YOUR QUESTION INTO THE WELL AND AN ANSWER WILL COME BACK.
WHY NOT FRIDAY?
FRIDAY IS YOUR DAY IN THE WELL.
© 1992 United Feature Syndicate, Inc.

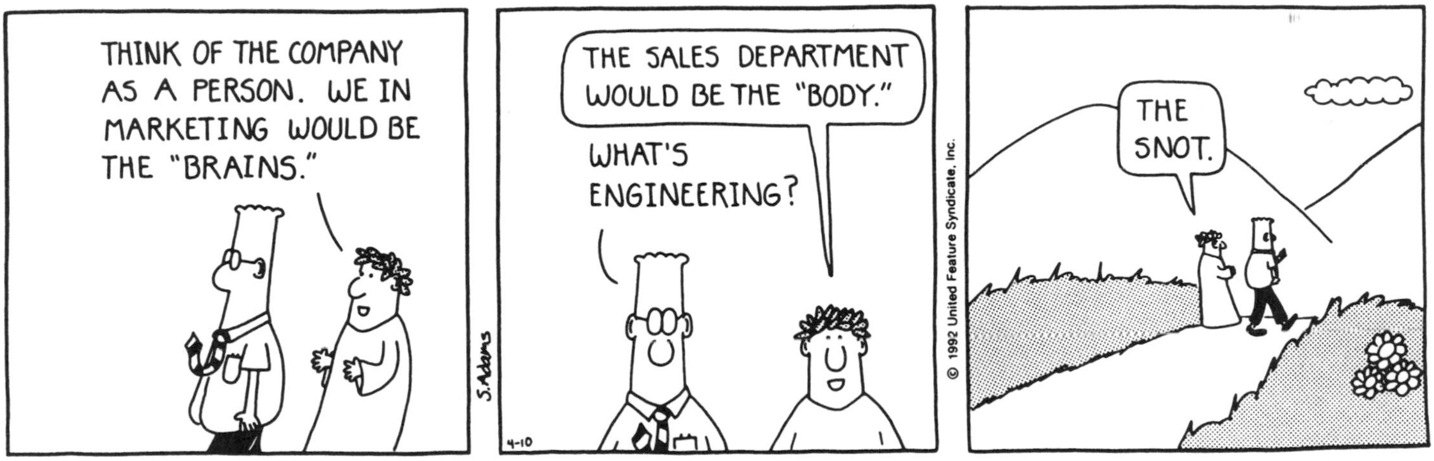
THINK OF THE COMPANY AS A PERSON. WE IN MARKETING WOULD BE THE "BRAINS."
THE SALES DEPARTMENT WOULD BE THE "BODY."
WHAT'S ENGINEERING?
THE SNOT.
© 1992 United Feature Syndicate, Inc.

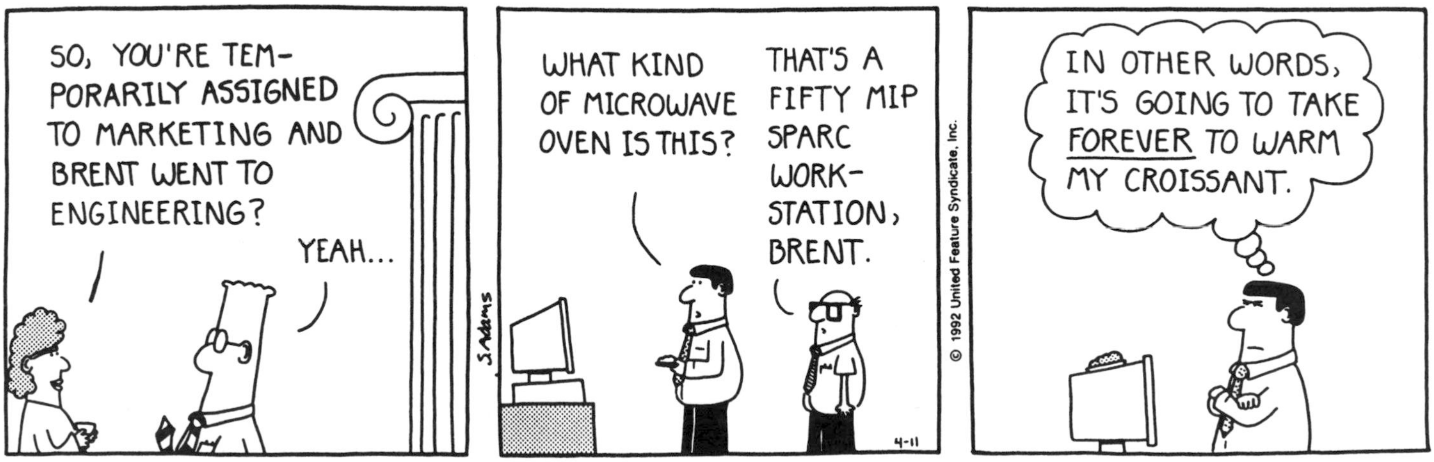
SO, YOU'RE TEMPORARILY ASSIGNED TO MARKETING AND BRENT WENT TO ENGINEERING?
YEAH...
WHAT KIND OF MICROWAVE OVEN IS THIS?
THAT'S A FIFTY MIP SPARC WORKSTATION, BRENT.
IN OTHER WORDS, IT'S GOING TO TAKE FOREVER TO WARM MY CROISSANT.
© 1992 United Feature Syndicate, Inc.

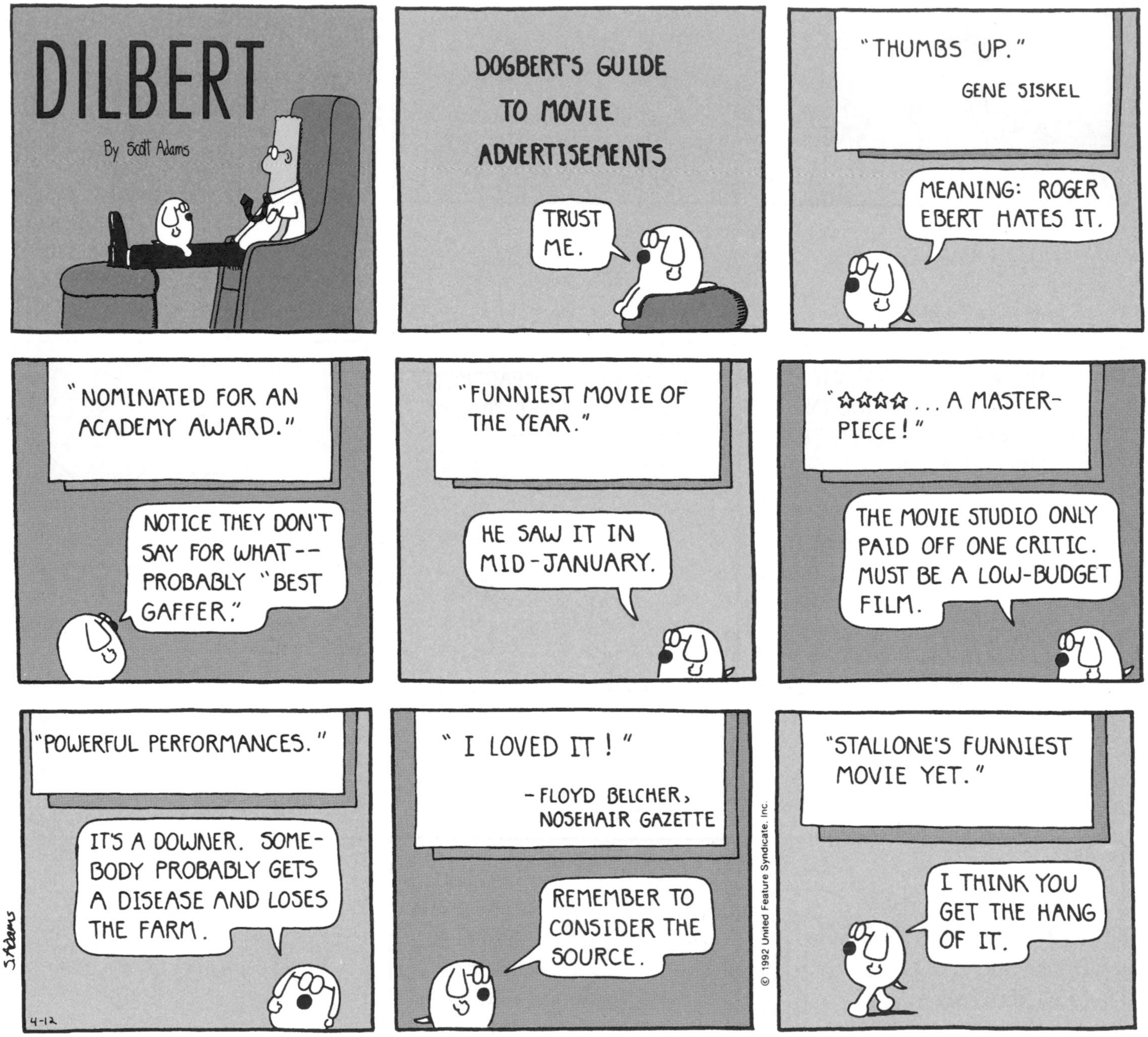
DILBERT
By Scott Adams
DOGBERT'S GUIDE TO MOVIE ADVERTISEMENTS
TRUST ME.
"THUMBS UP."
GENE SISKEL
MEANING: ROGER EBERT HATES IT.
"NOMINATED FOR AN ACADEMY AWARD."
NOTICE THEY DON'T SAY FOR WHAT-- PROBABLY "BEST GAFFER."
"FUNNIEST MOVIE OF THE YEAR."
HE SAW IT IN MID-JANUARY.
"☆☆☆☆ . . . A MASTER-PIECE!"
THE MOVIE STUDIO ONLY PAID OFF ONE CRITIC. MUST BE A LOW-BUDGET FILM.
"POWERFUL PERFORMANCES."
IT'S A DOWNER. SOMEBODY PROBABLY GETS A DISEASE AND LOSES THE FARM.
S.Adams
4-12
"I LOVED IT!"
-FLOYD BELCHER, NOSEHAIR GAZETTE
REMEMBER TO CONSIDER THE SOURCE.
© 1992 United Feature Syndicate, Inc.
"STALLONE'S FUNNIEST MOVIE YET."
I THINK YOU GET THE HANG OF IT.

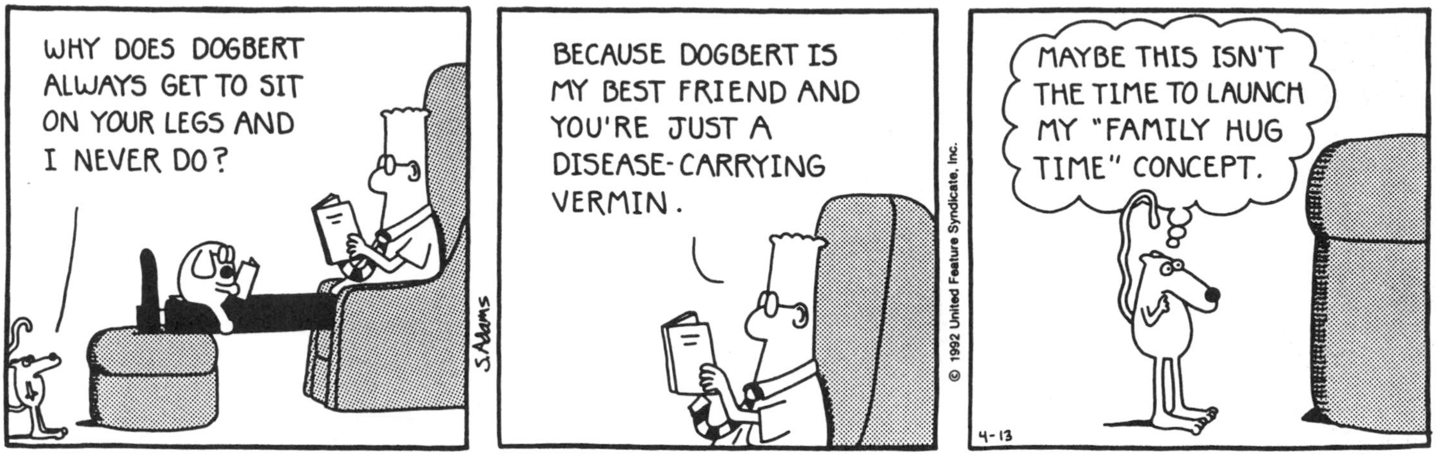
WHY DOES DOGBERT ALWAYS GET TO SIT ON YOUR LEGS AND I NEVER DO?
BECAUSE DOGBERT IS MY BEST FRIEND AND YOU'RE JUST A DISEASE-CARRYING VERMIN.
MAYBE THIS ISN'T THE TIME TO LAUNCH MY "FAMILY HUG TIME" CONCEPT.
© 1992 United Feature Syndicate, Inc.

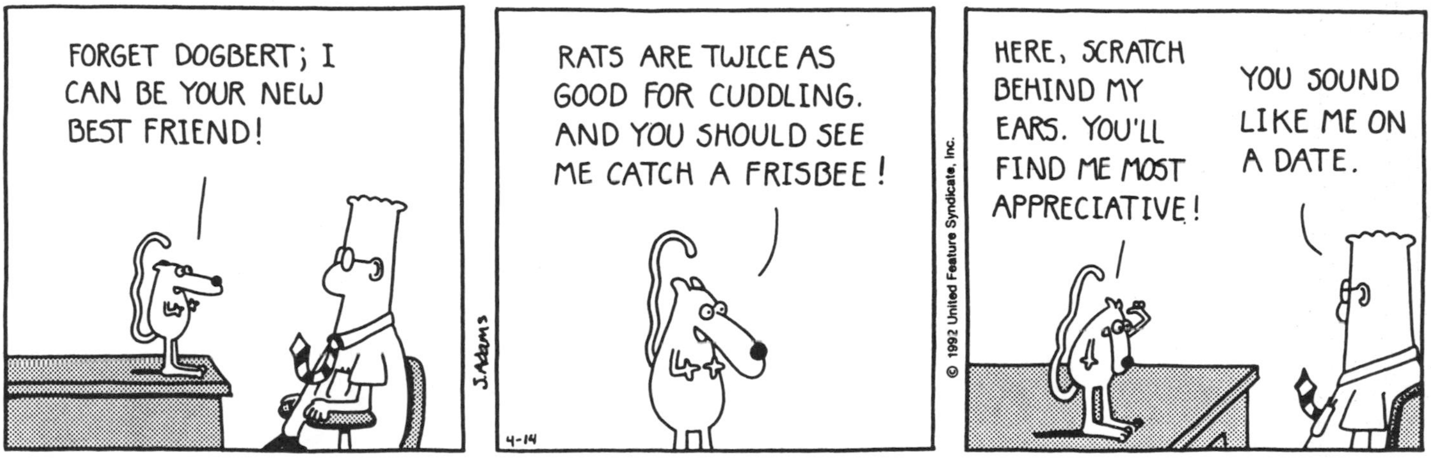
FORGET DOGBERT; I CAN BE YOUR NEW BEST FRIEND!
RATS ARE TWICE AS GOOD FOR CUDDLING. AND YOU SHOULD SEE ME CATCH A FRISBEE!
HERE, SCRATCH BEHIND MY EARS. YOU'LL FIND ME MOST APPRECIATIVE!
YOU SOUND LIKE ME ON A DATE.
© 1992 United Feature Syndicate, Inc.

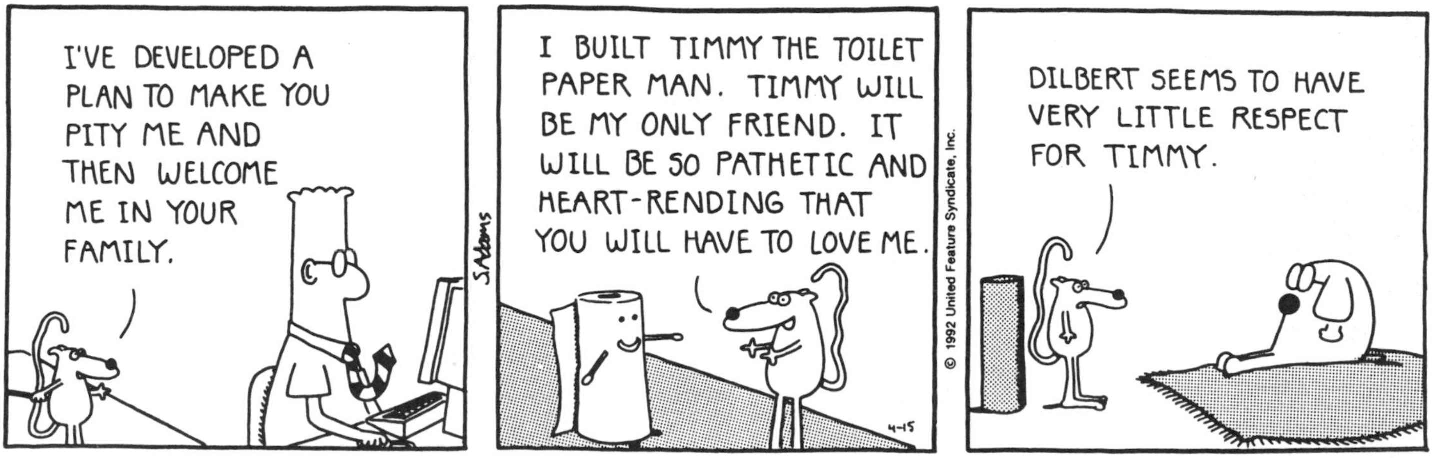
I'VE DEVELOPED A PLAN TO MAKE YOU PITY ME AND THEN WELCOME ME IN YOUR FAMILY.
I BUILT TIMMY THE TOILET PAPER MAN. TIMMY WILL BE MY ONLY FRIEND. IT WILL BE SO PATHETIC AND HEART-RENDING THAT YOU WILL HAVE TO LOVE ME.
DILBERT SEEMS TO HAVE VERY LITTLE RESPECT FOR TIMMY.
© 1992 United Feature Syndicate, Inc.

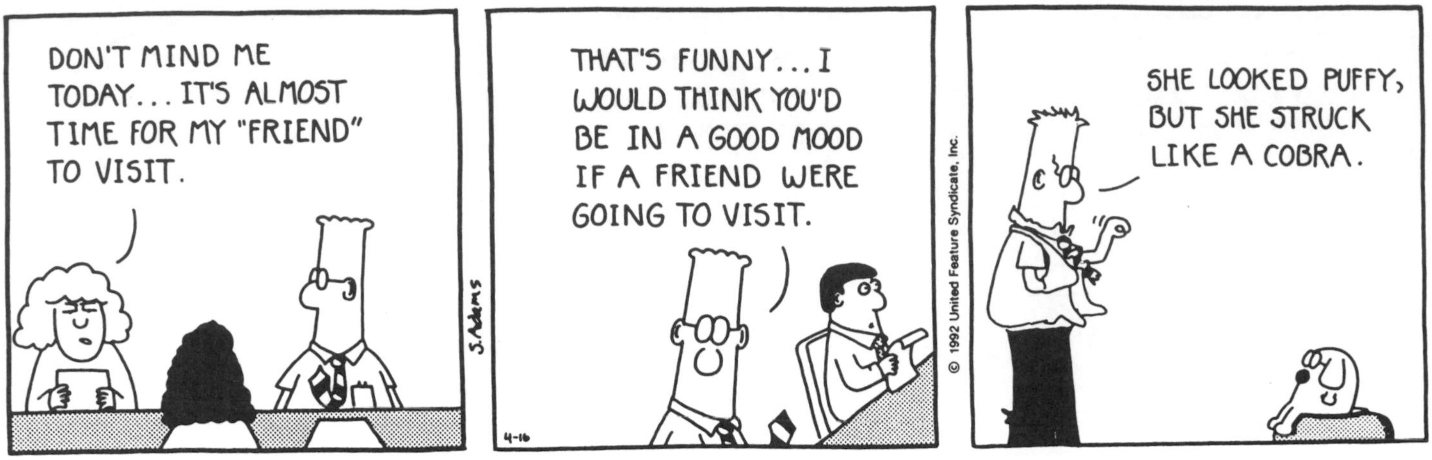
DON'T MIND ME TODAY... IT'S ALMOST TIME FOR MY "FRIEND" TO VISIT.
THAT'S FUNNY... I WOULD THINK YOU'D BE IN A GOOD MOOD IF A FRIEND WERE GOING TO VISIT.
SHE LOOKED PUFFY, BUT SHE STRUCK LIKE A COBRA.
S. Adams
4-16
© 1992 United Feature Syndicate, Inc.

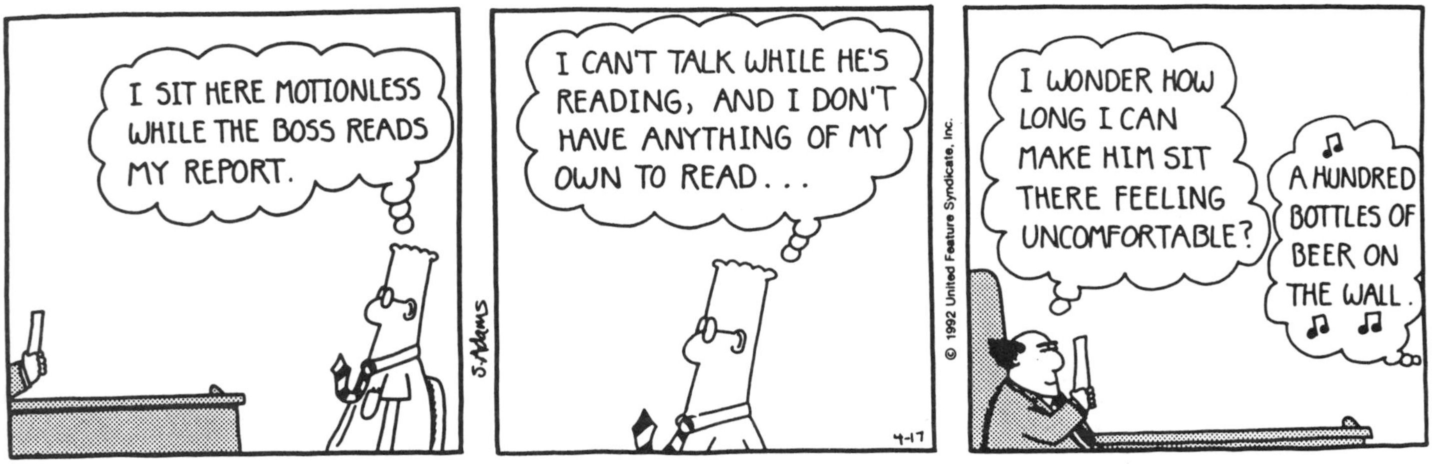
I SIT HERE MOTIONLESS WHILE THE BOSS READS MY REPORT.
I CAN'T TALK WHILE HE'S READING, AND I DON'T HAVE ANYTHING OF MY OWN TO READ...
I WONDER HOW LONG I CAN MAKE HIM SIT THERE FEELING UNCOMFORTABLE?
A HUNDRED BOTTLES OF BEER ON THE WALL.
S. Adams
4-17
© 1992 United Feature Syndicate, Inc.

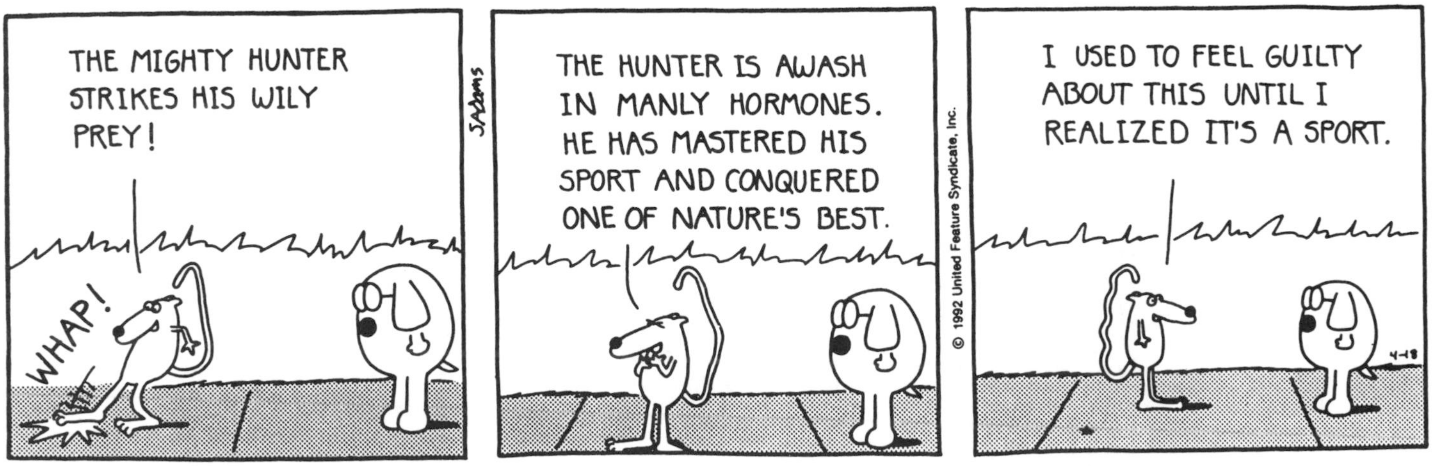
THE MIGHTY HUNTER STRIKES HIS WILY PREY!
WHAP!
THE HUNTER IS AWASH IN MANLY HORMONES. HE HAS MASTERED HIS SPORT AND CONQUERED ONE OF NATURE'S BEST.
I USED TO FEEL GUILTY ABOUT THIS UNTIL I REALIZED IT'S A SPORT.
S. Adams
4-18
© 1992 United Feature Syndicate, Inc.

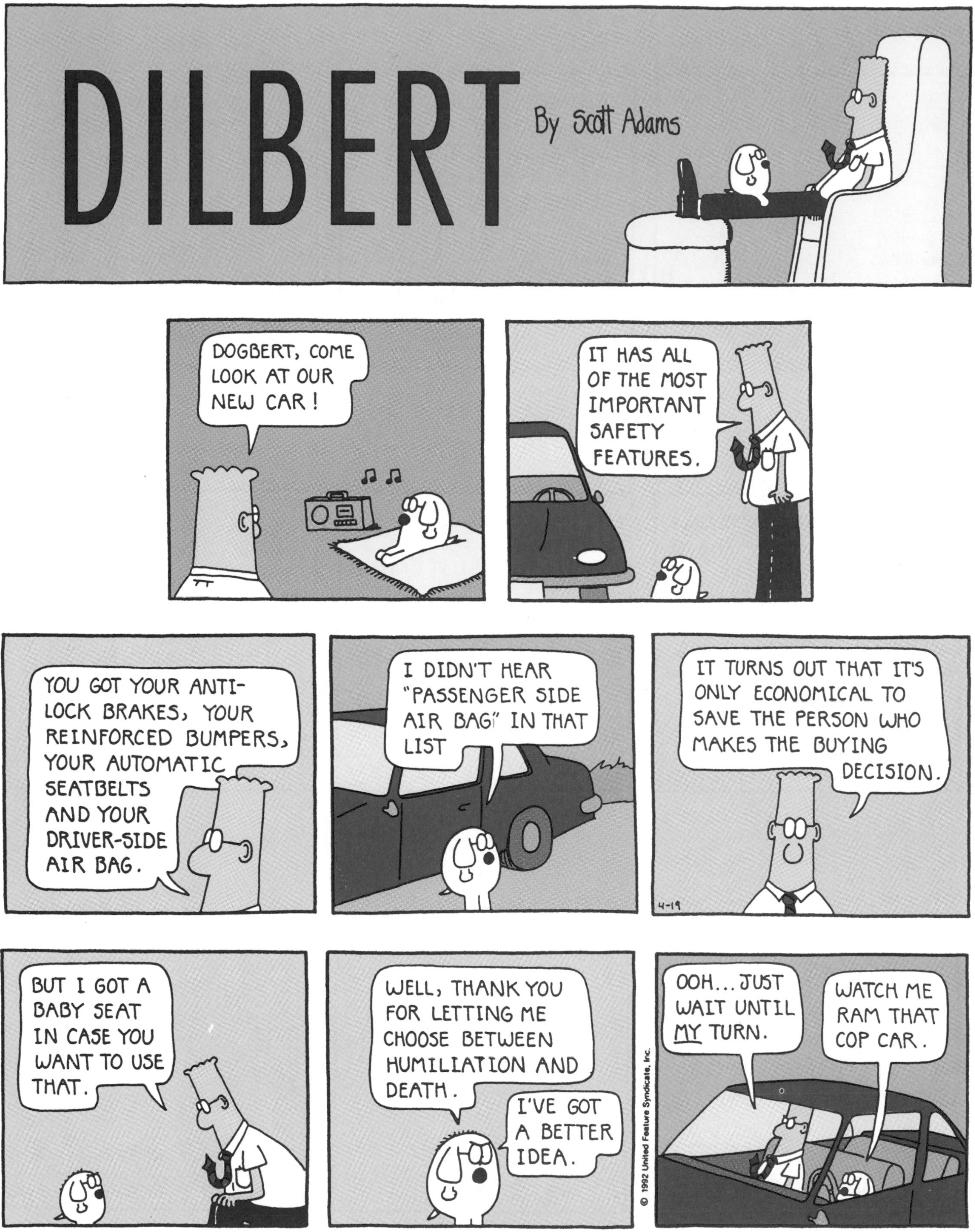
DILBERT
By Scott Adams
DOGBERT, COME LOOK AT OUR NEW CAR!
IT HAS ALL OF THE MOST IMPORTANT SAFETY FEATURES.
YOU GOT YOUR ANTI-LOCK BRAKES, YOUR REINFORCED BUMPERS, YOUR AUTOMATIC SEATBELTS AND YOUR DRIVER-SIDE AIR BAG.
I DIDN'T HEAR "PASSENGER SIDE AIR BAG" IN THAT LIST
IT TURNS OUT THAT IT'S ONLY ECONOMICAL TO SAVE THE PERSON WHO MAKES THE BUYING DECISION.
4-19
BUT I GOT A BABY SEAT IN CASE YOU WANT TO USE THAT.
S. Adams
WELL, THANK YOU FOR LETTING ME CHOOSE BETWEEN HUMILIATION AND DEATH.
I'VE GOT A BETTER IDEA.
© 1992 United Feature Syndicate, Inc.
OOH... JUST WAIT UNTIL MY TURN.
WATCH ME RAM THAT COP CAR.

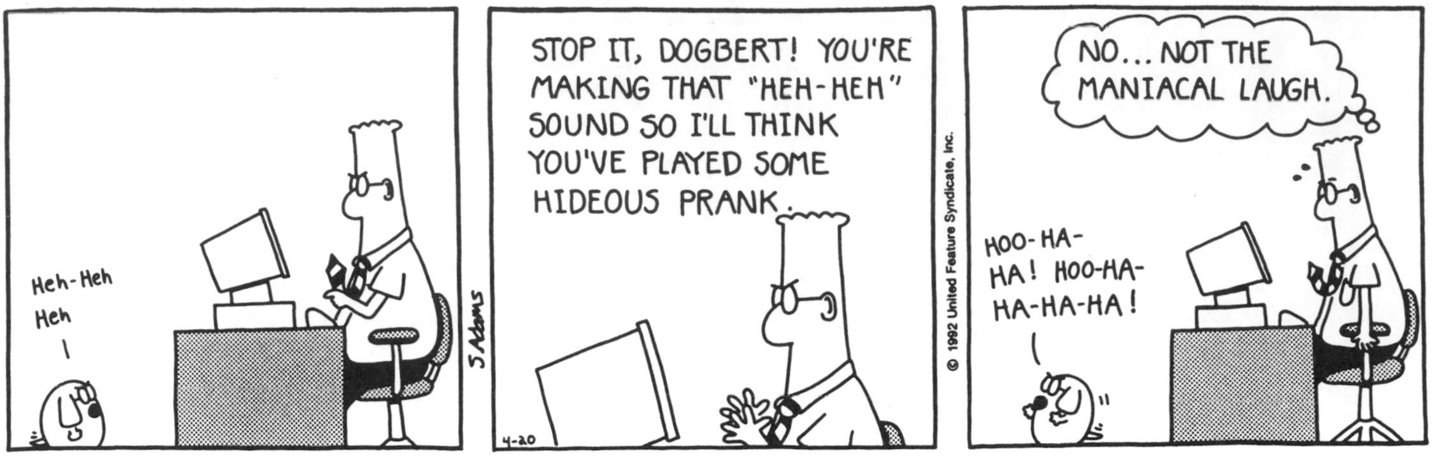
Heh-Heh
Heh
S. Adams
STOP IT, DOGBERT! YOU'RE MAKING THAT "HEH-HEH" SOUND SO I'LL THINK YOU'VE PLAYED SOME HIDEOUS PRANK.
4-20
© 1992 United Feature Syndicate, Inc.
NO... NOT THE MANIACAL LAUGH.
HOO-HA-HA! HOO-HA-HA-HA-HA!

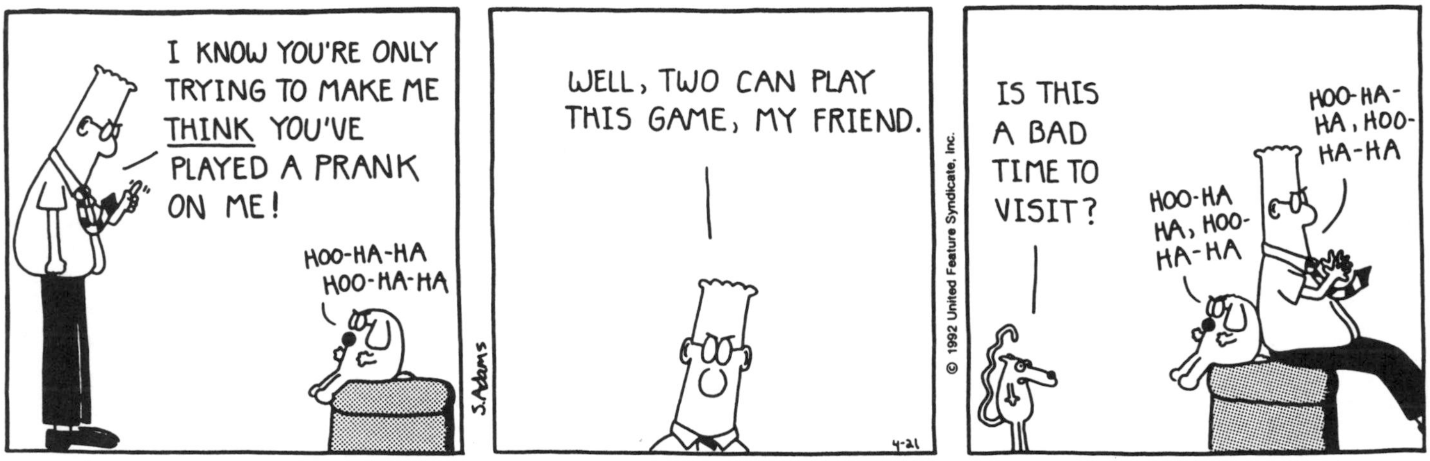
I KNOW YOU'RE ONLY TRYING TO MAKE ME THINK YOU'VE PLAYED A PRANK ON ME!
HOO-HA-HA HOO-HA-HA
S. Adams
WELL, TWO CAN PLAY THIS GAME, MY FRIEND.
4-21
© 1992 United Feature Syndicate, Inc.
IS THIS A BAD TIME TO VISIT?
HOO-HA HA, HOO-HA-HA
HOO-HA-HA, HOO-HA-HA

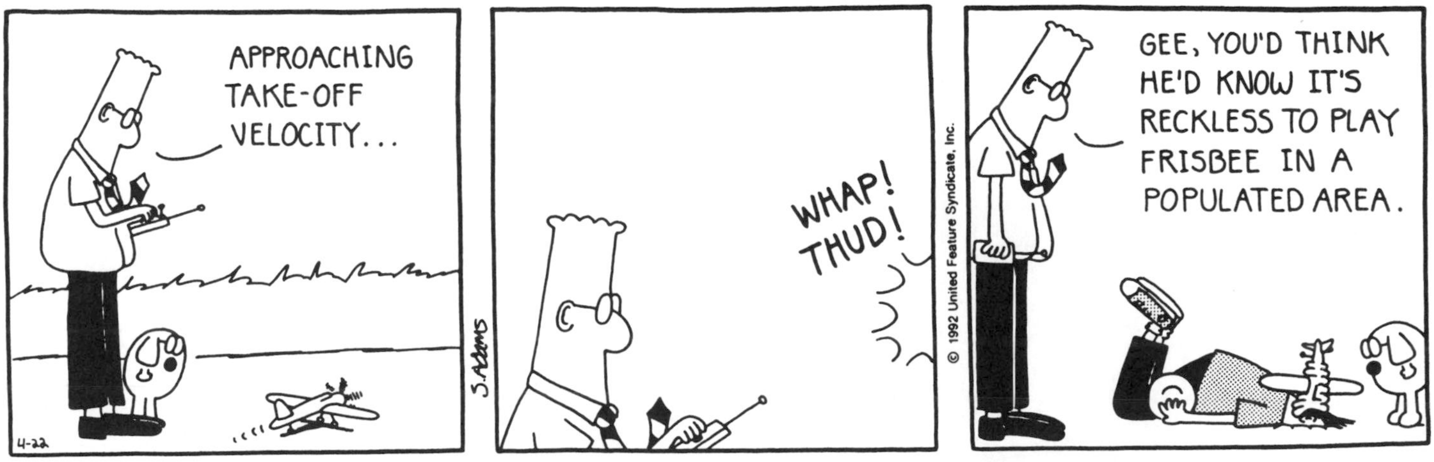
APPROACHING TAKE-OFF VELOCITY...
4-22
S. Adams
WHAP! THUD!
© 1992 United Feature Syndicate, Inc.
GEE, YOU'D THINK HE'D KNOW IT'S RECKLESS TO PLAY FRISBEE IN A POPULATED AREA.

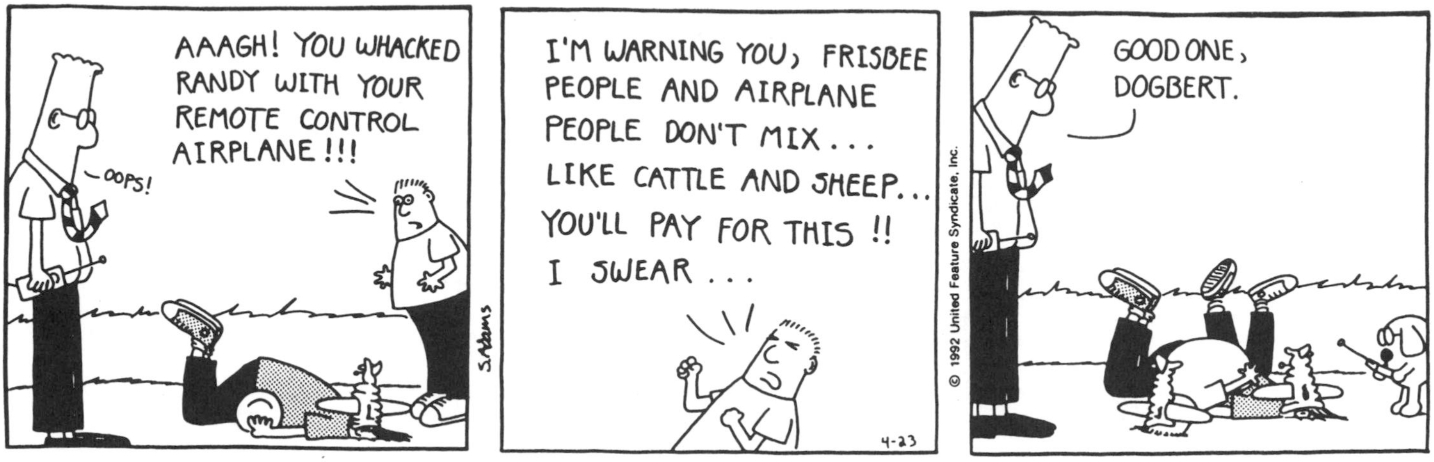
AAAGH! YOU WHACKED RANDY WITH YOUR REMOTE CONTROL AIRPLANE!!!
OOPS!
S.Adams
I'M WARNING YOU, FRISBEE PEOPLE AND AIRPLANE PEOPLE DON'T MIX... LIKE CATTLE AND SHEEP... YOU'LL PAY FOR THIS!! I SWEAR...
4-23
© 1992 United Feature Syndicate, Inc.
GOOD ONE, DOGBERT.

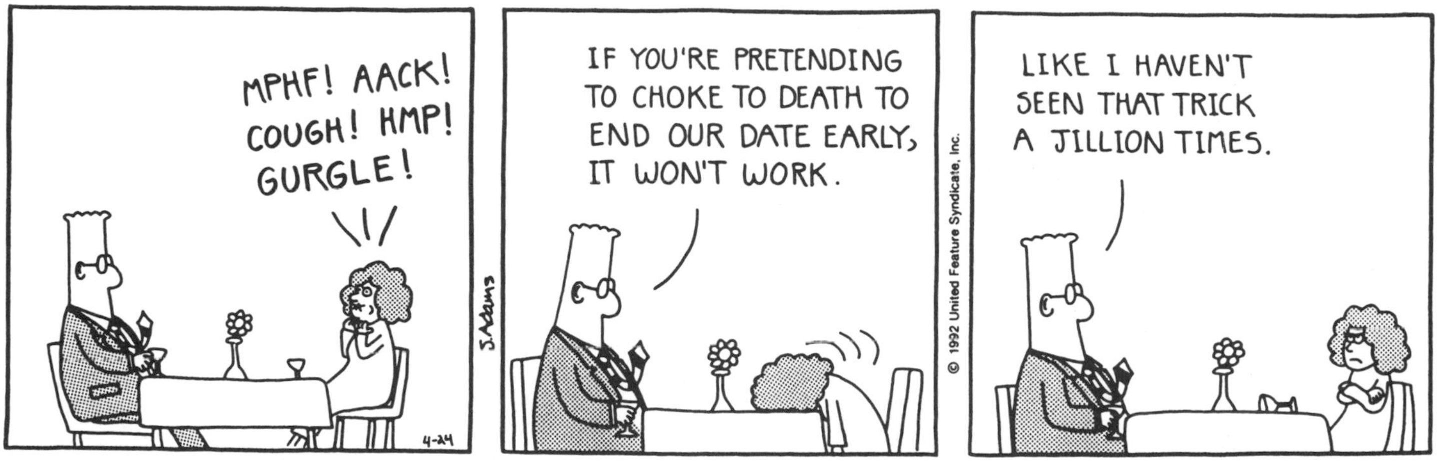
MPHF! AACK! COUGH! HMP! GURGLE!
S.Adams
4-24
IF YOU'RE PRETENDING TO CHOKE TO DEATH TO END OUR DATE EARLY, IT WON'T WORK.
© 1992 United Feature Syndicate, Inc.
LIKE I HAVEN'T SEEN THAT TRICK A JILLION TIMES.

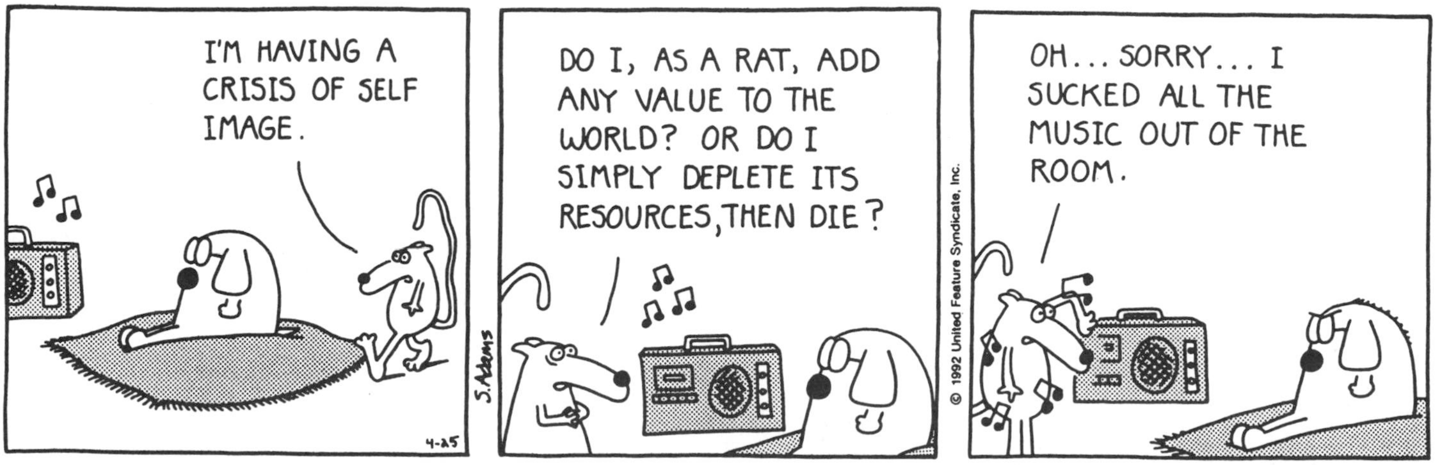
I'M HAVING A CRISIS OF SELF IMAGE.
S.Adams
4-25
DO I, AS A RAT, ADD ANY VALUE TO THE WORLD? OR DO I SIMPLY DEPLETE ITS RESOURCES, THEN DIE?
© 1992 United Feature Syndicate, Inc.
OH... SORRY... I SUCKED ALL THE MUSIC OUT OF THE ROOM.

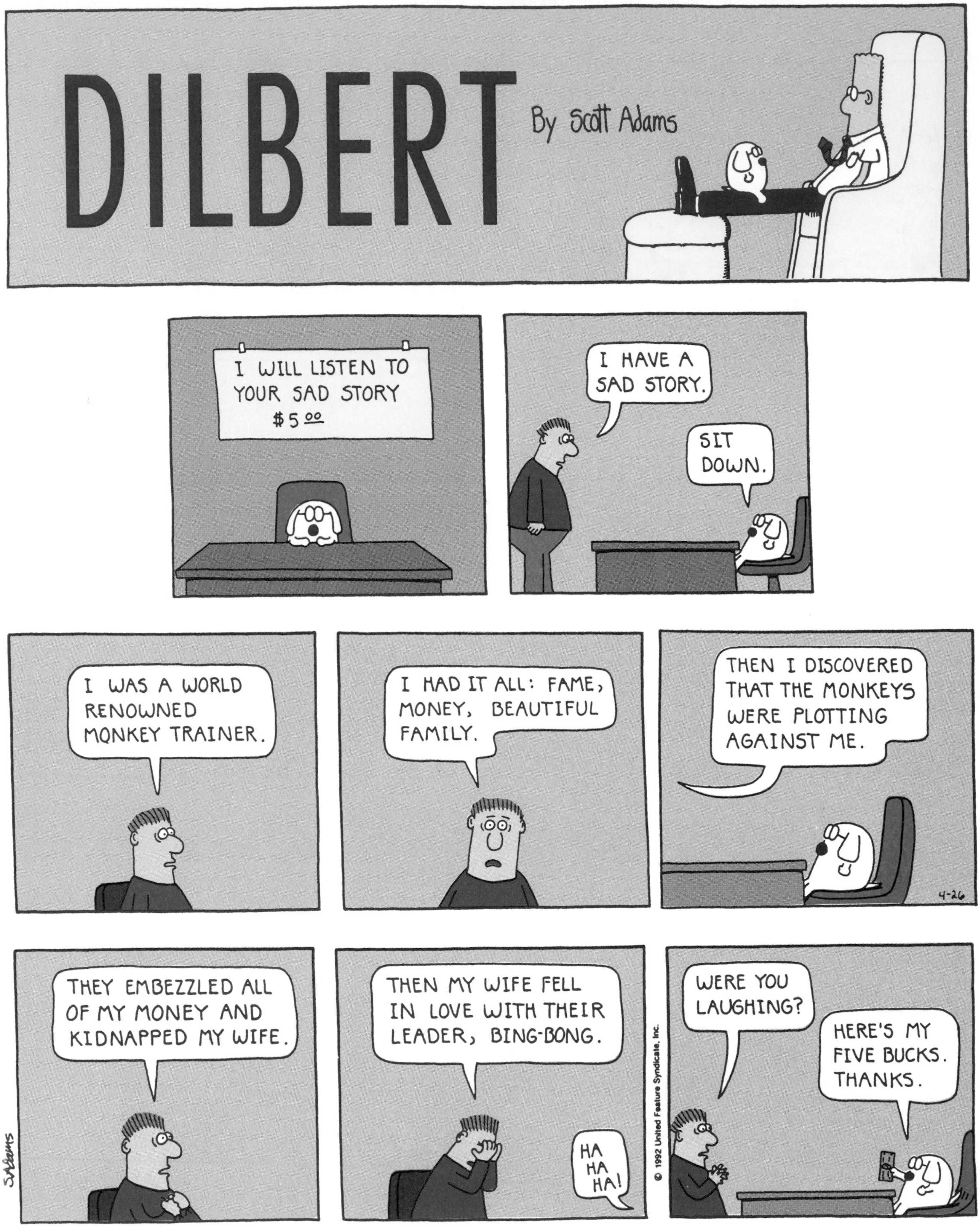
DILBERT
By Scott Adams
I WILL LISTEN TO YOUR SAD STORY $5.00
I HAVE A SAD STORY.
SIT DOWN.
I WAS A WORLD RENOWNED MONKEY TRAINER.
I HAD IT ALL: FAME, MONEY, BEAUTIFUL FAMILY.
THEN I DISCOVERED THAT THE MONKEYS WERE PLOTTING AGAINST ME.
4-26
THEY EMBEZZLED ALL OF MY MONEY AND KIDNAPPED MY WIFE.
THEN MY WIFE FELL IN LOVE WITH THEIR LEADER, BING-BONG.
HA HA HA!
© 1992 United Feature Syndicate, Inc.
WERE YOU LAUGHING?
HERE'S MY FIVE BUCKS. THANKS.

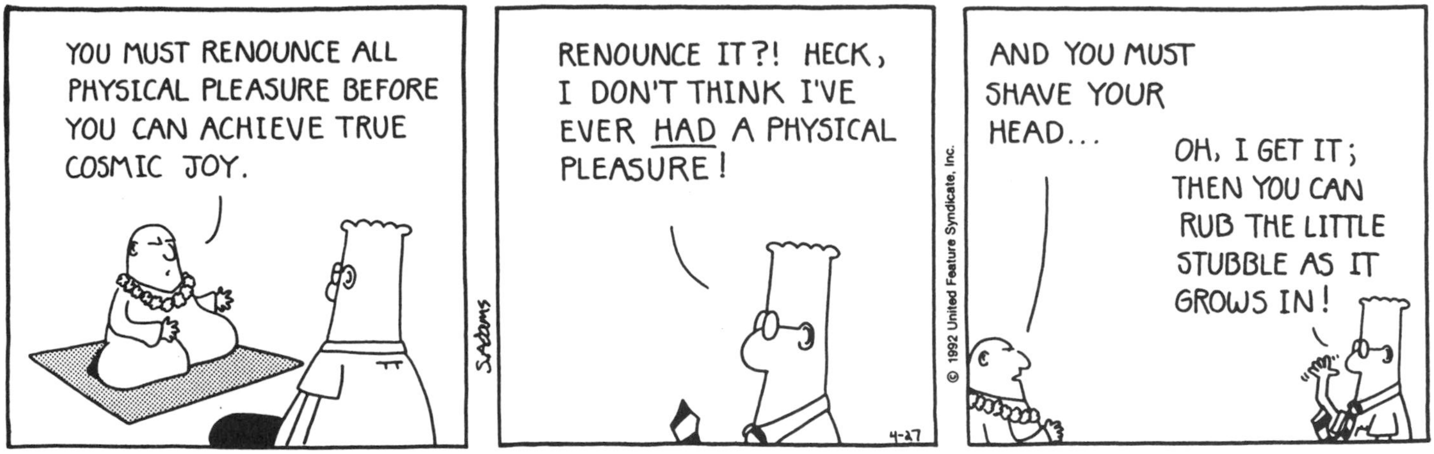
YOU MUST RENOUNCE ALL PHYSICAL PLEASURE BEFORE YOU CAN ACHIEVE TRUE COSMIC JOY.
S.Adams
RENOUNCE IT?! HECK, I DON'T THINK I'VE EVER HAD A PHYSICAL PLEASURE!
4-27
© 1992 United Feature Syndicate, Inc.
AND YOU MUST SHAVE YOUR HEAD...
OH, I GET IT; THEN YOU CAN RUB THE LITTLE STUBBLE AS IT GROWS IN!

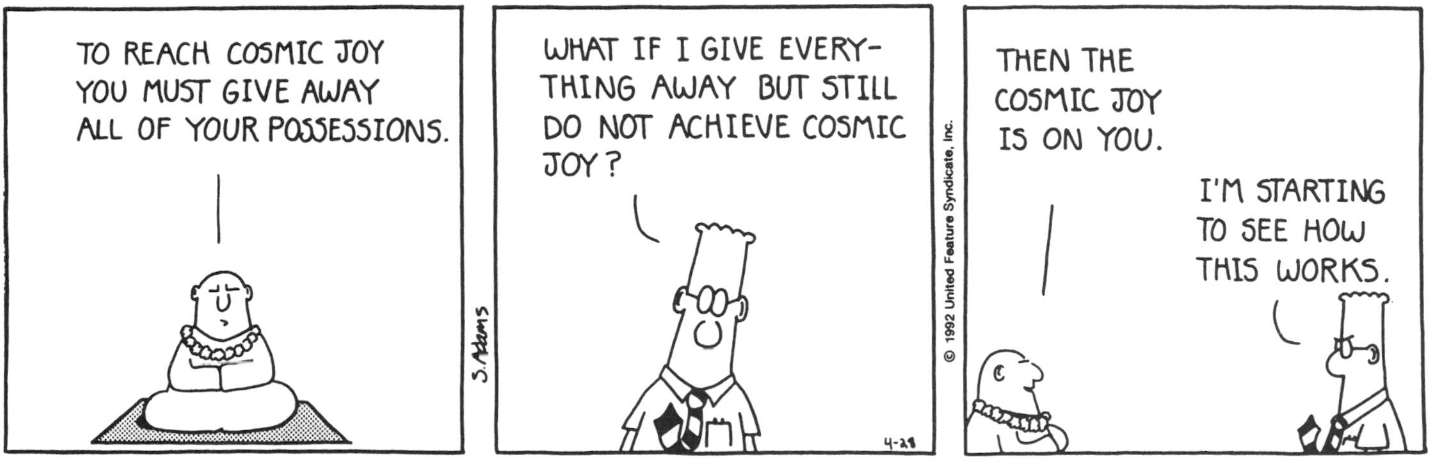
TO REACH COSMIC JOY YOU MUST GIVE AWAY ALL OF YOUR POSSESSIONS.
S.Adams
WHAT IF I GIVE EVERYTHING AWAY BUT STILL DO NOT ACHIEVE COSMIC JOY?
4-28
© 1992 United Feature Syndicate, Inc.
THEN THE COSMIC JOY IS ON YOU.
I'M STARTING TO SEE HOW THIS WORKS.

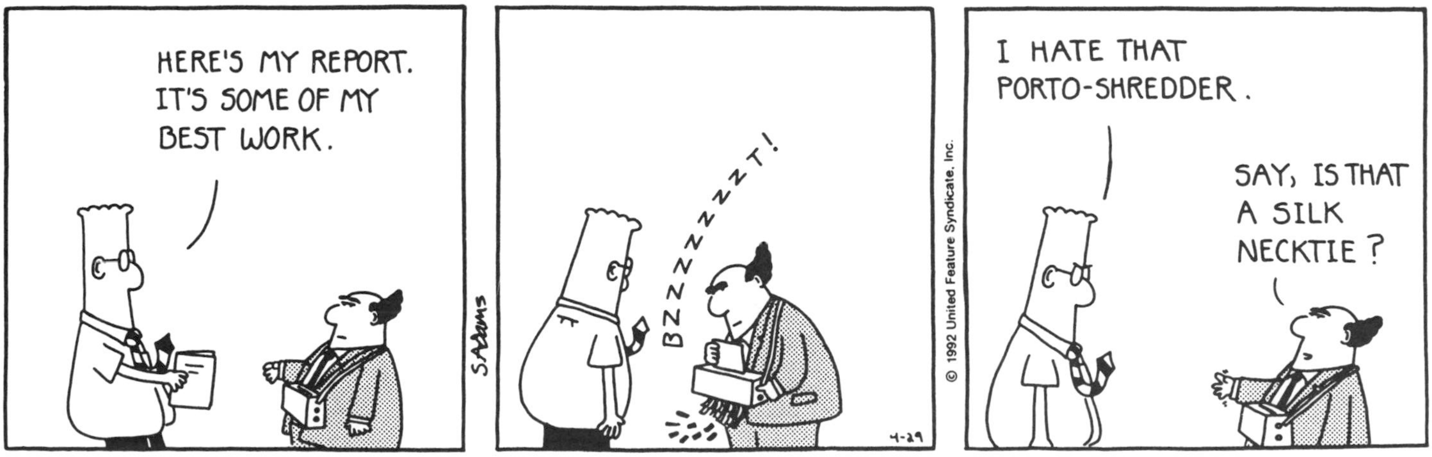
HERE'S MY REPORT. IT'S SOME OF MY BEST WORK.
S.Adams
BZZZZZZZZT!
4-29
© 1992 United Feature Syndicate, Inc.
I HATE THAT PORTO-SHREDDER.
SAY, IS THAT A SILK NECKTIE?

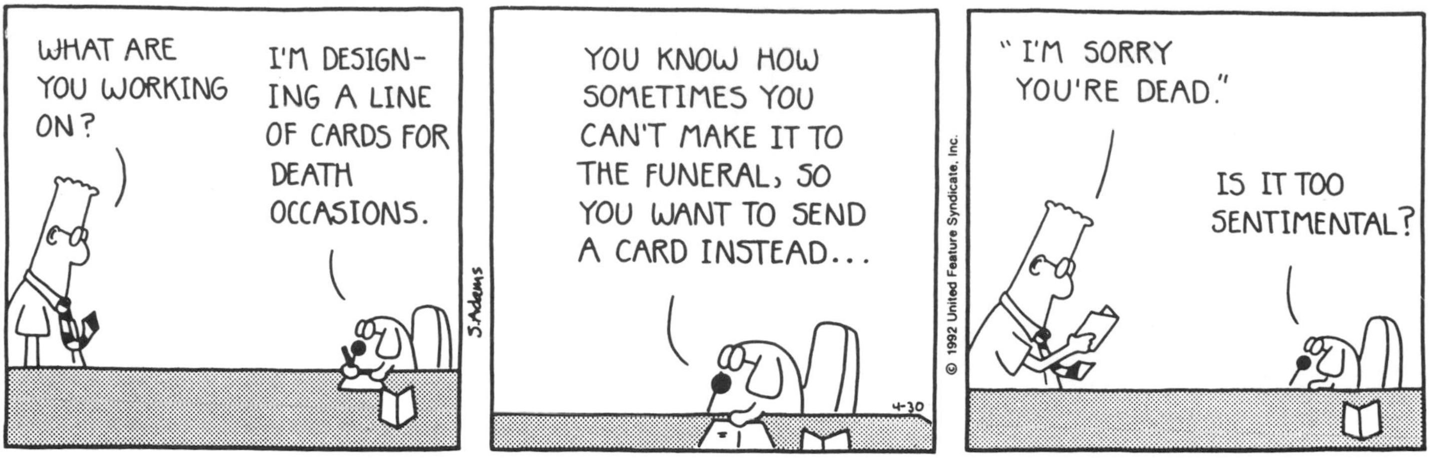
WHAT ARE YOU WORKING ON?
I'M DESIGNING A LINE OF CARDS FOR DEATH OCCASIONS.
YOU KNOW HOW SOMETIMES YOU CAN'T MAKE IT TO THE FUNERAL, SO YOU WANT TO SEND A CARD INSTEAD...
"I'M SORRY YOU'RE DEAD."
IS IT TOO SENTIMENTAL?
© 1992 United Feature Syndicate, Inc.

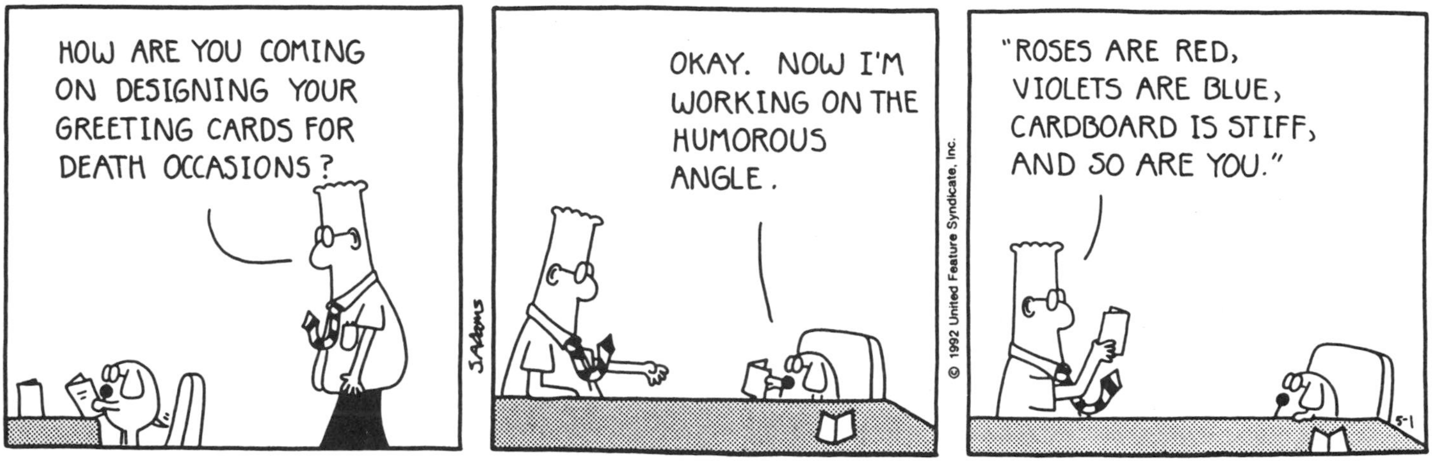
HOW ARE YOU COMING ON DESIGNING YOUR GREETING CARDS FOR DEATH OCCASIONS?
OKAY. NOW I'M WORKING ON THE HUMOROUS ANGLE.
"ROSES ARE RED, VIOLETS ARE BLUE, CARDBOARD IS STIFF, AND SO ARE YOU."
© 1992 United Feature Syndicate, Inc.

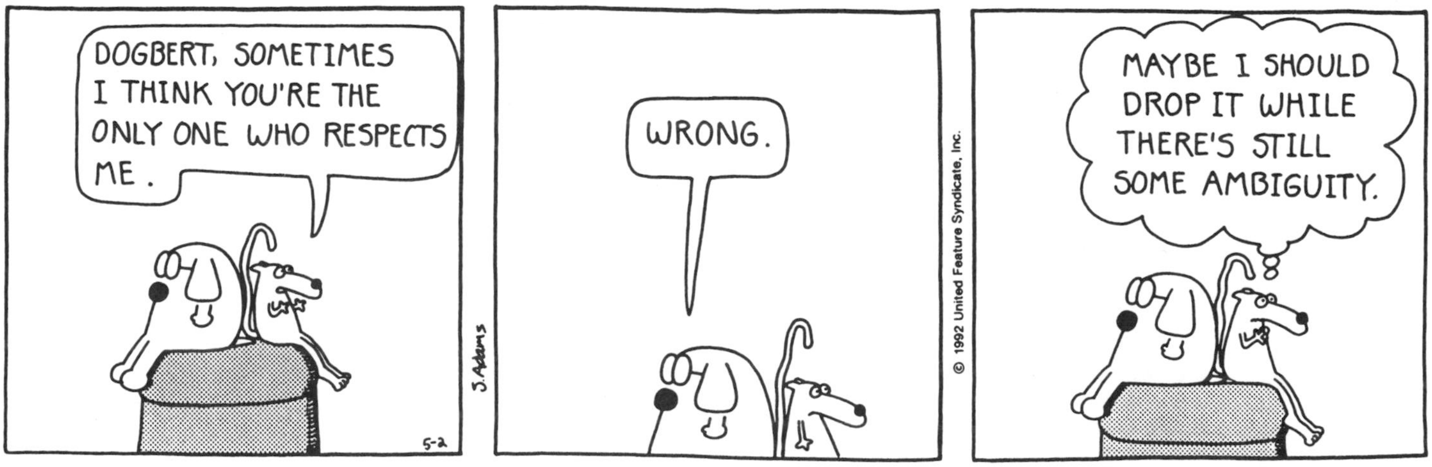
DOGBERT, SOMETIMES I THINK YOU'RE THE ONLY ONE WHO RESPECTS ME.
WRONG.
MAYBE I SHOULD DROP IT WHILE THERE'S STILL SOME AMBIGUITY.
© 1992 United Feature Syndicate, Inc.

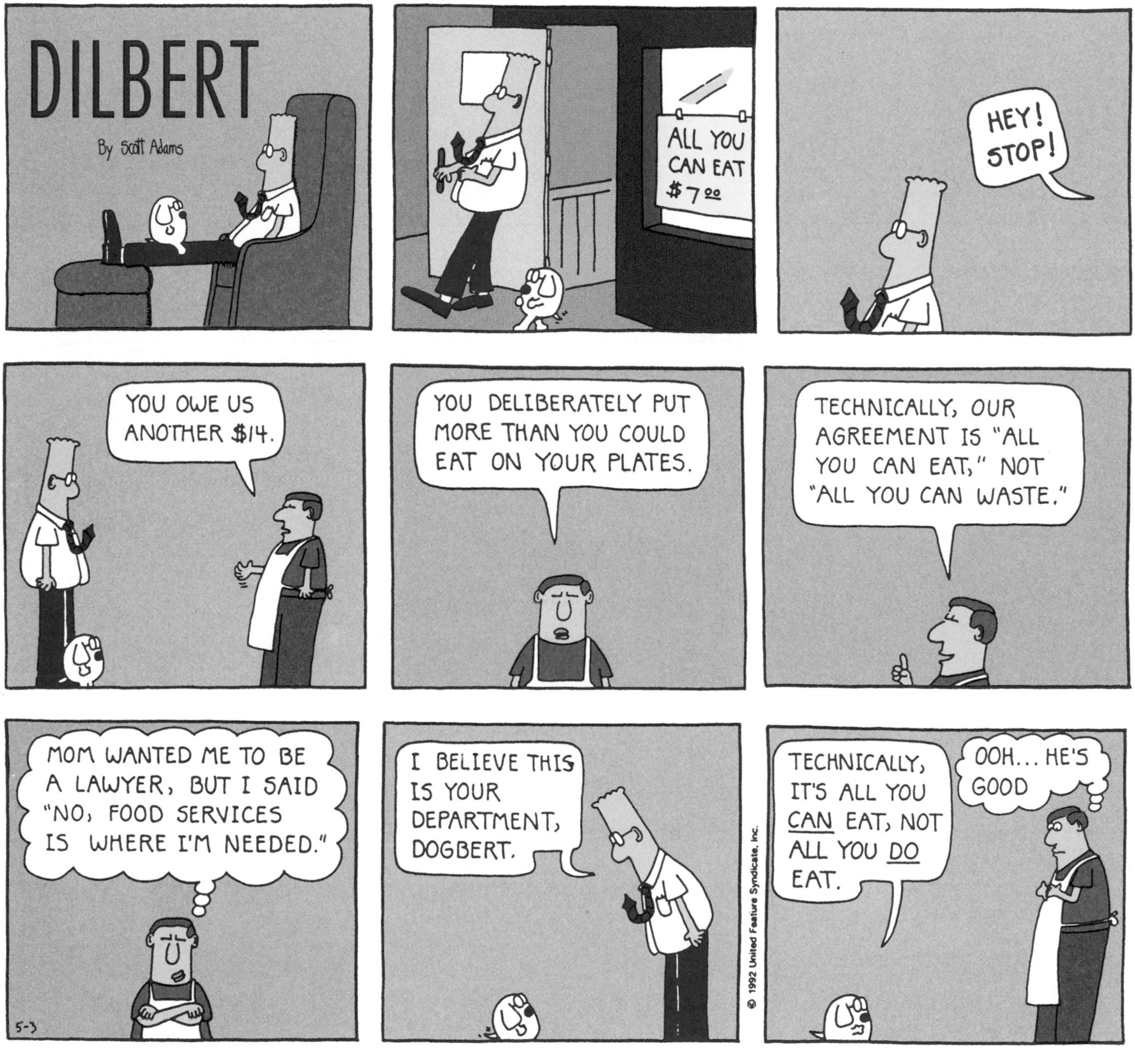
DILBERT
By Scott Adams
ALL YOU CAN EAT $7.00
HEY! STOP!
YOU OWE US ANOTHER $14.
YOU DELIBERATELY PUT MORE THAN YOU COULD EAT ON YOUR PLATES.
TECHNICALLY, OUR AGREEMENT IS "ALL YOU CAN EAT," NOT "ALL YOU CAN WASTE."
MOM WANTED ME TO BE A LAWYER, BUT I SAID "NO, FOOD SERVICES IS WHERE I'M NEEDED."
I BELIEVE THIS IS YOUR DEPARTMENT, DOGBERT.
TECHNICALLY, IT'S ALL YOU CAN EAT, NOT ALL YOU DO EAT.
OOH... HE'S GOOD
S.Adams
5-3
© 1992 United Feature Syndicate, Inc.

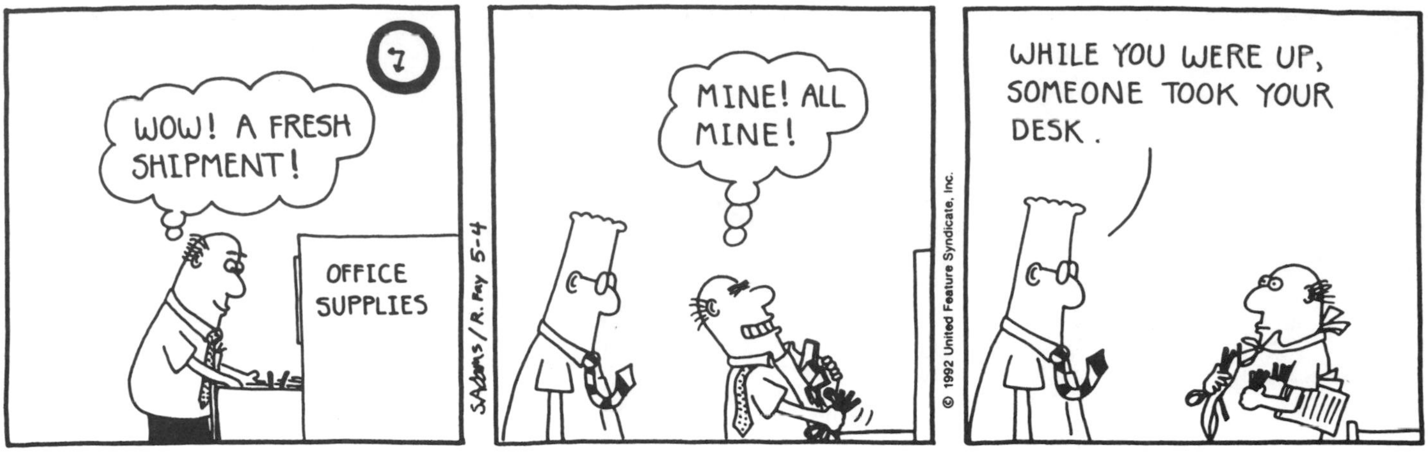
WOW! A FRESH SHIPMENT!
OFFICE SUPPLIES
S.Adams / R. Fay 5-4
MINE! ALL MINE!
© 1992 United Feature Syndicate, Inc.
WHILE YOU WERE UP, SOMEONE TOOK YOUR DESK.

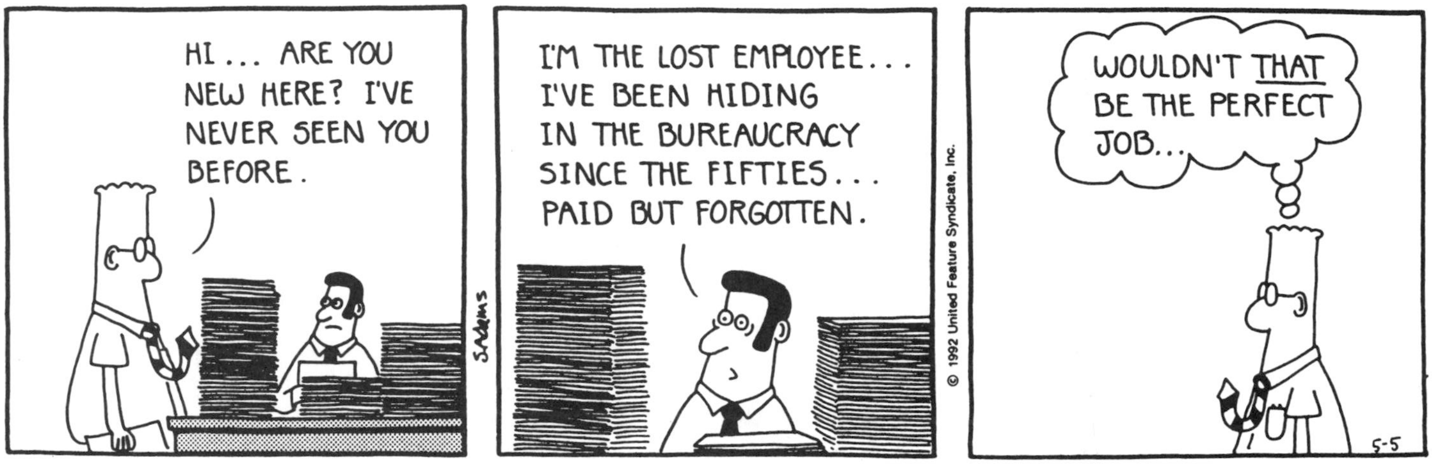
HI ... ARE YOU NEW HERE? I'VE NEVER SEEN YOU BEFORE.
S.Adams
I'M THE LOST EMPLOYEE... I'VE BEEN HIDING IN THE BUREAUCRACY SINCE THE FIFTIES... PAID BUT FORGOTTEN.
© 1992 United Feature Syndicate, Inc.
WOULDN'T THAT BE THE PERFECT JOB...
5-5

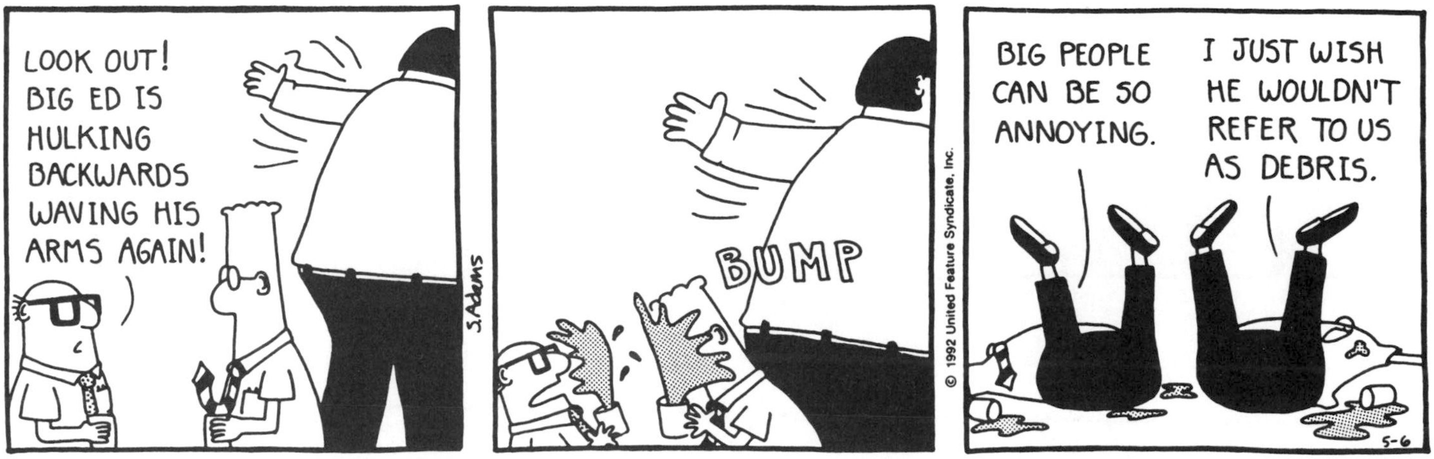
LOOK OUT! BIG ED IS HULKING BACKWARDS WAVING HIS ARMS AGAIN!
S.Adams
BUMP
© 1992 United Feature Syndicate, Inc.
BIG PEOPLE CAN BE SO ANNOYING.
I JUST WISH HE WOULDN'T REFER TO US AS DEBRIS.
5-6

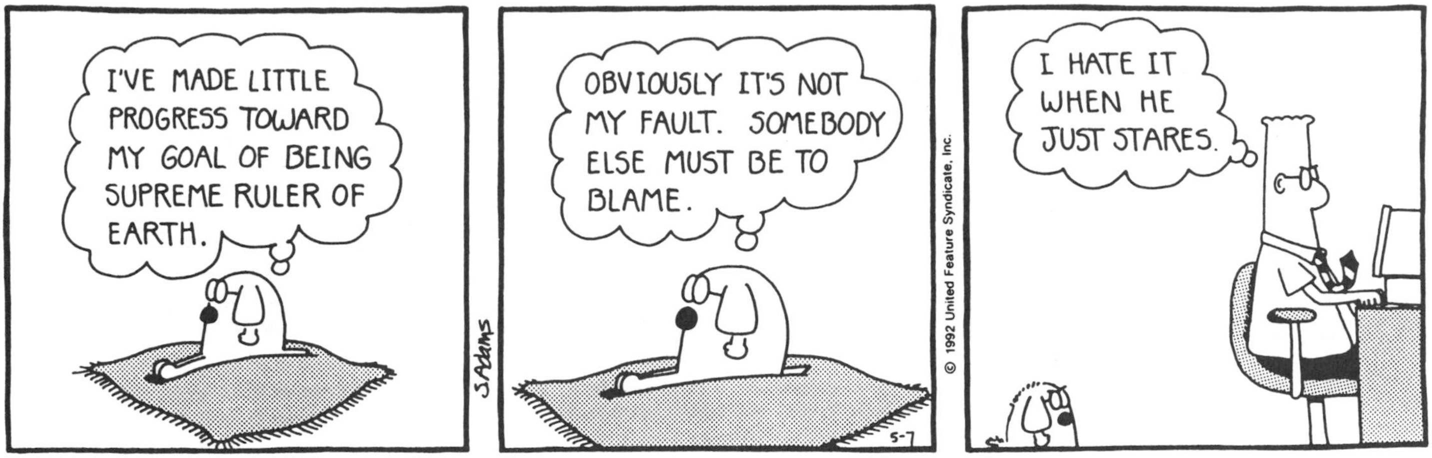
I'VE MADE LITTLE PROGRESS TOWARD MY GOAL OF BEING SUPREME RULER OF EARTH.
OBVIOUSLY IT'S NOT MY FAULT. SOMEBODY ELSE MUST BE TO BLAME.
I HATE IT WHEN HE JUST STARES.
S.ADAMS
5-7
© 1992 United Feature Syndicate, Inc.

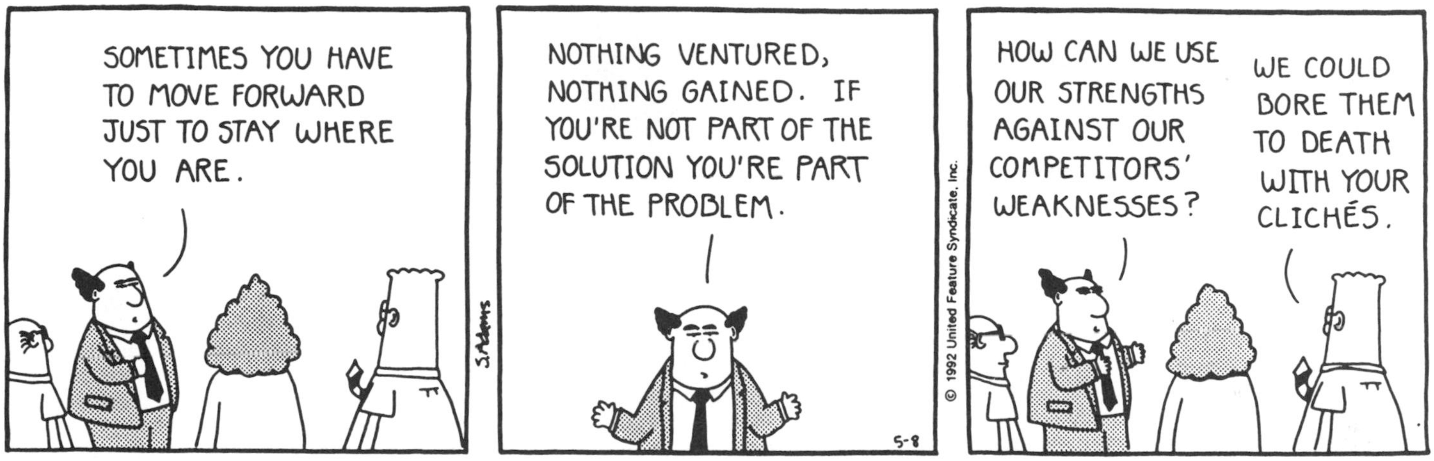
SOMETIMES YOU HAVE TO MOVE FORWARD JUST TO STAY WHERE YOU ARE.
NOTHING VENTURED, NOTHING GAINED. IF YOU'RE NOT PART OF THE SOLUTION YOU'RE PART OF THE PROBLEM.
HOW CAN WE USE OUR STRENGTHS AGAINST OUR COMPETITORS' WEAKNESSES?
WE COULD BORE THEM TO DEATH WITH YOUR CLICHÉS.
S.Adams
5-8
© 1992 United Feature Syndicate, Inc.

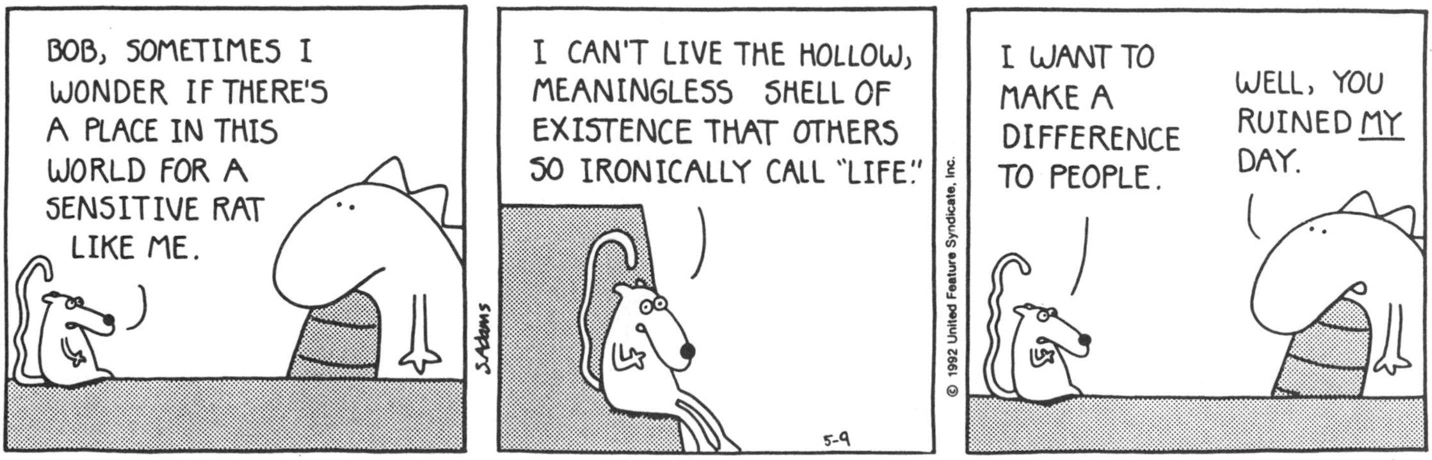
BOB, SOMETIMES I WONDER IF THERE'S A PLACE IN THIS WORLD FOR A SENSITIVE RAT LIKE ME.
I CAN'T LIVE THE HOLLOW, MEANINGLESS SHELL OF EXISTENCE THAT OTHERS SO IRONICALLY CALL "LIFE."
I WANT TO MAKE A DIFFERENCE TO PEOPLE.
WELL, YOU RUINED MY DAY.
S.Adams
5-9
© 1992 United Feature Syndicate, Inc.

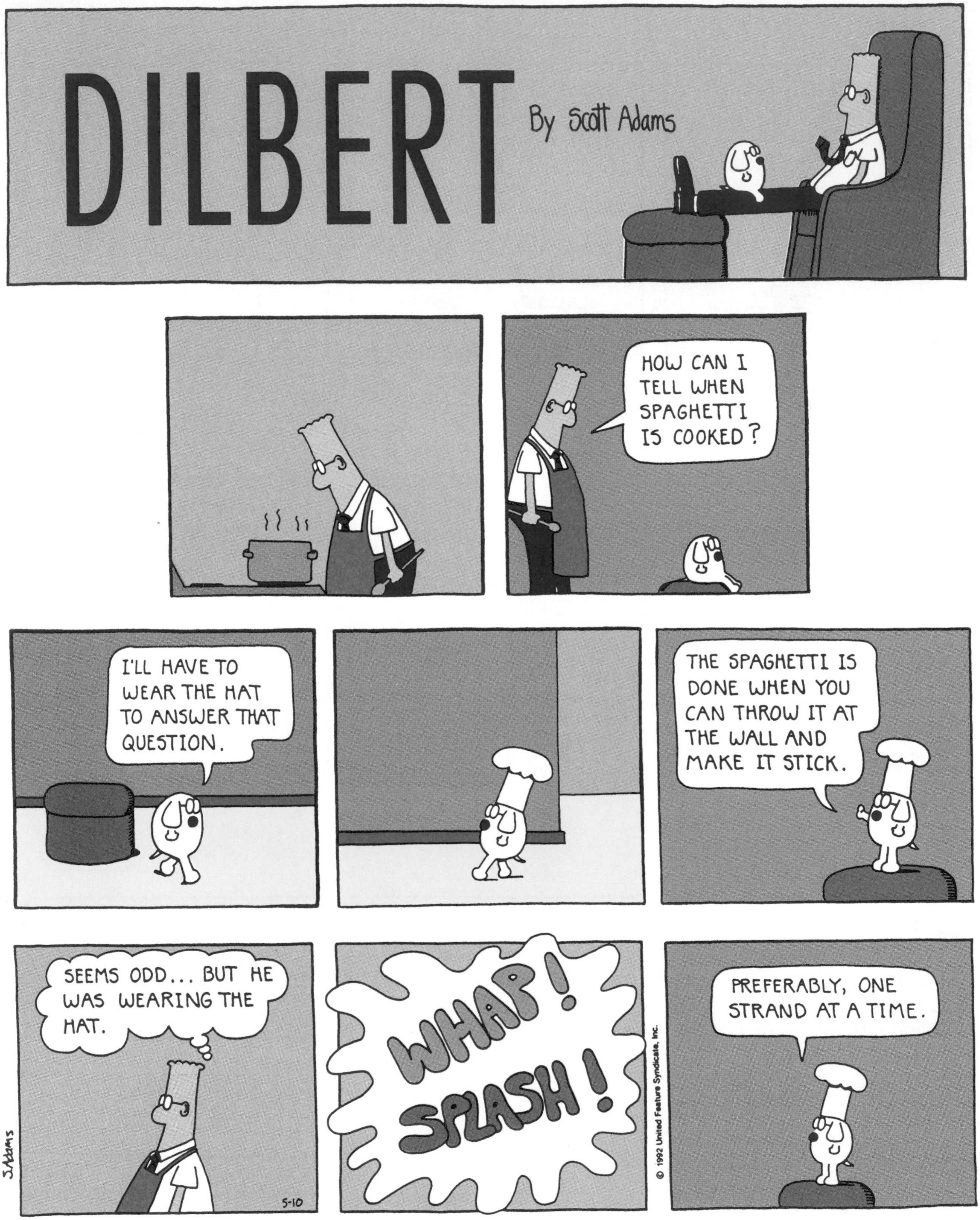
DILBERT
By Scott Adams
HOW CAN I TELL WHEN SPAGHETTI IS COOKED?
I'LL HAVE TO WEAR THE HAT TO ANSWER THAT QUESTION.
THE SPAGHETTI IS DONE WHEN YOU CAN THROW IT AT THE WALL AND MAKE IT STICK.
SEEMS ODD... BUT HE WAS WEARING THE HAT.
S.Adams
5-10
WHAP!
SPLASH!
© 1992 United Feature Syndicate, Inc.
PREFERABLY, ONE STRAND AT A TIME.

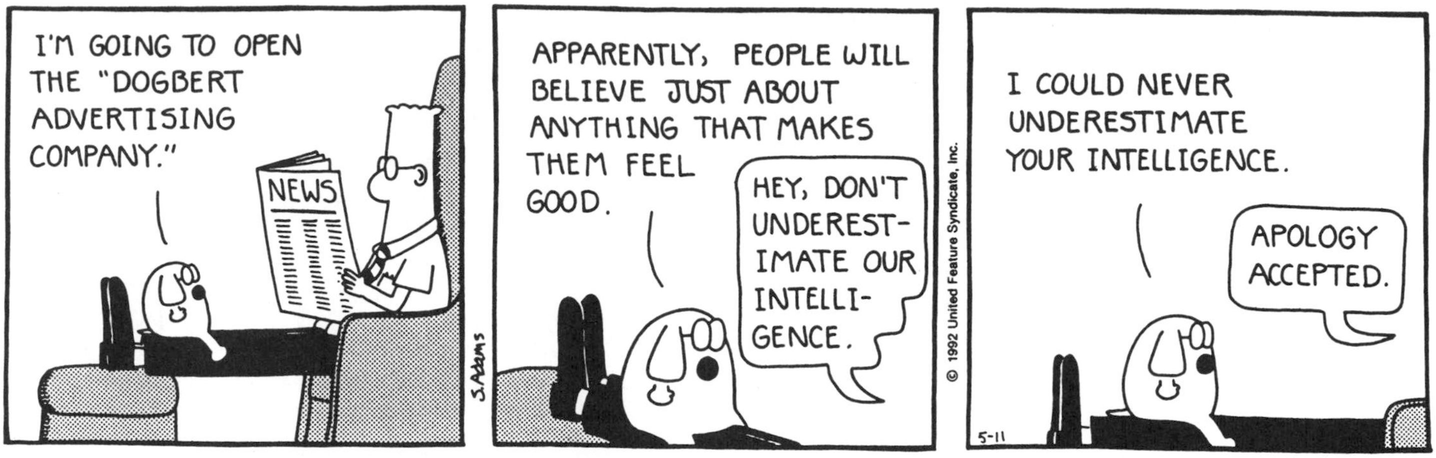
I'M GOING TO OPEN THE "DOGBERT ADVERTISING COMPANY."
NEWS
S. Adams
APPARENTLY, PEOPLE WILL BELIEVE JUST ABOUT ANYTHING THAT MAKES THEM FEEL GOOD.
HEY, DON'T UNDEREST-IMATE OUR INTELLI-GENCE.
© 1992 United Feature Syndicate, Inc.
I COULD NEVER UNDERESTIMATE YOUR INTELLIGENCE.
APOLOGY ACCEPTED.
5-11

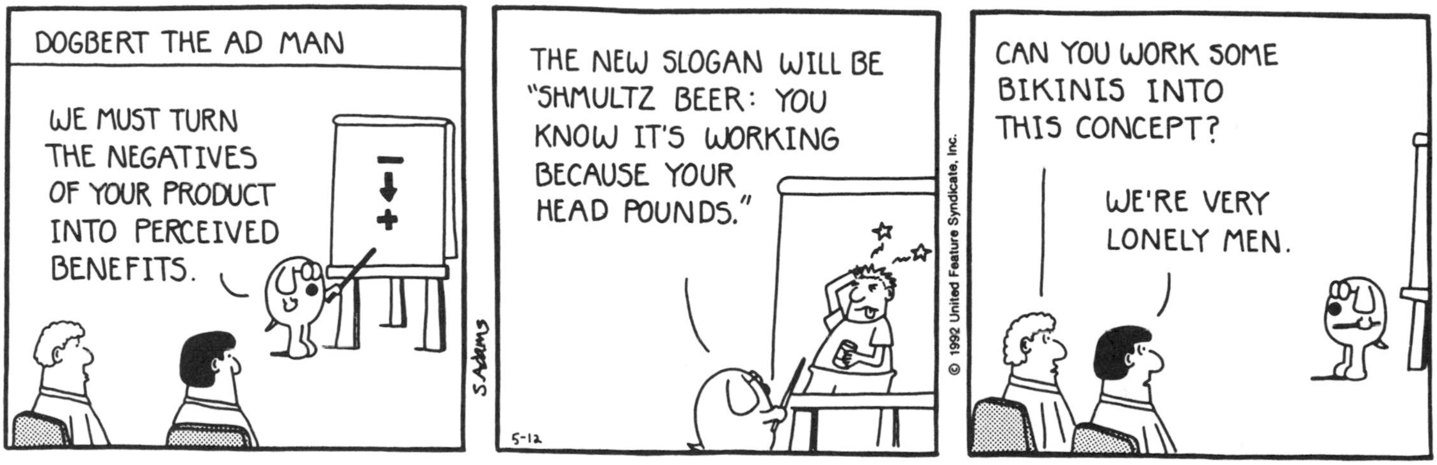
DOGBERT THE AD MAN
WE MUST TURN THE NEGATIVES OF YOUR PRODUCT INTO PERCEIVED BENEFITS.
S. Adams
5-12
THE NEW SLOGAN WILL BE "SHMULTZ BEER: YOU KNOW IT'S WORKING BECAUSE YOUR HEAD POUNDS."
© 1992 United Feature Syndicate, Inc.
CAN YOU WORK SOME BIKINIS INTO THIS CONCEPT?
WE'RE VERY LONELY MEN.

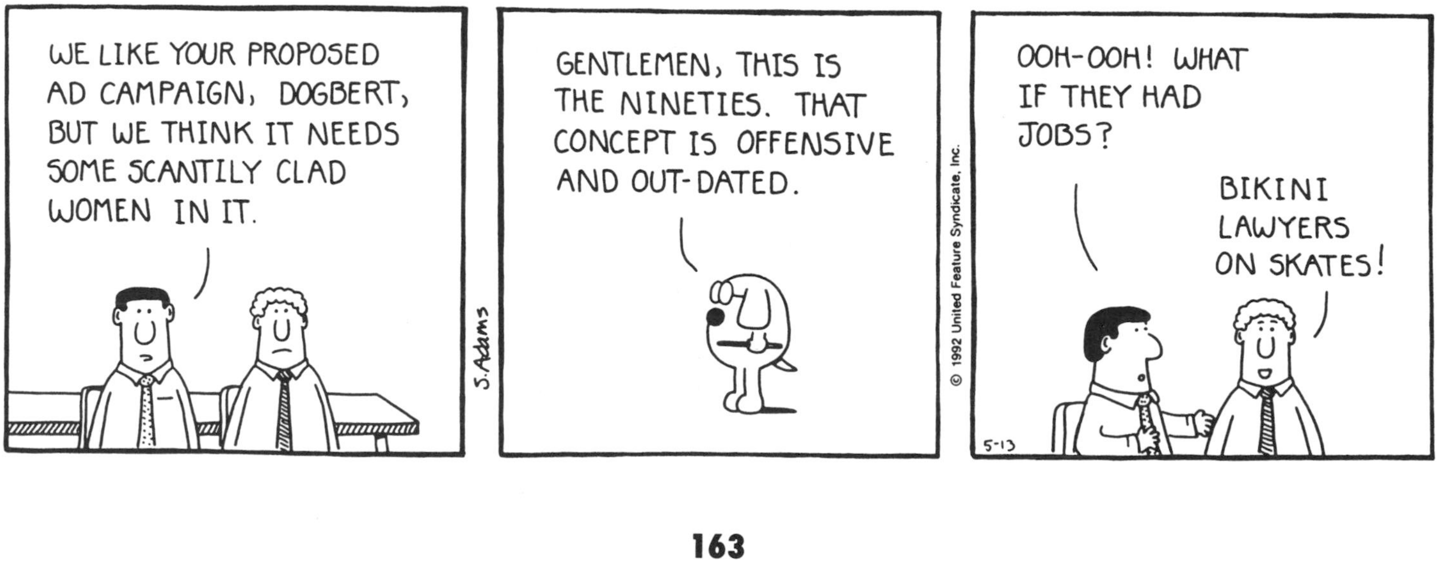
WE LIKE YOUR PROPOSED AD CAMPAIGN, DOGBERT, BUT WE THINK IT NEEDS SOME SCANTILY CLAD WOMEN IN IT.
S. Adams
GENTLEMEN, THIS IS THE NINETIES. THAT CONCEPT IS OFFENSIVE AND OUT-DATED.
© 1992 United Feature Syndicate, Inc.
OOH-OOH! WHAT IF THEY HAD JOBS?
BIKINI LAWYERS ON SKATES!
5-13

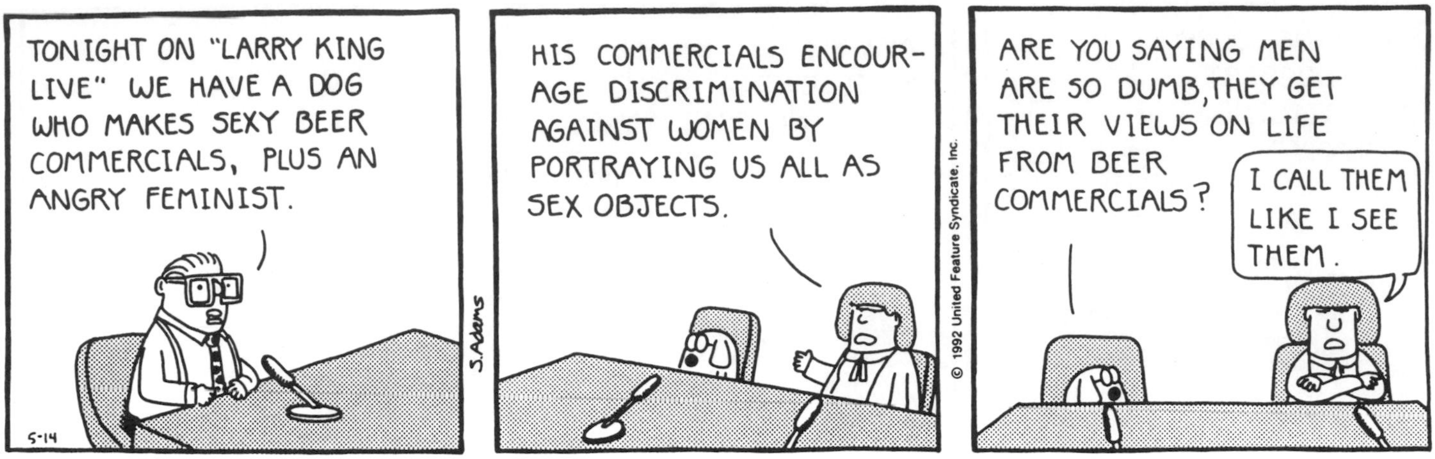
TONIGHT ON "LARRY KING LIVE" WE HAVE A DOG WHO MAKES SEXY BEER COMMERCIALS, PLUS AN ANGRY FEMINIST.
5-14
S. Adams
HIS COMMERCIALS ENCOURAGE DISCRIMINATION AGAINST WOMEN BY PORTRAYING US ALL AS SEX OBJECTS.
© 1992 United Feature Syndicate, Inc.
ARE YOU SAYING MEN ARE SO DUMB, THEY GET THEIR VIEWS ON LIFE FROM BEER COMMERCIALS?
I CALL THEM LIKE I SEE THEM.

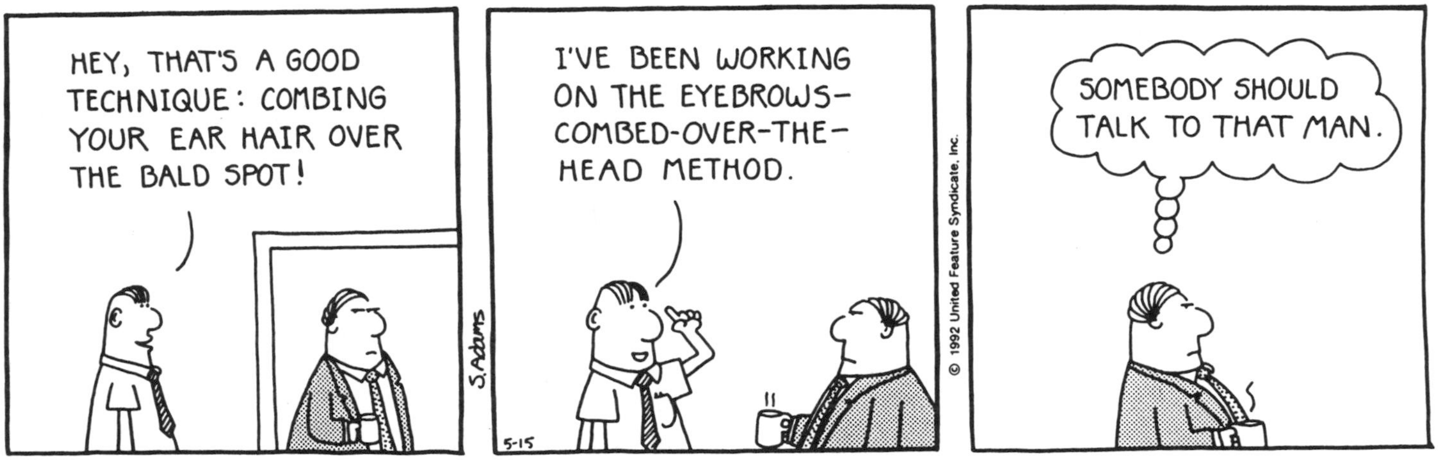
HEY, THAT'S A GOOD TECHNIQUE: COMBING YOUR EAR HAIR OVER THE BALD SPOT!
S. Adams
I'VE BEEN WORKING ON THE EYEBROWS-COMBED-OVER-THE-HEAD METHOD.
5-15
© 1992 United Feature Syndicate, Inc.
SOMEBODY SHOULD TALK TO THAT MAN.

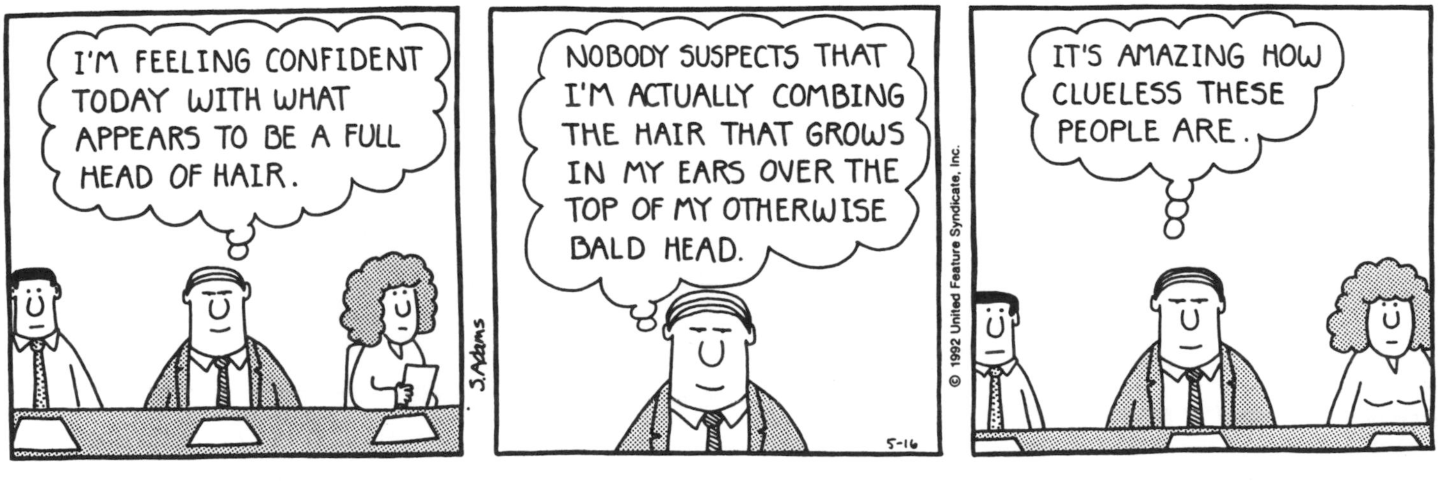
I'M FEELING CONFIDENT TODAY WITH WHAT APPEARS TO BE A FULL HEAD OF HAIR.
S. Adams
NOBODY SUSPECTS THAT I'M ACTUALLY COMBING THE HAIR THAT GROWS IN MY EARS OVER THE TOP OF MY OTHERWISE BALD HEAD.
5-16
© 1992 United Feature Syndicate, Inc.
IT'S AMAZING HOW CLUELESS THESE PEOPLE ARE.

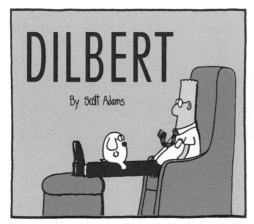

DILBERT
By Scott Adams
TENNIS RACKETS ON SALE
I'M LOOKING FOR A NEW RACKET.
YOU'RE PROBABLY INTERESTED IN OUR COLORFUL ALL-PLASTIC RACKETS FOR PATHETIC BEGINNERS.
NO, ACTUALLY I'M INTERESTED IN THE TITANIUM ALLOY DEATHSTICK 3000.
HA HA! AS IF A DUMPY LITTLE POOCH COULD HANDLE THAT KIND OF POWER ON THE COURT!
HERE... YOU CAN TOUCH IT, BUT I'M ONLY HUMORING YOU.
S.Adams
BOOM!
© 1992 United Feature Syndicate, Inc.
THIS IS THE PERFECT RACKET FOR THOSE WHO DON'T TAKE LOSING GRACEFULLY.
5-17

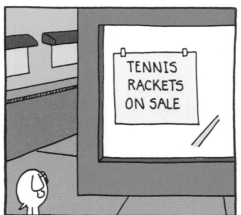

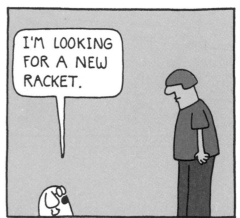

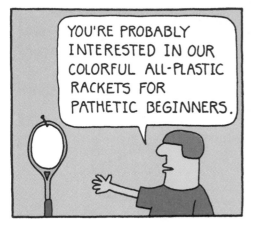

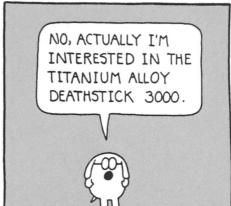

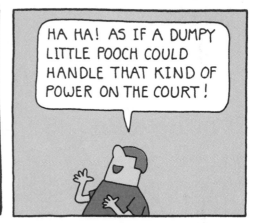

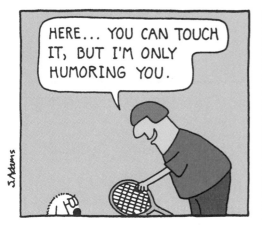

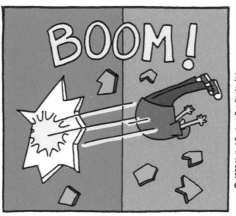

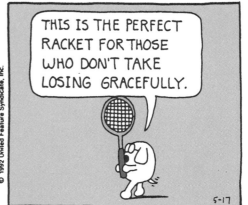

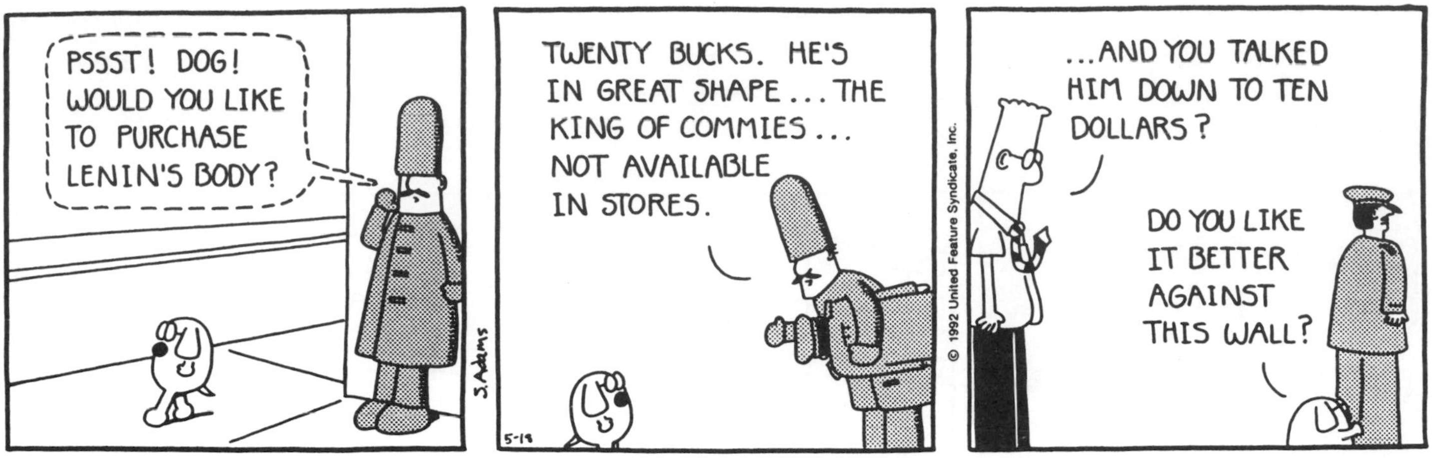
PSSST! DOG! WOULD YOU LIKE TO PURCHASE LENIN'S BODY?
S. Adams
TWENTY BUCKS. HE'S IN GREAT SHAPE... THE KING OF COMMIES... NOT AVAILABLE IN STORES.
5-18
© 1992 United Feature Syndicate, Inc.
...AND YOU TALKED HIM DOWN TO TEN DOLLARS?
DO YOU LIKE IT BETTER AGAINST THIS WALL?

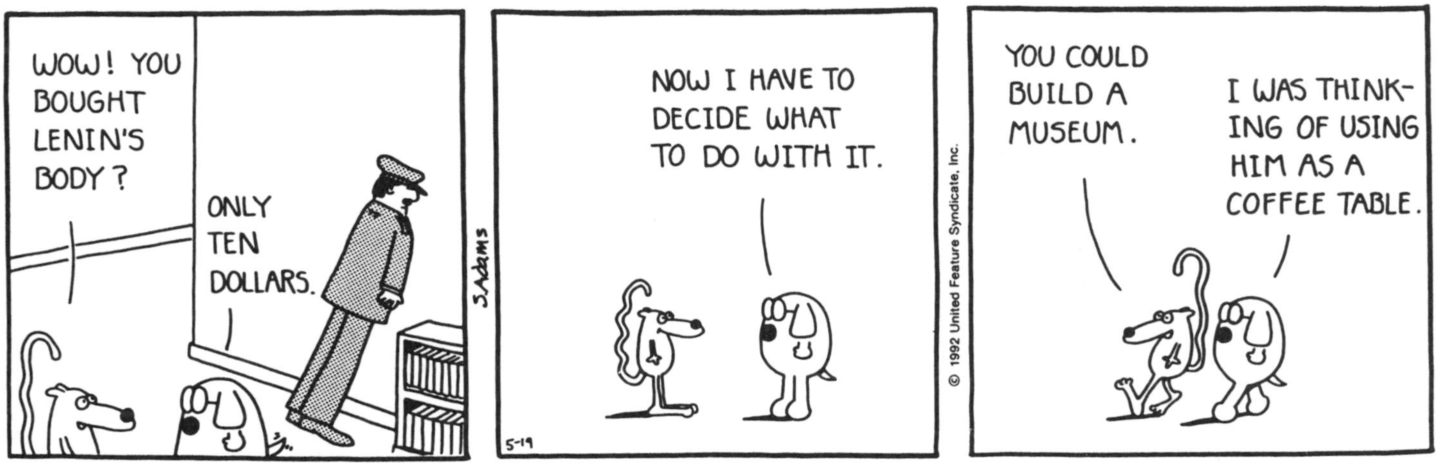
WOW! YOU BOUGHT LENIN'S BODY?
ONLY TEN DOLLARS.
S. Adams
NOW I HAVE TO DECIDE WHAT TO DO WITH IT.
5-19
© 1992 United Feature Syndicate, Inc.
YOU COULD BUILD A MUSEUM.
I WAS THINKING OF USING HIM AS A COFFEE TABLE.

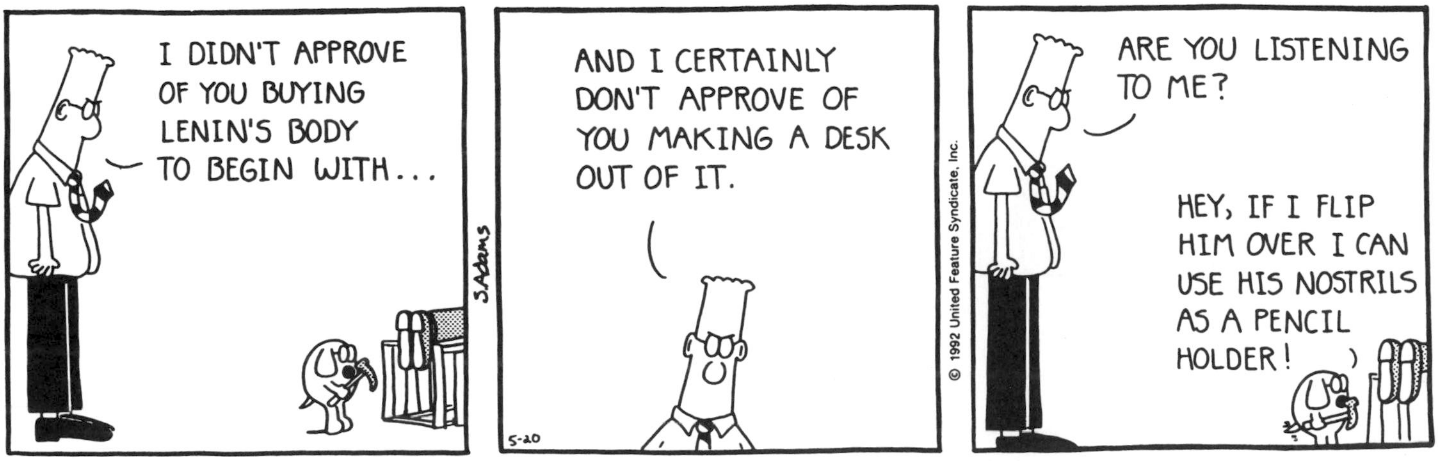
I DIDN'T APPROVE OF YOU BUYING LENIN'S BODY TO BEGIN WITH...
S. Adams
AND I CERTAINLY DON'T APPROVE OF YOU MAKING A DESK OUT OF IT.
5-20
© 1992 United Feature Syndicate, Inc.
ARE YOU LISTENING TO ME?
HEY, IF I FLIP HIM OVER I CAN USE HIS NOSTRILS AS A PENCIL HOLDER!

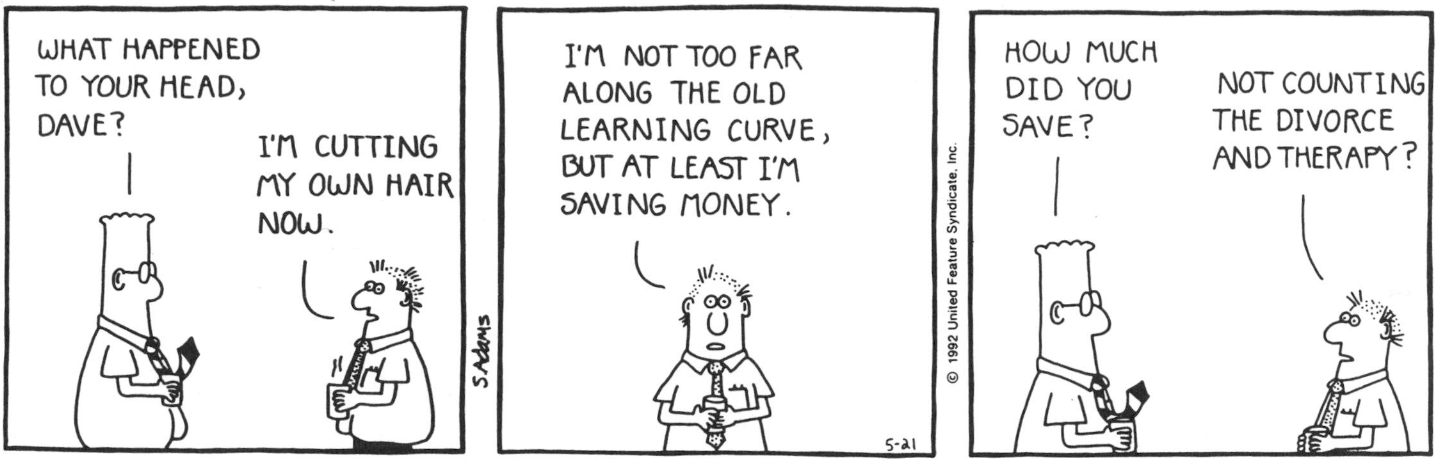
WHAT HAPPENED TO YOUR HEAD, DAVE?
I'M CUTTING MY OWN HAIR NOW.
I'M NOT TOO FAR ALONG THE OLD LEARNING CURVE, BUT AT LEAST I'M SAVING MONEY.
© 1992 United Feature Syndicate, Inc.
HOW MUCH DID YOU SAVE?
NOT COUNTING THE DIVORCE AND THERAPY?

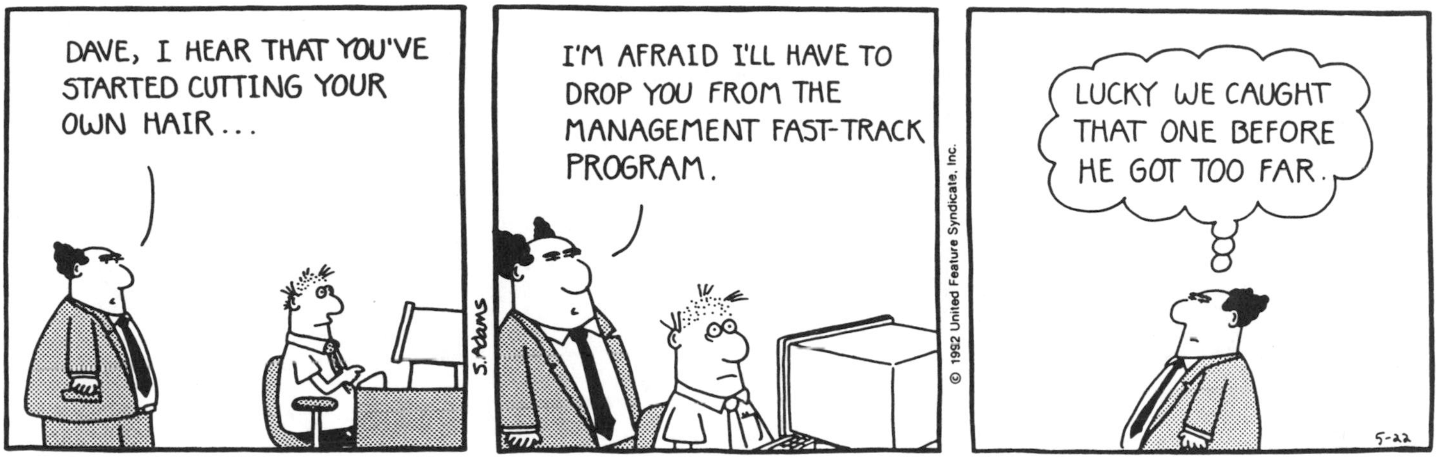
DAVE, I HEAR THAT YOU'VE STARTED CUTTING YOUR OWN HAIR...
I'M AFRAID I'LL HAVE TO DROP YOU FROM THE MANAGEMENT FAST-TRACK PROGRAM.
© 1992 United Feature Syndicate, Inc.
LUCKY WE CAUGHT THAT ONE BEFORE HE GOT TOO FAR.

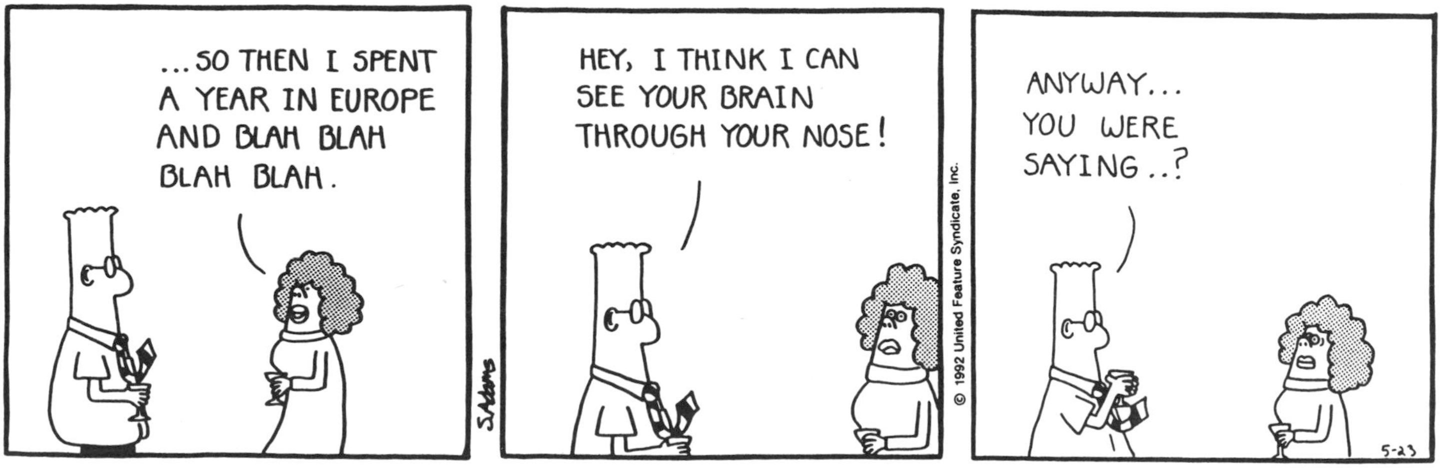
...SO THEN I SPENT A YEAR IN EUROPE AND BLAH BLAH BLAH BLAH.
HEY, I THINK I CAN SEE YOUR BRAIN THROUGH YOUR NOSE!
© 1992 United Feature Syndicate, Inc.
ANYWAY... YOU WERE SAYING..?

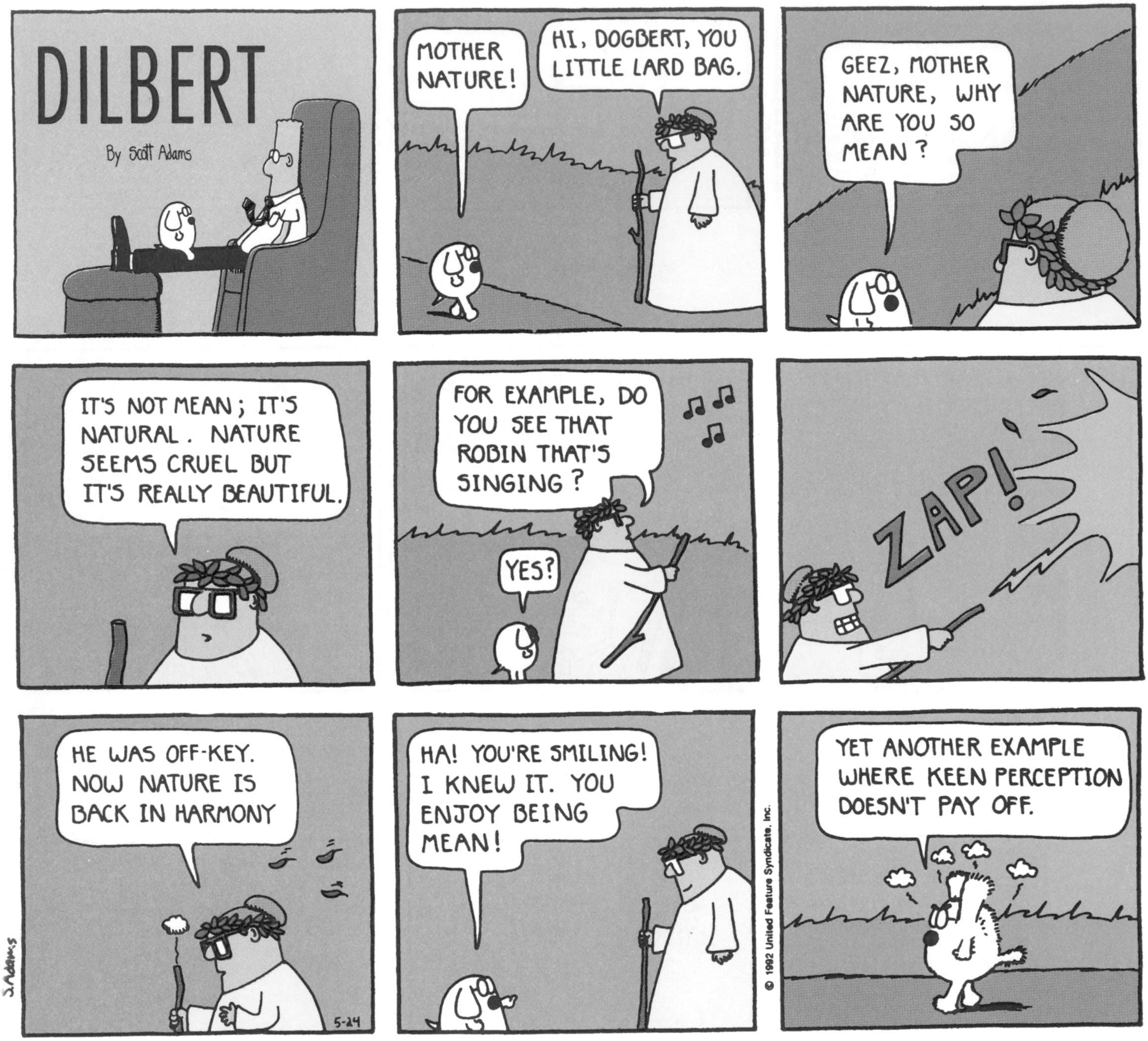
DILBERT
By Scott Adams
MOTHER NATURE!
HI, DOGBERT, YOU LITTLE LARD BAG.
GEEZ, MOTHER NATURE, WHY ARE YOU SO MEAN?
IT'S NOT MEAN; IT'S NATURAL. NATURE SEEMS CRUEL BUT IT'S REALLY BEAUTIFUL.
FOR EXAMPLE, DO YOU SEE THAT ROBIN THAT'S SINGING?
YES?
ZAP!
HE WAS OFF-KEY. NOW NATURE IS BACK IN HARMONY
S. ADAMS
5-24
HA! YOU'RE SMILING! I KNEW IT. YOU ENJOY BEING MEAN!
© 1992 United Feature Syndicate, Inc.
YET ANOTHER EXAMPLE WHERE KEEN PERCEPTION DOESN'T PAY OFF.

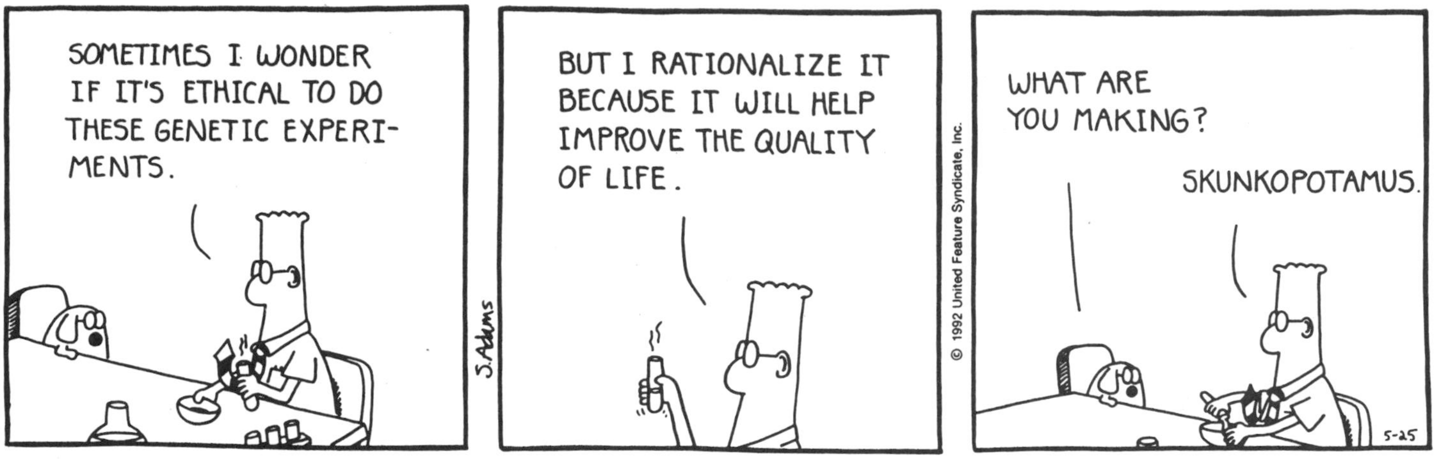
SOMETIMES I WONDER IF IT'S ETHICAL TO DO THESE GENETIC EXPERIMENTS.
BUT I RATIONALIZE IT BECAUSE IT WILL HELP IMPROVE THE QUALITY OF LIFE.
WHAT ARE YOU MAKING?
SKUNKOPOTAMUS.
S. Adams
© 1992 United Feature Syndicate, Inc.
5-25

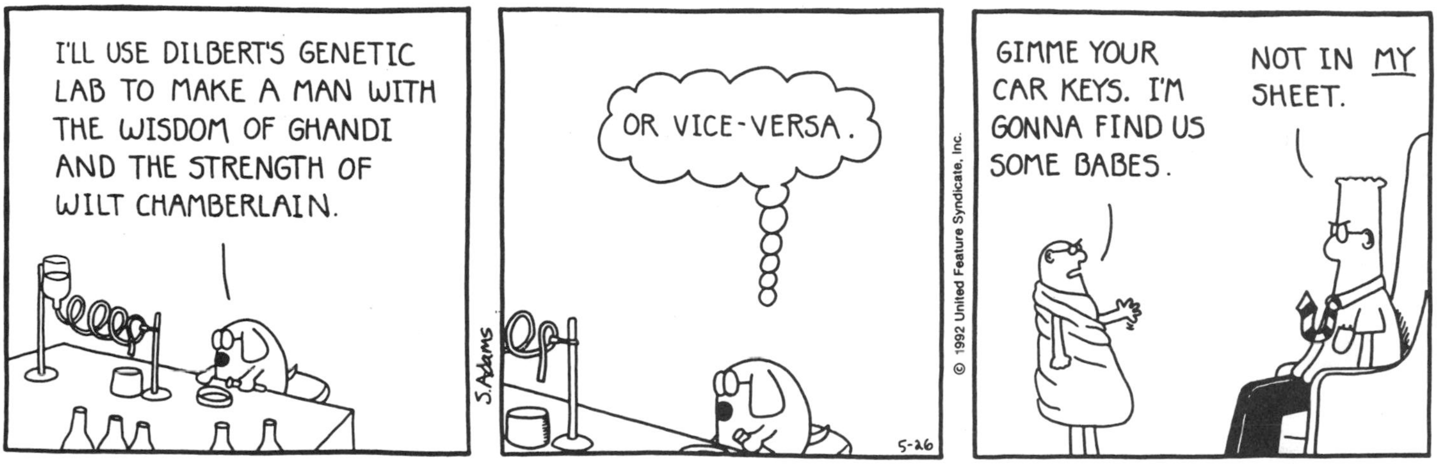
I'LL USE DILBERT'S GENETIC LAB TO MAKE A MAN WITH THE WISDOM OF GHANDI AND THE STRENGTH OF WILT CHAMBERLAIN.
OR VICE-VERSA.
GIMME YOUR CAR KEYS. I'M GONNA FIND US SOME BABES.
NOT IN MY SHEET.
S. Adams
© 1992 United Feature Syndicate, Inc.
5-26

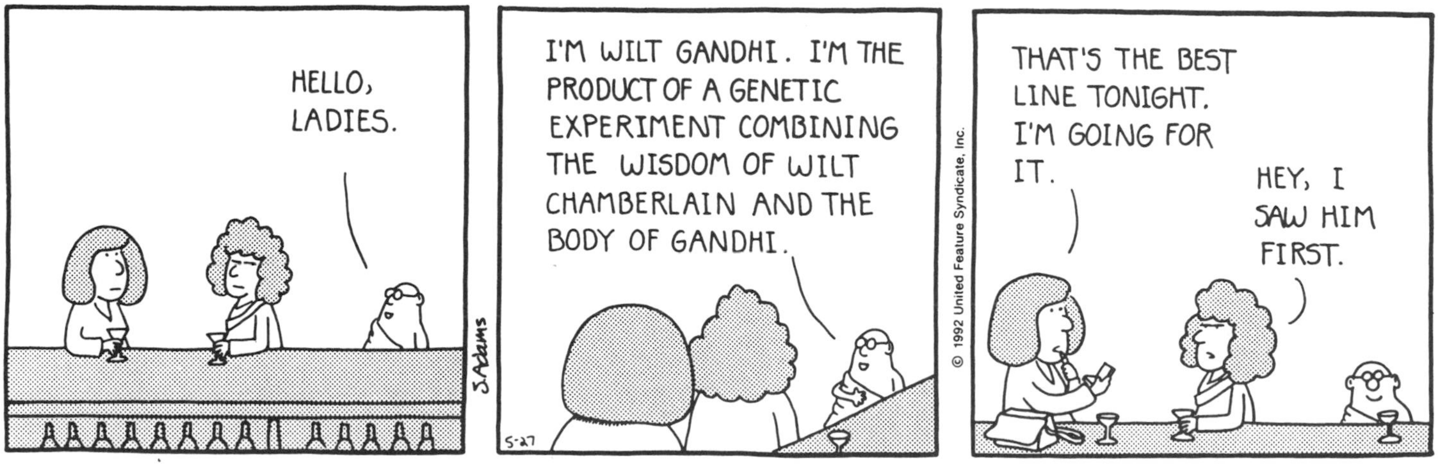
HELLO, LADIES.
I'M WILT GANDHI. I'M THE PRODUCT OF A GENETIC EXPERIMENT COMBINING THE WISDOM OF WILT CHAMBERLAIN AND THE BODY OF GANDHI.
THAT'S THE BEST LINE TONIGHT. I'M GOING FOR IT.
HEY, I SAW HIM FIRST.
S. Adams
© 1992 United Feature Syndicate, Inc.
5-27

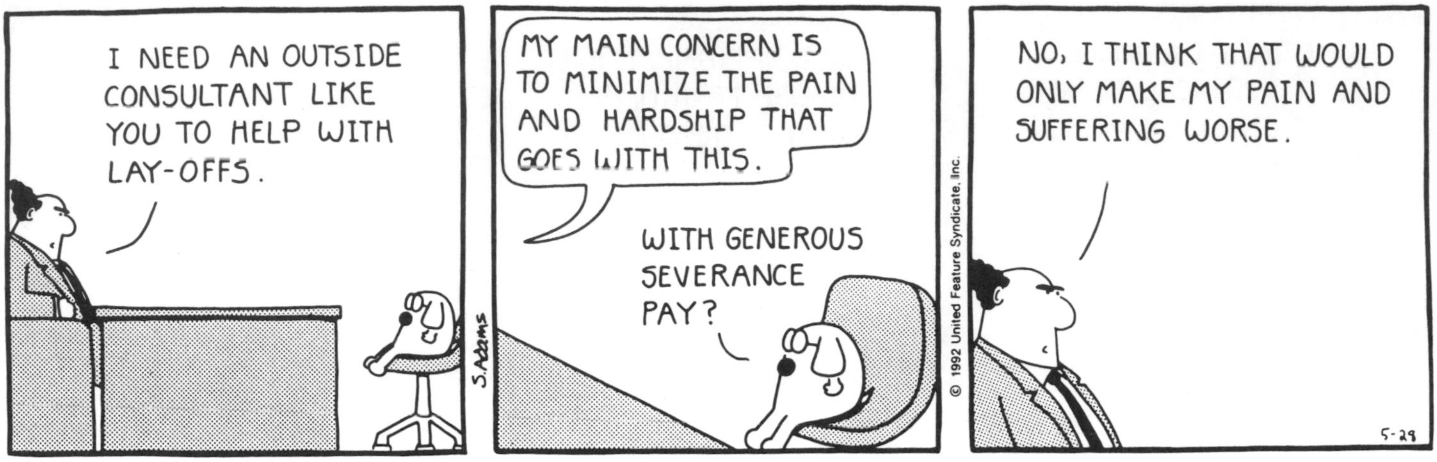
I NEED AN OUTSIDE CONSULTANT LIKE YOU TO HELP WITH LAY-OFFS.
S.Adams
MY MAIN CONCERN IS TO MINIMIZE THE PAIN AND HARDSHIP THAT GOES WITH THIS.
WITH GENEROUS SEVERANCE PAY?
© 1992 United Feature Syndicate, Inc.
NO, I THINK THAT WOULD ONLY MAKE MY PAIN AND SUFFERING WORSE.
5-29

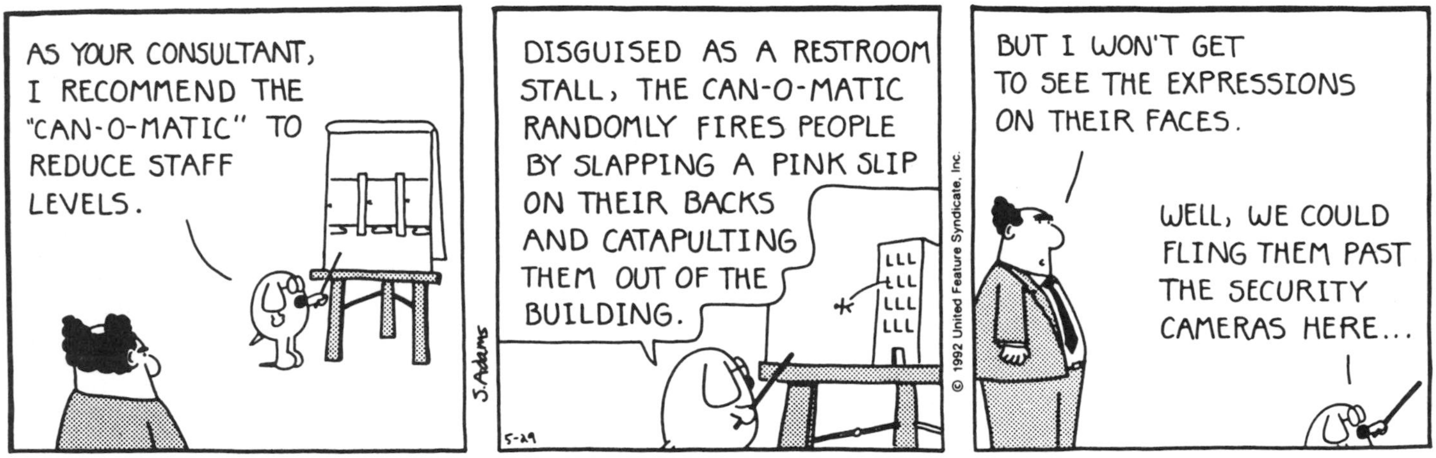
AS YOUR CONSULTANT, I RECOMMEND THE "CAN-O-MATIC" TO REDUCE STAFF LEVELS.
S.Adams
DISGUISED AS A RESTROOM STALL, THE CAN-O-MATIC RANDOMLY FIRES PEOPLE BY SLAPPING A PINK SLIP ON THEIR BACKS AND CATAPULTING THEM OUT OF THE BUILDING.
5-29
© 1992 United Feature Syndicate, Inc.
BUT I WON'T GET TO SEE THE EXPRESSIONS ON THEIR FACES.
WELL, WE COULD FLING THEM PAST THE SECURITY CAMERAS HERE...

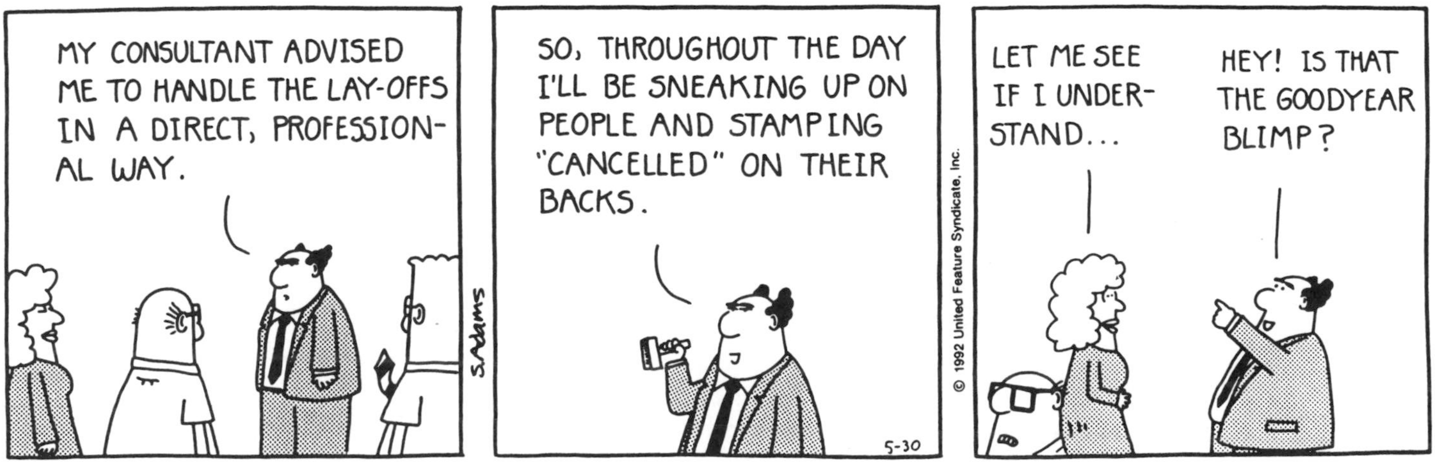
MY CONSULTANT ADVISED ME TO HANDLE THE LAY-OFFS IN A DIRECT, PROFESSION-AL WAY.
S.Adams
SO, THROUGHOUT THE DAY I'LL BE SNEAKING UP ON PEOPLE AND STAMPING "CANCELLED" ON THEIR BACKS.
5-30
© 1992 United Feature Syndicate, Inc.
LET ME SEE IF I UNDER-STAND...
HEY! IS THAT THE GOODYEAR BLIMP?

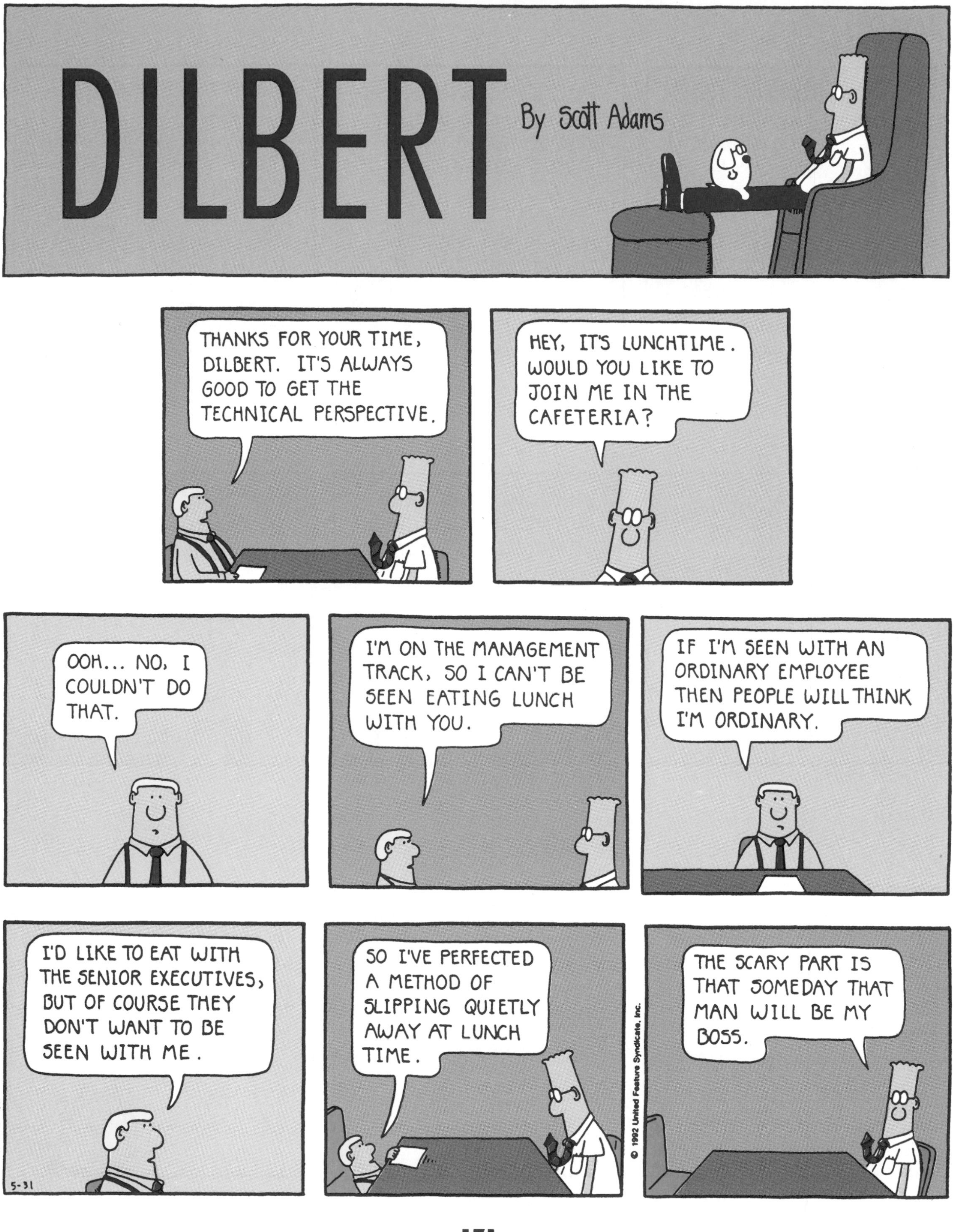
DILBERT
By Scott Adams
THANKS FOR YOUR TIME, DILBERT. IT'S ALWAYS GOOD TO GET THE TECHNICAL PERSPECTIVE.
HEY, IT'S LUNCHTIME. WOULD YOU LIKE TO JOIN ME IN THE CAFETERIA?
OOH... NO, I COULDN'T DO THAT.
I'M ON THE MANAGEMENT TRACK, SO I CAN'T BE SEEN EATING LUNCH WITH YOU.
IF I'M SEEN WITH AN ORDINARY EMPLOYEE THEN PEOPLE WILL THINK I'M ORDINARY.
I'D LIKE TO EAT WITH THE SENIOR EXECUTIVES, BUT OF COURSE THEY DON'T WANT TO BE SEEN WITH ME.
S.Adams
5-31
SO I'VE PERFECTED A METHOD OF SLIPPING QUIETLY AWAY AT LUNCH TIME.
© 1992 United Feature Syndicate, Inc.
THE SCARY PART IS THAT SOMEDAY THAT MAN WILL BE MY BOSS.

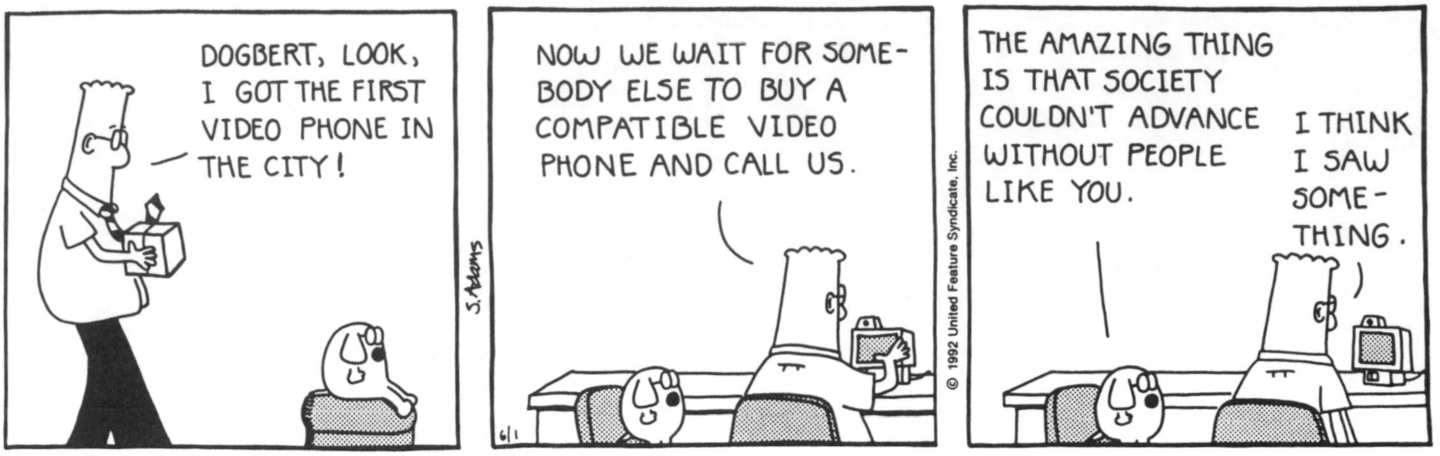
DOGBERT, LOOK, I GOT THE FIRST VIDEO PHONE IN THE CITY!
S. Adams
6/1
NOW WE WAIT FOR SOMEBODY ELSE TO BUY A COMPATIBLE VIDEO PHONE AND CALL US.
© 1992 United Feature Syndicate, Inc.
THE AMAZING THING IS THAT SOCIETY COULDN'T ADVANCE WITHOUT PEOPLE LIKE YOU.
I THINK I SAW SOMETHING.

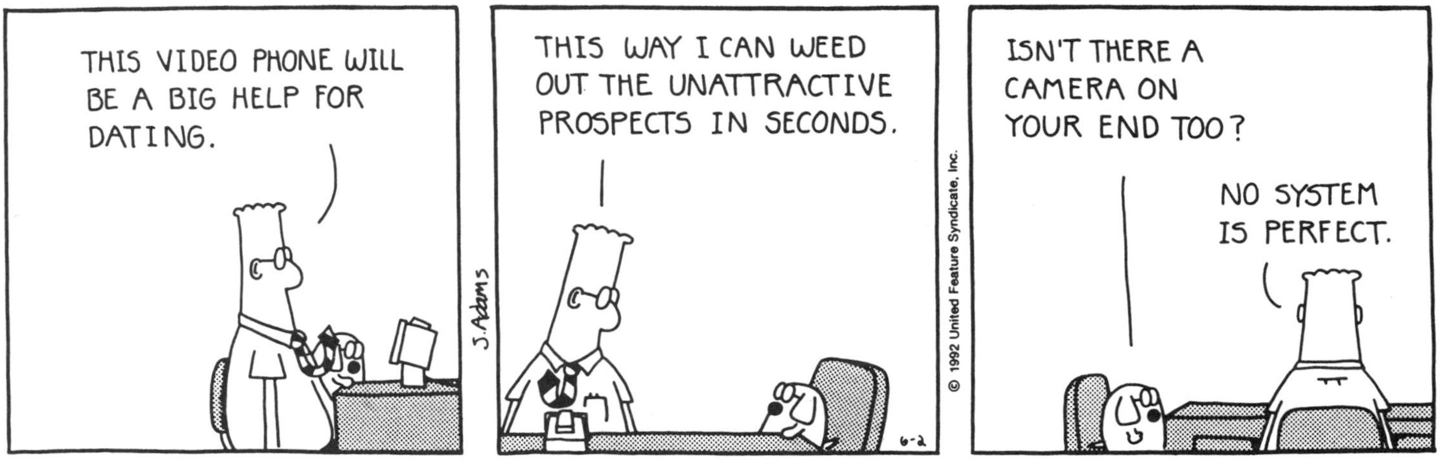
THIS VIDEO PHONE WILL BE A BIG HELP FOR DATING.
S. Adams
THIS WAY I CAN WEED OUT THE UNATTRACTIVE PROSPECTS IN SECONDS.
6-2
© 1992 United Feature Syndicate, Inc.
ISN'T THERE A CAMERA ON YOUR END TOO?
NO SYSTEM IS PERFECT.

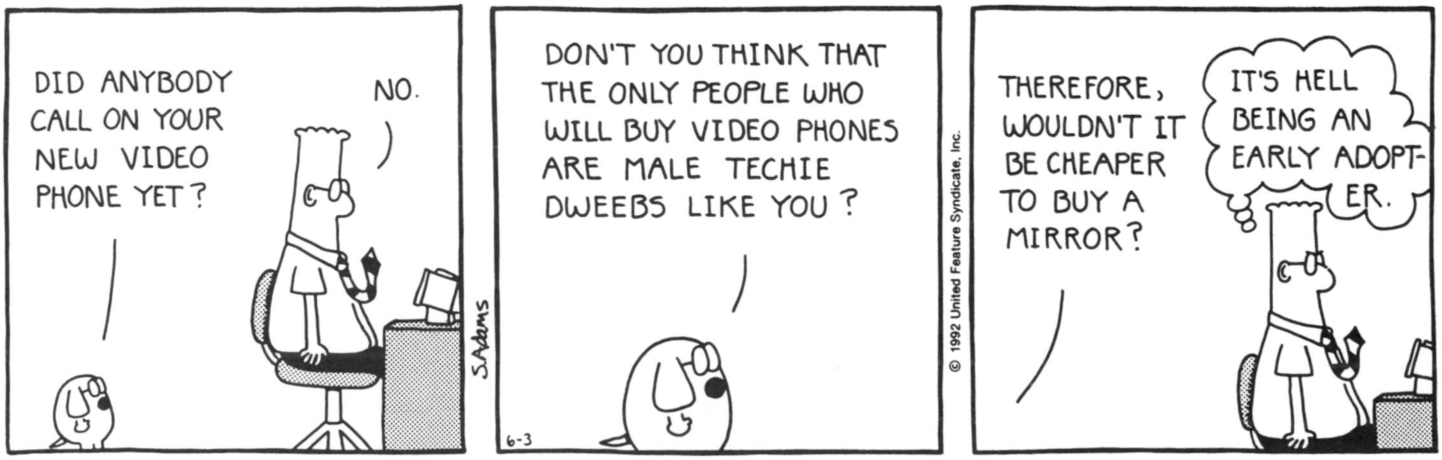
DID ANYBODY CALL ON YOUR NEW VIDEO PHONE YET?
NO.
S. Adams
DON'T YOU THINK THAT THE ONLY PEOPLE WHO WILL BUY VIDEO PHONES ARE MALE TECHIE DWEEBS LIKE YOU?
6-3
© 1992 United Feature Syndicate, Inc.
THEREFORE, WOULDN'T IT BE CHEAPER TO BUY A MIRROR?
IT'S HELL BEING AN EARLY ADOPTER.

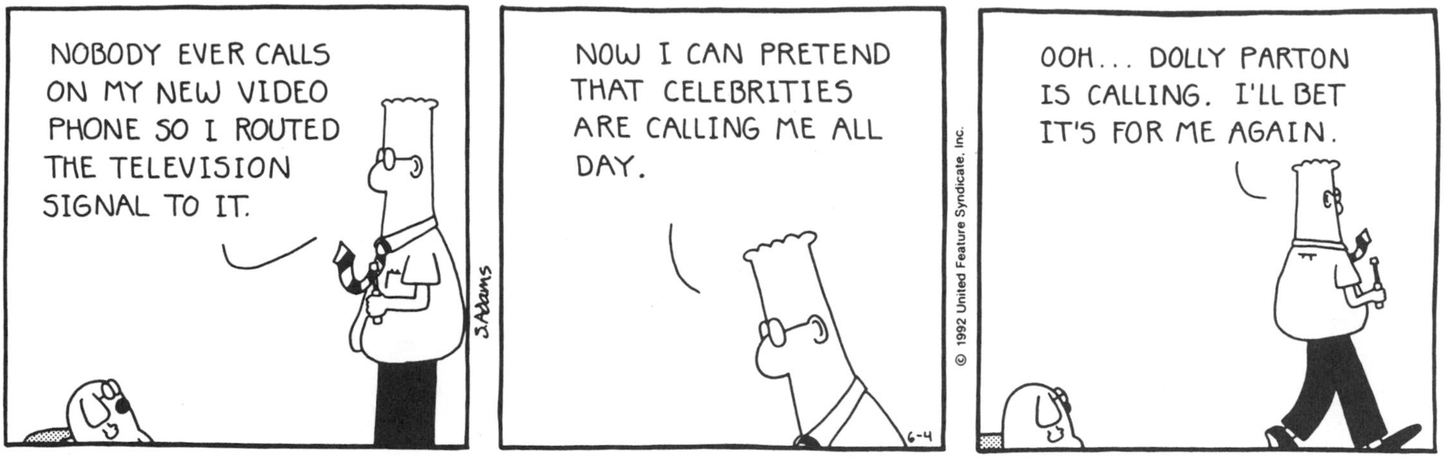
NOBODY EVER CALLS ON MY NEW VIDEO PHONE SO I ROUTED THE TELEVISION SIGNAL TO IT.
S.Adams
NOW I CAN PRETEND THAT CELEBRITIES ARE CALLING ME ALL DAY.
6-4
© 1992 United Feature Syndicate, Inc.
OOH... DOLLY PARTON IS CALLING. I'LL BET IT'S FOR ME AGAIN.

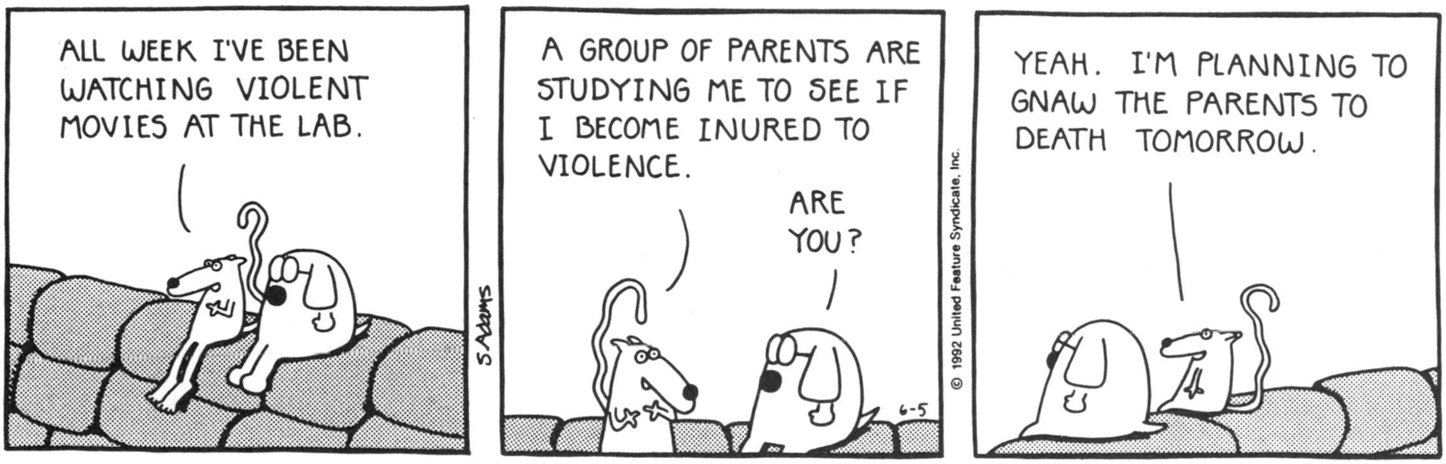
ALL WEEK I'VE BEEN WATCHING VIOLENT MOVIES AT THE LAB.
S.Adams
A GROUP OF PARENTS ARE STUDYING ME TO SEE IF I BECOME INURED TO VIOLENCE.
ARE YOU?
6-5
© 1992 United Feature Syndicate, Inc.
YEAH. I'M PLANNING TO GNAW THE PARENTS TO DEATH TOMORROW.

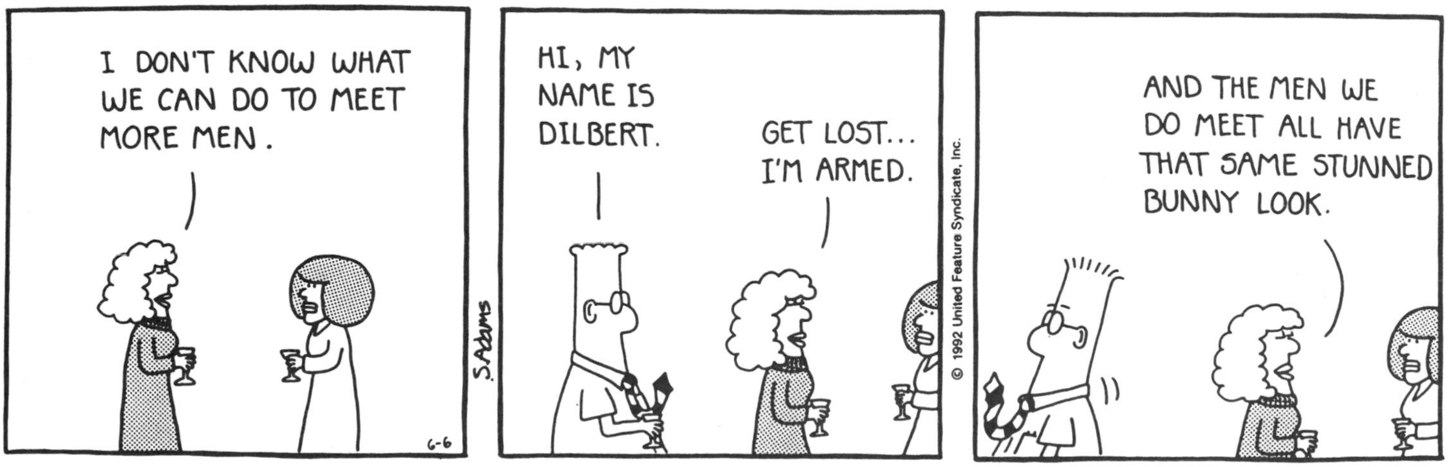
I DON'T KNOW WHAT WE CAN DO TO MEET MORE MEN.
6-6
S.Adams
HI, MY NAME IS DILBERT.
GET LOST... I'M ARMED.
© 1992 United Feature Syndicate, Inc.
AND THE MEN WE DO MEET ALL HAVE THAT SAME STUNNED BUNNY LOOK.

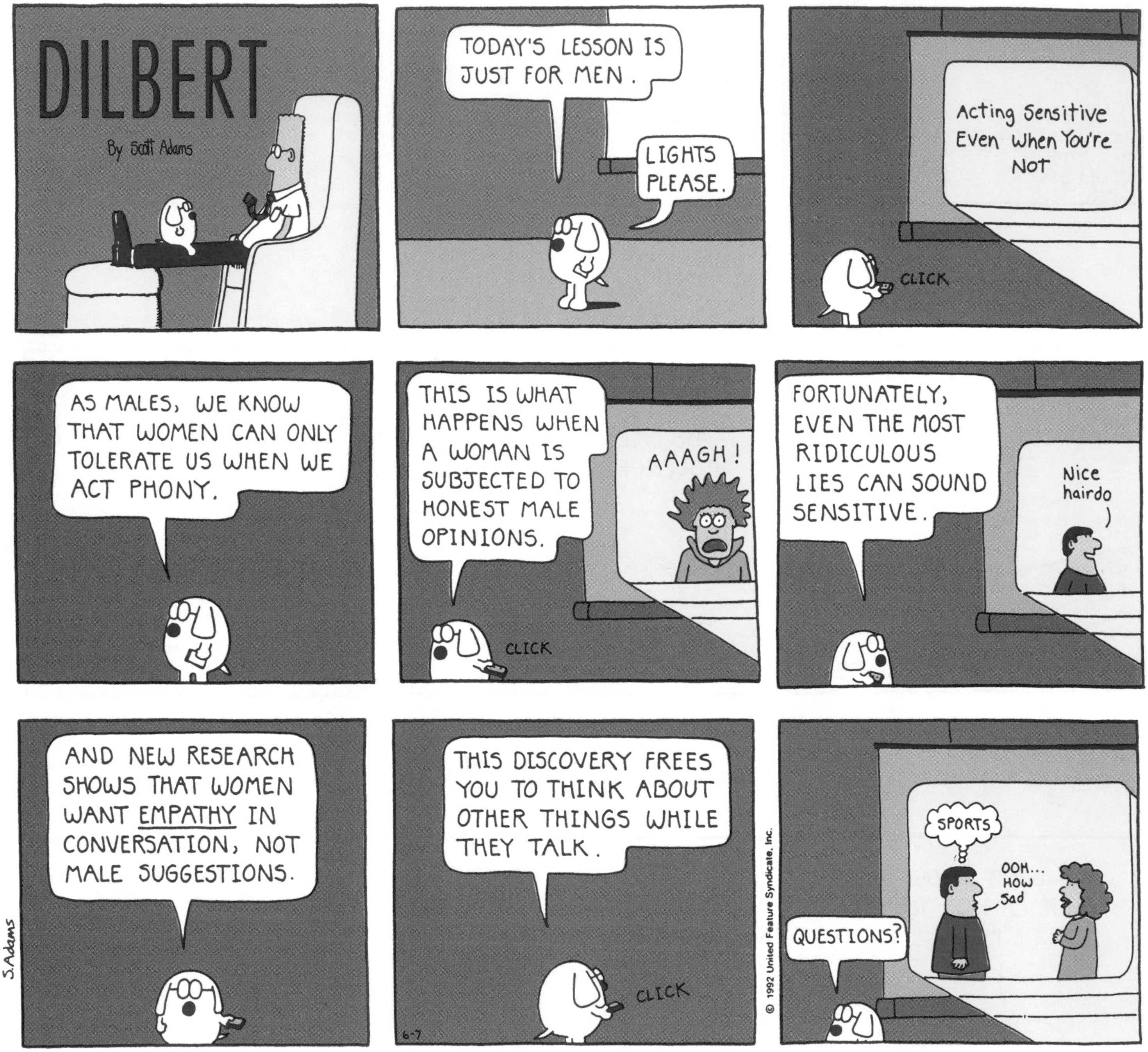
DILBERT
By Scott Adams
TODAY'S LESSON IS JUST FOR MEN.
LIGHTS PLEASE.
Acting Sensitive Even When You're Not
CLICK
AS MALES, WE KNOW THAT WOMEN CAN ONLY TOLERATE US WHEN WE ACT PHONY.
THIS IS WHAT HAPPENS WHEN A WOMAN IS SUBJECTED TO HONEST MALE OPINIONS.
AAAGH!
CLICK
FORTUNATELY, EVEN THE MOST RIDICULOUS LIES CAN SOUND SENSITIVE.
Nice hairdo
AND NEW RESEARCH SHOWS THAT WOMEN WANT EMPATHY IN CONVERSATION, NOT MALE SUGGESTIONS.
S.Adams
THIS DISCOVERY FREES YOU TO THINK ABOUT OTHER THINGS WHILE THEY TALK.
CLICK
6-7
© 1992 United Feature Syndicate, Inc.
SPORTS
OOH... HOW Sad
QUESTIONS?

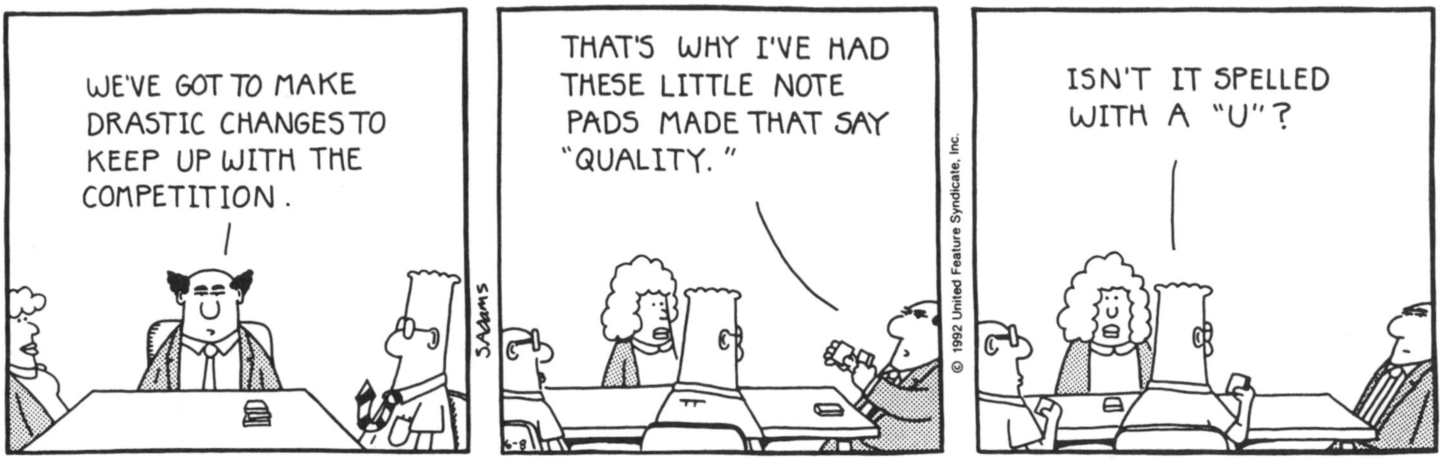

WE'VE GOT TO MAKE DRASTIC CHANGES TO KEEP UP WITH THE COMPETITION.
S.Adams
6-8
THAT'S WHY I'VE HAD THESE LITTLE NOTE PADS MADE THAT SAY "QUALITY."
© 1992 United Feature Syndicate, Inc.
ISN'T IT SPELLED WITH A "U"?

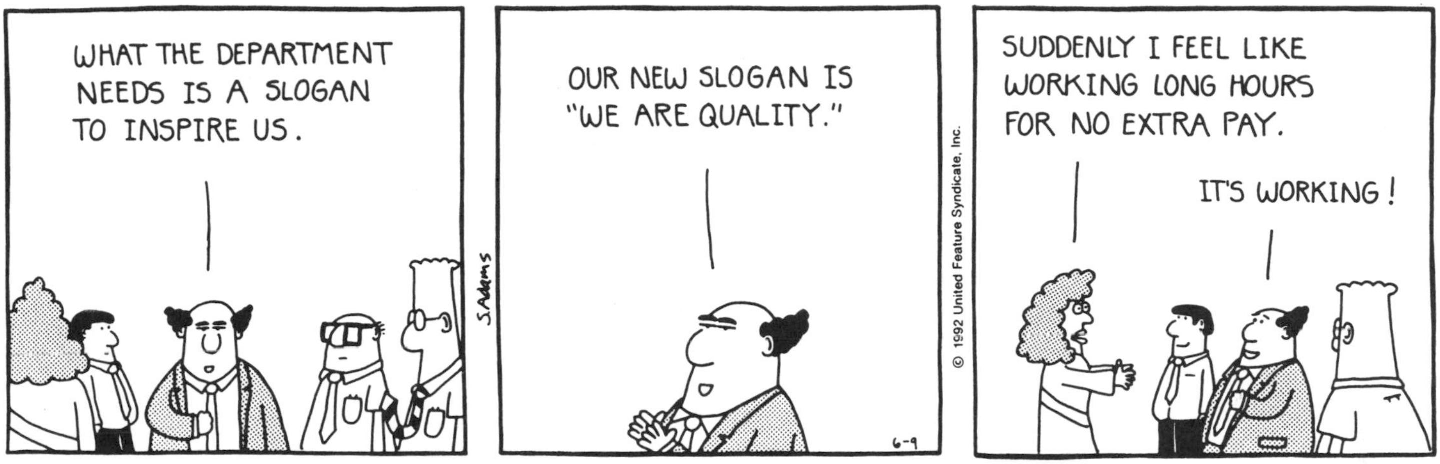

WHAT THE DEPARTMENT NEEDS IS A SLOGAN TO INSPIRE US.
S.Adams
OUR NEW SLOGAN IS "WE ARE QUALITY."
6-9
© 1992 United Feature Syndicate, Inc.
SUDDENLY I FEEL LIKE WORKING LONG HOURS FOR NO EXTRA PAY.
IT'S WORKING!

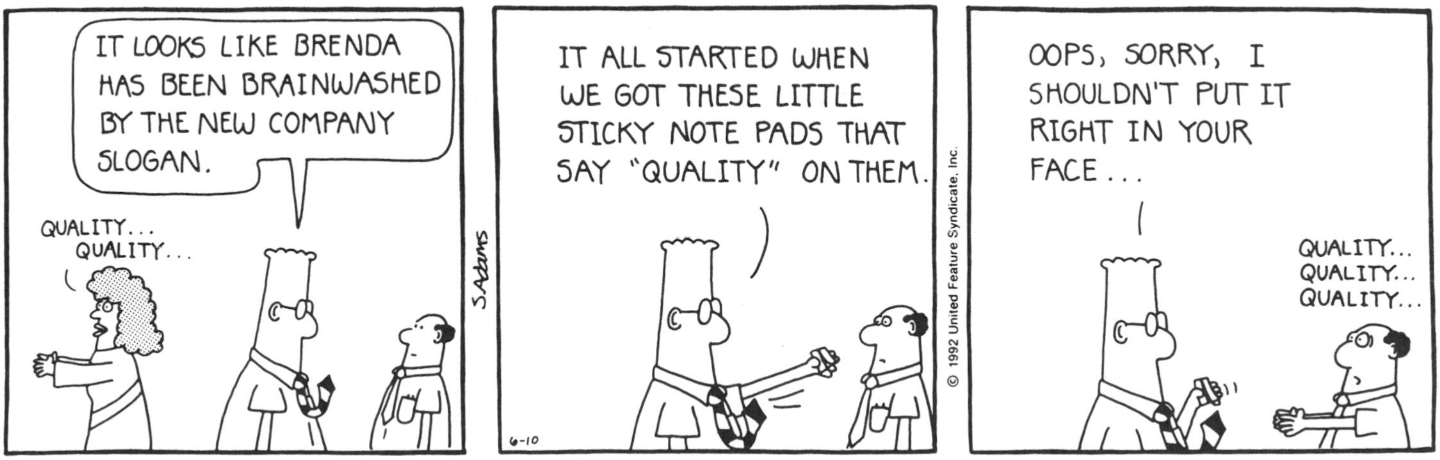

IT LOOKS LIKE BRENDA HAS BEEN BRAINWASHED BY THE NEW COMPANY SLOGAN.
QUALITY... QUALITY...
S.Adams
IT ALL STARTED WHEN WE GOT THESE LITTLE STICKY NOTE PADS THAT SAY "QUALITY" ON THEM.
6-10
© 1992 United Feature Syndicate, Inc.
OOPS, SORRY, I SHOULDN'T PUT IT RIGHT IN YOUR FACE...
QUALITY... QUALITY... QUALITY...

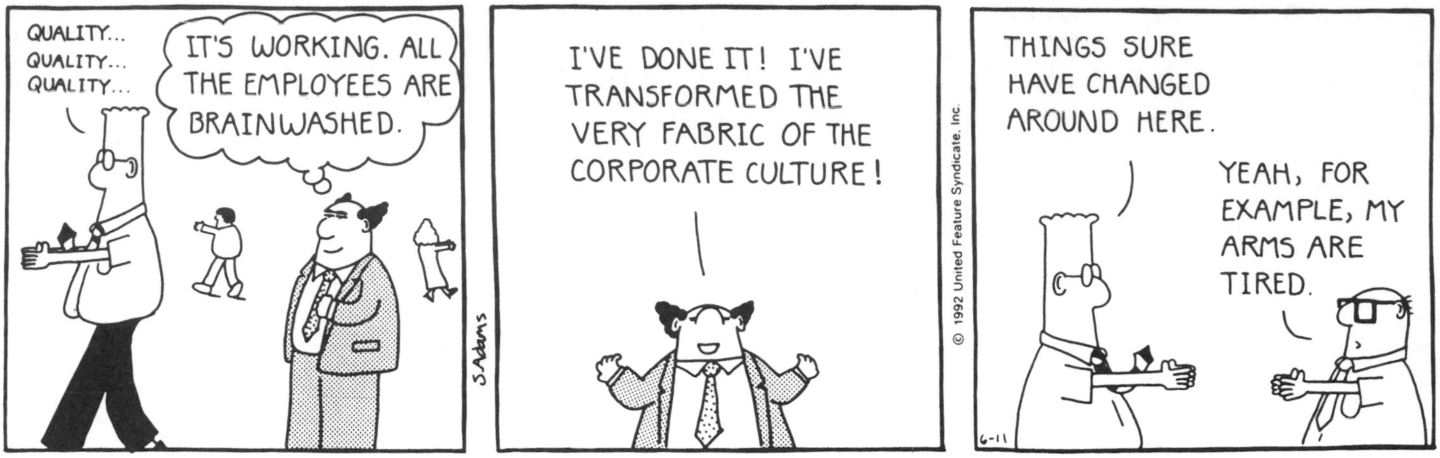
QUALITY... QUALITY... QUALITY...
IT'S WORKING. ALL THE EMPLOYEES ARE BRAINWASHED.
S. Adams
I'VE DONE IT! I'VE TRANSFORMED THE VERY FABRIC OF THE CORPORATE CULTURE!
© 1992 United Feature Syndicate, Inc.
THINGS SURE HAVE CHANGED AROUND HERE.
YEAH, FOR EXAMPLE, MY ARMS ARE TIRED.
6-11

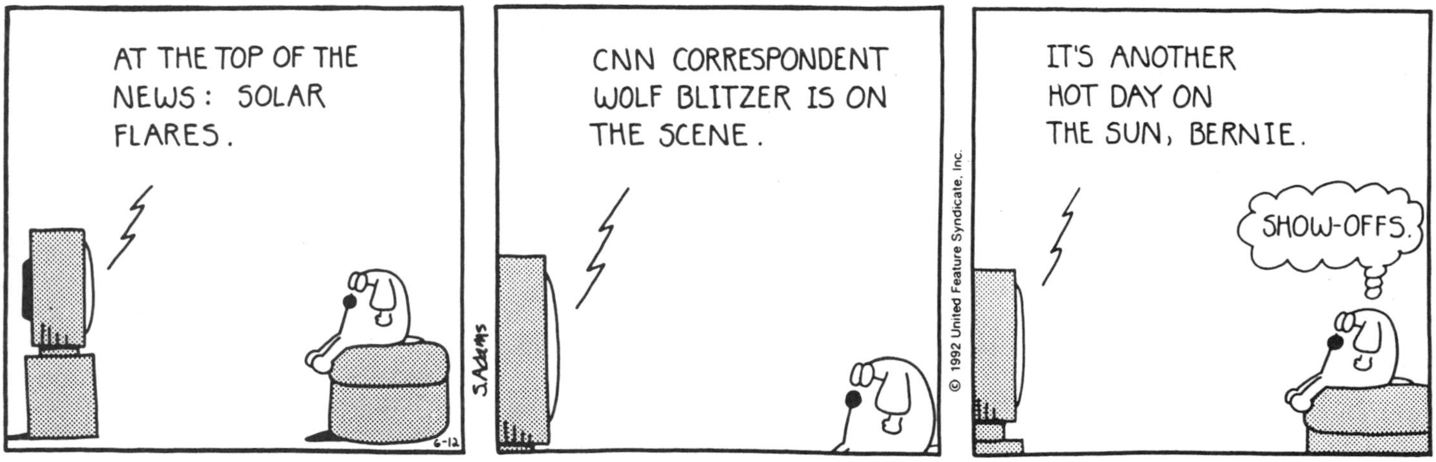
AT THE TOP OF THE NEWS: SOLAR FLARES.
6-12
S. Adams
CNN CORRESPONDENT WOLF BLITZER IS ON THE SCENE.
© 1992 United Feature Syndicate, Inc.
IT'S ANOTHER HOT DAY ON THE SUN, BERNIE.
SHOW-OFFS.

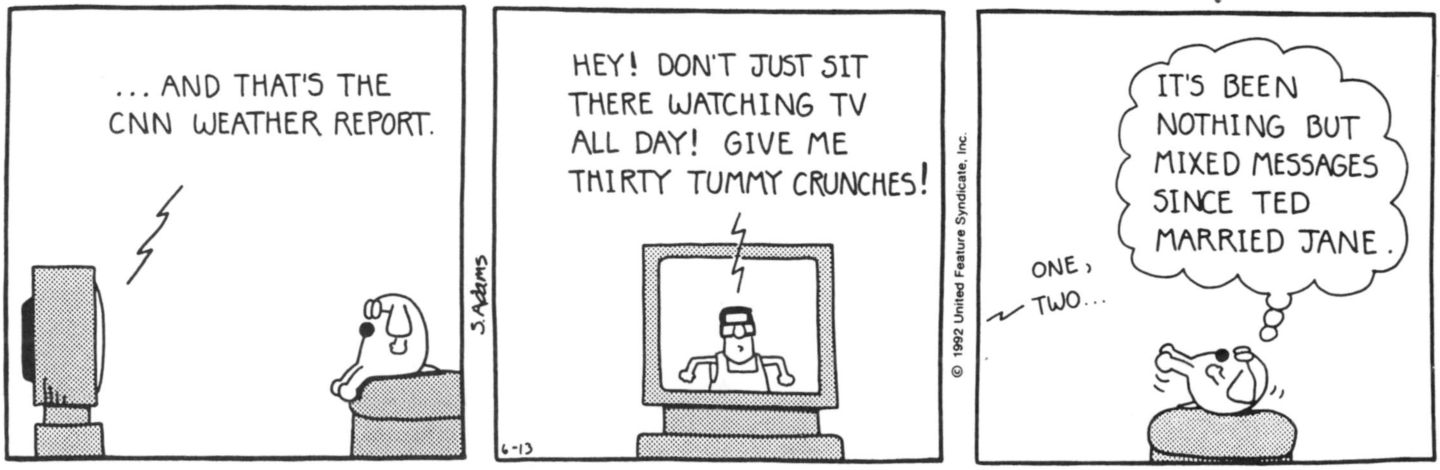
... AND THAT'S THE CNN WEATHER REPORT.
S. Adams
HEY! DON'T JUST SIT THERE WATCHING TV ALL DAY! GIVE ME THIRTY TUMMY CRUNCHES!
6-13
© 1992 United Feature Syndicate, Inc.
ONE, TWO...
IT'S BEEN NOTHING BUT MIXED MESSAGES SINCE TED MARRIED JANE.

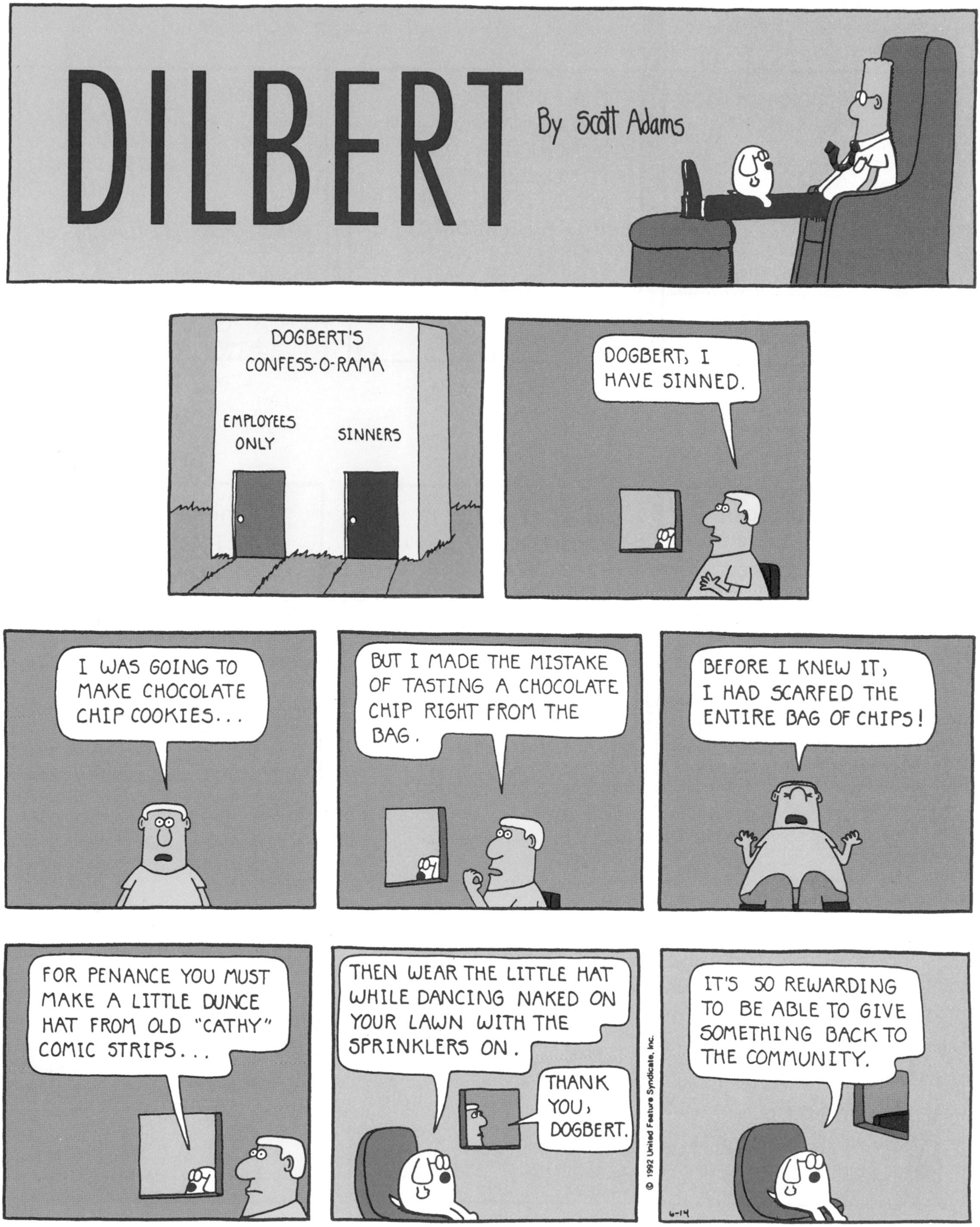
DILBERT
By Scott Adams
DOGBERT'S CONFESS-O-RAMA
EMPLOYEES ONLY
SINNERS
DOGBERT, I HAVE SINNED.
I WAS GOING TO MAKE CHOCOLATE CHIP COOKIES...
BUT I MADE THE MISTAKE OF TASTING A CHOCOLATE CHIP RIGHT FROM THE BAG.
BEFORE I KNEW IT, I HAD SCARFED THE ENTIRE BAG OF CHIPS!
FOR PENANCE YOU MUST MAKE A LITTLE DUNCE HAT FROM OLD "CATHY" COMIC STRIPS...
THEN WEAR THE LITTLE HAT WHILE DANCING NAKED ON YOUR LAWN WITH THE SPRINKLERS ON.
THANK YOU, DOGBERT.
IT'S SO REWARDING TO BE ABLE TO GIVE SOMETHING BACK TO THE COMMUNITY.
S.Adams
© 1992 United Feature Syndicate, Inc.
6-14

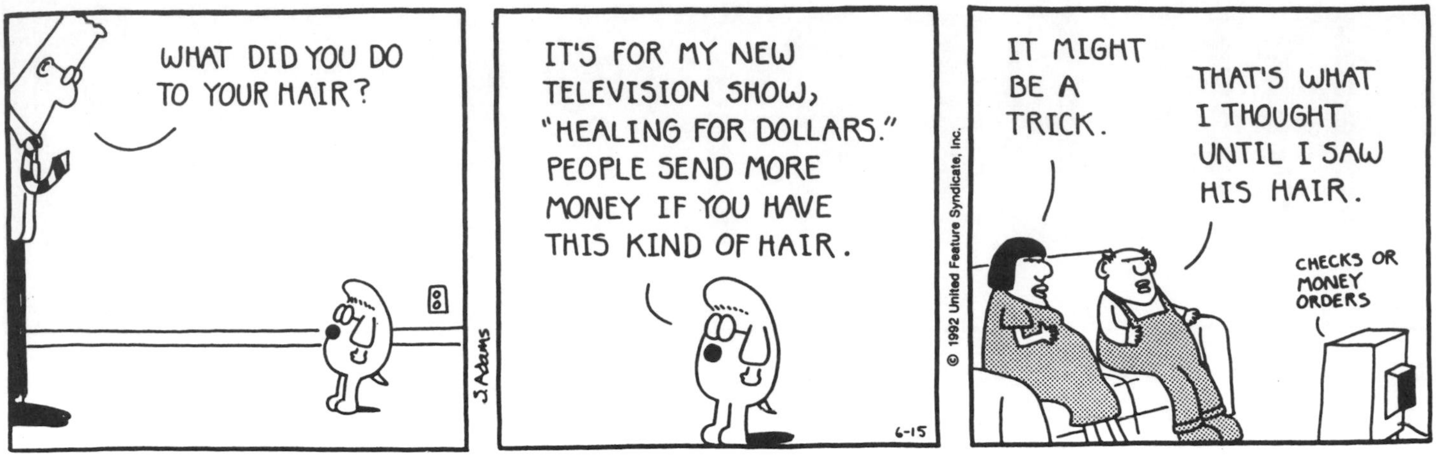
WHAT DID YOU DO TO YOUR HAIR?
IT'S FOR MY NEW TELEVISION SHOW, "HEALING FOR DOLLARS." PEOPLE SEND MORE MONEY IF YOU HAVE THIS KIND OF HAIR.
IT MIGHT BE A TRICK.
THAT'S WHAT I THOUGHT UNTIL I SAW HIS HAIR.
CHECKS OR MONEY ORDERS
S. Adams
6-15
© 1992 United Feature Syndicate, Inc.

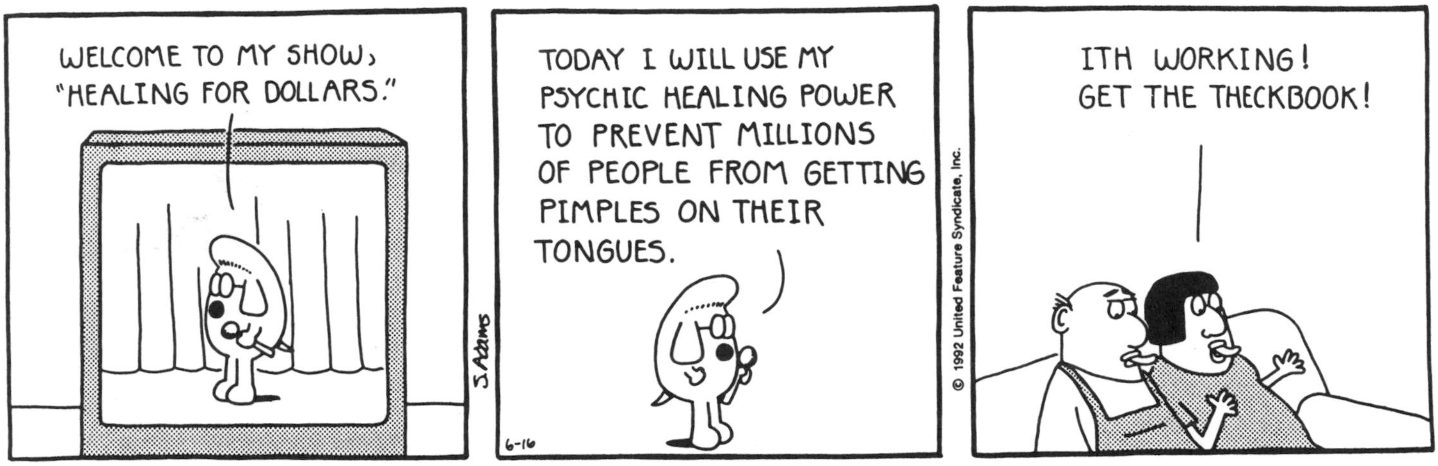
WELCOME TO MY SHOW, "HEALING FOR DOLLARS."
TODAY I WILL USE MY PSYCHIC HEALING POWER TO PREVENT MILLIONS OF PEOPLE FROM GETTING PIMPLES ON THEIR TONGUES.
ITH WORKING! GET THE THECKBOOK!
S. Adams
6-16
© 1992 United Feature Syndicate, Inc.

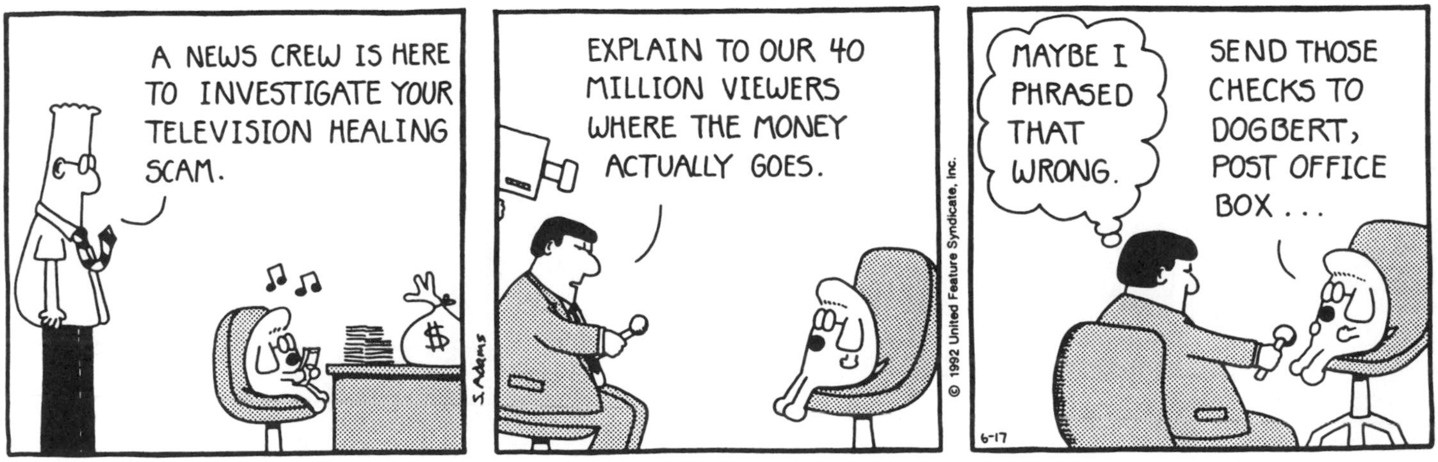
A NEWS CREW IS HERE TO INVESTIGATE YOUR TELEVISION HEALING SCAM.
$
EXPLAIN TO OUR 40 MILLION VIEWERS WHERE THE MONEY ACTUALLY GOES.
MAYBE I PHRASED THAT WRONG.
SEND THOSE CHECKS TO DOGBERT, POST OFFICE BOX . . .
S. Adams
6-17
© 1992 United Feature Syndicate, Inc.

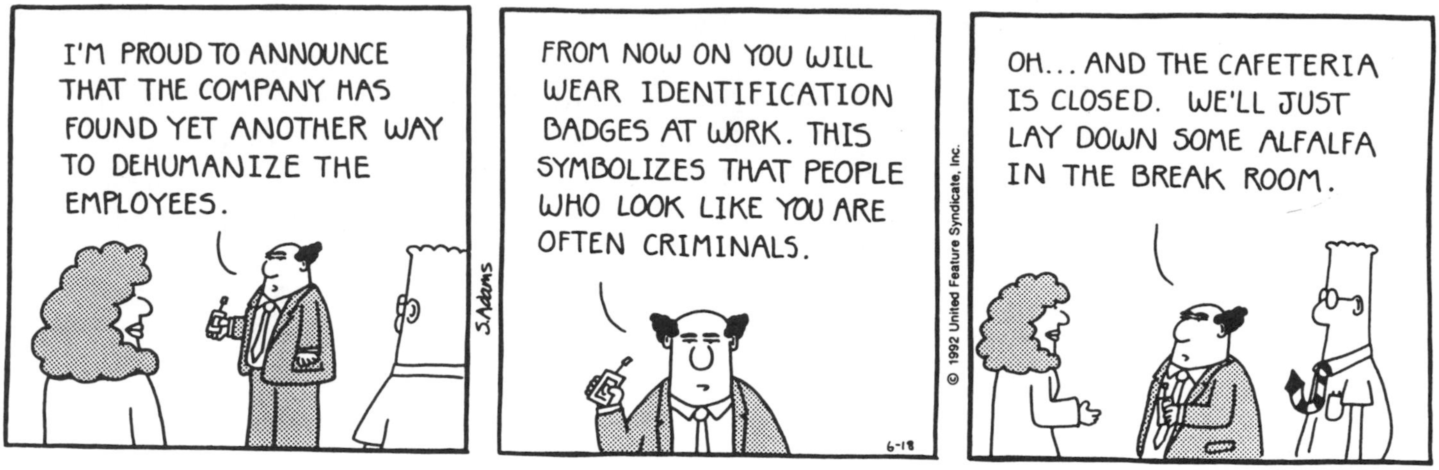
I'M PROUD TO ANNOUNCE THAT THE COMPANY HAS FOUND YET ANOTHER WAY TO DEHUMANIZE THE EMPLOYEES.
S.Adams
FROM NOW ON YOU WILL WEAR IDENTIFICATION BADGES AT WORK. THIS SYMBOLIZES THAT PEOPLE WHO LOOK LIKE YOU ARE OFTEN CRIMINALS.
6-18
© 1992 United Feature Syndicate, Inc.
OH... AND THE CAFETERIA IS CLOSED. WE'LL JUST LAY DOWN SOME ALFALFA IN THE BREAK ROOM.

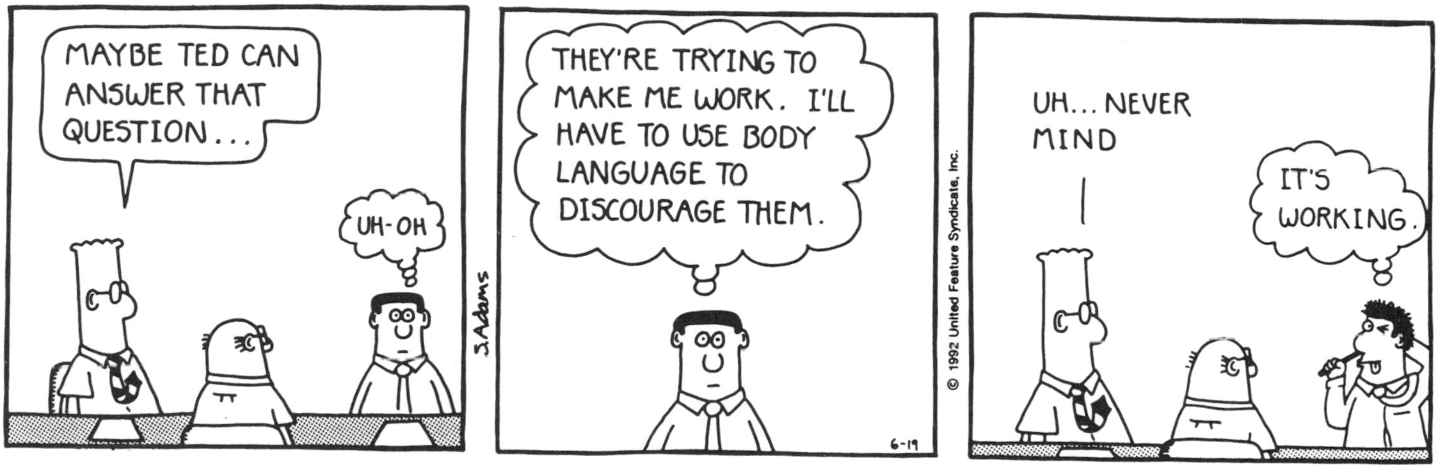
MAYBE TED CAN ANSWER THAT QUESTION...
UH-OH
S.Adams
THEY'RE TRYING TO MAKE ME WORK. I'LL HAVE TO USE BODY LANGUAGE TO DISCOURAGE THEM.
6-19
© 1992 United Feature Syndicate, Inc.
UH... NEVER MIND
IT'S WORKING.

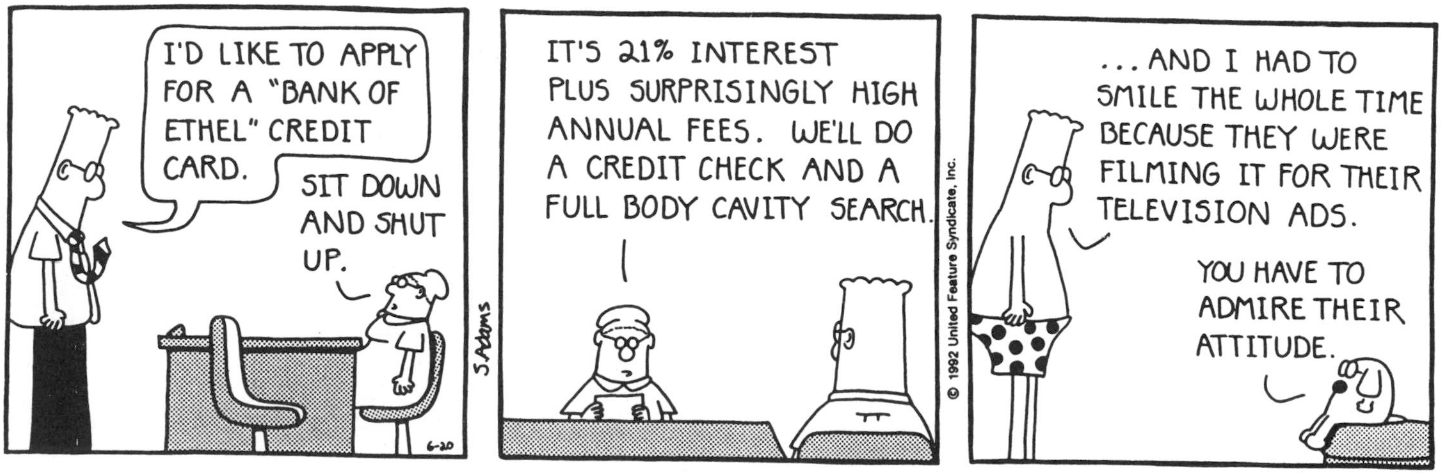
I'D LIKE TO APPLY FOR A "BANK OF ETHEL" CREDIT CARD.
SIT DOWN AND SHUT UP.
6-20
S.Adams
IT'S 21% INTEREST PLUS SURPRISINGLY HIGH ANNUAL FEES. WE'LL DO A CREDIT CHECK AND A FULL BODY CAVITY SEARCH.
© 1992 United Feature Syndicate, Inc.
...AND I HAD TO SMILE THE WHOLE TIME BECAUSE THEY WERE FILMING IT FOR THEIR TELEVISION ADS.
YOU HAVE TO ADMIRE THEIR ATTITUDE.

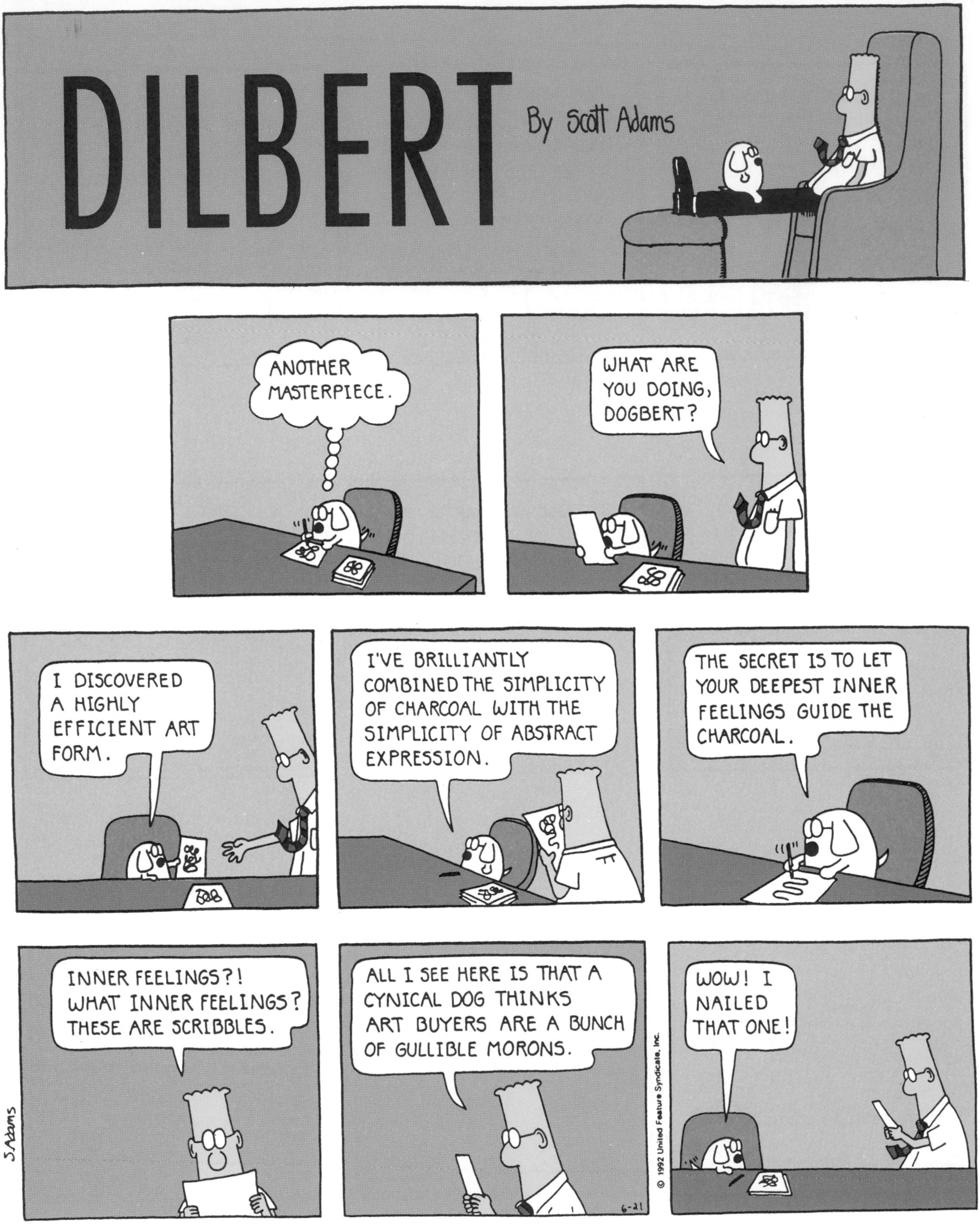
DILBERT
By Scott Adams
ANOTHER MASTERPIECE.
WHAT ARE YOU DOING, DOGBERT?
I DISCOVERED A HIGHLY EFFICIENT ART FORM.
I'VE BRILLIANTLY COMBINED THE SIMPLICITY OF CHARCOAL WITH THE SIMPLICITY OF ABSTRACT EXPRESSION.
THE SECRET IS TO LET YOUR DEEPEST INNER FEELINGS GUIDE THE CHARCOAL.
INNER FEELINGS?! WHAT INNER FEELINGS? THESE ARE SCRIBBLES.
ALL I SEE HERE IS THAT A CYNICAL DOG THINKS ART BUYERS ARE A BUNCH OF GULLIBLE MORONS.
WOW! I NAILED THAT ONE!
S. Adams
6-21
© 1992 United Feature Syndicate, Inc.

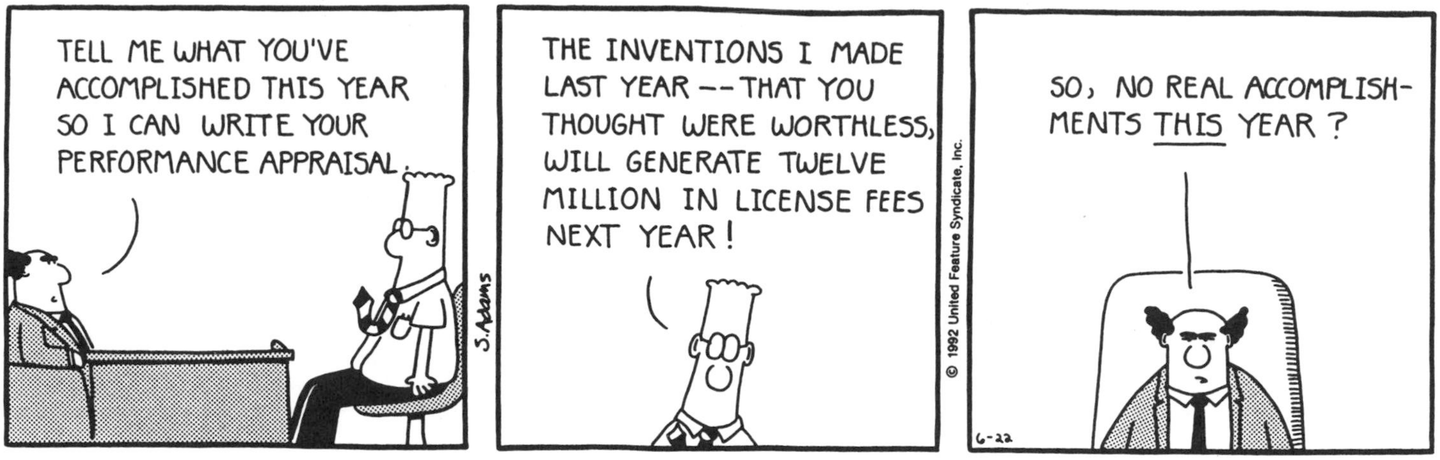
TELL ME WHAT YOU'VE ACCOMPLISHED THIS YEAR SO I CAN WRITE YOUR PERFORMANCE APPRAISAL.
S. Adams
THE INVENTIONS I MADE LAST YEAR -- THAT YOU THOUGHT WERE WORTHLESS, WILL GENERATE TWELVE MILLION IN LICENSE FEES NEXT YEAR!
© 1992 United Feature Syndicate, Inc.
SO, NO REAL ACCOMPLISHMENTS THIS YEAR?
6-22

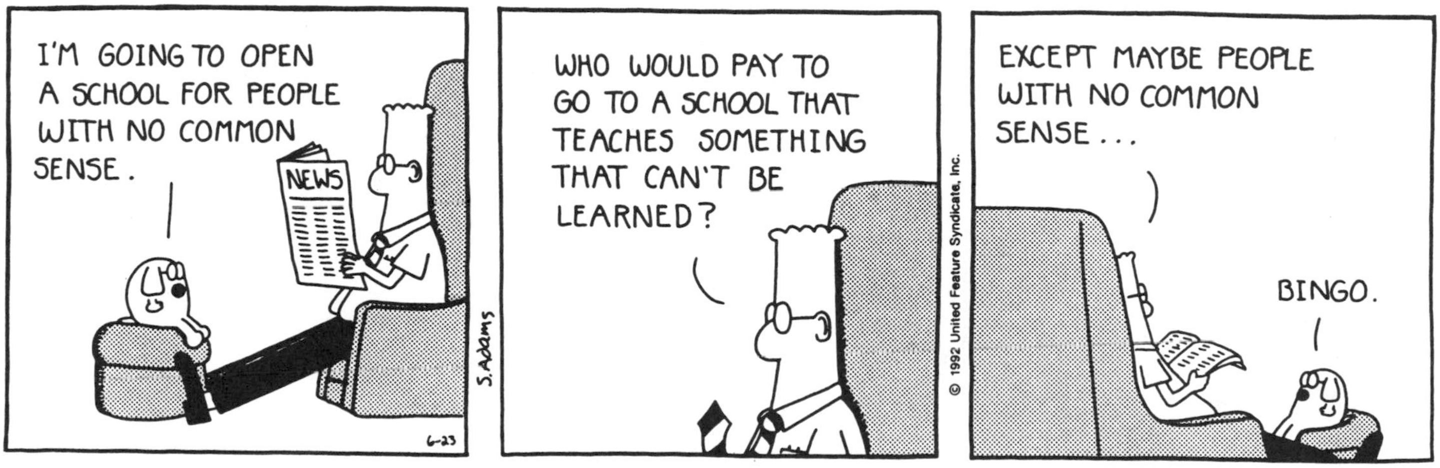
I'M GOING TO OPEN A SCHOOL FOR PEOPLE WITH NO COMMON SENSE.
NEWS
6-23
S. Adams
WHO WOULD PAY TO GO TO A SCHOOL THAT TEACHES SOMETHING THAT CAN'T BE LEARNED?
© 1992 United Feature Syndicate, Inc.
EXCEPT MAYBE PEOPLE WITH NO COMMON SENSE...
BINGO.

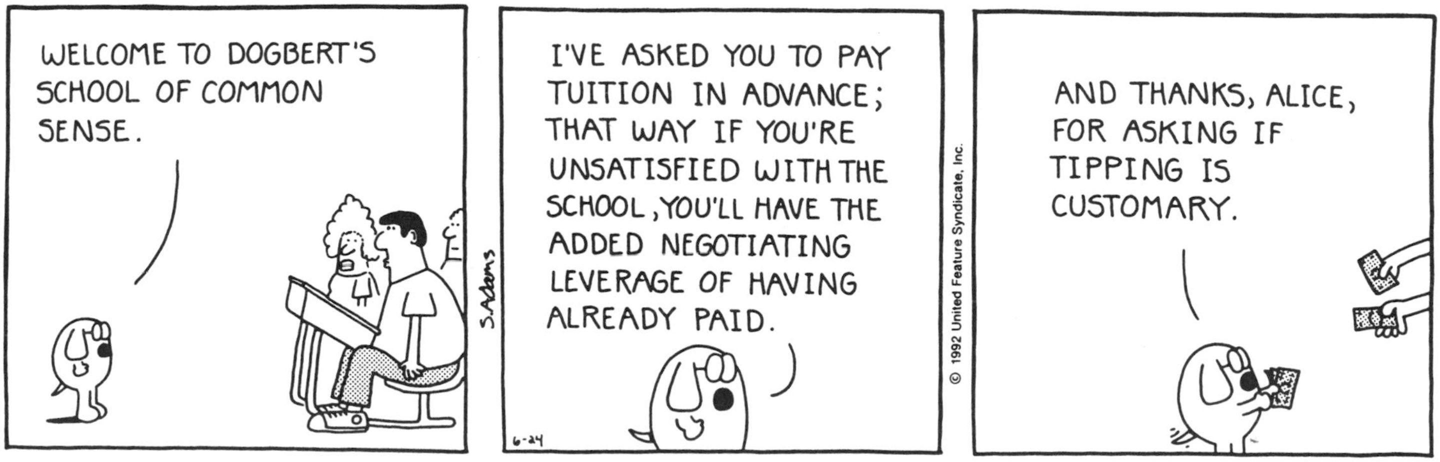
WELCOME TO DOGBERT'S SCHOOL OF COMMON SENSE.
S. Adams
I'VE ASKED YOU TO PAY TUITION IN ADVANCE; THAT WAY IF YOU'RE UNSATISFIED WITH THE SCHOOL, YOU'LL HAVE THE ADDED NEGOTIATING LEVERAGE OF HAVING ALREADY PAID.
6-24
© 1992 United Feature Syndicate, Inc.
AND THANKS, ALICE, FOR ASKING IF TIPPING IS CUSTOMARY.

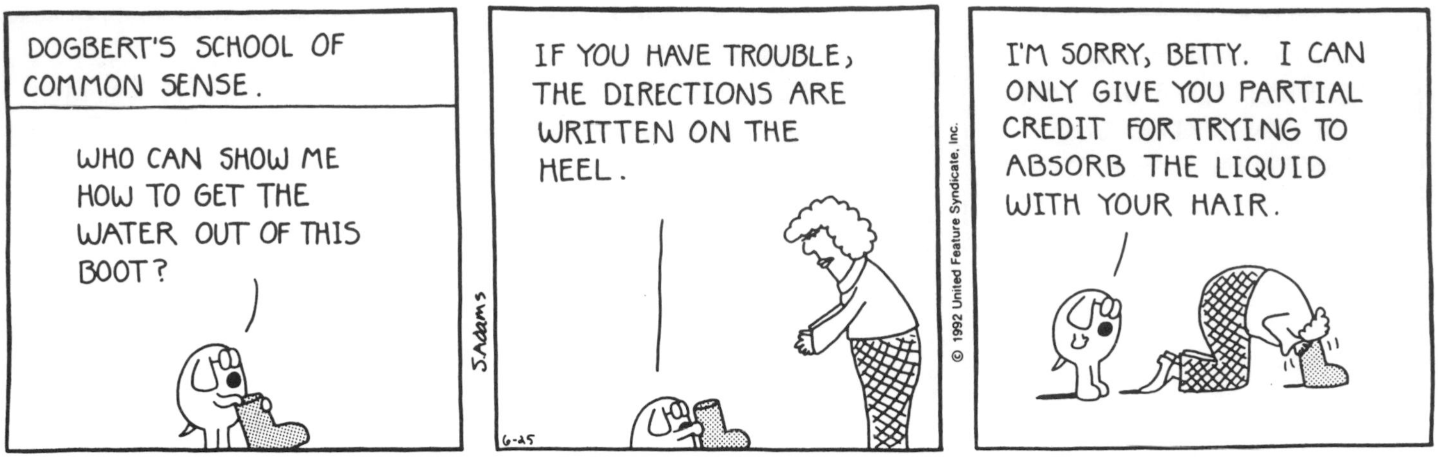
DOGBERT'S SCHOOL OF COMMON SENSE.
WHO CAN SHOW ME HOW TO GET THE WATER OUT OF THIS BOOT?
IF YOU HAVE TROUBLE, THE DIRECTIONS ARE WRITTEN ON THE HEEL.
S.Adams
6-25
© 1992 United Feature Syndicate, Inc.
I'M SORRY, BETTY. I CAN ONLY GIVE YOU PARTIAL CREDIT FOR TRYING TO ABSORB THE LIQUID WITH YOUR HAIR.

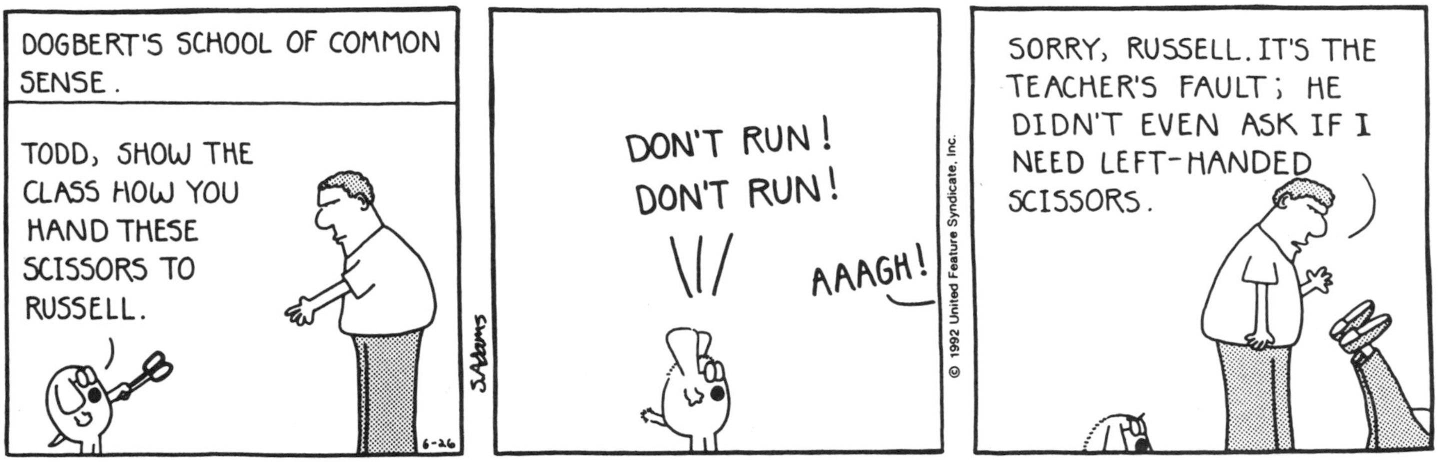
DOGBERT'S SCHOOL OF COMMON SENSE.
TODD, SHOW THE CLASS HOW YOU HAND THESE SCISSORS TO RUSSELL.
6-26
S.Adams
DON'T RUN! DON'T RUN!
AAAGH!
© 1992 United Feature Syndicate, Inc.
SORRY, RUSSELL. IT'S THE TEACHER'S FAULT; HE DIDN'T EVEN ASK IF I NEED LEFT-HANDED SCISSORS.

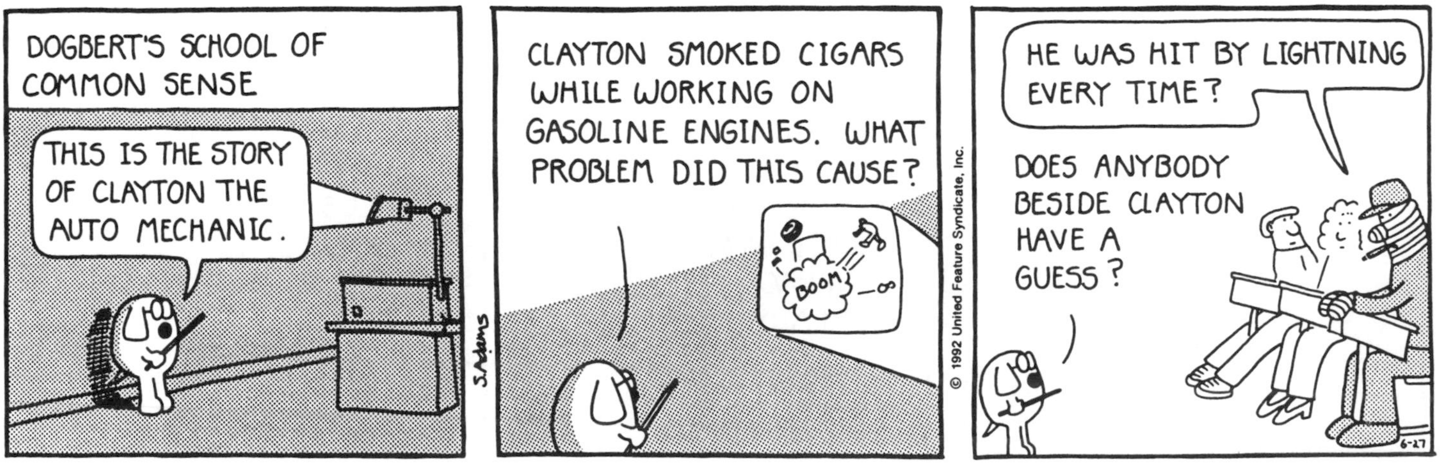
DOGBERT'S SCHOOL OF COMMON SENSE
THIS IS THE STORY OF CLAYTON THE AUTO MECHANIC.
S.Adams
CLAYTON SMOKED CIGARS WHILE WORKING ON GASOLINE ENGINES. WHAT PROBLEM DID THIS CAUSE?
BOOM
© 1992 United Feature Syndicate, Inc.
HE WAS HIT BY LIGHTNING EVERY TIME?
DOES ANYBODY BESIDE CLAYTON HAVE A GUESS?
6-27

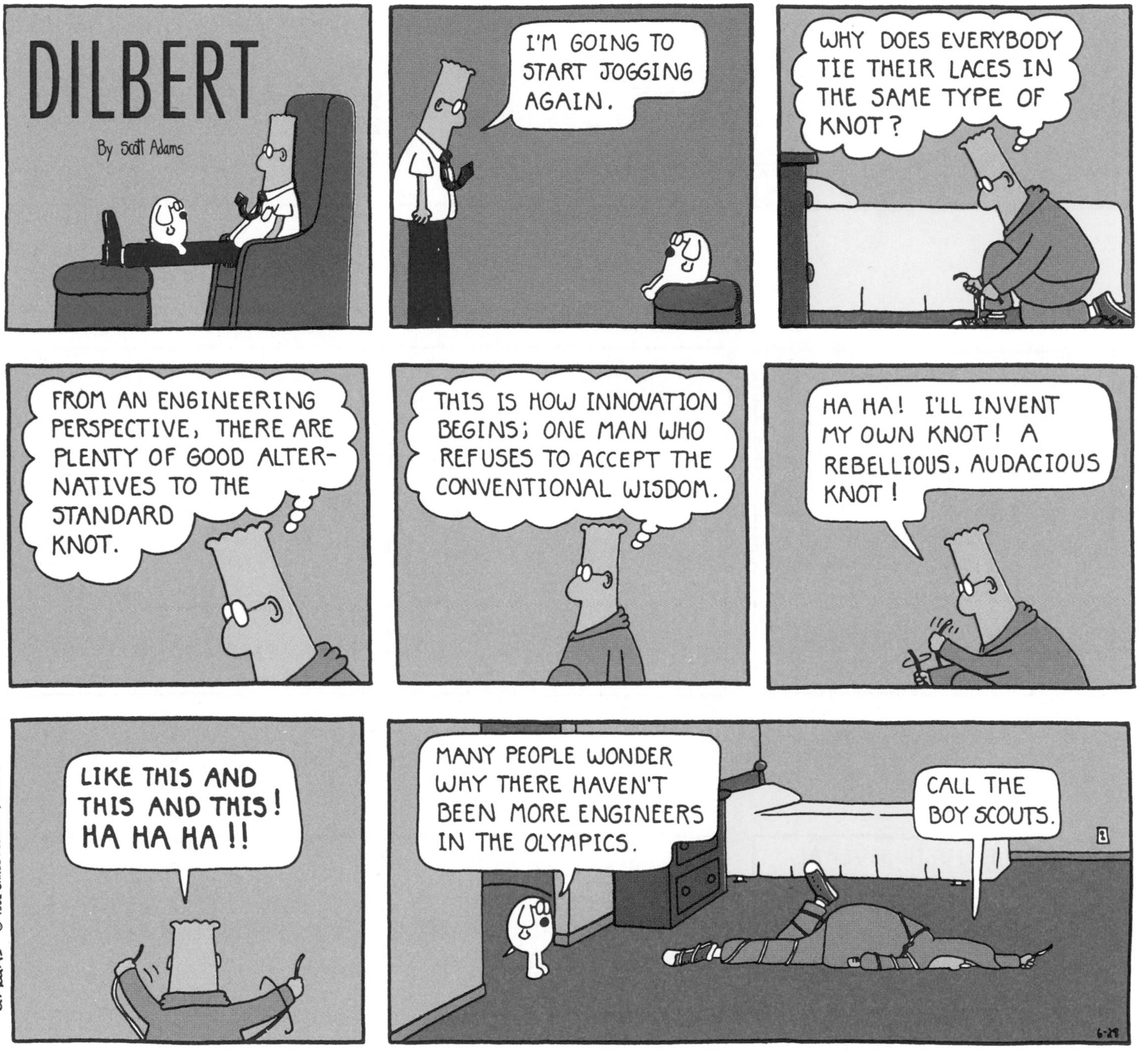
DILBERT
By Scott Adams
I'M GOING TO START JOGGING AGAIN.
WHY DOES EVERYBODY TIE THEIR LACES IN THE SAME TYPE OF KNOT?
FROM AN ENGINEERING PERSPECTIVE, THERE ARE PLENTY OF GOOD ALTERNATIVES TO THE STANDARD KNOT.
THIS IS HOW INNOVATION BEGINS; ONE MAN WHO REFUSES TO ACCEPT THE CONVENTIONAL WISDOM.
HA HA! I'LL INVENT MY OWN KNOT! A REBELLIOUS, AUDACIOUS KNOT!
LIKE THIS AND THIS AND THIS! HA HA HA!!
MANY PEOPLE WONDER WHY THERE HAVEN'T BEEN MORE ENGINEERS IN THE OLYMPICS.
CALL THE BOY SCOUTS.
S. Adams © 1992 United Feature Syndicate, Inc.
6-28

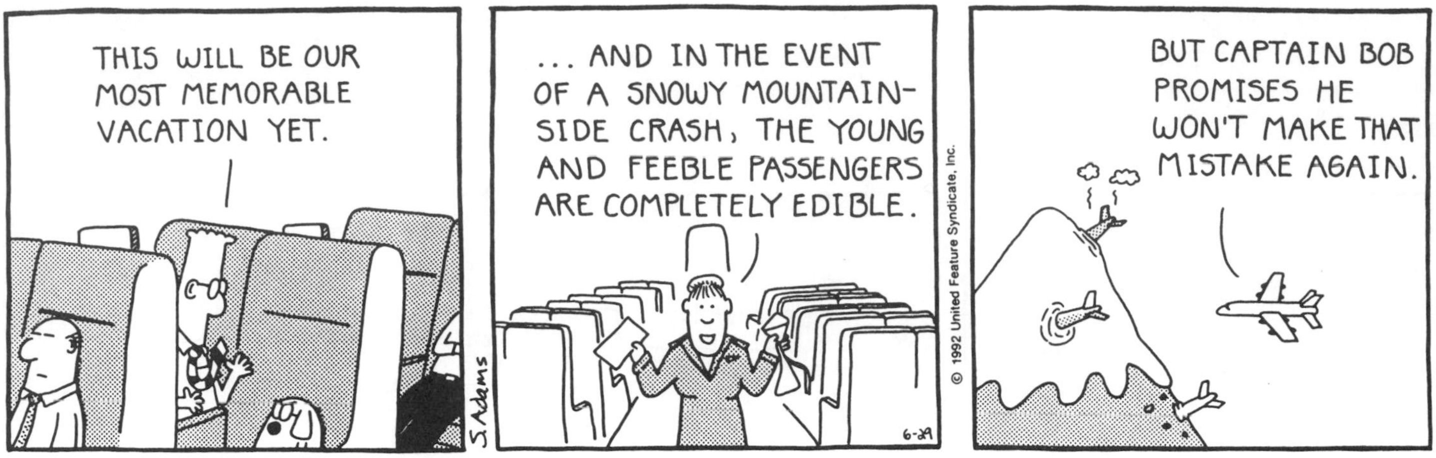
THIS WILL BE OUR MOST MEMORABLE VACATION YET.
S. Adams
... AND IN THE EVENT OF A SNOWY MOUNTAIN-SIDE CRASH, THE YOUNG AND FEEBLE PASSENGERS ARE COMPLETELY EDIBLE.
6-29
© 1992 United Feature Syndicate, Inc.
BUT CAPTAIN BOB PROMISES HE WON'T MAKE THAT MISTAKE AGAIN.

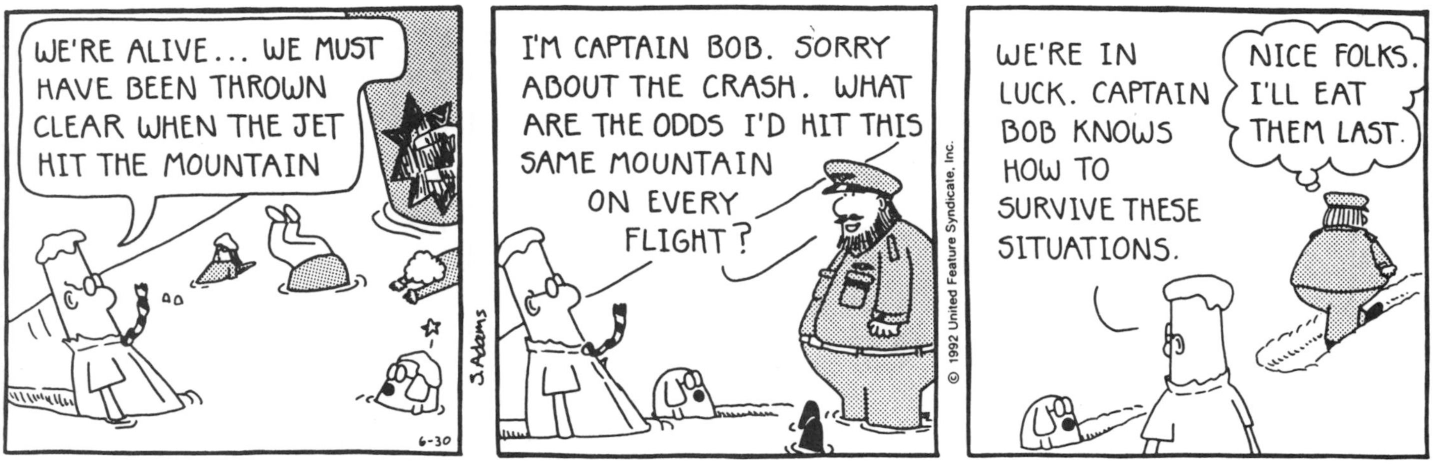
WE'RE ALIVE... WE MUST HAVE BEEN THROWN CLEAR WHEN THE JET HIT THE MOUNTAIN
6-30
S. Adams
I'M CAPTAIN BOB. SORRY ABOUT THE CRASH. WHAT ARE THE ODDS I'D HIT THIS SAME MOUNTAIN ON EVERY FLIGHT?
© 1992 United Feature Syndicate, Inc.
WE'RE IN LUCK. CAPTAIN BOB KNOWS HOW TO SURVIVE THESE SITUATIONS.
NICE FOLKS. I'LL EAT THEM LAST.

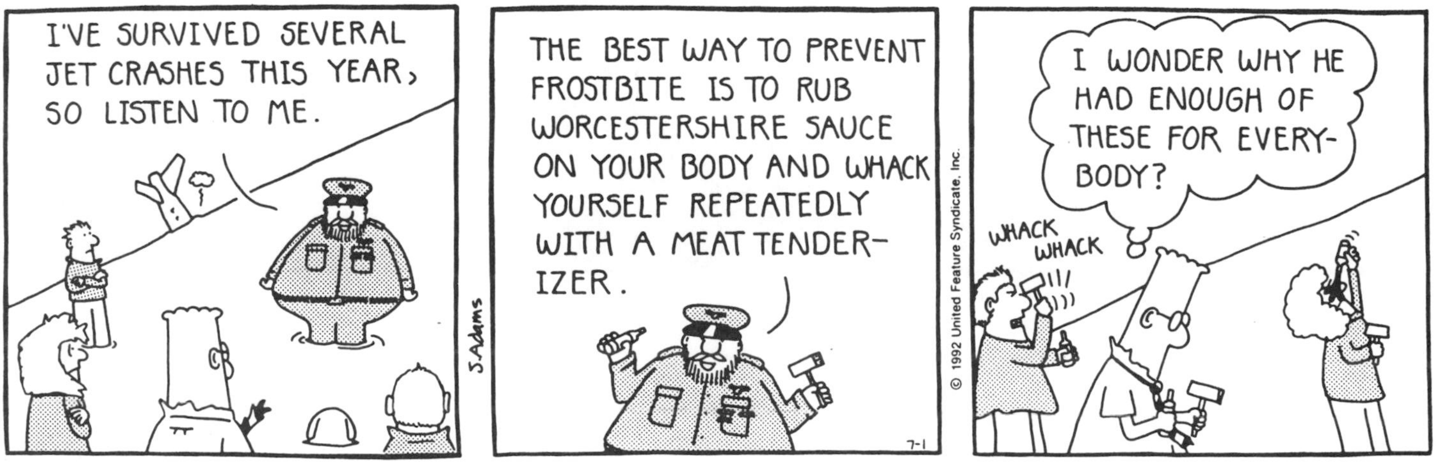
I'VE SURVIVED SEVERAL JET CRASHES THIS YEAR, SO LISTEN TO ME.
S. Adams
THE BEST WAY TO PREVENT FROSTBITE IS TO RUB WORCESTERSHIRE SAUCE ON YOUR BODY AND WHACK YOURSELF REPEATEDLY WITH A MEAT TENDER-IZER.
7-1
© 1992 United Feature Syndicate, Inc.
WHACK
WHACK
I WONDER WHY HE HAD ENOUGH OF THESE FOR EVERY-BODY?

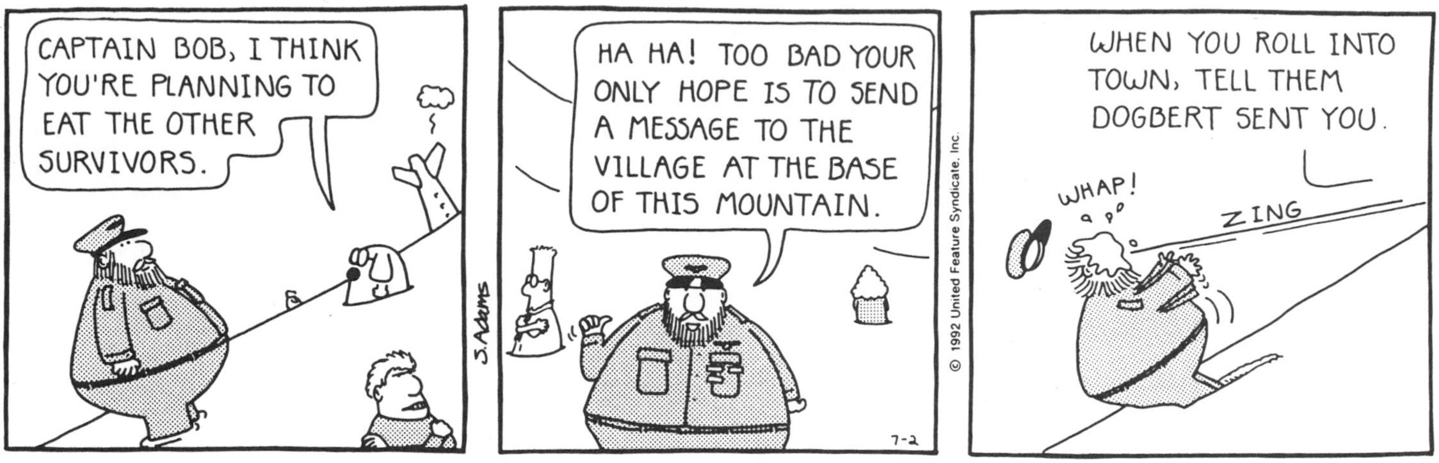
CAPTAIN BOB, I THINK YOU'RE PLANNING TO EAT THE OTHER SURVIVORS.
S.Adams
HA HA! TOO BAD YOUR ONLY HOPE IS TO SEND A MESSAGE TO THE VILLAGE AT THE BASE OF THIS MOUNTAIN.
7-2
© 1992 United Feature Syndicate, Inc.
WHEN YOU ROLL INTO TOWN, TELL THEM DOGBERT SENT YOU.
WHAP!
ZING

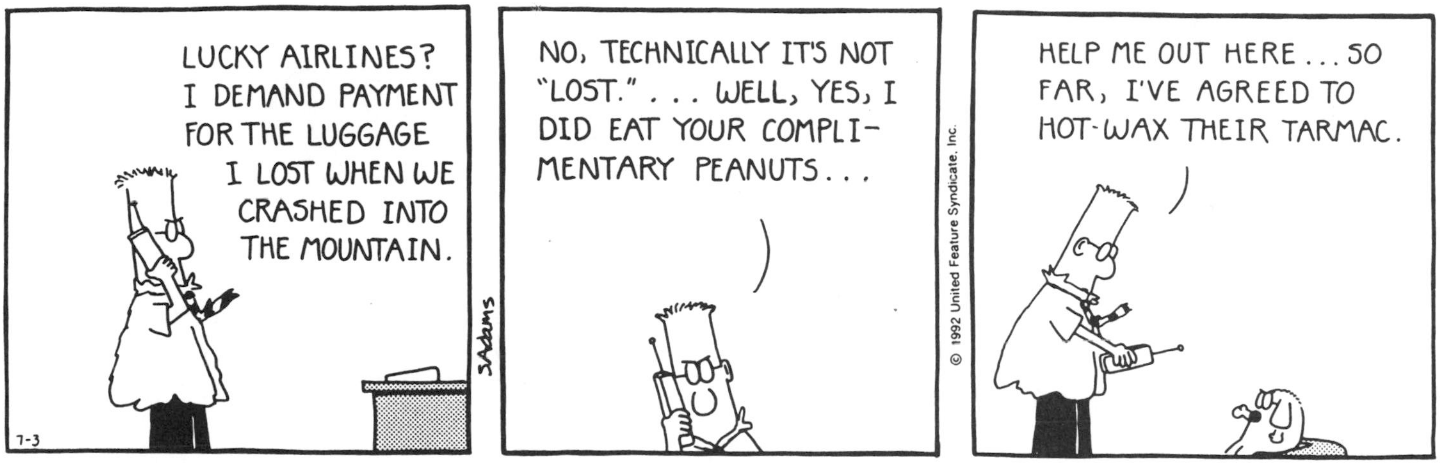
LUCKY AIRLINES? I DEMAND PAYMENT FOR THE LUGGAGE I LOST WHEN WE CRASHED INTO THE MOUNTAIN.
7-3
S.Adams
NO, TECHNICALLY IT'S NOT "LOST." . . . WELL, YES, I DID EAT YOUR COMPLIMENTARY PEANUTS . . .
© 1992 United Feature Syndicate, Inc.
HELP ME OUT HERE . . . SO FAR, I'VE AGREED TO HOT-WAX THEIR TARMAC.

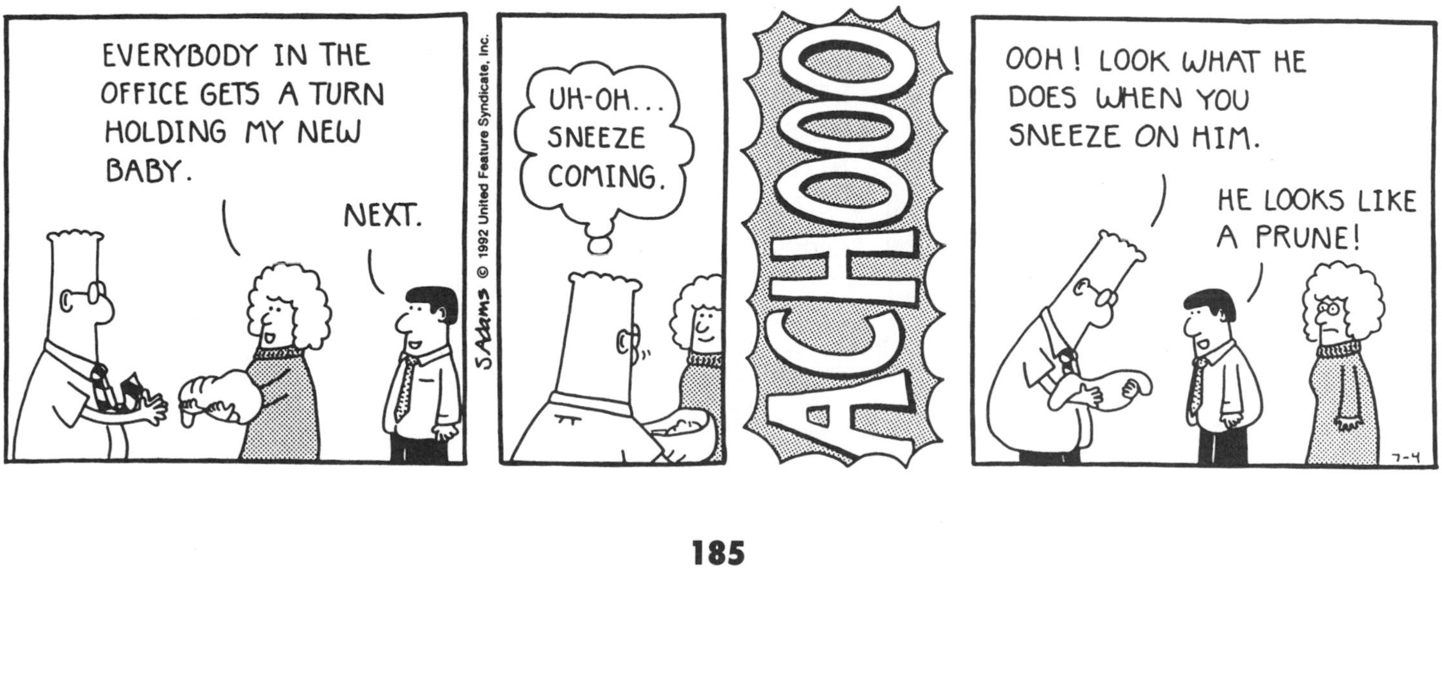
EVERYBODY IN THE OFFICE GETS A TURN HOLDING MY NEW BABY.
NEXT.
S.Adams © 1992 United Feature Syndicate, Inc.
UH-OH... SNEEZE COMING.
ACHOOO
OOH! LOOK WHAT HE DOES WHEN YOU SNEEZE ON HIM.
HE LOOKS LIKE A PRUNE!
7-4

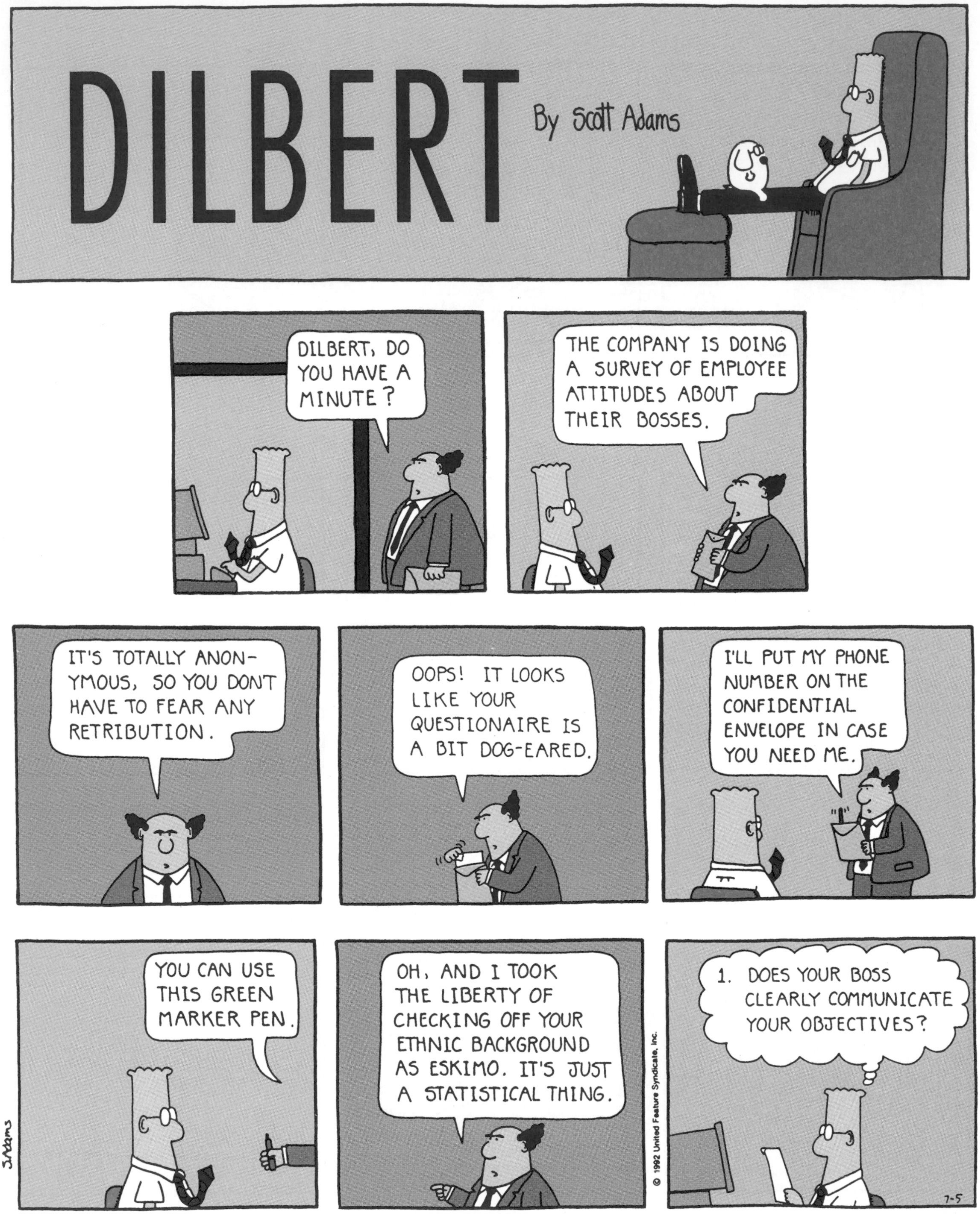

DILBERT
By Scott Adams
DILBERT, DO YOU HAVE A MINUTE?
THE COMPANY IS DOING A SURVEY OF EMPLOYEE ATTITUDES ABOUT THEIR BOSSES.
IT'S TOTALLY ANONYMOUS, SO YOU DON'T HAVE TO FEAR ANY RETRIBUTION.
OOPS! IT LOOKS LIKE YOUR QUESTIONAIRE IS A BIT DOG-EARED.
I'LL PUT MY PHONE NUMBER ON THE CONFIDENTIAL ENVELOPE IN CASE YOU NEED ME.
YOU CAN USE THIS GREEN MARKER PEN.
OH, AND I TOOK THE LIBERTY OF CHECKING OFF YOUR ETHNIC BACKGROUND AS ESKIMO. IT'S JUST A STATISTICAL THING.
1. DOES YOUR BOSS CLEARLY COMMUNICATE YOUR OBJECTIVES?
© 1992 United Feature Syndicate, Inc.
7-5

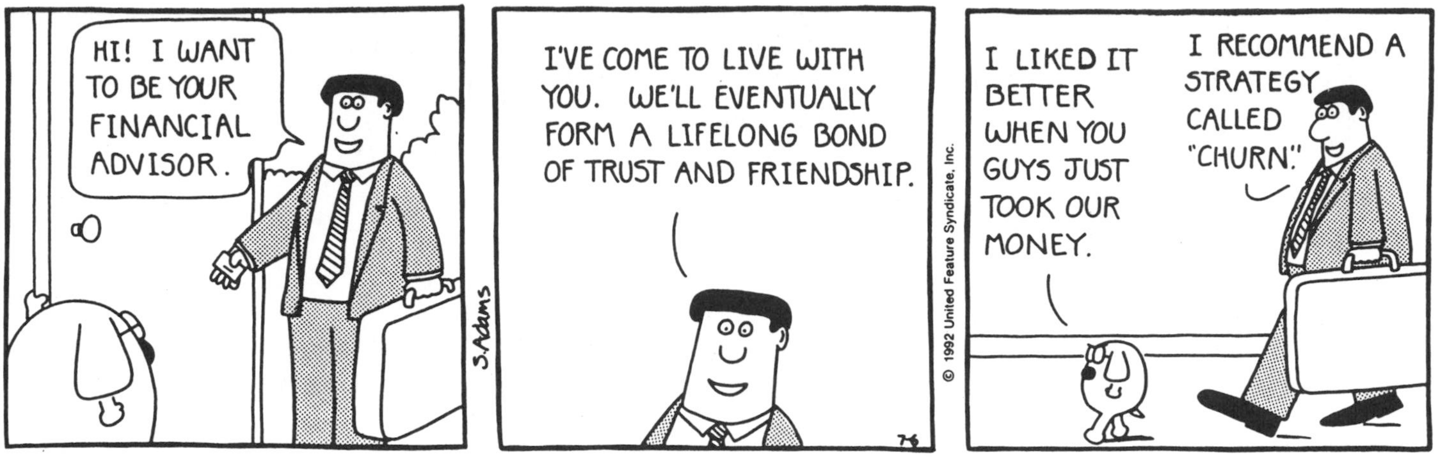
HI! I WANT TO BE YOUR FINANCIAL ADVISOR.
S. Adams
I'VE COME TO LIVE WITH YOU. WE'LL EVENTUALLY FORM A LIFELONG BOND OF TRUST AND FRIENDSHIP.
© 1992 United Feature Syndicate, Inc.
I LIKED IT BETTER WHEN YOU GUYS JUST TOOK OUR MONEY.
I RECOMMEND A STRATEGY CALLED "CHURN."

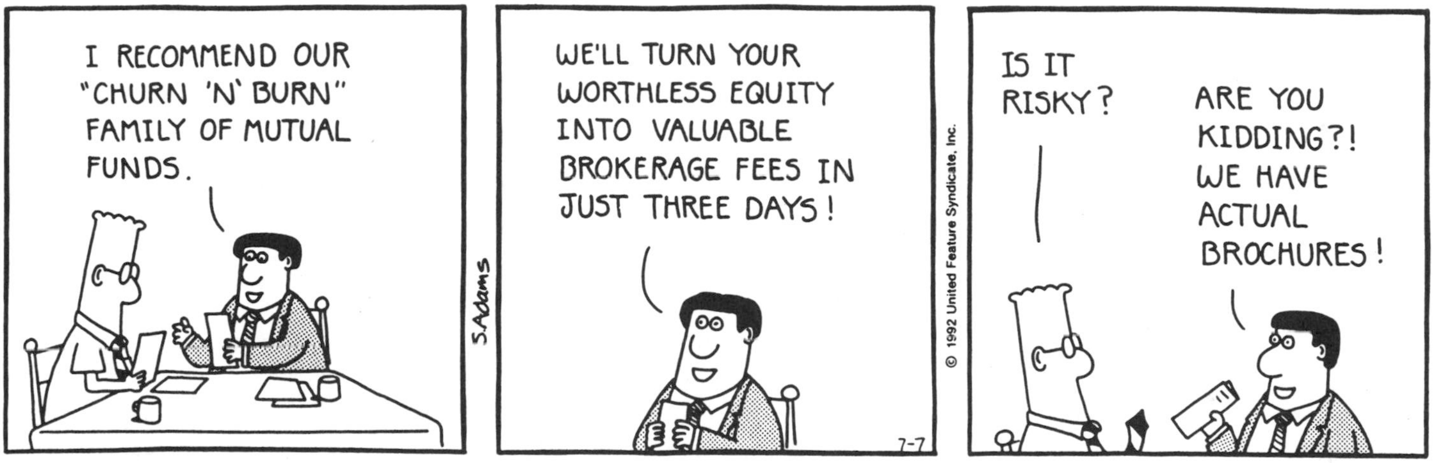
I RECOMMEND OUR "CHURN 'N' BURN" FAMILY OF MUTUAL FUNDS.
S. Adams
WE'LL TURN YOUR WORTHLESS EQUITY INTO VALUABLE BROKERAGE FEES IN JUST THREE DAYS!
7-7
© 1992 United Feature Syndicate, Inc.
IS IT RISKY?
ARE YOU KIDDING?! WE HAVE ACTUAL BROCHURES!

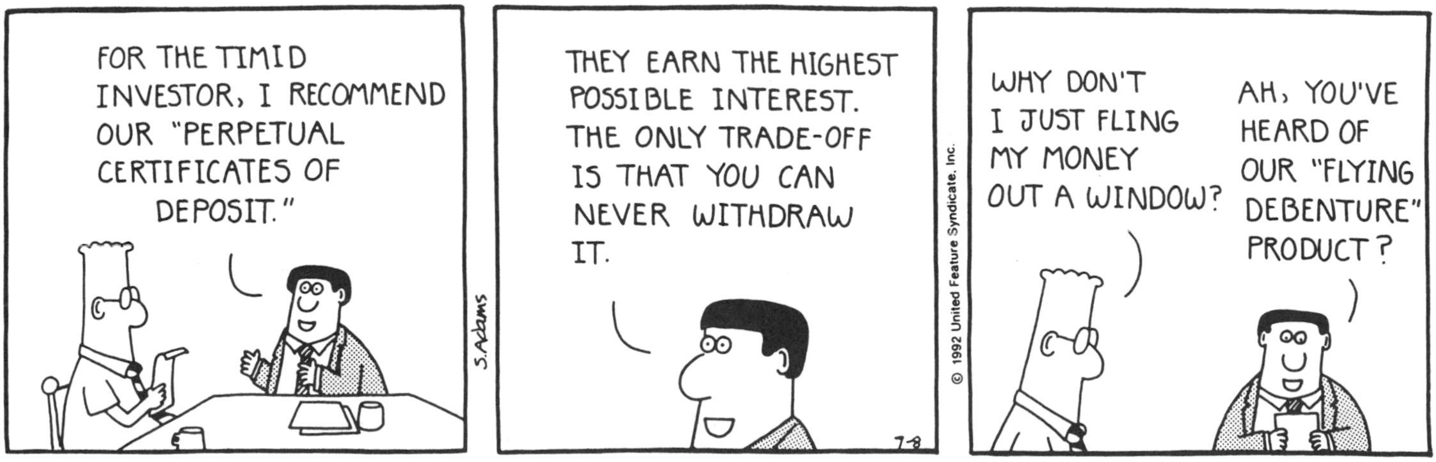
FOR THE TIMID INVESTOR, I RECOMMEND OUR "PERPETUAL CERTIFICATES OF DEPOSIT."
S. Adams
THEY EARN THE HIGHEST POSSIBLE INTEREST. THE ONLY TRADE-OFF IS THAT YOU CAN NEVER WITHDRAW IT.
7-8
© 1992 United Feature Syndicate, Inc.
WHY DON'T I JUST FLING MY MONEY OUT A WINDOW?
AH, YOU'VE HEARD OF OUR "FLYING DEBENTURE" PRODUCT?

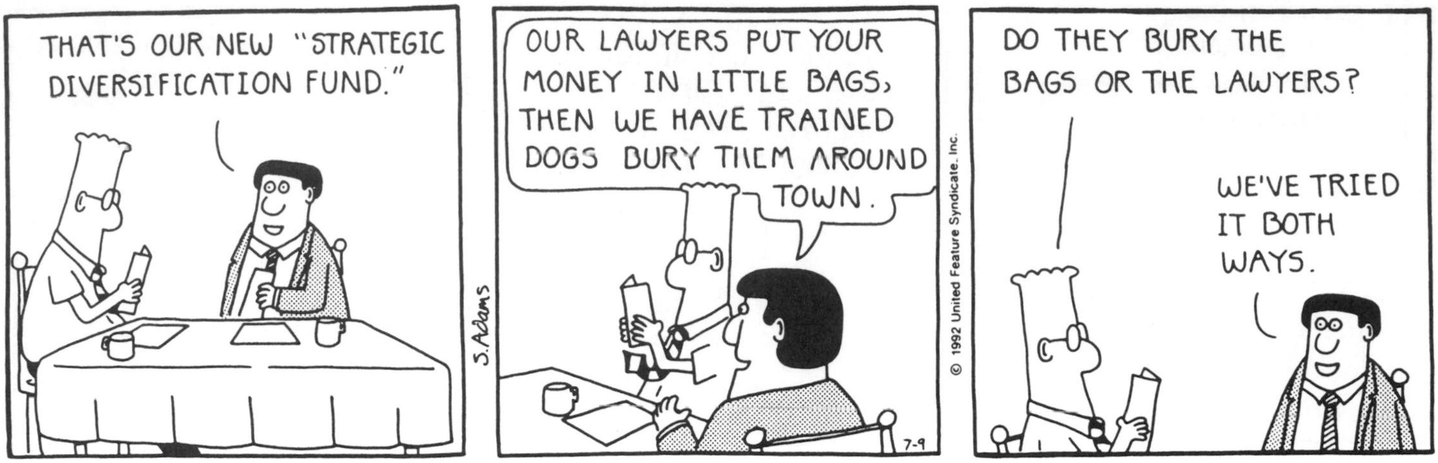
THAT'S OUR NEW "STRATEGIC DIVERSIFICATION FUND."
S. Adams
OUR LAWYERS PUT YOUR MONEY IN LITTLE BAGS, THEN WE HAVE TRAINED DOGS BURY THEM AROUND TOWN.
7-9
© 1992 United Feature Syndicate, Inc.
DO THEY BURY THE BAGS OR THE LAWYERS?
WE'VE TRIED IT BOTH WAYS.

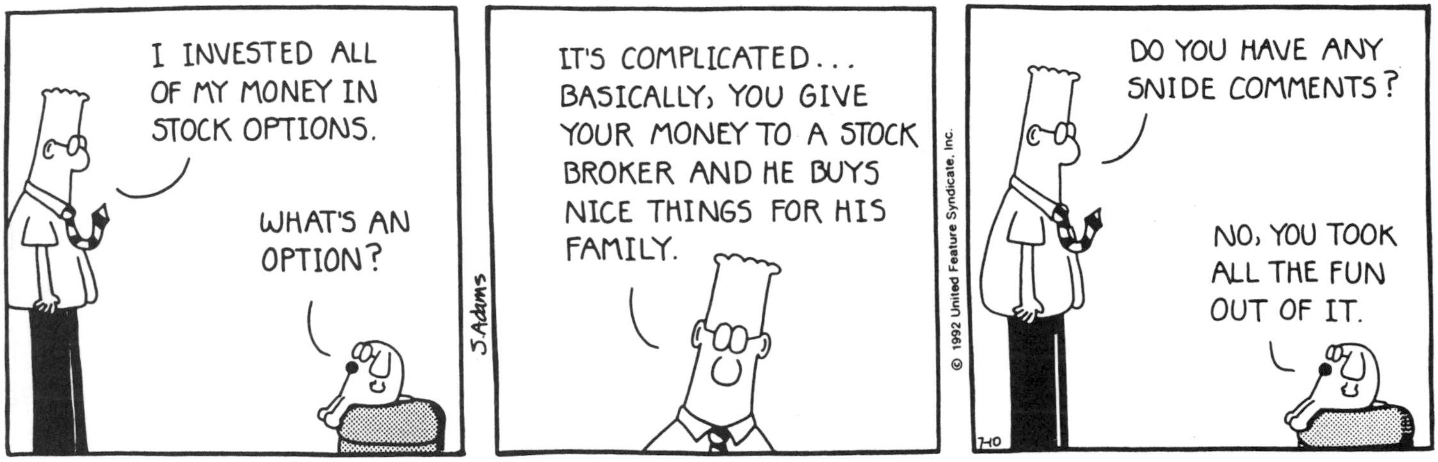
I INVESTED ALL OF MY MONEY IN STOCK OPTIONS.
WHAT'S AN OPTION?
S. Adams
IT'S COMPLICATED... BASICALLY, YOU GIVE YOUR MONEY TO A STOCK BROKER AND HE BUYS NICE THINGS FOR HIS FAMILY.
© 1992 United Feature Syndicate, Inc.
DO YOU HAVE ANY SNIDE COMMENTS?
NO, YOU TOOK ALL THE FUN OUT OF IT.
7-10

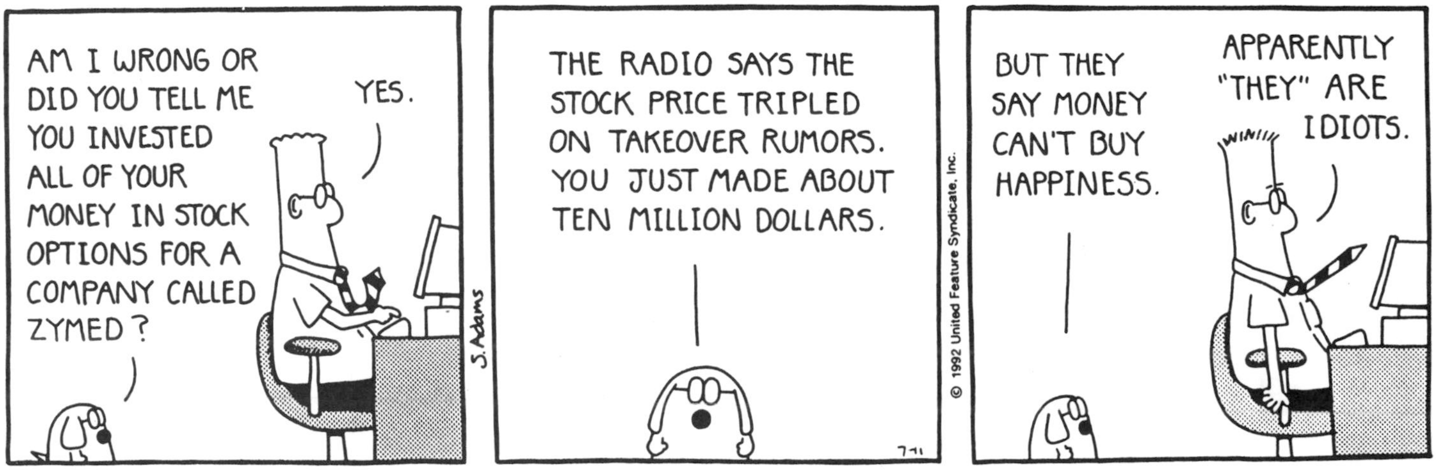
AM I WRONG OR DID YOU TELL ME YOU INVESTED ALL OF YOUR MONEY IN STOCK OPTIONS FOR A COMPANY CALLED ZYMED?
YES.
S. Adams
THE RADIO SAYS THE STOCK PRICE TRIPLED ON TAKEOVER RUMORS. YOU JUST MADE ABOUT TEN MILLION DOLLARS.
7-11
© 1992 United Feature Syndicate, Inc.
BUT THEY SAY MONEY CAN'T BUY HAPPINESS.
APPARENTLY "THEY" ARE IDIOTS.

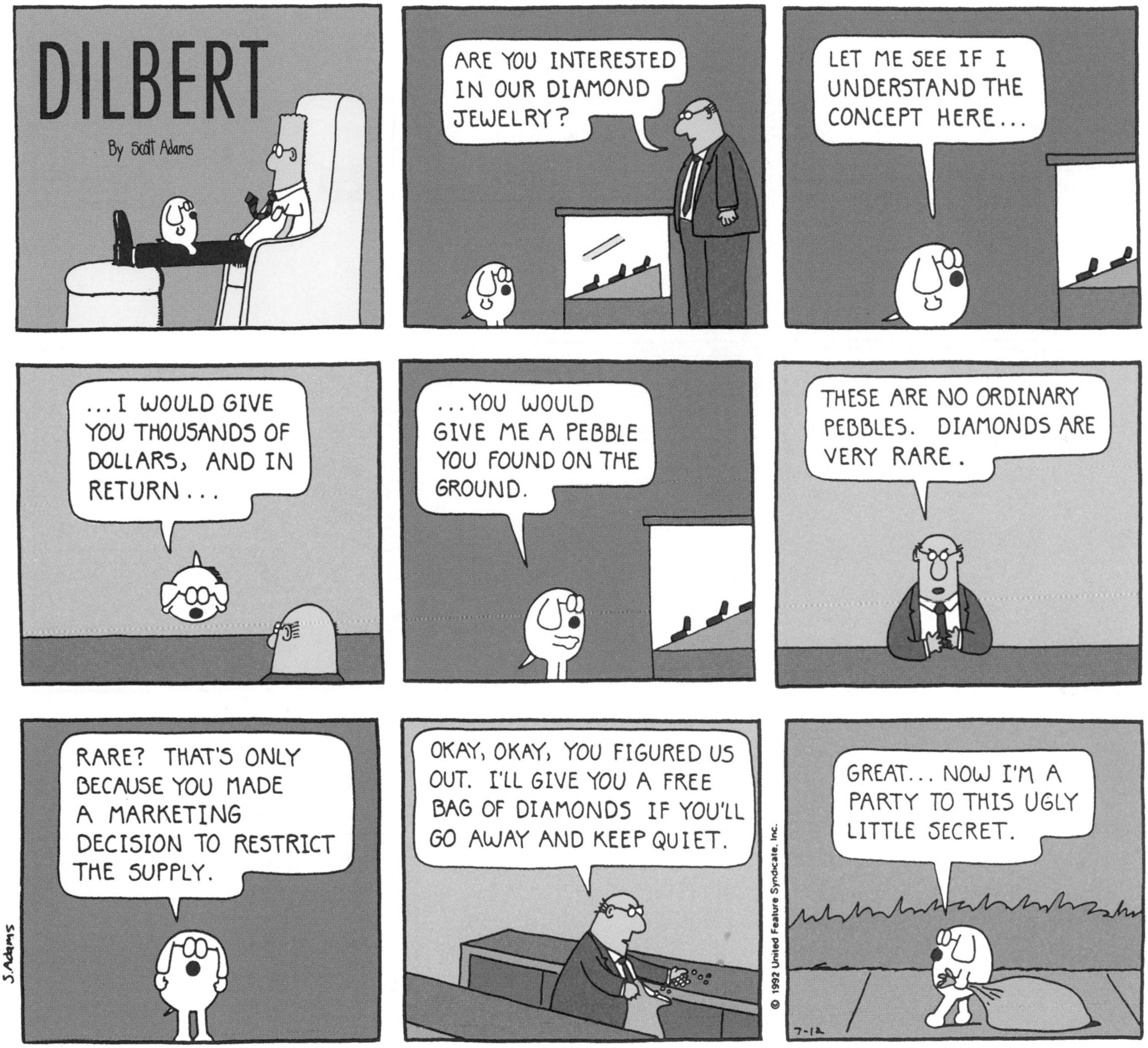
DILBERT
By Scott Adams
ARE YOU INTERESTED IN OUR DIAMOND JEWELRY?
LET ME SEE IF I UNDERSTAND THE CONCEPT HERE...
...I WOULD GIVE YOU THOUSANDS OF DOLLARS, AND IN RETURN...
...YOU WOULD GIVE ME A PEBBLE YOU FOUND ON THE GROUND.
THESE ARE NO ORDINARY PEBBLES. DIAMONDS ARE VERY RARE.
RARE? THAT'S ONLY BECAUSE YOU MADE A MARKETING DECISION TO RESTRICT THE SUPPLY.
S.Adams
OKAY, OKAY, YOU FIGURED US OUT. I'LL GIVE YOU A FREE BAG OF DIAMONDS IF YOU'LL GO AWAY AND KEEP QUIET.
© 1992 United Feature Syndicate, Inc.
GREAT... NOW I'M A PARTY TO THIS UGLY LITTLE SECRET.
7-12

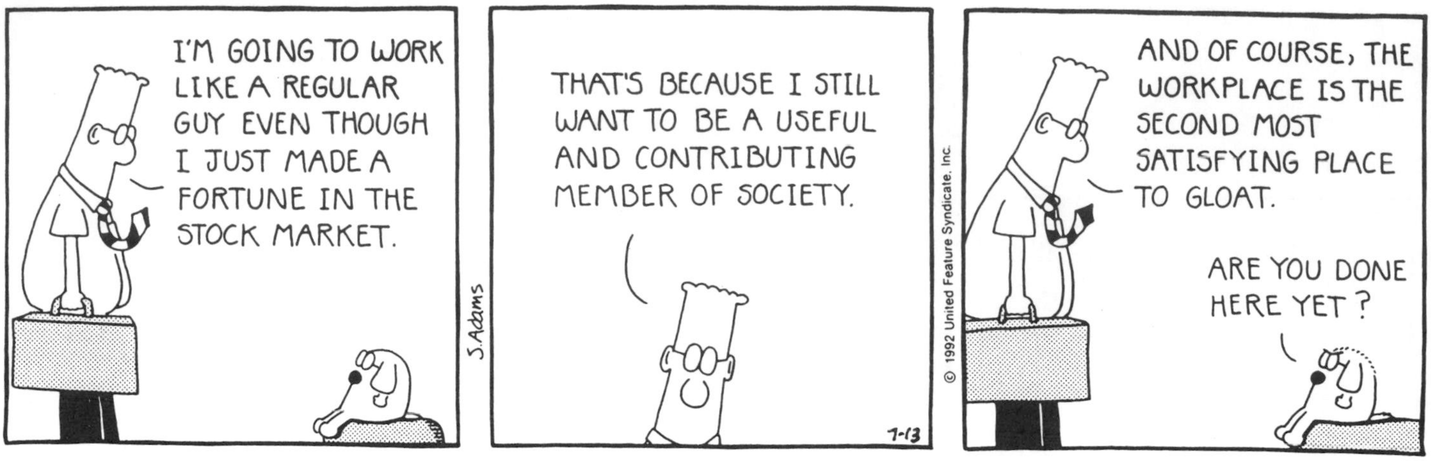
I'M GOING TO WORK LIKE A REGULAR GUY EVEN THOUGH I JUST MADE A FORTUNE IN THE STOCK MARKET.
S. Adams
THAT'S BECAUSE I STILL WANT TO BE A USEFUL AND CONTRIBUTING MEMBER OF SOCIETY.
7-13
© 1992 United Feature Syndicate, Inc.
AND OF COURSE, THE WORKPLACE IS THE SECOND MOST SATISFYING PLACE TO GLOAT.
ARE YOU DONE HERE YET ?

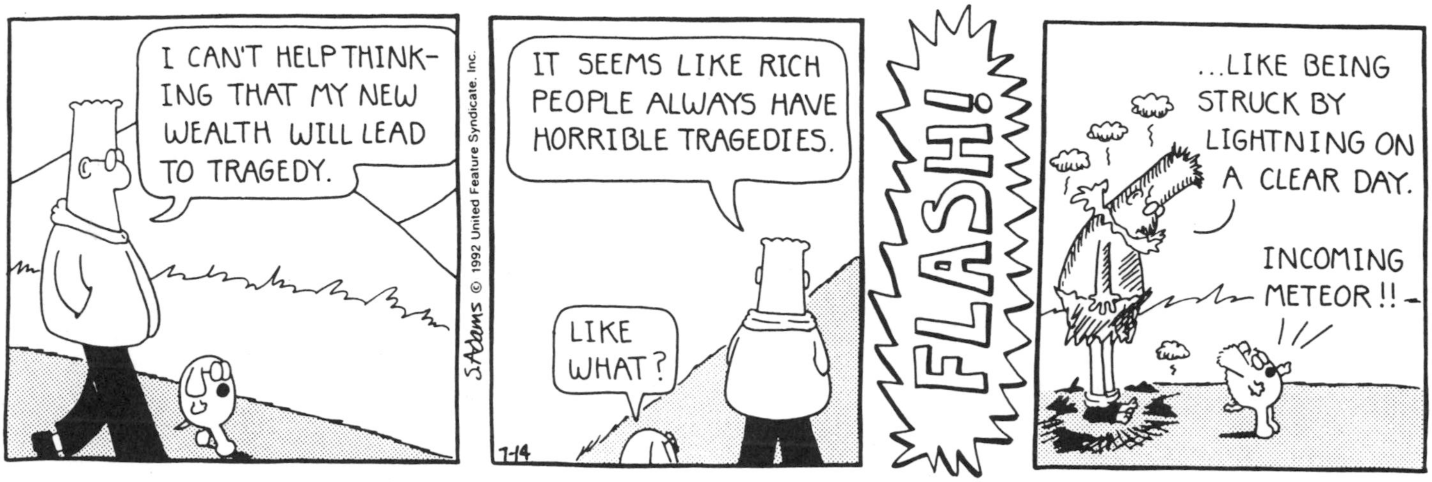
I CAN'T HELP THINKING THAT MY NEW WEALTH WILL LEAD TO TRAGEDY.
S. Adams © 1992 United Feature Syndicate, Inc.
IT SEEMS LIKE RICH PEOPLE ALWAYS HAVE HORRIBLE TRAGEDIES.
LIKE WHAT?
7-14
FLASH!
...LIKE BEING STRUCK BY LIGHTNING ON A CLEAR DAY.
INCOMING METEOR !!

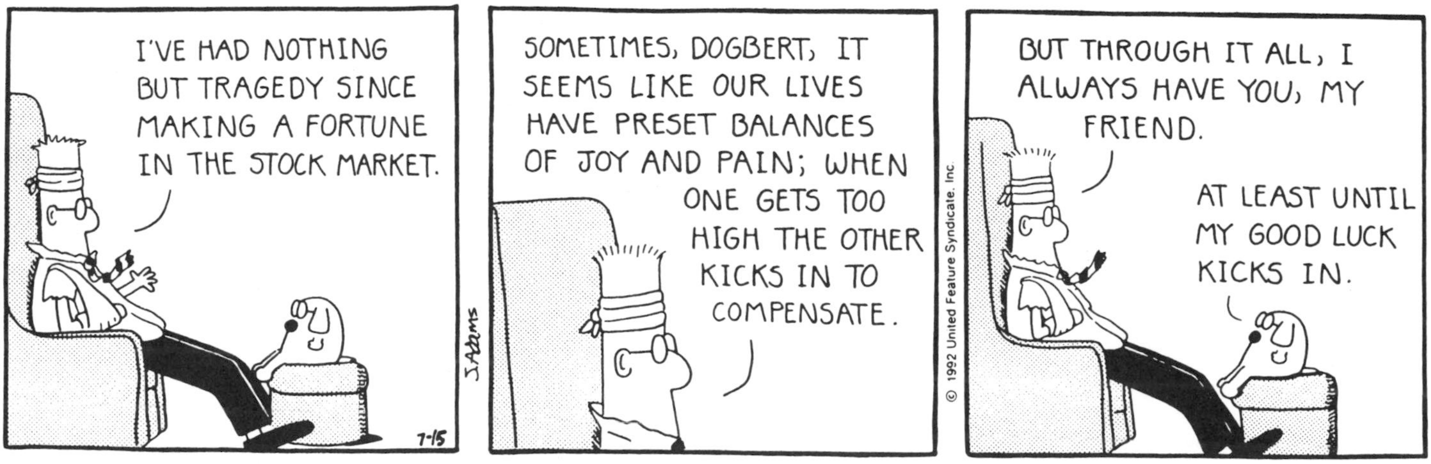
I'VE HAD NOTHING BUT TRAGEDY SINCE MAKING A FORTUNE IN THE STOCK MARKET.
7-15
S. Adams
SOMETIMES, DOGBERT, IT SEEMS LIKE OUR LIVES HAVE PRESET BALANCES OF JOY AND PAIN; WHEN ONE GETS TOO HIGH THE OTHER KICKS IN TO COMPENSATE.
© 1992 United Feature Syndicate, Inc.
BUT THROUGH IT ALL, I ALWAYS HAVE YOU, MY FRIEND.
AT LEAST UNTIL MY GOOD LUCK KICKS IN.

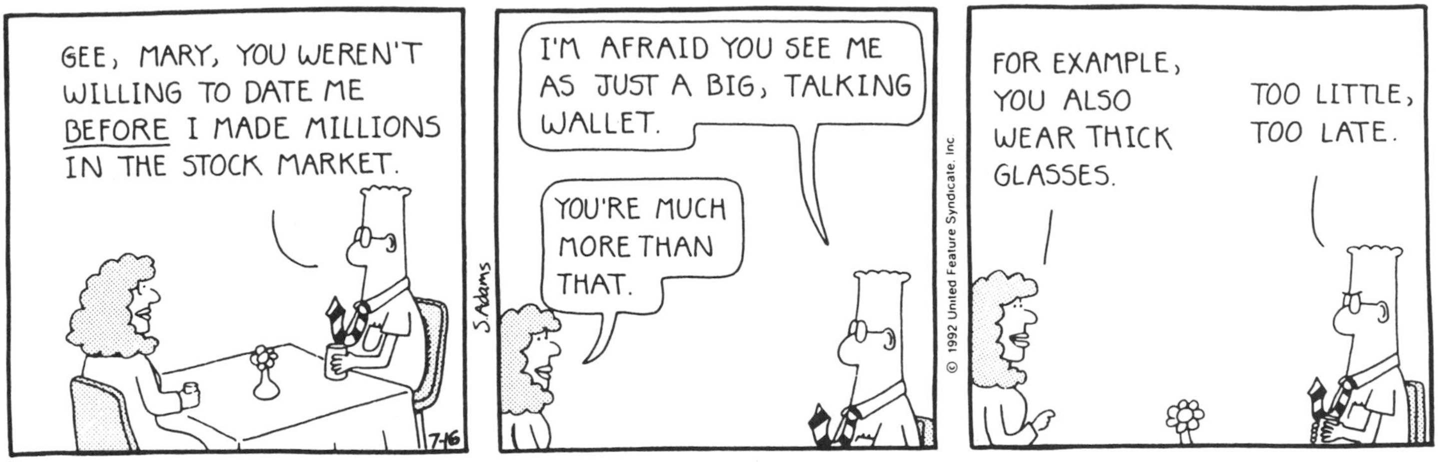
GEE, MARY, YOU WEREN'T WILLING TO DATE ME BEFORE I MADE MILLIONS IN THE STOCK MARKET.
7-16
S. Adams
I'M AFRAID YOU SEE ME AS JUST A BIG, TALKING WALLET.
YOU'RE MUCH MORE THAN THAT.
© 1992 United Feature Syndicate, Inc.
FOR EXAMPLE, YOU ALSO WEAR THICK GLASSES.
TOO LITTLE, TOO LATE.

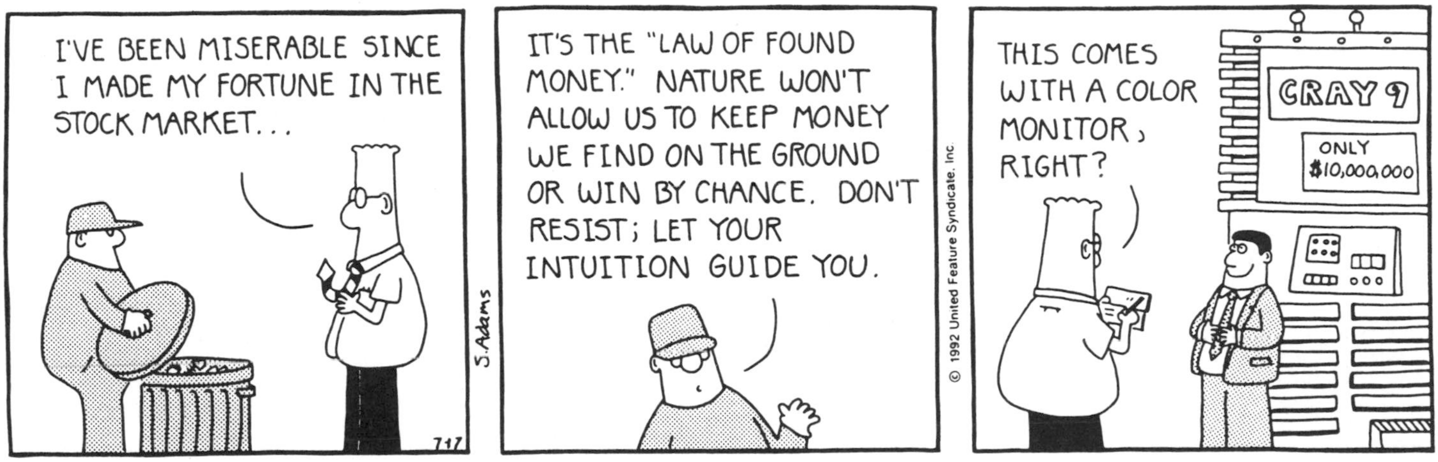
I'VE BEEN MISERABLE SINCE I MADE MY FORTUNE IN THE STOCK MARKET...
7-17
S. Adams
IT'S THE "LAW OF FOUND MONEY." NATURE WON'T ALLOW US TO KEEP MONEY WE FIND ON THE GROUND OR WIN BY CHANCE. DON'T RESIST; LET YOUR INTUITION GUIDE YOU.
© 1992 United Feature Syndicate, Inc.
THIS COMES WITH A COLOR MONITOR, RIGHT?
CRAY 9
ONLY $10,000,000

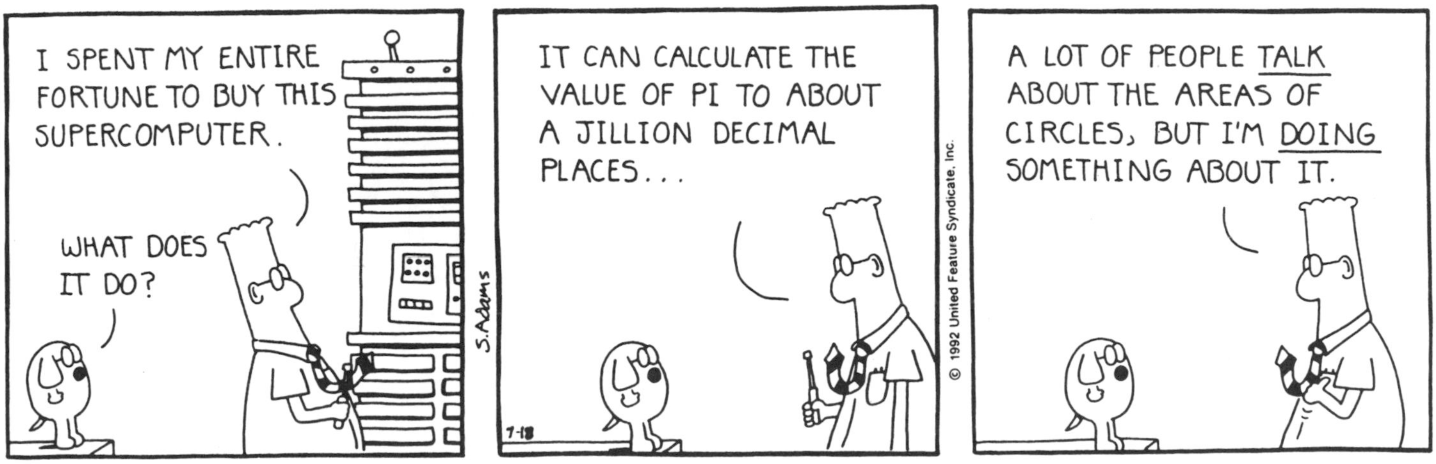
I SPENT MY ENTIRE FORTUNE TO BUY THIS SUPERCOMPUTER.
WHAT DOES IT DO?
S. Adams
IT CAN CALCULATE THE VALUE OF PI TO ABOUT A JILLION DECIMAL PLACES...
7-18
© 1992 United Feature Syndicate, Inc.
A LOT OF PEOPLE TALK ABOUT THE AREAS OF CIRCLES, BUT I'M DOING SOMETHING ABOUT IT.

DILBERT

By Scott Adams

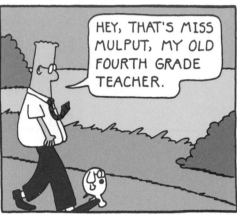

HEY, THAT'S MISS MULPUT, MY OLD FOURTH GRADE TEACHER.

HI, MISS MULPUT! DO YOU REMEMBER ME — DILBERT?

NO.

YOU USED TO MAKE ME WRITE ON THE BOARD A THOUSAND TIMES "I WILL NOT BE HOMELY IN CLASS."

OH, YEAH. THAT WAS A GOOD ONE.

AT THE TIME IT SEEMED LIKE PRETTY STRICT PUNISHMENT FOR CHEWING GUM.

BUT THAT EXPERIENCE MADE ME WHAT I AM TODAY...

AN ANGRY ADULT, OBSESSED WITH THOUGHTS OF REVENGE.

7-19

YOU KNOW, MISS "MOLEPIT," IF MY DOG HAD YOUR FACE I'D SHAVE HIS HINEY AND MAKE HIM WALK BACKWARD.

LEAVE ME OUT OF THIS.

S.Adams

© 1992 United Feature Syndicate, Inc.

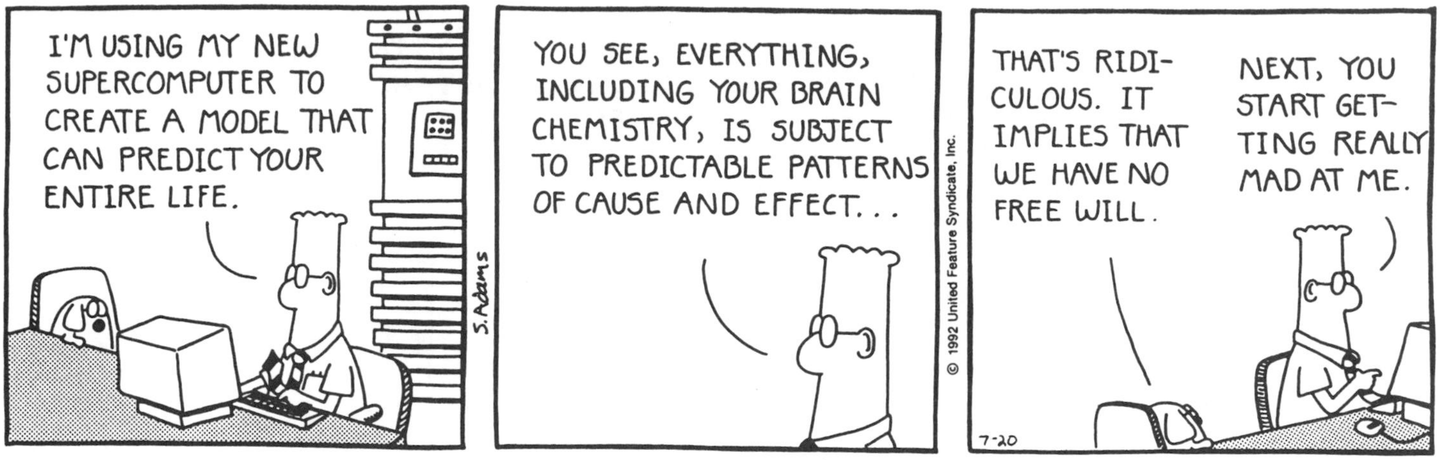
I'M USING MY NEW SUPERCOMPUTER TO CREATE A MODEL THAT CAN PREDICT YOUR ENTIRE LIFE.
S. Adams
YOU SEE, EVERYTHING, INCLUDING YOUR BRAIN CHEMISTRY, IS SUBJECT TO PREDICTABLE PATTERNS OF CAUSE AND EFFECT...
© 1992 United Feature Syndicate, Inc.
THAT'S RIDICULOUS. IT IMPLIES THAT WE HAVE NO FREE WILL.
NEXT, YOU START GETTING REALLY MAD AT ME.
7-20

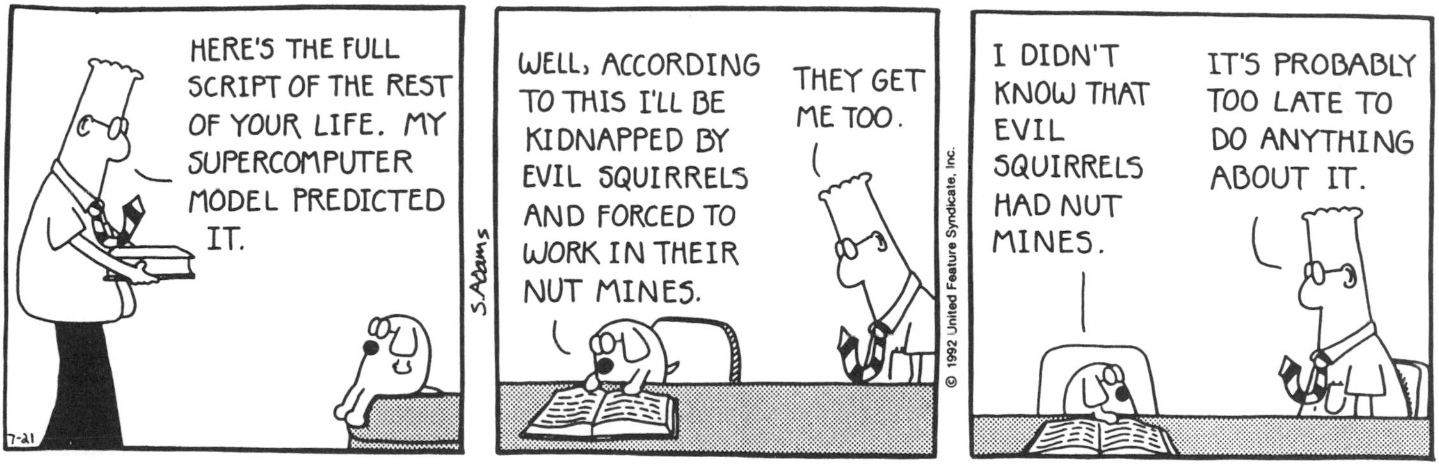
HERE'S THE FULL SCRIPT OF THE REST OF YOUR LIFE. MY SUPERCOMPUTER MODEL PREDICTED IT.
7-21
S. Adams
WELL, ACCORDING TO THIS I'LL BE KIDNAPPED BY EVIL SQUIRRELS AND FORCED TO WORK IN THEIR NUT MINES.
THEY GET ME TOO.
© 1992 United Feature Syndicate, Inc.
I DIDN'T KNOW THAT EVIL SQUIRRELS HAD NUT MINES.
IT'S PROBABLY TOO LATE TO DO ANYTHING ABOUT IT.

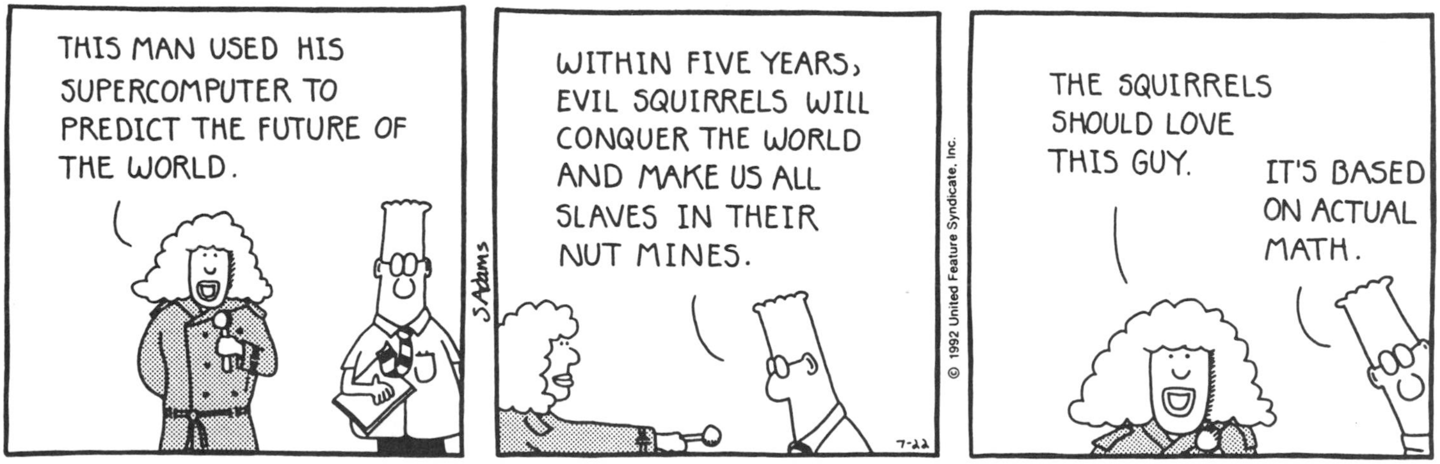
THIS MAN USED HIS SUPERCOMPUTER TO PREDICT THE FUTURE OF THE WORLD.
S. Adams
WITHIN FIVE YEARS, EVIL SQUIRRELS WILL CONQUER THE WORLD AND MAKE US ALL SLAVES IN THEIR NUT MINES.
7-22
© 1992 United Feature Syndicate, Inc.
THE SQUIRRELS SHOULD LOVE THIS GUY.
IT'S BASED ON ACTUAL MATH.

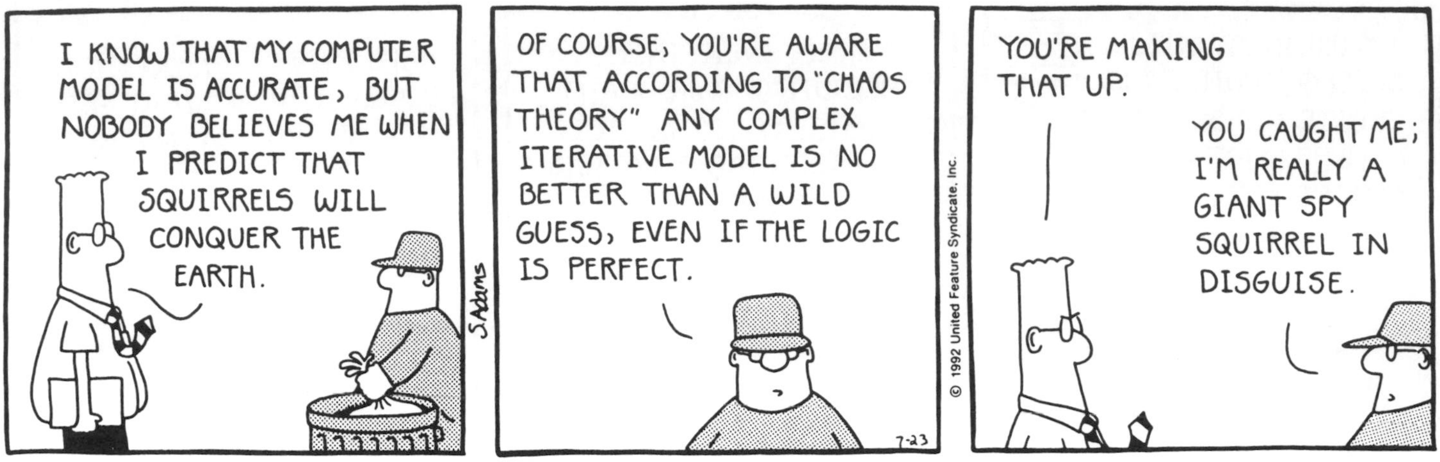
I KNOW THAT MY COMPUTER MODEL IS ACCURATE, BUT NOBODY BELIEVES ME WHEN I PREDICT THAT SQUIRRELS WILL CONQUER THE EARTH.
OF COURSE, YOU'RE AWARE THAT ACCORDING TO "CHAOS THEORY" ANY COMPLEX ITERATIVE MODEL IS NO BETTER THAN A WILD GUESS, EVEN IF THE LOGIC IS PERFECT.
YOU'RE MAKING THAT UP.
YOU CAUGHT ME; I'M REALLY A GIANT SPY SQUIRREL IN DISGUISE.
© 1992 United Feature Syndicate, Inc.

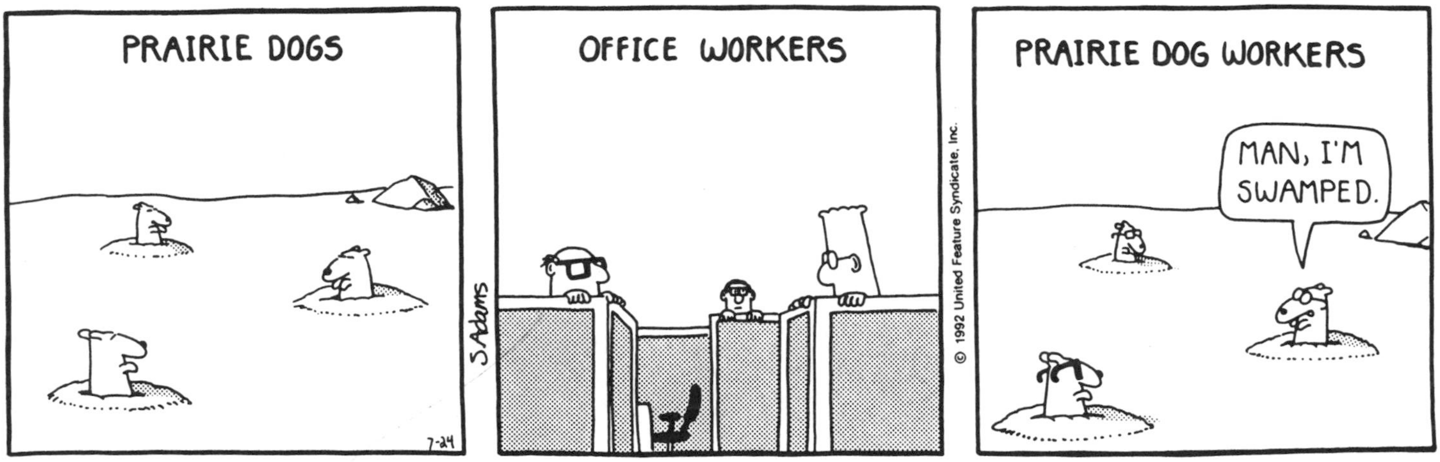
PRAIRIE DOGS
OFFICE WORKERS
PRAIRIE DOG WORKERS
MAN, I'M SWAMPED.
© 1992 United Feature Syndicate, Inc.

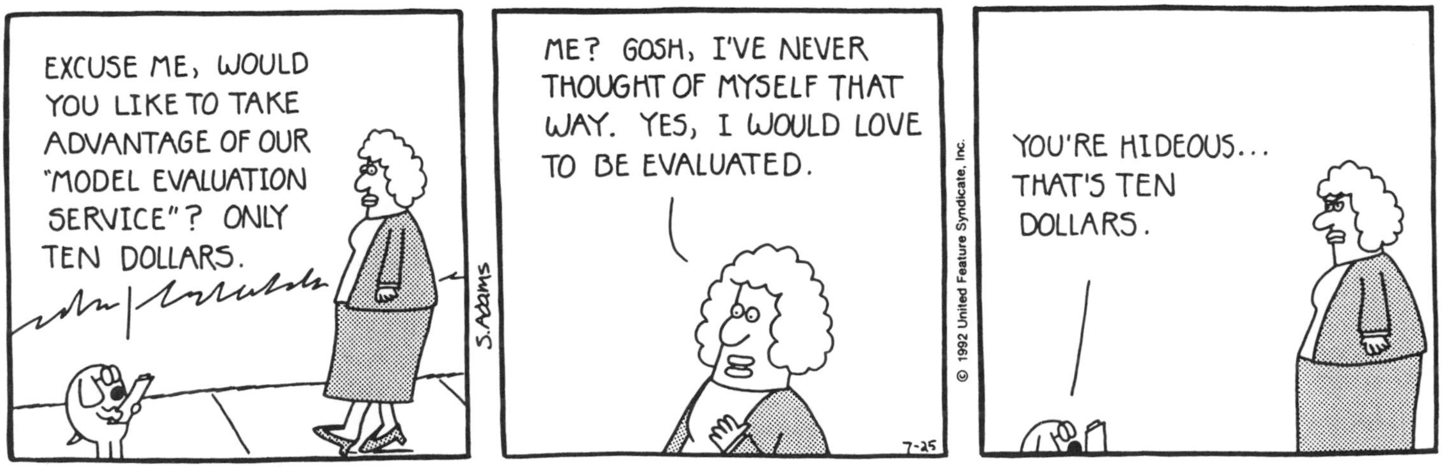
EXCUSE ME, WOULD YOU LIKE TO TAKE ADVANTAGE OF OUR "MODEL EVALUATION SERVICE"? ONLY TEN DOLLARS.
ME? GOSH, I'VE NEVER THOUGHT OF MYSELF THAT WAY. YES, I WOULD LOVE TO BE EVALUATED.
YOU'RE HIDEOUS... THAT'S TEN DOLLARS.
© 1992 United Feature Syndicate, Inc.

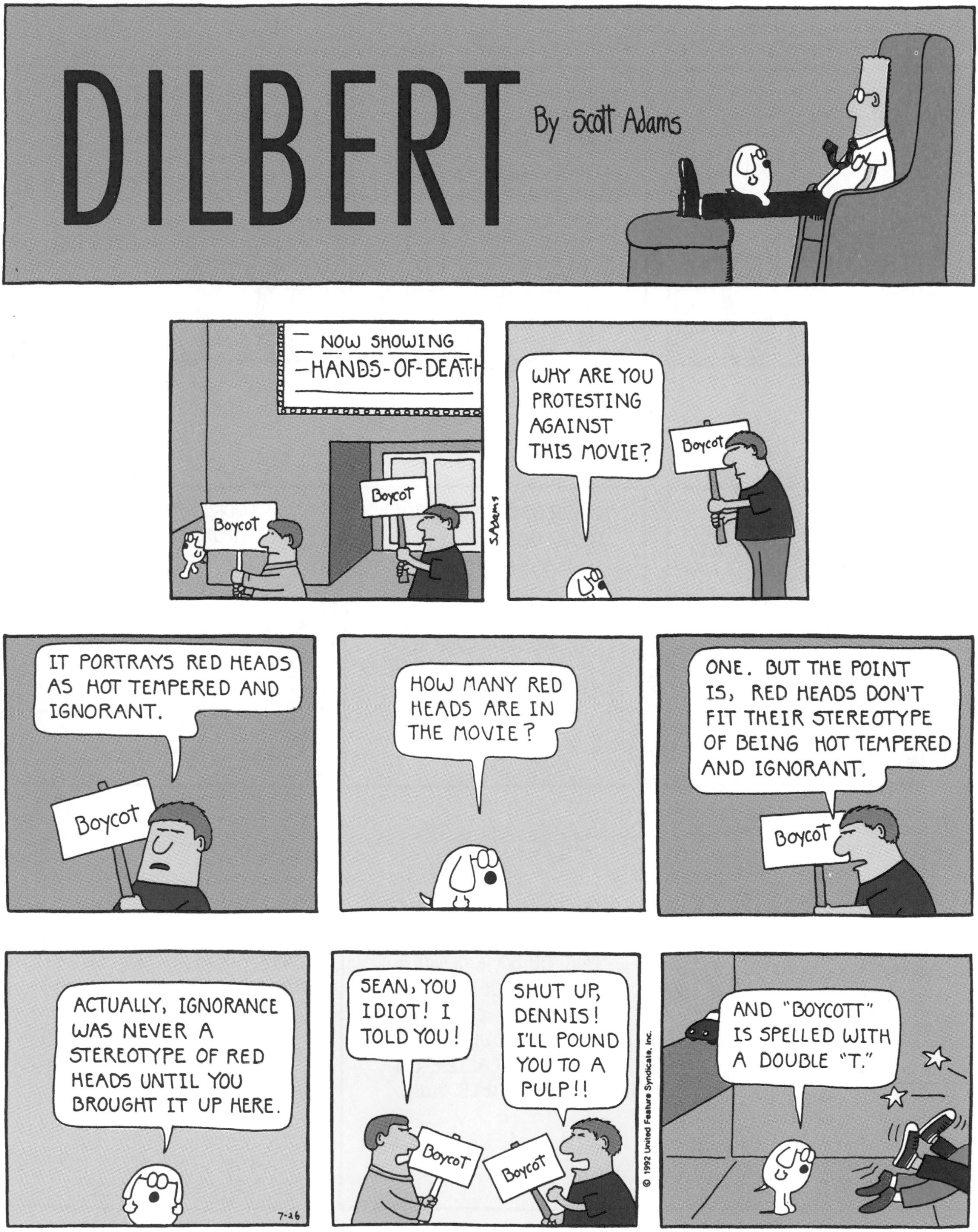
DILBERT
By Scott Adams
NOW SHOWING
HANDS-OF-DEATH
Boycot
Boycot
WHY ARE YOU PROTESTING AGAINST THIS MOVIE?
Boycot
IT PORTRAYS RED HEADS AS HOT TEMPERED AND IGNORANT.
Boycot
HOW MANY RED HEADS ARE IN THE MOVIE?
ONE. BUT THE POINT IS, RED HEADS DON'T FIT THEIR STEREOTYPE OF BEING HOT TEMPERED AND IGNORANT.
Boycot
ACTUALLY, IGNORANCE WAS NEVER A STEREOTYPE OF RED HEADS UNTIL YOU BROUGHT IT UP HERE.
SEAN, YOU IDIOT! I TOLD YOU!
SHUT UP, DENNIS! I'LL POUND YOU TO A PULP!!
Boycot
Boycot
© 1992 United Feature Syndicate, Inc.
AND "BOYCOTT" IS SPELLED WITH A DOUBLE "T."

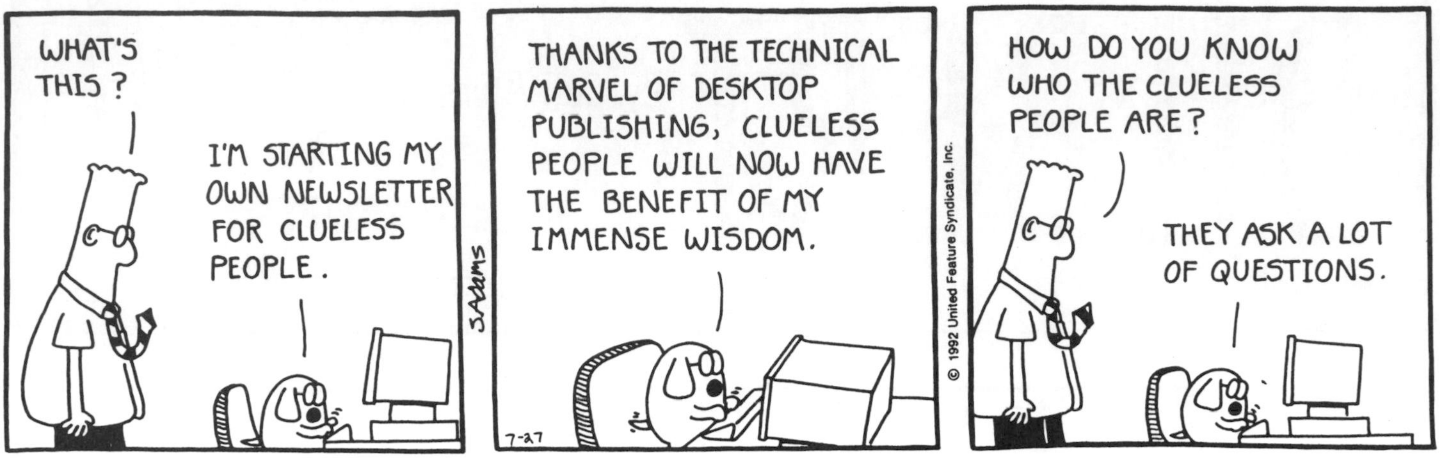
WHAT'S THIS?
I'M STARTING MY OWN NEWSLETTER FOR CLUELESS PEOPLE.
THANKS TO THE TECHNICAL MARVEL OF DESKTOP PUBLISHING, CLUELESS PEOPLE WILL NOW HAVE THE BENEFIT OF MY IMMENSE WISDOM.
© 1992 United Feature Syndicate, Inc.
HOW DO YOU KNOW WHO THE CLUELESS PEOPLE ARE?
THEY ASK A LOT OF QUESTIONS.

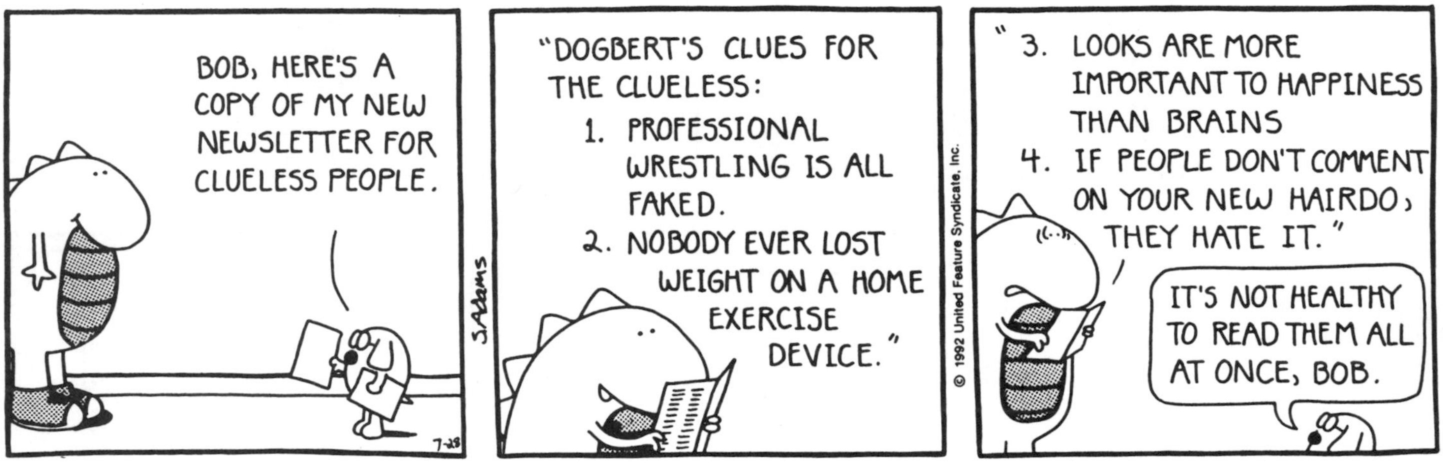
BOB, HERE'S A COPY OF MY NEW NEWSLETTER FOR CLUELESS PEOPLE.
"DOGBERT'S CLUES FOR THE CLUELESS:
1. PROFESSIONAL WRESTLING IS ALL FAKED.
2. NOBODY EVER LOST WEIGHT ON A HOME EXERCISE DEVICE."
© 1992 United Feature Syndicate, Inc.
" 3. LOOKS ARE MORE IMPORTANT TO HAPPINESS THAN BRAINS
4. IF PEOPLE DON'T COMMENT ON YOUR NEW HAIRDO, THEY HATE IT."
IT'S NOT HEALTHY TO READ THEM ALL AT ONCE, BOB.

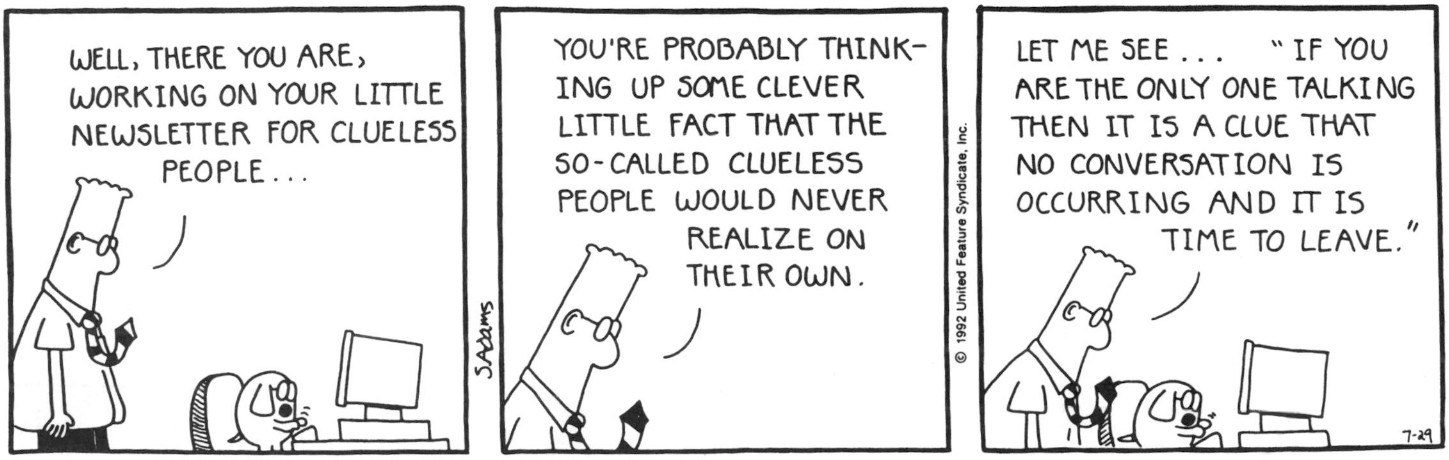
WELL, THERE YOU ARE, WORKING ON YOUR LITTLE NEWSLETTER FOR CLUELESS PEOPLE...
YOU'RE PROBABLY THINKING UP SOME CLEVER LITTLE FACT THAT THE SO-CALLED CLUELESS PEOPLE WOULD NEVER REALIZE ON THEIR OWN.
© 1992 United Feature Syndicate, Inc.
LET ME SEE... "IF YOU ARE THE ONLY ONE TALKING THEN IT IS A CLUE THAT NO CONVERSATION IS OCCURRING AND IT IS TIME TO LEAVE."

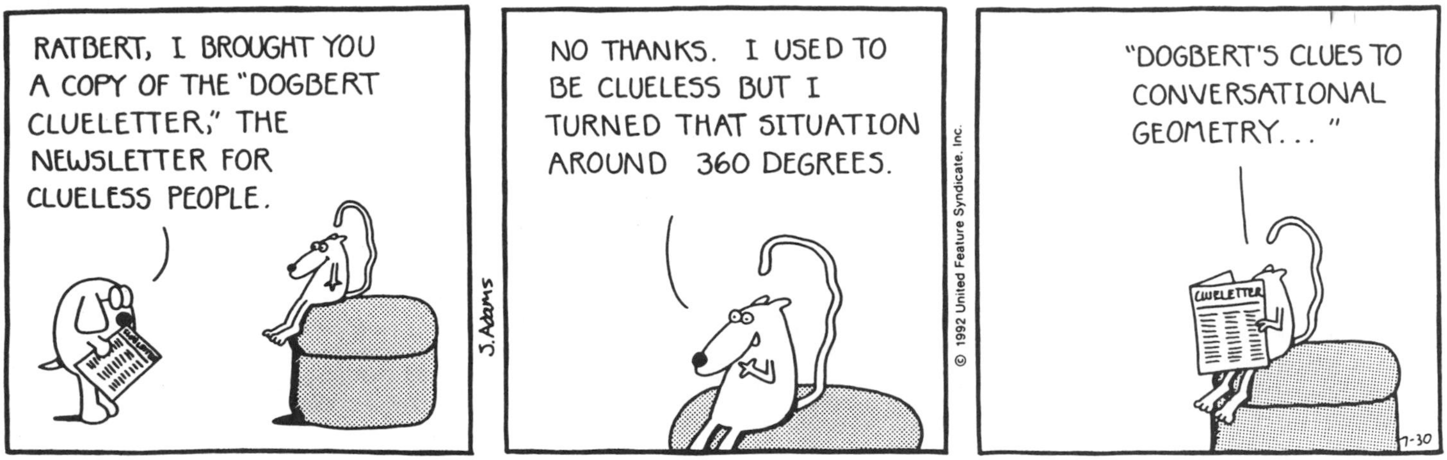
RATBERT, I BROUGHT YOU A COPY OF THE "DOGBERT CLUELETTER," THE NEWSLETTER FOR CLUELESS PEOPLE.
S. Adams
NO THANKS. I USED TO BE CLUELESS BUT I TURNED THAT SITUATION AROUND 360 DEGREES.
© 1992 United Feature Syndicate, Inc.
"DOGBERT'S CLUES TO CONVERSATIONAL GEOMETRY..."
CLUELETTER
7-30

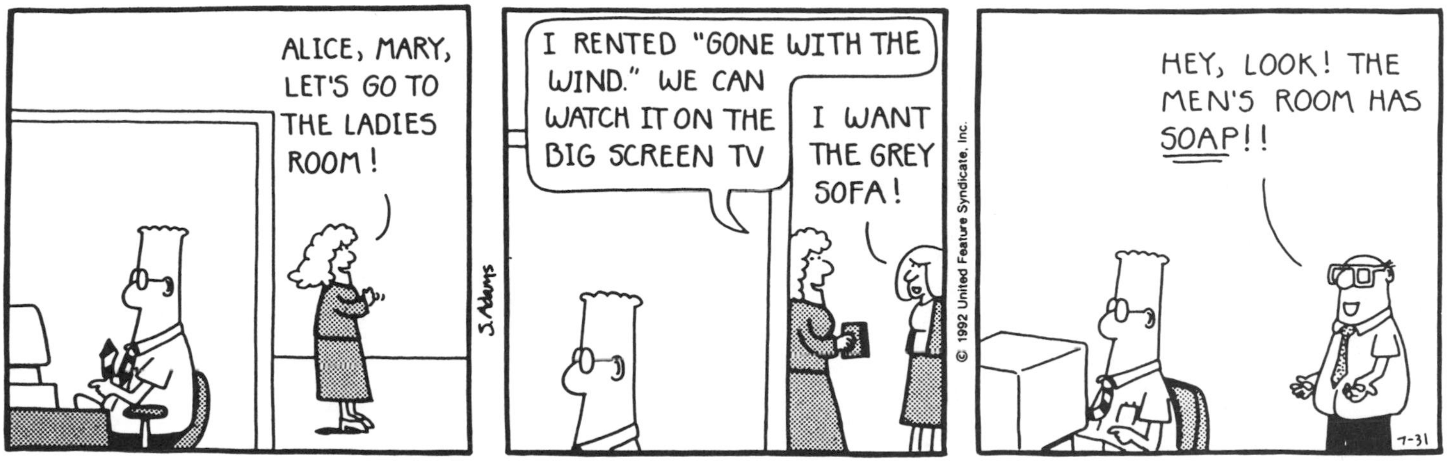
ALICE, MARY, LET'S GO TO THE LADIES ROOM!
S. Adams
I RENTED "GONE WITH THE WIND." WE CAN WATCH IT ON THE BIG SCREEN TV
I WANT THE GREY SOFA!
© 1992 United Feature Syndicate, Inc.
HEY, LOOK! THE MEN'S ROOM HAS SOAP!!
7-31

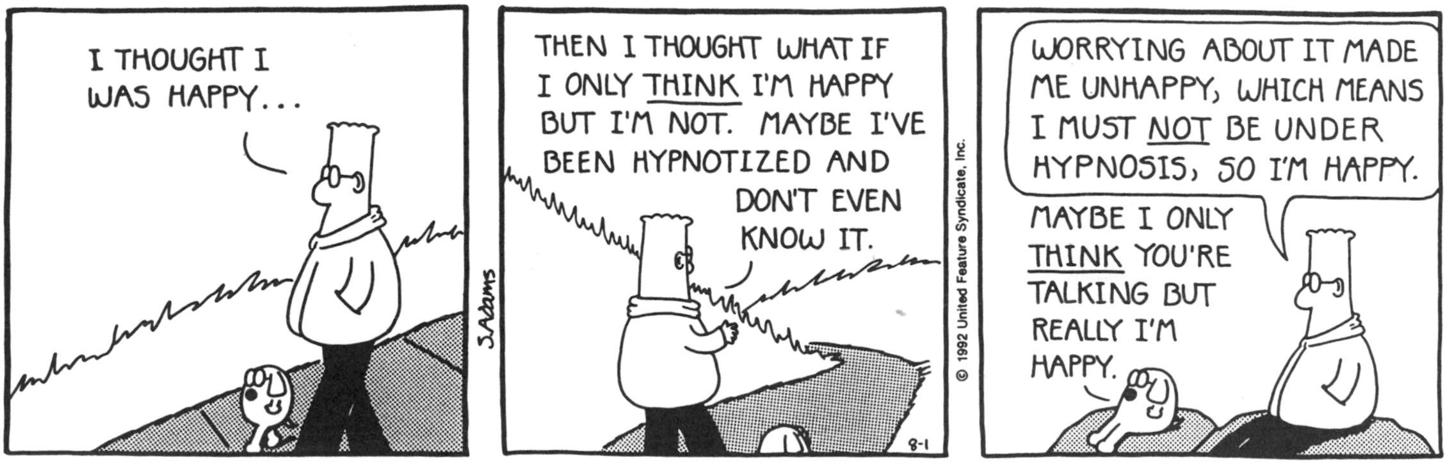
I THOUGHT I WAS HAPPY...
S. Adams
THEN I THOUGHT WHAT IF I ONLY THINK I'M HAPPY BUT I'M NOT. MAYBE I'VE BEEN HYPNOTIZED AND DON'T EVEN KNOW IT.
8-1
© 1992 United Feature Syndicate, Inc.
WORRYING ABOUT IT MADE ME UNHAPPY, WHICH MEANS I MUST NOT BE UNDER HYPNOSIS, SO I'M HAPPY.
MAYBE I ONLY THINK YOU'RE TALKING BUT REALLY I'M HAPPY.

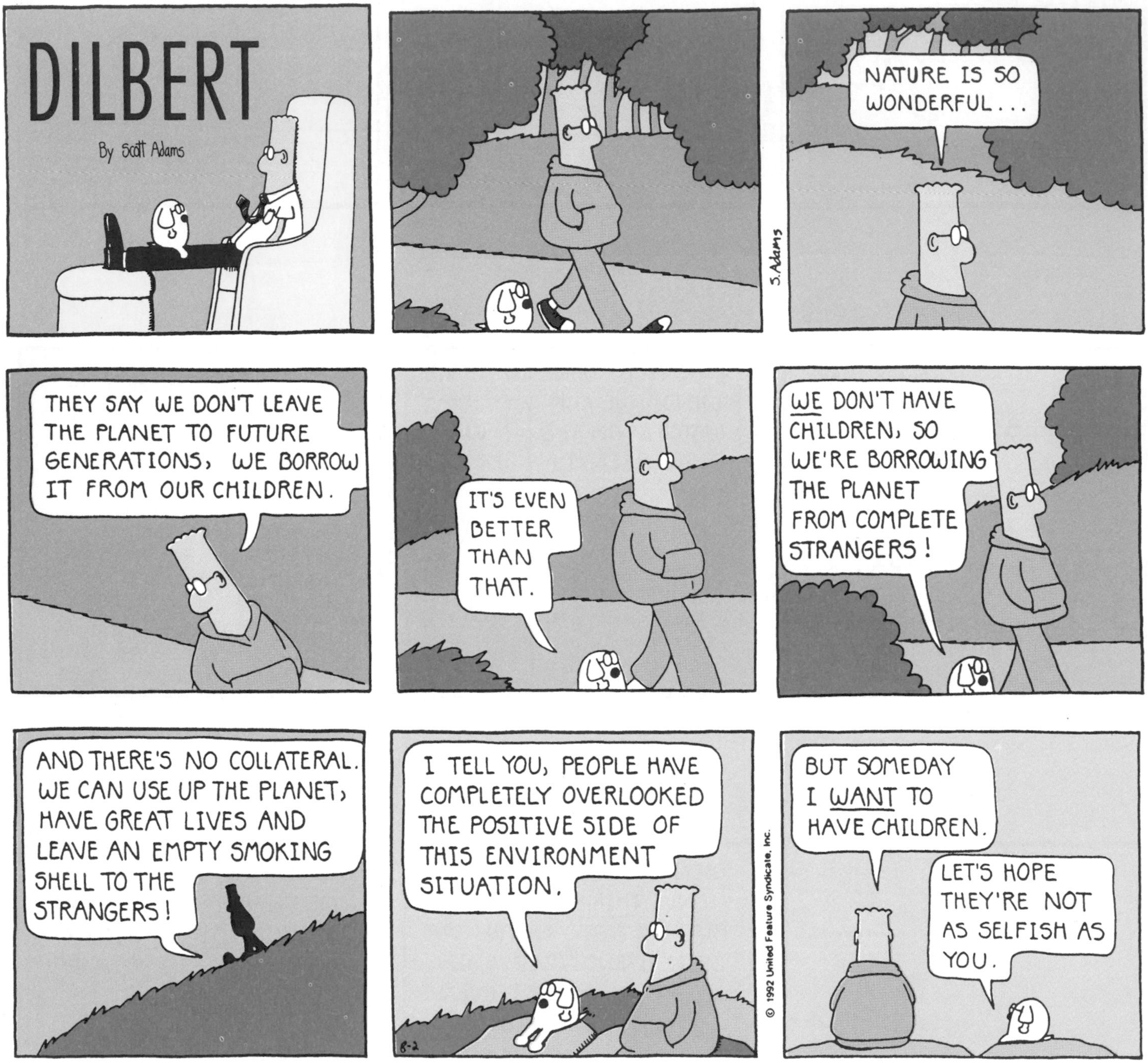

DILBERT
By Scott Adams
S. Adams
NATURE IS SO WONDERFUL . . .
THEY SAY WE DON'T LEAVE THE PLANET TO FUTURE GENERATIONS, WE BORROW IT FROM OUR CHILDREN.
IT'S EVEN BETTER THAN THAT.
WE DON'T HAVE CHILDREN, SO WE'RE BORROWING THE PLANET FROM COMPLETE STRANGERS!
AND THERE'S NO COLLATERAL. WE CAN USE UP THE PLANET, HAVE GREAT LIVES AND LEAVE AN EMPTY SMOKING SHELL TO THE STRANGERS!
I TELL YOU, PEOPLE HAVE COMPLETELY OVERLOOKED THE POSITIVE SIDE OF THIS ENVIRONMENT SITUATION.
8-2
© 1992 United Feature Syndicate, Inc.
BUT SOMEDAY I WANT TO HAVE CHILDREN.
LET'S HOPE THEY'RE NOT AS SELFISH AS YOU.

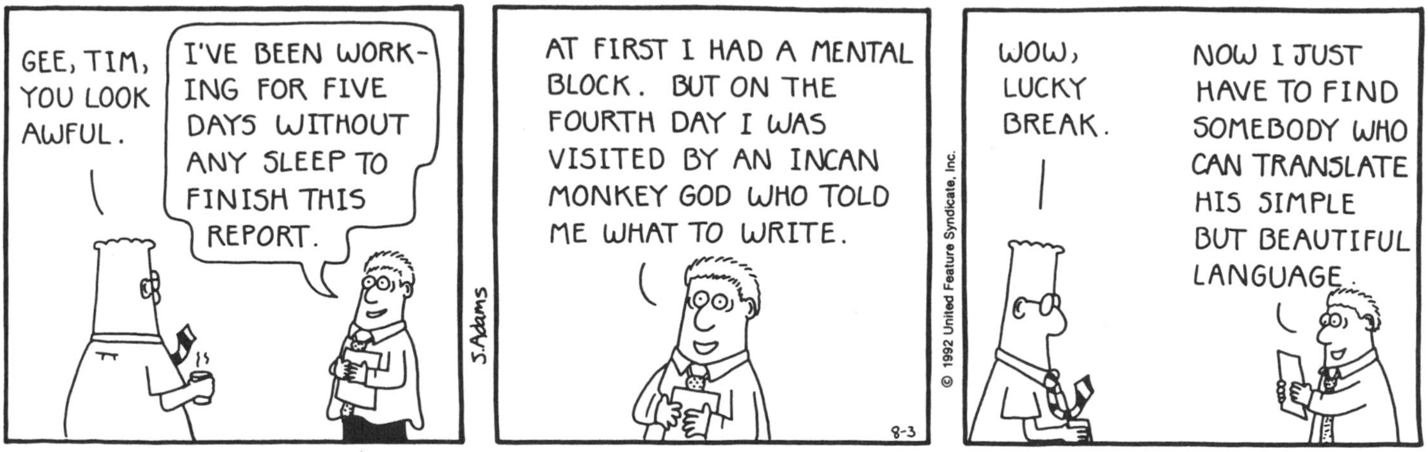
GEE, TIM, YOU LOOK AWFUL.
I'VE BEEN WORKING FOR FIVE DAYS WITHOUT ANY SLEEP TO FINISH THIS REPORT.
S. Adams
AT FIRST I HAD A MENTAL BLOCK. BUT ON THE FOURTH DAY I WAS VISITED BY AN INCAN MONKEY GOD WHO TOLD ME WHAT TO WRITE.
8-3
© 1992 United Feature Syndicate, Inc.
WOW, LUCKY BREAK.
NOW I JUST HAVE TO FIND SOMEBODY WHO CAN TRANSLATE HIS SIMPLE BUT BEAUTIFUL LANGUAGE.

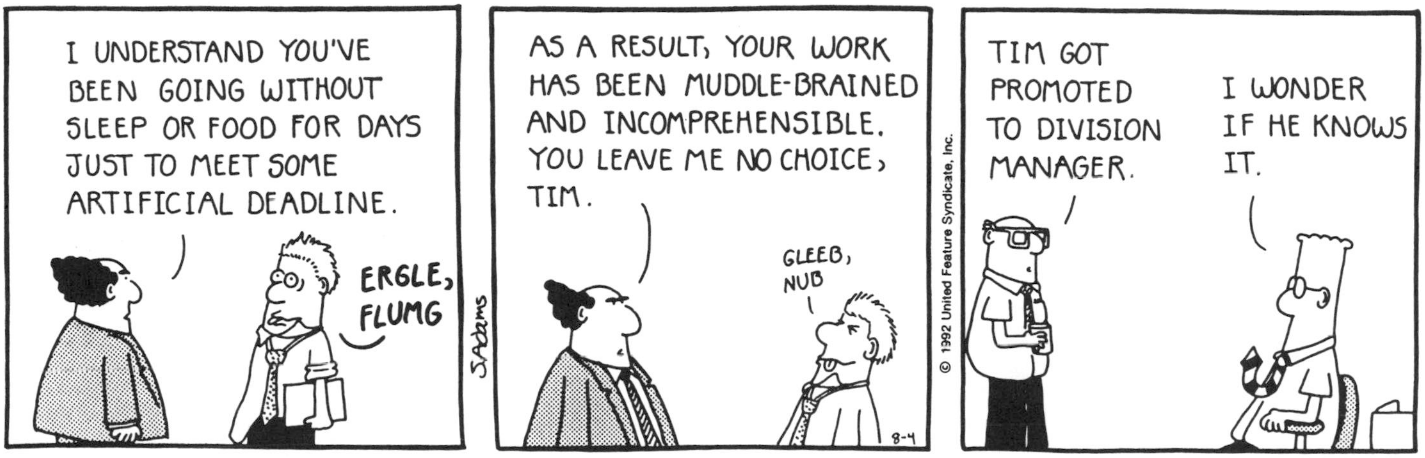
I UNDERSTAND YOU'VE BEEN GOING WITHOUT SLEEP OR FOOD FOR DAYS JUST TO MEET SOME ARTIFICIAL DEADLINE.
ERGLE, FLUMG
S. Adams
AS A RESULT, YOUR WORK HAS BEEN MUDDLE-BRAINED AND INCOMPREHENSIBLE. YOU LEAVE ME NO CHOICE, TIM.
GLEEB, NUB
8-4
© 1992 United Feature Syndicate, Inc.
TIM GOT PROMOTED TO DIVISION MANAGER.
I WONDER IF HE KNOWS IT.

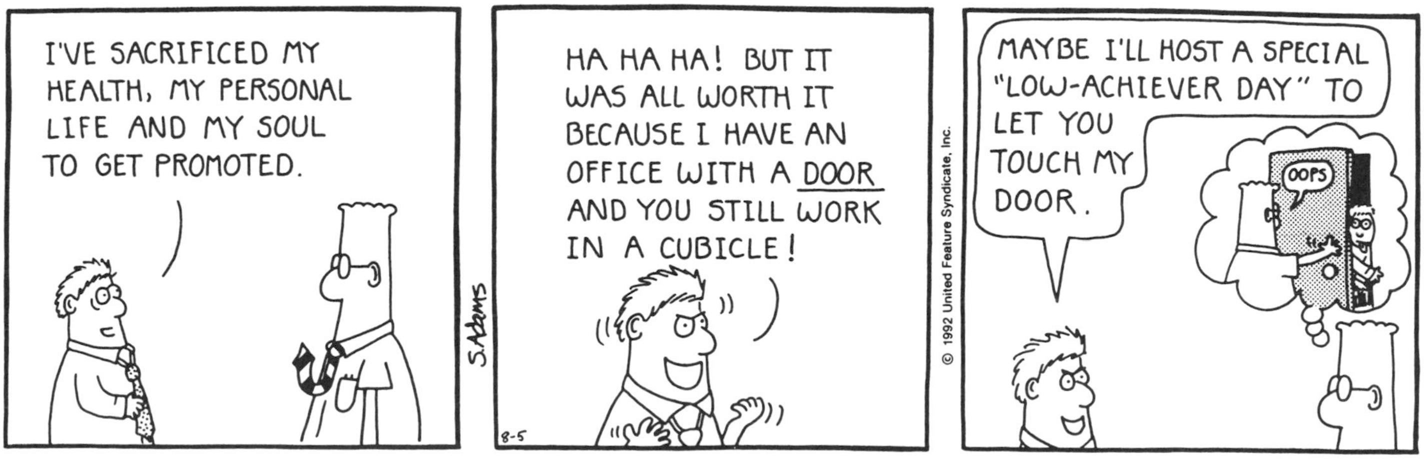
I'VE SACRIFICED MY HEALTH, MY PERSONAL LIFE AND MY SOUL TO GET PROMOTED.
S. Adams
8-5
HA HA HA! BUT IT WAS ALL WORTH IT BECAUSE I HAVE AN OFFICE WITH A DOOR AND YOU STILL WORK IN A CUBICLE!
© 1992 United Feature Syndicate, Inc.
MAYBE I'LL HOST A SPECIAL "LOW-ACHIEVER DAY" TO LET YOU TOUCH MY DOOR.
OOPS

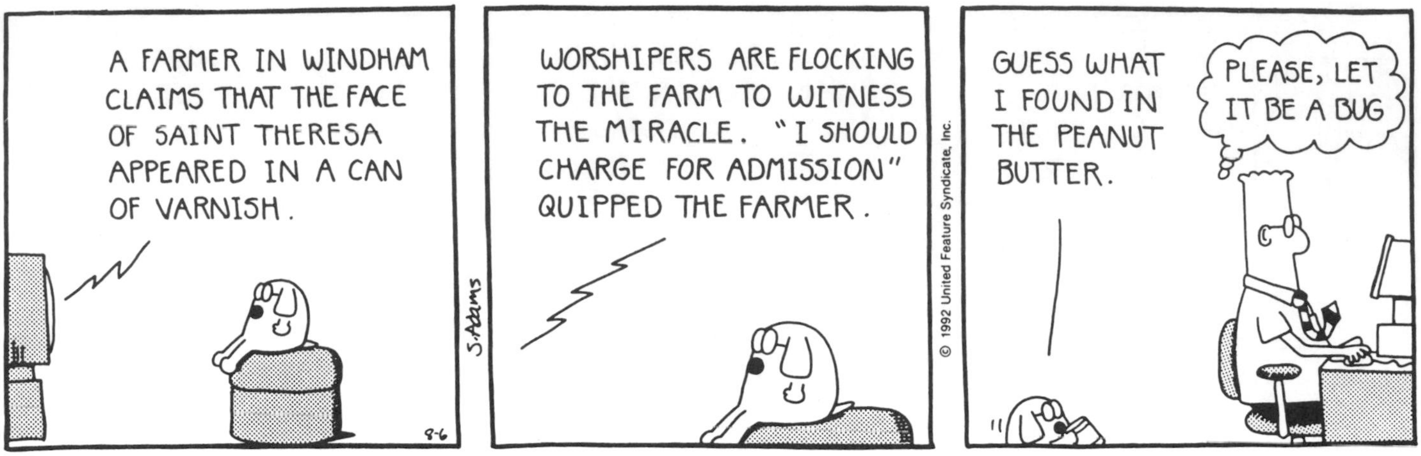
A FARMER IN WINDHAM CLAIMS THAT THE FACE OF SAINT THERESA APPEARED IN A CAN OF VARNISH.
WORSHIPERS ARE FLOCKING TO THE FARM TO WITNESS THE MIRACLE. "I SHOULD CHARGE FOR ADMISSION" QUIPPED THE FARMER.
GUESS WHAT I FOUND IN THE PEANUT BUTTER.
PLEASE, LET IT BE A BUG
© 1992 United Feature Syndicate, Inc.
S. Adams
8-6

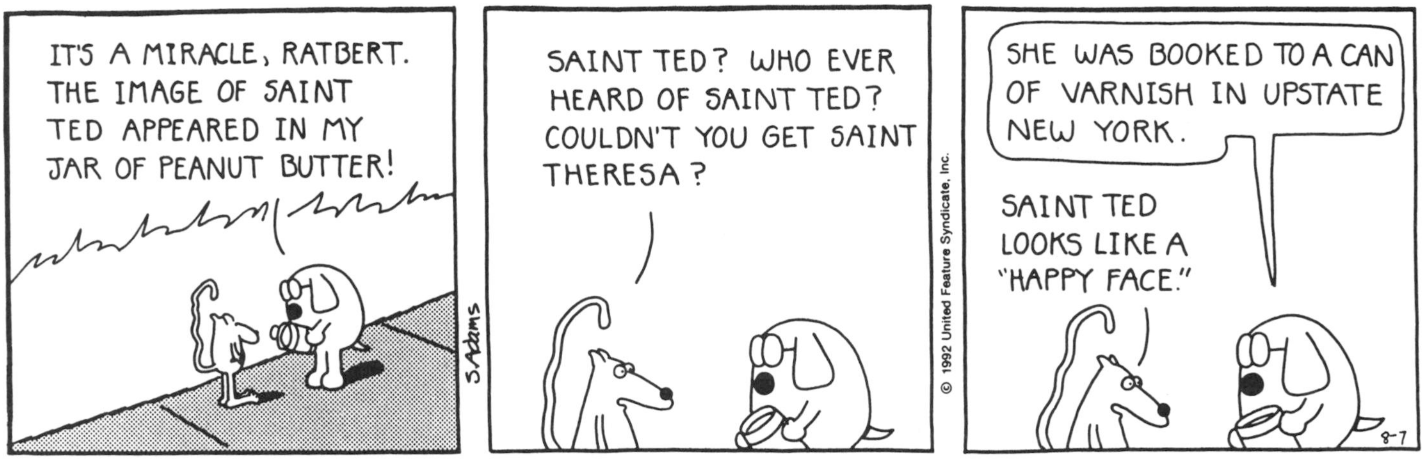
IT'S A MIRACLE, RATBERT. THE IMAGE OF SAINT TED APPEARED IN MY JAR OF PEANUT BUTTER!
SAINT TED? WHO EVER HEARD OF SAINT TED? COULDN'T YOU GET SAINT THERESA?
SHE WAS BOOKED TO A CAN OF VARNISH IN UPSTATE NEW YORK.
SAINT TED LOOKS LIKE A "HAPPY FACE."
© 1992 United Feature Syndicate, Inc.
S. Adams
8-7

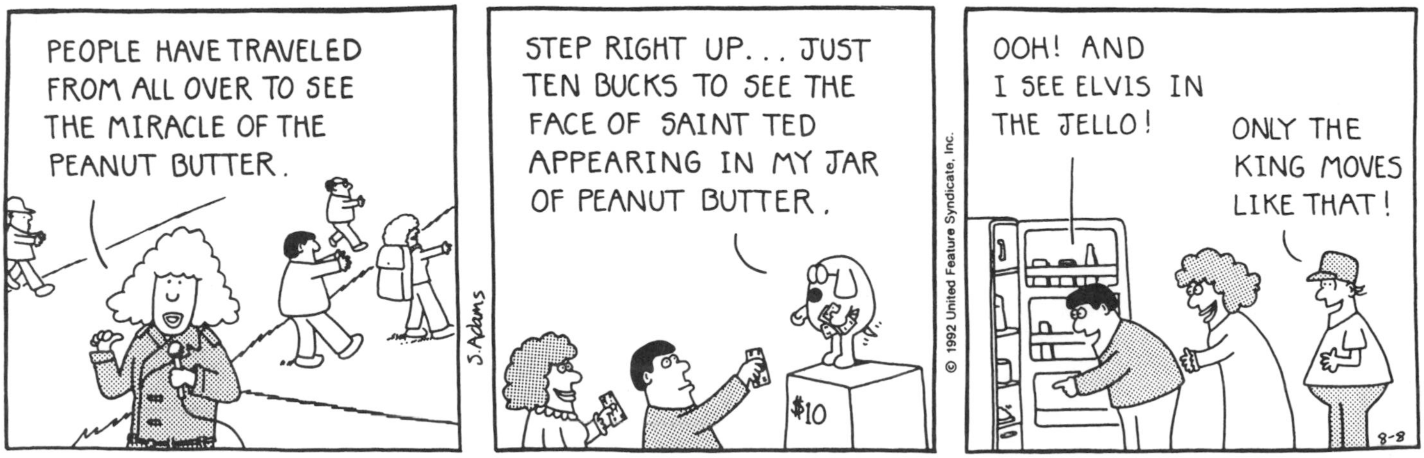
PEOPLE HAVE TRAVELED FROM ALL OVER TO SEE THE MIRACLE OF THE PEANUT BUTTER.
STEP RIGHT UP... JUST TEN BUCKS TO SEE THE FACE OF SAINT TED APPEARING IN MY JAR OF PEANUT BUTTER.
$10
OOH! AND I SEE ELVIS IN THE JELLO!
ONLY THE KING MOVES LIKE THAT!
© 1992 United Feature Syndicate, Inc.
S. Adams
8-8

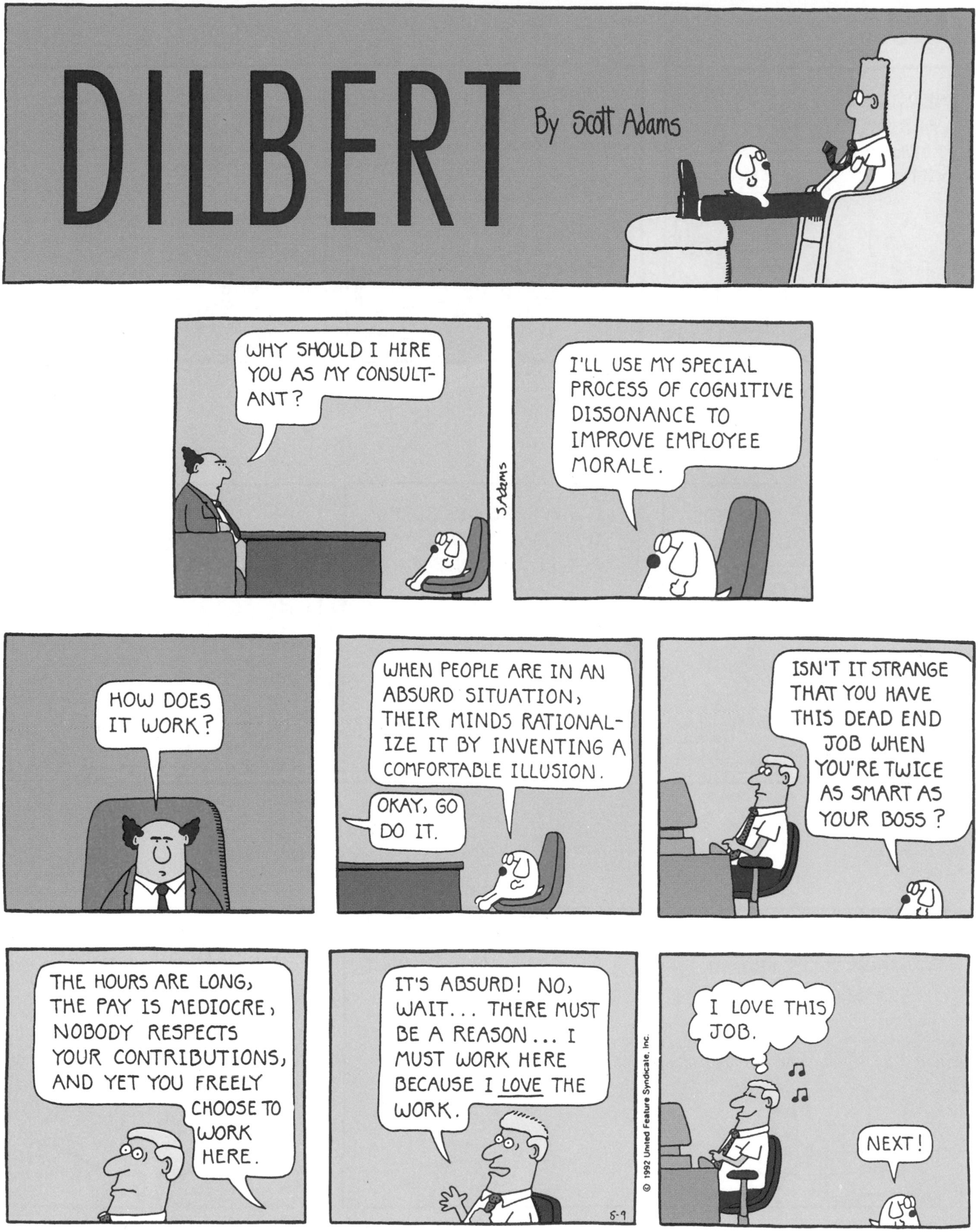
DILBERT
By Scott Adams
WHY SHOULD I HIRE YOU AS MY CONSULT-ANT?
S.ADAMS
I'LL USE MY SPECIAL PROCESS OF COGNITIVE DISSONANCE TO IMPROVE EMPLOYEE MORALE.
HOW DOES IT WORK?
WHEN PEOPLE ARE IN AN ABSURD SITUATION, THEIR MINDS RATIONAL-IZE IT BY INVENTING A COMFORTABLE ILLUSION.
OKAY, GO DO IT.
ISN'T IT STRANGE THAT YOU HAVE THIS DEAD END JOB WHEN YOU'RE TWICE AS SMART AS YOUR BOSS?
THE HOURS ARE LONG, THE PAY IS MEDIOCRE, NOBODY RESPECTS YOUR CONTRIBUTIONS, AND YET YOU FREELY CHOOSE TO WORK HERE.
IT'S ABSURD! NO, WAIT... THERE MUST BE A REASON... I MUST WORK HERE BECAUSE I LOVE THE WORK.
© 1992 United Feature Syndicate, Inc.
8-9
I LOVE THIS JOB.
NEXT!

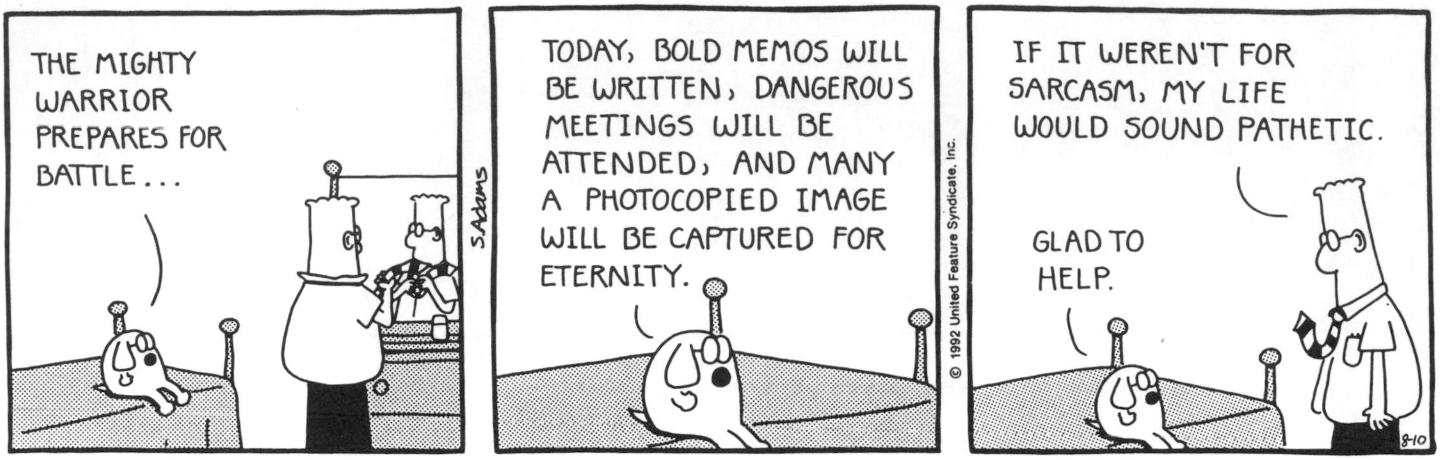
THE MIGHTY WARRIOR PREPARES FOR BATTLE...
S.Adams
TODAY, BOLD MEMOS WILL BE WRITTEN, DANGEROUS MEETINGS WILL BE ATTENDED, AND MANY A PHOTOCOPIED IMAGE WILL BE CAPTURED FOR ETERNITY.
© 1992 United Feature Syndicate, Inc.
IF IT WEREN'T FOR SARCASM, MY LIFE WOULD SOUND PATHETIC.
GLAD TO HELP.
8-10

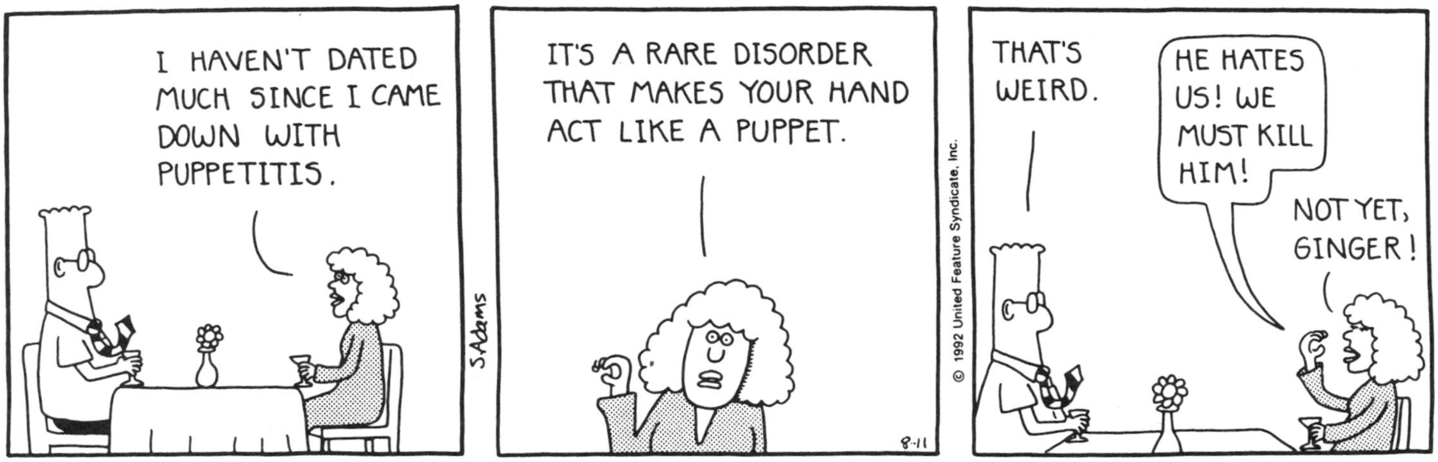
I HAVEN'T DATED MUCH SINCE I CAME DOWN WITH PUPPETITIS.
S.Adams
IT'S A RARE DISORDER THAT MAKES YOUR HAND ACT LIKE A PUPPET.
8-11
© 1992 United Feature Syndicate, Inc.
THAT'S WEIRD.
HE HATES US! WE MUST KILL HIM!
NOT YET, GINGER!

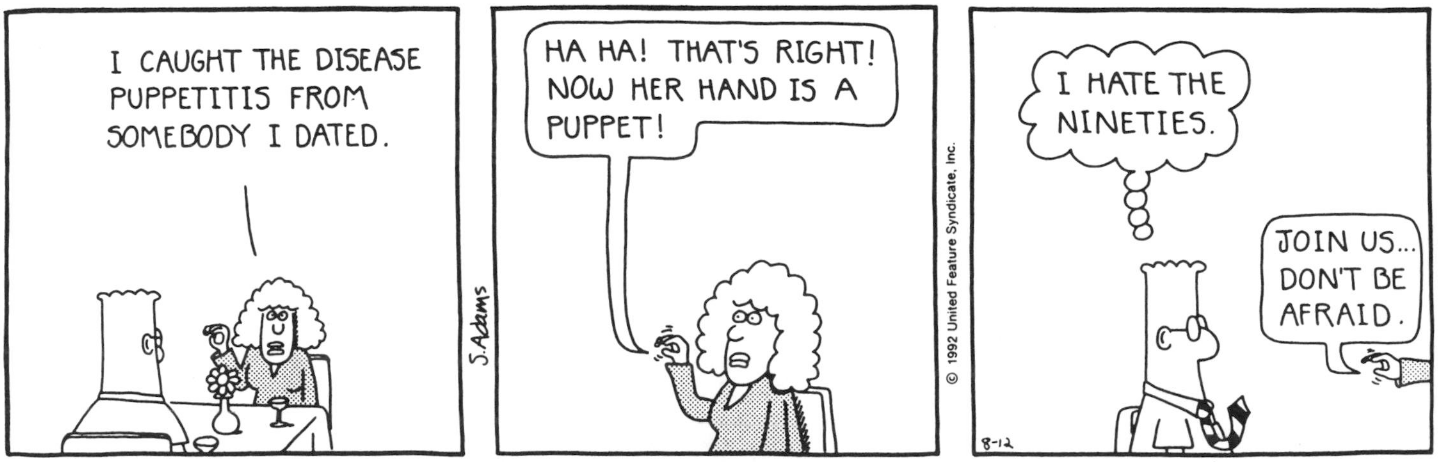
I CAUGHT THE DISEASE PUPPETITIS FROM SOMEBODY I DATED.
S.Adams
HA HA! THAT'S RIGHT! NOW HER HAND IS A PUPPET!
© 1992 United Feature Syndicate, Inc.
I HATE THE NINETIES.
JOIN US... DON'T BE AFRAID.
8-12

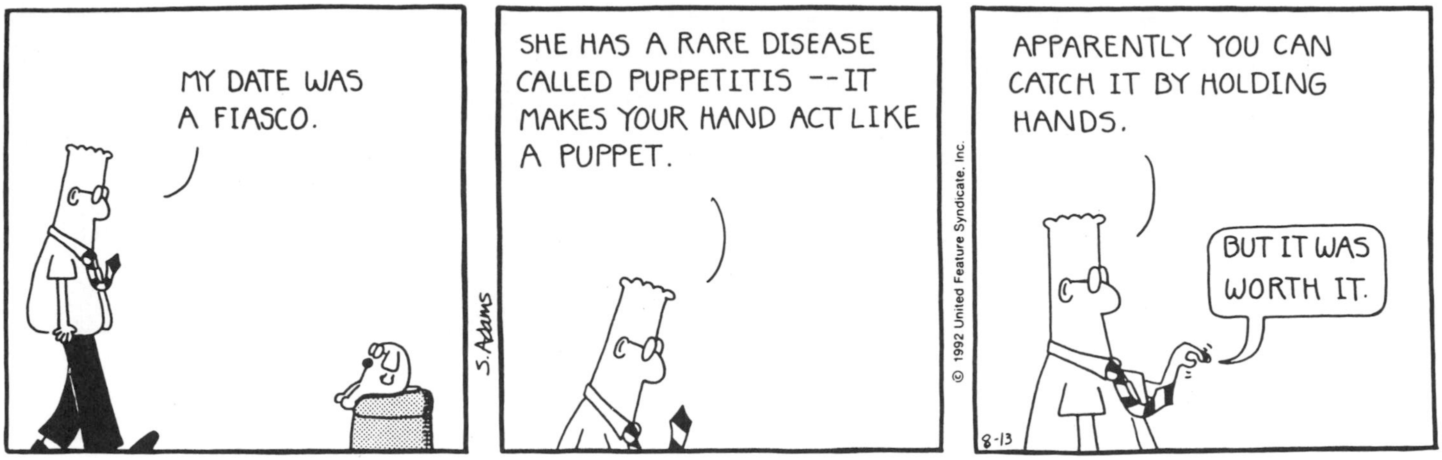
MY DATE WAS A FIASCO.
SHE HAS A RARE DISEASE CALLED PUPPETITIS --IT MAKES YOUR HAND ACT LIKE A PUPPET.
APPARENTLY YOU CAN CATCH IT BY HOLDING HANDS.
BUT IT WAS WORTH IT.
S. Adams
© 1992 United Feature Syndicate, Inc.
8-13

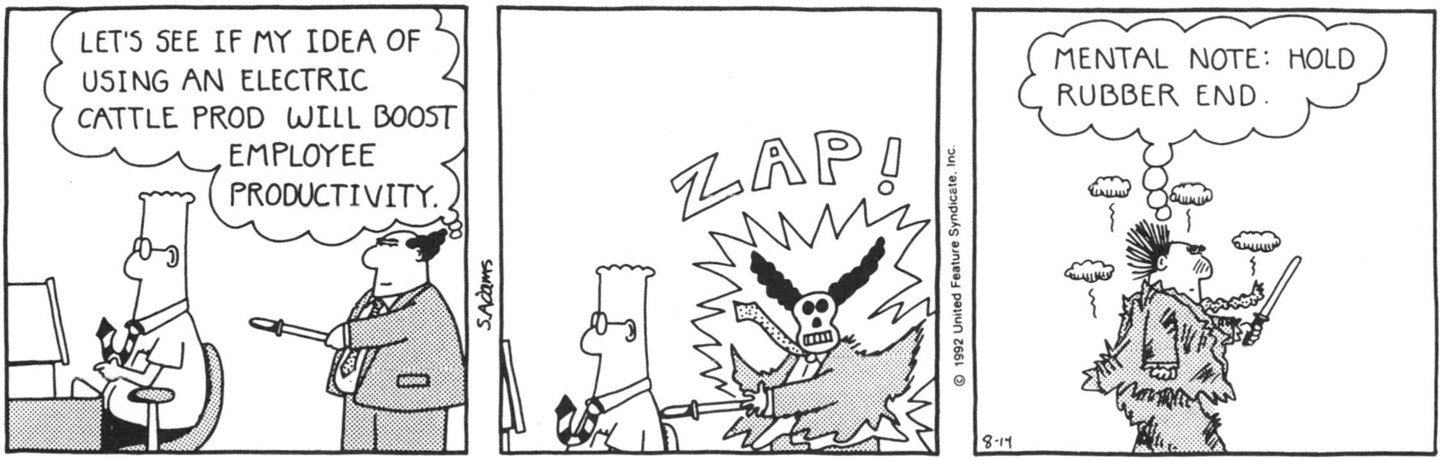
LET'S SEE IF MY IDEA OF USING AN ELECTRIC CATTLE PROD WILL BOOST EMPLOYEE PRODUCTIVITY.
ZAP!
MENTAL NOTE: HOLD RUBBER END.
S. Adams
© 1992 United Feature Syndicate, Inc.
8-14

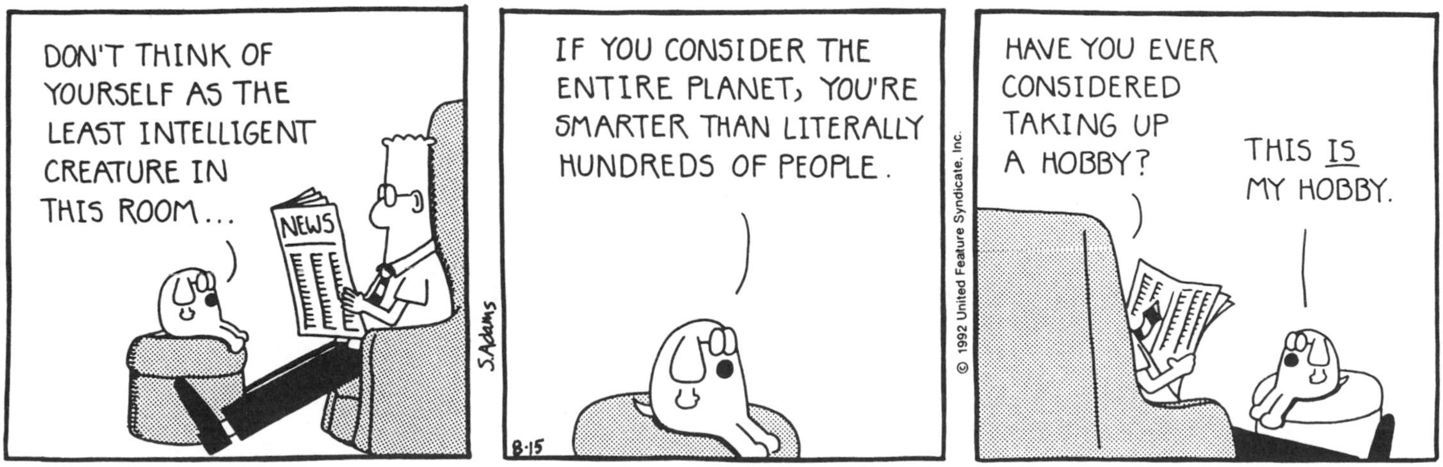
DON'T THINK OF YOURSELF AS THE LEAST INTELLIGENT CREATURE IN THIS ROOM...
NEWS
IF YOU CONSIDER THE ENTIRE PLANET, YOU'RE SMARTER THAN LITERALLY HUNDREDS OF PEOPLE.
HAVE YOU EVER CONSIDERED TAKING UP A HOBBY?
THIS IS MY HOBBY.
S. Adams
© 1992 United Feature Syndicate, Inc.
8-15

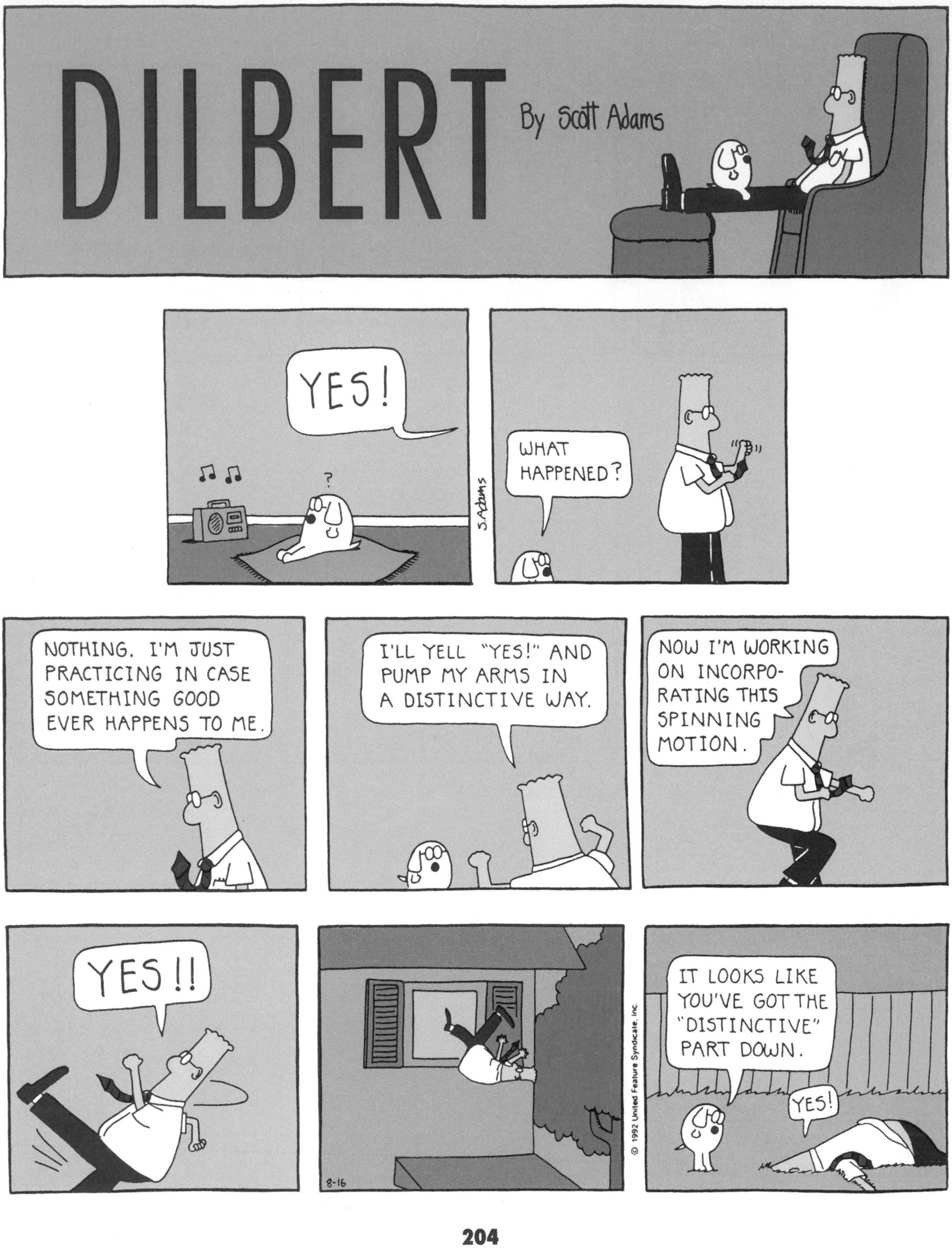
DILBERT
By Scott Adams
YES!
S. Adams
WHAT HAPPENED?
NOTHING. I'M JUST PRACTICING IN CASE SOMETHING GOOD EVER HAPPENS TO ME.
I'LL YELL "YES!" AND PUMP MY ARMS IN A DISTINCTIVE WAY.
NOW I'M WORKING ON INCORPO-RATING THIS SPINNING MOTION.
YES!!
8-16
© 1992 United Feature Syndicate, Inc.
IT LOOKS LIKE YOU'VE GOT THE "DISTINCTIVE" PART DOWN.
YES!

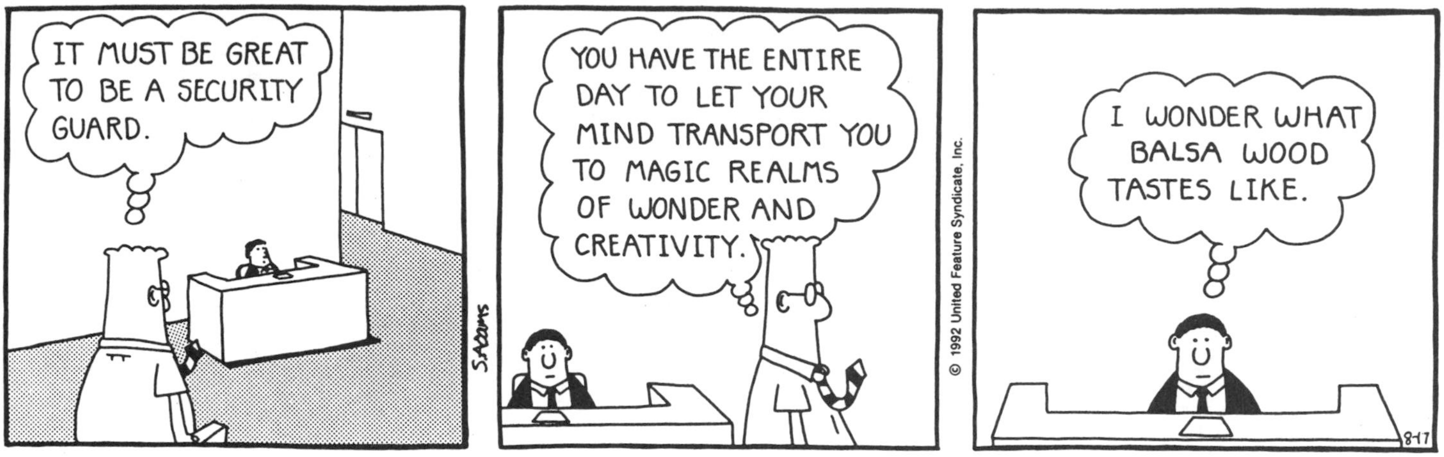
IT MUST BE GREAT TO BE A SECURITY GUARD.
S.ADAMS
YOU HAVE THE ENTIRE DAY TO LET YOUR MIND TRANSPORT YOU TO MAGIC REALMS OF WONDER AND CREATIVITY.
© 1992 United Feature Syndicate, Inc.
I WONDER WHAT BALSA WOOD TASTES LIKE.
8-17

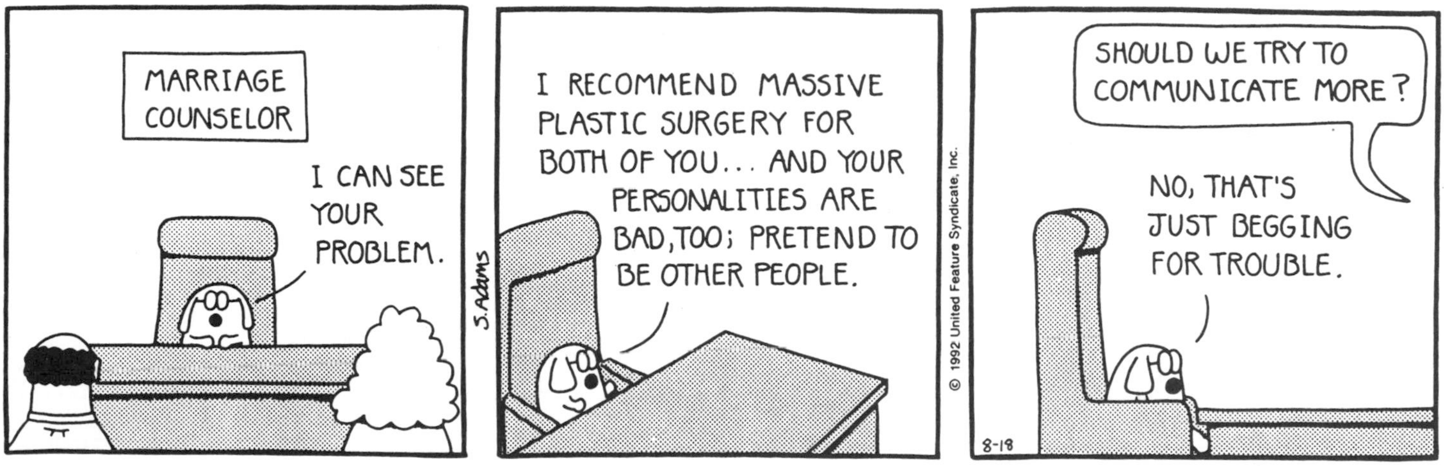
MARRIAGE COUNSELOR
I CAN SEE YOUR PROBLEM.
S.ADAMS
I RECOMMEND MASSIVE PLASTIC SURGERY FOR BOTH OF YOU... AND YOUR PERSONALITIES ARE BAD, TOO; PRETEND TO BE OTHER PEOPLE.
© 1992 United Feature Syndicate, Inc.
SHOULD WE TRY TO COMMUNICATE MORE?
NO, THAT'S JUST BEGGING FOR TROUBLE.
8-18

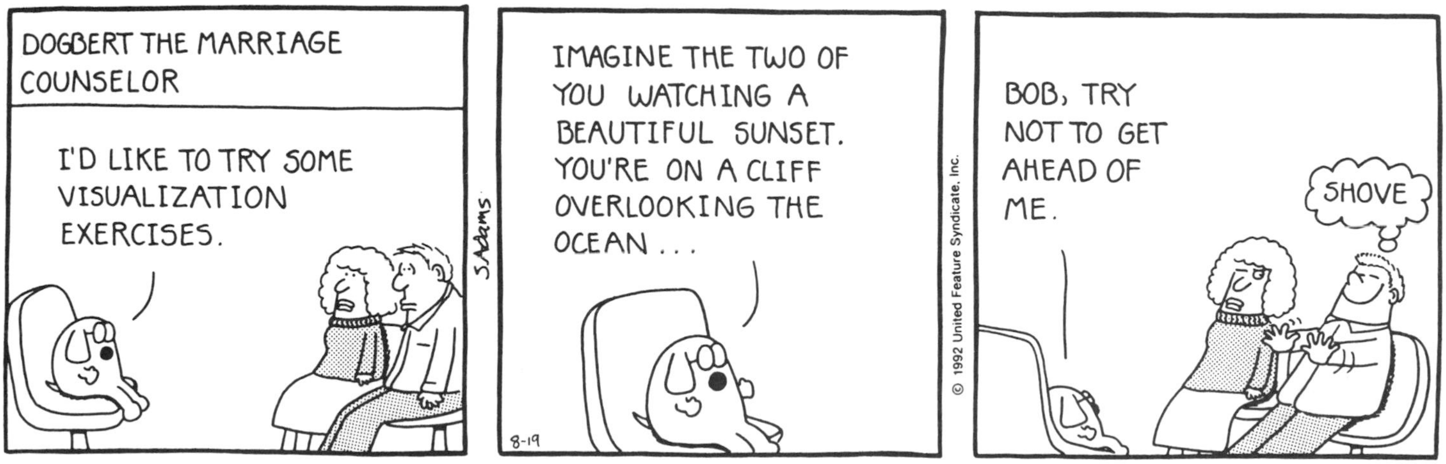
DOGBERT THE MARRIAGE COUNSELOR
I'D LIKE TO TRY SOME VISUALIZATION EXERCISES.
S.ADAMS
IMAGINE THE TWO OF YOU WATCHING A BEAUTIFUL SUNSET. YOU'RE ON A CLIFF OVERLOOKING THE OCEAN...
8-19
© 1992 United Feature Syndicate, Inc.
BOB, TRY NOT TO GET AHEAD OF ME.
SHOVE

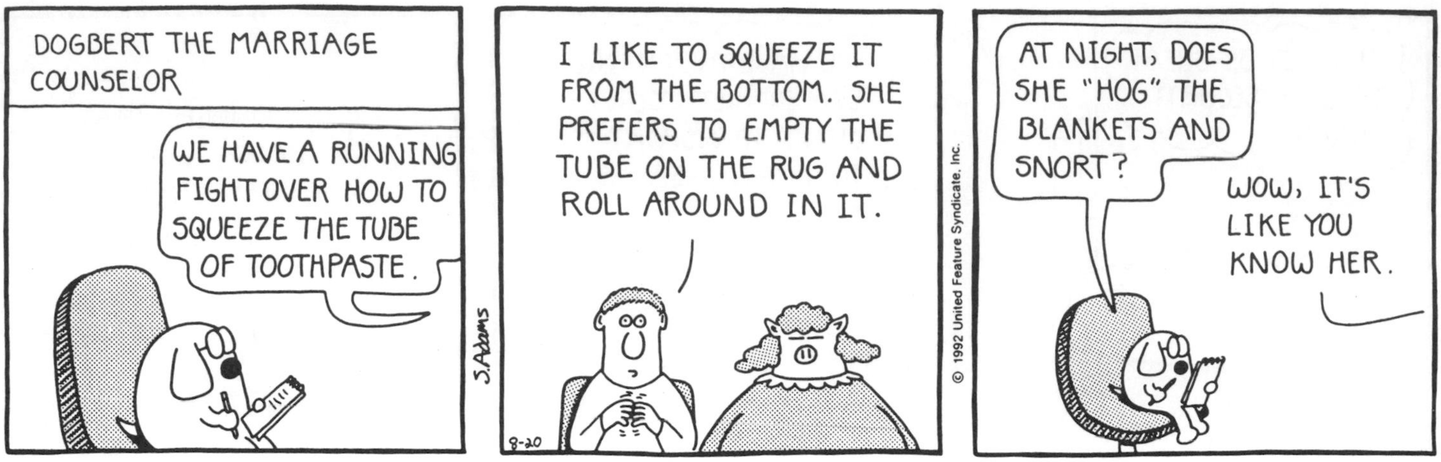
DOGBERT THE MARRIAGE COUNSELOR
WE HAVE A RUNNING FIGHT OVER HOW TO SQUEEZE THE TUBE OF TOOTHPASTE.
S. Adams
I LIKE TO SQUEEZE IT FROM THE BOTTOM. SHE PREFERS TO EMPTY THE TUBE ON THE RUG AND ROLL AROUND IN IT.
8-20
© 1992 United Feature Syndicate, Inc.
AT NIGHT, DOES SHE "HOG" THE BLANKETS AND SNORT?
WOW, IT'S LIKE YOU KNOW HER.

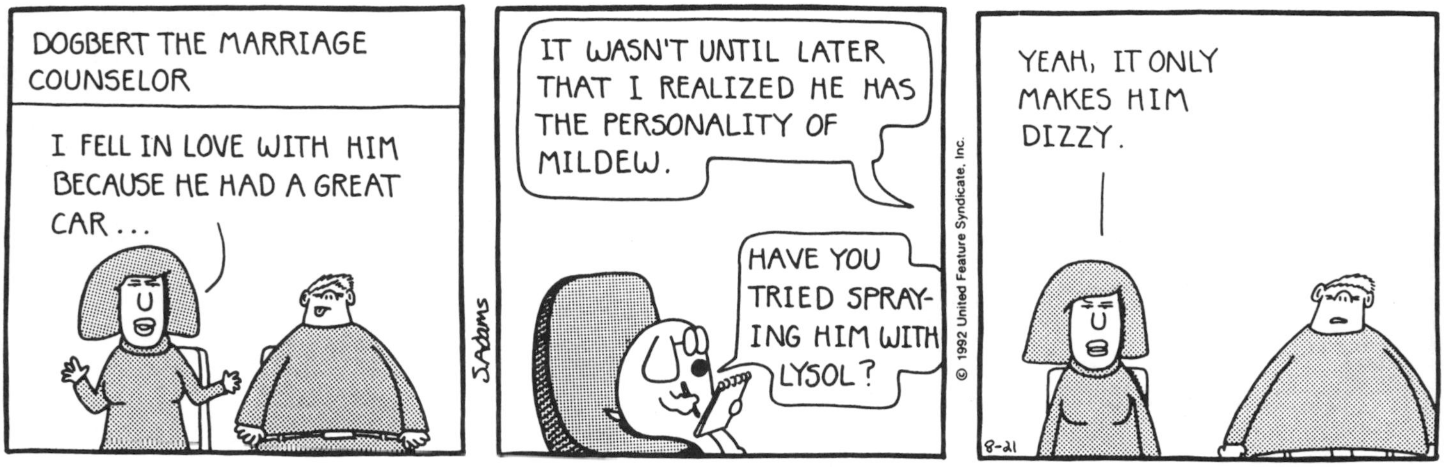
DOGBERT THE MARRIAGE COUNSELOR
I FELL IN LOVE WITH HIM BECAUSE HE HAD A GREAT CAR...
S. Adams
IT WASN'T UNTIL LATER THAT I REALIZED HE HAS THE PERSONALITY OF MILDEW.
HAVE YOU TRIED SPRAYING HIM WITH LYSOL?
© 1992 United Feature Syndicate, Inc.
YEAH, IT ONLY MAKES HIM DIZZY.
8-21

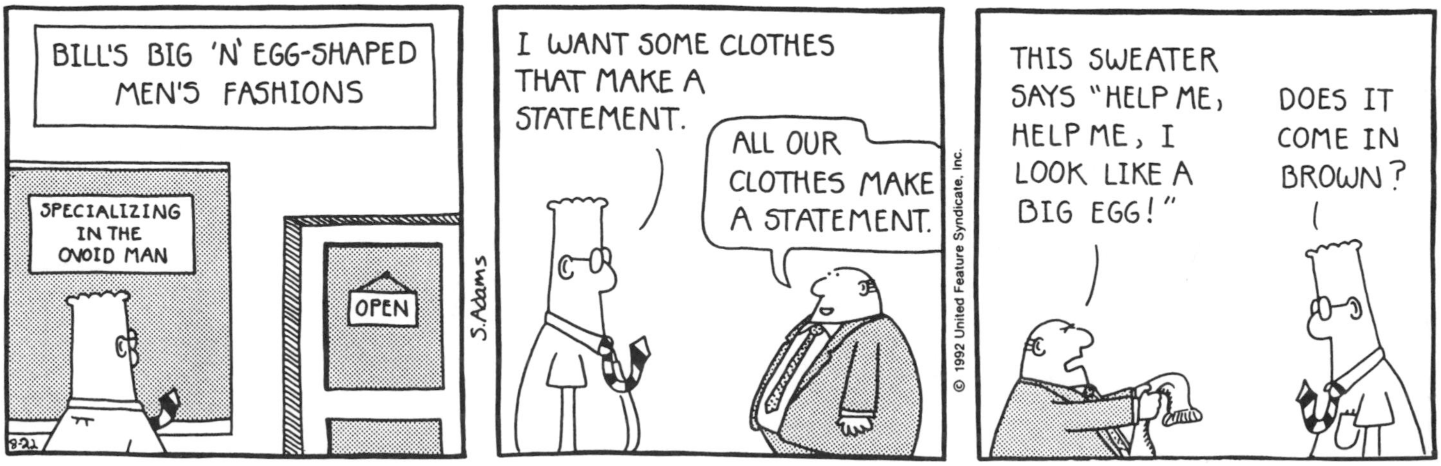
BILL'S BIG 'N' EGG-SHAPED MEN'S FASHIONS
SPECIALIZING IN THE OVOID MAN
OPEN
8-22
S. Adams
I WANT SOME CLOTHES THAT MAKE A STATEMENT.
ALL OUR CLOTHES MAKE A STATEMENT.
© 1992 United Feature Syndicate, Inc.
THIS SWEATER SAYS "HELP ME, HELP ME, I LOOK LIKE A BIG EGG!"
DOES IT COME IN BROWN?

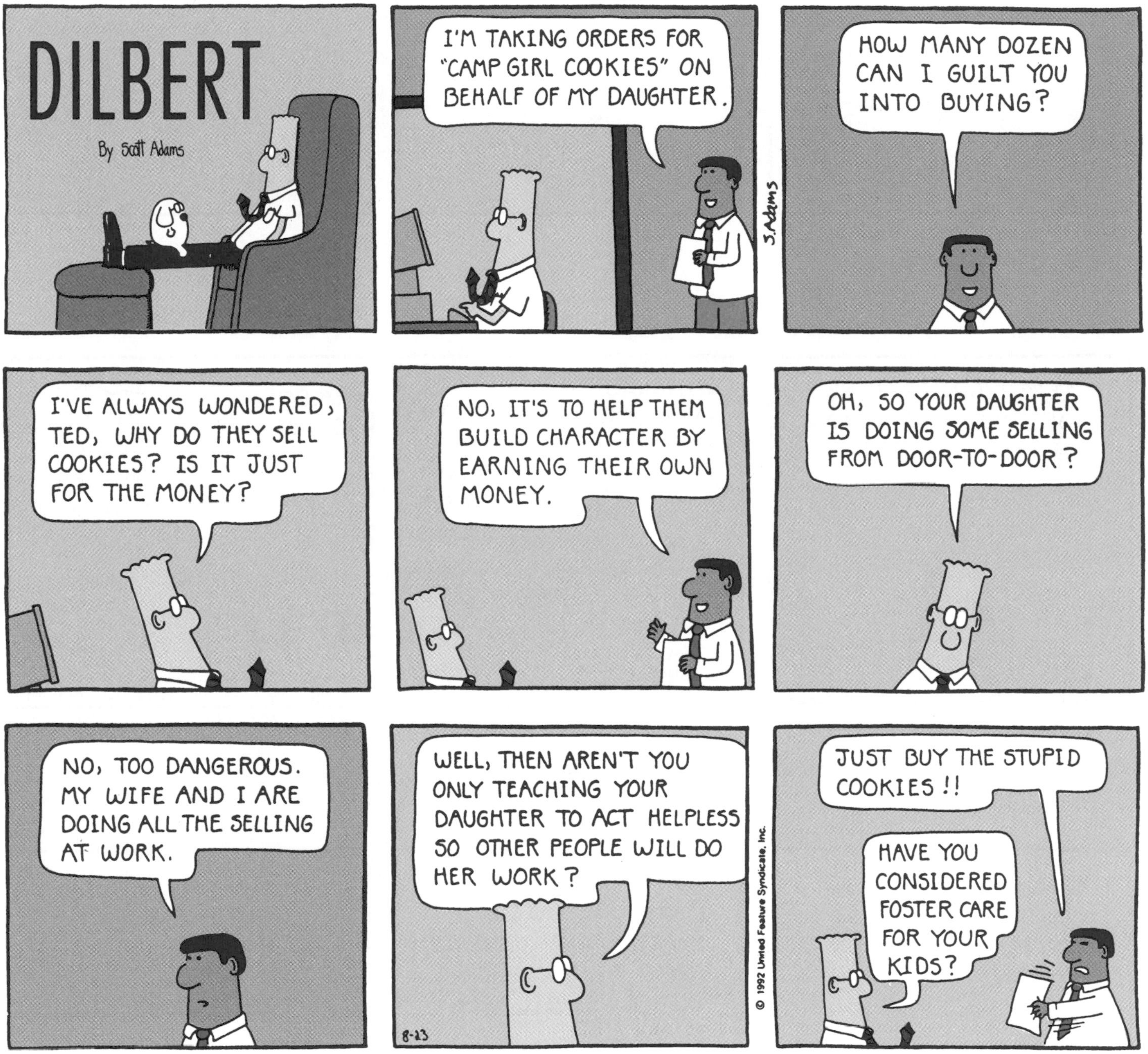
DILBERT
By Scott Adams
I'M TAKING ORDERS FOR "CAMP GIRL COOKIES" ON BEHALF OF MY DAUGHTER.
S. Adams
HOW MANY DOZEN CAN I GUILT YOU INTO BUYING?
I'VE ALWAYS WONDERED, TED, WHY DO THEY SELL COOKIES? IS IT JUST FOR THE MONEY?
NO, IT'S TO HELP THEM BUILD CHARACTER BY EARNING THEIR OWN MONEY.
OH, SO YOUR DAUGHTER IS DOING SOME SELLING FROM DOOR-TO-DOOR?
NO, TOO DANGEROUS. MY WIFE AND I ARE DOING ALL THE SELLING AT WORK.
WELL, THEN AREN'T YOU ONLY TEACHING YOUR DAUGHTER TO ACT HELPLESS SO OTHER PEOPLE WILL DO HER WORK?
8-23
© 1992 United Feature Syndicate, Inc.
JUST BUY THE STUPID COOKIES!!
HAVE YOU CONSIDERED FOSTER CARE FOR YOUR KIDS?

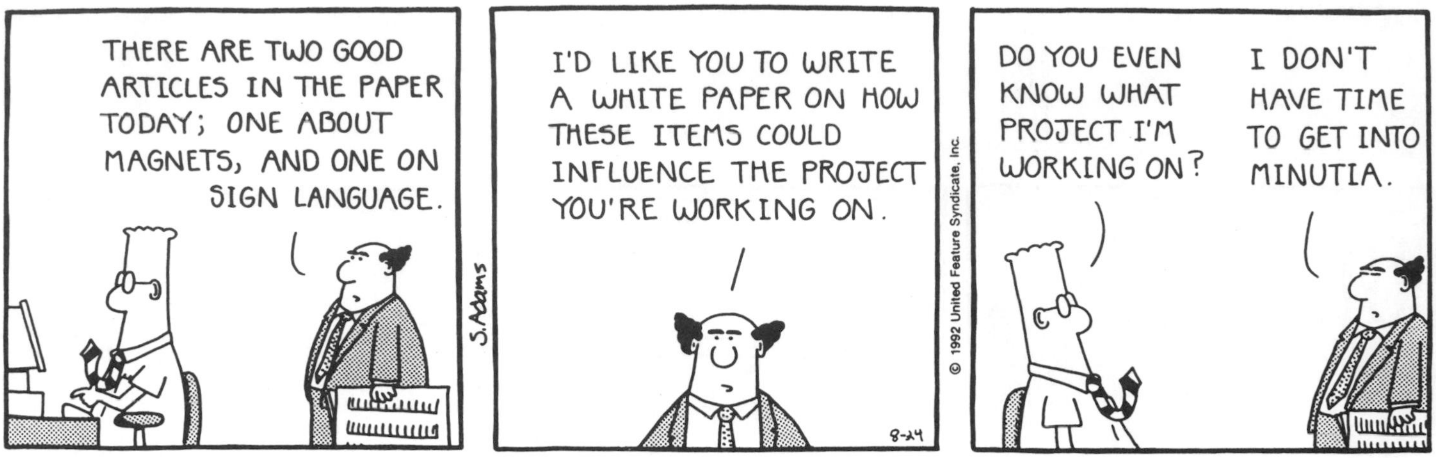
THERE ARE TWO GOOD ARTICLES IN THE PAPER TODAY; ONE ABOUT MAGNETS, AND ONE ON SIGN LANGUAGE.
S. Adams
I'D LIKE YOU TO WRITE A WHITE PAPER ON HOW THESE ITEMS COULD INFLUENCE THE PROJECT YOU'RE WORKING ON.
8-24
© 1992 United Feature Syndicate, Inc.
DO YOU EVEN KNOW WHAT PROJECT I'M WORKING ON?
I DON'T HAVE TIME TO GET INTO MINUTIA.

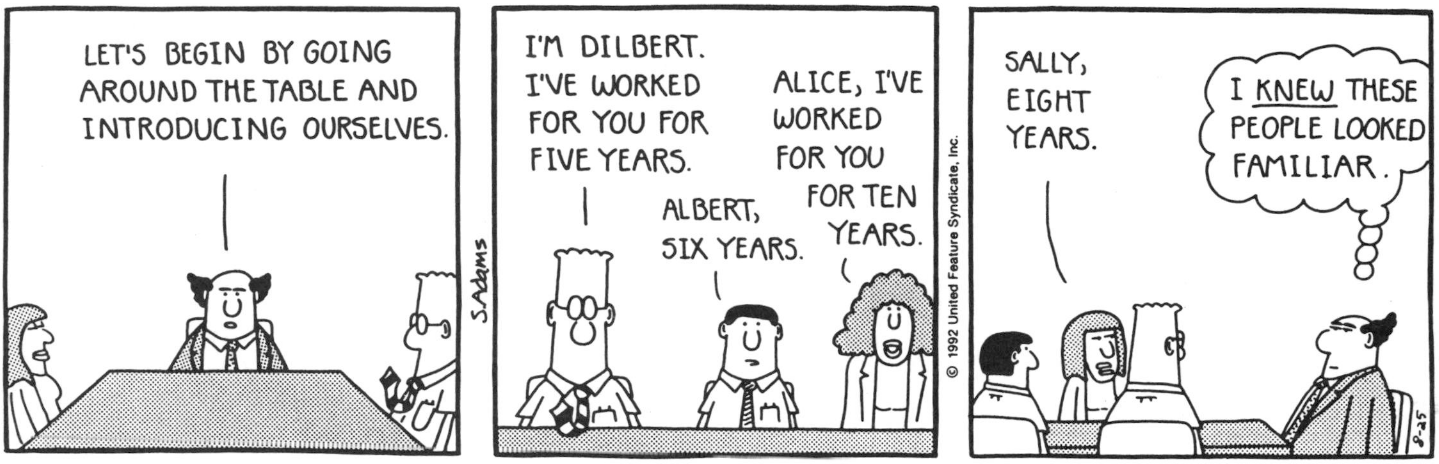
LET'S BEGIN BY GOING AROUND THE TABLE AND INTRODUCING OURSELVES.
S. Adams
I'M DILBERT. I'VE WORKED FOR YOU FOR FIVE YEARS.
ALBERT, SIX YEARS.
ALICE, I'VE WORKED FOR YOU FOR TEN YEARS.
© 1992 United Feature Syndicate, Inc.
SALLY, EIGHT YEARS.
I KNEW THESE PEOPLE LOOKED FAMILIAR.
8-25

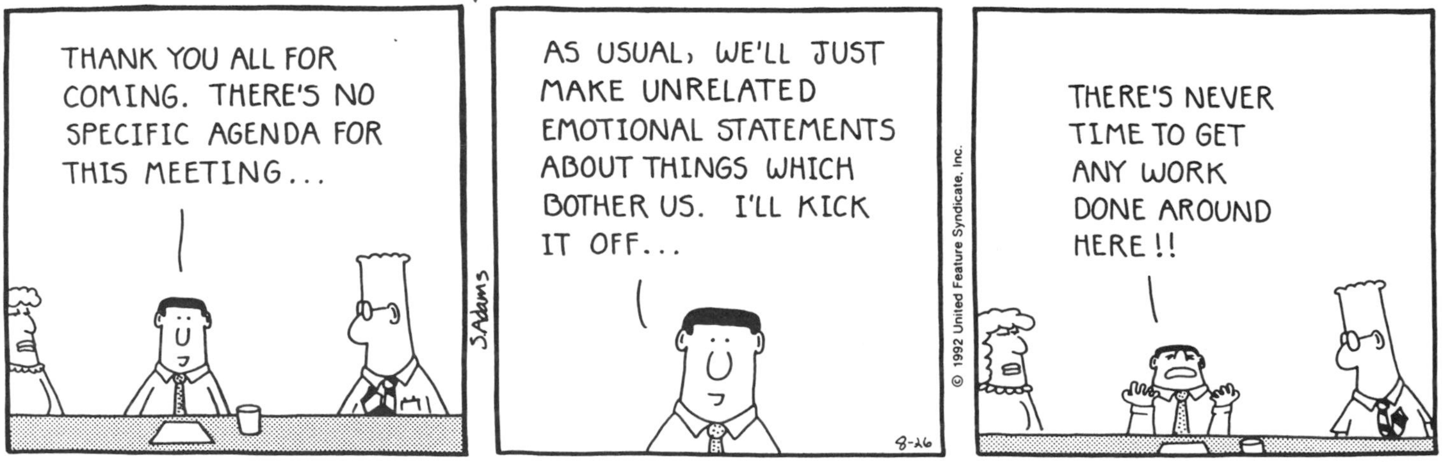
THANK YOU ALL FOR COMING. THERE'S NO SPECIFIC AGENDA FOR THIS MEETING...
S. Adams
AS USUAL, WE'LL JUST MAKE UNRELATED EMOTIONAL STATEMENTS ABOUT THINGS WHICH BOTHER US. I'LL KICK IT OFF...
8-26
© 1992 United Feature Syndicate, Inc.
THERE'S NEVER TIME TO GET ANY WORK DONE AROUND HERE!!

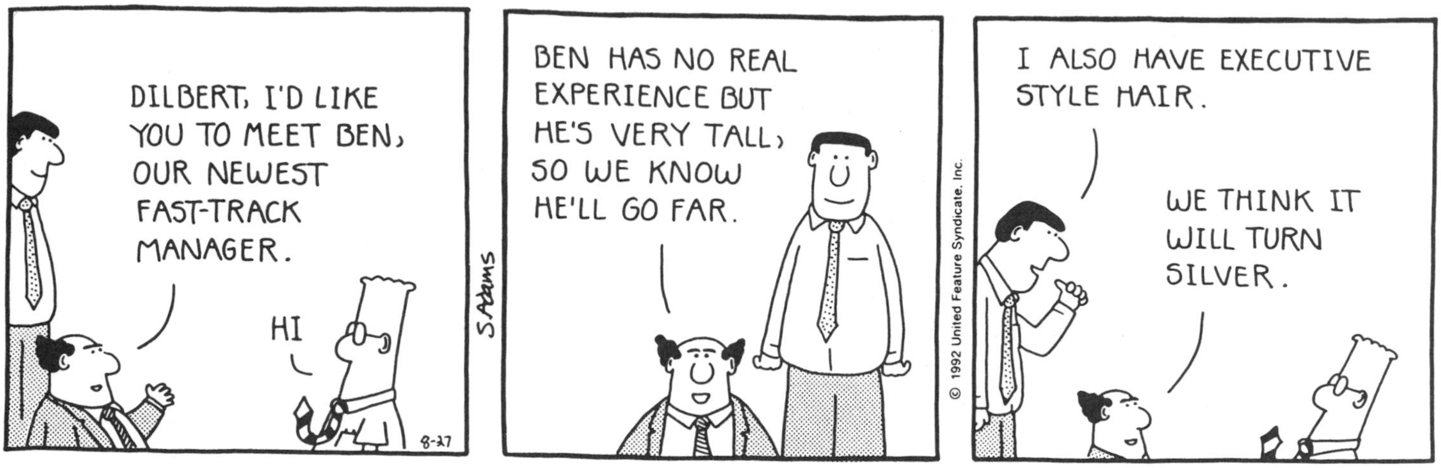

DILBERT, I'D LIKE YOU TO MEET BEN, OUR NEWEST FAST-TRACK MANAGER.
HI
8-27
S.Adams
BEN HAS NO REAL EXPERIENCE BUT HE'S VERY TALL, SO WE KNOW HE'LL GO FAR.
© 1992 United Feature Syndicate, Inc.
I ALSO HAVE EXECUTIVE STYLE HAIR.
WE THINK IT WILL TURN SILVER.

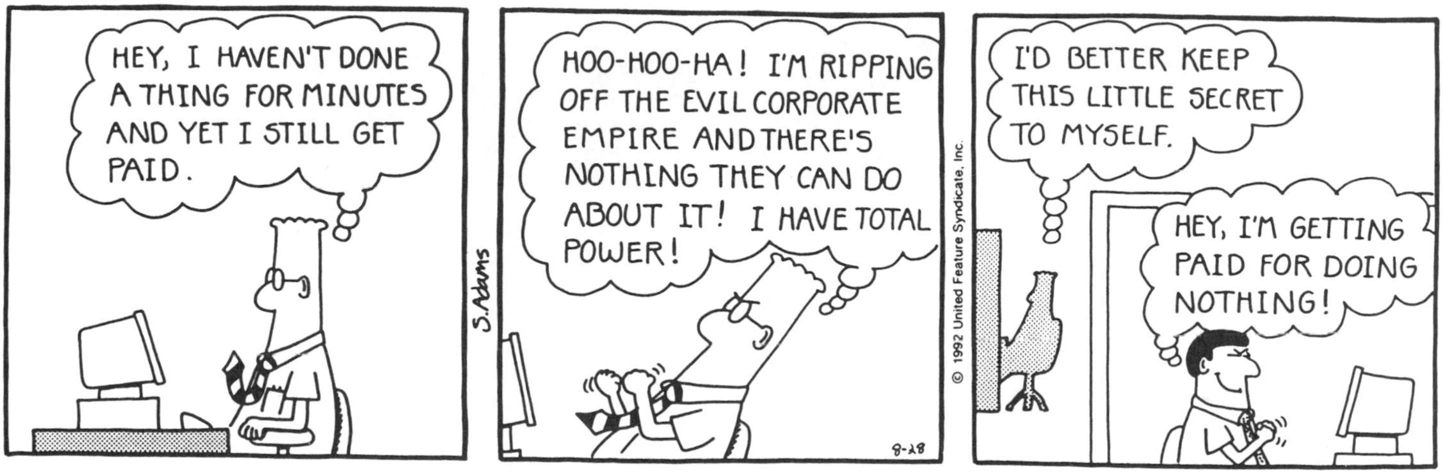

HEY, I HAVEN'T DONE A THING FOR MINUTES AND YET I STILL GET PAID.
S.Adams
HOO-HOO-HA! I'M RIPPING OFF THE EVIL CORPORATE EMPIRE AND THERE'S NOTHING THEY CAN DO ABOUT IT! I HAVE TOTAL POWER!
8-28
© 1992 United Feature Syndicate, Inc.
I'D BETTER KEEP THIS LITTLE SECRET TO MYSELF.
HEY, I'M GETTING PAID FOR DOING NOTHING!

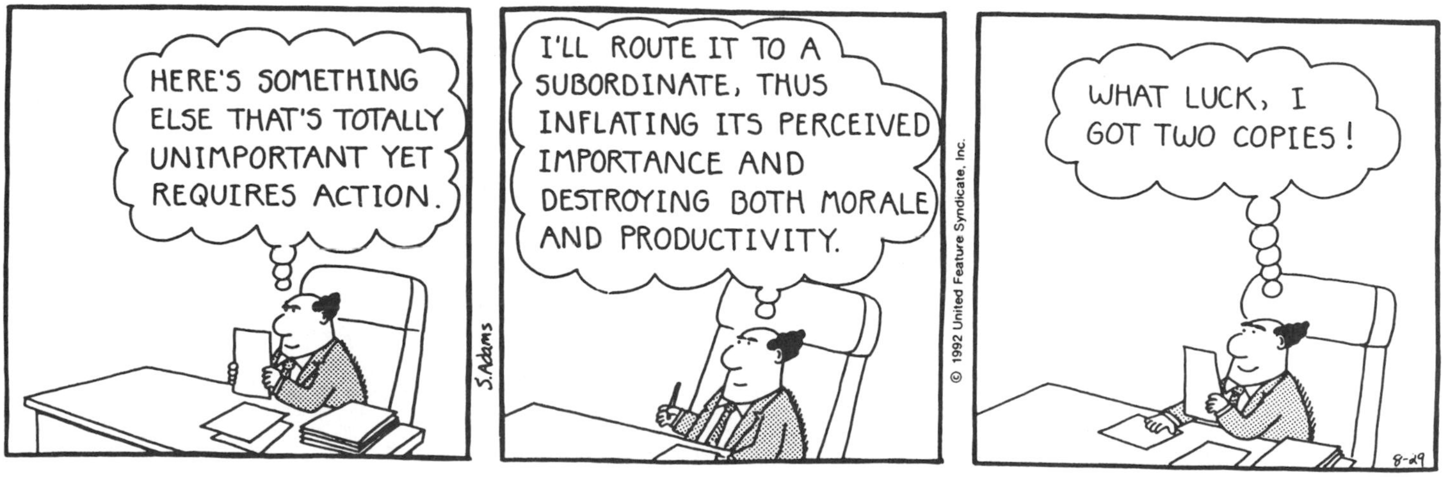

HERE'S SOMETHING ELSE THAT'S TOTALLY UNIMPORTANT YET REQUIRES ACTION.
S.Adams
I'LL ROUTE IT TO A SUBORDINATE, THUS INFLATING ITS PERCEIVED IMPORTANCE AND DESTROYING BOTH MORALE AND PRODUCTIVITY.
© 1992 United Feature Syndicate, Inc.
WHAT LUCK, I GOT TWO COPIES!
8-29

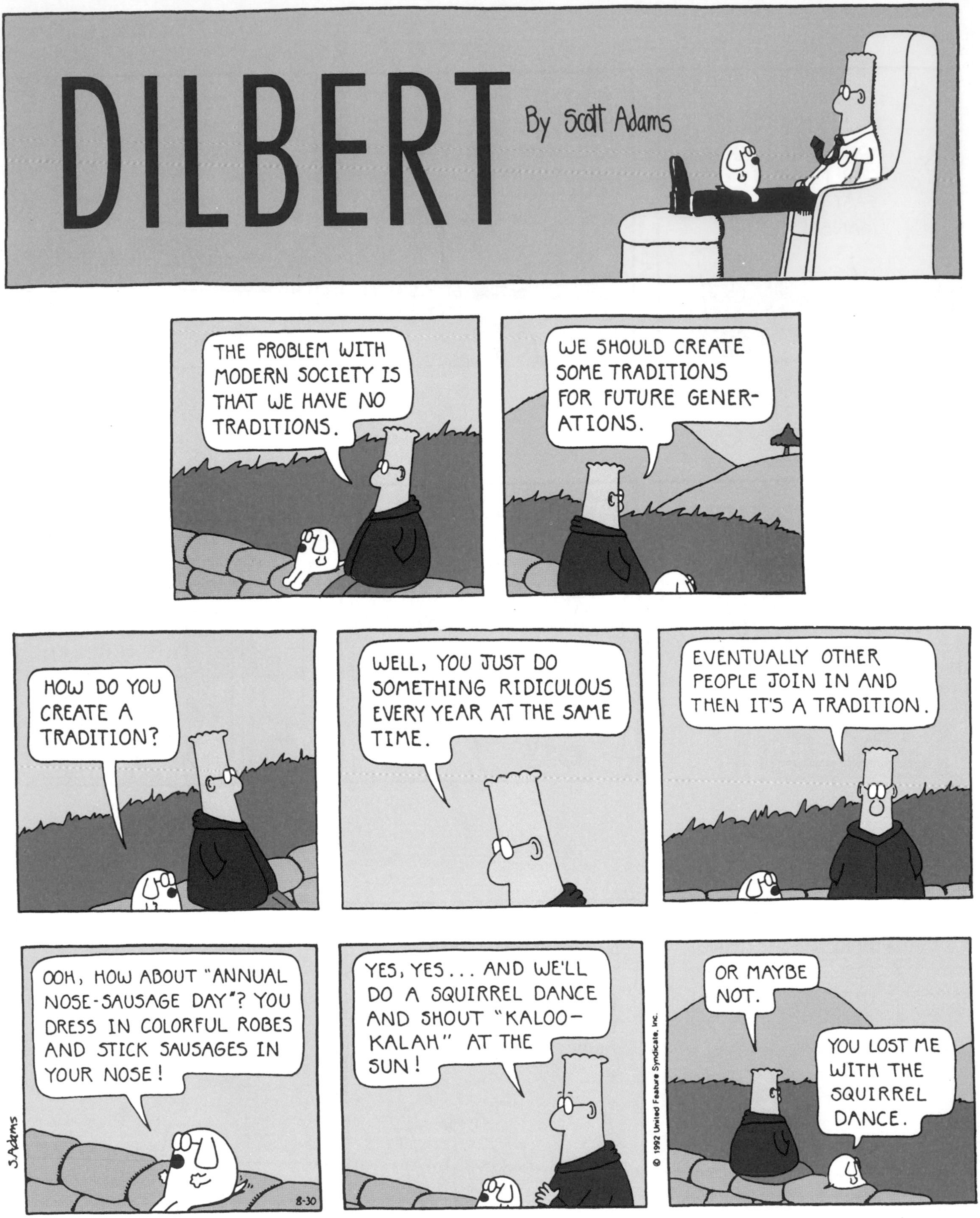
DILBERT
By Scott Adams
THE PROBLEM WITH MODERN SOCIETY IS THAT WE HAVE NO TRADITIONS.
WE SHOULD CREATE SOME TRADITIONS FOR FUTURE GENER-ATIONS.
HOW DO YOU CREATE A TRADITION?
WELL, YOU JUST DO SOMETHING RIDICULOUS EVERY YEAR AT THE SAME TIME.
EVENTUALLY OTHER PEOPLE JOIN IN AND THEN IT'S A TRADITION.
OOH, HOW ABOUT "ANNUAL NOSE-SAUSAGE DAY"? YOU DRESS IN COLORFUL ROBES AND STICK SAUSAGES IN YOUR NOSE!
S.Adams
8-30
YES, YES... AND WE'LL DO A SQUIRREL DANCE AND SHOUT "KALOO-KALAH" AT THE SUN!
© 1992 United Feature Syndicate, Inc.
OR MAYBE NOT.
YOU LOST ME WITH THE SQUIRREL DANCE.

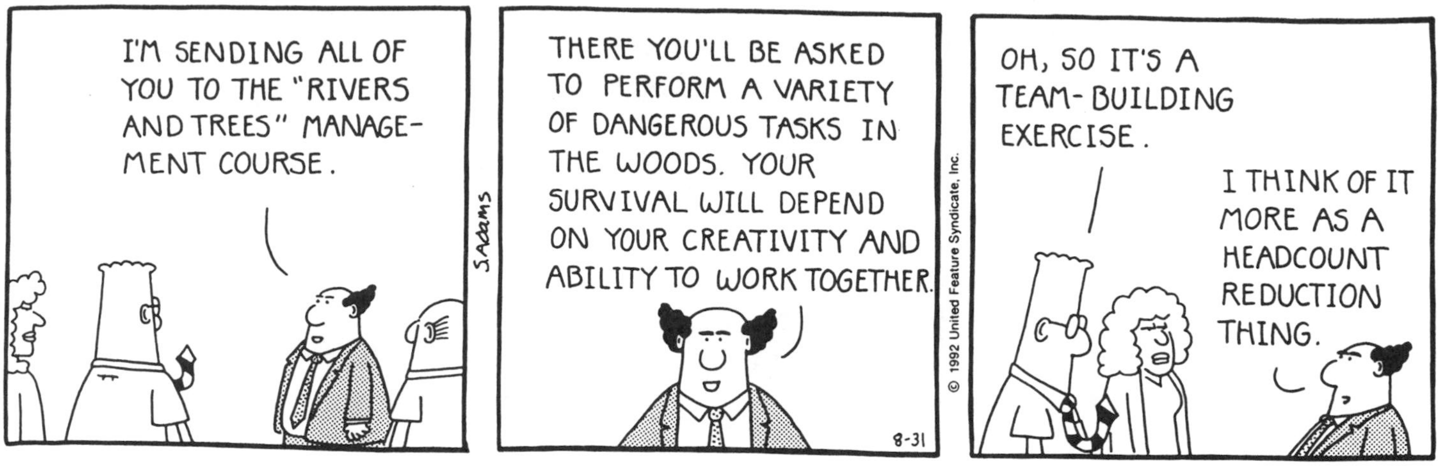
I'M SENDING ALL OF YOU TO THE "RIVERS AND TREES" MANAGEMENT COURSE.
S. ADAMS
THERE YOU'LL BE ASKED TO PERFORM A VARIETY OF DANGEROUS TASKS IN THE WOODS. YOUR SURVIVAL WILL DEPEND ON YOUR CREATIVITY AND ABILITY TO WORK TOGETHER.
8-31
© 1992 United Feature Syndicate, Inc.
OH, SO IT'S A TEAM-BUILDING EXERCISE.
I THINK OF IT MORE AS A HEADCOUNT REDUCTION THING.

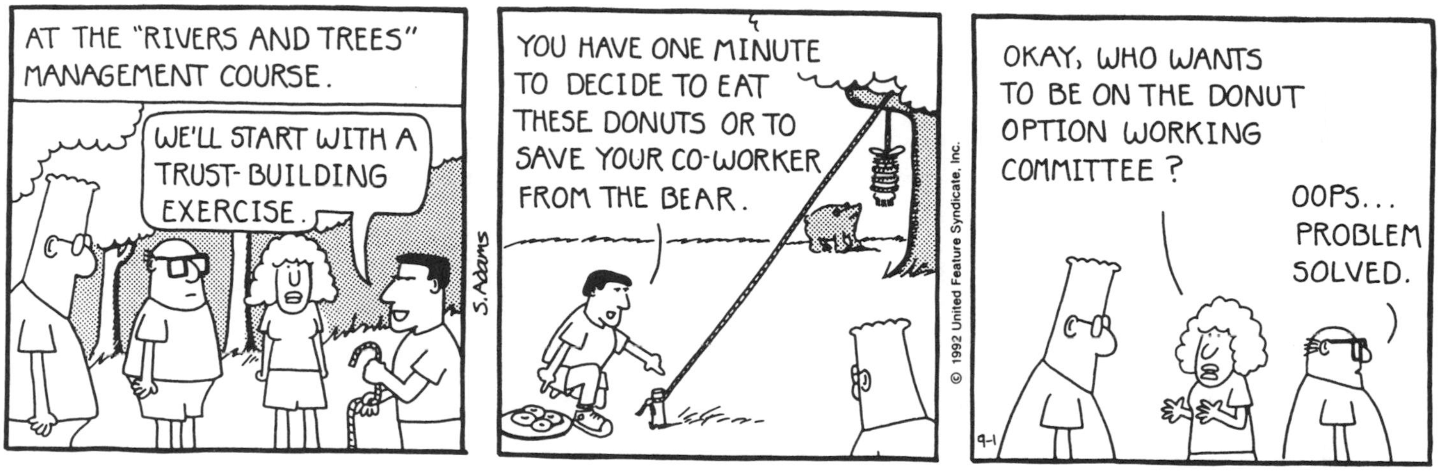
AT THE "RIVERS AND TREES" MANAGEMENT COURSE.
WE'LL START WITH A TRUST-BUILDING EXERCISE.
S. ADAMS
YOU HAVE ONE MINUTE TO DECIDE TO EAT THESE DONUTS OR TO SAVE YOUR CO-WORKER FROM THE BEAR.
© 1992 United Feature Syndicate, Inc.
OKAY, WHO WANTS TO BE ON THE DONUT OPTION WORKING COMMITTEE?
OOPS... PROBLEM SOLVED.
9-1

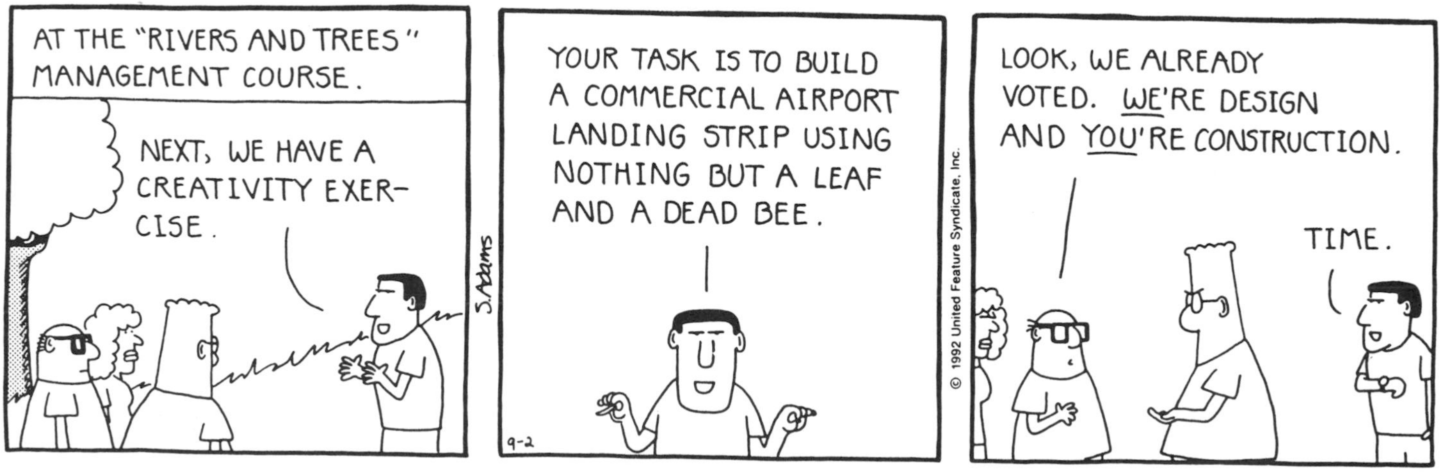
AT THE "RIVERS AND TREES" MANAGEMENT COURSE.
NEXT, WE HAVE A CREATIVITY EXERCISE.
S. ADAMS
YOUR TASK IS TO BUILD A COMMERCIAL AIRPORT LANDING STRIP USING NOTHING BUT A LEAF AND A DEAD BEE.
9-2
© 1992 United Feature Syndicate, Inc.
LOOK, WE ALREADY VOTED. WE'RE DESIGN AND YOU'RE CONSTRUCTION.
TIME.

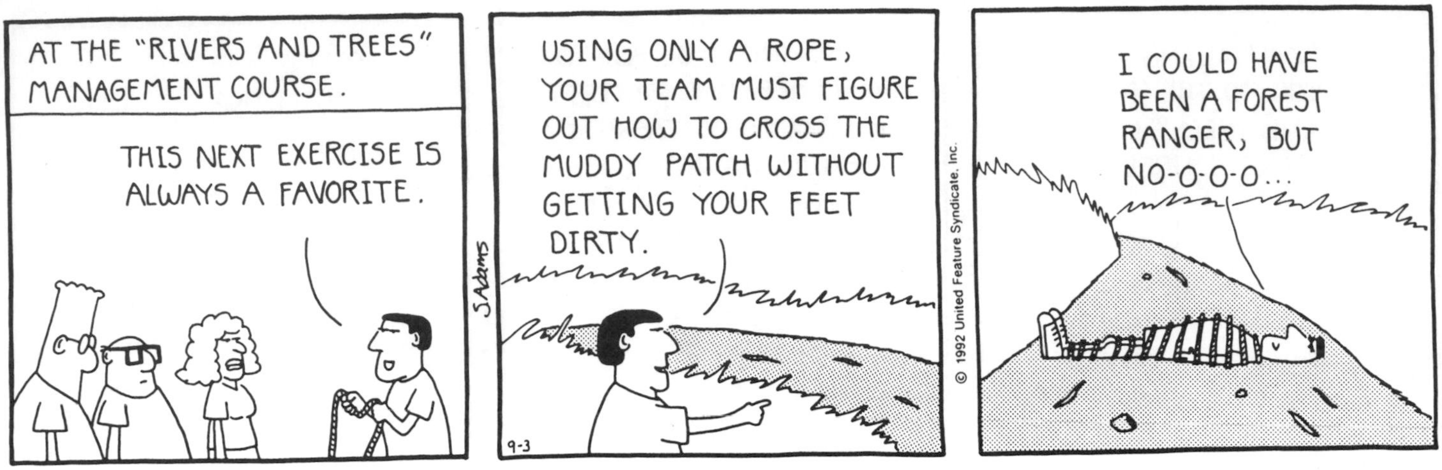
AT THE "RIVERS AND TREES" MANAGEMENT COURSE.
THIS NEXT EXERCISE IS ALWAYS A FAVORITE.
S.Adams
USING ONLY A ROPE, YOUR TEAM MUST FIGURE OUT HOW TO CROSS THE MUDDY PATCH WITHOUT GETTING YOUR FEET DIRTY.
9-3
© 1992 United Feature Syndicate, Inc.
I COULD HAVE BEEN A FOREST RANGER, BUT NO-O-O-O...

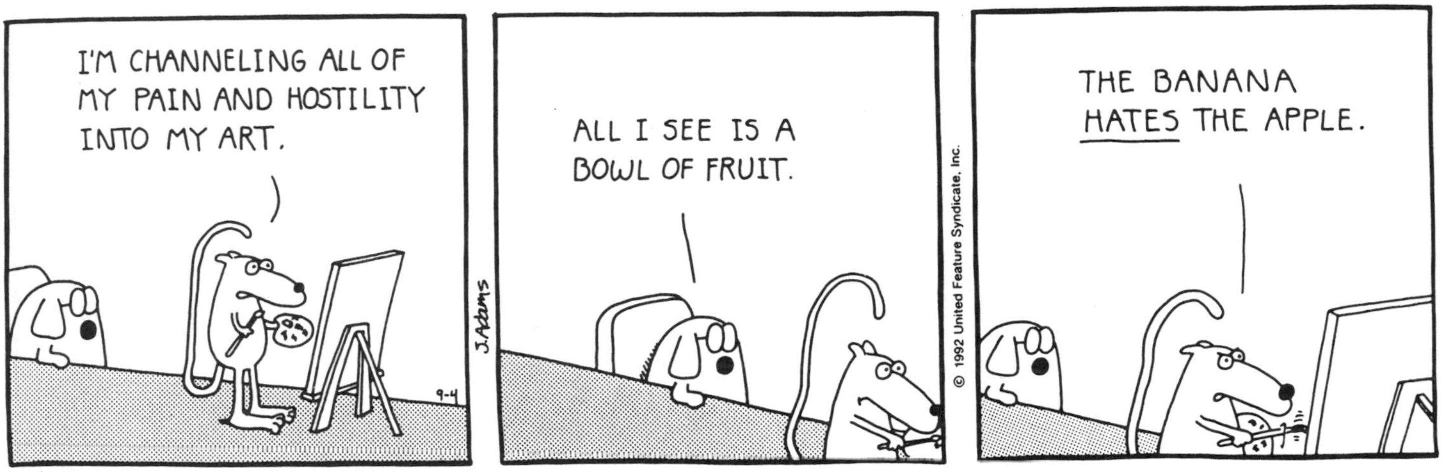
I'M CHANNELING ALL OF MY PAIN AND HOSTILITY INTO MY ART.
9-4
S.Adams
ALL I SEE IS A BOWL OF FRUIT.
© 1992 United Feature Syndicate, Inc.
THE BANANA HATES THE APPLE.

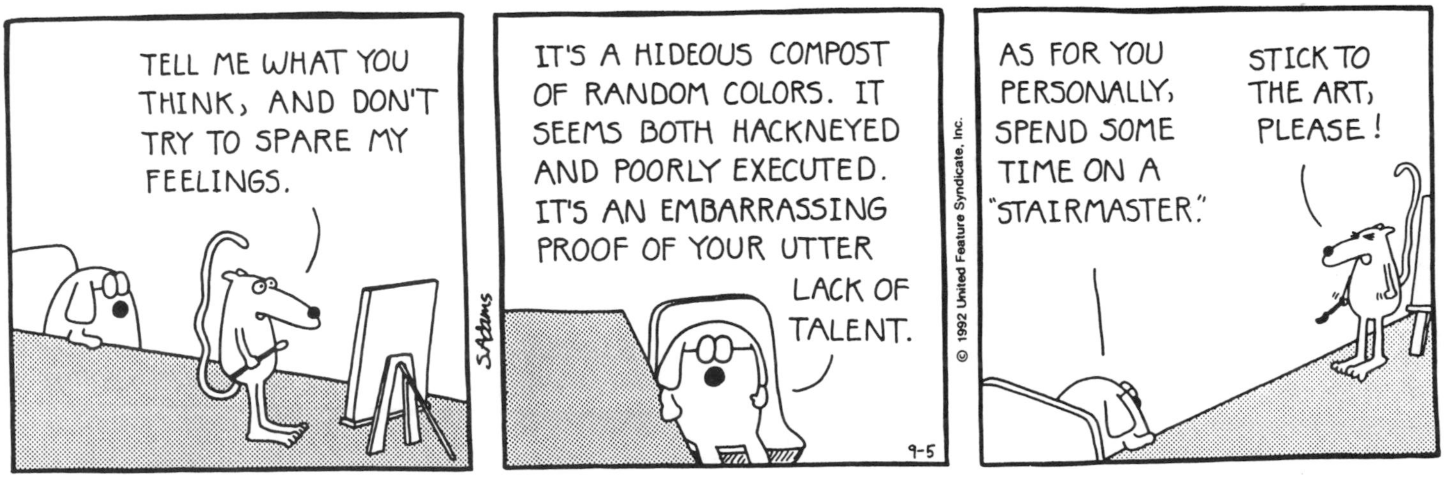
TELL ME WHAT YOU THINK, AND DON'T TRY TO SPARE MY FEELINGS.
S.Adams
IT'S A HIDEOUS COMPOST OF RANDOM COLORS. IT SEEMS BOTH HACKNEYED AND POORLY EXECUTED. IT'S AN EMBARRASSING PROOF OF YOUR UTTER
LACK OF TALENT.
9-5
© 1992 United Feature Syndicate, Inc.
AS FOR YOU PERSONALLY, SPEND SOME TIME ON A "STAIRMASTER."
STICK TO THE ART, PLEASE!

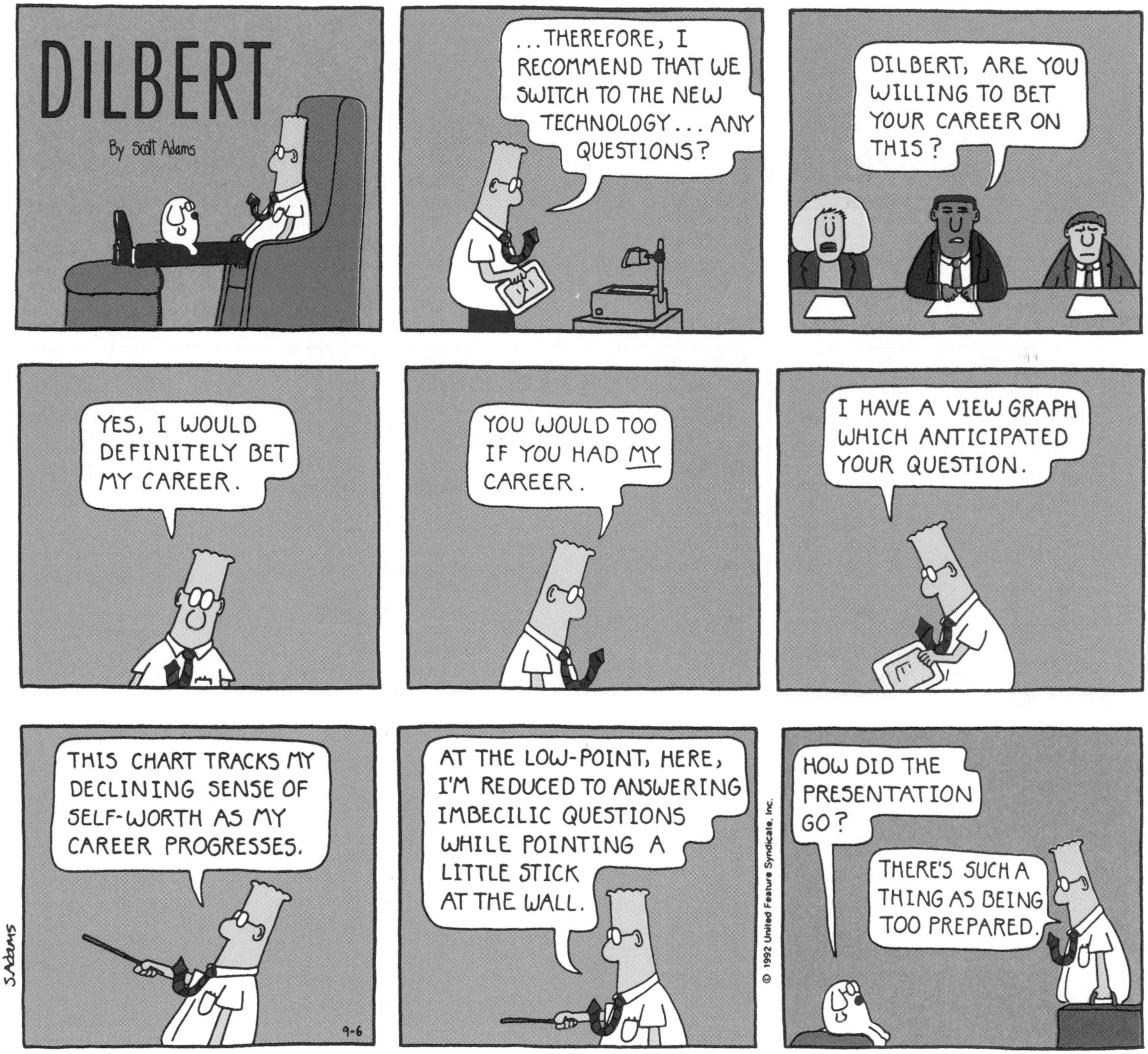
DILBERT
By Scott Adams
...THEREFORE, I RECOMMEND THAT WE SWITCH TO THE NEW TECHNOLOGY... ANY QUESTIONS?
DILBERT, ARE YOU WILLING TO BET YOUR CAREER ON THIS?
YES, I WOULD DEFINITELY BET MY CAREER.
YOU WOULD TOO IF YOU HAD MY CAREER.
I HAVE A VIEW GRAPH WHICH ANTICIPATED YOUR QUESTION.
THIS CHART TRACKS MY DECLINING SENSE OF SELF-WORTH AS MY CAREER PROGRESSES.
S.ADAMS
9-6
AT THE LOW-POINT, HERE, I'M REDUCED TO ANSWERING IMBECILIC QUESTIONS WHILE POINTING A LITTLE STICK AT THE WALL.
© 1992 United Feature Syndicate, Inc.
HOW DID THE PRESENTATION GO?
THERE'S SUCH A THING AS BEING TOO PREPARED.

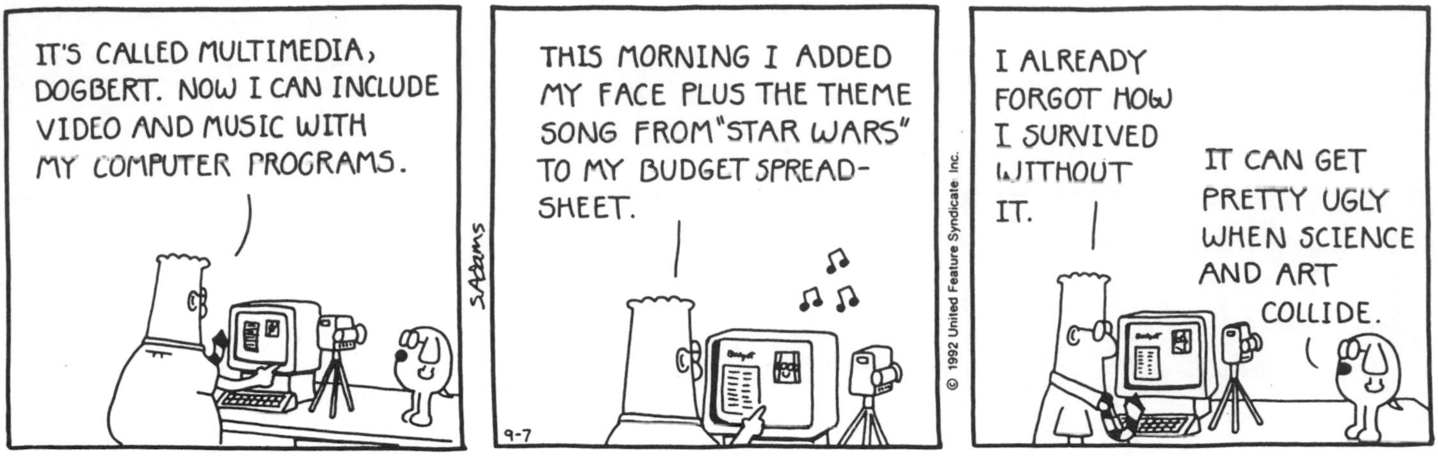
IT'S CALLED MULTIMEDIA, DOGBERT. NOW I CAN INCLUDE VIDEO AND MUSIC WITH MY COMPUTER PROGRAMS.
S.Adams
THIS MORNING I ADDED MY FACE PLUS THE THEME SONG FROM "STAR WARS" TO MY BUDGET SPREAD-SHEET.
9-7
© 1992 United Feature Syndicate, Inc.
I ALREADY FORGOT HOW I SURVIVED WITHOUT IT.
IT CAN GET PRETTY UGLY WHEN SCIENCE AND ART COLLIDE.

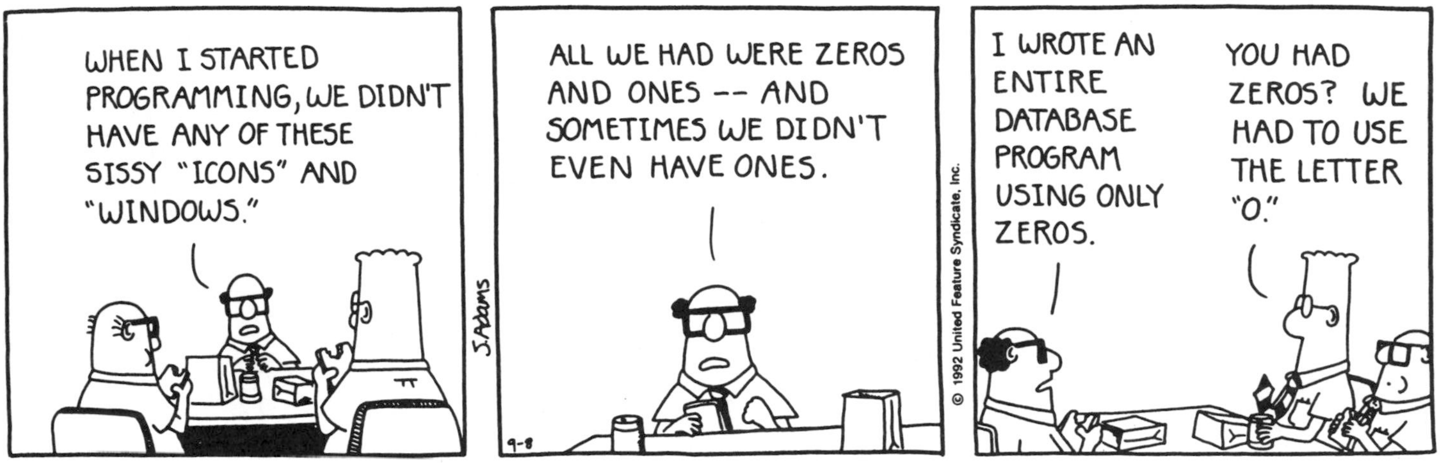
WHEN I STARTED PROGRAMMING, WE DIDN'T HAVE ANY OF THESE SISSY "ICONS" AND "WINDOWS."
S.Adams
ALL WE HAD WERE ZEROS AND ONES -- AND SOMETIMES WE DIDN'T EVEN HAVE ONES.
9-8
© 1992 United Feature Syndicate, Inc.
I WROTE AN ENTIRE DATABASE PROGRAM USING ONLY ZEROS.
YOU HAD ZEROS? WE HAD TO USE THE LETTER "O."

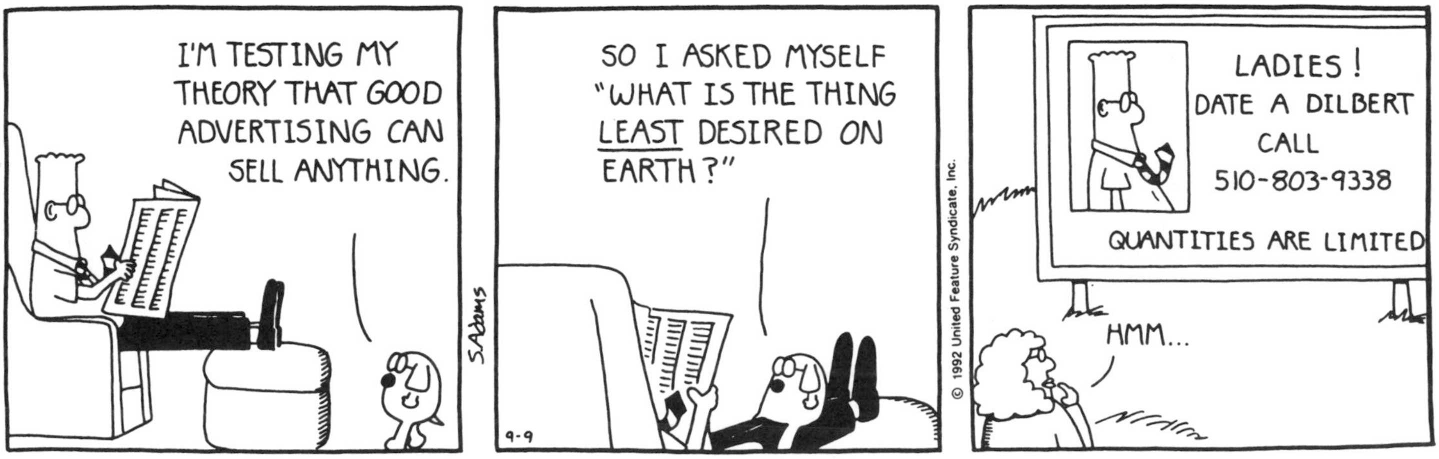
I'M TESTING MY THEORY THAT GOOD ADVERTISING CAN SELL ANYTHING.
S.Adams
SO I ASKED MYSELF "WHAT IS THE THING LEAST DESIRED ON EARTH?"
9-9
© 1992 United Feature Syndicate, Inc.
LADIES! DATE A DILBERT CALL 510-803-9338
QUANTITIES ARE LIMITED
HMM...

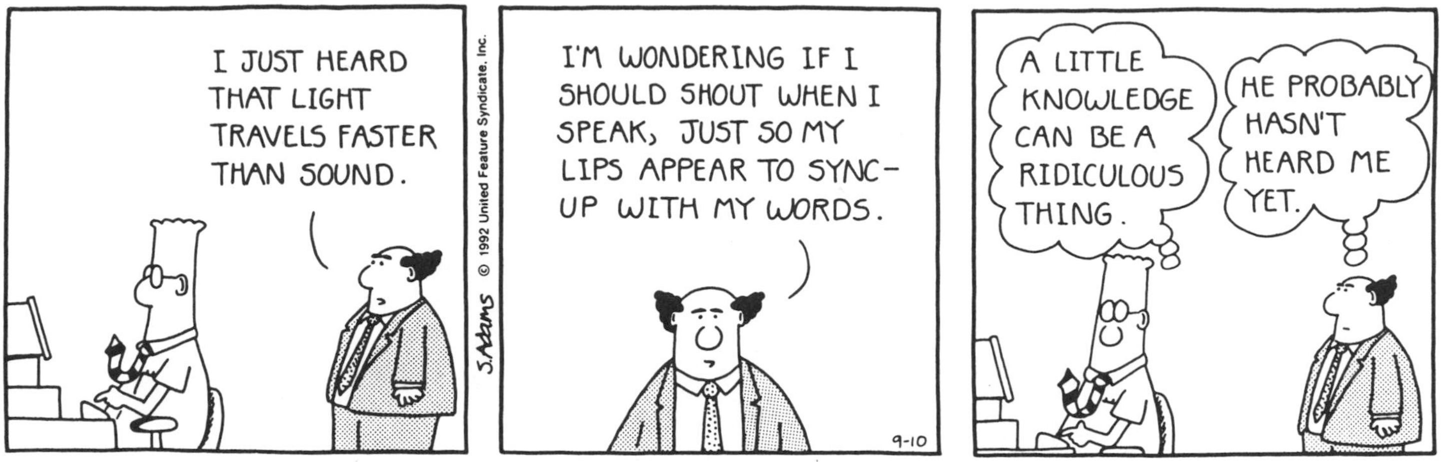
I JUST HEARD THAT LIGHT TRAVELS FASTER THAN SOUND.
S.Adams © 1992 United Feature Syndicate, Inc.
I'M WONDERING IF I SHOULD SHOUT WHEN I SPEAK, JUST SO MY LIPS APPEAR TO SYNC-UP WITH MY WORDS.
9-10
A LITTLE KNOWLEDGE CAN BE A RIDICULOUS THING.
HE PROBABLY HASN'T HEARD ME YET.

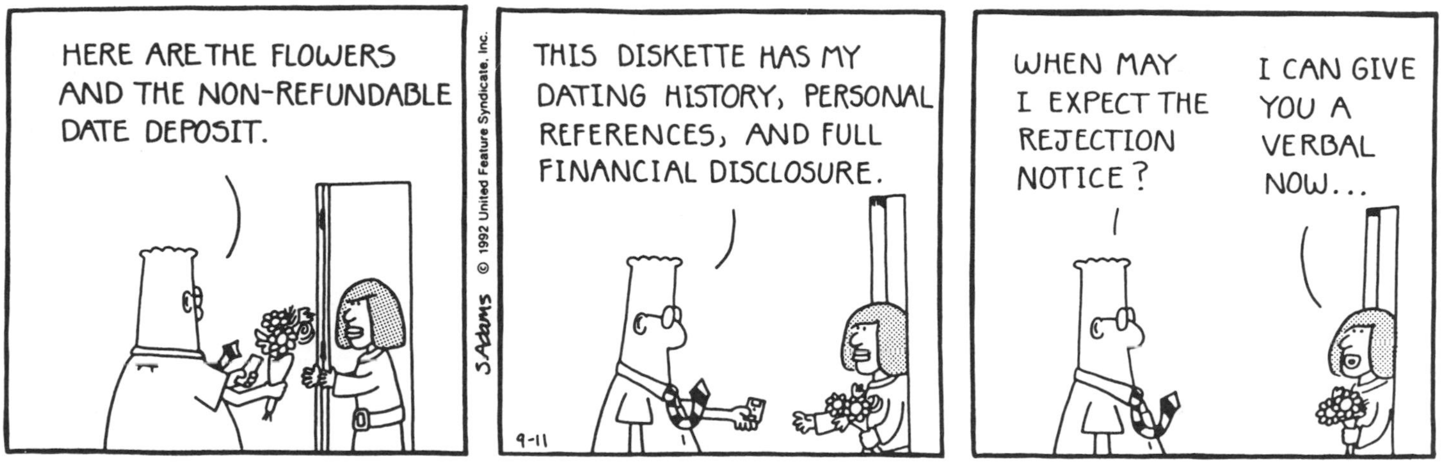
HERE ARE THE FLOWERS AND THE NON-REFUNDABLE DATE DEPOSIT.
S.Adams © 1992 United Feature Syndicate, Inc.
THIS DISKETTE HAS MY DATING HISTORY, PERSONAL REFERENCES, AND FULL FINANCIAL DISCLOSURE.
9-11
WHEN MAY I EXPECT THE REJECTION NOTICE?
I CAN GIVE YOU A VERBAL NOW...

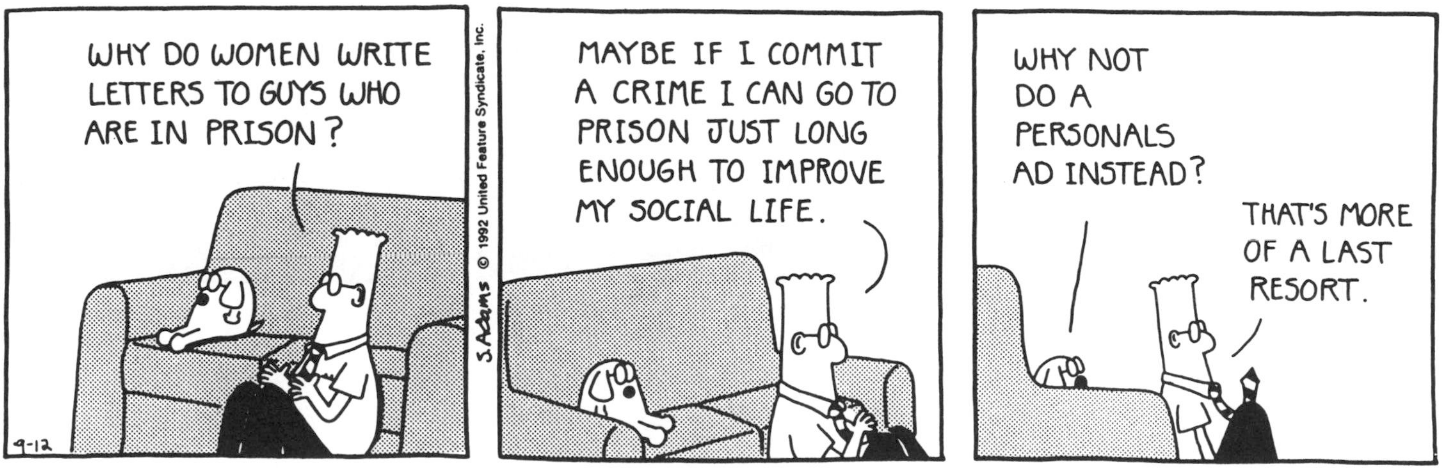
WHY DO WOMEN WRITE LETTERS TO GUYS WHO ARE IN PRISON?
9-12
S.Adams © 1992 United Feature Syndicate, Inc.
MAYBE IF I COMMIT A CRIME I CAN GO TO PRISON JUST LONG ENOUGH TO IMPROVE MY SOCIAL LIFE.
WHY NOT DO A PERSONALS AD INSTEAD?
THAT'S MORE OF A LAST RESORT.

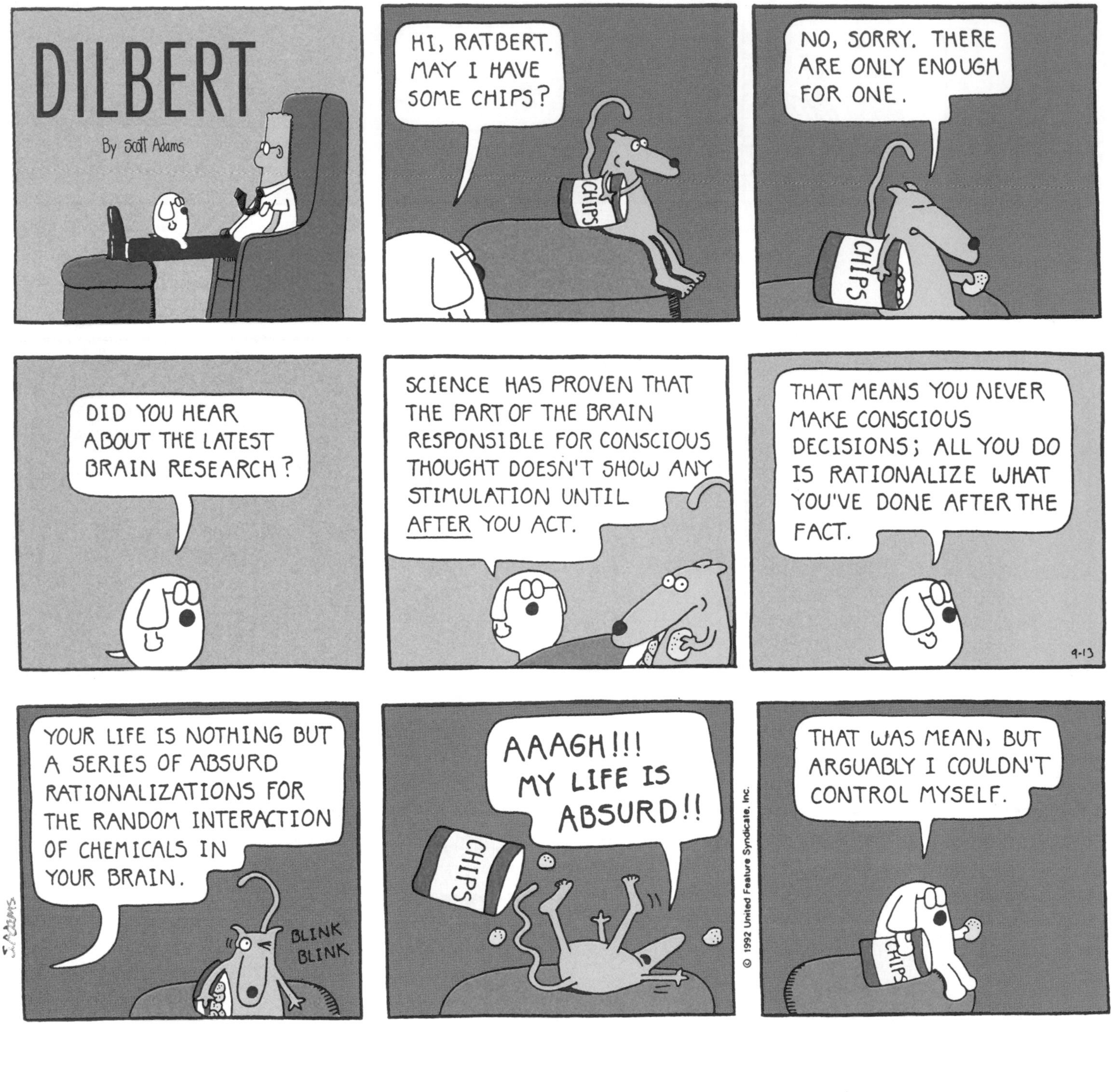
DILBERT
By Scott Adams
HI, RATBERT. MAY I HAVE SOME CHIPS?
CHIPS
NO, SORRY. THERE ARE ONLY ENOUGH FOR ONE.
CHIPS
DID YOU HEAR ABOUT THE LATEST BRAIN RESEARCH?
SCIENCE HAS PROVEN THAT THE PART OF THE BRAIN RESPONSIBLE FOR CONSCIOUS THOUGHT DOESN'T SHOW ANY STIMULATION UNTIL AFTER YOU ACT.
THAT MEANS YOU NEVER MAKE CONSCIOUS DECISIONS; ALL YOU DO IS RATIONALIZE WHAT YOU'VE DONE AFTER THE FACT.
9-13
YOUR LIFE IS NOTHING BUT A SERIES OF ABSURD RATIONALIZATIONS FOR THE RANDOM INTERACTION OF CHEMICALS IN YOUR BRAIN.
BLINK BLINK
AAAGH!!! MY LIFE IS ABSURD!!
CHIPS
© 1992 United Feature Syndicate, Inc.
THAT WAS MEAN, BUT ARGUABLY I COULDN'T CONTROL MYSELF.
CHIPS

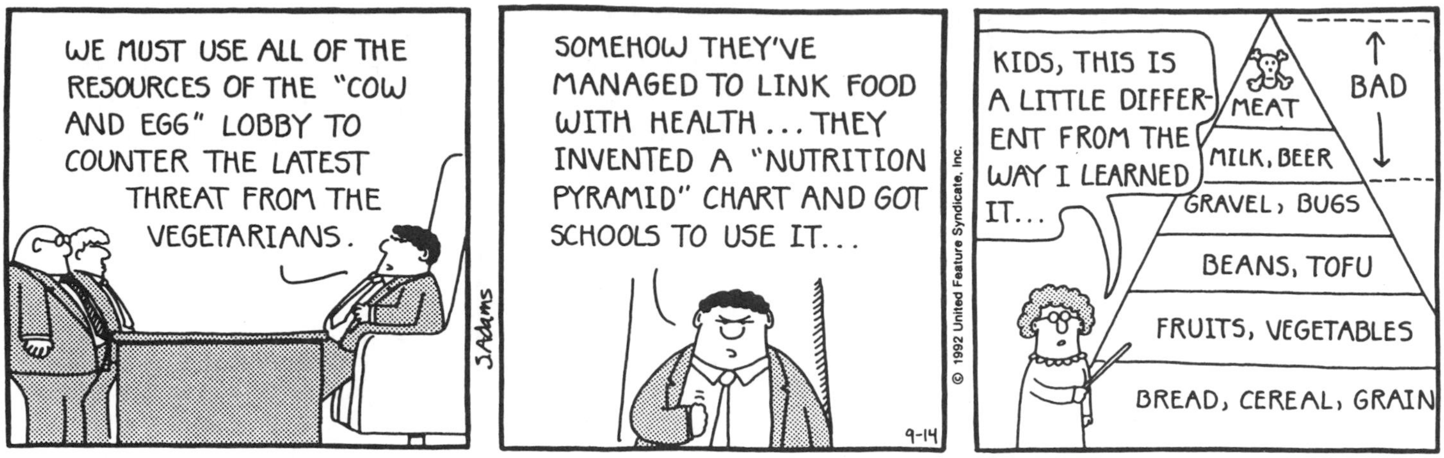
WE MUST USE ALL OF THE RESOURCES OF THE "COW AND EGG" LOBBY TO COUNTER THE LATEST THREAT FROM THE VEGETARIANS.
S.Adams
SOMEHOW THEY'VE MANAGED TO LINK FOOD WITH HEALTH ... THEY INVENTED A "NUTRITION PYRAMID" CHART AND GOT SCHOOLS TO USE IT...
9-14
© 1992 United Feature Syndicate, Inc.
KIDS, THIS IS A LITTLE DIFFERENT FROM THE WAY I LEARNED IT...
MEAT
MILK, BEER
GRAVEL, BUGS
BEANS, TOFU
FRUITS, VEGETABLES
BREAD, CEREAL, GRAIN
BAD

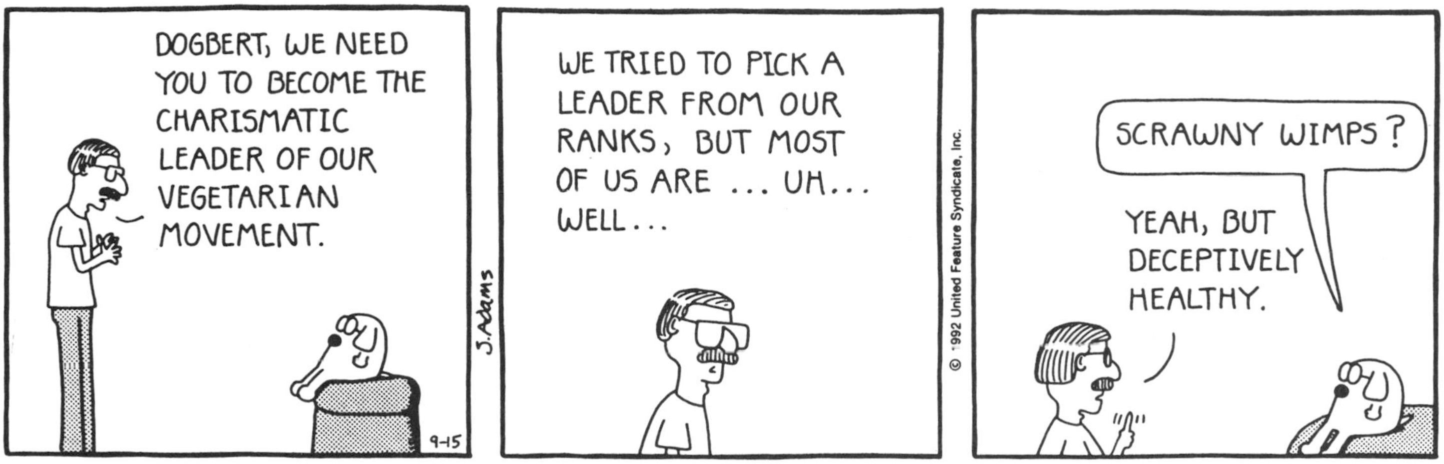
DOGBERT, WE NEED YOU TO BECOME THE CHARISMATIC LEADER OF OUR VEGETARIAN MOVEMENT.
9-15
S.Adams
WE TRIED TO PICK A LEADER FROM OUR RANKS, BUT MOST OF US ARE ... UH... WELL...
© 1992 United Feature Syndicate, Inc.
SCRAWNY WIMPS?
YEAH, BUT DECEPTIVELY HEALTHY.

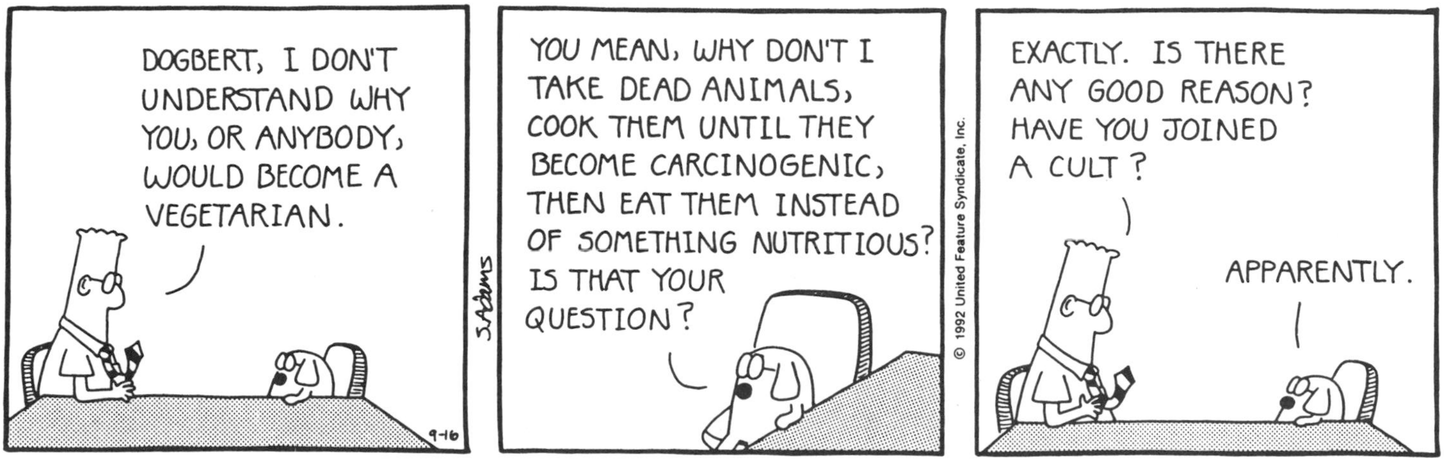
DOGBERT, I DON'T UNDERSTAND WHY YOU, OR ANYBODY, WOULD BECOME A VEGETARIAN.
9-16
S.Adams
YOU MEAN, WHY DON'T I TAKE DEAD ANIMALS, COOK THEM UNTIL THEY BECOME CARCINOGENIC, THEN EAT THEM INSTEAD OF SOMETHING NUTRITIOUS? IS THAT YOUR QUESTION?
© 1992 United Feature Syndicate, Inc.
EXACTLY. IS THERE ANY GOOD REASON? HAVE YOU JOINED A CULT?
APPARENTLY.

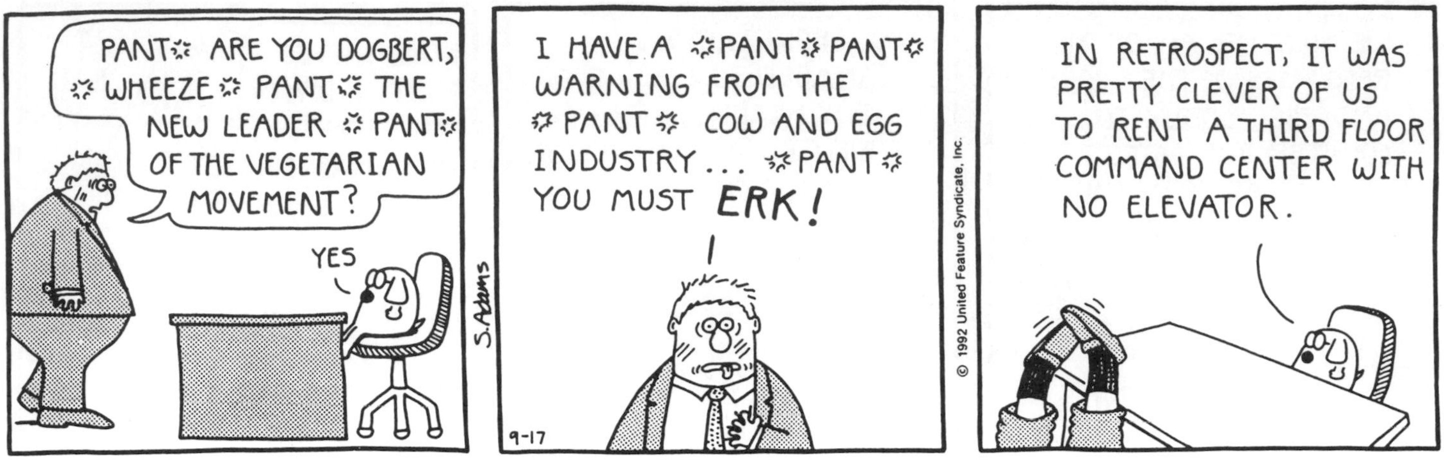
PANT ARE YOU DOGBERT, WHEEZE PANT THE NEW LEADER PANT OF THE VEGETARIAN MOVEMENT?
YES
S. Adams
I HAVE A PANT PANT WARNING FROM THE PANT COW AND EGG INDUSTRY... PANT YOU MUST ERK!
9-17
© 1992 United Feature Syndicate, Inc.
IN RETROSPECT, IT WAS PRETTY CLEVER OF US TO RENT A THIRD FLOOR COMMAND CENTER WITH NO ELEVATOR.

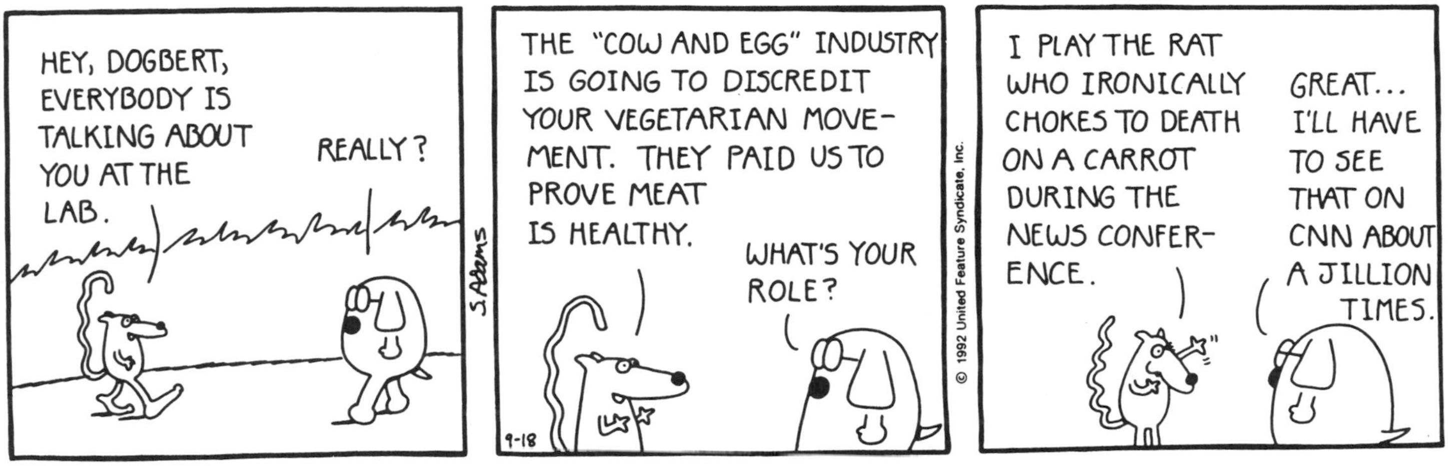
HEY, DOGBERT, EVERYBODY IS TALKING ABOUT YOU AT THE LAB.
REALLY?
S. Adams
THE "COW AND EGG" INDUSTRY IS GOING TO DISCREDIT YOUR VEGETARIAN MOVEMENT. THEY PAID US TO PROVE MEAT IS HEALTHY.
WHAT'S YOUR ROLE?
9-18
© 1992 United Feature Syndicate, Inc.
I PLAY THE RAT WHO IRONICALLY CHOKES TO DEATH ON A CARROT DURING THE NEWS CONFERENCE.
GREAT... I'LL HAVE TO SEE THAT ON CNN ABOUT A JILLION TIMES.

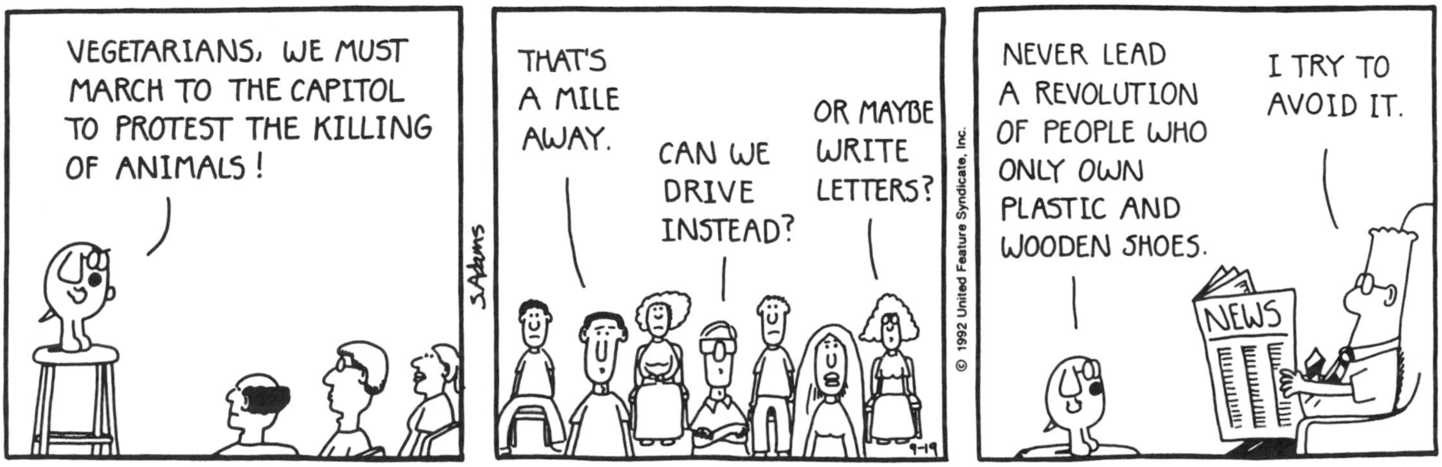
VEGETARIANS, WE MUST MARCH TO THE CAPITOL TO PROTEST THE KILLING OF ANIMALS!
S. Adams
THAT'S A MILE AWAY.
CAN WE DRIVE INSTEAD?
OR MAYBE WRITE LETTERS?
9-19
© 1992 United Feature Syndicate, Inc.
NEVER LEAD A REVOLUTION OF PEOPLE WHO ONLY OWN PLASTIC AND WOODEN SHOES.
I TRY TO AVOID IT.
NEWS

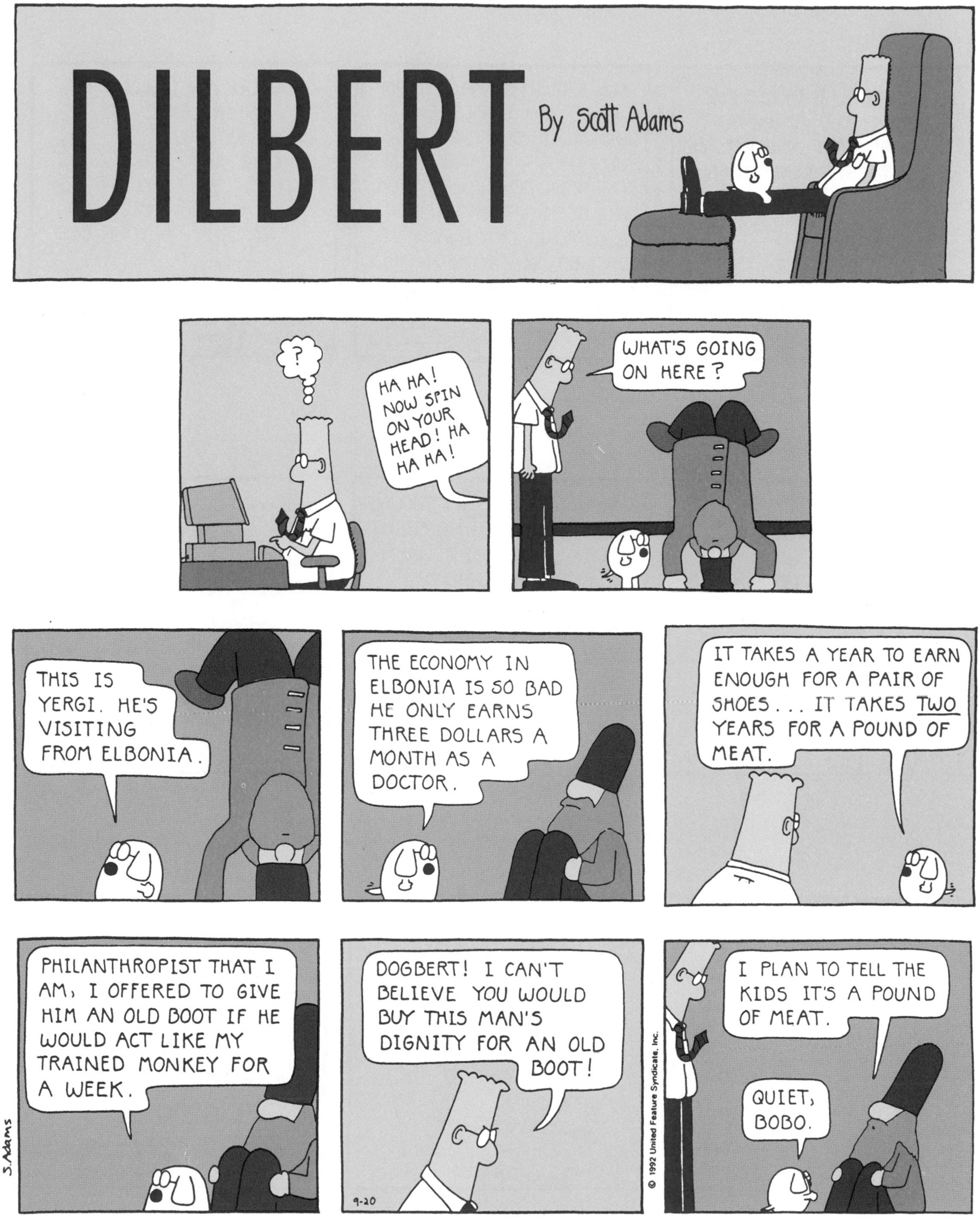
DILBERT
By Scott Adams
?
HA HA! NOW SPIN ON YOUR HEAD! HA HA HA!
WHAT'S GOING ON HERE?
THIS IS YERGI. HE'S VISITING FROM ELBONIA.
THE ECONOMY IN ELBONIA IS SO BAD HE ONLY EARNS THREE DOLLARS A MONTH AS A DOCTOR.
IT TAKES A YEAR TO EARN ENOUGH FOR A PAIR OF SHOES . . . IT TAKES TWO YEARS FOR A POUND OF MEAT.
PHILANTHROPIST THAT I AM, I OFFERED TO GIVE HIM AN OLD BOOT IF HE WOULD ACT LIKE MY TRAINED MONKEY FOR A WEEK.
S. Adams
DOGBERT! I CAN'T BELIEVE YOU WOULD BUY THIS MAN'S DIGNITY FOR AN OLD BOOT!
9-20
© 1992 United Feature Syndicate, Inc.
I PLAN TO TELL THE KIDS IT'S A POUND OF MEAT.
QUIET, BOBO.

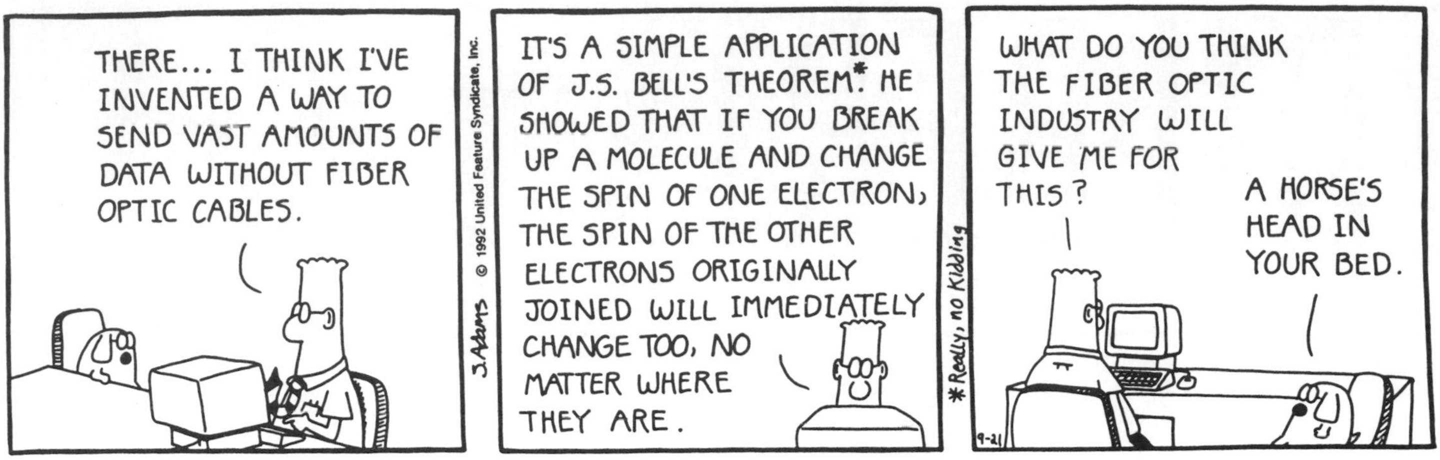
THERE... I THINK I'VE INVENTED A WAY TO SEND VAST AMOUNTS OF DATA WITHOUT FIBER OPTIC CABLES.
IT'S A SIMPLE APPLICATION OF J.S. BELL'S THEOREM.* HE SHOWED THAT IF YOU BREAK UP A MOLECULE AND CHANGE THE SPIN OF ONE ELECTRON, THE SPIN OF THE OTHER ELECTRONS ORIGINALLY JOINED WILL IMMEDIATELY CHANGE TOO, NO MATTER WHERE THEY ARE.
* Really, no kidding
WHAT DO YOU THINK THE FIBER OPTIC INDUSTRY WILL GIVE ME FOR THIS?
A HORSE'S HEAD IN YOUR BED.
S. Adams
© 1992 United Feature Syndicate, Inc.
9-21

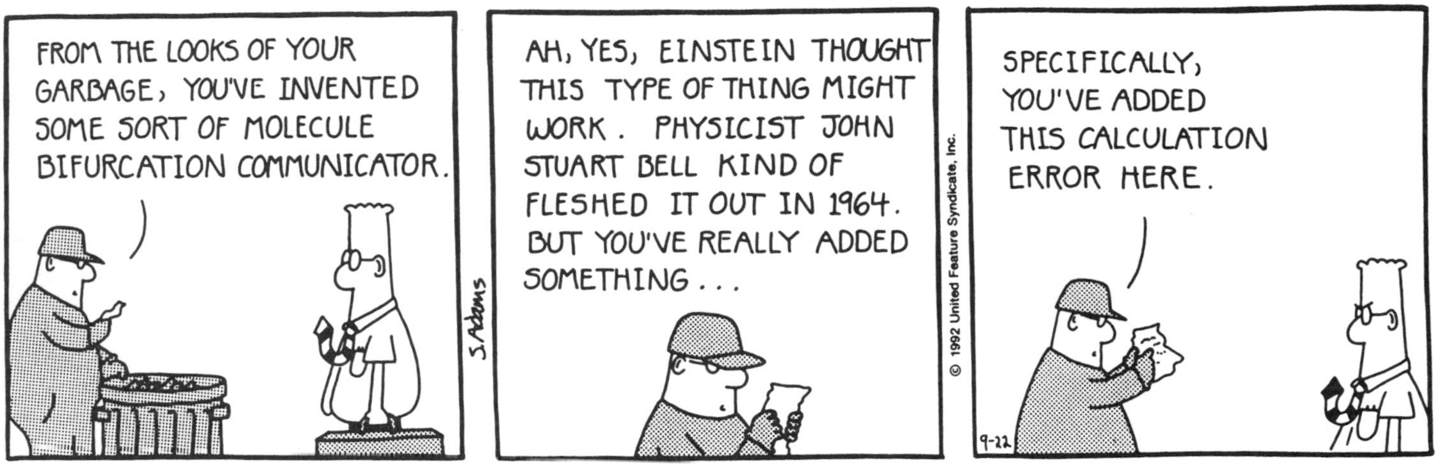
FROM THE LOOKS OF YOUR GARBAGE, YOU'VE INVENTED SOME SORT OF MOLECULE BIFURCATION COMMUNICATOR.
AH, YES, EINSTEIN THOUGHT THIS TYPE OF THING MIGHT WORK. PHYSICIST JOHN STUART BELL KIND OF FLESHED IT OUT IN 1964. BUT YOU'VE REALLY ADDED SOMETHING...
SPECIFICALLY, YOU'VE ADDED THIS CALCULATION ERROR HERE.
S. Adams
© 1992 United Feature Syndicate, Inc.
9-22

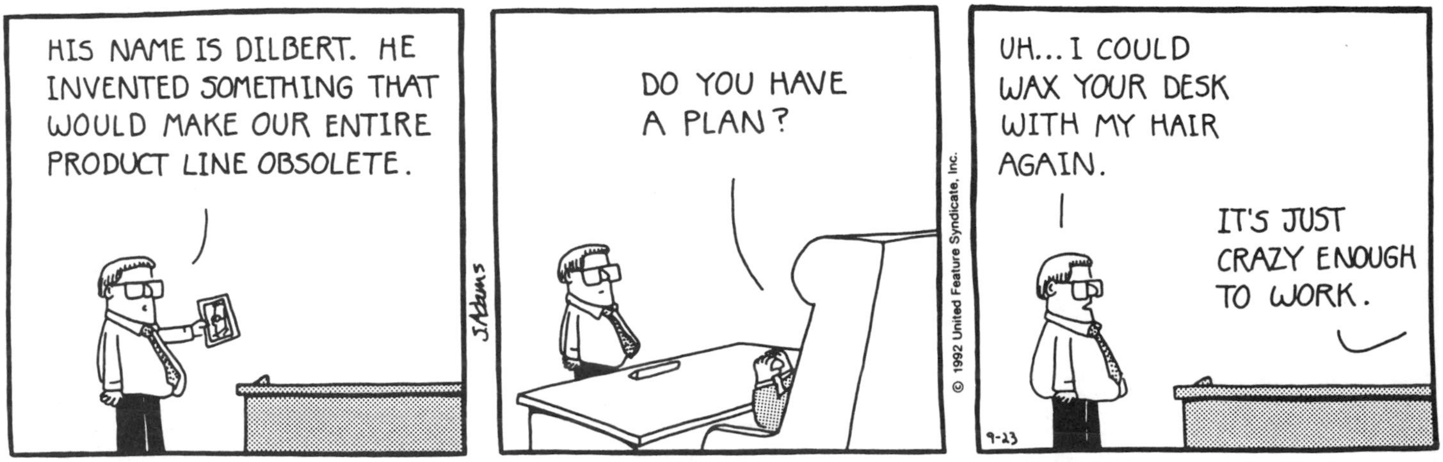
HIS NAME IS DILBERT. HE INVENTED SOMETHING THAT WOULD MAKE OUR ENTIRE PRODUCT LINE OBSOLETE.
DO YOU HAVE A PLAN?
UH... I COULD WAX YOUR DESK WITH MY HAIR AGAIN.
IT'S JUST CRAZY ENOUGH TO WORK.
S. Adams
© 1992 United Feature Syndicate, Inc.
9-23

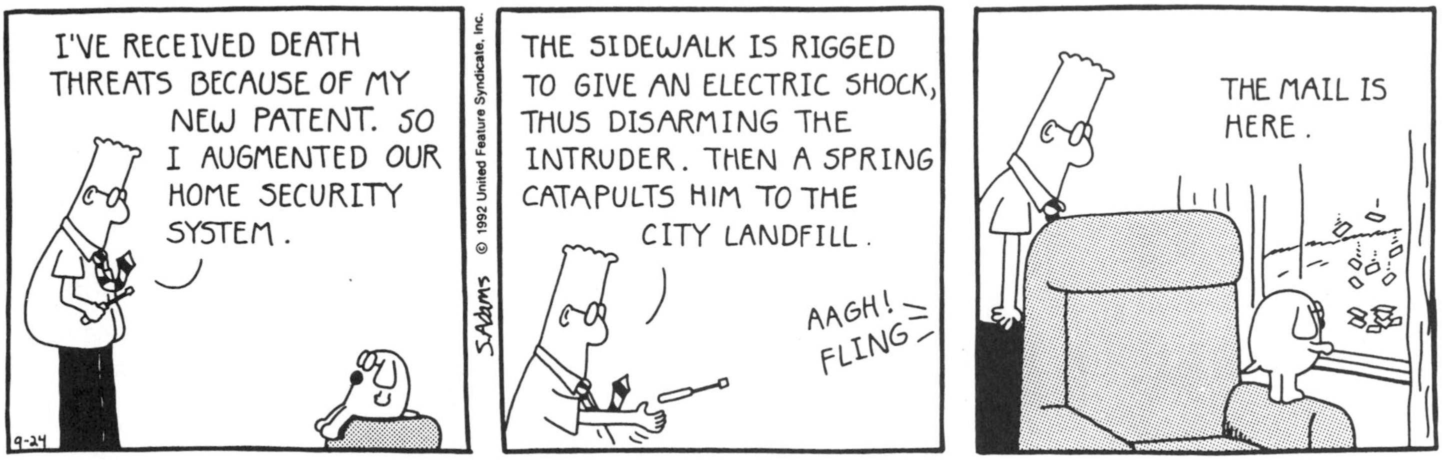
I'VE RECEIVED DEATH THREATS BECAUSE OF MY NEW PATENT. SO I AUGMENTED OUR HOME SECURITY SYSTEM.
9-24
S.Adams © 1992 United Feature Syndicate, Inc.
THE SIDEWALK IS RIGGED TO GIVE AN ELECTRIC SHOCK, THUS DISARMING THE INTRUDER. THEN A SPRING CATAPULTS HIM TO THE CITY LANDFILL.
AAGH!
FLING
THE MAIL IS HERE.

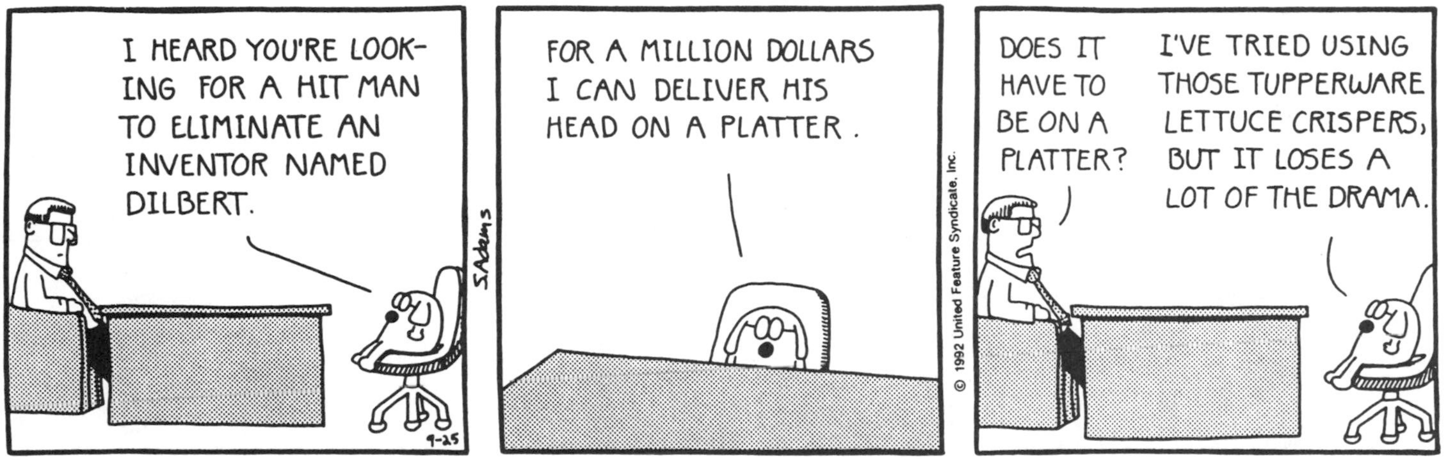
I HEARD YOU'RE LOOKING FOR A HIT MAN TO ELIMINATE AN INVENTOR NAMED DILBERT.
9-25
S.Adams
FOR A MILLION DOLLARS I CAN DELIVER HIS HEAD ON A PLATTER.
© 1992 United Feature Syndicate, Inc.
DOES IT HAVE TO BE ON A PLATTER?
I'VE TRIED USING THOSE TUPPERWARE LETTUCE CRISPERS, BUT IT LOSES A LOT OF THE DRAMA.

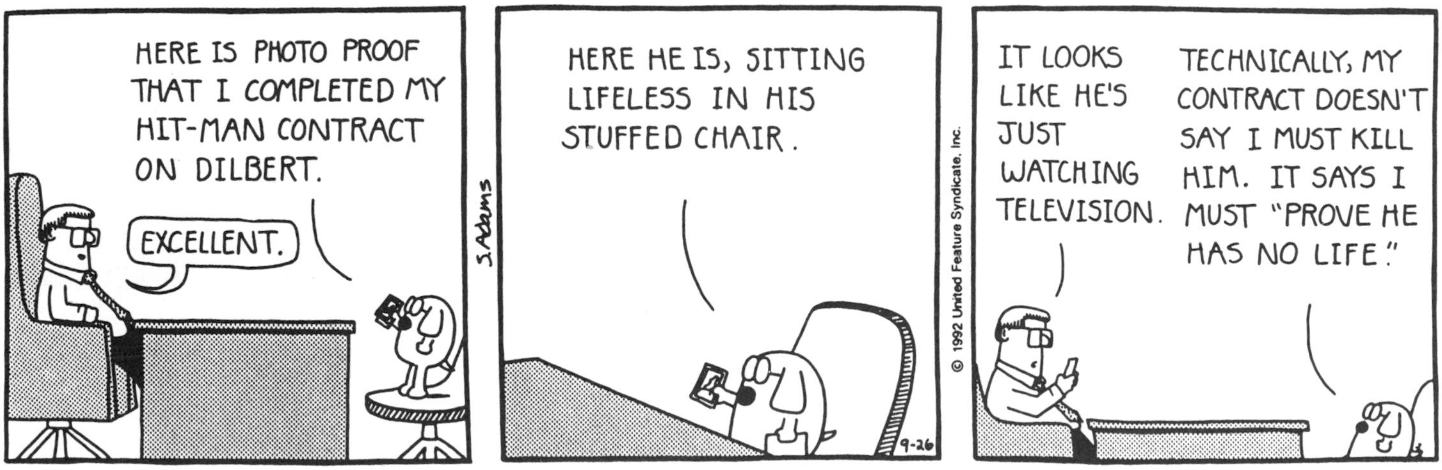
HERE IS PHOTO PROOF THAT I COMPLETED MY HIT-MAN CONTRACT ON DILBERT.
EXCELLENT.
S.Adams
HERE HE IS, SITTING LIFELESS IN HIS STUFFED CHAIR.
9-26
© 1992 United Feature Syndicate, Inc.
IT LOOKS LIKE HE'S JUST WATCHING TELEVISION.
TECHNICALLY, MY CONTRACT DOESN'T SAY I MUST KILL HIM. IT SAYS I MUST "PROVE HE HAS NO LIFE."

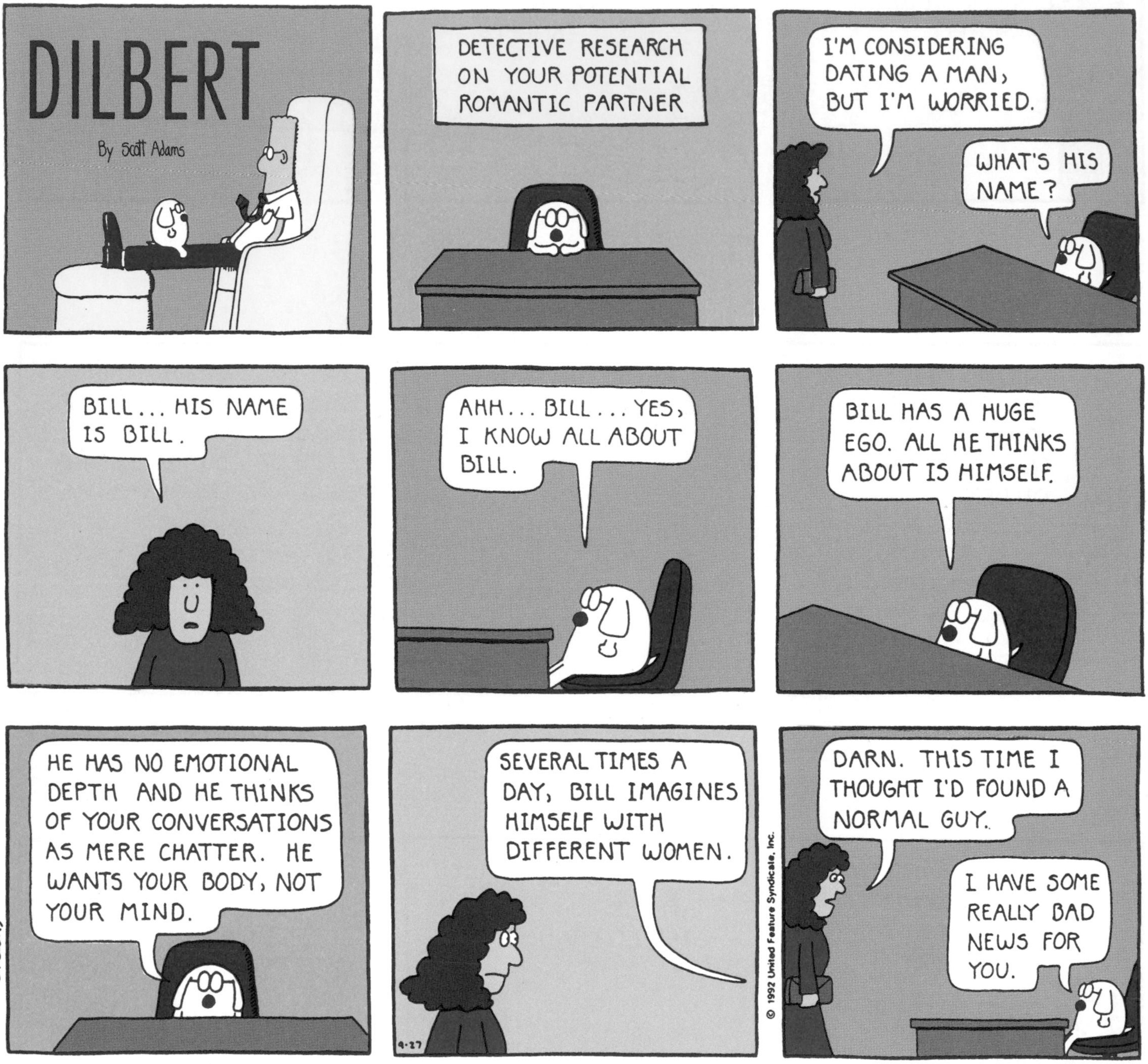

DILBERT
By Scott Adams
DETECTIVE RESEARCH ON YOUR POTENTIAL ROMANTIC PARTNER
I'M CONSIDERING DATING A MAN, BUT I'M WORRIED.
WHAT'S HIS NAME?
BILL... HIS NAME IS BILL.
AHH... BILL... YES, I KNOW ALL ABOUT BILL.
BILL HAS A HUGE EGO. ALL HE THINKS ABOUT IS HIMSELF.
HE HAS NO EMOTIONAL DEPTH AND HE THINKS OF YOUR CONVERSATIONS AS MERE CHATTER. HE WANTS YOUR BODY, NOT YOUR MIND.
S.Adams
SEVERAL TIMES A DAY, BILL IMAGINES HIMSELF WITH DIFFERENT WOMEN.
9-27
© 1992 United Feature Syndicate, Inc.
DARN. THIS TIME I THOUGHT I'D FOUND A NORMAL GUY.
I HAVE SOME REALLY BAD NEWS FOR YOU.

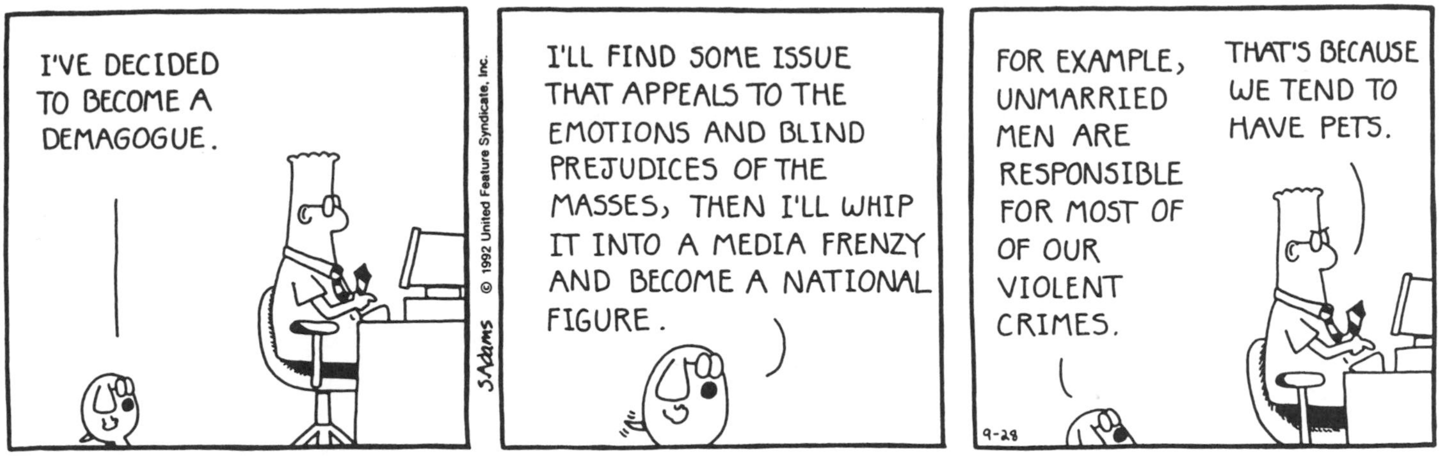
I'VE DECIDED TO BECOME A DEMAGOGUE.
© 1992 United Feature Syndicate, Inc.
S.Adams
I'LL FIND SOME ISSUE THAT APPEALS TO THE EMOTIONS AND BLIND PREJUDICES OF THE MASSES, THEN I'LL WHIP IT INTO A MEDIA FRENZY AND BECOME A NATIONAL FIGURE.
FOR EXAMPLE, UNMARRIED MEN ARE RESPONSIBLE FOR MOST OF OF OUR VIOLENT CRIMES.
THAT'S BECAUSE WE TEND TO HAVE PETS.
9-28

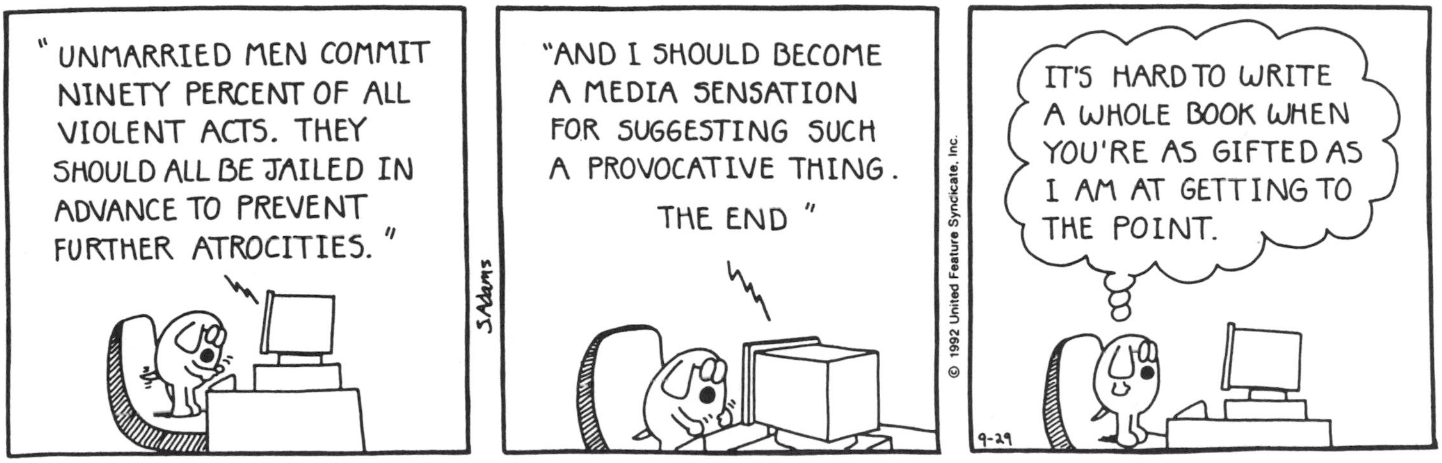
"UNMARRIED MEN COMMIT NINETY PERCENT OF ALL VIOLENT ACTS. THEY SHOULD ALL BE JAILED IN ADVANCE TO PREVENT FURTHER ATROCITIES."
S.Adams
"AND I SHOULD BECOME A MEDIA SENSATION FOR SUGGESTING SUCH A PROVOCATIVE THING.
THE END"
© 1992 United Feature Syndicate, Inc.
IT'S HARD TO WRITE A WHOLE BOOK WHEN YOU'RE AS GIFTED AS I AM AT GETTING TO THE POINT.
9-29

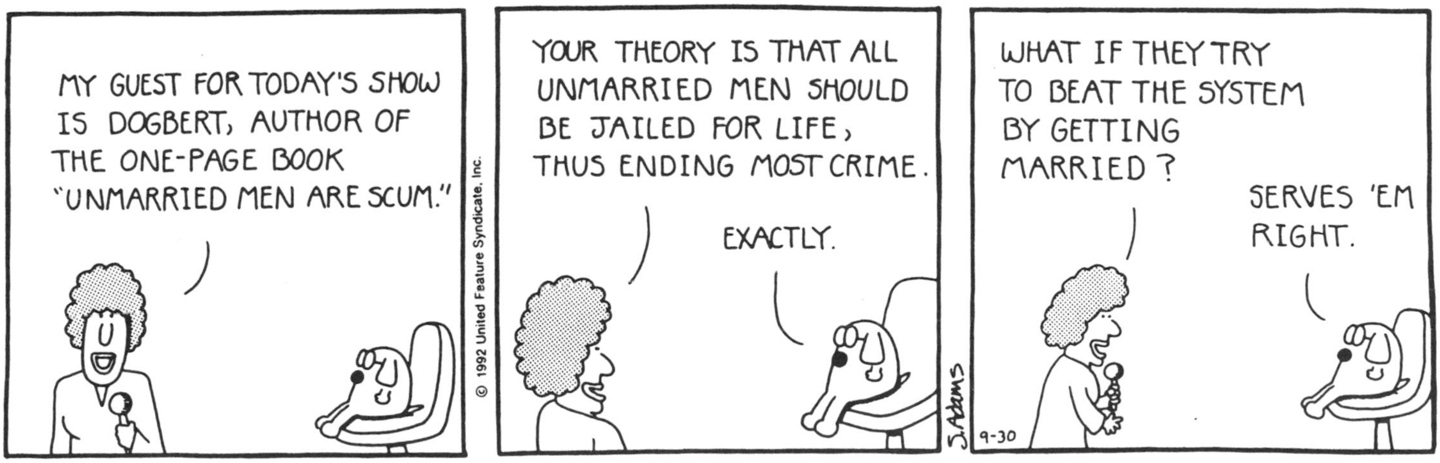
MY GUEST FOR TODAY'S SHOW IS DOGBERT, AUTHOR OF THE ONE-PAGE BOOK "UNMARRIED MEN ARE SCUM."
© 1992 United Feature Syndicate, Inc.
YOUR THEORY IS THAT ALL UNMARRIED MEN SHOULD BE JAILED FOR LIFE, THUS ENDING MOST CRIME.
EXACTLY.
S.Adams
WHAT IF THEY TRY TO BEAT THE SYSTEM BY GETTING MARRIED?
SERVES 'EM RIGHT.
9-30

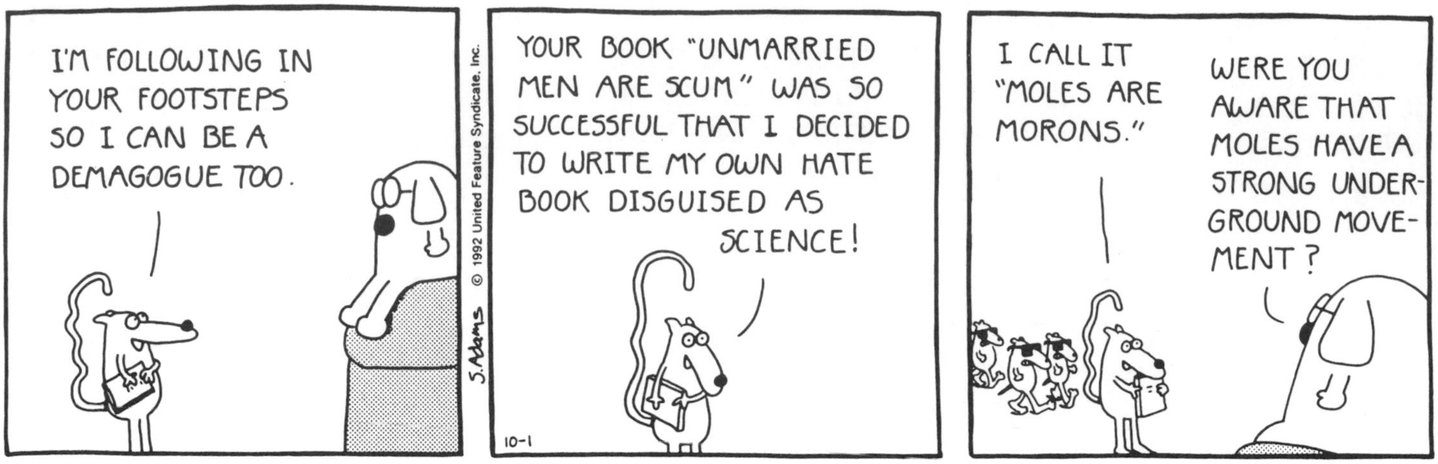
I'M FOLLOWING IN YOUR FOOTSTEPS SO I CAN BE A DEMAGOGUE TOO.
S. Adams © 1992 United Feature Syndicate, Inc.
YOUR BOOK "UNMARRIED MEN ARE SCUM" WAS SO SUCCESSFUL THAT I DECIDED TO WRITE MY OWN HATE BOOK DISGUISED AS SCIENCE!
10-1
I CALL IT "MOLES ARE MORONS."
WERE YOU AWARE THAT MOLES HAVE A STRONG UNDERGROUND MOVEMENT?

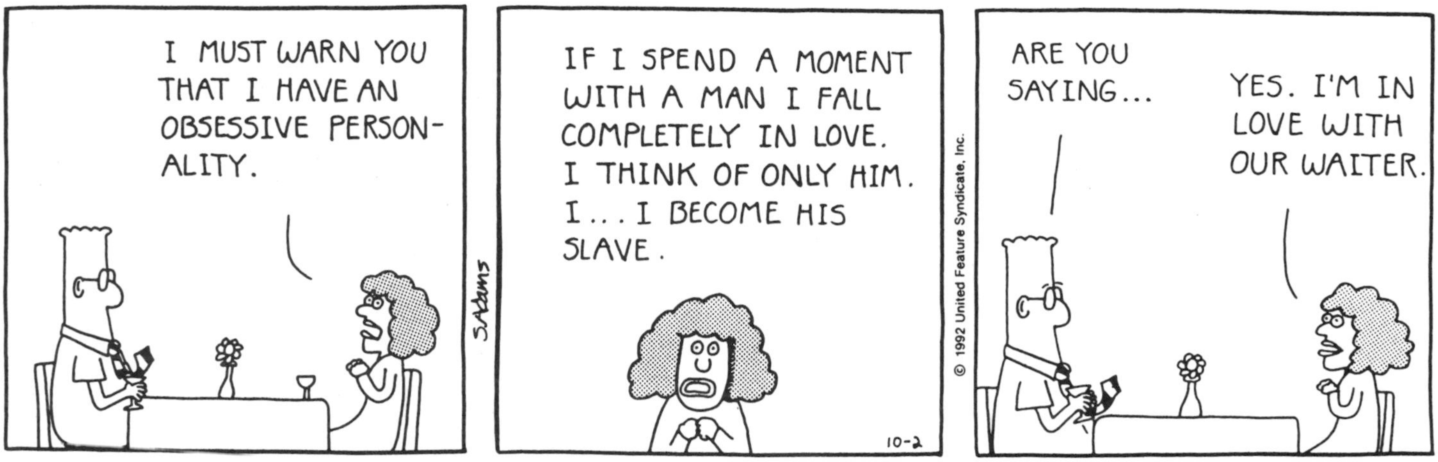
I MUST WARN YOU THAT I HAVE AN OBSESSIVE PERSONALITY.
S. Adams
IF I SPEND A MOMENT WITH A MAN I FALL COMPLETELY IN LOVE. I THINK OF ONLY HIM. I... I BECOME HIS SLAVE.
10-2
© 1992 United Feature Syndicate, Inc.
ARE YOU SAYING...
YES. I'M IN LOVE WITH OUR WAITER.

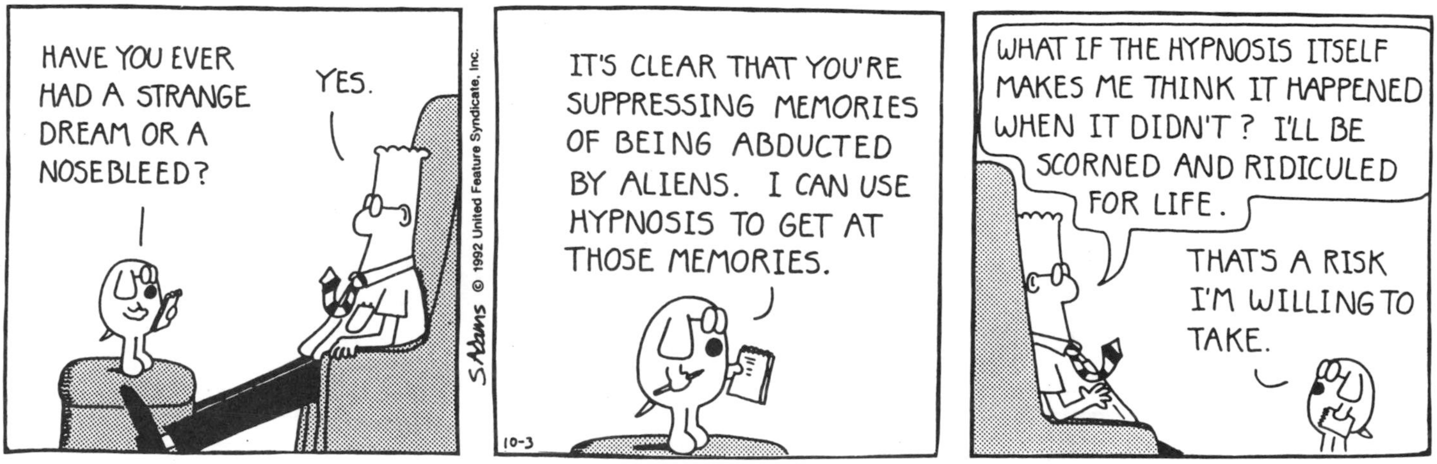
HAVE YOU EVER HAD A STRANGE DREAM OR A NOSEBLEED?
YES.
S. Adams © 1992 United Feature Syndicate, Inc.
IT'S CLEAR THAT YOU'RE SUPPRESSING MEMORIES OF BEING ABDUCTED BY ALIENS. I CAN USE HYPNOSIS TO GET AT THOSE MEMORIES.
10-3
WHAT IF THE HYPNOSIS ITSELF MAKES ME THINK IT HAPPENED WHEN IT DIDN'T? I'LL BE SCORNED AND RIDICULED FOR LIFE.
THAT'S A RISK I'M WILLING TO TAKE.

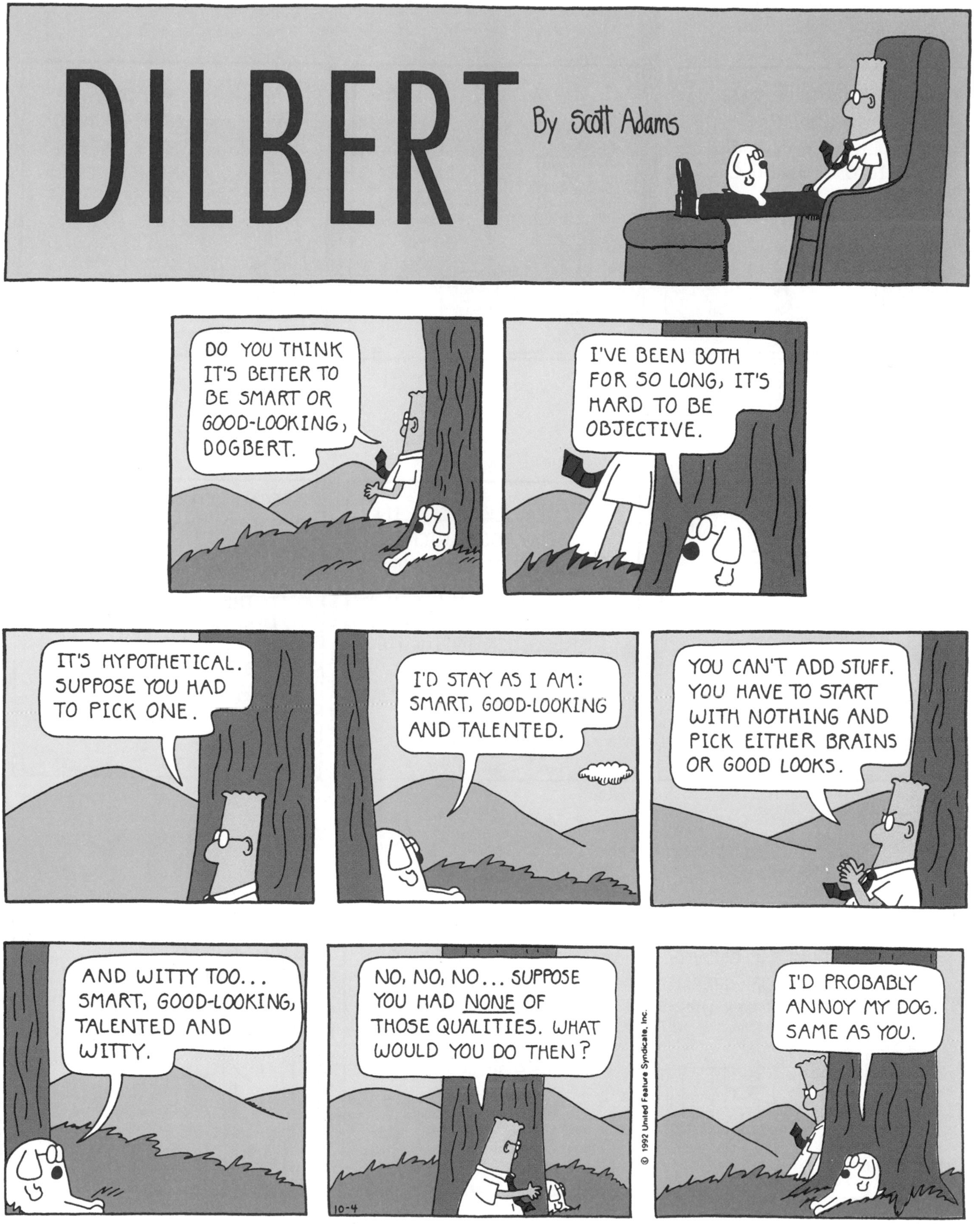
DILBERT
By Scott Adams
DO YOU THINK IT'S BETTER TO BE SMART OR GOOD-LOOKING, DOGBERT.
I'VE BEEN BOTH FOR SO LONG, IT'S HARD TO BE OBJECTIVE.
IT'S HYPOTHETICAL. SUPPOSE YOU HAD TO PICK ONE.
I'D STAY AS I AM: SMART, GOOD-LOOKING AND TALENTED.
YOU CAN'T ADD STUFF. YOU HAVE TO START WITH NOTHING AND PICK EITHER BRAINS OR GOOD LOOKS.
AND WITTY TOO... SMART, GOOD-LOOKING, TALENTED AND WITTY.
NO, NO, NO... SUPPOSE YOU HAD NONE OF THOSE QUALITIES. WHAT WOULD YOU DO THEN?
I'D PROBABLY ANNOY MY DOG. SAME AS YOU.
S. Adams
10-4
© 1992 United Feature Syndicate, Inc.

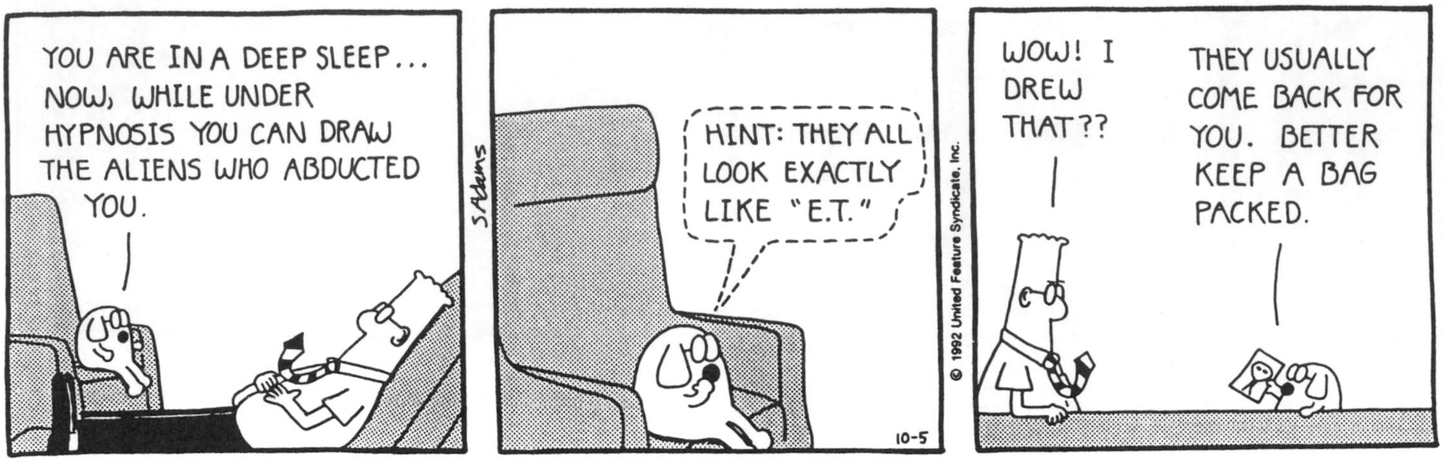
YOU ARE IN A DEEP SLEEP... NOW, WHILE UNDER HYPNOSIS YOU CAN DRAW THE ALIENS WHO ABDUCTED YOU.
S. Adams
HINT: THEY ALL LOOK EXACTLY LIKE "E.T."
10-5
© 1992 United Feature Syndicate, Inc.
WOW! I DREW THAT??
THEY USUALLY COME BACK FOR YOU. BETTER KEEP A BAG PACKED.

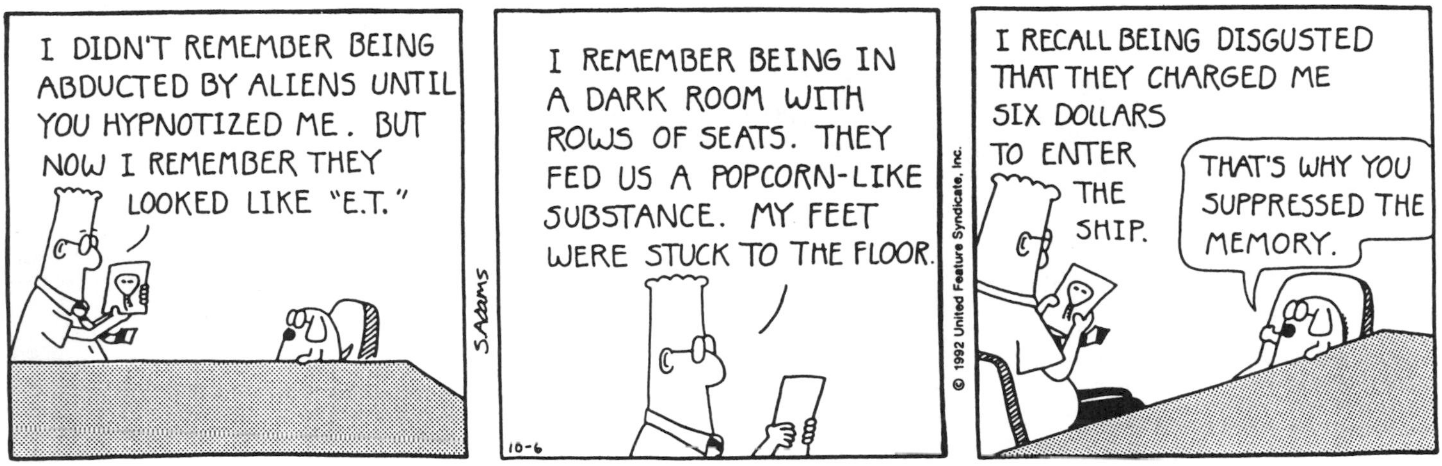
I DIDN'T REMEMBER BEING ABDUCTED BY ALIENS UNTIL YOU HYPNOTIZED ME. BUT NOW I REMEMBER THEY LOOKED LIKE "E.T."
S. Adams
I REMEMBER BEING IN A DARK ROOM WITH ROWS OF SEATS. THEY FED US A POPCORN-LIKE SUBSTANCE. MY FEET WERE STUCK TO THE FLOOR.
10-6
© 1992 United Feature Syndicate, Inc.
I RECALL BEING DISGUSTED THAT THEY CHARGED ME SIX DOLLARS TO ENTER THE SHIP.
THAT'S WHY YOU SUPPRESSED THE MEMORY.

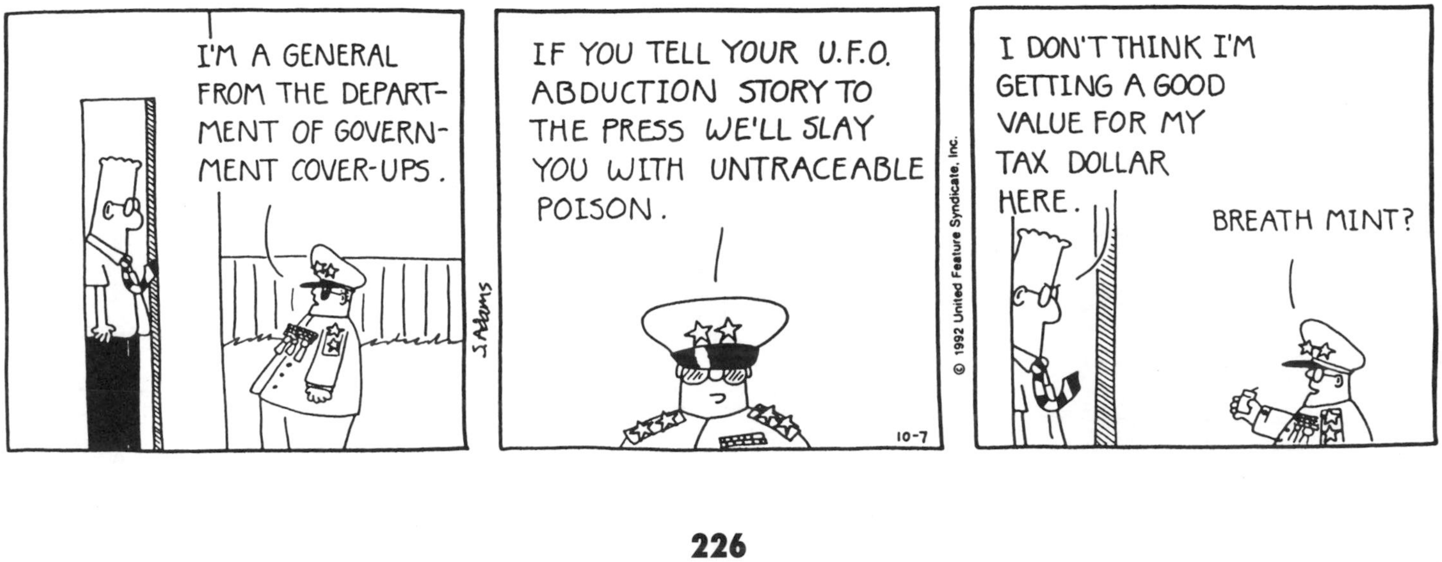
I'M A GENERAL FROM THE DEPARTMENT OF GOVERNMENT COVER-UPS.
S. Adams
IF YOU TELL YOUR U.F.O. ABDUCTION STORY TO THE PRESS WE'LL SLAY YOU WITH UNTRACEABLE POISON.
10-7
© 1992 United Feature Syndicate, Inc.
I DON'T THINK I'M GETTING A GOOD VALUE FOR MY TAX DOLLAR HERE.
BREATH MINT?

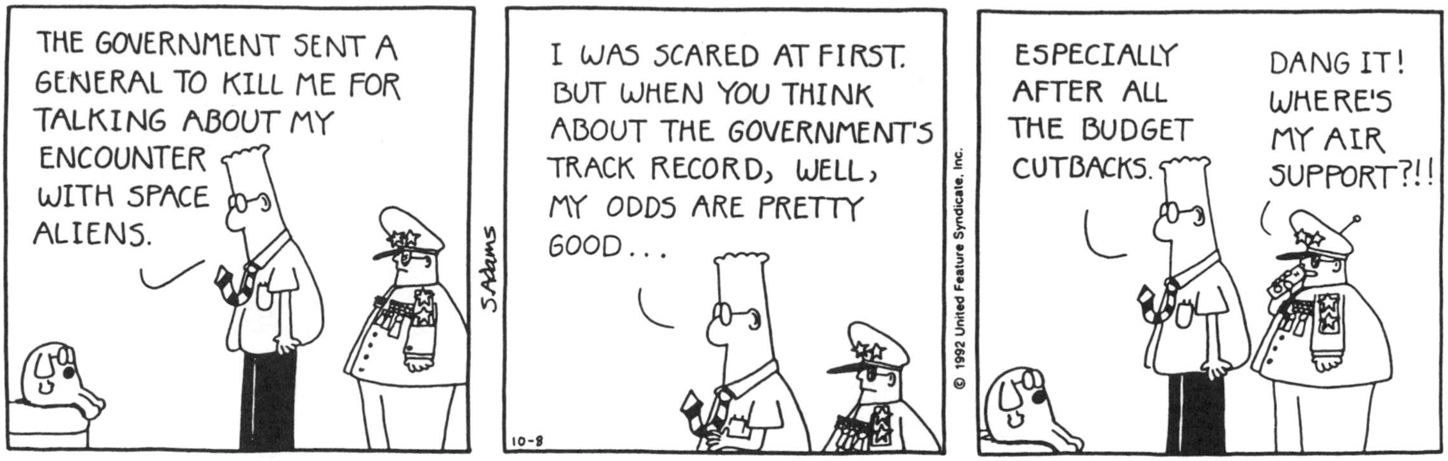
THE GOVERNMENT SENT A GENERAL TO KILL ME FOR TALKING ABOUT MY ENCOUNTER WITH SPACE ALIENS.
S.Adams
I WAS SCARED AT FIRST. BUT WHEN YOU THINK ABOUT THE GOVERNMENT'S TRACK RECORD, WELL, MY ODDS ARE PRETTY GOOD...
10-8
© 1992 United Feature Syndicate, Inc.
ESPECIALLY AFTER ALL THE BUDGET CUTBACKS.
DANG IT! WHERE'S MY AIR SUPPORT?!!

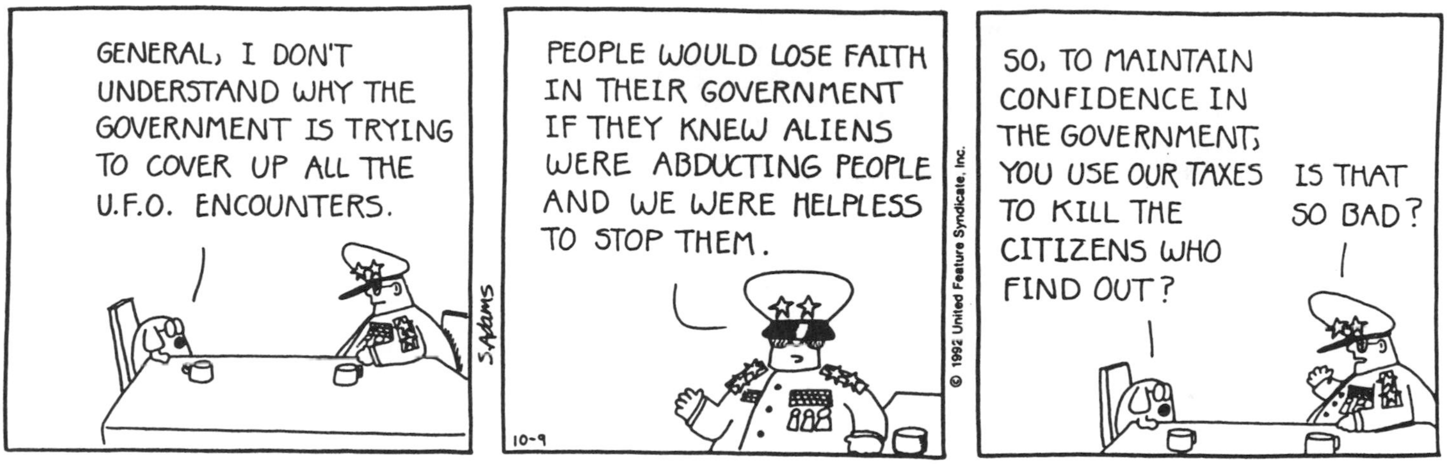
GENERAL, I DON'T UNDERSTAND WHY THE GOVERNMENT IS TRYING TO COVER UP ALL THE U.F.O. ENCOUNTERS.
S.Adams
PEOPLE WOULD LOSE FAITH IN THEIR GOVERNMENT IF THEY KNEW ALIENS WERE ABDUCTING PEOPLE AND WE WERE HELPLESS TO STOP THEM.
10-9
© 1992 United Feature Syndicate, Inc.
SO, TO MAINTAIN CONFIDENCE IN THE GOVERNMENT, YOU USE OUR TAXES TO KILL THE CITIZENS WHO FIND OUT?
IS THAT SO BAD?

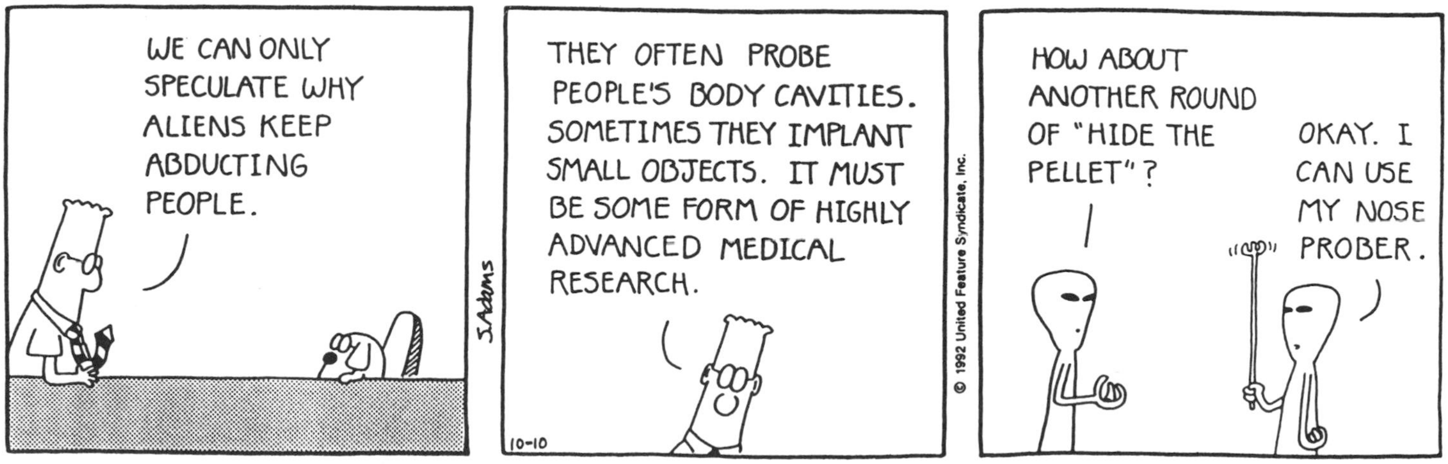
WE CAN ONLY SPECULATE WHY ALIENS KEEP ABDUCTING PEOPLE.
S.Adams
THEY OFTEN PROBE PEOPLE'S BODY CAVITIES. SOMETIMES THEY IMPLANT SMALL OBJECTS. IT MUST BE SOME FORM OF HIGHLY ADVANCED MEDICAL RESEARCH.
10-10
© 1992 United Feature Syndicate, Inc.
HOW ABOUT ANOTHER ROUND OF "HIDE THE PELLET"?
OKAY. I CAN USE MY NOSE PROBER.

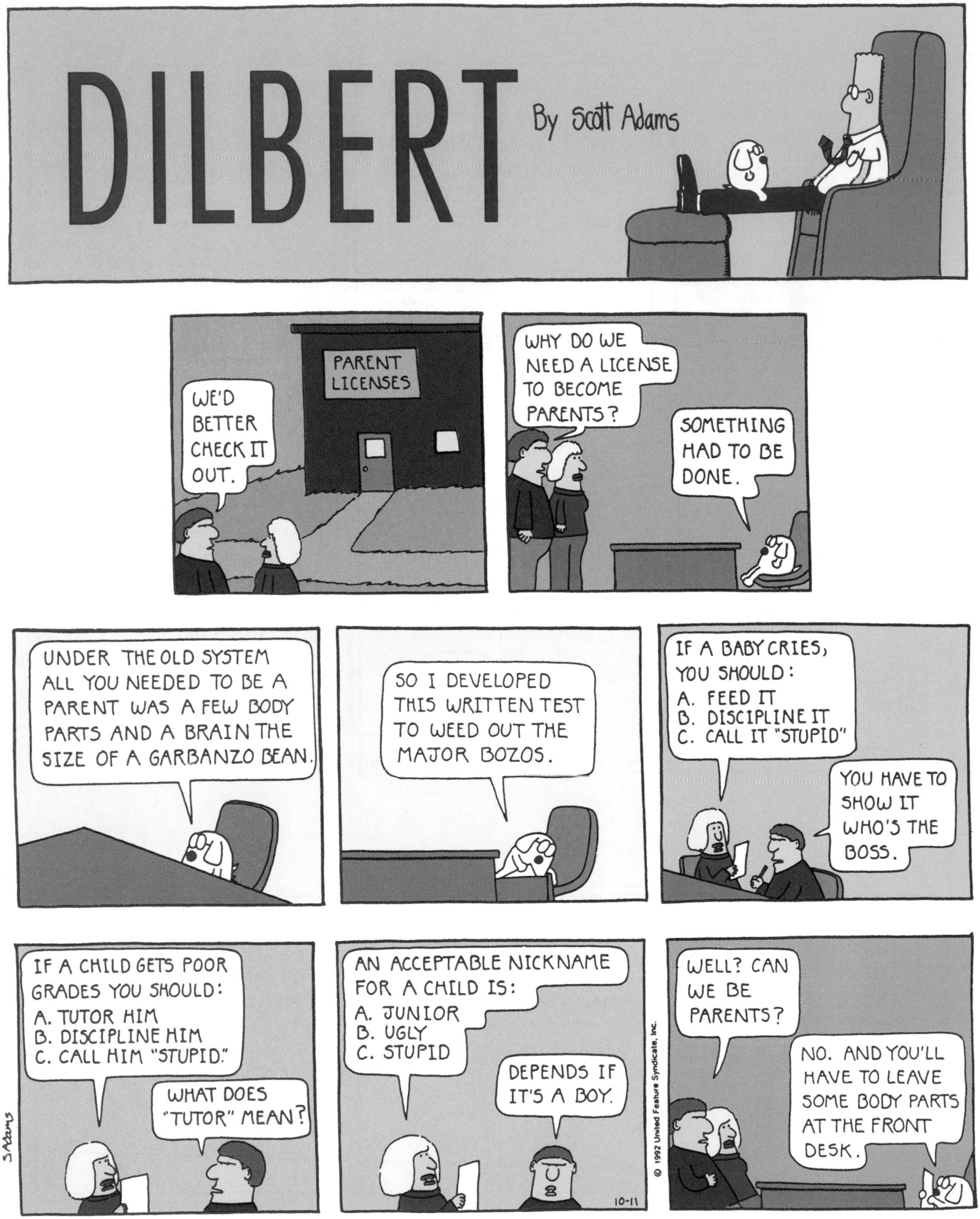
DILBERT
By Scott Adams
PARENT LICENSES
WE'D BETTER CHECK IT OUT.
WHY DO WE NEED A LICENSE TO BECOME PARENTS?
SOMETHING HAD TO BE DONE.
UNDER THE OLD SYSTEM ALL YOU NEEDED TO BE A PARENT WAS A FEW BODY PARTS AND A BRAIN THE SIZE OF A GARBANZO BEAN.
SO I DEVELOPED THIS WRITTEN TEST TO WEED OUT THE MAJOR BOZOS.
IF A BABY CRIES, YOU SHOULD: A. FEED IT B. DISCIPLINE IT C. CALL IT "STUPID"
YOU HAVE TO SHOW IT WHO'S THE BOSS.
IF A CHILD GETS POOR GRADES YOU SHOULD: A. TUTOR HIM B. DISCIPLINE HIM C. CALL HIM "STUPID."
WHAT DOES "TUTOR" MEAN?
AN ACCEPTABLE NICKNAME FOR A CHILD IS: A. JUNIOR B. UGLY C. STUPID
DEPENDS IF IT'S A BOY.
© 1992 United Feature Syndicate, Inc.
10-11
WELL? CAN WE BE PARENTS?
NO. AND YOU'LL HAVE TO LEAVE SOME BODY PARTS AT THE FRONT DESK.

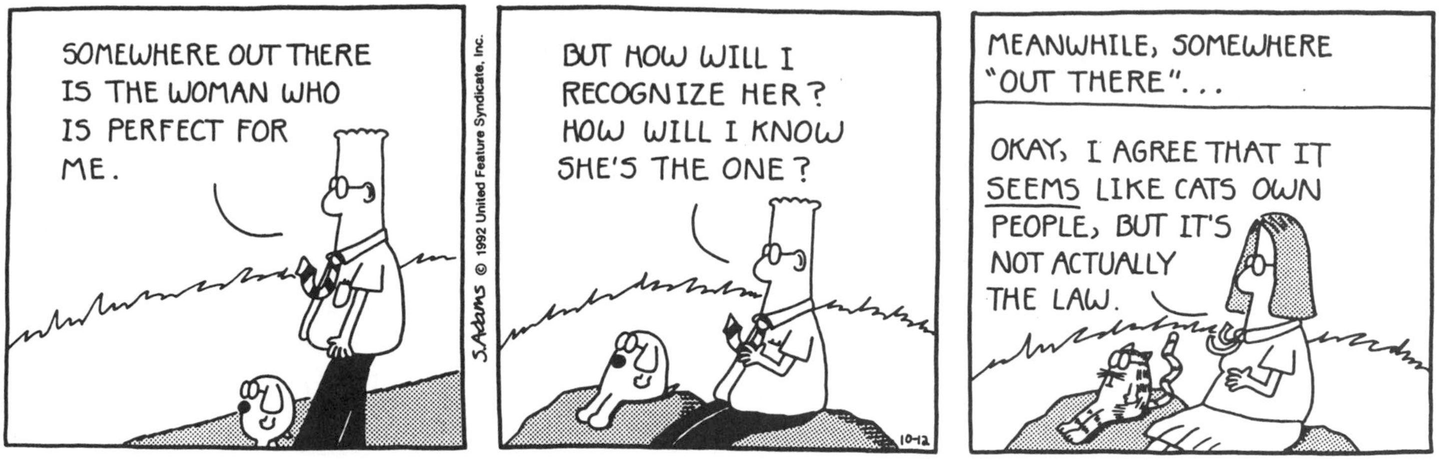
SOMEWHERE OUT THERE IS THE WOMAN WHO IS PERFECT FOR ME.
BUT HOW WILL I RECOGNIZE HER? HOW WILL I KNOW SHE'S THE ONE?
MEANWHILE, SOMEWHERE "OUT THERE"...
OKAY, I AGREE THAT IT SEEMS LIKE CATS OWN PEOPLE, BUT IT'S NOT ACTUALLY THE LAW.
S. Adams © 1992 United Feature Syndicate, Inc.
10-12

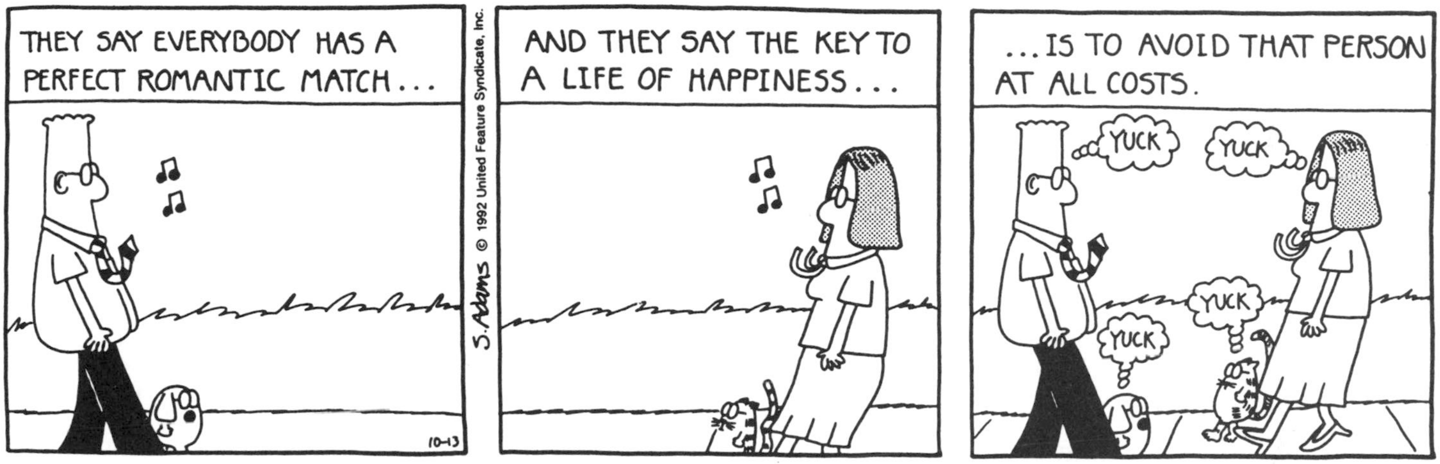
THEY SAY EVERYBODY HAS A PERFECT ROMANTIC MATCH...
AND THEY SAY THE KEY TO A LIFE OF HAPPINESS...
...IS TO AVOID THAT PERSON AT ALL COSTS.
YUCK
YUCK
YUCK
YUCK
S. Adams © 1992 United Feature Syndicate, Inc.
10-13

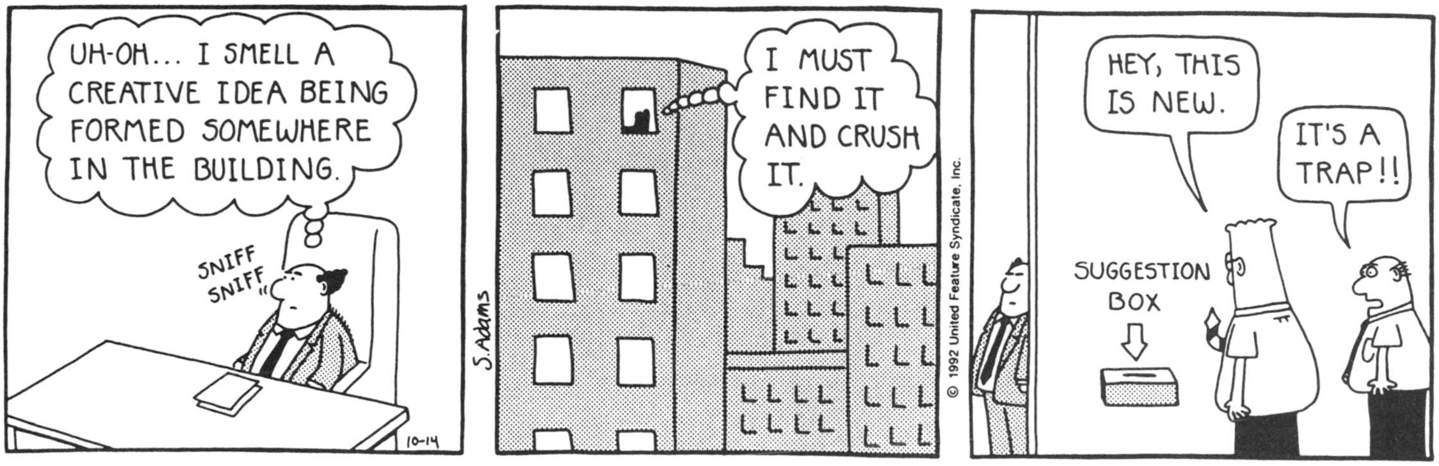
UH-OH... I SMELL A CREATIVE IDEA BEING FORMED SOMEWHERE IN THE BUILDING.
SNIFF SNIFF
I MUST FIND IT AND CRUSH IT.
HEY, THIS IS NEW.
SUGGESTION BOX
IT'S A TRAP!!
S. Adams © 1992 United Feature Syndicate, Inc.
10-14

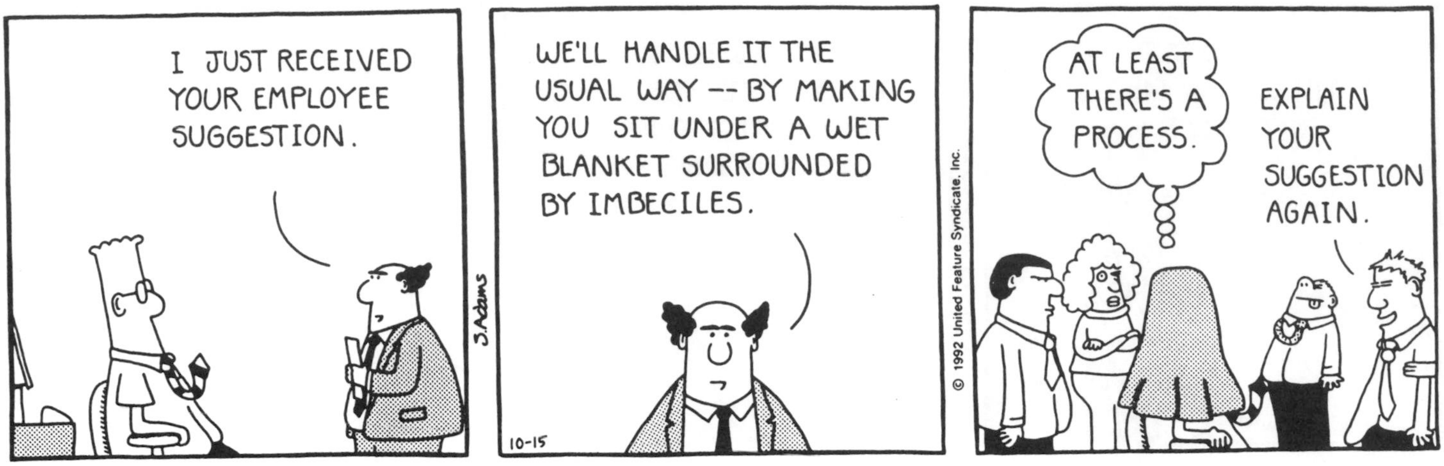
I JUST RECEIVED YOUR EMPLOYEE SUGGESTION.
S.Adams
WE'LL HANDLE IT THE USUAL WAY -- BY MAKING YOU SIT UNDER A WET BLANKET SURROUNDED BY IMBECILES.
10-15
© 1992 United Feature Syndicate, Inc.
AT LEAST THERE'S A PROCESS.
EXPLAIN YOUR SUGGESTION AGAIN.

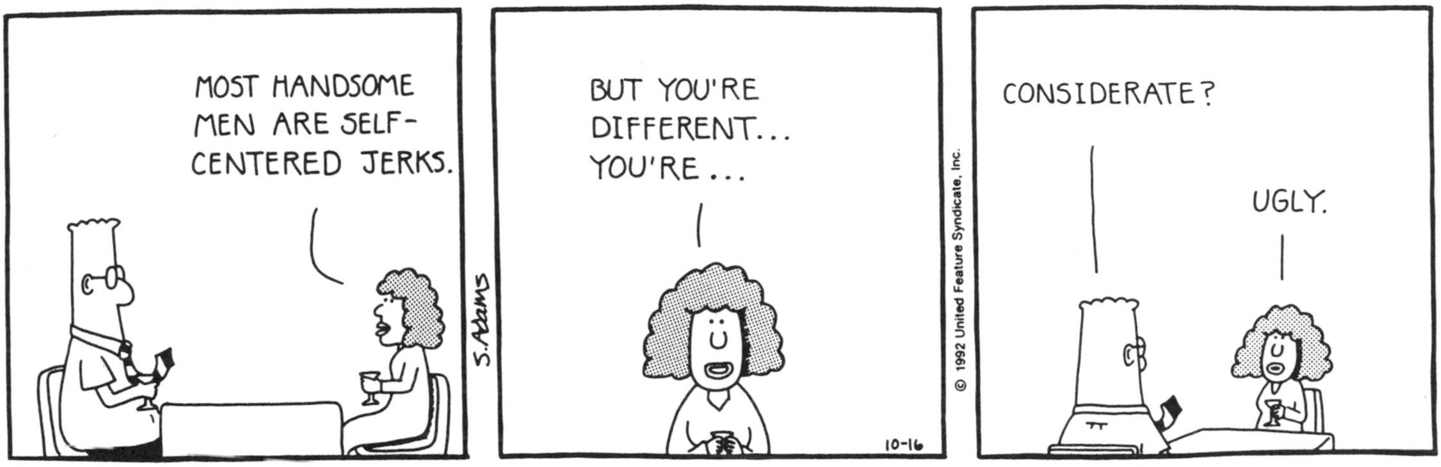
MOST HANDSOME MEN ARE SELF-CENTERED JERKS.
S.Adams
BUT YOU'RE DIFFERENT... YOU'RE...
10-16
© 1992 United Feature Syndicate, Inc.
CONSIDERATE?
UGLY.

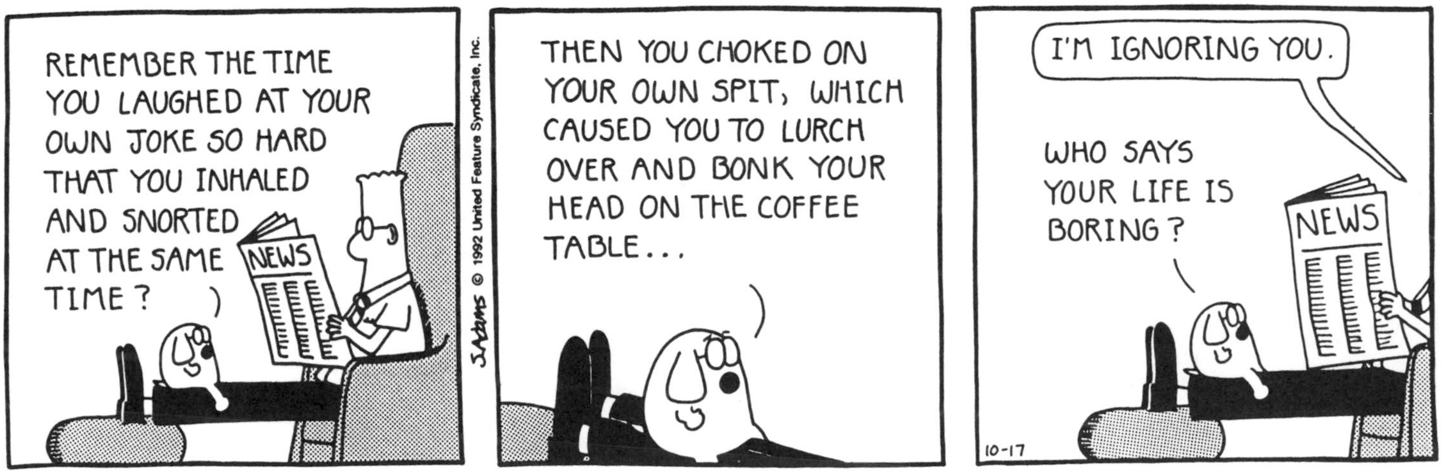
REMEMBER THE TIME YOU LAUGHED AT YOUR OWN JOKE SO HARD THAT YOU INHALED AND SNORTED AT THE SAME TIME?
NEWS
S.Adams © 1992 United Feature Syndicate, Inc.
THEN YOU CHOKED ON YOUR OWN SPIT, WHICH CAUSED YOU TO LURCH OVER AND BONK YOUR HEAD ON THE COFFEE TABLE...
I'M IGNORING YOU.
WHO SAYS YOUR LIFE IS BORING?
NEWS
10-17

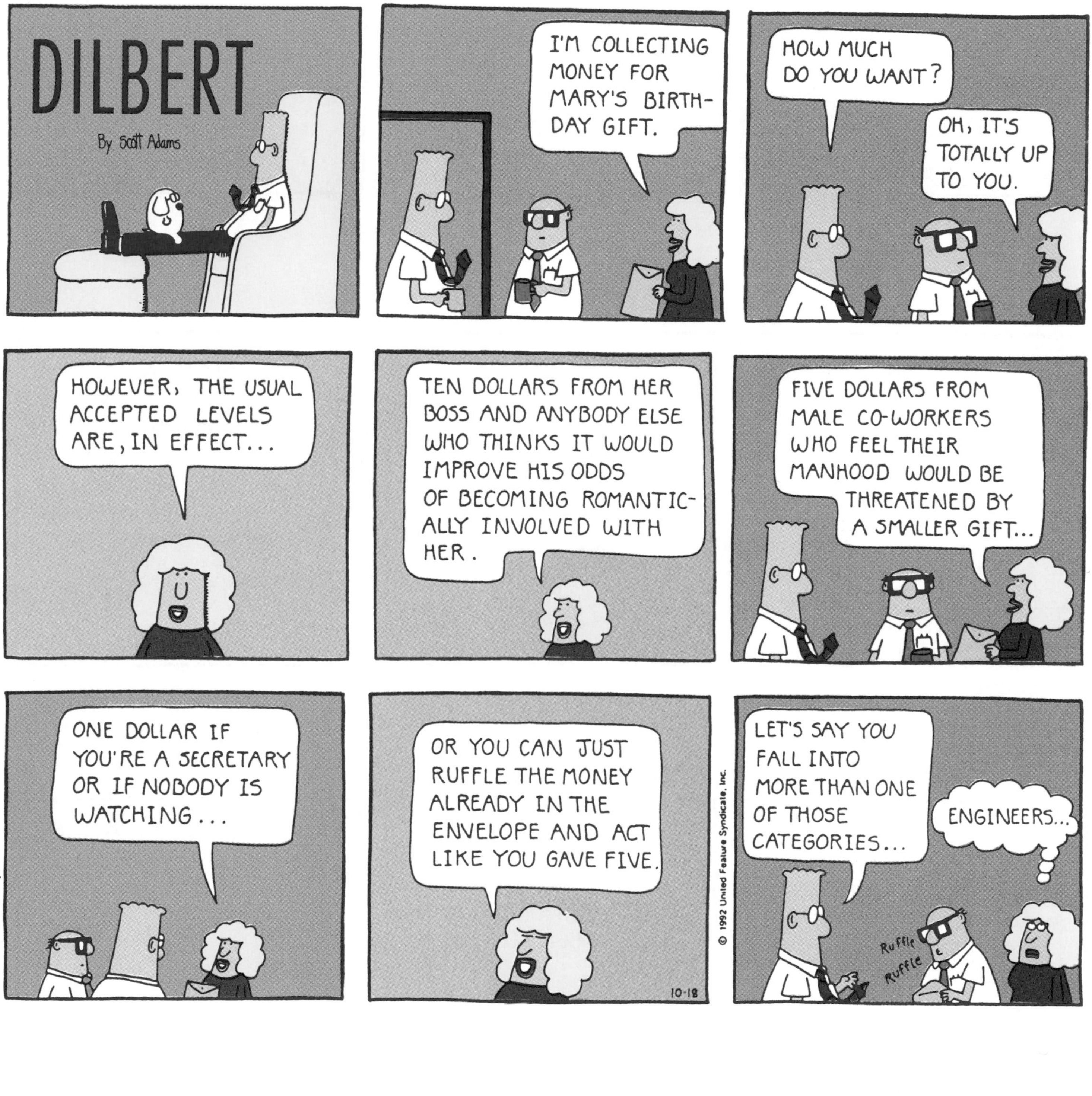

DILBERT
By Scott Adams
I'M COLLECTING MONEY FOR MARY'S BIRTH-DAY GIFT.
HOW MUCH DO YOU WANT?
OH, IT'S TOTALLY UP TO YOU.
HOWEVER, THE USUAL ACCEPTED LEVELS ARE, IN EFFECT...
TEN DOLLARS FROM HER BOSS AND ANYBODY ELSE WHO THINKS IT WOULD IMPROVE HIS ODDS OF BECOMING ROMANTIC-ALLY INVOLVED WITH HER.
FIVE DOLLARS FROM MALE CO-WORKERS WHO FEEL THEIR MANHOOD WOULD BE THREATENED BY A SMALLER GIFT...
ONE DOLLAR IF YOU'RE A SECRETARY OR IF NOBODY IS WATCHING...
S.Adams
OR YOU CAN JUST RUFFLE THE MONEY ALREADY IN THE ENVELOPE AND ACT LIKE YOU GAVE FIVE.
10-18
© 1992 United Feature Syndicate, Inc.
LET'S SAY YOU FALL INTO MORE THAN ONE OF THOSE CATEGORIES...
ENGINEERS...
Ruffle
Ruffle

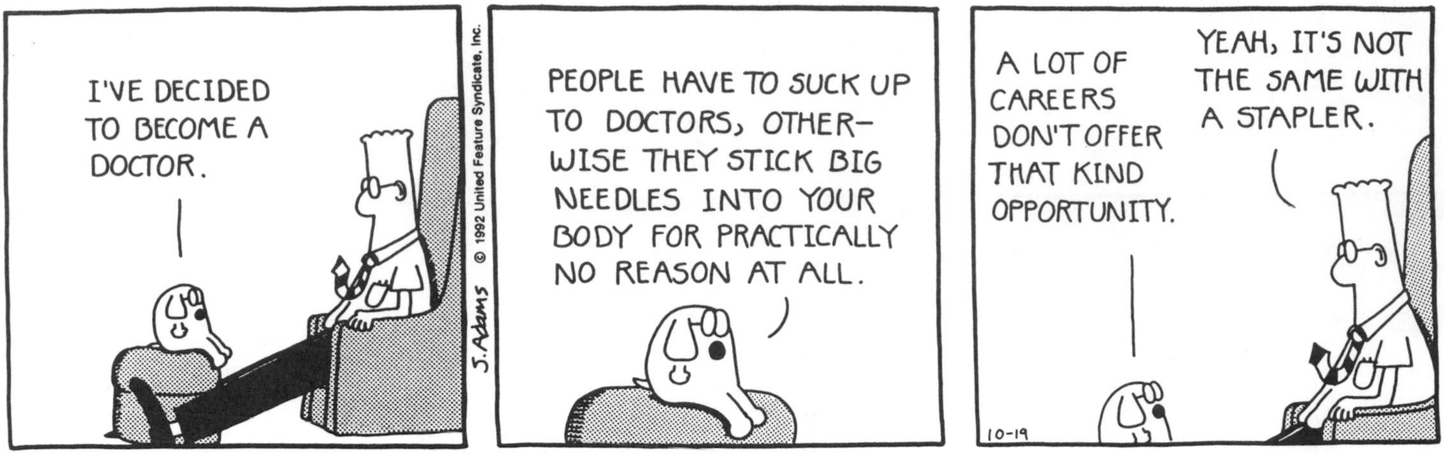
I'VE DECIDED TO BECOME A DOCTOR.
S. Adams
© 1992 United Feature Syndicate, Inc.
PEOPLE HAVE TO SUCK UP TO DOCTORS, OTHER-WISE THEY STICK BIG NEEDLES INTO YOUR BODY FOR PRACTICALLY NO REASON AT ALL.
A LOT OF CAREERS DON'T OFFER THAT KIND OPPORTUNITY.
YEAH, IT'S NOT THE SAME WITH A STAPLER.
10-19

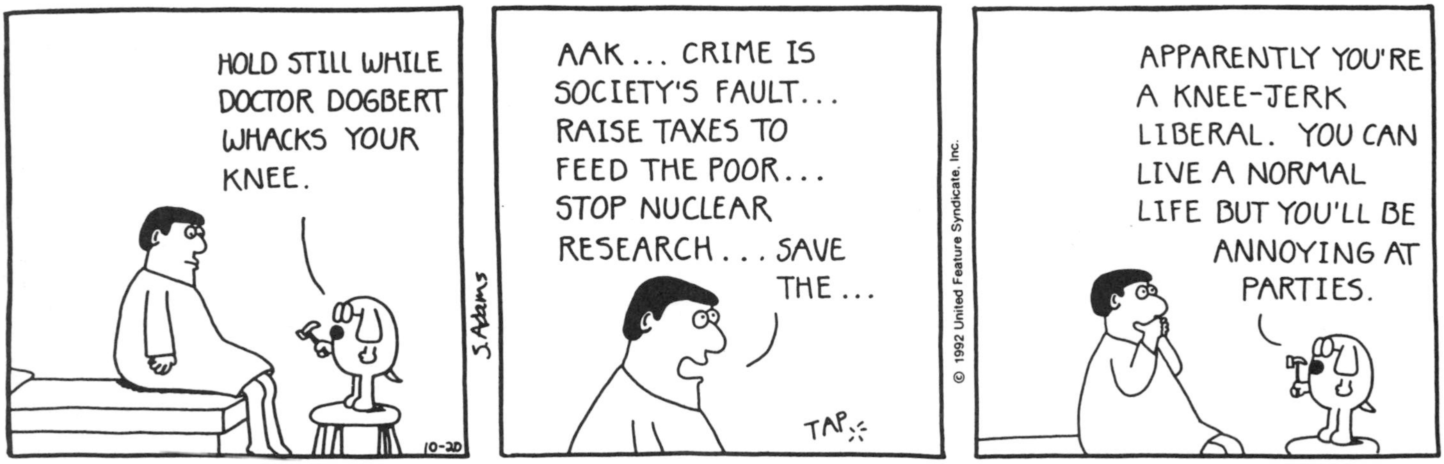
HOLD STILL WHILE DOCTOR DOGBERT WHACKS YOUR KNEE.
10-20
S. Adams
AAK... CRIME IS SOCIETY'S FAULT... RAISE TAXES TO FEED THE POOR... STOP NUCLEAR RESEARCH... SAVE THE...
TAP
© 1992 United Feature Syndicate, Inc.
APPARENTLY YOU'RE A KNEE-JERK LIBERAL. YOU CAN LIVE A NORMAL LIFE BUT YOU'LL BE ANNOYING AT PARTIES.

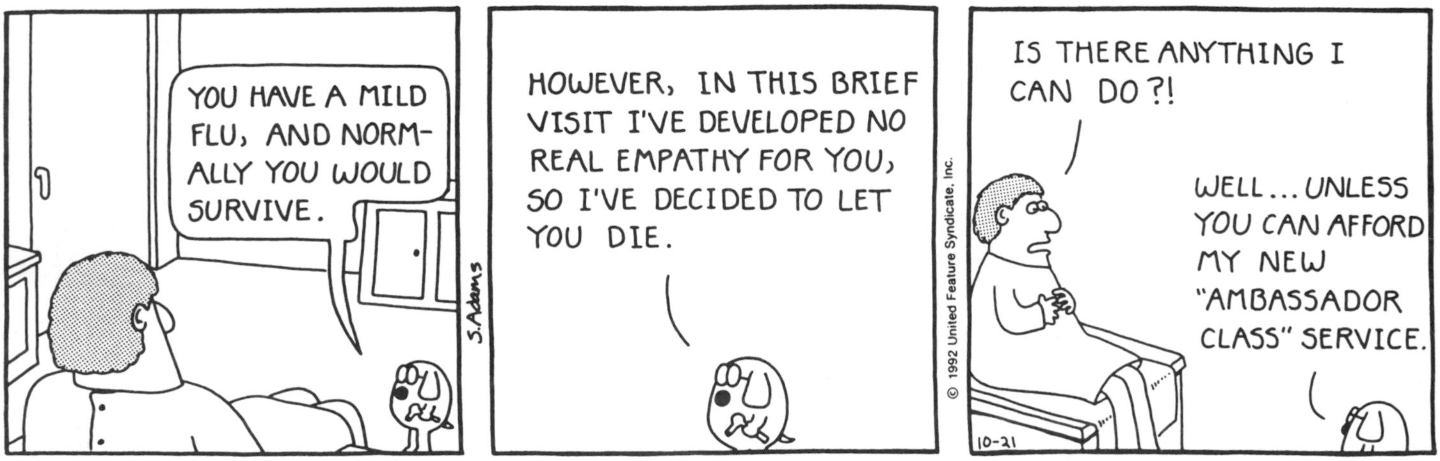
YOU HAVE A MILD FLU, AND NORM-ALLY YOU WOULD SURVIVE.
S. Adams
HOWEVER, IN THIS BRIEF VISIT I'VE DEVELOPED NO REAL EMPATHY FOR YOU, SO I'VE DECIDED TO LET YOU DIE.
© 1992 United Feature Syndicate, Inc.
IS THERE ANYTHING I CAN DO?!
WELL... UNLESS YOU CAN AFFORD MY NEW "AMBASSADOR CLASS" SERVICE.
10-21

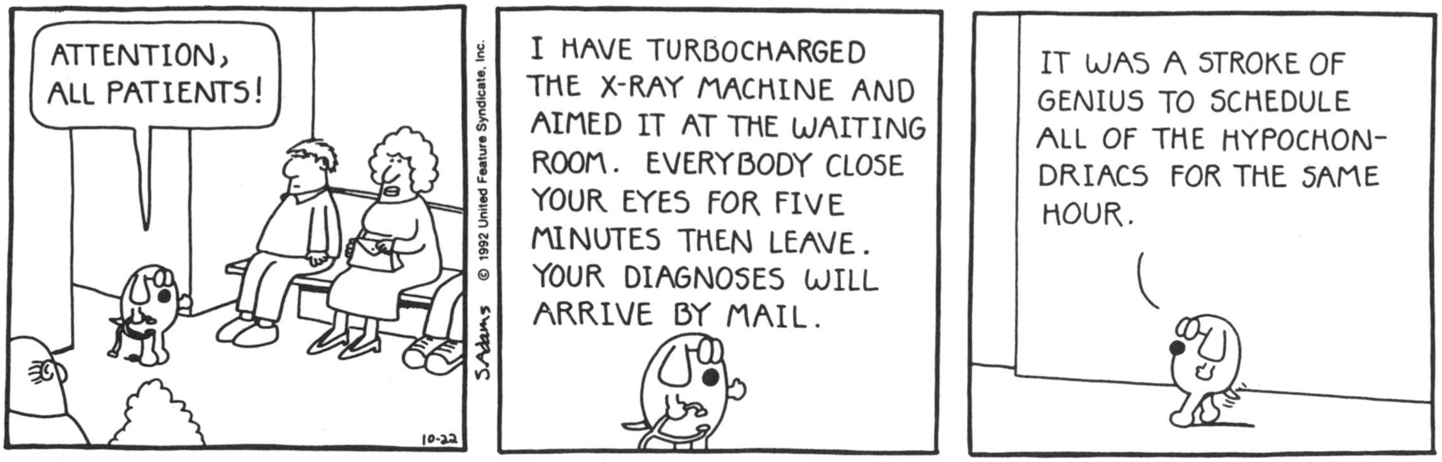
ATTENTION, ALL PATIENTS!
I HAVE TURBOCHARGED THE X-RAY MACHINE AND AIMED IT AT THE WAITING ROOM. EVERYBODY CLOSE YOUR EYES FOR FIVE MINUTES THEN LEAVE. YOUR DIAGNOSES WILL ARRIVE BY MAIL.
IT WAS A STROKE OF GENIUS TO SCHEDULE ALL OF THE HYPOCHONDRIACS FOR THE SAME HOUR.
© 1992 United Feature Syndicate, Inc.
10-22

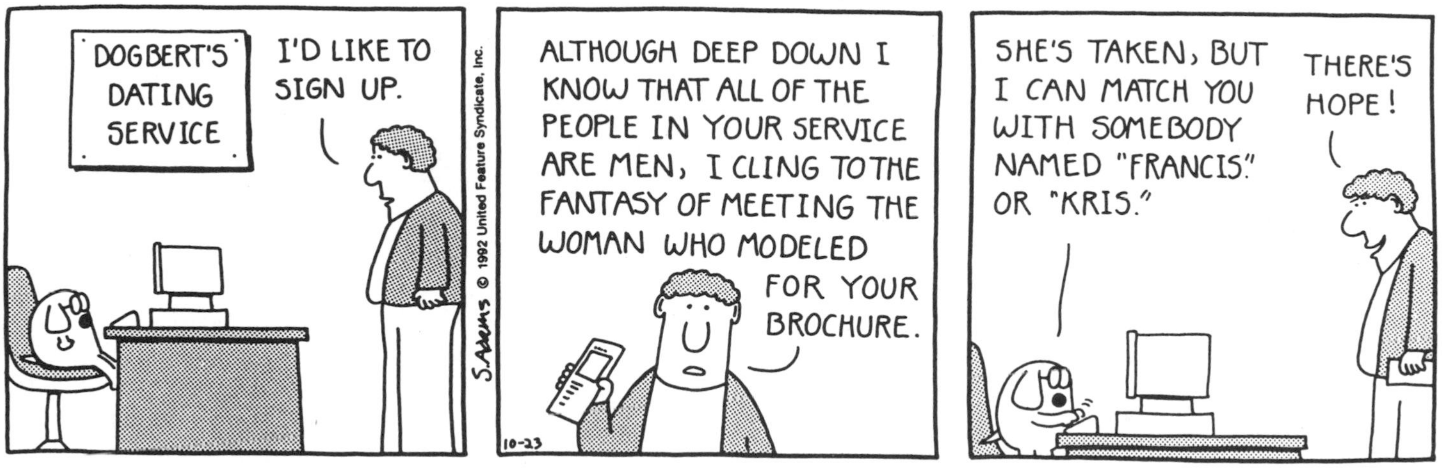
DOGBERT'S DATING SERVICE
I'D LIKE TO SIGN UP.
ALTHOUGH DEEP DOWN I KNOW THAT ALL OF THE PEOPLE IN YOUR SERVICE ARE MEN, I CLING TO THE FANTASY OF MEETING THE WOMAN WHO MODELED FOR YOUR BROCHURE.
SHE'S TAKEN, BUT I CAN MATCH YOU WITH SOMEBODY NAMED "FRANCIS" OR "KRIS."
THERE'S HOPE!
© 1992 United Feature Syndicate, Inc.
10-23

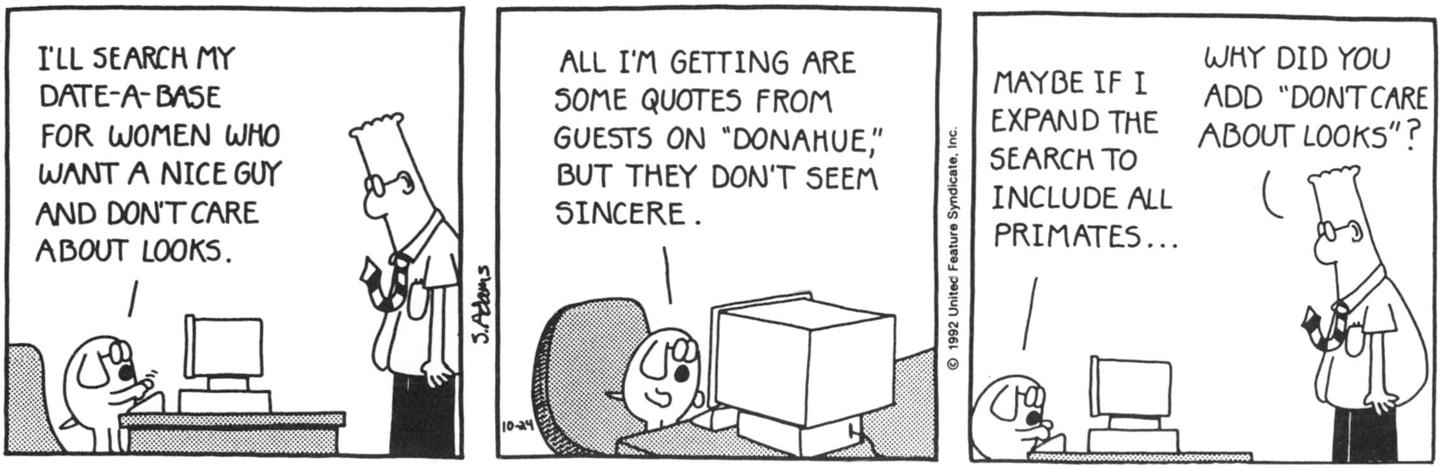
I'LL SEARCH MY DATE-A-BASE FOR WOMEN WHO WANT A NICE GUY AND DON'T CARE ABOUT LOOKS.
ALL I'M GETTING ARE SOME QUOTES FROM GUESTS ON "DONAHUE," BUT THEY DON'T SEEM SINCERE.
MAYBE IF I EXPAND THE SEARCH TO INCLUDE ALL PRIMATES...
WHY DID YOU ADD "DON'T CARE ABOUT LOOKS"?
© 1992 United Feature Syndicate, Inc.
10-24

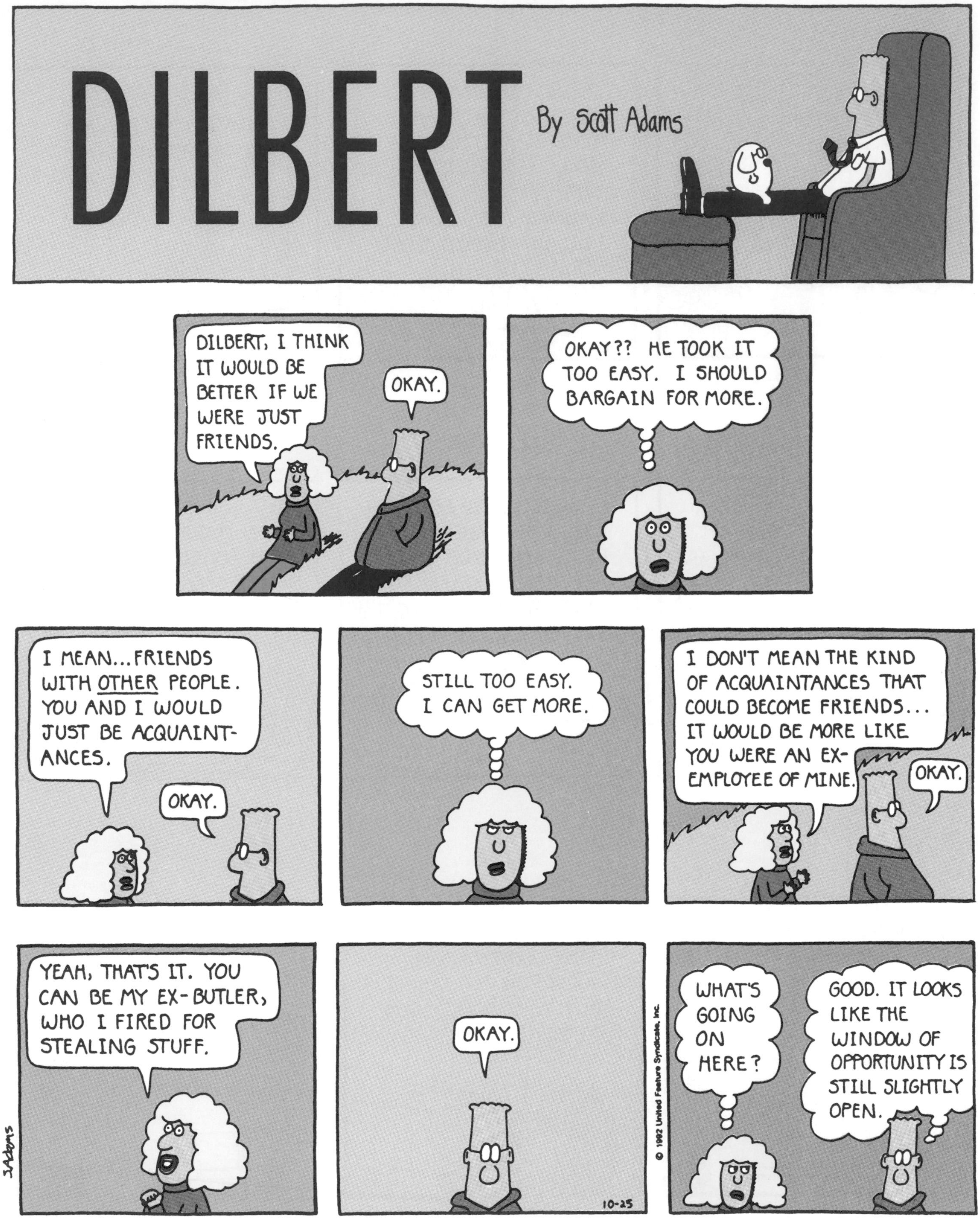
DILBERT
By Scott Adams
DILBERT, I THINK IT WOULD BE BETTER IF WE WERE JUST FRIENDS.
OKAY.
OKAY?? HE TOOK IT TOO EASY. I SHOULD BARGAIN FOR MORE.
I MEAN...FRIENDS WITH OTHER PEOPLE. YOU AND I WOULD JUST BE ACQUAINT-ANCES.
OKAY.
STILL TOO EASY. I CAN GET MORE.
I DON'T MEAN THE KIND OF ACQUAINTANCES THAT COULD BECOME FRIENDS... IT WOULD BE MORE LIKE YOU WERE AN EX-EMPLOYEE OF MINE.
OKAY.
YEAH, THAT'S IT. YOU CAN BE MY EX-BUTLER, WHO I FIRED FOR STEALING STUFF.
OKAY.
WHAT'S GOING ON HERE?
GOOD. IT LOOKS LIKE THE WINDOW OF OPPORTUNITY IS STILL SLIGHTLY OPEN.
© 1992 United Feature Syndicate, Inc.
10-25

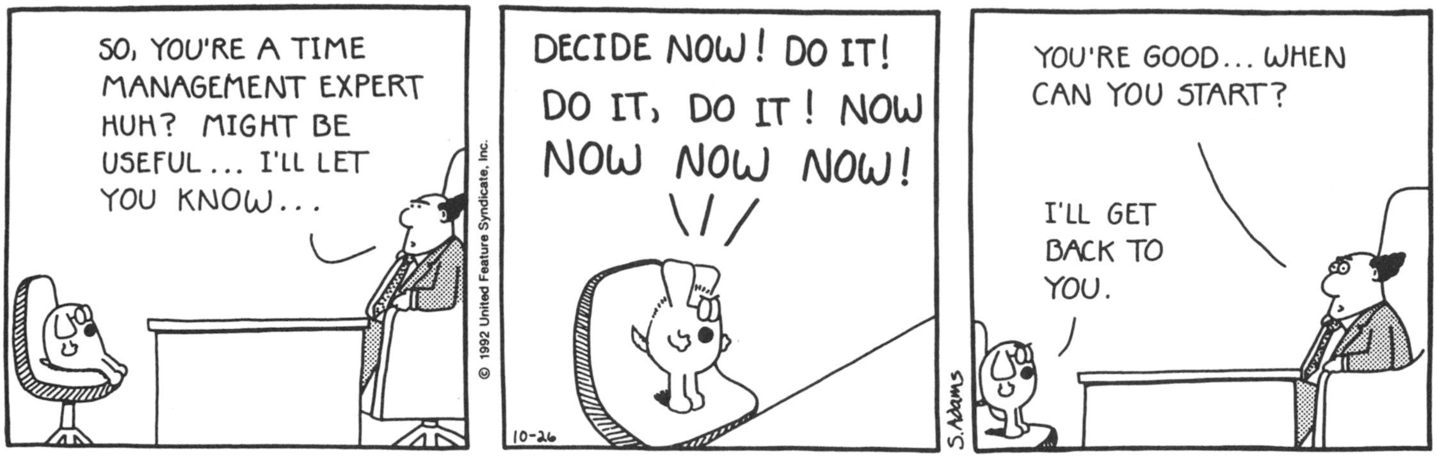
SO, YOU'RE A TIME MANAGEMENT EXPERT HUH? MIGHT BE USEFUL... I'LL LET YOU KNOW...
© 1992 United Feature Syndicate, Inc.
DECIDE NOW! DO IT! DO IT, DO IT! NOW NOW NOW NOW!
10-26
YOU'RE GOOD... WHEN CAN YOU START?
I'LL GET BACK TO YOU.
S. Adams

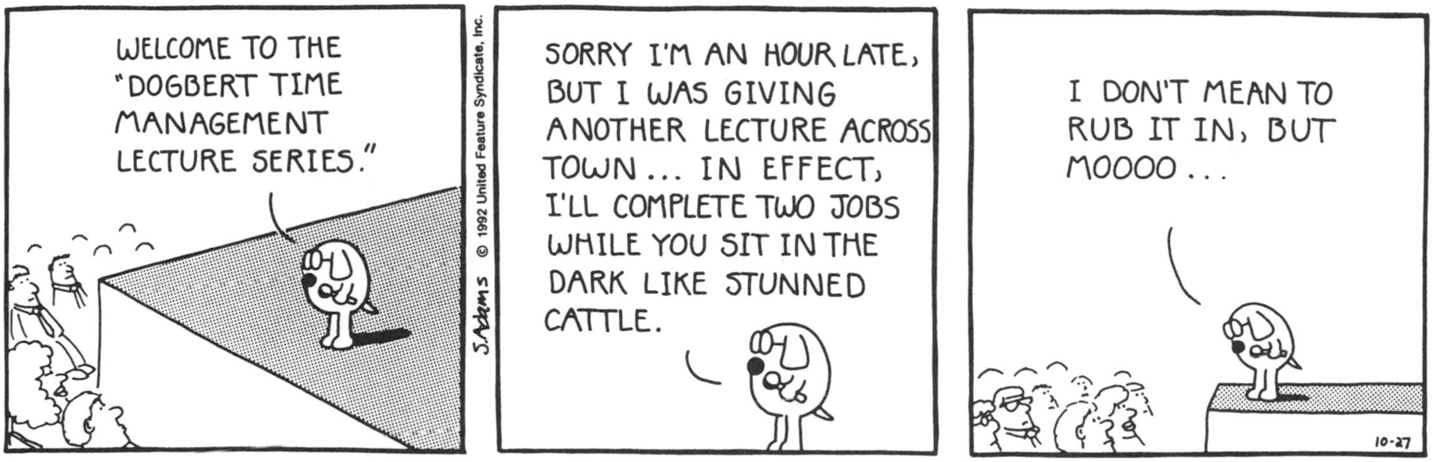
WELCOME TO THE "DOGBERT TIME MANAGEMENT LECTURE SERIES."
S. Adams © 1992 United Feature Syndicate, Inc.
SORRY I'M AN HOUR LATE, BUT I WAS GIVING ANOTHER LECTURE ACROSS TOWN... IN EFFECT, I'LL COMPLETE TWO JOBS WHILE YOU SIT IN THE DARK LIKE STUNNED CATTLE.
I DON'T MEAN TO RUB IT IN, BUT MOOOO...
10-27

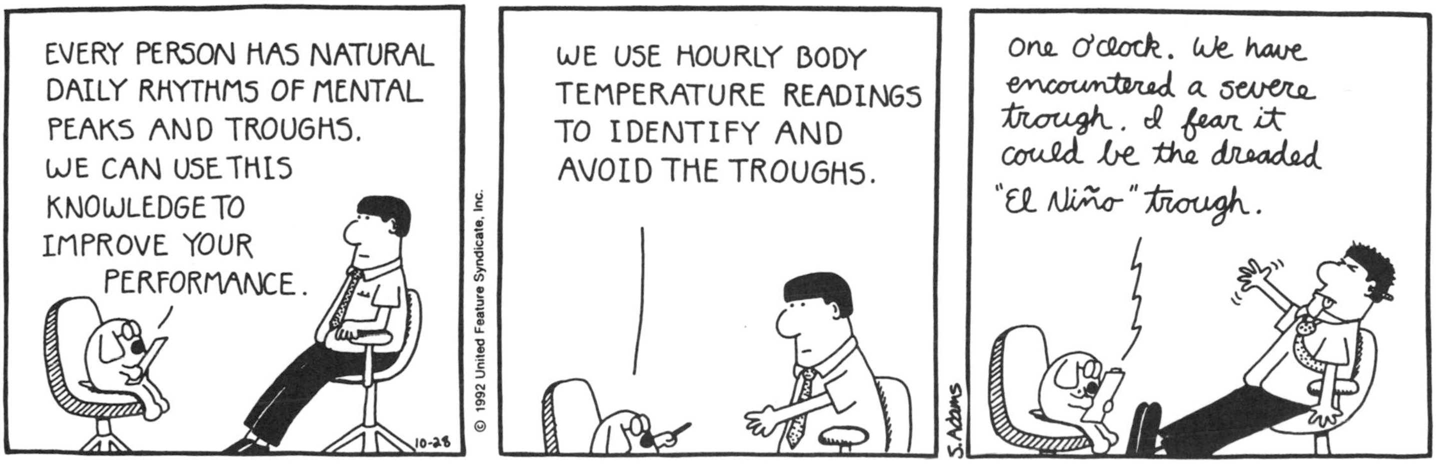
EVERY PERSON HAS NATURAL DAILY RHYTHMS OF MENTAL PEAKS AND TROUGHS. WE CAN USE THIS KNOWLEDGE TO IMPROVE YOUR PERFORMANCE.
10-28
© 1992 United Feature Syndicate, Inc.
WE USE HOURLY BODY TEMPERATURE READINGS TO IDENTIFY AND AVOID THE TROUGHS.
S. Adams
One O'clock. We have encountered a severe trough. I fear it could be the dreaded "El Niño" trough.

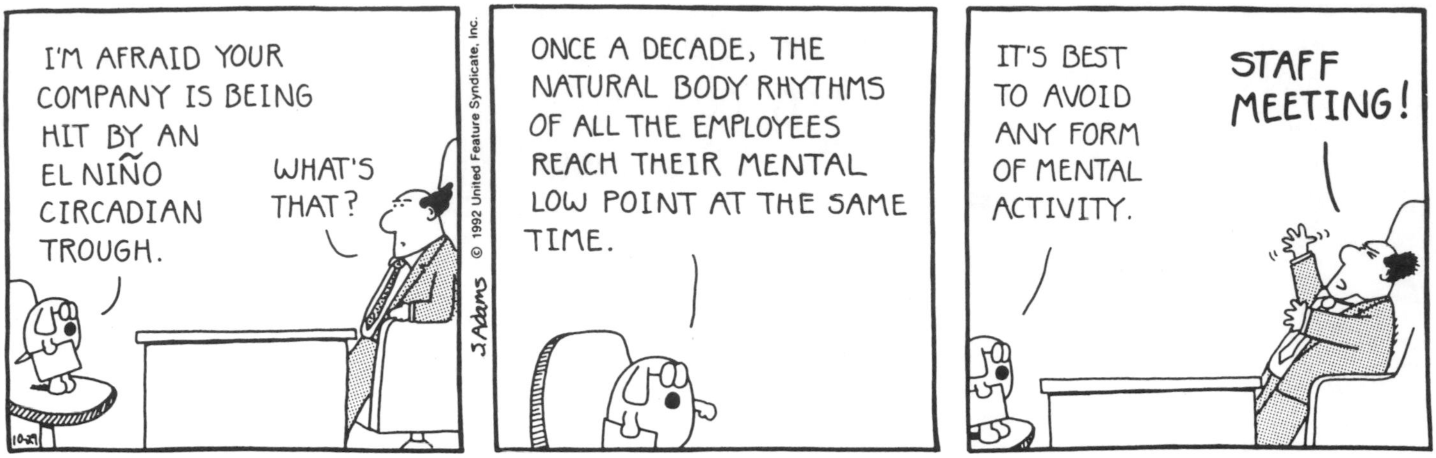
I'M AFRAID YOUR COMPANY IS BEING HIT BY AN EL NIÑO CIRCADIAN TROUGH.
WHAT'S THAT?
ONCE A DECADE, THE NATURAL BODY RHYTHMS OF ALL THE EMPLOYEES REACH THEIR MENTAL LOW POINT AT THE SAME TIME.
IT'S BEST TO AVOID ANY FORM OF MENTAL ACTIVITY.
STAFF MEETING!
© 1992 United Feature Syndicate, Inc.

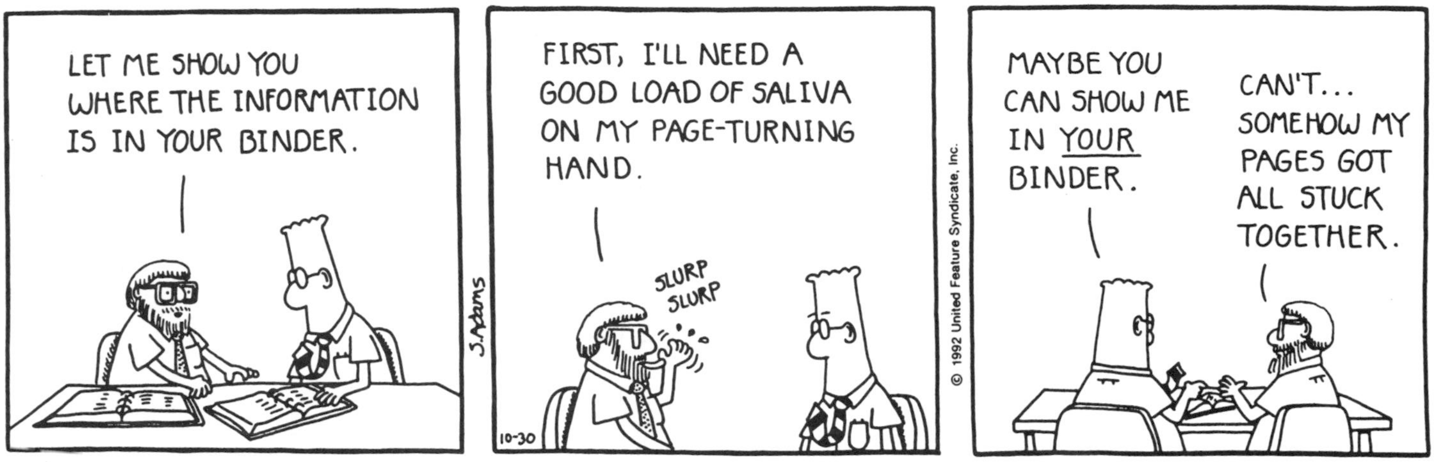
LET ME SHOW YOU WHERE THE INFORMATION IS IN YOUR BINDER.
FIRST, I'LL NEED A GOOD LOAD OF SALIVA ON MY PAGE-TURNING HAND.
SLURP SLURP
MAYBE YOU CAN SHOW ME IN YOUR BINDER.
CAN'T... SOMEHOW MY PAGES GOT ALL STUCK TOGETHER.
© 1992 United Feature Syndicate, Inc.

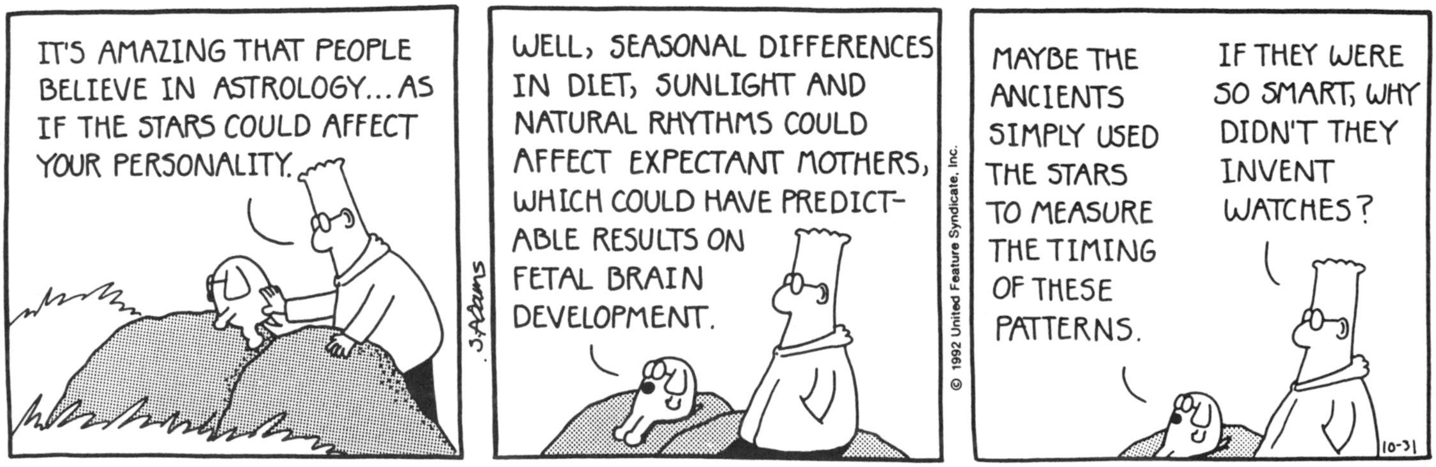
IT'S AMAZING THAT PEOPLE BELIEVE IN ASTROLOGY... AS IF THE STARS COULD AFFECT YOUR PERSONALITY.
WELL, SEASONAL DIFFERENCES IN DIET, SUNLIGHT AND NATURAL RHYTHMS COULD AFFECT EXPECTANT MOTHERS, WHICH COULD HAVE PREDICTABLE RESULTS ON FETAL BRAIN DEVELOPMENT.
MAYBE THE ANCIENTS SIMPLY USED THE STARS TO MEASURE THE TIMING OF THESE PATTERNS.
IF THEY WERE SO SMART, WHY DIDN'T THEY INVENT WATCHES?
© 1992 United Feature Syndicate, Inc.

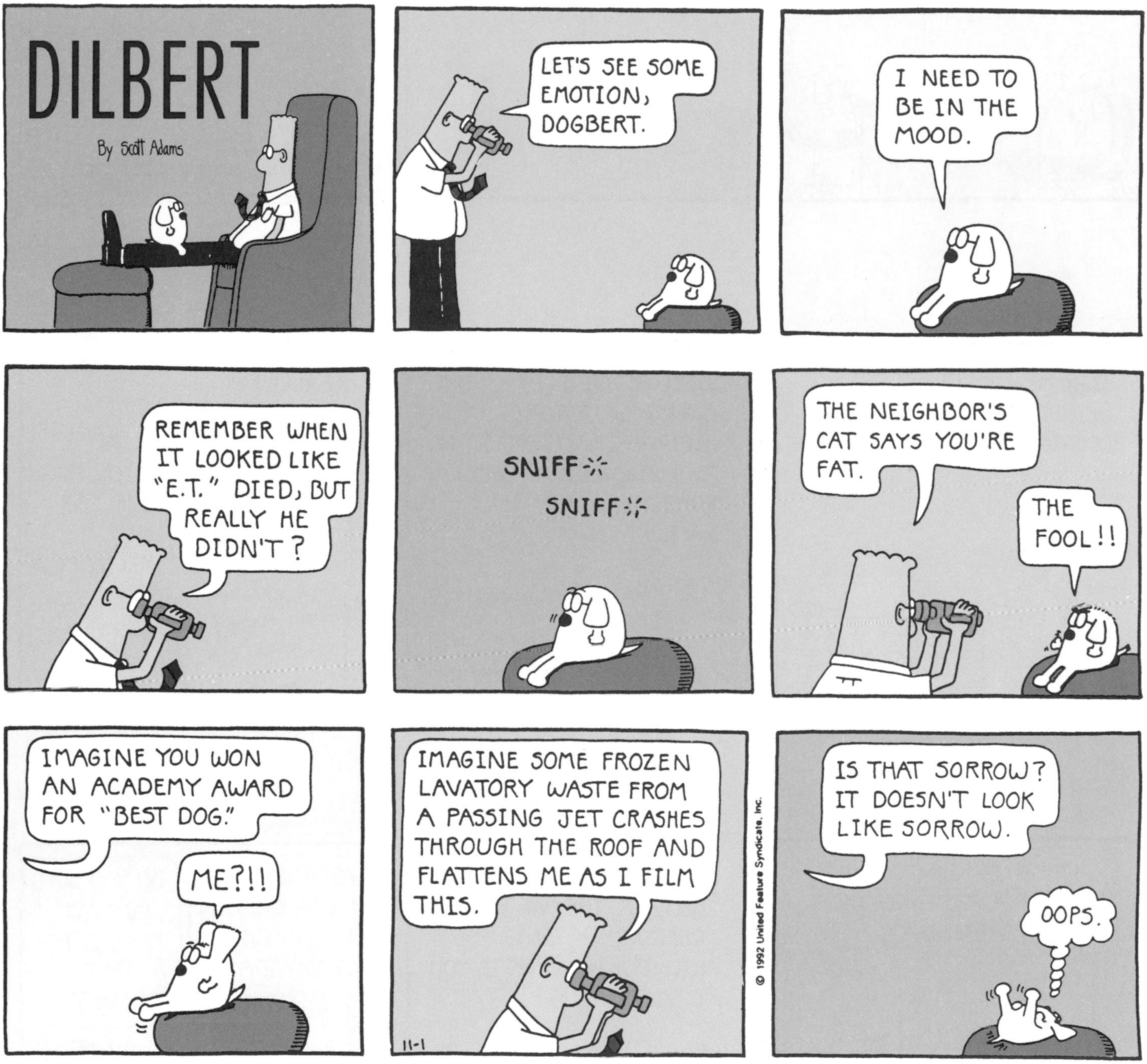
DILBERT
By Scott Adams
LET'S SEE SOME EMOTION, DOGBERT.
I NEED TO BE IN THE MOOD.
REMEMBER WHEN IT LOOKED LIKE "E.T." DIED, BUT REALLY HE DIDN'T?
SNIFF
SNIFF
THE NEIGHBOR'S CAT SAYS YOU'RE FAT.
THE FOOL!!
IMAGINE YOU WON AN ACADEMY AWARD FOR "BEST DOG."
ME?!!
IMAGINE SOME FROZEN LAVATORY WASTE FROM A PASSING JET CRASHES THROUGH THE ROOF AND FLATTENS ME AS I FILM THIS.
IS THAT SORROW? IT DOESN'T LOOK LIKE SORROW.
OOPS.
S. Adams
11-1
© 1992 United Feature Syndicate, Inc.

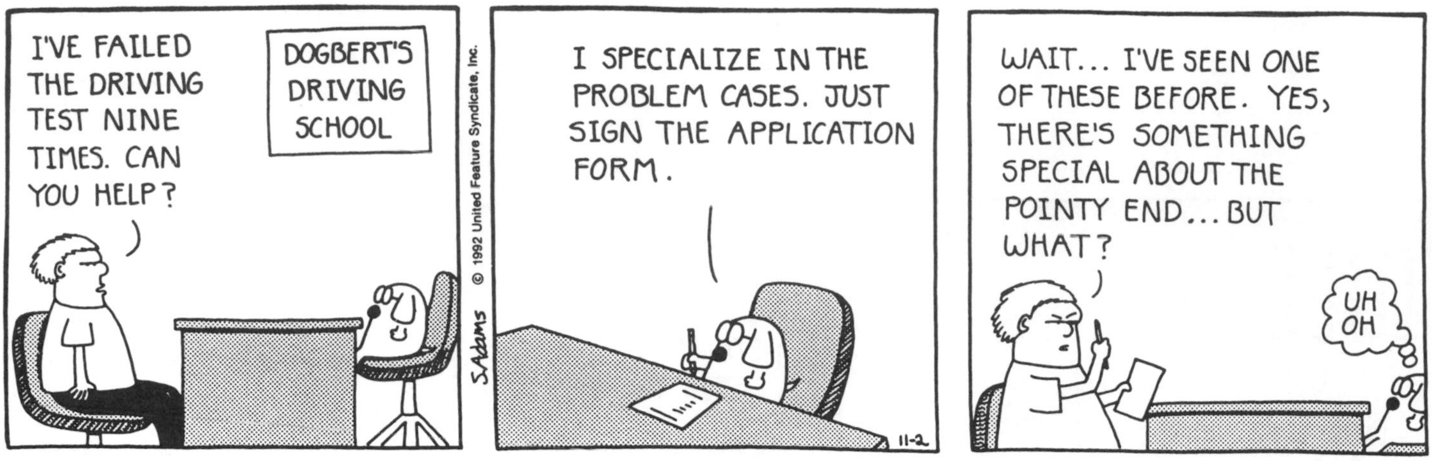
I'VE FAILED THE DRIVING TEST NINE TIMES. CAN YOU HELP?
DOGBERT'S DRIVING SCHOOL
S.Adams
© 1992 United Feature Syndicate, Inc.
I SPECIALIZE IN THE PROBLEM CASES. JUST SIGN THE APPLICATION FORM.
11-2
WAIT... I'VE SEEN ONE OF THESE BEFORE. YES, THERE'S SOMETHING SPECIAL ABOUT THE POINTY END... BUT WHAT?
UH OH

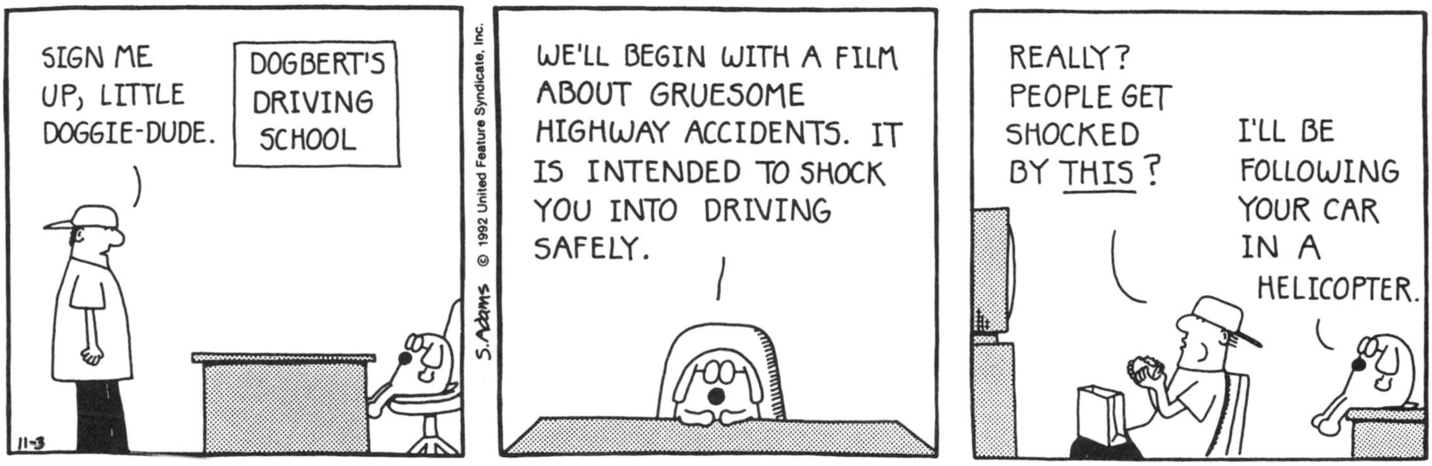
SIGN ME UP, LITTLE DOGGIE-DUDE.
DOGBERT'S DRIVING SCHOOL
11-3
S.Adams
© 1992 United Feature Syndicate, Inc.
WE'LL BEGIN WITH A FILM ABOUT GRUESOME HIGHWAY ACCIDENTS. IT IS INTENDED TO SHOCK YOU INTO DRIVING SAFELY.
REALLY? PEOPLE GET SHOCKED BY THIS?
I'LL BE FOLLOWING YOUR CAR IN A HELICOPTER.

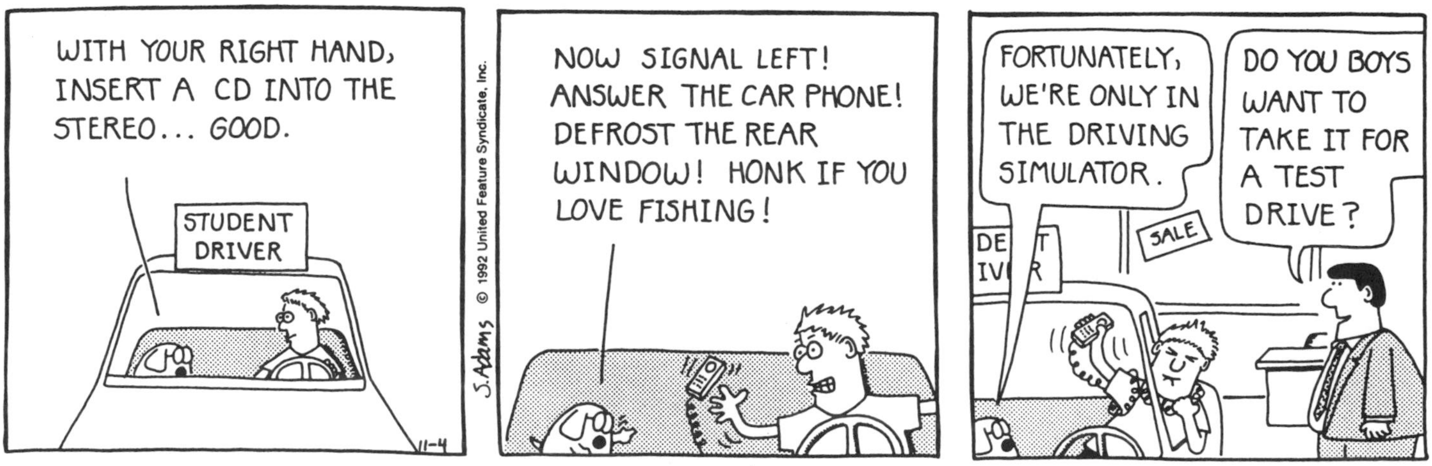
WITH YOUR RIGHT HAND, INSERT A CD INTO THE STEREO... GOOD.
STUDENT DRIVER
11-4
S.Adams
© 1992 United Feature Syndicate, Inc.
NOW SIGNAL LEFT! ANSWER THE CAR PHONE! DEFROST THE REAR WINDOW! HONK IF YOU LOVE FISHING!
FORTUNATELY, WE'RE ONLY IN THE DRIVING SIMULATOR.
DO YOU BOYS WANT TO TAKE IT FOR A TEST DRIVE?
SALE

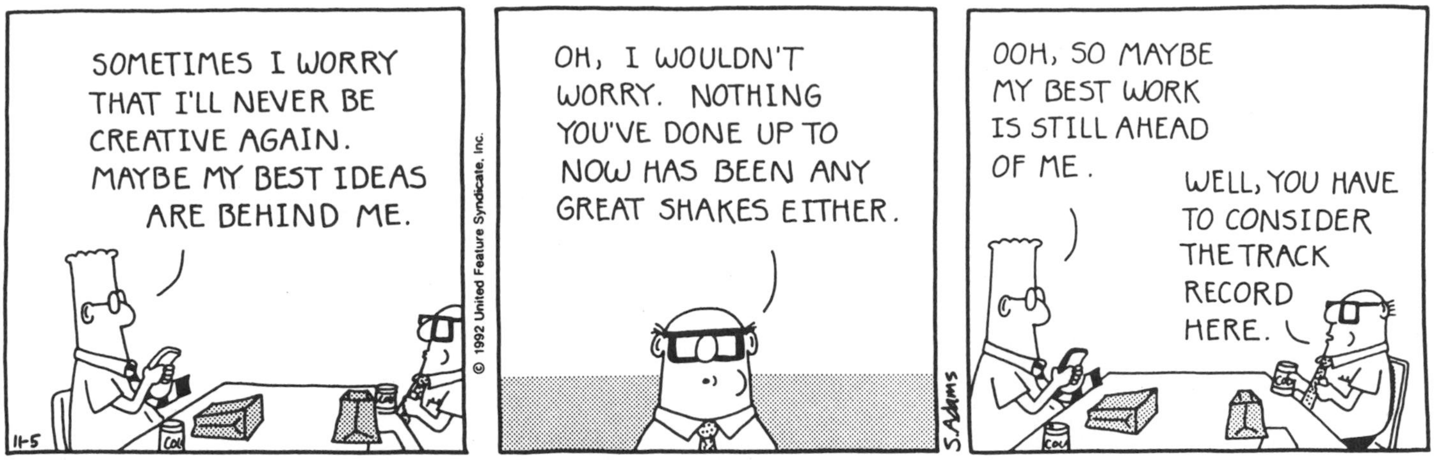
SOMETIMES I WORRY THAT I'LL NEVER BE CREATIVE AGAIN. MAYBE MY BEST IDEAS ARE BEHIND ME.
OH, I WOULDN'T WORRY. NOTHING YOU'VE DONE UP TO NOW HAS BEEN ANY GREAT SHAKES EITHER.
OOH, SO MAYBE MY BEST WORK IS STILL AHEAD OF ME.
WELL, YOU HAVE TO CONSIDER THE TRACK RECORD HERE.
11-5
© 1992 United Feature Syndicate, Inc.
S.Adams

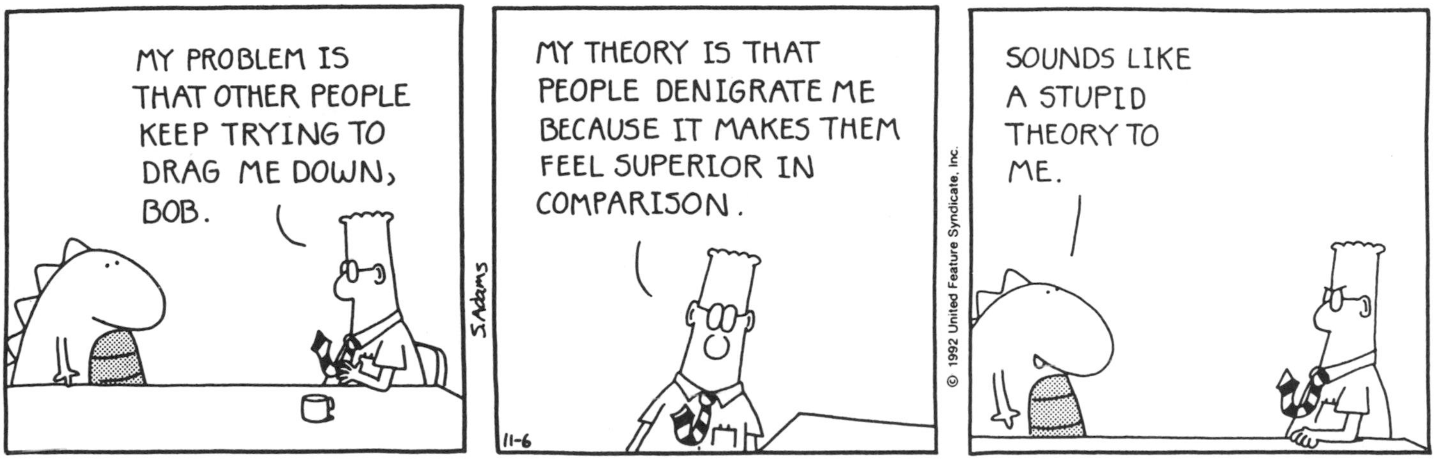
MY PROBLEM IS THAT OTHER PEOPLE KEEP TRYING TO DRAG ME DOWN, BOB.
MY THEORY IS THAT PEOPLE DENIGRATE ME BECAUSE IT MAKES THEM FEEL SUPERIOR IN COMPARISON.
SOUNDS LIKE A STUPID THEORY TO ME.
11-6
S.Adams
© 1992 United Feature Syndicate, Inc.

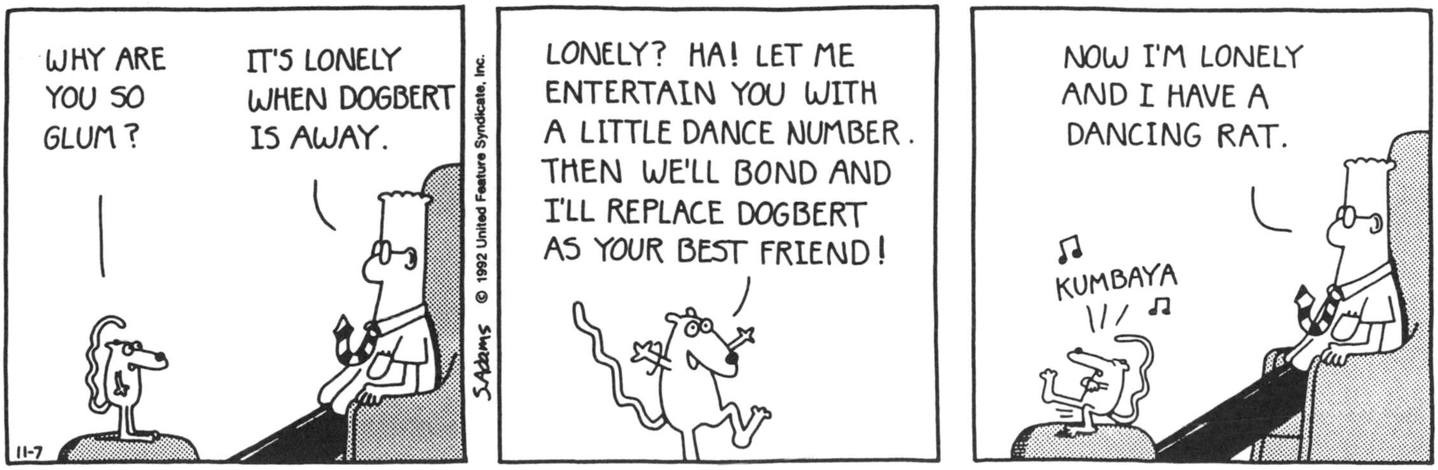
WHY ARE YOU SO GLUM?
IT'S LONELY WHEN DOGBERT IS AWAY.
LONELY? HA! LET ME ENTERTAIN YOU WITH A LITTLE DANCE NUMBER. THEN WE'LL BOND AND I'LL REPLACE DOGBERT AS YOUR BEST FRIEND!
KUMBAYA
NOW I'M LONELY AND I HAVE A DANCING RAT.
11-7
S.Adams
© 1992 United Feature Syndicate, Inc.

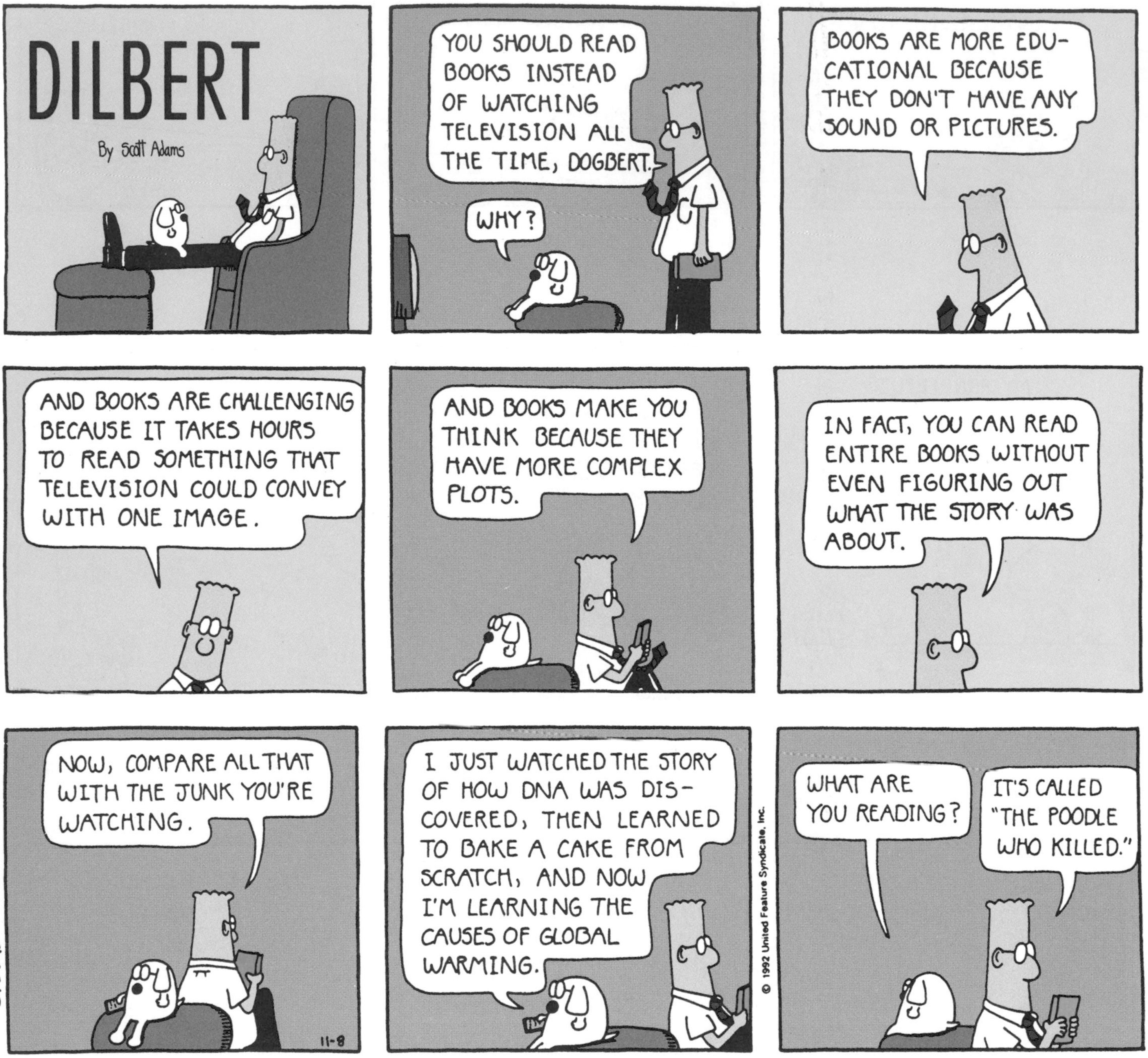
DILBERT
By Scott Adams
YOU SHOULD READ BOOKS INSTEAD OF WATCHING TELEVISION ALL THE TIME, DOGBERT.
WHY?
BOOKS ARE MORE EDUCATIONAL BECAUSE THEY DON'T HAVE ANY SOUND OR PICTURES.
AND BOOKS ARE CHALLENGING BECAUSE IT TAKES HOURS TO READ SOMETHING THAT TELEVISION COULD CONVEY WITH ONE IMAGE.
AND BOOKS MAKE YOU THINK BECAUSE THEY HAVE MORE COMPLEX PLOTS.
IN FACT, YOU CAN READ ENTIRE BOOKS WITHOUT EVEN FIGURING OUT WHAT THE STORY WAS ABOUT.
NOW, COMPARE ALL THAT WITH THE JUNK YOU'RE WATCHING.
S.Adams
11-8
I JUST WATCHED THE STORY OF HOW DNA WAS DISCOVERED, THEN LEARNED TO BAKE A CAKE FROM SCRATCH, AND NOW I'M LEARNING THE CAUSES OF GLOBAL WARMING.
© 1992 United Feature Syndicate, Inc.
WHAT ARE YOU READING?
IT'S CALLED "THE POODLE WHO KILLED."

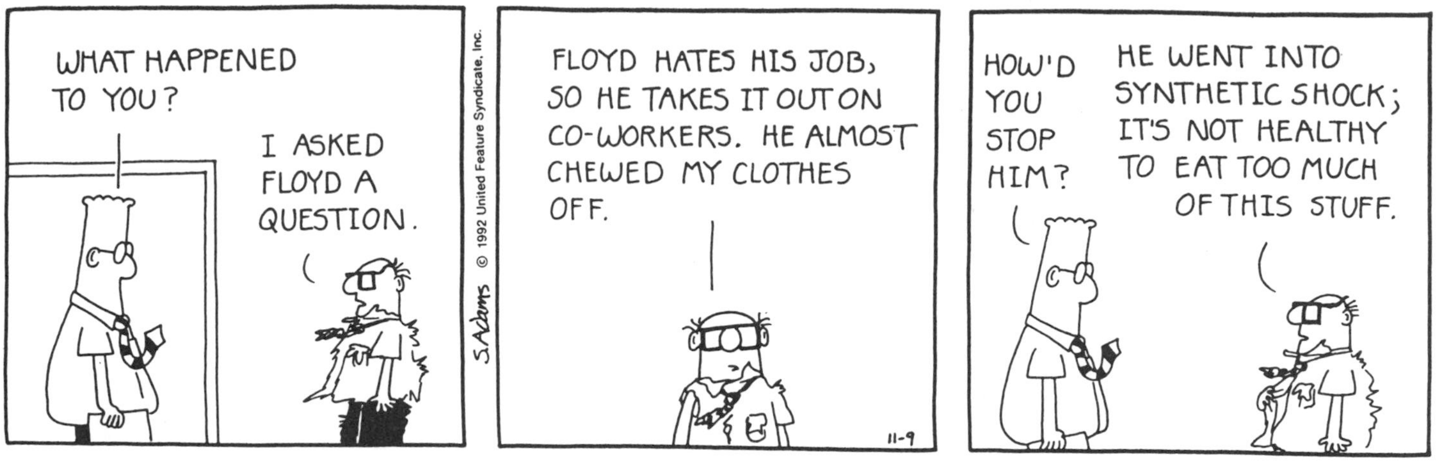
WHAT HAPPENED TO YOU?
I ASKED FLOYD A QUESTION.
S. Adams © 1992 United Feature Syndicate, Inc.
FLOYD HATES HIS JOB, SO HE TAKES IT OUT ON CO-WORKERS. HE ALMOST CHEWED MY CLOTHES OFF.
11-9
HOW'D YOU STOP HIM?
HE WENT INTO SYNTHETIC SHOCK; IT'S NOT HEALTHY TO EAT TOO MUCH OF THIS STUFF.

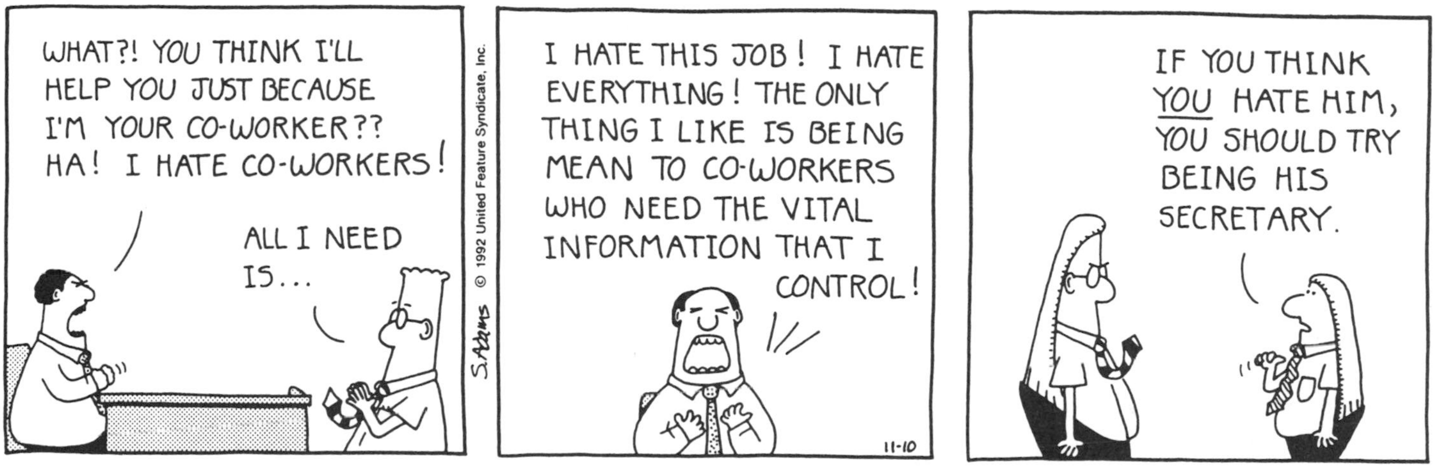
WHAT?! YOU THINK I'LL HELP YOU JUST BECAUSE I'M YOUR CO-WORKER?? HA! I HATE CO-WORKERS!
ALL I NEED IS...
S. Adams © 1992 United Feature Syndicate, Inc.
I HATE THIS JOB! I HATE EVERYTHING! THE ONLY THING I LIKE IS BEING MEAN TO CO-WORKERS WHO NEED THE VITAL INFORMATION THAT I CONTROL!
11-10
IF YOU THINK YOU HATE HIM, YOU SHOULD TRY BEING HIS SECRETARY.

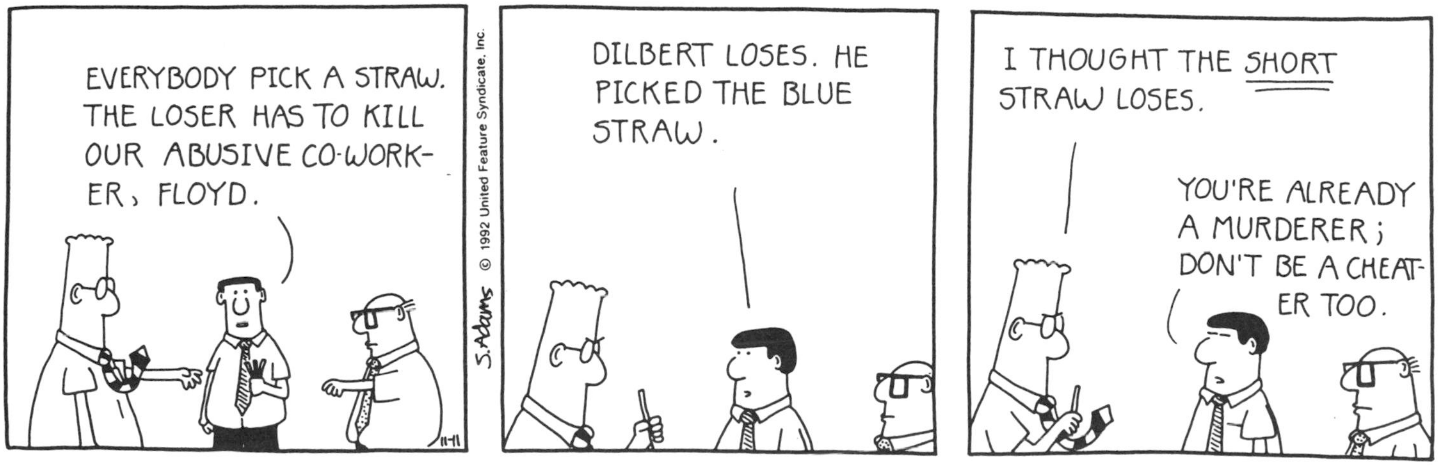
EVERYBODY PICK A STRAW. THE LOSER HAS TO KILL OUR ABUSIVE CO-WORKER, FLOYD.
11-11
S. Adams © 1992 United Feature Syndicate, Inc.
DILBERT LOSES. HE PICKED THE BLUE STRAW.
I THOUGHT THE SHORT STRAW LOSES.
YOU'RE ALREADY A MURDERER; DON'T BE A CHEATER TOO.

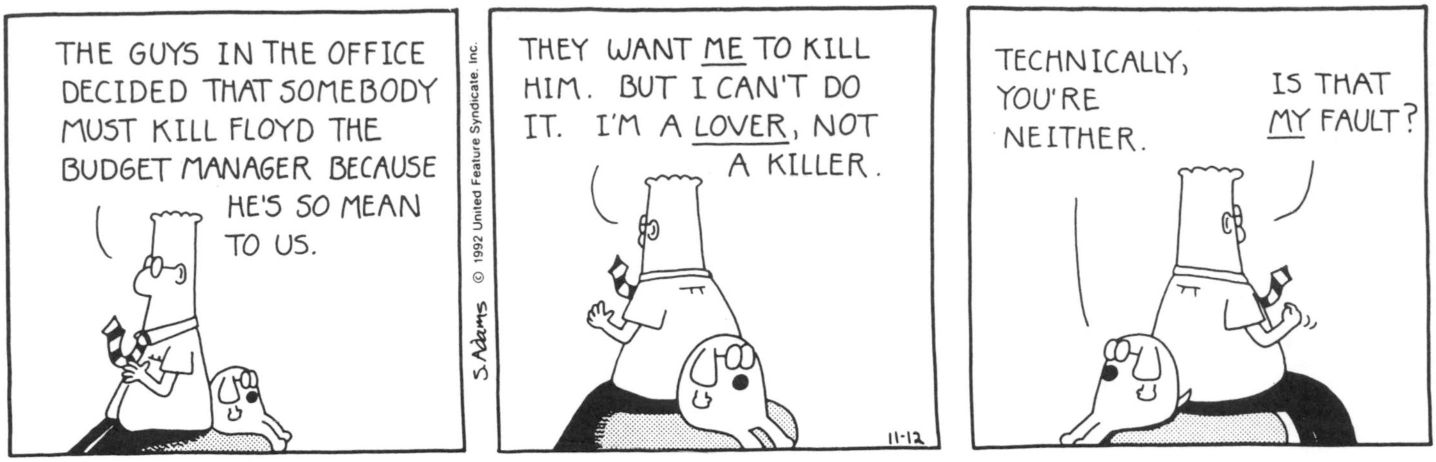
THE GUYS IN THE OFFICE DECIDED THAT SOMEBODY MUST KILL FLOYD THE BUDGET MANAGER BECAUSE HE'S SO MEAN TO US.
© 1992 United Feature Syndicate, Inc.
S. Adams
THEY WANT ME TO KILL HIM. BUT I CAN'T DO IT. I'M A LOVER, NOT A KILLER.
11-12
TECHNICALLY, YOU'RE NEITHER.
IS THAT MY FAULT?

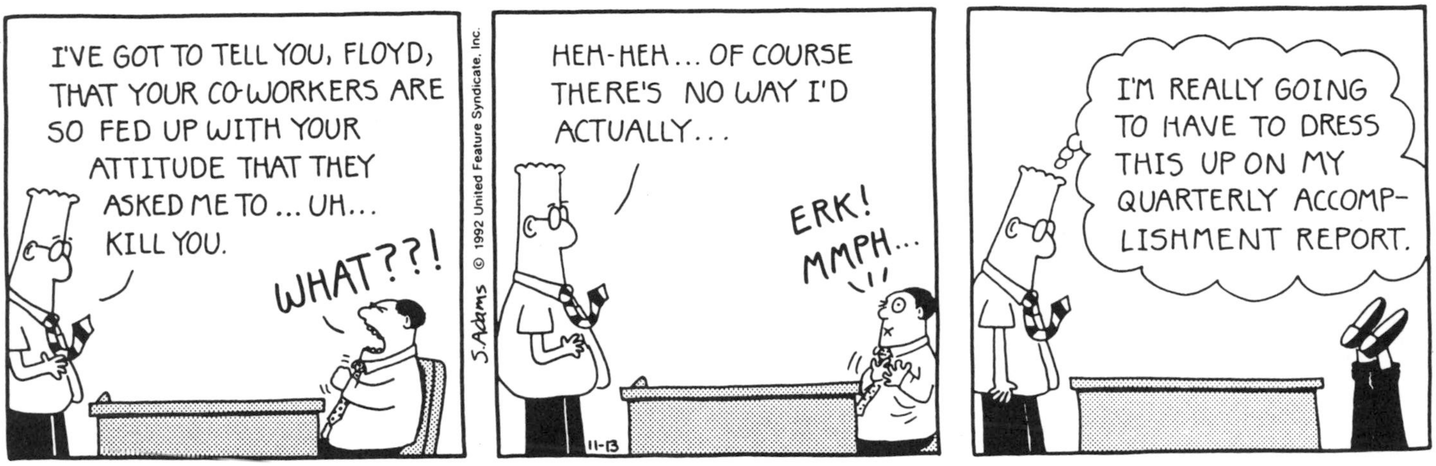
I'VE GOT TO TELL YOU, FLOYD, THAT YOUR CO-WORKERS ARE SO FED UP WITH YOUR ATTITUDE THAT THEY ASKED ME TO ... UH... KILL YOU.
WHAT??!
© 1992 United Feature Syndicate, Inc.
S. Adams
HEH-HEH... OF COURSE THERE'S NO WAY I'D ACTUALLY...
ERK! MMPH...
11-13
I'M REALLY GOING TO HAVE TO DRESS THIS UP ON MY QUARTERLY ACCOMPLISHMENT REPORT.

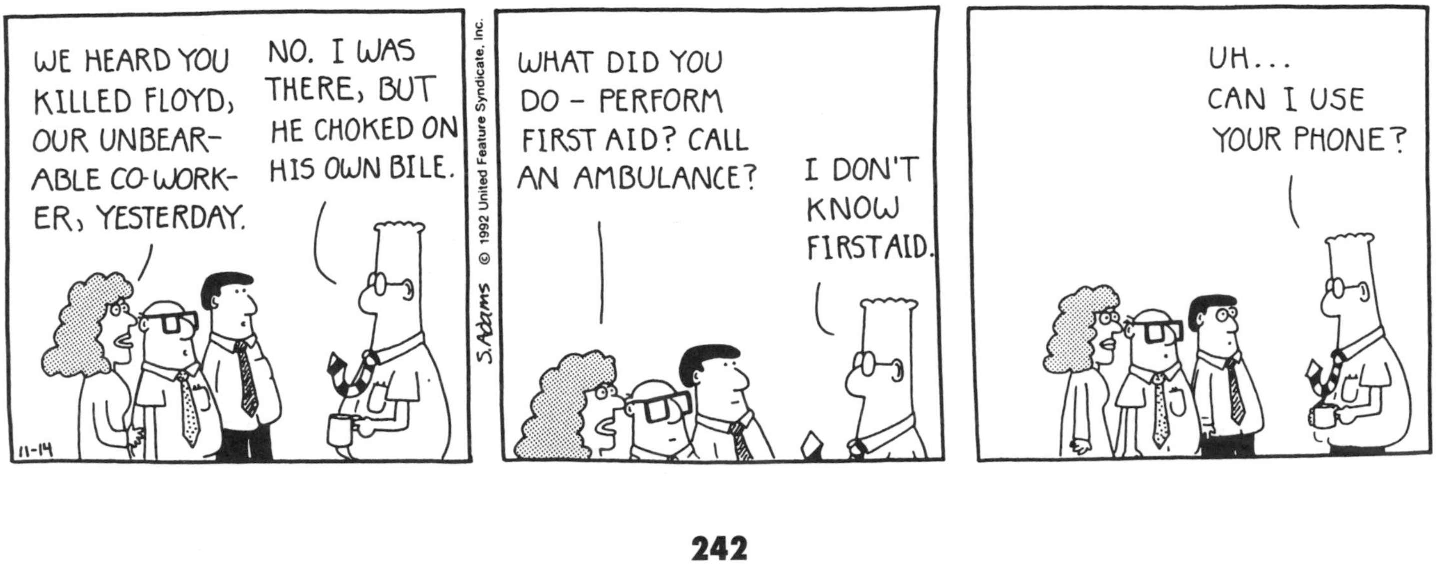
WE HEARD YOU KILLED FLOYD, OUR UNBEARABLE CO-WORKER, YESTERDAY.
NO. I WAS THERE, BUT HE CHOKED ON HIS OWN BILE.
11-14
© 1992 United Feature Syndicate, Inc.
S. Adams
WHAT DID YOU DO – PERFORM FIRST AID? CALL AN AMBULANCE?
I DON'T KNOW FIRST AID.
UH... CAN I USE YOUR PHONE?

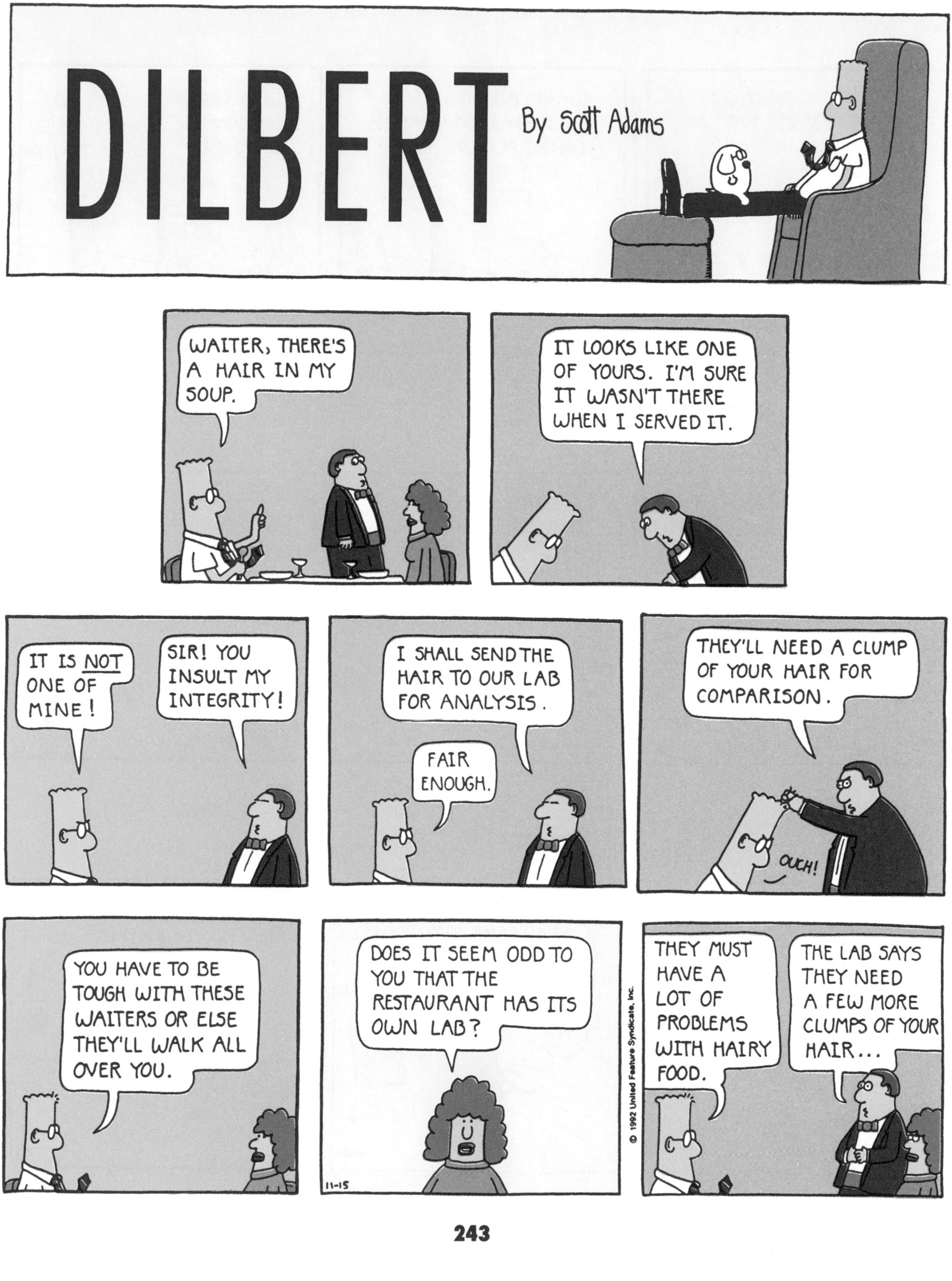
DILBERT
By Scott Adams
WAITER, THERE'S A HAIR IN MY SOUP.
IT LOOKS LIKE ONE OF YOURS. I'M SURE IT WASN'T THERE WHEN I SERVED IT.
IT IS NOT ONE OF MINE!
SIR! YOU INSULT MY INTEGRITY!
I SHALL SEND THE HAIR TO OUR LAB FOR ANALYSIS.
FAIR ENOUGH.
THEY'LL NEED A CLUMP OF YOUR HAIR FOR COMPARISON.
OUCH!
YOU HAVE TO BE TOUGH WITH THESE WAITERS OR ELSE THEY'LL WALK ALL OVER YOU.
S. Adams
DOES IT SEEM ODD TO YOU THAT THE RESTAURANT HAS ITS OWN LAB?
11-15
© 1992 United Feature Syndicate, Inc.
THEY MUST HAVE A LOT OF PROBLEMS WITH HAIRY FOOD.
THE LAB SAYS THEY NEED A FEW MORE CLUMPS OF YOUR HAIR...

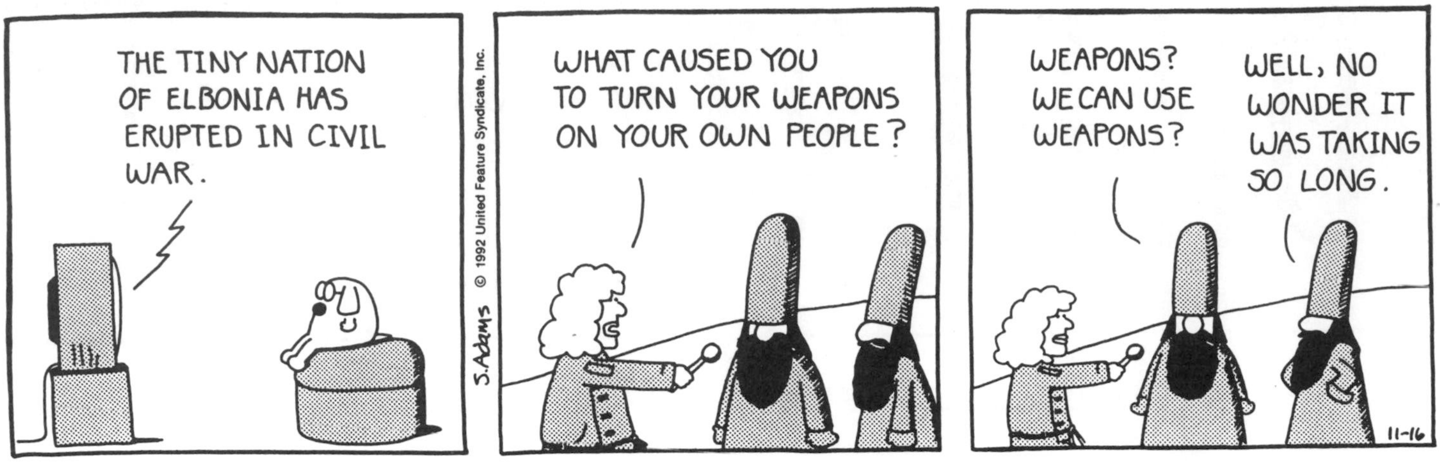
THE TINY NATION OF ELBONIA HAS ERUPTED IN CIVIL WAR.
S. Adams © 1992 United Feature Syndicate, Inc.
WHAT CAUSED YOU TO TURN YOUR WEAPONS ON YOUR OWN PEOPLE?
WEAPONS? WE CAN USE WEAPONS?
WELL, NO WONDER IT WAS TAKING SO LONG.
11-16

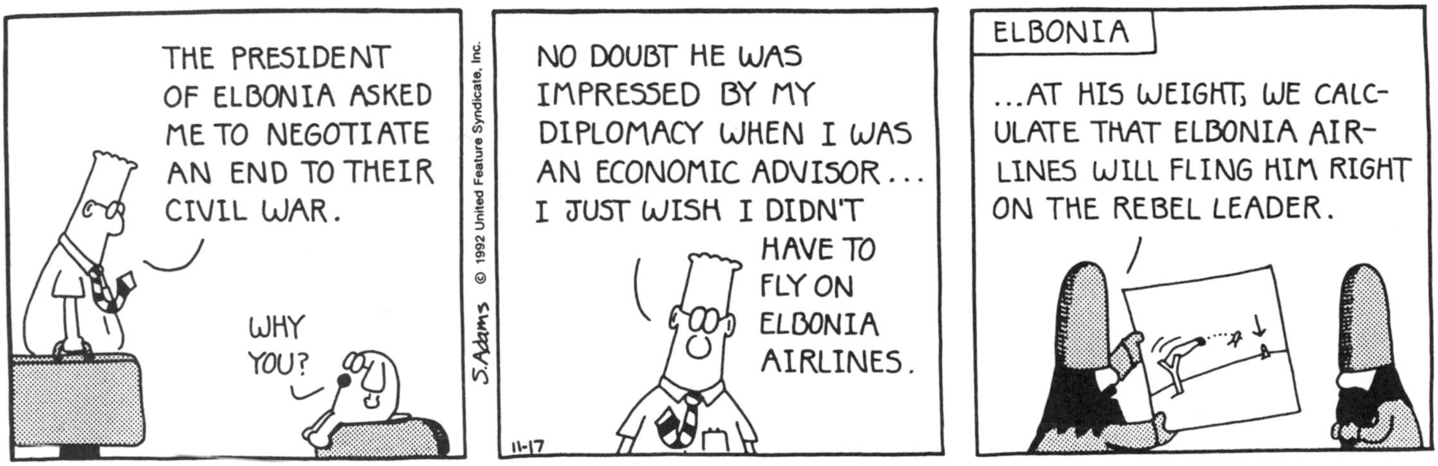
THE PRESIDENT OF ELBONIA ASKED ME TO NEGOTIATE AN END TO THEIR CIVIL WAR.
WHY YOU?
S. Adams © 1992 United Feature Syndicate, Inc.
NO DOUBT HE WAS IMPRESSED BY MY DIPLOMACY WHEN I WAS AN ECONOMIC ADVISOR... I JUST WISH I DIDN'T HAVE TO FLY ON ELBONIA AIRLINES.
11-17
ELBONIA
...AT HIS WEIGHT, WE CALCULATE THAT ELBONIA AIRLINES WILL FLING HIM RIGHT ON THE REBEL LEADER.

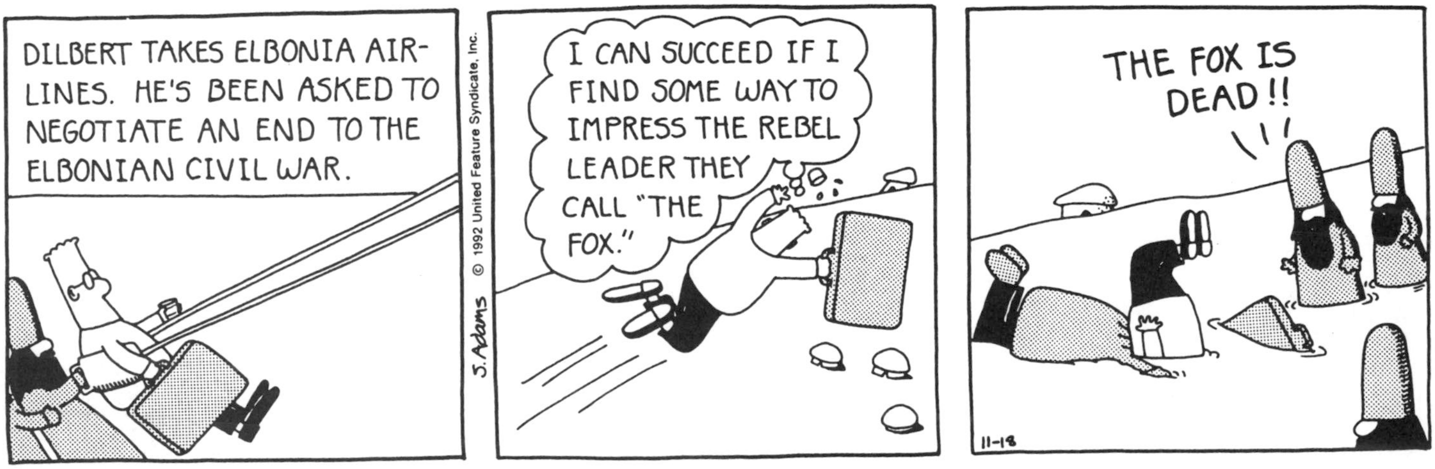
DILBERT TAKES ELBONIA AIRLINES. HE'S BEEN ASKED TO NEGOTIATE AN END TO THE ELBONIAN CIVIL WAR.
S. Adams © 1992 United Feature Syndicate, Inc.
I CAN SUCCEED IF I FIND SOME WAY TO IMPRESS THE REBEL LEADER THEY CALL "THE FOX."
THE FOX IS DEAD!!
11-18

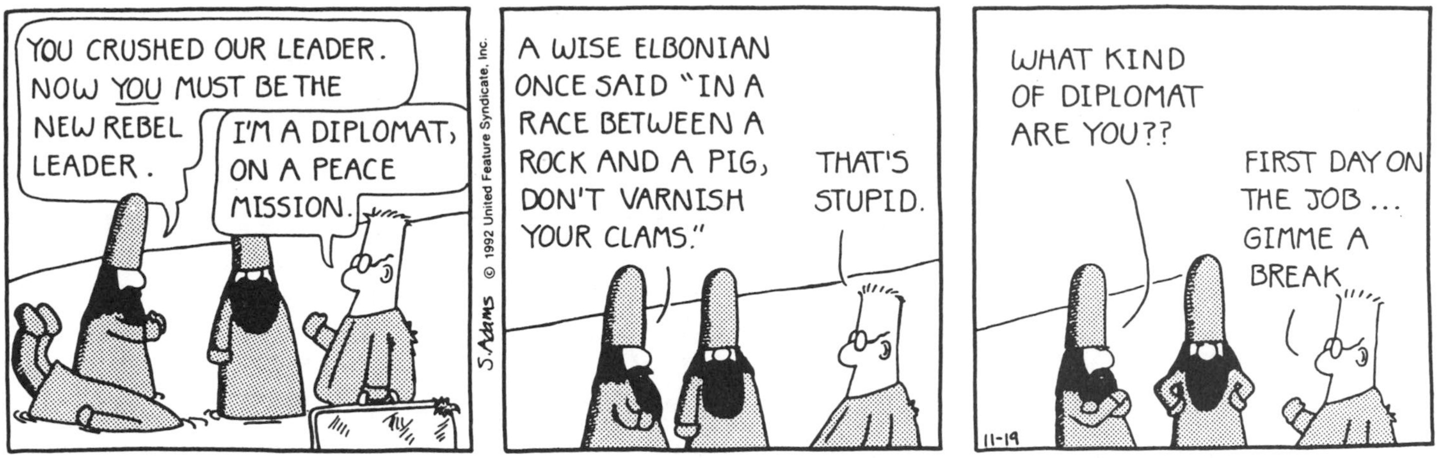
YOU CRUSHED OUR LEADER. NOW YOU MUST BE THE NEW REBEL LEADER.
I'M A DIPLOMAT, ON A PEACE MISSION.
S.Adams © 1992 United Feature Syndicate, Inc.
A WISE ELBONIAN ONCE SAID "IN A RACE BETWEEN A ROCK AND A PIG, DON'T VARNISH YOUR CLAMS."
THAT'S STUPID.
WHAT KIND OF DIPLOMAT ARE YOU??
FIRST DAY ON THE JOB... GIMME A BREAK
11-19

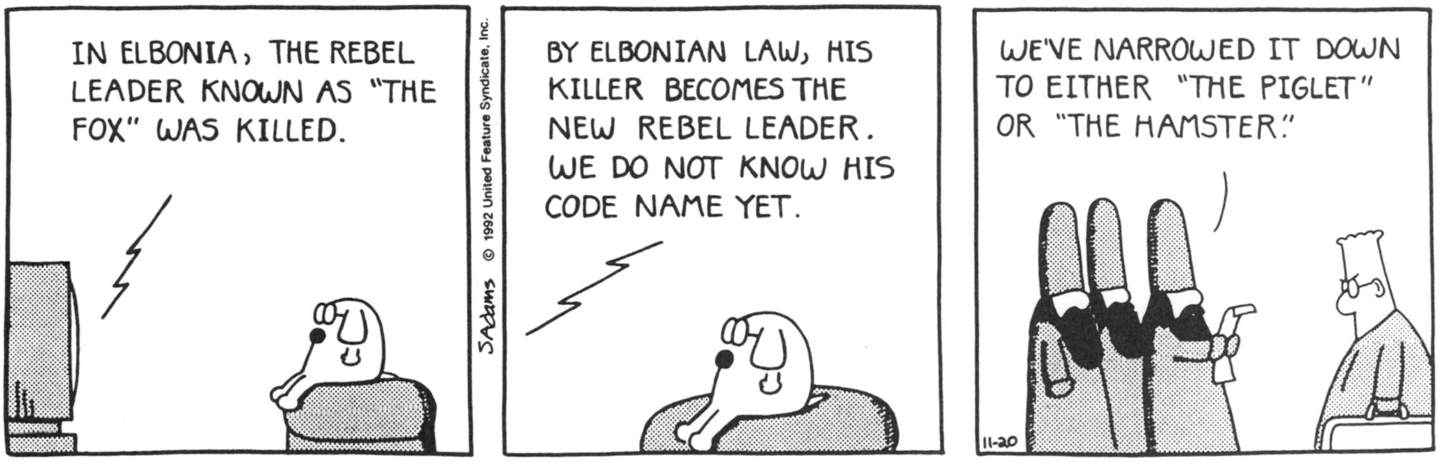
IN ELBONIA, THE REBEL LEADER KNOWN AS "THE FOX" WAS KILLED.
S.Adams © 1992 United Feature Syndicate, Inc.
BY ELBONIAN LAW, HIS KILLER BECOMES THE NEW REBEL LEADER. WE DO NOT KNOW HIS CODE NAME YET.
WE'VE NARROWED IT DOWN TO EITHER "THE PIGLET" OR "THE HAMSTER."
11-20

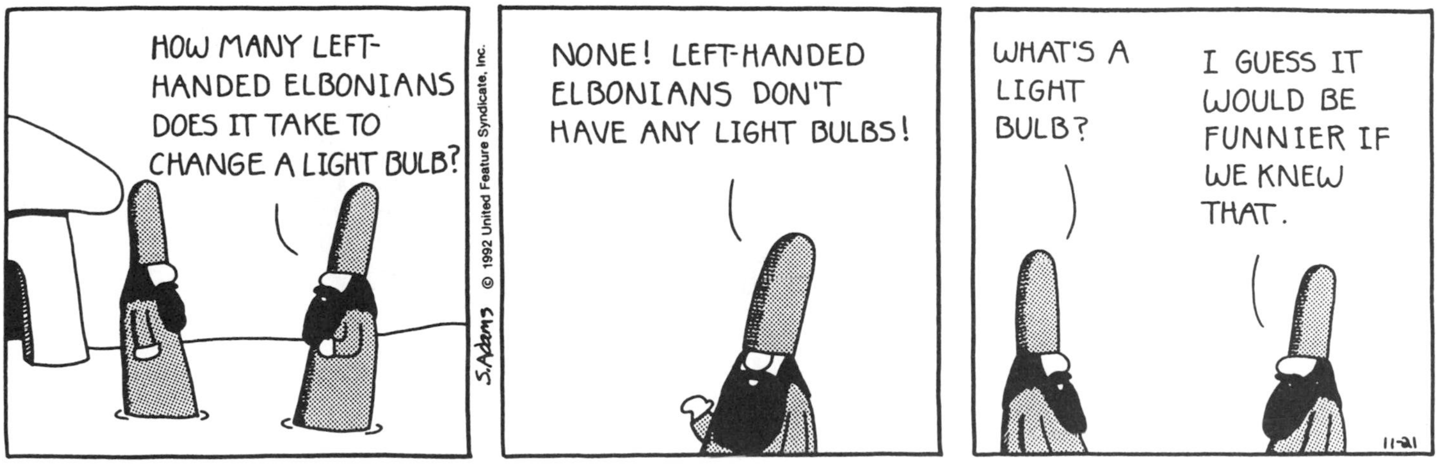
HOW MANY LEFT-HANDED ELBONIANS DOES IT TAKE TO CHANGE A LIGHT BULB?
S.Adams © 1992 United Feature Syndicate, Inc.
NONE! LEFT-HANDED ELBONIANS DON'T HAVE ANY LIGHT BULBS!
WHAT'S A LIGHT BULB?
I GUESS IT WOULD BE FUNNIER IF WE KNEW THAT.
11-21

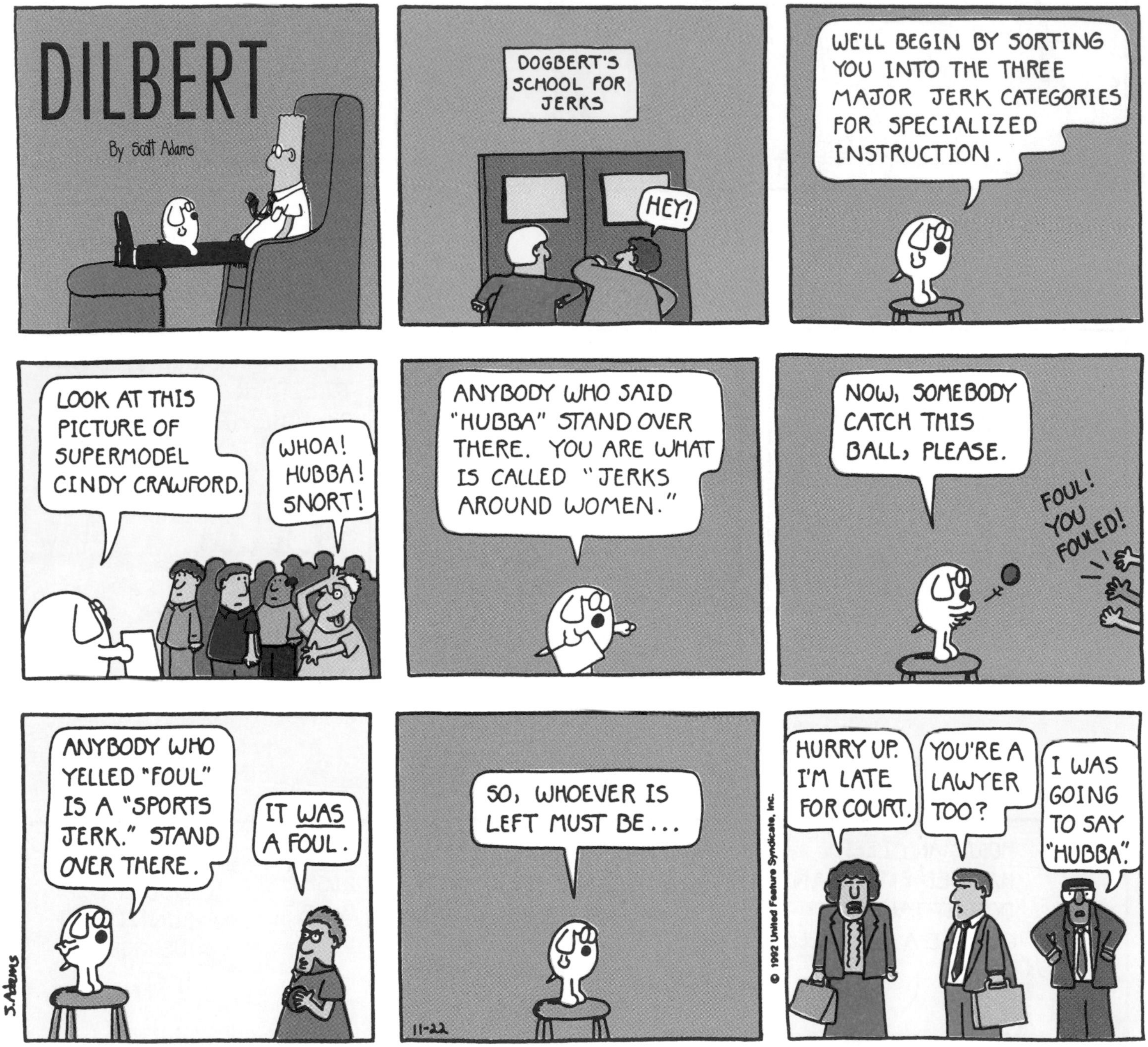
DILBERT
By Scott Adams
DOGBERT'S SCHOOL FOR JERKS
HEY!
WE'LL BEGIN BY SORTING YOU INTO THE THREE MAJOR JERK CATEGORIES FOR SPECIALIZED INSTRUCTION.
LOOK AT THIS PICTURE OF SUPERMODEL CINDY CRAWFORD.
WHOA! HUBBA! SNORT!
ANYBODY WHO SAID "HUBBA" STAND OVER THERE. YOU ARE WHAT IS CALLED "JERKS AROUND WOMEN."
NOW, SOMEBODY CATCH THIS BALL, PLEASE.
FOUL! YOU FOULED!
ANYBODY WHO YELLED "FOUL" IS A "SPORTS JERK." STAND OVER THERE.
IT WAS A FOUL.
S. Adams
SO, WHOEVER IS LEFT MUST BE...
11-22
© 1992 United Feature Syndicate, Inc.
HURRY UP. I'M LATE FOR COURT.
YOU'RE A LAWYER TOO?
I WAS GOING TO SAY "HUBBA".

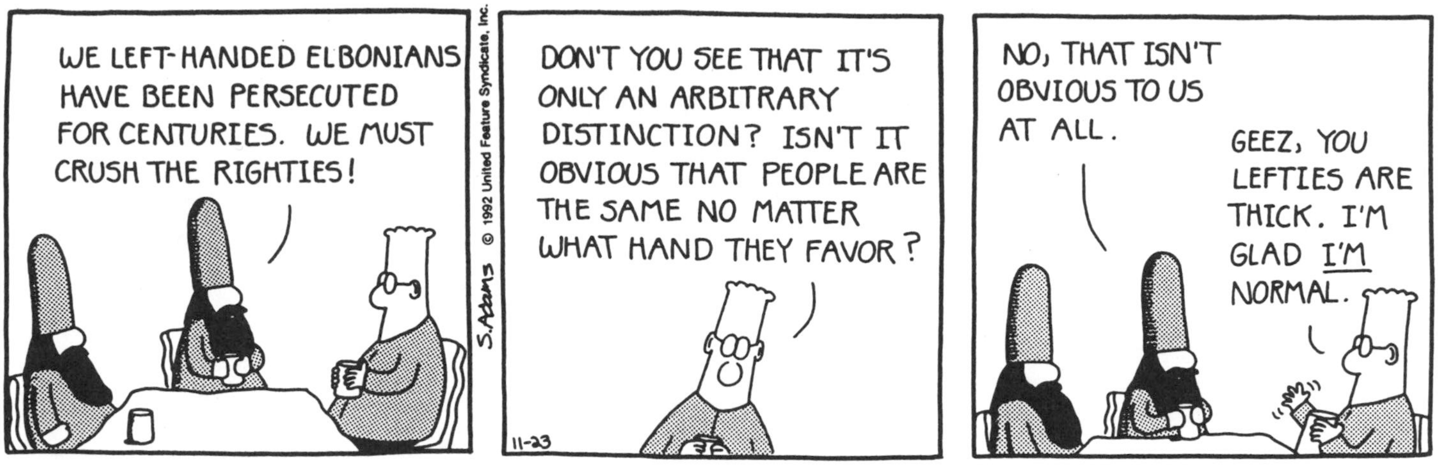
WE LEFT-HANDED ELBONIANS HAVE BEEN PERSECUTED FOR CENTURIES. WE MUST CRUSH THE RIGHTIES!
S. Adams © 1992 United Feature Syndicate, Inc.
DON'T YOU SEE THAT IT'S ONLY AN ARBITRARY DISTINCTION? ISN'T IT OBVIOUS THAT PEOPLE ARE THE SAME NO MATTER WHAT HAND THEY FAVOR?
11-23
NO, THAT ISN'T OBVIOUS TO US AT ALL.
GEEZ, YOU LEFTIES ARE THICK. I'M GLAD I'M NORMAL.

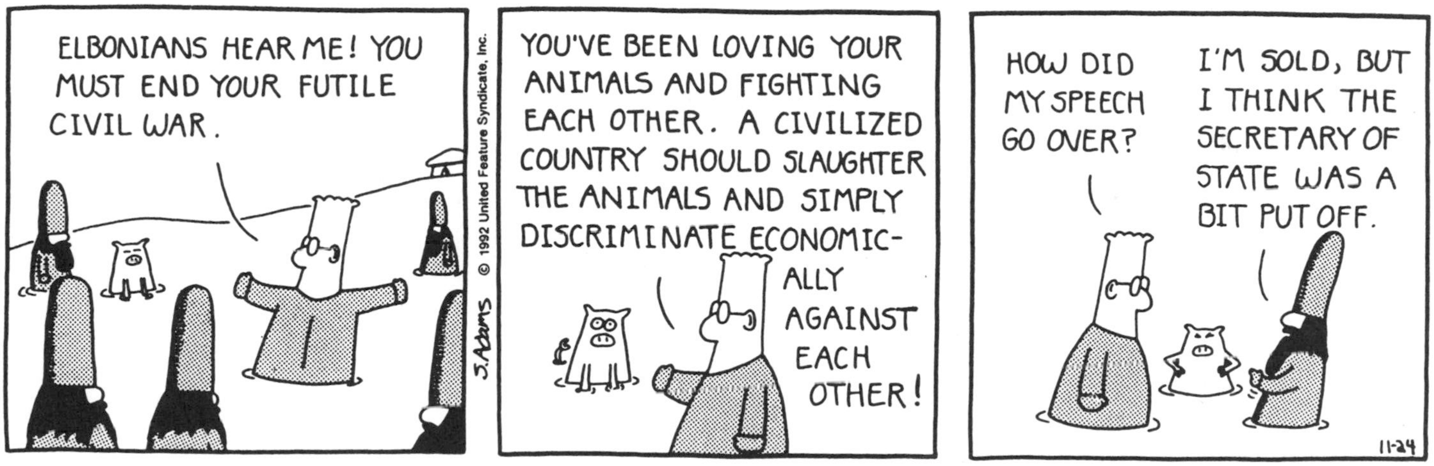
ELBONIANS HEAR ME! YOU MUST END YOUR FUTILE CIVIL WAR.
S. Adams © 1992 United Feature Syndicate, Inc.
YOU'VE BEEN LOVING YOUR ANIMALS AND FIGHTING EACH OTHER. A CIVILIZED COUNTRY SHOULD SLAUGHTER THE ANIMALS AND SIMPLY DISCRIMINATE ECONOMICALLY AGAINST EACH OTHER!
HOW DID MY SPEECH GO OVER?
I'M SOLD, BUT I THINK THE SECRETARY OF STATE WAS A BIT PUT OFF.
11-24

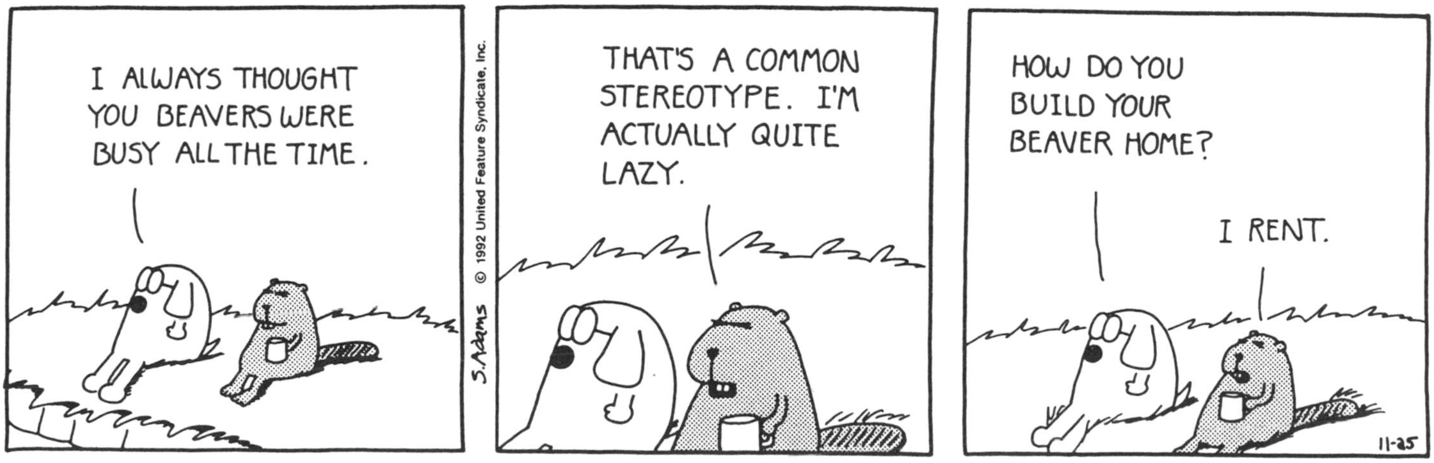
I ALWAYS THOUGHT YOU BEAVERS WERE BUSY ALL THE TIME.
S. Adams © 1992 United Feature Syndicate, Inc.
THAT'S A COMMON STEREOTYPE. I'M ACTUALLY QUITE LAZY.
HOW DO YOU BUILD YOUR BEAVER HOME?
I RENT.
11-25

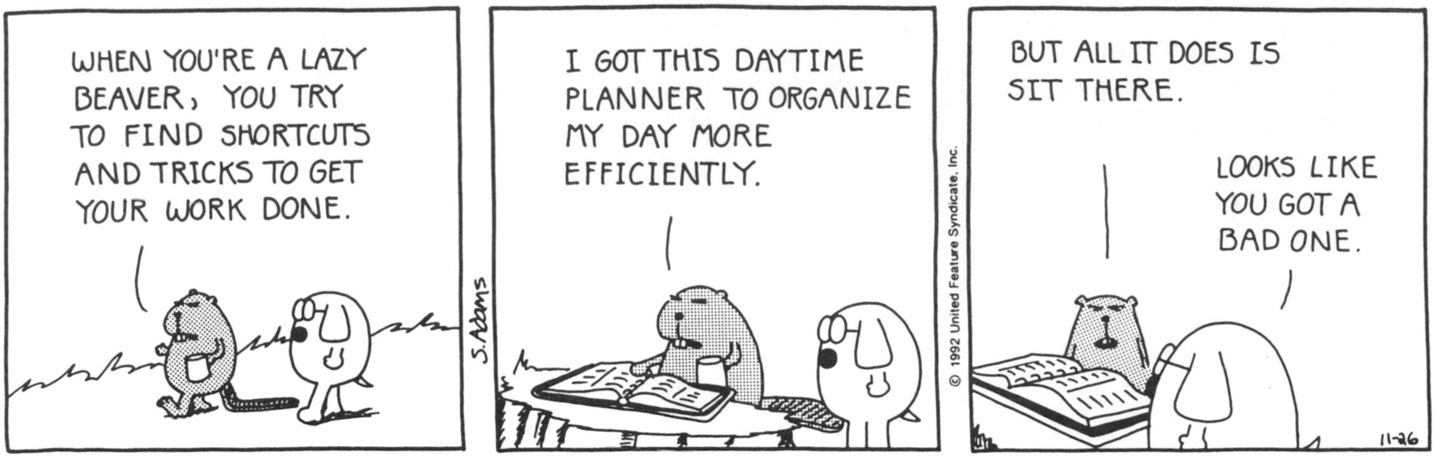
WHEN YOU'RE A LAZY BEAVER, YOU TRY TO FIND SHORTCUTS AND TRICKS TO GET YOUR WORK DONE.
S. Adams
I GOT THIS DAYTIME PLANNER TO ORGANIZE MY DAY MORE EFFICIENTLY.
© 1992 United Feature Syndicate, Inc.
BUT ALL IT DOES IS SIT THERE.
LOOKS LIKE YOU GOT A BAD ONE.
11-26

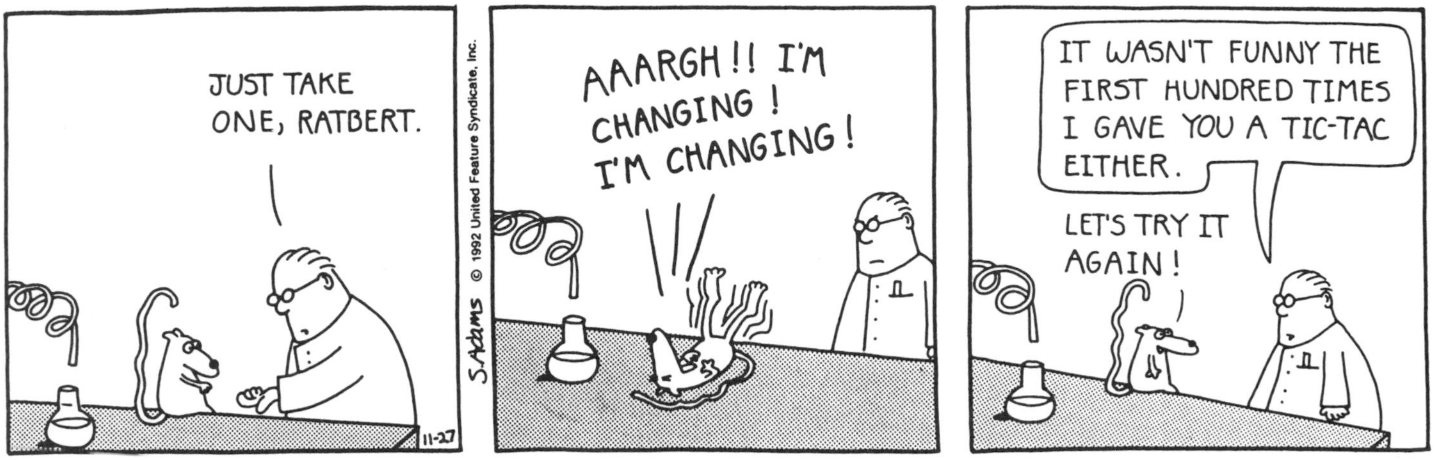
JUST TAKE ONE, RATBERT.
11-27
S. Adams © 1992 United Feature Syndicate, Inc.
AAARGH!! I'M CHANGING! I'M CHANGING!
IT WASN'T FUNNY THE FIRST HUNDRED TIMES I GAVE YOU A TIC-TAC EITHER.
LET'S TRY IT AGAIN!

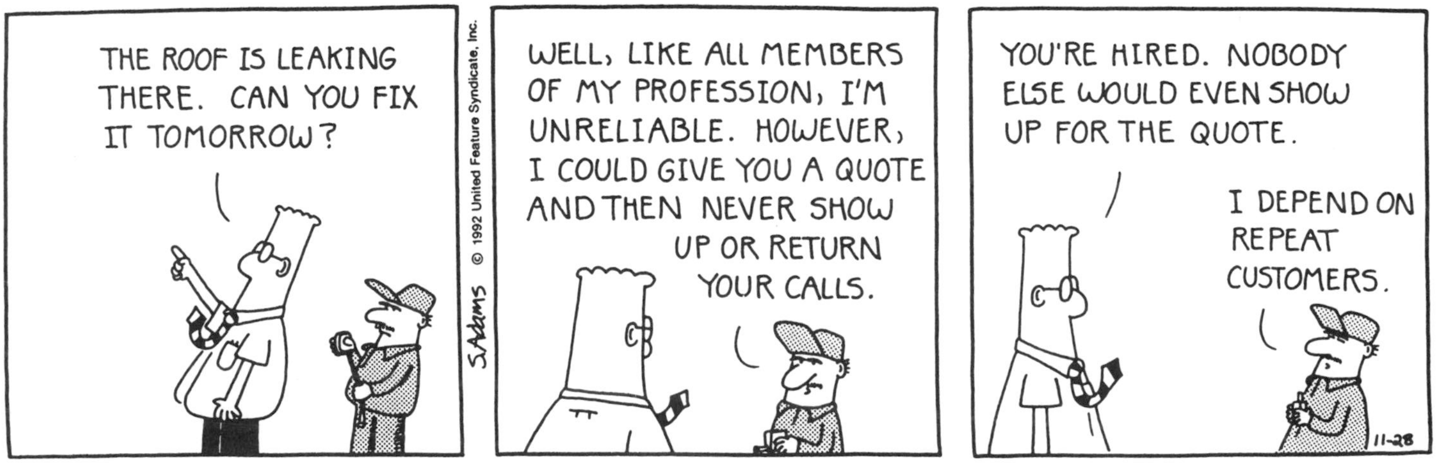
THE ROOF IS LEAKING THERE. CAN YOU FIX IT TOMORROW?
S. Adams © 1992 United Feature Syndicate, Inc.
WELL, LIKE ALL MEMBERS OF MY PROFESSION, I'M UNRELIABLE. HOWEVER, I COULD GIVE YOU A QUOTE AND THEN NEVER SHOW UP OR RETURN YOUR CALLS.
YOU'RE HIRED. NOBODY ELSE WOULD EVEN SHOW UP FOR THE QUOTE.
I DEPEND ON REPEAT CUSTOMERS.
11-28

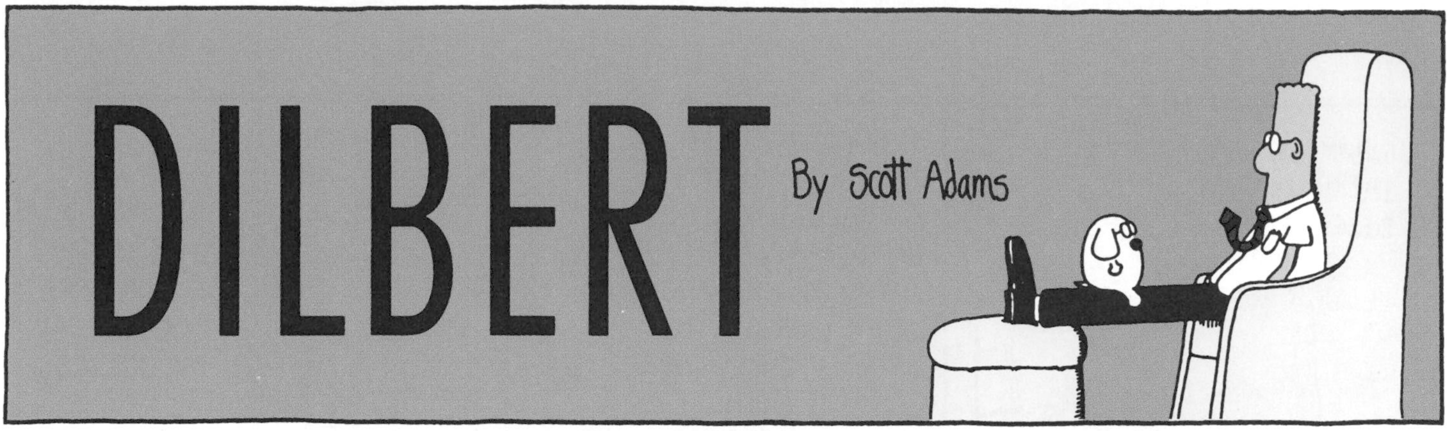
DILBERT
By Scott Adams

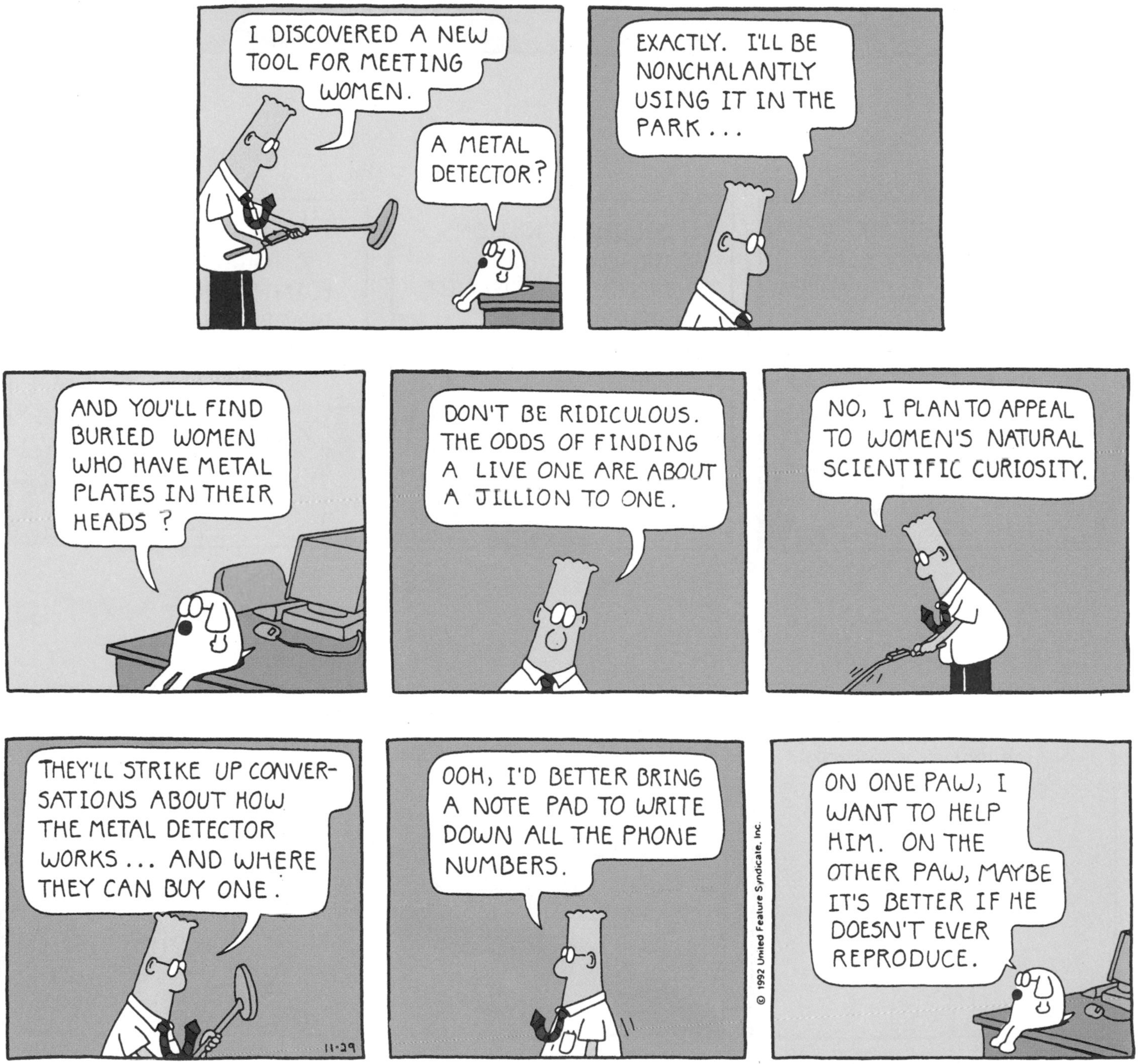
I DISCOVERED A NEW TOOL FOR MEETING WOMEN.
A METAL DETECTOR?
EXACTLY. I'LL BE NONCHALANTLY USING IT IN THE PARK . . .
AND YOU'LL FIND BURIED WOMEN WHO HAVE METAL PLATES IN THEIR HEADS ?
DON'T BE RIDICULOUS. THE ODDS OF FINDING A LIVE ONE ARE ABOUT A JILLION TO ONE.
NO, I PLAN TO APPEAL TO WOMEN'S NATURAL SCIENTIFIC CURIOSITY.
THEY'LL STRIKE UP CONVERSATIONS ABOUT HOW THE METAL DETECTOR WORKS . . . AND WHERE THEY CAN BUY ONE.
S. Adams
11-29
OOH, I'D BETTER BRING A NOTE PAD TO WRITE DOWN ALL THE PHONE NUMBERS.
© 1992 United Feature Syndicate, Inc.
ON ONE PAW, I WANT TO HELP HIM. ON THE OTHER PAW, MAYBE IT'S BETTER IF HE DOESN'T EVER REPRODUCE.

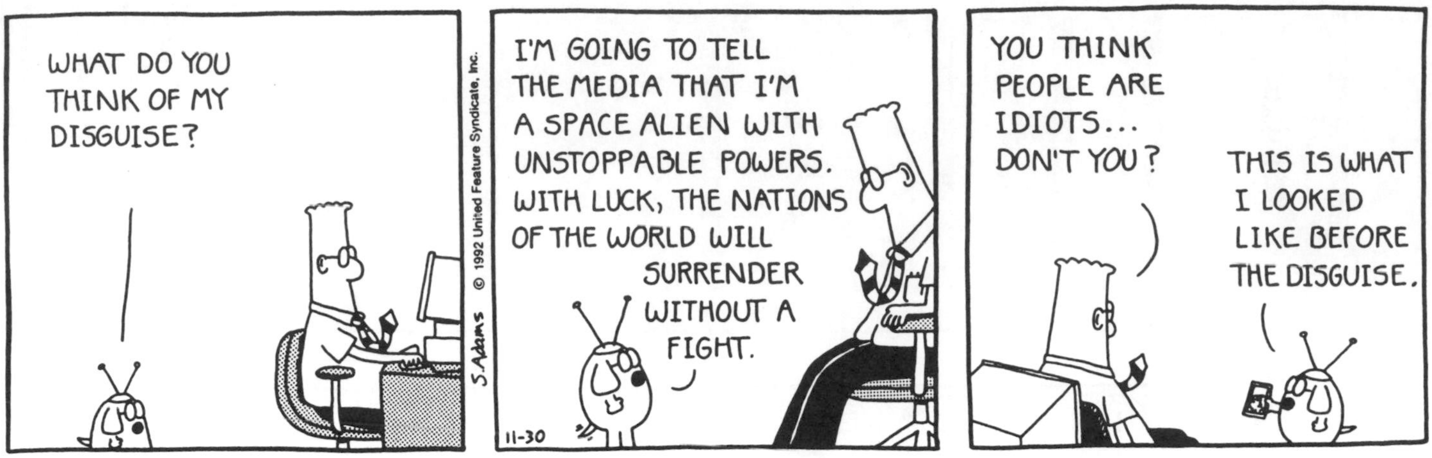
WHAT DO YOU THINK OF MY DISGUISE?
I'M GOING TO TELL THE MEDIA THAT I'M A SPACE ALIEN WITH UNSTOPPABLE POWERS. WITH LUCK, THE NATIONS OF THE WORLD WILL SURRENDER WITHOUT A FIGHT.
YOU THINK PEOPLE ARE IDIOTS... DON'T YOU?
THIS IS WHAT I LOOKED LIKE BEFORE THE DISGUISE.
S.Adams © 1992 United Feature Syndicate, Inc.
11-30

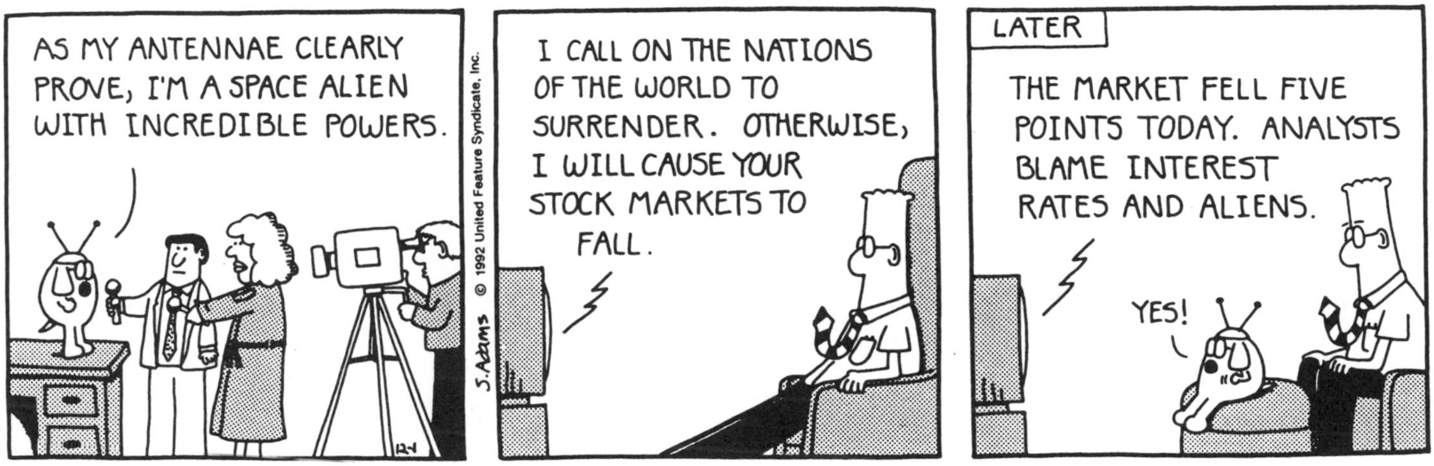
AS MY ANTENNAE CLEARLY PROVE, I'M A SPACE ALIEN WITH INCREDIBLE POWERS.
I CALL ON THE NATIONS OF THE WORLD TO SURRENDER. OTHERWISE, I WILL CAUSE YOUR STOCK MARKETS TO FALL.
LATER
THE MARKET FELL FIVE POINTS TODAY. ANALYSTS BLAME INTEREST RATES AND ALIENS.
YES!
S.Adams © 1992 United Feature Syndicate, Inc.

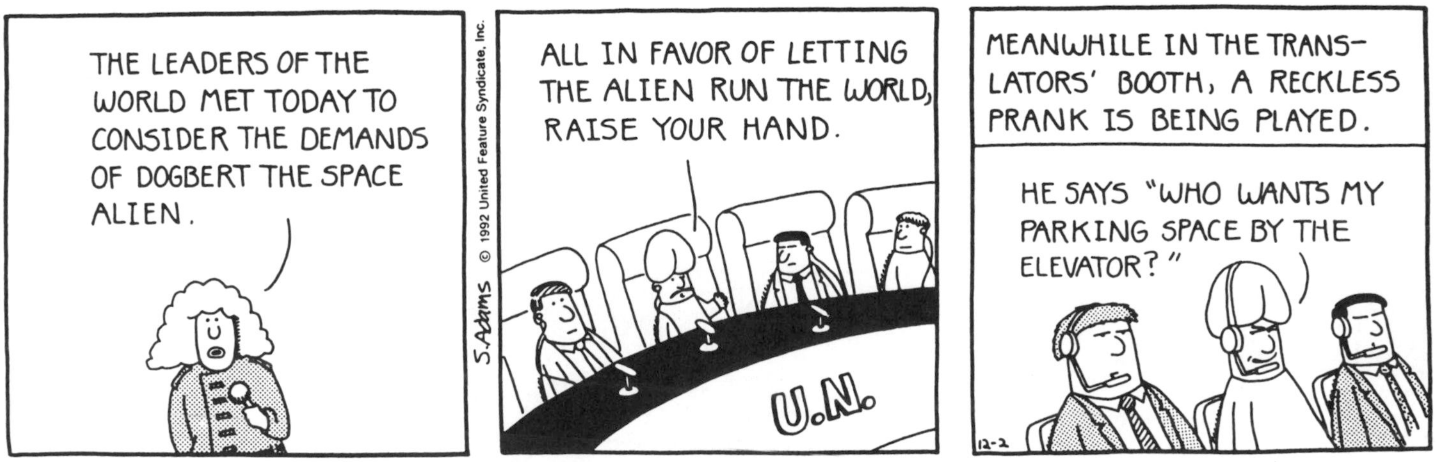
THE LEADERS OF THE WORLD MET TODAY TO CONSIDER THE DEMANDS OF DOGBERT THE SPACE ALIEN.
ALL IN FAVOR OF LETTING THE ALIEN RUN THE WORLD, RAISE YOUR HAND.
U.N.
MEANWHILE IN THE TRANSLATORS' BOOTH, A RECKLESS PRANK IS BEING PLAYED.
HE SAYS "WHO WANTS MY PARKING SPACE BY THE ELEVATOR?"
S.Adams © 1992 United Feature Syndicate, Inc.
12-2

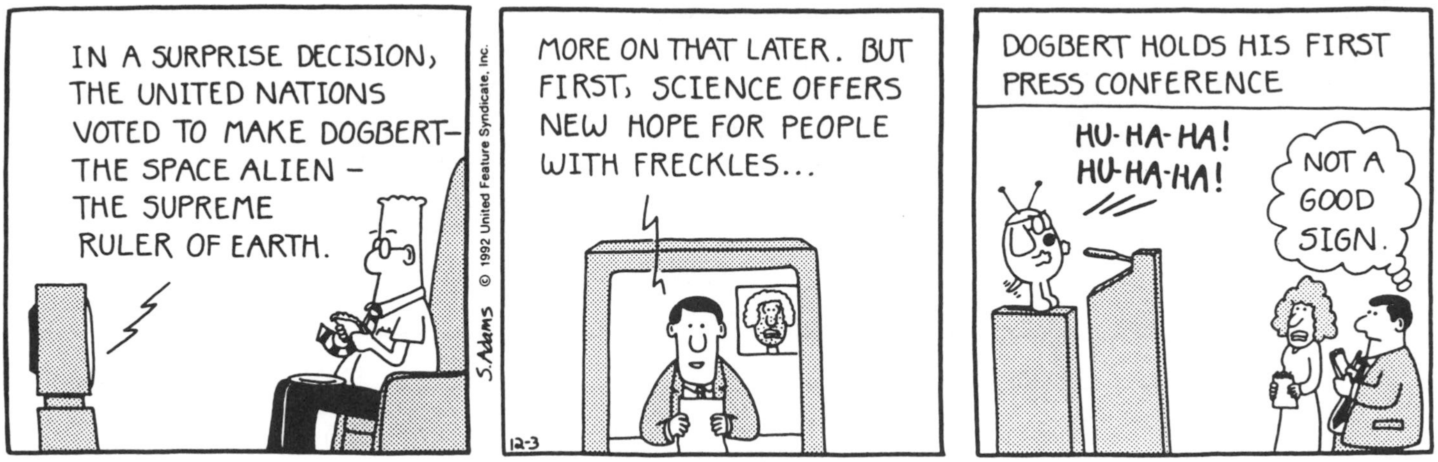
IN A SURPRISE DECISION, THE UNITED NATIONS VOTED TO MAKE DOGBERT– THE SPACE ALIEN – THE SUPREME RULER OF EARTH.
S. Adams © 1992 United Feature Syndicate, Inc.
MORE ON THAT LATER. BUT FIRST, SCIENCE OFFERS NEW HOPE FOR PEOPLE WITH FRECKLES...
12-3
DOGBERT HOLDS HIS FIRST PRESS CONFERENCE
HU-HA-HA! HU-HA-HA!
NOT A GOOD SIGN.

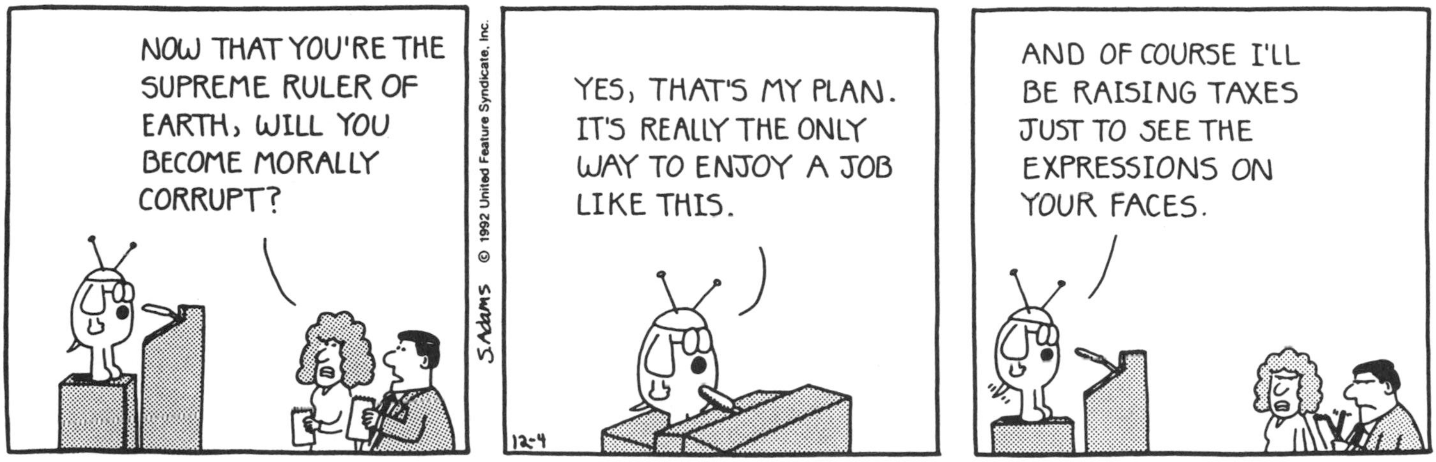
NOW THAT YOU'RE THE SUPREME RULER OF EARTH, WILL YOU BECOME MORALLY CORRUPT?
S. Adams © 1992 United Feature Syndicate, Inc.
YES, THAT'S MY PLAN. IT'S REALLY THE ONLY WAY TO ENJOY A JOB LIKE THIS.
12-4
AND OF COURSE I'LL BE RAISING TAXES JUST TO SEE THE EXPRESSIONS ON YOUR FACES.

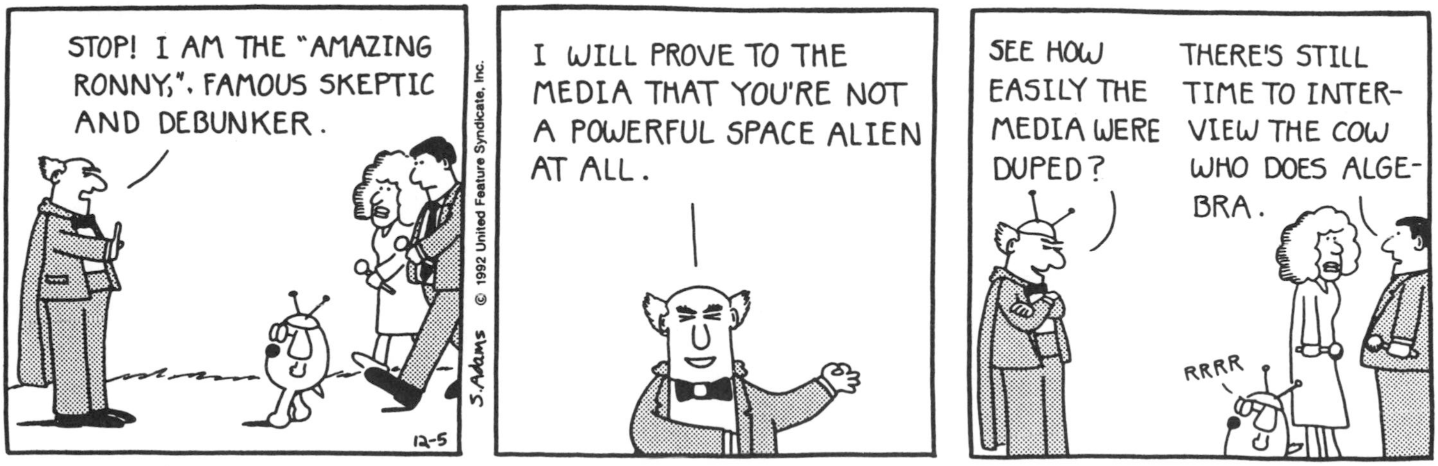
STOP! I AM THE "AMAZING RONNY,". FAMOUS SKEPTIC AND DEBUNKER.
12-5
S. Adams © 1992 United Feature Syndicate, Inc.
I WILL PROVE TO THE MEDIA THAT YOU'RE NOT A POWERFUL SPACE ALIEN AT ALL.
SEE HOW EASILY THE MEDIA WERE DUPED?
THERE'S STILL TIME TO INTERVIEW THE COW WHO DOES ALGEBRA.
RRRR

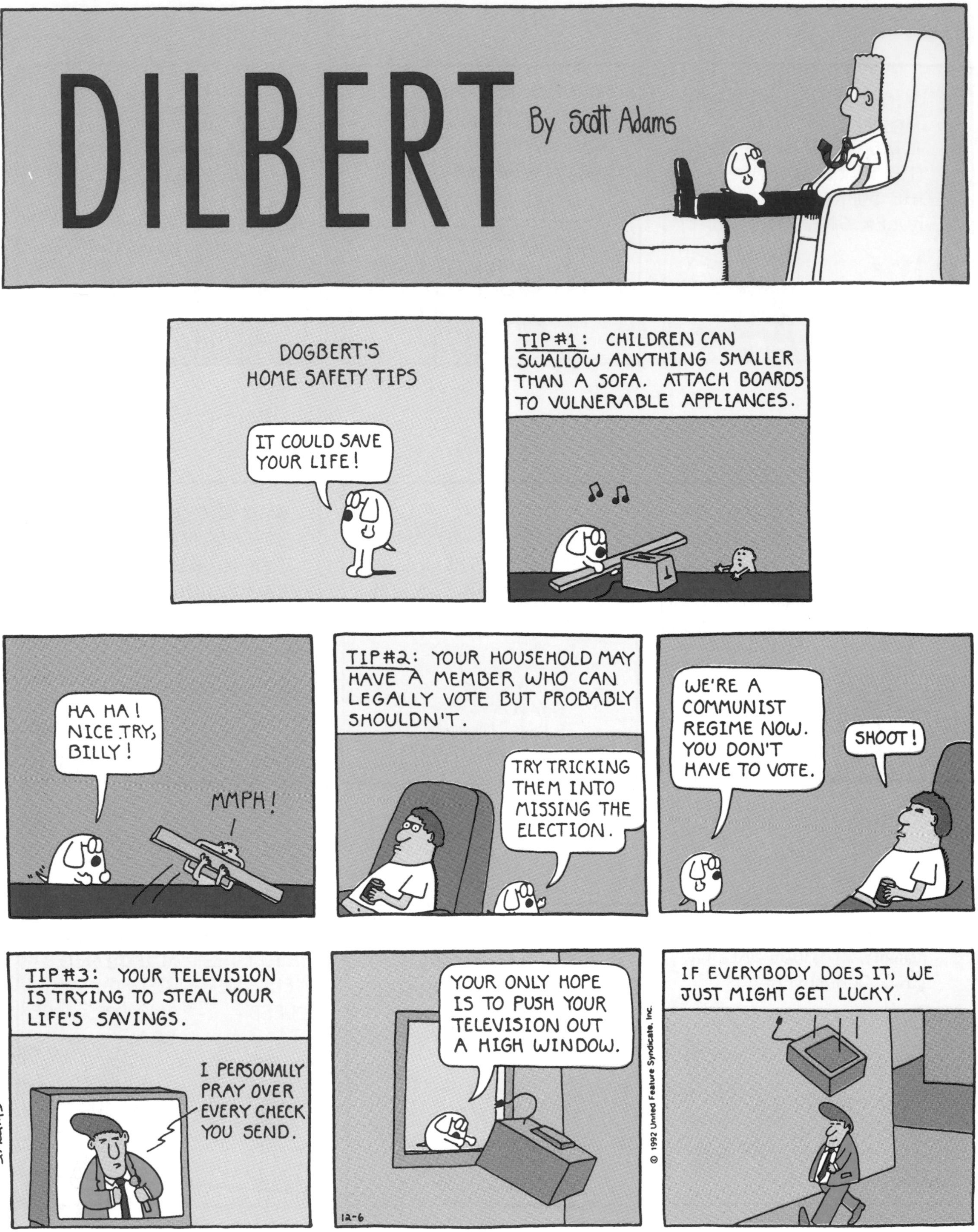
DILBERT
By Scott Adams
DOGBERT'S HOME SAFETY TIPS
IT COULD SAVE YOUR LIFE!
TIP #1: CHILDREN CAN SWALLOW ANYTHING SMALLER THAN A SOFA. ATTACH BOARDS TO VULNERABLE APPLIANCES.
HA HA! NICE TRY, BILLY!
MMPH!
TIP #2: YOUR HOUSEHOLD MAY HAVE A MEMBER WHO CAN LEGALLY VOTE BUT PROBABLY SHOULDN'T.
TRY TRICKING THEM INTO MISSING THE ELECTION.
WE'RE A COMMUNIST REGIME NOW. YOU DON'T HAVE TO VOTE.
SHOOT!
TIP #3: YOUR TELEVISION IS TRYING TO STEAL YOUR LIFE'S SAVINGS.
I PERSONALLY PRAY OVER EVERY CHECK YOU SEND.
S. Adams
YOUR ONLY HOPE IS TO PUSH YOUR TELEVISION OUT A HIGH WINDOW.
12-6
© 1992 United Feature Syndicate, Inc.
IF EVERYBODY DOES IT, WE JUST MIGHT GET LUCKY.

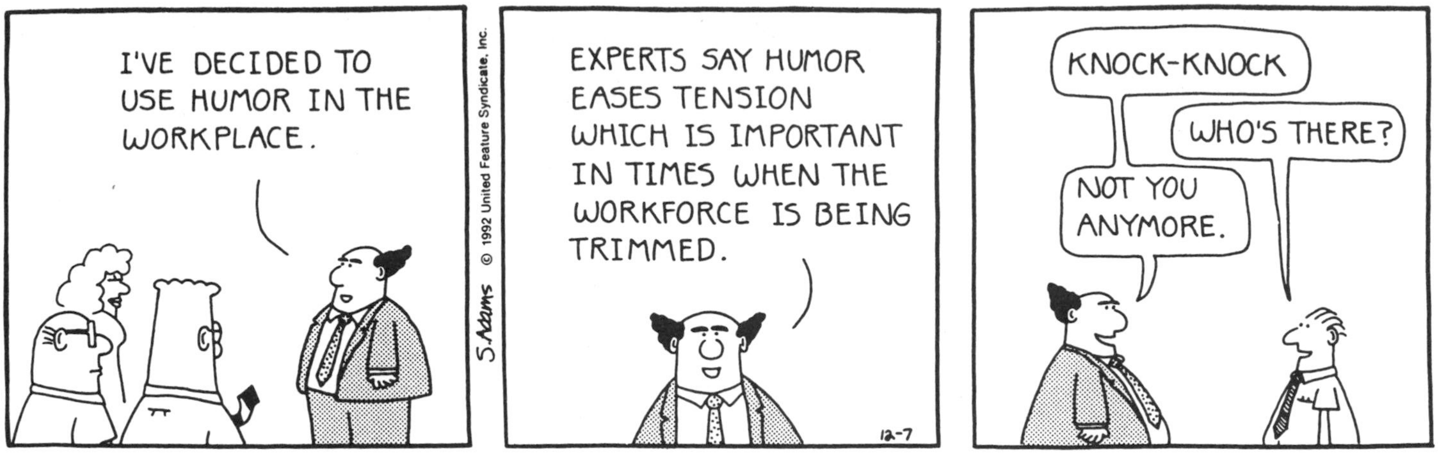
I'VE DECIDED TO USE HUMOR IN THE WORKPLACE.
© 1992 United Feature Syndicate, Inc.
S. Adams
EXPERTS SAY HUMOR EASES TENSION WHICH IS IMPORTANT IN TIMES WHEN THE WORKFORCE IS BEING TRIMMED.
12-7
KNOCK-KNOCK
WHO'S THERE?
NOT YOU ANYMORE.

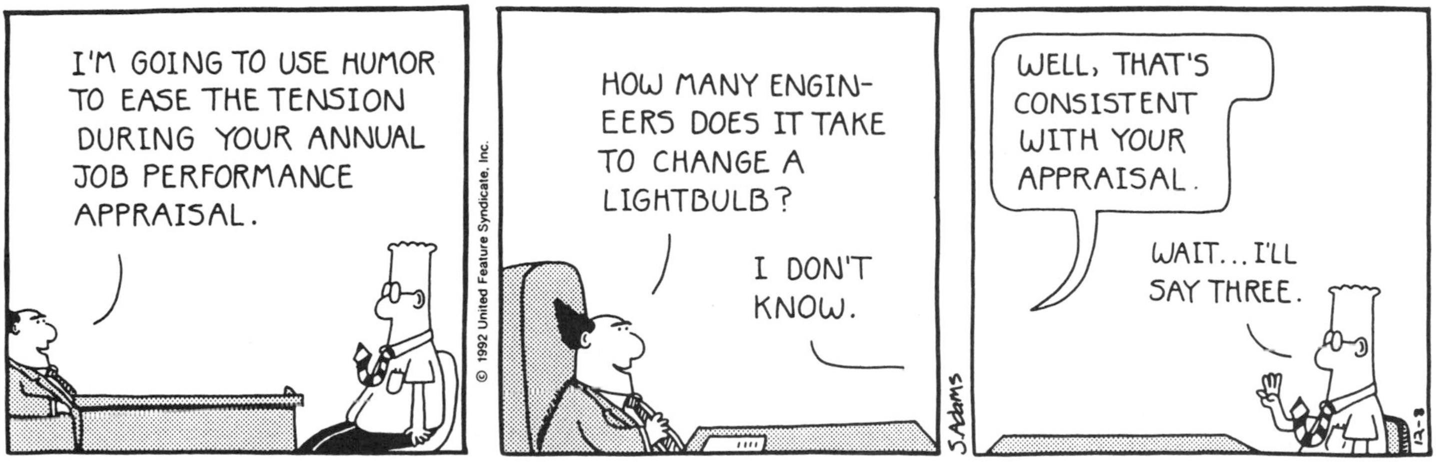
I'M GOING TO USE HUMOR TO EASE THE TENSION DURING YOUR ANNUAL JOB PERFORMANCE APPRAISAL.
© 1992 United Feature Syndicate, Inc.
HOW MANY ENGINEERS DOES IT TAKE TO CHANGE A LIGHTBULB?
I DON'T KNOW.
S. Adams
WELL, THAT'S CONSISTENT WITH YOUR APPRAISAL.
WAIT... I'LL SAY THREE.
12-8

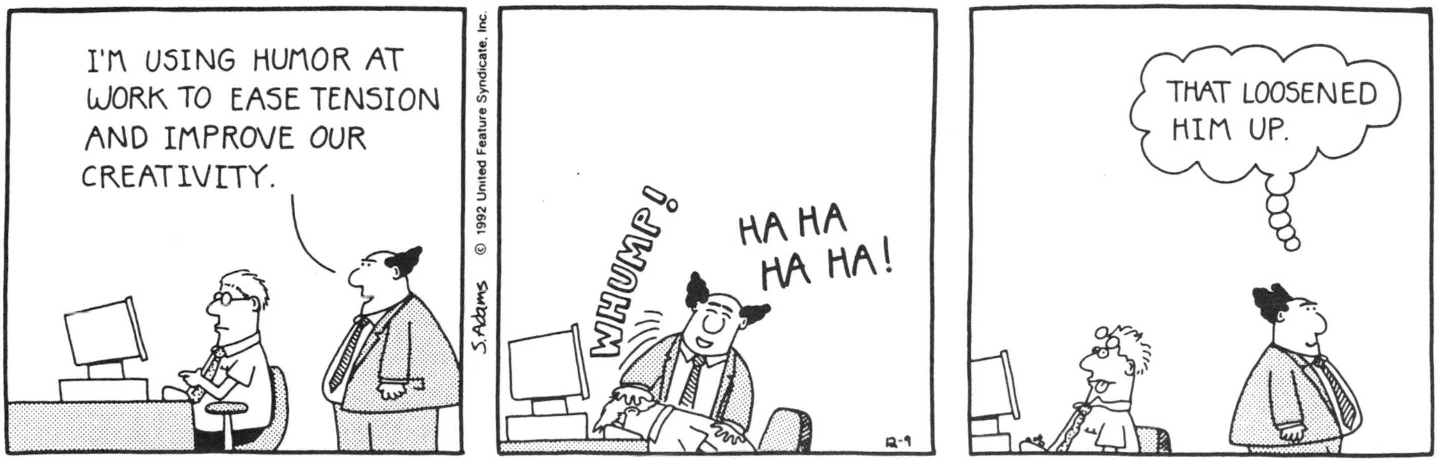
I'M USING HUMOR AT WORK TO EASE TENSION AND IMPROVE OUR CREATIVITY.
© 1992 United Feature Syndicate, Inc.
S. Adams
WHUMP!
HA HA HA HA!
12-9
THAT LOOSENED HIM UP.

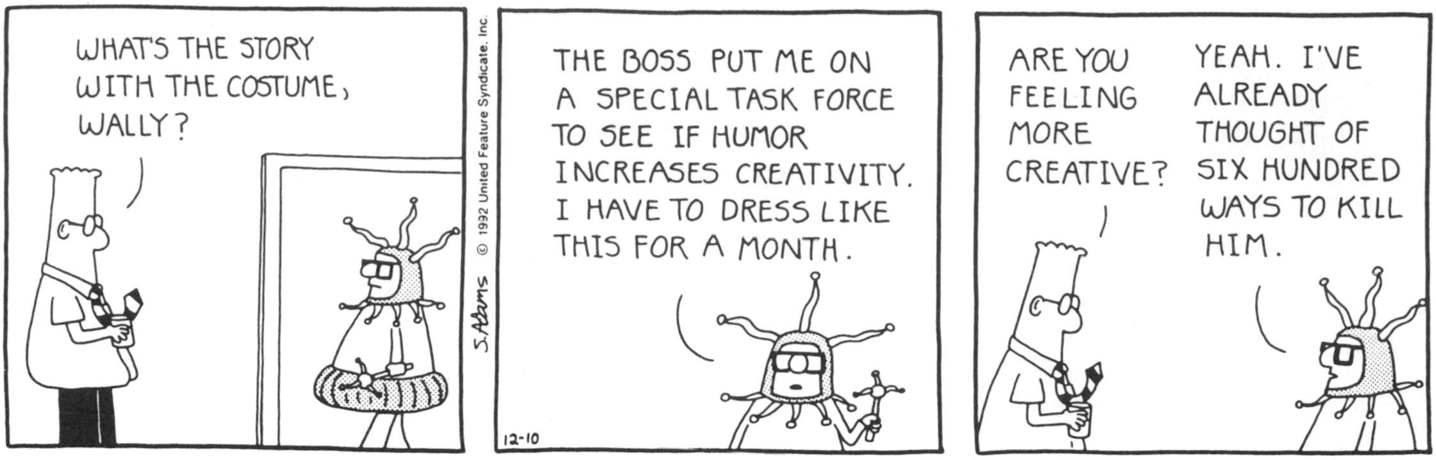
WHAT'S THE STORY WITH THE COSTUME, WALLY?
S. Adams © 1992 United Feature Syndicate, Inc.
THE BOSS PUT ME ON A SPECIAL TASK FORCE TO SEE IF HUMOR INCREASES CREATIVITY. I HAVE TO DRESS LIKE THIS FOR A MONTH.
12-10
ARE YOU FEELING MORE CREATIVE?
YEAH. I'VE ALREADY THOUGHT OF SIX HUNDRED WAYS TO KILL HIM.

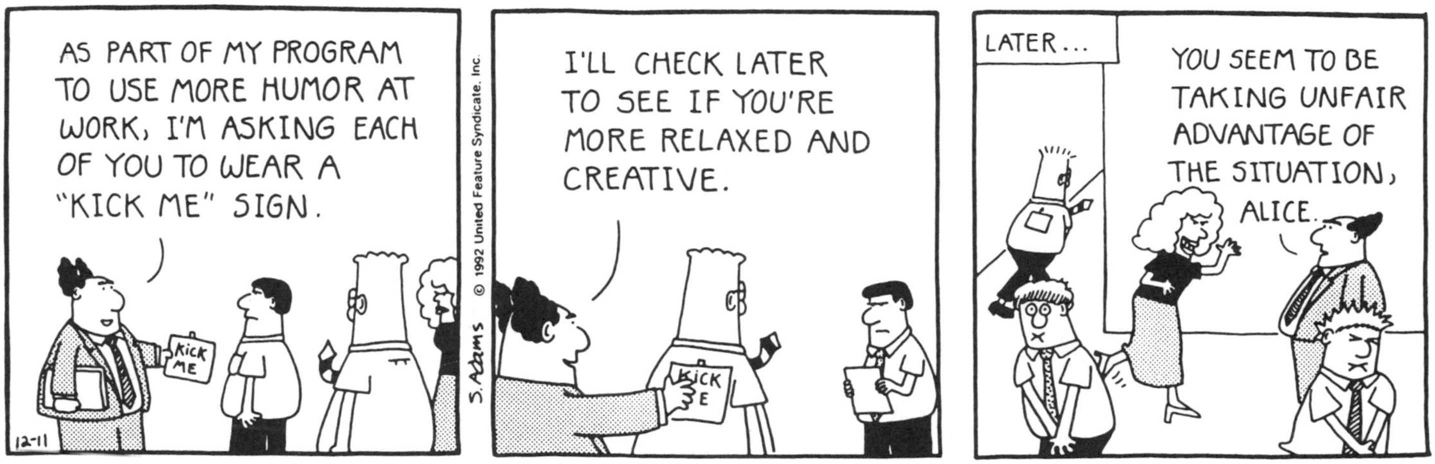
AS PART OF MY PROGRAM TO USE MORE HUMOR AT WORK, I'M ASKING EACH OF YOU TO WEAR A "KICK ME" SIGN.
KICK ME
12-11
S. Adams © 1992 United Feature Syndicate, Inc.
I'LL CHECK LATER TO SEE IF YOU'RE MORE RELAXED AND CREATIVE.
LATER...
YOU SEEM TO BE TAKING UNFAIR ADVANTAGE OF THE SITUATION, ALICE.

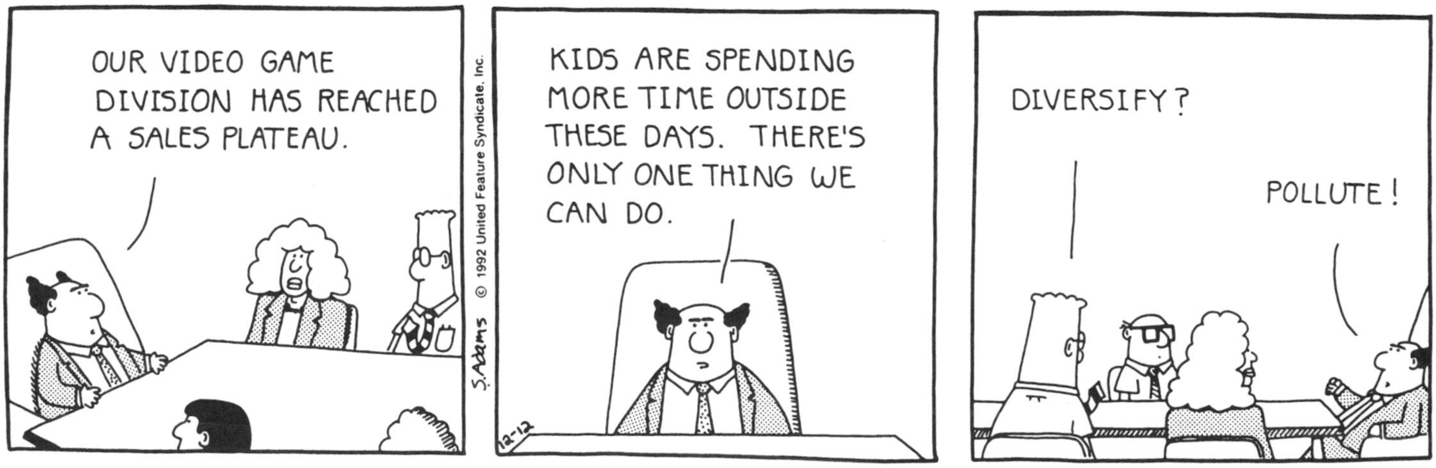
OUR VIDEO GAME DIVISION HAS REACHED A SALES PLATEAU.
S. Adams © 1992 United Feature Syndicate, Inc.
KIDS ARE SPENDING MORE TIME OUTSIDE THESE DAYS. THERE'S ONLY ONE THING WE CAN DO.
12-12
DIVERSIFY?
POLLUTE!

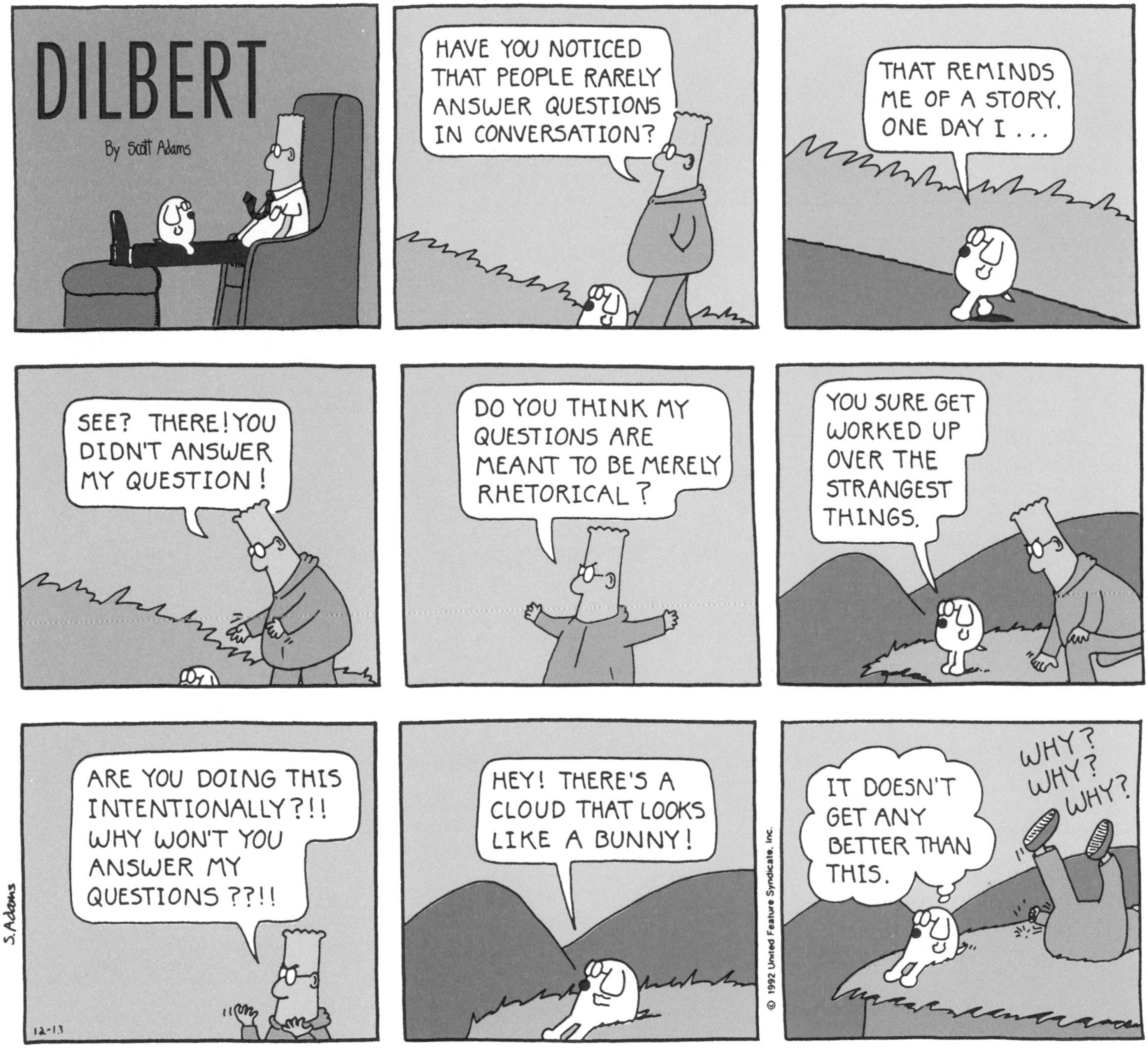
DILBERT
By Scott Adams
HAVE YOU NOTICED THAT PEOPLE RARELY ANSWER QUESTIONS IN CONVERSATION?
THAT REMINDS ME OF A STORY. ONE DAY I . . .
SEE? THERE! YOU DIDN'T ANSWER MY QUESTION!
DO YOU THINK MY QUESTIONS ARE MEANT TO BE MERELY RHETORICAL?
YOU SURE GET WORKED UP OVER THE STRANGEST THINGS.
ARE YOU DOING THIS INTENTIONALLY?!! WHY WON'T YOU ANSWER MY QUESTIONS??!!
S. Adams
12-13
HEY! THERE'S A CLOUD THAT LOOKS LIKE A BUNNY!
© 1992 United Feature Syndicate, Inc.
IT DOESN'T GET ANY BETTER THAN THIS.
WHY? WHY? WHY?